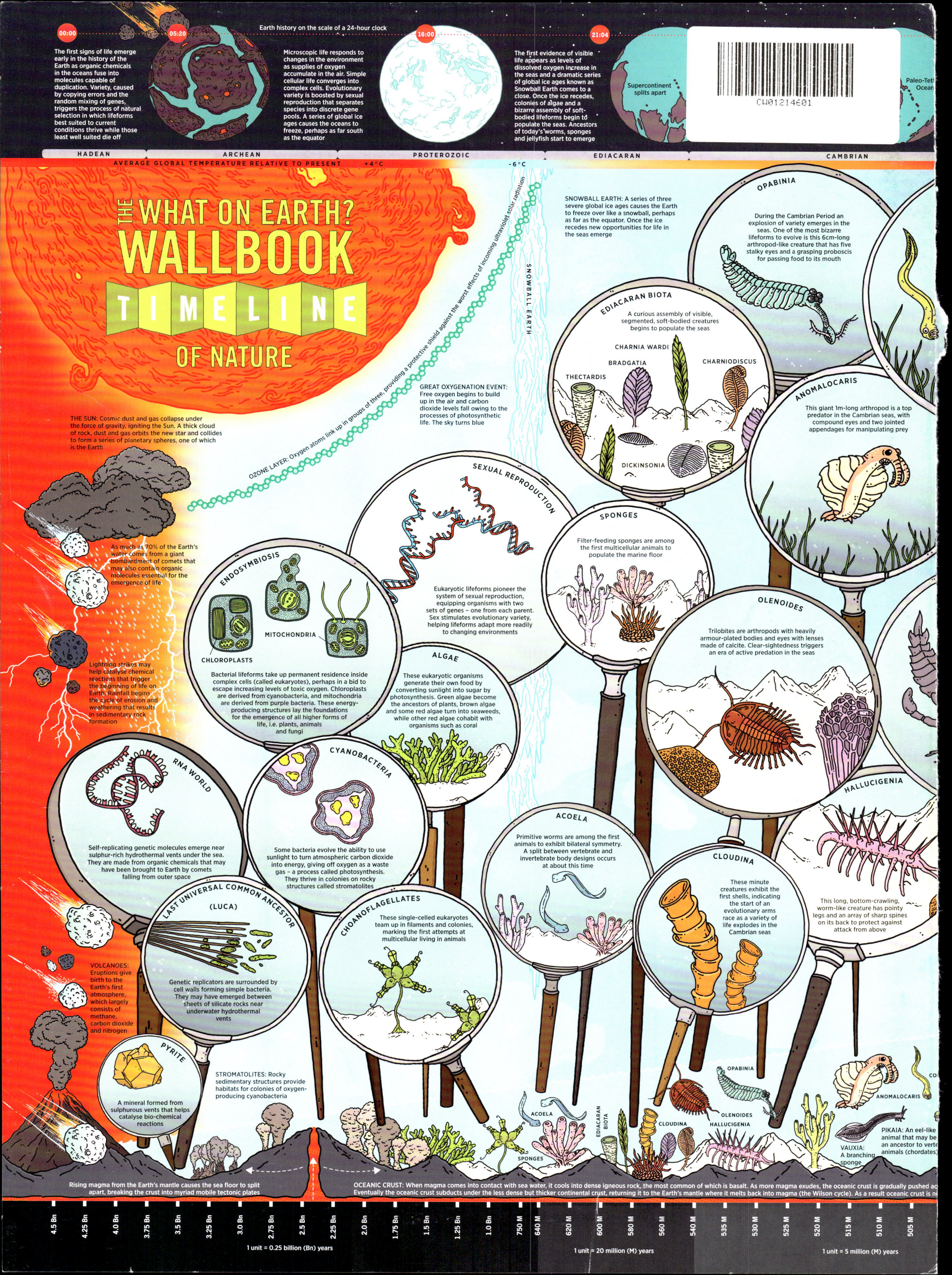

Earth history on the scale of a 24-hour clock
00:00
The first signs of life emerge early in the history of the Earth as organic chemicals in the oceans fuse into molecules capable of duplication. Variety, caused by copying errors and the random mixing of genes, triggers the process of natural selection in which lifeforms best suited to current conditions thrive while those least well suited die off
05:20
Microscopic life responds to changes in the environment as supplies of oxygen accumulate in the air. Simple cellular life converges into complex cells. Evolutionary variety is boosted by sexual reproduction that separates species into discrete gene pools. A series of global ice ages causes the oceans to freeze, perhaps as far south as the equator
16:00
21:04
The first evidence of visible life appears as levels of dissolved oxygen increase in the seas and a dramatic series of global ice ages known as Snowball Earth comes to a close. Once the ice recedes, colonies of algae and a bizarre assembly of soft-bodied lifeforms begin to populate the seas. Ancestors of today's worms, sponges and jellyfish start to emerge
Supercontinent splits apart
Paleo-Tet
Ocean
HADEAN
ARCHEAN
PROTEROZOIC
EDIACARAN
CAMBRIAN
AVERAGE GLOBAL TEMPERATURE RELATIVE TO PRESENT
+4°C
-6°C
THE WHAT ON EARTH? WALLBOOK TIMELINE OF NATURE
THE SUN: Cosmic dust and gas collapse under the force of gravity, igniting the Sun. A thick cloud of rock, dust and gas orbits the new star and collides to form a series of planetary spheres, one of which is the Earth
As much as 70% of the Earth's water comes from a giant bombardment of comets that may also contain organic molecules essential for the emergence of life
Lightning strikes may help catalyse chemical reactions that trigger the beginning of life on Earth. Rainfall begins the cycle of erosion and weathering that results in sedimentary rock formation
VOLCANOES: Eruptions give birth to the Earth's first atmosphere, which largely consists of methane, carbon dioxide and nitrogen
OZONE LAYER: Oxygen atoms link up in groups of three, providing a protective shield against the worst effects of incoming ultraviolet solar radiation
GREAT OXYGENATION EVENT: Free oxygen begins to build up in the air and carbon dioxide levels fall owing to the processes of photosynthetic life. The sky turns blue
SNOWBALL EARTH
SNOWBALL EARTH: A series of three severe global ice ages causes the Earth to freeze over like a snowball, perhaps as far as the equator. Once the ice recedes new opportunities for life in the seas emerge
OPABINIA
During the Cambrian Period an explosion of variety emerges in the seas. One of the most bizarre lifeforms to evolve is this 6cm-long arthropod-like creature that has five stalky eyes and a grasping proboscis for passing food to its mouth
EDIACARAN BIOTA
A curious assembly of visible, segmented, soft-bodied creatures begins to populate the seas
CHARNIA WARDI
BRADGATIA
CHARNIODISCUS
THECTARDIS
DICKINSONIA
ANOMALOCARIS
This giant 1m-long arthropod is a top predator in the Cambrian seas, with compound eyes and two jointed appendages for manipulating prey
SEXUAL REPRODUCTION
Eukaryotic lifeforms pioneer the system of sexual reproduction, equipping organisms with two sets of genes – one from each parent. Sex stimulates evolutionary variety, helping lifeforms adapt more readily to changing environments
SPONGES
Filter-feeding sponges are among the first multicellular animals to populate the marine floor
ENDOSYMBIOSIS
MITOCHONDRIA
CHLOROPLASTS
Bacterial lifeforms take up permanent residence inside complex cells (called eukaryotes), perhaps in a bid to escape increasing levels of toxic oxygen. Chloroplasts are derived from cyanobacteria, and mitochondria are derived from purple bacteria. These energy-producing structures lay the foundations for the emergence of all higher forms of life, i.e. plants, animals and fungi
ALGAE
These eukaryotic organisms generate their own food by converting sunlight into sugar by photosynthesis. Green algae become the ancestors of plants, brown algae and some red algae turn into seaweeds, while other red algae cohabit with organisms such as coral
OLENOIDES
Trilobites are arthropods with heavily armour-plated bodies and eyes with lenses made of calcite. Clear-sightedness triggers an era of active predation in the seas
RNA WORLD
Self-replicating genetic molecules emerge near sulphur-rich hydrothermal vents under the sea. They are made from organic chemicals that may have been brought to Earth by comets falling from outer space
CYANOBACTERIA
Some bacteria evolve the ability to use sunlight to turn atmospheric carbon dioxide into energy, giving off oxygen as a waste gas – a process called photosynthesis. They thrive in colonies on rocky structures called stromatolites
ACOELA
Primitive worms are among the first animals to exhibit bilateral symmetry. A split between vertebrate and invertebrate body designs occurs at about this time
HALLUCIGENIA
This long, bottom-crawling, worm-like creature has pointy legs and an array of sharp spines on its back to protect against attack from above
CLOUDINA
These minute creatures exhibit the first shells, indicating the start of an evolutionary arms race as a variety of life explodes in the Cambrian seas
LAST UNIVERSAL COMMON ANCESTOR (LUCA)
Genetic replicators are surrounded by cell walls forming simple bacteria. They may have emerged between sheets of silicate rocks near underwater hydrothermal vents
CHOANOFLAGELLATES
These single-celled eukaryotes team up in filaments and colonies, marking the first attempts at multicellular living in animals
PYRITE
A mineral formed from sulphurous vents that helps catalyse bio-chemical reactions
STROMATOLITES: Rocky sedimentary structures provide habitats for colonies of oxygen-producing cyanobacteria
ACOELA
SPONGES
EDIACARAN BIOTA
CLOUDINA
OPABINIA
OLENOIDES
HALLUCIGENIA
ANOMALOCARIS
CO
VAUXIA: A branching sponge
PIKAIA: An eel-like animal that may be an ancestor to verte animals (chordates)
Rising magma from the Earth's mantle causes the sea floor to split apart, breaking the crust into myriad mobile tectonic plates
OCEANIC CRUST: When magma comes into contact with sea water, it cools into dense igneous rock, the most common of which is basalt. As more magma exudes, the oceanic crust is gradually pushed ac Eventually the oceanic crust subducts under the less dense but thicker continental crust, returning it to the Earth's mantle where it melts back into magma (the Wilson cycle). As a result oceanic crust is n
4.5 Bn
4.25 Bn
4.0 Bn
3.75 Bn
3.5 Bn
3.25 Bn
3.0 Bn
2.75 Bn
2.5 Bn
2.25 Bn
2.0 Bn
1.75 Bn
1.5 Bn
1.25 Bn
1.0 Bn
750 M
640 M
620 M
600 M
580 M
560 M
540 M
535 M
530 M
525 M
520 M
515 M
510 M
505 M
1 unit = 0.25 billion (Bn) years
1 unit = 20 million (M) years
1 unit = 5 million (M) years

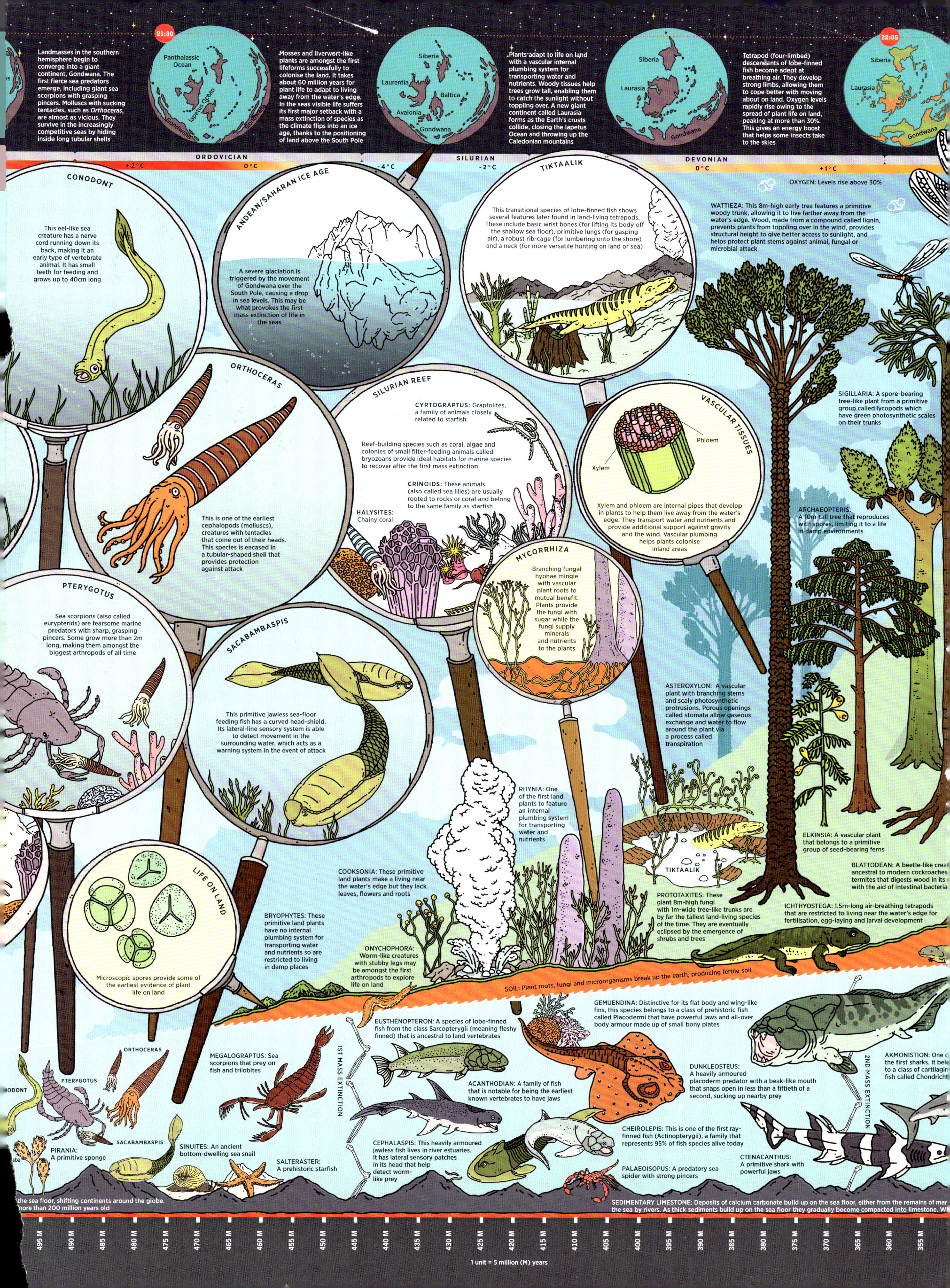
21:30
Landmasses in the southern hemisphere begin to converge into a giant continent, Gondwana. The first fierce sea predators emerge, including giant sea scorpions with grasping pincers. Molluscs with sucking tentacles, such as Orthoceras, are almost as vicious. They survive in the increasingly competitive seas by hiding inside long tubular shells
Panthalassic Ocean
Iapetus Ocean
Gondwana
Gondwana
Mosses and liverwort-like plants are amongst the first lifeforms successfully to colonise the land. It takes about 60 million years for plant life to adapt to living away from the water's edge. In the seas visible life suffers its first major setback with a mass extinction of species as the climate flips into an ice age, thanks to the positioning of land above the South Pole
Siberia
Laurentia
Baltica
Avalonia
Gondwana
Plants adapt to life on land with a vascular internal plumbing system for transporting water and nutrients. Woody tissues help trees grow tall, enabling them to catch the sunlight without toppling over. A new giant continent called Laurasia forms as the Earth's crusts collide, closing the Iapetus Ocean and throwing up the Caledonian mountains
Siberia
Laurasia
Gondwana
Tetrapod (four-limbed) descendants of lobe-finned fish become adept at breathing air. They develop strong limbs, allowing them to cope better with moving about on land. Oxygen levels rapidly rise owing to the spread of plant life on land, peaking at more than 30%. This gives an energy boost that helps some insects take to the skies
22:05
Siberia
Laurasia
Gondwana
ORDOVICIAN
+2°C
0°C
-4°C
SILURIAN
-2°C
DEVONIAN
0°C
+1°C
OXYGEN: Levels rise above 30%
CONODONT
This eel-like sea creature has a nerve cord running down its back, making it an early type of vertebrate animal. It has small teeth for feeding and grows up to 40cm long
ANDEAN/SAHARAN ICE AGE
A severe glaciation is triggered by the movement of Gondwana over the South Pole, causing a drop in sea levels. This may be what provokes the first mass extinction of life in the seas
TIKTAALIK
This transitional species of lobe-finned fish shows several features later found in land-living tetrapods. These include basic wrist bones (for lifting its body off the shallow sea floor), primitive lungs (for gasping air), a robust rib-cage (for lumbering onto the shore) and a neck (for more versatile hunting on land or sea)
WATTIEZA: This 8m-high early tree features a primitive woody trunk, allowing it to live farther away from the water's edge. Wood, made from a compound called lignin, prevents plants from toppling over in the wind, provides structural height to give better access to sunlight, and helps protect plant stems against animal, fungal or microbial attack
ORTHOCERAS
This is one of the earliest cephalopods (molluscs), creatures with tentacles that come out of their heads. This species is encased in a tubular-shaped shell that provides protection against attack
SILURIAN REEF
CYRTOGRAPTUS: Graptolites, a family of animals closely related to starfish
Reef-building species such as coral, algae and colonies of small filter-feeding animals called bryozoans provide ideal habitats for marine species to recover after the first mass extinction
CRINOIDS: These animals (also called sea lilies) are usually rooted to rocks or coral and belong to the same family as starfish
HALYSITES: Chainy coral
VASCULAR TISSUES
Phloem
Xylem
Xylem and phloem are internal pipes that develop in plants to help them live away from the water's edge. They transport water and nutrients and provide additional support against gravity and the wind. Vascular plumbing helps plants colonise inland areas
SIGILLARIA: A spore-bearing tree-like plant from a primitive group called lycopods which have green photosynthetic scales on their trunks
ARCHAEOPTERIS: A 10m-tall tree that reproduces with spores, limiting it to a life in damp environments
MYCORRHIZA
Branching fungal hyphae mingle with vascular plant roots to mutual benefit. Plants provide the fungi with sugar while the fungi supply minerals and nutrients to the plants
PTERYGOTUS
Sea scorpions (also called eurypterids) are fearsome marine predators with sharp, grasping pincers. Some grow more than 2m long, making them amongst the biggest arthropods of all time
SACABAMBASPIS
This primitive jawless sea-floor feeding fish has a curved head-shield. Its lateral-line sensory system is able to detect movement in the surrounding water, which acts as a warning system in the event of attack
ASTEROXYLON: A vascular plant with branching stems and scaly photosynthetic protrusions. Porous openings called stomata allow gaseous exchange and water to flow around the plant via a process called transpiration
RHYNIA: One of the first land plants to feature an internal plumbing system for transporting water and nutrients
TIKTAALIK
ELKINSIA: A vascular plant that belongs to a primitive group of seed-bearing ferns
BLATTODEAN: A beetle-like crea
ancestral to modern cockroaches
termites that digests wood in its
with the aid of intestinal bacteria
LIFE ON LAND
Microscopic spores provide some of the earliest evidence of plant life on land
COOKSONIA: These primitive land plants make a living near the water's edge but they lack leaves, flowers and roots
BRYOPHYTES: These primitive land plants have no internal plumbing system for transporting water and nutrients so are restricted to living in damp places
ONYCHOPHORA: Worm-like creatures with stubby legs may be amongst the first arthropods to explore life on land
PROTOTAXITES: These giant 8m-high fungi with 1m-wide tree-like trunks are by far the tallest land-living species of the time. They are eventually eclipsed by the emergence of shrubs and trees
ICHTHYOSTEGA: 1.5m-long air-breathing tetrapods that are restricted to living near the water's edge for fertilisation, egg-laying and larval development
SOIL: Plant roots, fungi and microorganisms break up the earth, producing fertile soil
ORTHOCERAS
PTERYGOTUS
ODONT
SACABAMBASPIS
PIRANIA: A primitive sponge
MEGALOGRAPTUS: Sea scorpions that prey on fish and trilobites
SINUITES: An ancient bottom-dwelling sea snail
SALTERASTER: A prehistoric starfish
1ST MASS EXTINCTION
EUSTHENOPTERON: A species of lobe-finned fish from the class Sarcopterygii (meaning fleshy finned) that is ancestral to land vertebrates
ACANTHODIAN: A family of fish that is notable for being the earliest known vertebrates to have jaws
CEPHALASPIS: This heavily armoured jawless fish lives in river estuaries. It has lateral sensory patches in its head that help detect worm-like prey
GEMUENDINA: Distinctive for its flat body and wing-like fins, this species belongs to a class of prehistoric fish called Placodermi that have powerful jaws and all-over body armour made up of small bony plates
DUNKLEOSTEUS: A heavily armoured placoderm predator with a beak-like mouth that snaps open in less than a fiftieth of a second, sucking up nearby prey
CHEIROLEPIS: This is one of the first ray-finned fish (Actinopterygii), a family that represents 95% of fish species alive today
PALAEOISOPUS: A predatory sea spider with strong pincers
CTENACANTHUS: A primitive shark with powerful jaws
2ND MASS EXTINCTION
AKMONISTION: One c
the first sharks. It bel
to a class of cartilagin
fish called Chondricht
the sea floor, shifting continents around the globe.
more than 200 million years old
SEDIMENTARY LIMESTONE: Deposits of calcium carbonate build up on the sea floor, either from the remains of mar
the sea by rivers. As thick sediments build up on the sea floor they gradually become compacted into limestone. W
495 M
490 M
485 M
480 M
475 M
470 M
465 M
460 M
455 M
450 M
445 M
440 M
435 M
430 M
425 M
420 M
415 M
410 M
405 M
400 M
395 M
390 M
385 M
380 M
375 M
370 M
365 M
360 M
355 M
1 unit = 5 million (M) years

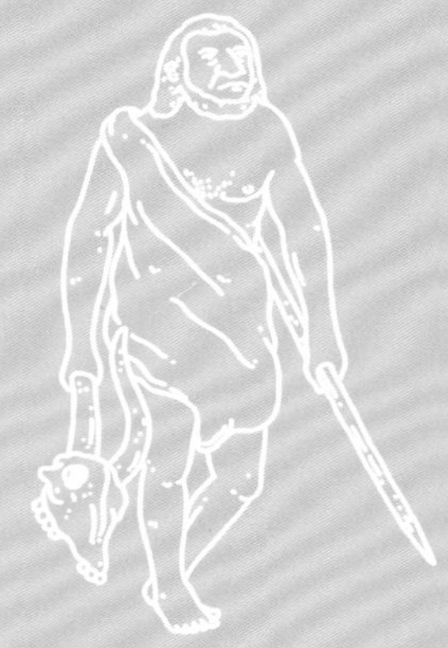

Huge millipede-like arthropods roam the land beneath a canopy of fast-growing, tall woody trees. Giant carnivorous dragonflies dominate the skies, their bodies swollen in size by high levels of atmospheric oxygen. Swamps are filled with half-decayed trees. These are eventually transformed by geological processes into seams of energy-rich coal
Siberia
Laurasia
Gondwana
Reptiles lay hard-shelled eggs, freeing them of the need to return to the water to breed. Water-tight skins also protect them from dehydration, making them perfectly suited to dominating life on land. Some larger reptiles have strange-looking sail-like backbones that help regulate their body temperature. Others adapt to eating vegetation not meat
Siberia
Laurasia
Gondwana
The Earth's landmasses converge into a giant supercontinent, Pangaea. A mass extinction, perhaps caused by a meteorite strike in Antarctica and/or an increase in volcanic activity, heats up the atmosphere, triggering the release of vast quantities of frozen methane from the sea floor. This gas reacts with oxygen, reducing levels to as little as 12%
22:40
Urals
Panthalassa
Pangaea
Slowly life recovers from the trauma of its worst ever mass extinction. Mammal-like reptiles such as *Lystrosaurus* are able to thrive thanks to their capacity for living in low-oxygen environments. Reptiles called archosaurs with larger, stronger jaw muscles gradually come to dominate life on land. Other reptiles experiment with returning to a life in the seas
Pangaea
Paleo-Tethys Ocean
CARBONIFEROUS
PERMIAN
TRIASSIC
-3°C
-2°C
+2°C
MEGANEURA: Giant dragonfly-like insects with wingspans of up to 75cm take to the skies and become top carnivorous predators. Increasing levels of atmospheric oxygen allow these creatures to grow bigger and make the air more dense, permitting easier flight
KAROO ICE AGE: Alpine glaciers spread out over highland areas, covering much of the southern hemisphere in ice
OXYGEN: Levels fall
PETEINOSAURUS: One of the first pterosaurs (flying reptiles) with a 60cm wingspan
PERMIAN MASS EXTINCTION: As many as 96% of marine species and 76% of land species die off. Victims include trilobites, sea scorpions, acanthodians, *Dimetrodon* and *Edaphosaurus*. *Calamites*, *Glossopteris* and *Lepidodendron* trees fall into decline
ROSAMYGALE: The first funnel-web spider
3RD MASS EXTINCTION
LEPIDODENDRON: These fast-growing trees dominate Carboniferous forests and grow up to 30m tall. They capture sunlight for photosynthesis using needle-like microphylls instead of true leaves
GLOSSOPTERIS: These 30m-high woody seed-ferns dominate forests across the southern hemisphere
CADDISFLIES: Moth-like insects with two pairs of hairy wings
PLEUROMEIA: A 2m-tall lycopod tree that thrives in saltmarshes
CYNOGNATHUS: A mammal-like reptile with worldwide distribution that can breathe and swallow simultaneously
CALAMITES: A 30m-high tree with needle-shaped leaves that's closely related to modern horsetails. It has a hollow trunk and vertical ribbing, making it look like bamboo
MEDULLOSA: A primitive seed-bearing tree. The extra food and protective casing of a seed means these plants can reproduce more effectively in dry, inland environments
DIMETRODON: This synapsid carnivorous predator is more like a mammal than a reptile, with an opening in the skull behind each eye. Its sail-like back may have helped it regulate body temperature
PULMONOSCORPIUS: A giant scorpion and top land predator that grows up to 1m long
EDAPHOSAURUS: A mammal-like reptile with a sail on its back. It is one of the earliest large plant-eating vertebrates, filling out the terrestrial ecosystem
THRINAXODON: This mammal-like reptile has molar and canine teeth for chewing and biting food. It feeds its young with milk
EORAPTOR: The oldest known saurischian dinosaur, a group with an offshoot that eventually evolves into birds
ARTHROPLEURA: A giant plant-eating arthropod from the myriapod family, which includes millipedes and centipedes. It grows to more than 2m in length owing to high concentrations of oxygen in the air
SCUTOSAURUS: A massive 2.5m-long armour-plated herbivorous reptile with flattened teeth that can grind up leaves. Bellowing noises are sounded as signals to mates or to warn against attack
HYLONOMUS: An early 20cm-long insect-eating reptile that lays hard-shelled eggs, allowing it to reproduce inland where the chances of survival are greater
EUPARKERIA: This small archosaur-like reptile, possibly ancestral to dinosaurs, is one of the first creatures to walk on two feet
The earliest known harvestman spider (opilionid)
EOPHALANGIUM SHEARI
ERYOPS: This 2m-long predatory amphibian is well adapted to living on land, with a strong backbone and recessed jawbones that make a rudimentary ear
LYSTROSAURUS: This mammal-like dicynodont reptile with a large lung capacity survives the trauma of the Permian Mass Extinction thanks to its ability to tolerate low oxygen environments
PISANOSAURUS: The oldest known beaked dinosaur (from a group called Ornithischians) with a bird-like hip joint and a downward-facing pubic bone
SPHENOPHYLLUM: A vine-like shrub with triangular leaves that resembles modern horsetails. It reproduces using cones and spores
DEAD WOOD: Half-rotten trunks of *Lepidodendron*, *Calamites* and *Glossopteris* gradually sink in swamps and are eventually crushed into energy-rich seams of coal
DIICTODON: A small mammal-like reptile that uses tusks to dig for food and to build burrows to shelter from the scorching sun
NOTOCUPOIDES: An early beetle
COAL SEAM
COAL SEAM
COAL GAP
TRIADOBATRACHUS: A primitive frog-like amphibian
BALANERPETON: A small, semi-aquatic creature with high-frequency hearing
ESSEXELLA: A jellyfish that captures prey using stinging tentacles
DIPLOCAULUS: A 1m-long newt-like creature with an arrow-shaped head that prevents predators from swallowing it too easily
LEAF BEETLE
Insects become premier pollinators for many plants and trees
Methane erupts from the sea floor as the global climate warms. It reacts with the air, reducing oxygen levels to as low as 12%, triggering a mass extinction of species
GNATHORHIZA: A lungfish that can survive in dried-out river estuaries and coastal regions
LIMULITELLA: An ancient horseshoe crab that ventures into rivers and estuaries
TANYSTROPHEUS: A semi-aquatic reptile with an enormously long neck for catching fish
CARDIOSUCTOR: A lobe-finned fish that resembles the modern coelacanth
BELETELSON: A shrimp-like crustacean
CERESIOSAURUS: This seal-like reptile is one of the first to re-adapt to living in the sea as well as on land
BELANTSEA: A leaf-shaped cartilaginous fish that feeds off sponges and sea lilies
GASTRIOCERAS: Ammonoid cephalopods (closely related to octopus and squid) first appear in the Devonian Period. They become highly successful thanks to their characteristic coiled shells that provide a safe place to hide when under attack
SAURICHTHYS: A ray-finned fish that feeds on the corpses of fish-eating pterosaurs. It is ancestral to modern sturgeons
CERATITES: A Triassic ammonoid
PUNCTARIOPSIS: Brown algae with leaf-like blades
TULLIMONSTRUM: A soft-bodied invertebrate that uses a long proboscis for teasing out food from beneath the sea floor
AVICULOPECTEN: Bivalve molluscs that belong to the same family as scallops, clams, oysters and mussels
e animals such as crinoids (sea lilies) and corals or via the precipitation of chemicals washed into
en limestone is crushed by further geological processes, it metamorphoses into marble
345 M
340 M
335 M
330 M
325 M
320 M
315 M
310 M
305 M
300 M
295 M
290 M
285 M
280 M
275 M
270 M
265 M
260 M
255 M
252 M
249 M
246 M
243 M
240 M
237 M
234 M
231 M
228 M
225 M
222 M
1 unit = 5 million (M) years
1 unit = 3 million (M) years

22:56
Archosaurs diversify into crocodile and lizard-like forms, the most successful of which are 'dinosaurs' (meaning 'terrible lizards'). For 175 million years these creatures, defined as land-living and with legs that point directly beneath their bodies, are the most successful on Earth. Mammals stay small, skulking in the shadows, keeping out of harm's way
Pangaea begins to split apart
A fourth mass extinction spells doom for many non-dinosaur archosaurs. More reptiles return to the seas where they evolve into fierce marine predators. Pterosaurs ('winged lizards') launch into the skies from the forests, where Carboniferous-era lycopods and clubmosses are slowly eclipsed by seed-bearing conifers, gingkos and cycads
Laurasia
Tethys Sea
Gondwana
Mammals survive in a world dominated by dinosaurs thanks to a range of adaptations. Fur insulates their bodies so they can hunt at night when the dinosaurs are asleep. Many give birth to live young, rather than lay eggs that might otherwise be eaten. Feeding with breast milk means they do not have to leave their offspring exposed when danger lurks
Laurasia
Tethys Sea
Gondwana
Giant sauropod dinosaurs such as *Diplodocus* roam the Cretaceous landscape. *Archaeopteryx*, the oldest known dinosaur with feathery wings, takes to the skies, ushering in the era of birds. The first flowering plants splash the landscape with colour, attracting insects, birds and mammals with their sugary nectar and juicy fruits
Tethys Sea
Gondwana splits up
Antarctica
0 °C
-1 °C
-2 °C
JURASSIC
SAWFLY: The earliest member of the order Hymenoptera, the family to which modern wasps, bees and ants belong
DIMORPHODON: A big-headed pterosaur with a wingspan of about 1.5m
ARAUCARIA: A tall monkey-puzzle tree with spiky, zaggedy branches designed to bamboozle the plant-eating, long-necked sauropods. Over millions of years the half-rotted remains of monkey puzzles are transformed into the easy-to-carve mineral jet
ARCHAEOPTERYX: A primitive bird about the size of a raven but with dinosaur features such as sharp teeth, three-fingered claws and a long bony tail
TEMPSKYA: A unique design of tree with a false trunk of branching stems
VOLATICOTHERIUM: An insect-eating mammal that glides through the air like a modern flying squirrel
IGUANODON: A bulky herbivorous dinosaur with vicious thumb spikes for warding off predators
RAUCARIOXYLON: hese massive 60m-high rees populate the north-west orner of Pangaea
m-high s its leaves ous), helps he warm
POSTOSUCHUS: An archosaur that has two holes on either side of its skull (diapsid). This allows a stronger, more muscular bite. Crocodiles, dinosaurs and birds all belong to this family
ARCHAEOLEPIS MANE: The earliest known member of the butterfly/moth family (Lepidoptera)
ALLOSAURUS: A giant 12m-high theropod dinosaur with one of the most powerful bites of any creature that has ever lived
DIPLODOCUS: At 27m long from head to tail, this sauropod giant feeds off trees, ferns and bushes. Its huge size provides protection against carnivore attack
GINGKO: These trees spread throughout the Jurassic but decline thereafter – only one species remains today
PLATEOSAURUS: An early herbivorous prosauropod dinosaur (one of the first long-necked species) and among the first to grow to a gigantic size (up to 10m long)
STEGOSAURUS: A 9m-long, heavily armoured herbivore with a spiked tail for whipping predators. Its 80g brain may be the smallest amongst dinosaurs
DILOPHOSAURUS: A 6m-long theropod with three toes on each foot and a pair of rounded crests on its head
MEGALOSAURUS: The first dinosaur – a large meat-eating theropod – to be discovered, described and named by humans
SCELIDOSAURUS: An early heavily armoured 4m-long herbivorous dinosaur with leaf-shaped teeth
KENTROSAURUS: A herbivorous stegosaurid dinosaur with a double row of spiky plates on its back to deter predators
ANTARTICYCAS: These shrubs are related to modern cycads. They are well adapted to living in polar regions where sunlight is dim
PLACERIAS: A herbivorous mammal-like reptile that belongs to the same group as *Lystrosaurus*
4TH MASS EXTINCTION
TYPOTHORAX: A heavily armoured 2.5m-long herbivorous reptile that searches for food by digging up soil
HETERODONTOSAURUS: A small, fast-moving herbivorous dinosaur with large canine teeth and five-fingered 'hands' for grasping food
HENKELOTHERIUM: A primitive mammal ancestral to placentals and marsupials that has good high-frequency hearing
ARCHIDERMAPTERA: The earliest form of earwig
MEGAZOSTRODON: The first true mammal. This small, furry animal hunts at night and eats insects and small lizards
FRUITAFOSSOR: A small, burrowing, ant-eating mammal
HALDANODON: A mouse-sized mammal with a long, narrow snout
TERMITES
Worker
Soldier
Queen
These nest-building insects are descended from cockroaches and develop complex social organisations. Their bodies adapt to perform different functions, such as worker (for building), soldier (for defending) or queen (for breeding)
LAPPARENTOPHIS: An early burrowing snake – reptiles that are descended from lizards
PARAPLACODUS: A 4.5m-long marine reptile with crushing toothplates that allow it to feed almost entirely on shellfish
PROSALIRUS: This frog-like amphibian appears 55 million years before *Sanyanlichan*, the first modern frog
STENEOSAURUS: A 4.8m crocodile with an elongated snout that attacks shoals of fish from below
CASTOROCAUDA: A small, semi-aquatic mammal that looks similar to the modern beaver, otter and platypus
STASAURUS: A large air-thing marine reptile that erficially resembles a dolphin
ICHTHYOSAURUS: A 2m-long marine reptile that gives birth to live young (viviparous)
DIATOMS
These microscopic algae form a major component of the sea's food chain, essential for the survival of many molluscs and fish. They are encased in porous cell walls made from silica. Some are cylindrical, others are elongated
PROTEROCTOPUS: A small, primitive octopus – the earliest that is known
HYBODUS: A 2m-long predatory shark with a varied diet and two rows of teeth
HYPERLIOCERAS: A Jurassic ammonite
BELEMNITE: A squid-like cephalopod with 10 arms but no tentacles. It uses a series of hooks for grabbing prey
DOLLOCARIS: A large crustacean with bulbous compound eyes
PLESIOSAURUS: A 5m-long marine reptile with a small head, long neck and turtle-shaped body that feeds off fish and belemnites
AEGER: Ancient prawns
PSEUDOGLYPHEA: A primitive lobster
BOSITRA: A small, well-protected clam that swims by clapping its shells
219 M
216 M
213 M
210 M
207 M
204 M
201 M
198 M
195 M
192 M
189 M
186 M
183 M
180 M
177 M
174 M
171 M
168 M
165 M
162 M
159 M
156 M
153 M
150 M
147 M
144 M
141 M
138 M
135 M
132 M
1 unit = 3 million (M) years

Rising magma in deep sea trenches forces parts of Gondwana to begin to split into Africa and South America, separated by a growing expanse of ocean. Animal and plant species are isolated on giant continental rafts, diversifying as climates change. 'Monocot' plants pioneer a radical new pattern of growth by sprouting outwards from a central bud
Pacific
Africa
Eurasia
Antarctica
Coccolithophores, microscopic lifeforms with calcium carbonate shells, proliferate in the Cretaceous seas, falling to the sea floor as sediment that eventually turns to chalk. The climate begins to cool as the continents slowly shuffle around the globe. Antarctica heads towards the South Pole while India breaks loose on a journey north-east
Eurasia
Africa
S America
India breaks off Africa
Antarctica
Tyrannosaurus and *Triceratops* are among the last 'terrible lizards' to wander the Earth as the world lurches towards a fifth mass extinction. This one wipes out all non-avian dinosaurs, pterosaurs and all the marine reptiles, but birds, crocodiles, turtles and mammals scramble through. The world now offers fresh ecological possibilities for the survivors
23:39
Eurasia
Atlantic
Africa
India
S America
Australia
Although fallout from the meteorite impact triggers an ecological catastrophe, small mammals seize the opportunities of a new dawn. Free from the fear of dinosaur attack, they now begin to grow larger, hunt in the daytime and diversify into forms we are familiar with today
India collides into Asia
Antarctica
CRETACEOUS
+1°C
PALAEOCENE
+0.5°C
MICRORAPTOR: A transitional species of theropod dinosaur that may have been able to glide through the air using four feathered limbs for lift
CONFUCIUSORNIS: A crow-sized bird with a toothless beak and a short tail
MONOCOTS VS DICOTS
Two different designs of flowering plants emerge. Dicots usually have leaves with networks of veins and petals in multiples of four or five. Monocots have leaves with parallel veins and petals in multiples of three
ACANTHISITTA: Ancestral songbirds (Passeriformes) emerge in New Zealand, a family that includes blackbirds, sparrows, robins, larks, finches, warblers and wrens
QUETZALCOATLUS: A toothless pterosaur with a long, stiff neck and a wingspan of about 11m
5TH MASS EXTINCTION: A giant meteorite strike (near Mexico) and a volcanic apocalypse (in India) provoke a mass extinction that kills off the non-avian dinosaurs, pterodactyls and mosasaurs
GLOBAL WARMING: The climate warms rapidly by as much as 6°C in 20,000 years, perhaps caused by a sudden release of methane from the sea floor
PRESBYORNIS: Anseriform birds that eventually diversify into ducks, geese, swans and waterfowl
PTERANODON: A large flying reptile with a toothless beak, large cranial crest and a wingspan of more than 5m
SINODELPHYS: The earliest known marsupial is an expert at climbing trees
OVIRAPTOR: A theropod dinosaur that broods over its eggs like a chicken
PARASAUROLOPHUS: Some hadrosaurs are notable for their distinctive head-ornaments – perhaps used for identifying species
OAKS: Wind-pollinated flowering trees spread throughout the northern hemisphere
BURMACULEX: A primitive mosquito. Females suck animal blood as a source of protein for egg-making. Males feed off pollen and nectar
FIRST FLOWERS BLOOM
Flowering plants rapidly spread throughout the world
Style
Anther
Stamen
Petal
Sepal
Stigma
Ovary
SABALITES: A monocot in the palm family Arecaceae. Palm leaves grow outwards from a central elevated bud, protecting their newest growth from being grazed by animals
FORMICIUM: These giant ants grow up to 3cm long and have a wingspan of 13cm across. Ants spread across the world boosted by the spread of flowering plants
MIACIS: A carnivorous distant ancestor to cats and dogs
SINOSAUROPTERYX: One of the first dinosaurs NOT in the class of birds to have feathers, probably for body insulation
VELOCIRAPTOR: A vicious two-legged, feathered, turkey-sized dinosaur with sickle-shaped claws and jagged teeth for ripping prey
DINOSAUR EXTINCTION
PHENACODUS: A small hoofed condylarth mammal and possible forerunner of odd-toed ungulates (mammals with hooves). Modern descendants include horses, tapirs and rhinos
DEINONYCHUS: An agile predator with a sickle-shaped second toe on its hind legs for kicking prey to death
PROTOCERATOPS: A herbivorous horned dinosaur that is about the size of a sheep, with a large frilly neck
TYRANNOSAURUS REX: A fierce bipedal carnivore with a massive skull and heavy tail
DIACODEXIS: A small fruit-eating mammal and the oldest known even-toed ungulate. Modern descendants include pigs, goats, sheep, camels, deer, giraffes and cows
POLLINATION
Flowering plants, insects and mammals co-evolve to mutual advantage. Flowers provide food and sugary fruits for animals, while animals spread the plants' pollen and seeds
TRICERATOPS: A three-horned herbivorous dinosaur with a large bony frill used for both protection against predators and courtship displays
NYPA: These early palms flourish in tropical swamps, near coasts and beside tidal rivers. Fossil remains found in London clays suggest that at this time Britain enjoys a tropical climate
PLESIADAPIS: A primate-like mammal, adept at climbing trees, that evolves in North America and crosses to Europe via Greenland
FICUS: Figs are one of the earliest flowering trees in the Rosid family. They co-evolve with small species of wasps that pollinate their flowers
AMBORELLA: One of the most primitive flowering plants
SUSISUCHUS: A fast-walking reptile ancestral to modern crocodiles
MAIASAURA: A large, duck-billed herbivorous dinosaur that raises its young in nesting colonies
CORYPHODON: A 2m-long herbivorous mammal – one of the largest of its day
SANYANLICHAN: The ancestor of modern frogs
PTILODUS: A small squirrel-like mammal
EOMAIA: An early placental mammal
MAGNOLIA: An ancient flower family
TYPHA: Primitive grasses thrive in wetlands
KOOLASUCHUS: A 5m-long temnospondyl amphibian that survives in Australia long after similar creatures become extinct
COCCOLITHOPHORES
These microscopic organisms secrete hard outer plate-like shells made from calcium carbonate
ARCHELON: A giant 4m-long, 5m-wide squid-eating sea turtle that is covered in a large leathery shell
GUARINISUCHUS: Crocodiles are one of the few large reptile families to survive the dinosaur mass extinction
WAIMANU: An ancestral penguin
FORAMINIFERA
NYMPHAEALES: Water lilies are one of the oldest orders of flowering plants (angiosperms)
LEPISOSTEUS: Primitive ray-finned fish with heavily armoured scales and sharp teeth
LYCOPTERA: A small freshwater fish that feeds off plankton
ANISOCERAS: A small, spiky, U-shaped ammonite
TYLOSAURUS: This giant 15m-long predatory marine lizard, called a mosasaur, has a crocodile-like bite and razor-sharp teeth
ELASMOSAURUS: A 14m-long plesiosaur with a giant neck containing 70 vertebrae, a record for animals with backbones
OIL DEPOSITS
The remains of marine life from the Tethys Sea is trapped beneath the Earth's crust, burying what become vast deposits of Middle Eastern oil and gas
Porous rock
Non-porous rock
Gas
Gas
Oil
DASYATIS: An ancient stingray with venomous spines on its tail that belongs to the cartilaginous fishes (Chondrichthyes) – the same class as sharks
CAMPANILE: A 60cm-long giant sea snail
CLADOCYCLUS: Primitive bony fish from the family Ichthyodectidae
KRONOSAURUS: A 10m-long marine predator belonging to a family of short-necked reptiles called pliosaurs
MICRASTER: A small sea urchin with five-fold symmetry
INOCERAMUS: A 1m-wide Cretaceous clam
LOPHIUS: A monkfish that hides in the sea bed before ambushing its prey
GAULT: An ancient crab ancestral to modern species
CHALK DEPOSITS: Coccolithophores have a cooling effect on the climate by depositing dissolved carbon from the atmosphere in calcium carbonate sediments that accumulate on the sea floor. Over millions of years, these sediments are compacted into chalk
129 M
126 M
123 M
120 M
117 M
114 M
111 M
108 M
105 M
102 M
99 M
96 M
93 M
90 M
87 M
84 M
81 M
78 M
75 M
72 M
69 M
65.5 M
64 M
62.5 M
61 M
59.5 M
58 M
56.5 M
55 M
53.5 M
1 unit = 3 million (M) years

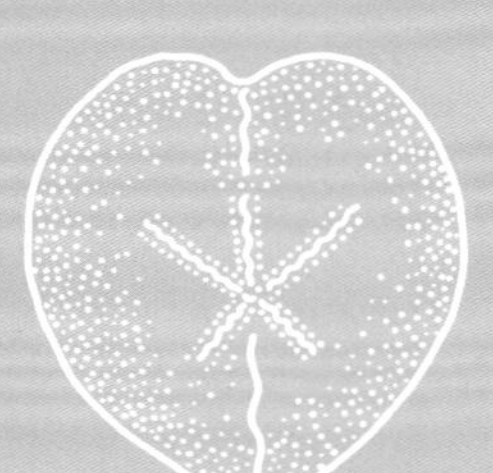

23:50
Atlantic
Tethys
Antarctic ice sheets begin to form
The climate cools further as massive volumes of atmospheric carbon dioxide dissolve in the monsoon rains thanks to the rise of the Himalayas. As Antarctica settles over the South Pole its climate is transformed from balmy warmth to deep freeze, smothering the continent in ice sheets more than 1 mile thick
Africa pushes north
Himalayas
Flowers bloom into the most successful group of plants on Earth, spreading out from the tropics. Some remain woodless and herby while others grow into tall, majestic trees. Insects diversify, often providing specialist plant pollination services. Mammals and birds eat juicy fruits, distributing the seeds of flowering plants far and wide in their nitrogen-rich dung
Pacific
Atlantic
Indian Ocean
Drake Passage
Certain types of grass adapt efficiently to a world with declining levels of atmospheric carbon dioxide. Their new process of photosynthesis, called C4, works especially well in times of drought. These and other plants eclipse many areas of forest, replacing them with grassland savannahs as the climate becomes cool and dry. Creatures adapt
Pacific
Atlantic
Indian Ocean
Antarctic ice-pack builds
EOCENE
OLIGOCENE
-1°C
MIOCENE
AEGIALORNIS: An ancestor to modern swifts and hummingbirds which is especially agile when flying
EUROPEAN ALPS: Mountains in Europe begin to rise as Africa pushes north
XENERODIOPS: Fish eating birds from the heron family
PANDION HOMALOPTERON: An early species of osprey, a large raptor with a 2m wingspan
RHIZOBIA
These symbiotic bacteria live in nodules on the roots of flowering plants from the Fabaceae family. They fertilise the plant using chemicals 'fixed' from nitrogen in the air
PRODRYAS: A North American Mapwing butterfly
PALAEOCHIROPTERYX: The first bat known to use basic echolocation (sound waves) to locate prey in the dark
GALLINULOIDES: A primitive galliform bird, an order that eventually includes turkeys, chickens, partridges and pheasants
ALPINE FLORA: Rhododendron and camellia bushes emerge in the foothills of the Himalayas
ROSACEAE: These flowering plants diversify into roses, apples, apricots, plums, cherries, peaches, pears, raspberries and strawberries
ASTERACEAE: Flowers with star-shaped, composite heads called capitulums (e.g. asters, daisies, dahlias and marigolds) spread worldwide
DEINOTHERIUM: A gigantic relative of modern elephants but with a short trunk and downward-curving tusks in the lower jaw
EUCALYPTUS: Aggressive flowering trees from the southern hemisphere that spring back to life after forest fires
PALAEOGLAUX: An ancient owl from the family of mostly nocturnal birds of prey called Strigiformes
PALAEOLAGUS: A primitive hare
ACACIA: From the Fabaceae family that also includes beans, pulses, peas, peanuts and liquorice
NOTHOFAGUS: Tall flowering trees that colonise the balmy climates of South America and Australia
PAMPAS: Grasses gradually replace forests as the Earth's climate cools and rainfall reduces
PARICTIS: The earliest known bear emerges in North America but eventually migrates to Europe, Asia and Africa when sea levels are low
BRANISELLA: New World monkeys evolve in South America and are distinctive for their flat noses and prehensile tails that they use for swinging from branches
GIRAFFOKERYX: A short-necked giraffe with two pairs of horn-like ossicones roams across Europe, Africa and Asia
PALAEOPYTHON: Snakes, like this early python, begin to diversify now the dinosaurs are extinct
DENDROPITHECUS: A gibbon-like ape that excels at swinging from the branches of trees
DARWINIUS: An early lemur-like primate in the family Adapidae
BALTIC AMBER
This sticky resin secreted from pine trees wards off infection. Over millions of years it fossilises to form amber, sometimes trapping and preserving ancient insects and flowers
DROMORNIS: This 3m-tall flightless Australian anseriform bird, related to modern geese, weighs more than half a ton
FOUR-CHAMBERED STOMACH
The ruminant digestive system allows deer, giraffes, sheep, cattle, elk, camels and bison to digest plant food more effectively
HERPETOTHERIUM: A pygmy marsupial, similar to some modern opossums that live in North America
ARSINOITHERIUM: This rhino-like herbivore has two enormous horns and lives in African swamps
DICROCERUS: This European deer may be one of the first ruminants with a four-chambered stomach
EOSIMIAS: Also known as 'dawn monkey', this primitive, small, tree-dwelling primate lives in Asia and feeds on insects
MIOHIPPUS: Horses with longer legs are better able to flee predators in more open environments
NIMRAVUS: An early sabre-toothed cat-like carnivore
PRISCILEO: This meat-eating marsupial lion inhabits Australia
HIPPARION: A modern-looking horse but with three hoofed toes on each foot – only the large middle toe reaches the ground
HARPAGOLESTES: A hyena-like placental carnivore belonging to a group of mammals called condylarths
HYAENODON: A fierce carnivorous mammal (from the order Creodonta) with a massive skull and small brain
SIVAPITHECUS: A likely ancestor to modern orangutans that spends time on the ground as well as in trees
EOMANIS: An early pangolin, the only mammal with scales, that eats termites with its very long tongue
APIDIUM: This small, fruit-eating monkey dwells in the forests of Africa
CHAMELEON: Reptiles that change their body colour
URSAVUS ELMENSIS: A European bear about the size of a small dog
PROCONSUL: A tail-less primate that resembles later apes
PAKICETUS: A carnivorous wolf-sized mammal that is ancestral to whales
PHOLIDOCERCUS: An early form of hedgehog covered in thin spines to protect it from attack
MOERITHERIUM: These hippo-like elephant relatives wallow in swamps and rivers
AMBULOCETUS: A transitional form of early whale that can walk as well as swim
PALAEOTRIONYX: A soft-shelled turtle
PEZOSIREN: A transitional species related to modern sea cows that can walk on land or swim under water
SQUALODON: A toothed whale that is able to communicate via echolocation
PUIJILA: An otter-like semi-aquatic mammal, ancestral to seals
KENTRIODON: A dolphin-like toothed whale capable of echolocation
BASILOSAURUS: A giant 18m-long ancestral whale that looks like an enormous snake. It is the largest animal of its day
MEGALODON: A giant 16m-long shark that feasts off whales
OBDURODON: A semi-aquatic mammal similar to a duck-billed platypus
CERATOICHTHYS: A prehistoric jackfish from an order called Perciformes (meaning perch-like) that includes 40% of all bony fish alive today
ANALECTIS: A brightly coloured bony fish that lives in the deep oceans
CETOTHERIUM: An early filter-feeding whale
EOBOTHUS: An early flatfish, ancestral to flounders, with both eyes on the left side of its head so it can lie hidden on the sea floor
ACORN BARNACLES: Crustaceans that attach themselves to rocks
ARCHITEUTHIS: This 13m-long squid is a deep sea giant with eight arms and two extremely long tentacles. They are hunted by sperm whales
PHYSETER: These 20m-long male sperm whales have giant heads used in courting contests.
CONTINENTAL CRUST: When two plates of continental crust collide, such as India and Asia, or Africa and Europe, the thickness of their silicate rock means they ruck upwards, creating mountain chains. Eventually these are eroded by wind and rain, often forming deserts nearby
TRIDACNA: Gigantic clams evolve in the Pacific
52 M
50.5 M
49 M
47.5 M
46 M
44.5 M
43 M
41.5 M
40 M
38.5 M
37 M
35.5 M
34 M
32.5 M
31 M
29.5 M
28 M
26.5 M
25 M
23.5 M
22 M
20.5 M
19 M
17.5 M
16 M
14.5 M
13 M
11.5 M
1 unit = 1.5 million (M) years

of apes evolves in
hat experiments with
upright in open
ds instead of
g from the branches
Walking helps them
lators at a distance,
etter across rivers and
od into storage. The
f their descendants
dramatic increase in
end possibly
d by toolmaking
The Earth starts to sink into a full-blown ice age as the joining up of North and South America whips up a new wind. The Gulf Stream causes snow to fall in the far north where a new polar ice cap forms. Subtle changes in the tilt of the Earth's axis and its orbit around the Sun provoke elongated bouts of bitter cold interspersed with shorter periods of warm weather
23:59
Gulf Stream
Creatures adapt to ice-age conditions. Some birds and butterflies (such as the Monarch) migrate, seeking better climates for breeding and feeding. Large mammals (megafauna) with tons of body fat fare best in the bitter cold. A new human species – *Homo erectus* – migrates out of Africa, across Europe and Asia, and masters the art of lighting and controlling fire
Homo erectus migrations
'Wise' people emerge in Africa, with brains four times the size of their upright walking ancestors. Bigger brains help this human species, *Homo sapiens*, become the most powerful on Earth. Despite, or possibly because of, a dramatic decline in its population these people develop a complex culture based on language, dancing, painting and music
Homo sapiens migrations
The last second
Homo sapie
last survivin
human on E
people fan
populating
Australia. B
years ago th
Americas, c
bridge whe
low. A serie
extinctions
of humans i
the America
PLIOCENE
0 °C
-3 °C
PLEISTOCENE
-3 °C
MESSINIAN SALINITY CRISIS
Africa cuts off what remains of the Tethys Sea into a basin (the Mediterranean) that dries up eight times in less than 1 million years, leaving vast deposits of salt on the sea floor
GREAT AMERICAN INTERCHANGE
As South America joins up with North America, placental mammals migrate southwards, leading to the extinction of many marsupial species. But some South American species also migrate north
SAGUARO CACTUS: This tree-sized cactus is mostly pollinated by bats and thrives in the arid deserts of North and Central America as the climate dries out
DANAUS PLEXIPPUS: Monarch butterflies migrate from Canada to Mexico and back each year, spanning as many as four butterfly generations along the way
ARCTIC TERN: A bird that migrates from pole to pole
TERATORNIS: A giant American bird of prey, related to the condor, with a wingspan of nearly 4m
MILANKOVITCH CYCLES
During the ice ages, variations in the Earth's orbit around the Sun and changes in its rotational axis trigger dramatic climate swings from interglacial hot house to glacial ice box roughly every 100,000 years
As glaci
they
of a
CASTOROIDES: A giant beaver – another example of North American ice-age megafauna
MAMMUT: Mastodons are elephant-like herbivores with giant tusks that roam freely throughout Europe and America
JRARCTOS: Ancestors
ne panda, these are
etarian bears from Asia
feast on bamboo
GIRAFFA: A deer-like ruminant with an exceptionally long neck that is useful for reaching leaves at the tops of trees
JOSEPHOARTIGASIA MONESI: A giant 3m-long rodent from South America
URSUS MARITIMUS: Polar bears emerge in the extreme north. They feast on seals
CAMELOPS: A camel that originates in North and Central America
MEGATHERIUM: A ground sloth the size of an elephant. It can stand on its hind legs to reach leaves high in the trees
MAMMUTHUS PRIMIGENIUS: Woolly mammoths, well adapted to ice-age conditions, are members of the elephant family that roam throughout the Americas, Europe and Asia
PLEISTOC
over-hunt
extinction
large man
BAMBOO: One of the fastest growing trees of all time (and member of the grass family, Poaceae) that can grow by as much as 1m a day
ELASMOTHERIUM: A giant rhino with a large horn on its forehead that lives in Europe and Asia
PROCOPTODON: A giant 2m-tall kangaroo
TOXODON: A large, hoofed mammal from South America. Charles Darwin discovers bones from this species during his round-the-world voyage on HMS *Beagle*
WONAMBI: A giant 6m-long snake that kills its prey by constriction
NYANZACHOERUS: Giant wild pigs emerge in Africa and Arabia
PANTHERA TIGRIS: Tigers emerge in Asia
MOUNT TOBA SUPERVOLCANO: A giant eruption in Sumatra plunges the Earth into a six- to nine-year-long volcanic winter
RODUS: A large, fierce
othed cat that roams
ut Europe, Asia, Africa
America
TITANIS: A giant flightless bird from North America
CHIMPANZEE: These great apes continue to live in the trees where they develop their own communications culture based on hand gestures
SYNCERUS: The African buffalo has never been successfully domesticated (unlike its distantly related Asian cousin, the water buffalo)
ORORAPITHECUS
SSINICUS: Gorillas
ve in Africa from an
estor they share
ith humans
HIPPOTRAGUS: A family of African antelope with backwardly curved horns
STRIPED HYENA: Dog-like scavengers become common throughout Europe, Asia and Africa
CANIS LEPOPHAGUS: A primitive species of wolf, possibly ancestral to grey wolves and coyotes
PANTHERA LEO: Lions emerge in Africa
HOMO ERECTUS: Humans with a brain size of about 900cm³. They migrate out of Africa and spread across Europe, Asia and the Middle East
SAHELANTHROPUS: An early hominin that may or may not have walked on two feet
HOMO HABILIS: Short humans with long arms and a brain size of about 600cm³. They make primitive tools using their freely available hands for skinning hides and butchering meat
FIRE: Humans thrive by keeping warm and cooking meat, killing harmful microbes
AUSTRALOPITHECUS AFARENSIS: These slender hominins emerge in Africa and are probably the first apes able to walk on two feet. Their brains are small (about 400cm³)
HOMO NEANDERTHALENSIS: These stocky humans are well adapted to living in cold north European ice-age climates. Their brain size is about 1,400cm³
HIPPOCAMPUS: Seahorses live in shallow, tropical waters
WHALESONG: Whales communicate over long distances using haunting song-like sounds
MEGALANIA: A giant 7m-long Australian lizard
REEF-BUILD
Tentacles
Stomach
Aquatic, flightless
vings adapted into
swimming
ORCINUS ORCA: Killer whales feed off fish, sharks and mammals (e.g. seals, walruses and even whales). They are highly social and evolve a sophisticated communications culture based on echolocation
BALAENOPTERA MUSCULUS: This filter-feeding blue whale grows to more than 33m long, making it the largest animal of all time
ONCORHYNCHUS: Plankton-eating salmon swim off the Pacific coast of North America
5.5 M
5.0 M
4.8 M
4.6 M
4.4 M
4.2 M
4.0 M
3.8 M
3.6 M
3.4 M
3.2 M
3.0 M
2.8 M
2.6 M
2.4 M
2.2 M
2.0 M
1.8 M
1.6 M
1.4 M
1.2 M
1.0 M
800 K
600 K
400 K
200 K
100 K
90 K
80 K
70 K
1 unit = 0.2 million (M) years
1 unit

23:59
59 secs
before midnight
s becomes the
species of
rth. These
ut of Africa,
urope, Asia and
about 14,000
ey reach the
ossing a land
sea levels are
of catastrophic
ollow the arrival
Australia and
Pleistocene extinctions
People living in river valleys master the art of growing food by cultivating crops and domesticating animals. Towns and cities spring up for storage and trade. Success for other species increasingly depends on pleasing humanity. Winners are those that taste good, provide material comfort, keep people company, instil pleasurable sensations, or look beautiful
Fertile Crescent
Waves of conquest result in the spread of species far from their natural habitats. Sugarcane, oranges, bananas, coffee and rice come across from Asia and Africa to Europe with the rise of Islam. European conquests diffuse peanuts, potatoes, tomatoes, squashes, sunflowers, tobacco, chocolate and maize from the Americas to Europe and Asia
Human populations, boosted by advanced agricultural techniques, artificial fertilisers and genetic modification, climb exponentially towards 7 billion individuals, growing at an average net increase of 219,000 every day. Such success comes at a great ecological cost, provoking what many experts claim is the start of a sixth mass extinction of species
HOLOCENE
ANTHROPOCENE
-4 °C
-1 °C
MEDIEVAL WARM PERIOD
0 °C
-2 °C
LITTLE ICE AGE
GLOBAL WARMING
U-SHAPED VALLEY
rs advance and recede
hange the contours
ine valleys from a
/ to a U shape
YOUNGER DRYAS EVENT: A sudden reversion to ice-age conditions lasts more than 1,000 years, triggering a food supply crisis. This may explain why Natufian people in the Middle East experiment with cultivating crops and taming animals for survival
HONEY BEES: Egyptian farmers keep bees in man-made hives for making honey
SMOG: Vast quantities of coal are burned for fuelling fires, powering trains and generating electricity. Smog becomes a major health hazard in big cities
FELIS SILVESTRIS: Cats protect people's grain supplies from attack by rodents. In return, people provide cats with food and shelter
FEUDALISM: Aristocratic landlords in medieval Europe bring extra land under cultivation as the climate warms. Populations increase
EARTHWORMS: Thanks to the fertilising power of earthworms, Egyptian farmers are able to take three months off each year to build funereal pyramids for their pharaohs
ORANGES AND LEMONS: Citrus fruits, originally from China, are brought to Europe by Portuguese explorers who cultivate the sweetest varieties
TOBACCO: An addictive Native American plant that unleashes a plague of cancer after it is transported by Europeans to populations worldwide
POPULATION BOOM: Modern high-rise cities such as London require farmland over 125 times bigger than the area of land they occupy to feed their enormous populations
SILKWORMS: Some Chinese people become rich after discovering how to turn the secretions of the caterpillar *Bombyx mori* into shimmering yarn for weaving silk
GRAPES: People grow specific varieties of the flowering plant *Vitis vinifera* to make wine
TEA LEAVES: Fabled Chinese emperor Shennong discovers the delights of drinking tea after a blast of wind blows a few leaves from a nearby camellia bush into his cup of hot water
OLIVE GROVES: This easy-to-grow fruit becomes the most valuable commodity in ancient Greece. Its oil is used for lighting lamps, keeping warm and cooking
DODO: European sailors hunt this flightless bird to extinction
POPPIES: British imperialists smuggle opium – extracted from poppies grown in Bengal – into China in exchange for porcelain and tea
'GREEN' REVOLUTION: Specially bred monocultures of dwarf wheat and drought-resistant rice help save the people of Mexico and India from mass famine and starvation
MEGALOCEROS GIGANTEUS: One of the largest ever deer with huge branching antlers that stretch nearly 4m across
PADDY FIELDS: Chinese peasants cultivate mutant varieties of wild rice with seeds that go soft when boiled
CHICKENS: These galliform birds are domesticated in the Far East. They become one of the world's most popular sources of protein
COFFEE: After seeing goat herder Kaldi and his flock whooping with excitement from the effects of eating coffee berries, a group of tenth-century monks in Ethiopia create a new hot drink to keep them awake for all-night prayers
SWEET AND SOUR: When Polynesian sugarcane reaches the Americas, plantations fuel demand for African slaves
CARBON DIOXIDE EMISSIONS
CO2 CONCENTRATIONS (PARTS PER MILLION)
380
320
260
0
1750
1850
2000
YEAR
FIRST FARMERS: People living in river valleys construct permanent settlements for managing farmland and storing food. They cultivate varieties of wheat with especially large seeds for grinding into flour to make bread
NE OVERKILL: A combination of
ng and climate change results in the
of as many as 33 out of 45 groups of
mals in Australia and the Americas
ARTIFICIAL FERTILISERS: German scientists pioneer the mass production of artificial fertilisers, triggering a rise in human populations
MAIZE: Native American farmers domesticate tomatoes and potatoes, and turn teosinte, a wild shrub from Mexico with hard, inedible seeds, into maize with its highly nutritious cob
COMBINE HARVESTER: Hedgerows and other ecosystems important for wildlife are cleared to make way for modern farm machinery
BANANAS: These seedless fruits spread west with the rise of Islam, eventually falling into the hands of Portuguese explorers who plant them in the Canaries and then in the Caribbean
EARLY TRACTOR: Diesel-powered machines become the new workhorses on modern farms
CANIS DOMESTICUS: People tame this sub-species of the grey wolf into a compliant animal that herds sheep, guards against attack and pulls sleds
CARROTS: Sixteenth-century Dutch botanists cross-breed yellow and purple varieties into deep orange in honour of their founder king, William of Orange
COWS: Wild aurochs are domesticated into cows. Those with the biggest udders are bred for producing milk. Those with the fleshiest rumps are turned into steaks
ULATION CRASH:
Toba eruption
account for the
uction of the
no sapiens
ulation in Africa
s few as 1,000
eding pairs
POWER STATIONS: Generating electricity by burning fossil fuels releases billions of tonnes of global warming gases, including carbon dioxide, into the atmosphere each year
SHEEP: The tamest flocks of sheep with the woolliest fleeces are carefully selected by farmers for making felt and woollen clothes. These animals are also popular to eat
CAMELS: These desert creatures are domesticated by Middle Eastern traders for transporting salt, spices and gold
MULES: Infertile crosses between horses and donkeys are especially robust, making them ideal beasts of burden
FULL STEAM AHEAD: Steam powers engines for ploughing, threshing and sewing, reducing a farmer's reliance on animal power and increasing agricultural yield
HOMO SAPIENS: A human species that emerges in Africa *c.* 160,000 years ago and eventually populates the entire world, displacing all other hominins. It develops a complex culture based on hunting, language, music, dancing and art
PIGS: Swineherds living in Asia and the Near East domesticate wild boars into pigs – creatures that become one of the most popular sources of protein
HORSES AND PLOUGHS: Collar harnesses from the Middle East and iron ploughs from China make horses the animals of choice for ploughing fields in medieval Europe
GOLD RUSH: Deep mines are dug to extract gold, diamonds, iron ore and coal across Europe, Africa, America, China and Australia
OIL RIG AND PIPELINE: Deep-sea drilling greatly increases the volume of oil and gas available to power the modern world, but ecological disasters like the Gulf of Mexico oil spill in 2010 are unintended consequences
BRONZE AGE
Middle Eastern metal-smiths discover that harder tools and weapons can be forged by smelting together copper and tin to make an alloy, bronze
COPPER AGE
People in Europe and the Middle East experiment with making tools out of smelted copper instead of stone. Their industry signals the beginning of mining the Earth for its mineral resources
IRON AGE
Crude techniques for smelting iron ore allow the creation of stronger metallic instruments for use in agriculture or war
Iron ore
Coal
Gold
KIMBERLITE PIPE: Source of diamond and other gemstones
QUARRIES: Clay dug from pits is used for baking bricks. Alum mined from quarries fixes colourful dyes for use on exotic cloths
NG CORAL POLYPS
louth
Colonies of coral polyps secrete outer skeletons that accumulate into reefs. Sometimes these structures emerge above the sea's surface, forming islands
BOTTOM TRAWLING: Diesel fishing vessels drag nets along the sea bed maximising the number of fish caught but destroying marine ecosystems
WHALING: Cosmetics and soap are made from oil extracted from the heads of sperm whales
GREAT BARRIER REEF: The world's largest living coral system emerges off the north-east coast of Australia. It eventually grows to cover 133,000 square miles, making it the only living structure clearly visible from outer space
FISH FINGERS: Cod off the east coast of America are so plentiful that fifteenth-century Basque fishermen scoop them up in buckets over the sides of their boats
60 K
50 K
40 K
30 K
20 K
10 K
9 K
8 K
7 K
6 K
5 K
4 K
3 K
2
200
400
600
800
1000
1200
1400
1600
1800
1900
1920
1940
1960
1980
2000
= 10,000 (10 K) years
1 unit = 1,000 years
Common Era (CE)
1 unit = 200 years
1 unit = 20 years

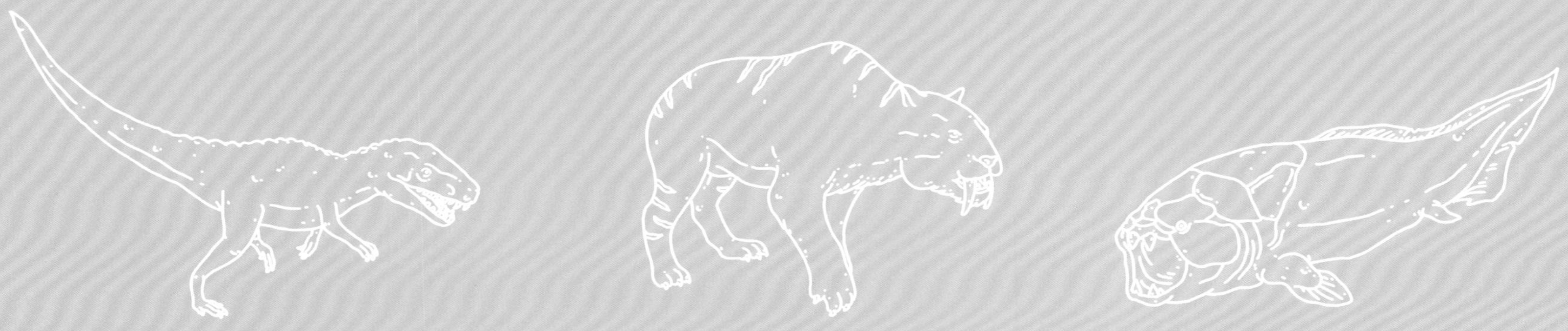

THE WALLBOOK CHRONICLE

AN EPIC EXPEDITION THROUGH THE HISTORY OF NATURAL SCIENCE

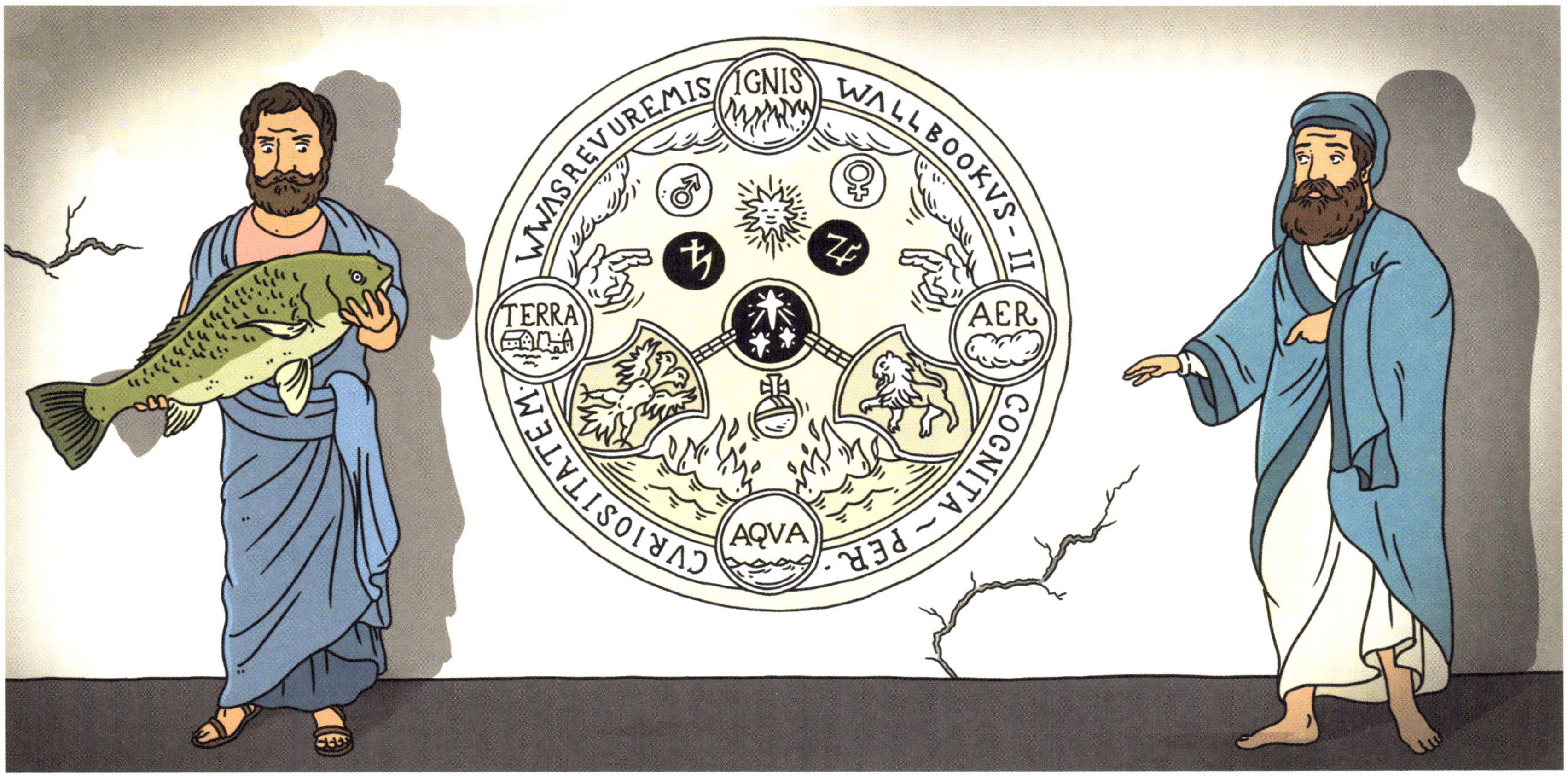

Verses tackle universal mysteries

Poet suggests that successful creatures are those best adapted for survival, and all physical matter is composed of four elements – earth, air, fire and water

BY OUR ANCIENT GREECE DESK, Sicily, c. 450 BC

WHERE DO WE come from? What is the Universe made of? These baffling questions are just a few of the topics addressed in an epic five thousand lines of poetry released yesterday by the multi-talented Greek scientist and philosopher Empedocles.

Mr Empedocles, who comes from Acragas on the southern coast of Sicily, has developed his ideas after studying the works of trailblazing philosophers such as Anaximander (died *c.*546 BC) and Pythagoras (died *c.*495 BC). Mr Anaximander, a scholar of the influential school at Miletus in Turkey, had argued that many natural phenomena could only be interpreted correctly through proper observation and investigation. He claimed that nature, like humanity, is controlled not by the will of the gods, but by a set of laws that keep the Universe in balance. By arguing that we can understand the natural world better by looking more closely at it, Mr Anaximander opened the way for major new theories, such as those now submitted by Mr Empedocles.

In his latest poem, *On Nature*, Mr Empedocles develops ideas taken from Mr Anaximander, proposing that fossils prove that animals, including humans, must in the past have come from the sea, shedding their scales along the way. He says some animals were created with strange and awkward features, such as arms without shoulders, but these died out because they were not built for survival, while others that had the right mix of body parts lived on.

One of the most important issues raised by Mr Empedocles is about the fundamental substance of the Universe. What is the real difference between iron and gold, or between a sparkling diamond and a lump of dull rock? Mr Empedocles suggests that everything in the Universe is made up of a set of basic building blocks – four elements – and that different combinations of these elements account for all the substances in the Universe. He names these four elements as earth, air, fire and water. For example, wood burns easily because it is made mostly of fire, while water and stone do not.

However, unlike Mr Anaximander, Mr Empedocles does not believe that observation alone is enough to reveal all the mysteries of the world. He maintains that we only ever see a very small part of reality, and that humans also have to think carefully to unlock the secrets underneath. Mr Empedocles believes this new rational approach will be vital if we wish better to understand the origins of the world and of ourselves.

Glorying in the natural world

Celebrated philosophers grapple with the mysteries of life during a unique summer vacation

BY OUR NATURE CORRESPONDENT,
Lesbos, 338 BC

EVERYONE KNOWS that the Greek islands are the perfect holiday destination for sunshine and sand, but few people realise that their most precious attraction may well be their indigenous flowers and animals. Our special nature correspondent caught up with the celebrated zoologist Mr Aristotle and the famous botanist Mr Theophrastus after they spent the summer investigating the Mediterranean flora and fauna.

In this imaginary conversation, he quizzes them about their recent research trip to the island of Lesbos, during which they made the first attempts to classify plants and animals. By doing so, they aim to help people to understand the richness and diversity of the natural world. He started by asking why they specifically chose Lesbos as the site of their scientific research.

Theophrastus: Well, Mr Aristotle and I met while we were both students at Mr Plato's Academy in Athens, but I'm actually a native of Lesbos, so it was my idea. I knew it would be a great place to work.

Aristotle: Things weren't going well for me at the Academy any more. After Mr Plato passed away there was a great deal of confusion and I simply couldn't get any work done. So it seemed the perfect time for a sabbatical, and just at that moment my old friend Mr Theophrastus appeared out of the blue and said, "Why don't you come to Lesbos?" The island, which is famous as the home of the love-poet Sappho, boasts a stunning lagoon, home to a huge variety of animal life. It was the perfect opportunity to get away from it all.

I was totally captivated by the lagoon. I started collecting specimens and quizzing the fishermen about the animals they came across. In the past I had followed in Mr Plato's footsteps, writing about philosophy and politics, but what struck me here was the sheer variety of species before me. I set about trying to understand all the creatures on the island and in the seas around it, putting them into categories based on their appearance and behaviour, and recording everything I could find.

Working on the island has led Mr Aristotle to some surprising conclusions. He realised that dolphins are not in fact fish but mammals – they breathe air and give birth to live young.

He has also spent time drawing and describing the biological structure of the animals he caught and dissected. He has even managed to look inside an egg and watch an embryo develop into a chick. Unlike his mentor, Mr Plato, Mr Aristotle has come to the conclusion that theory and reason can only take scholars so far, and that to test out their ideas scholars must make observations and carry out experiments to understand the world.

Meanwhile, as Mr Aristotle was in hot pursuit of creatures, Mr Theophrastus was busy making a detailed study of the island's plants.

Theophrastus: I placed them in categories and made notes about their reproductive cycles, how they were used on the island and even how they tasted. A lot of these plants were used by the islanders for healthcare, so I felt it was especially important to make a list of how to grow and produce medicines.

Mr Theophrastus hopes that this medical information might prove useful to future physicians and perhaps even save lives. His work also includes a theory on 'grafting' which will be of great interest to farmers. It allows a 'copy' of a plant with desirable features to be grown by attaching a cutting of it to the roots of another plant.

Mr Aristotle has now been called back to his homeland to teach the young prince Alexander of Macedon how to be a leader, but he and Mr Theophrastus haven't ruled out one day setting up an academy of their own.

Insatiable curiosity kills man of nature

Leading scientist's body discovered amongst thousands slaughtered by appalling volcano

BY OUR ROMAN EDITOR,
Naples, AD 79

THE DEVASTATING VOLCANIC eruption which destroyed the towns of Pompeii and Herculaneum is now known to have claimed the life of one of the Roman Empire's leading naturalists, Gaius Plinius Secundus.

Pliny, as he is better known, made lasting contributions to the field of natural philosophy through his scientific and philosophical works.

When Mount Vesuvius blew its top, it spewed out hot gas, stones and ash into the air, forming a terrifying dark cloud that fell on the land below, bombarding the densely populated region around the Bay of Naples with a hail of pumice stones. Whole cities have been buried in the thick ash.

After watching the growing cloud above Vesuvius, Mr Pliny, who was a Roman naval commander stationed on the coast, set out with his ships in a bid to try to help those fleeing the disaster. Yesterday, his body was found on a beach at Stabiae, where he had apparently died from asphyxiation. We spoke to his nephew, also called Pliny, about his famous uncle.

"It was part rescue mission, part research trip," said the younger Mr Pliny. "My uncle had friends near Vesuvius and he knew he had to help, but the eruption was also an opportunity to observe an incredible natural phenomenon close up. He even took his scribe with him to take notes along the way, right into the heart of the fire and ash. Ultimately, I guess you could say he was a victim of his own curiosity, but that was what made him so special."

The elder Mr Pliny's thirst for knowledge manifested itself in an epic thirty-seven-volume work, *Naturalis Historiae*, which has catalogued the latest scientific discoveries across a wide range of subjects including geography, geology, medicine, botany and zoology, to name just a few. Scholars regularly rank it alongside the great works of the ancient Greeks for its scientific value. Topics covered by the encyclopaedia include the organised societies of bees, and the octahedral shape and extreme hardness of natural substances such as diamonds. His book is the first to describe amber as the fossilised resin of trees and to categorise minerals into different groups. He even outlines the manufacture of perfumes from exotic plants and spices. He has devoted sixteen volumes of the encyclopaedia to botany, the study of plants.

Mr Pliny's work is a testament to his towering intellect and his insatiable passion for discovery. Although he will be much missed, his thirst for knowledge and the sheer breadth of his interests have left a lasting legacy in his unique encyclopaedia of nature.

Gladiators hold keys to medical science

BY OUR MEDICAL EDITOR,
Pergamon, AD 161

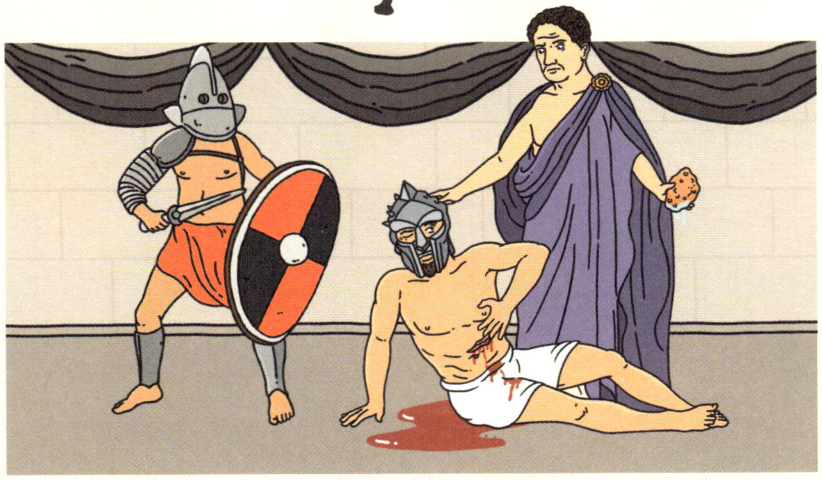

ROME'S MOST infamous and grisly entertainment, gladiatorial combat, has become the surprising source of major breakthroughs in medicine and surgery. The injuries sustained by the brave fighters are giving the medical genius Galen a close-up view on the inner workings of the human body at a time when cutting up corpses is illegal throughout the Roman Empire.

Mr Galen was born in the Greek city of Pergamon and learned his trade there in the temple of Asclepius, the god of medicine. He soon began travelling around the Roman Empire, selling his skills to the wealthy and picking up local medical techniques and theories wherever he went.

Mr Galen says that many of his medical discoveries have come from dissecting animals such as apes and pigs, but that to truly understand the human anatomy scientists need to study human bodies. So when he was offered a position as chief physician for gladiators, Mr Galen saw the chance for some exciting new research.

"Looking after the gladiators is great for my work," he says. "I get to treat all kinds of nasty wounds and disabilities you just wouldn't otherwise come across. By treating these ailments, I have learned a great deal about the body and what happens when you experiment with it."

Through observing the exhausting and dangerous lives of the gladiators, Mr Galen has come to understand the importance of proper diet and hygiene for health. He has also devised new ways of helping broken bones heal after injuries in the arena. Gladiators say they are lucky to have him – since he started looking after them four years ago, only five have died, which is a significant improvement on the record of his predecessor, during whose time sixty of their comrades died.

Mr Galen believes that good doctors should also be good philosophers. In one of his most controversial works, a study of the heart, he claims that this mysterious organ isn't the seat of the soul, as many others believe, but rather operates as a powerful pump that sends blood around the body.

Mr Galen's medical knowledge is now in hot demand. Even the Emperor, Marcus Aurelius, has said he is "*Primum sane medicorum esse, philosophorum autem solum*" – "First among doctors, unique among philosophers".

Unlocking the scientific secrets of sight

FROM OUR MAN IN THE MAGHREB,
Cairo, 1021

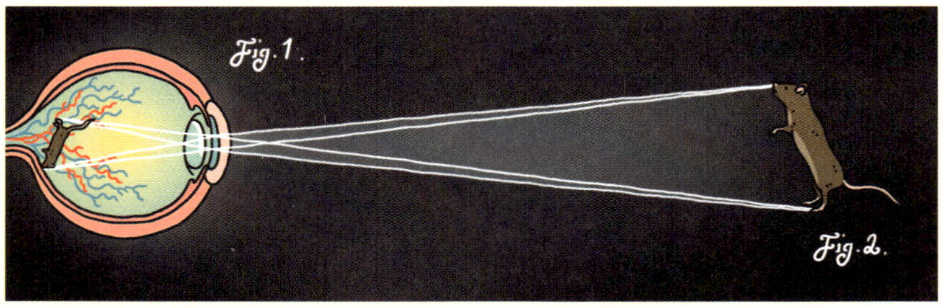

IMAGINE A TECHNOLOGY that would allow humans to zoom in so they could see the Moon and stars close up – as if they were in space! The scientist Ibn al-Haytham believes one day such a technology may be possible.

In his recent *Book of Optics*, the Muslim scholar puts forward a new theory explaining the science of how people see. Scholars believe his ideas may one day lead to the development of techniques for viewing distant objects, perhaps even the stars, close up.

Mr al-Haytham disagrees with the classical philosophers Euclid and Ptolemy, who argued that our eyes shoot out particles of light that illuminate objects, allowing us to see them. Instead, he says some objects reflect light from the Sun while others absorb it. Either way, the light that reaches our eyes is what creates the images we see. He points to the implausible notion that the eyes could light up an area as big as the night sky when they are open; it is much more likely, he says, that the Sun, Moon and stars are shining down on us.

Mr al-Haytham also discusses the concept of magnification, which has excited many scientists. Using this technique, he believes it will one day be possible to bend light so that objects look closer. Scholars hope that it might also be employed for viewing distant, mysterious objects or observing tiny creatures in fine detail.

Mr al-Haytham began his career as an engineer in Cairo, working for the Caliph. He started experimenting with optics after the failure of a huge project to control the flooding of the River Nile. After avoiding the Caliph's wrath, by pretending to be mad, Mr al-Haytham was able to focus his curiosity on the scientific investigations that have led to his groundbreaking *Book of Optics*.

House of Wisdom leaves Europe in dark

Baghdad becomes new seat of learning after caliphs order translation of ancient texts

BY OUR MIDDLE EAST EDITOR,
Baghdad, 1025

THE REDISCOVERY of ancient Greek and Roman wisdom is spurring new discoveries in medical and scientific thought throughout the Middle East. While much of Europe has been prey to intellectual drought since the fall of the Roman Empire, scholars across the Muslim world are busily translating, studying and developing ideas based on these classical ancient texts.

In Baghdad, a scholarly institution supported by the caliphate known as the House of Wisdom is now one of the largest repositories of knowledge from the ancient world. Since the introduction of convenient, affordable papermaking techniques from China, the caliphs have commissioned the translation of hundreds of texts into Arabic, ensuring that the study of science is a priority under their rule.

The works of Greek philosopher Aristotle were amongst the first to be translated, and his philosophy is now basic reading for all Muslim scholars.

Earlier this year, a doctor from Persia called Avicenna announced the release of his fourteen-volume *Canon of Medicine*. This encyclopaedia draws upon the discoveries and ideas of Aristotle and Galen to investigate the body and its various illnesses. It also details suggestions for healing and maintaining good health.

Mr Avicenna believes that exercise is key to healthy living, helping to stave off disease. He also provides information on how plants and herbs can be used as painkillers, medicines or even contraceptives.

Mr Avicenna says rigorous testing must be carried out before using any new drug or medicine. Perhaps most importantly, Mr Avicenna says new drugs should be tested on humans, not just animals, since he believes that what is good for an animal is not necessarily good for a human.

Mr Avicenna's discoveries about the human body are already being taught in libraries and schools across the Muslim world.

Other Greek, Roman, Persian and Indian works have also been translated and spread across the Arab world, leading to the rise of other centres of Muslim scholarship, for example in Córdoba in Andalucía. Here a rival government to the rulers of Baghdad was established in 756 by Abd ar-Rahman, a prince of the deposed Umayyad royal family who refused to recognise the authority of the Abbasid caliph in Damascus.

New irrigation techniques are now being deployed across Iberia to improve harvests and enable the cultivation of new crops such as watermelons, rice and bananas. Commentators consider that ever since the collapse of the Roman Empire in the fifth century AD, Christian Europe has been left far behind the Muslim world in terms of scientific understanding.

Bleeding and plants are keys to healthy life

BY OUR MEDICAL EDITOR,
Bingen, Germany, 1150

A VISIONARY female theologian, the poet and scientist Hildegard of Bingen, has just completed a new work on the human body and its ailments. The work promises to help alleviate many of the world's most pernicious afflictions and diseases.

Ms Hildegard has already proved her ample knowledge of the natural world in Physika, *a work that focuses on the medicinal properties of plants, minerals and animals. Ms Hildegard's latest work,* Causes and Cures, *lays out her specialist medical and anatomical thinking.*

In her work, Ms Hildegard recommends 'bleeding' a patient as a cure for many conditions. This technique, which involves letting bad blood flow out, has been in use since ancient Greek times, but Ms Hildegard describes in great detail how it should be done, including how much blood to take and even which phase of the Moon it should be performed under. She also presents remedies for burns, fractures, dislocations and cuts.

Ms Hildegard's strong belief is that since everything was put on Earth by God for humans to use, it is no wonder that cures for a wide variety of diseases can be found in various plants and minerals. In her book, Ms Hildegard has developed a classification system for all the organisms mentioned in the Book of Genesis.

Ms Hildegard says her inspiration has come from a series of visions that she has experienced throughout her life, as well as through the five senses – sight, hearing, taste, smell and touch – all of which she claims are gifts from God.

Renaissance man says fossils no proof of Biblical flood

BY OUR RESIDENT POLYMATH,
Monte Rosa, Switzerland, 1510

WHAT'S A FOSSIL? The origin of these strange shapes found in rocks around the globe is a mystery that has long puzzled scientists. Often they take the shape of animals and plants not found living on the Earth, seemingly frozen in time. Now a new explanation has been proffered by the celebrated Italian polymath, Leonardo da Vinci.

Mr da Vinci has dedicated much of his professional career to drawing diagrams for bizarre inventions such as helicopters, steam-powered cannons and mechanical soldiers. Now he has turned his curiosity to the natural sciences, observing birds in order to design his own flying machines and, through fossils, studying the ancient history of the Earth itself.

Perplexed by the many fossilised marine molluscs that are found high in the Alps bordering Switzerland and Italy, Mr da Vinci has pondered how these sea creatures came to be so far from water. Two common explanations exist: that a great flood sent by God submerged the mountains; or that these are formations that have simply grown in the rocks. Mr da Vinci disagrees with both theories.

"A worldwide flood is quite simply an impossibility," he says dismissively. "Where did all the water go? And as for these being an ordinary feature of the landscape, one can clearly see from the distinct layers of rock, which are laid down throughout Earth's life, that these creatures appear only at a certain time in history and bear a similarity to fossils found by the coasts."

Mr da Vinci maintains that these mountains were not always mountains – long ago this was an area of coastline or ocean, now raised high. In his view, fossils provide evidence to suggest that the Earth's shape is constantly changing.

Mr da Vinci has also been studying human anatomy, even creating the first study of a foetus in the womb, all to help him improve his painting.

"As an artist," he says, "understanding the skeleton and muscles to draw realistic figures is just as important as it is for a doctor to give the proper medicine. I have been working with physicians across Italy to create detailed drawings of the human body that will not only inform my work but also, I hope, further medical knowledge."

Dissections reveal body's secrets

THE GRUESOME DISSECTION of a human corpse took place yesterday in Basel, Switzerland, when radical surgeon Andreas Vesalius invited the public to watch him explain the inner workings of the human body. Mr Vesalius cut open the cadaver of local criminal Jakob Karrer von Gebweiler, preserving the skeleton for public display, *writes our medical editor from Switzerland on 13 May 1543.*

Mr Vesalius claims that dissecting humans, which is a long-standing taboo in many European countries, is a necessary technique for the proper study of anatomy. The Belgian surgeon hit the headlines two years ago when he pointed out that the anatomical works of the Greek physician Galen, long considered the ultimate authority, are based on flawed animal dissections.

In Mr Galen's time, the Roman Empire banned all dissection of human bodies but now, although controversial, such research is permitted. Thanks to his human dissections, Mr Vesalius has identified errors in Mr Galen's work.

For example, he has found that human jawbones are made of one hinged bone, not two as proposed by Mr Galen. As a result of Mr Galen's failings Mr Vesalius is now sceptical of relying too heavily on the classical thinkers, feeling that their lack of carefully repeated examination, and their merging of philosophy and medicine, has led to serious mistakes.

Mr Vesalius has also debunked some common misunderstandings about the body, including the belief that men have one rib fewer than women, a myth originating with the story of Adam and Eve. Mr Vesalius plans to publish his discoveries accompanied by detailed illustrations.

Pope puts man of science under arrest for astronomical challenge

BY OUR VATICAN EDITOR,
Rome, June 1633

FOR MANY CENTURIES people have considered themselves to be at the centre of God's creation, the Universe. How else could it be? Every morning the Sun appears to rise in the east and set in the west, while the Earth remains stationary at the centre.

But, astonishing as it sounds, even this most apparently obvious fact may not be what it seems. Scientific discoveries are causing some scholars to claim that the Earth is a single planet in a vast solar system, and that our globe may itself be spinning round on its axis once a day and orbiting the Sun every year. In other words, the Earth is going round the Sun, not the Sun circling the Earth!

Such beliefs are causing uproar in ecclesiastical circles, as the Italian physicist and philosopher Galileo Galilei found out yesterday, when he was arrested by Church officials who are trying to halt the spread of these new ideas. The Catholic Church first declared 'heliocentricity' – the belief that the Earth orbits the Sun – to be heretical in 1616. Officials fear such ideas may shake the very foundations of Christianity, since Church teachings have always stated that the Earth is stationary in the centre of the Universe, a concept known as 'geocentricity'.

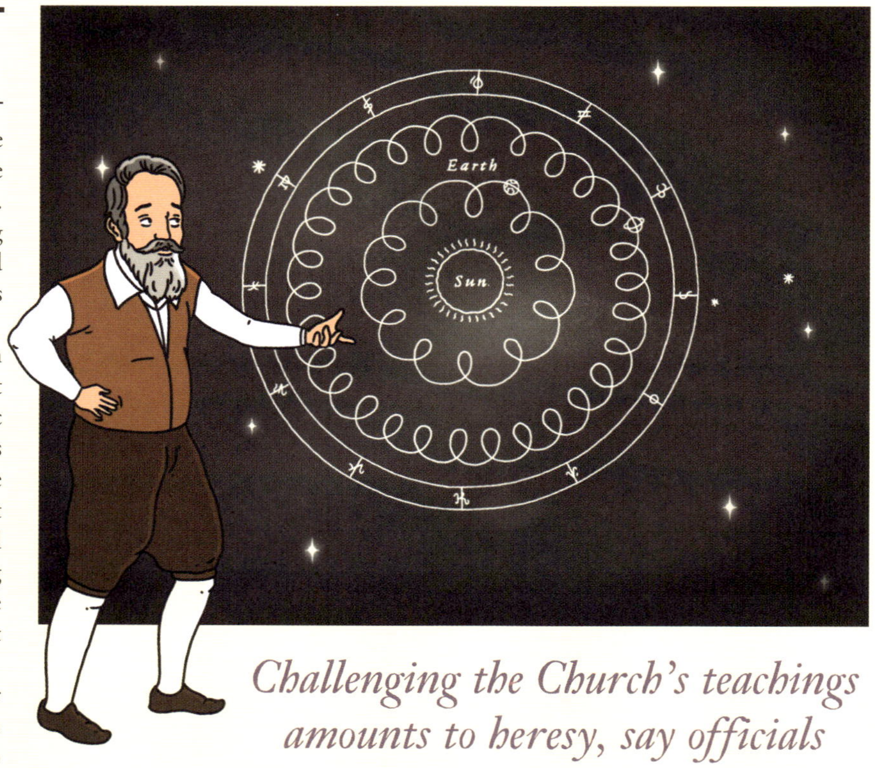

Challenging the Church's teachings amounts to heresy, say officials

Mr Galilei is not the first expert to argue against such a system. Much of his work is based on that of the Polish astronomer Nicolaus Copernicus ninety years ago. But now, thanks to major developments in telescope technology, Mr Galilei has made discoveries that help prove the heliocentric model to be correct. His observations of Venus and its changing phases show that it orbits the Sun, not the Earth. Other discoveries include a series of moons circling round the giant planet Jupiter, and mountains and canyons criss-crossing the surface of the Moon.

Mr Galilei has now united his ideas in a new work, *Dialogue Concerning the Two Chief World Systems*, which firmly supports heliocentricity. He uses the character of a fool, called Simplicio, to recite the Church's arguments for the Sun going round the Earth. The Church has responded decisively to the inflammatory work, arresting Mr Galilei and placing him indefinitely under house arrest.

The Church sees heliocentricity as a threat to many of its teachings. Officials say that God made man in His own image, separate from other living things and superior to them. It thus follows that the Earth, as man's home, must be at the very centre of God's Universe. The suggestion that the Church may be mistaken in its teachings is, say religious officials, tantamount to heresy.

LIFE ON MARS?
Find Out!
WITH GALILEO'S FANTASTIC OPTICAL ENHANCERS!
UP TO 30x Magnification!
VIA DEL PIERO, PADUA, ITALIA

Miniature world revealed

BY OUR OPTICAL CORRESPONDENT,
Amsterdam, 1677

A MINIATURE WORLD of living creatures and plants has been discovered by the Dutch scientist Antonie van Leeuwenhoek using rapidly improving 'microscope' technology. Mr van Leeuwenhoek says he can observe living organisms and their components on a scale far too small for the naked eye to see.

The microscope's potential was first demonstrated by the English scientist Robert Hooke in his 1665 work *Micrographia*, a book of spectacularly intricate drawings of minute living things. For example, one picture has to be folded out over four pages, revealing the image of a flea on which every hair is visible.

Through his observations, Mr Hooke investigated the functioning of life on this small scale, coining the term 'cell' for the tiny structures that are visible in all living things when they are viewed under a microscope. He suggested these cells act as building blocks, binding together like a honeycomb to form the body tissues of plants and animals.

Now Mr van Leeuwenhoek has looked even closer at these cells with a new generation of still more powerful microscopes. In a vial of slimy pond water he found mesmerising microscopic algae and protozoa swimming through the use of tiny hairs. Observing yeast, which is used to make alcohol and bread, he saw that each granule was in fact a minuscule plant-like organism.

He has also debunked the myth of spontaneous generation, whereby living things are thought to emerge out of inert chemicals, by observing that in almost all species males and females are both necessary for successful fertilisation and birth.

Mr van Leeuwenhoek made his most exciting discovery earlier this year when he discovered what look like tiny creatures in human semen. He called them 'animalcules' – Latin for 'little animals'. At first he was not sure where they came from, thinking they were perhaps some kind of parasite. However, the widespread appearance of these animalcules in both sick and healthy subjects showed they were something more. Now he says these tiny swimming cells are integral to fertilisation and the creation of new life.

Wise man gives humans a new name

BY OUR TAXONOMY CORRESPONDENT,
Stockholm, 1758

AS EVER MORE NEW SPECIES are found in far-flung corners of the globe, one botanist has pioneered a method of categorising living things so they can be arranged in groups based on related observable features. This naming system is now beginning to catch on among scientists all over the world, creating a new standard form of nomenclature or taxonomy.

The Swedish botanist Carolus Linnaeus says his system helps show the close relationships between living things, including humans, even if their natural habitats are thousands of miles apart.

Past naturalists such as the British plantsman John Ray (1627–1705) have tried to organise the natural world into an understandable, structured order. The current cumbersome system uses a series of scientific names for each species, typically consisting of a description of the organism in Latin. Sometimes these can be many words long, making them almost impossible to remember and tedious to write down.

Mr Linnaeus' system uses a maximum of two words for each species. The first word acts like a surname and places the organism in a group with similar animals or plants. The second word is always used to distinguish it from other members of the group. For example, the hooded crow, in Mr Linnaeus' system, is *Corvus cornix*, while the more common carrion crow is *Corvus corone*, sharing the same group name.

Scientists say the benefits of this system are significant. Clear, two-word names are easy to remember and overcome the problem of different names being used by scientists from different places. It also provides a framework for naming the countless new species currently being discovered, as well as an easy way to rectify mistakes. For example, if an organism turns out to have been placed in the wrong group, scientists simply change the group name and transfer the animal or plant to its new family.

Mr Linnaeus has made regular expeditions into the isolated reaches of his homeland of Sweden in search of new species. In 1753 he published *Species Plantarum*, an extensive catalogue of plants, in which he used his new system of taxonomy to name and describe more than seven thousand species. Now in its tenth edition, today's updated *Systema Naturae* describes and names all forms of known plant and animal life, including people.

Humans are grouped, according to Mr Linnaeus, beside apes and monkeys in the category he initially named *Anthropomorpha* – 'man-like'. While scientists are applauding Mr Linnaeus for establishing such a superb naming convention, some are sceptical of man's inclusion in a book of natural history.

Religious leaders have made it clear that man is above nature, not a part of it, and is unique in God's creation. Mr Linnaeus has restated his belief that significant similarities do exist between people and apes. In response to criticism, he has now placed humanity in its own separate group, labelling it *Homo sapiens* – 'wise man'. In a further controversial move, Mr Linnaeus has further subdivided humans based upon race, drawing divisions between people from different regions around the world.

Plants key to imperial success

FOLLOWING THE DISCOVERY of Australia, rich in its own unique flora and fauna, botanists have been looking for ways to exploit new species for the benefit of the British Empire, *reports our industrial correspondent from London in 1789.*

President of the Royal Society Sir Joseph Banks has led the way. He first made a name for himself on Captain Cook's first voyage to Australia on the *Endeavour*. Sir Joseph brought back numerous plant specimens from this trip, the most important being eucalyptus, a gum-producing tree native to the new continent. Rapidly growing eucalyptus plantations now provide much-needed wood and charcoal for Britain's ever-expanding industries.

The Royal Botanical Gardens at Kew, in London, are being developed to ensure Britain's botanical pre-eminence. Promising species include Assam tea, indigo, coffee, chocolate, vanilla and cotton.

New map of Britain rocks

BY OUR GEOLOGY EDITOR,
Bath, 1815

A NEW MAP OF BRITAIN aims to reveal the unseen world beneath our feet. Surveyor William Smith's geological map displays the material make-up of the land with a simple colour-coding system. The new map matters because as people mine deeper and deeper in search of materials to drive the nation's industrial revolution, understanding our geology has become more important than ever.

Mr Smith began his investigations while working for coal companies in Somerset, observing the layers of rock in the construction of the Somerset Coal Canal. As his work took him across Britain, he kept detailed accounts of the local geology wherever he went. He realised that fossils held the key to understanding the layers of rock. Since species change over time, Mr Smith discovered that he could use fossils as a way to date layers of rock. He reasoned that if the same species of fossils occur in rocks located at different places throughout the country, they must be of the same age. By using this method Mr Smith was able to develop a geological map of the area around Bath, near where he lived.

Now Mr Smith has made a similar map for England, Wales and part of Scotland. This fascinating document marks the extents of different rock formations, with each type of rock shown in a different colour. Some scientists have been dismissive of Mr Smith's map, however, claiming that he lacks sufficient education and training to be responsible for such an ambitious project.

Earth is much older than you think, says geological man of Principles

BY OUR EARTH SCIENCE EDITOR,
London, January 1830

HOW OLD IS EARTH? Ask a priest and a scientist and you will get very different answers. Nearly two hundred years ago, following a detailed study of the Old Testament, the Irish archbishop James Ussher pronounced the Earth's date of birth – the night of Sunday 22 October, 4004 BC.

However, scientists are beginning to question this date. By examining shifts in the Earth's rocks, they have concluded that our planet may in fact be far more than a few thousand years old. The latest study, *Principles of Geology*, released yesterday by geologist Charles Lyell, estimates that Earth must be many hundreds of millions of years old if science is to account for some of the rock formations that puncture the world's landscape.

Mr Lyell's work builds on centuries of study of the Earth's geological history. Some of the earliest revelations came from fossil studies undertaken in Italy by the Dane Nicolaus Steno in the seventeenth century. After examining the remains of a huge shark caught off Tuscany, Mr Steno noticed that its teeth looked very similar to triangular shapes sometimes found in rock. At the time it was believed that these formed naturally, but Mr Steno realised that they must be the remains of these ancient marine creatures, encased in the layers of rock.

After further studying the rock layers or 'strata' of the Italian hills, Mr Steno made a radical proposal: these layers had not always been here, they had changed over time. He proposed that each layer had once been 'fluid', gradually settling into a solid state. Living creatures have been encased within each layer, says Mr Steno, with each new layer settling successively on top. Deeper layers therefore represent the most ancient rocks as they contain the oldest fossils.

Mr Steno's theories then caught the attention of Scottish geologist James Hutton, whose work in the eighteenth century helped to establish geology as a proper field of scientific study. Mr Hutton realised that processes responsible for rock formation are still taking place, and therefore the Earth today is, as it has always been, in a state of perpetual creation.

By understanding these processes and looking at clues hidden in the layers of rocks and fossils, geologists believe they can learn about the natural history of the Earth and even decipher its age.

Mr Hutton was also the first naturalist to suggest that the Earth has a molten core. He divided rocks into three types. Firstly, *sedimentary* rock – this is rock laid down as it precipitates out of water, mixing with silt and dead creatures to form limestone and sandstone. Secondly, *igneous* rock – this is molten rock that bubbles up from beneath the Earth's surface, hardening into stones such as basalt and granite, often lifting up and shaping the sedimentary rocks. Finally, *metamorphic* rock – this is created from intense heat and pressure squeezing other rock layers into new forms such as marble and slate.

Mr Lyell's new text develops and builds on Mr Hutton's theories, and further divides the Earth's history into clearly defined geological epochs.

Most importantly, Mr Lyell supports the scientific notion known as 'uniformitarianism', which proposes that the processes shaping the world today are the same ones that have shaped it in the past and will shape it in the future. This idea has significance far beyond geology, and is inspiring scientists in all fields to look to nature to better understand both the history and the future of our precious planet.

Life on Earth theory about the survival of the fittest

"From so simple a beginning endless forms most beautiful and most wonderful have been, and are being, evolved," says author

BY OUR NATURE CORRESPONDENT,
Downe, Kent, 25 November 1859

A REMARKABLE NEW book has sparked heated scientific and religious debate about the origins of life on Earth. *On the Origin of Species by Means of Natural Selection* by the naturalist Charles Darwin, published yesterday, suggests that all forms of life – including humans – are related to one another and that they have, over millions of years, diversified into myriad species thanks to a mechanism that Mr Darwin refers to as evolution by 'natural selection'.

Mr Darwin is already well known for the popular account of his five-year voyage around South America and the Pacific aboard HMS *Beagle*. This long journey provided much of the inspiration for his new work, allowing him to observe at first hand the incredible variety of life on the planet.

On the Galápagos Islands, hundreds of miles off the western coast of South America, Mr Darwin studied the subtly different species around the archipelago. When visiting the islands, Mr Darwin observed slight variations in species of giant tortoises, finches and mockingbirds.

His explanation for such diversity is that slightly differing environmental conditions on each island have, over many years, led to the variation in the species he observed. Over time, those creatures with the most favourable attributes to the prevailing conditions thrived (he calls them the 'fittest') while those least well suited to the local conditions have declined. Over many generations this mechanism, which Mr Darwin calls 'natural selection', has accounted for the different species of birds and tortoises on each of the islands.

Although Mr Darwin is not the first to suggest that evolution is the dominant process in the creation of life, he is amongst the first to develop the theory of 'natural selection' as the mechanism that governs it.

Mr Darwin has published his evolutionary theory after presenting evidence in a paper last year in collaboration with fellow naturalist Alfred Russel Wallace. Mr Wallace's research dealt with a curious division of plant species between Indonesia and Australia along a natural border now known as the 'Wallace Line'. This division led Mr Wallace to draw the same conclusions as Mr Darwin that the evolution of species is related to their environmental conditions and circumstances.

Many people are finding the idea that all living things are related to each other profoundly disturbing. Anglican priests are amongst those who have denounced Mr Darwin's ideas from the pulpit, since traditional Church teachings suggest that humanity is unique and separate from any form of evolutionary hierarchy. Mr Darwin believes humans have evolved from great apes, a charge many people today would utterly refute.

Potty monk in inheritance laws breakthrough

BY OUR HORTICULTURAL EDITOR,
Brno, 9 February 1865

THE HUMBLE PEA may hold the key to understanding how children inherit features from their parents. In a paper presented yesterday, Austrian friar Gregor Mendel describes how experiments in his monastic garden have helped him develop a basic set of rules which explain how characteristics from one generation are passed on to the next.

In an extraordinary display of methodological persistence, Friar Mendel, working at the abbey in Brno, in the Austrian Empire, has studied the development of more than 29,000 pea plants. His research focuses on seven characteristics, such as the colour of the pods and how high the plant grows, and observes how these traits do or do not reappear in subsequent generations.

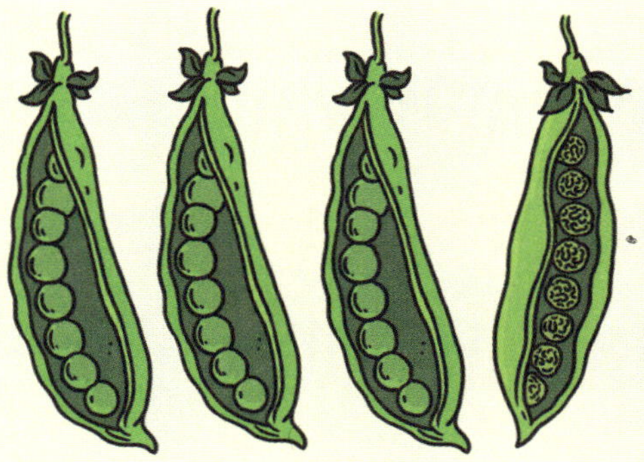

Through his work with the pea plants, Friar Mendel found that some characteristics were passed down to the next generation immediately, while others did not appear until subsequent generations. For example, he found that when breeding a plant that produces yellow peas with one that produces green peas, its offspring produced only yellow peas. However, in the next generation, the plants produced yellow and green peas in a ratio of one green to every three yellows.

Friar Mendel proposes that the yellow colour, therefore, is 'dominant', while the green is 'recessive', which is why it appears only in certain circumstances. He suggests that this mechanism of dominant and recessive characteristics can be seen at work across all the plants he has studied.

Friar Mendel's hypothesis contradicts the scientific consensus of today – that parents' traits are 'blended' in their offspring, producing something in between the parents' characteristics. Friar Mendel's experiments seem to show that certain traits are capable of 'pushing out' others, although the trait pushed into the background ('recessive') may resurface in later generations. With interest in evolutionary theory more widespread than ever, Friar Mendel's research will inspire fresh debate about the powerful processes that influence new life.

Dinosaur museum established as a 'cathedral to nature'

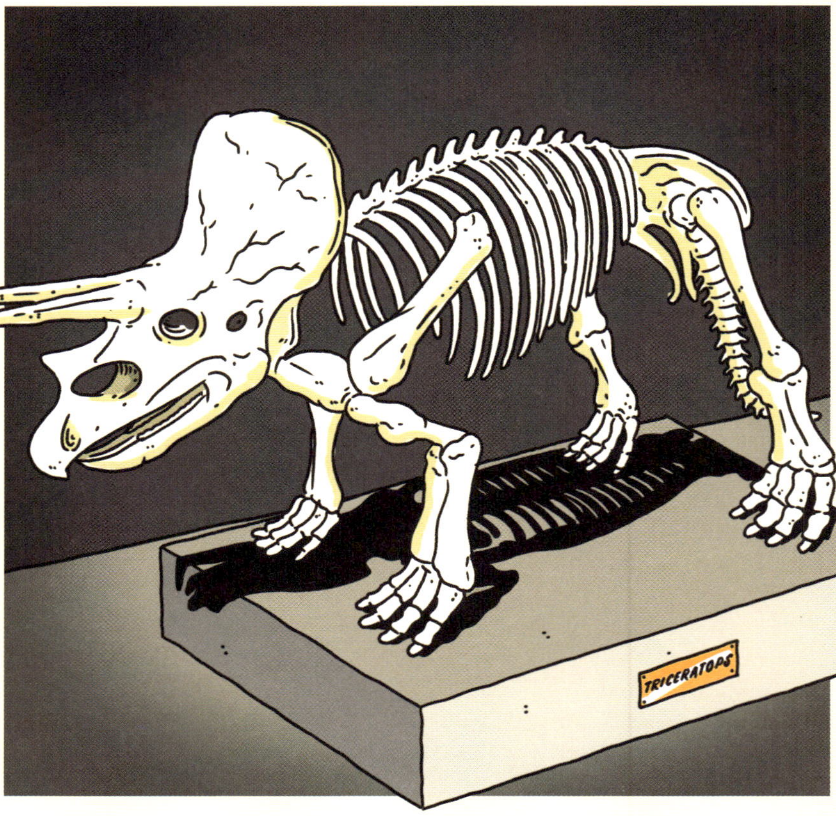

BY OUR MUSEUMS EDITOR,
London, 19 April 1881

A STUNNING MUSEUM, devoted to the history of the natural world, opened its doors to the public in London yesterday. The British Museum (Natural History) in South Kensington has been designed as a 'cathedral to nature', magnificently decorated with stained-glass windows and terracotta tiles depicting living and long-extinct lifeforms from around the globe.

The new museum is the brainchild of the British naturalist Richard Owen. Previously, fossils and other natural history exhibits had been kept in the British Museum, but Mr Owen has campaigned long and hard for these precious objects to be housed in their own dedicated museum space. He is convinced that growing interest in new species being discovered across the British Empire, and new theories about the natural world, warrant the construction of a new museum.

Ever since the publication of Charles Darwin's groundbreaking *On the Origin of Species* a little more than twenty years ago, theories about life's origins have fascinated people in all realms of society. Despite his own objection to many of Mr Darwin's evolutionary theories, Mr Owen felt that this 'mystery of mysteries' needed its own space, where it could be contemplated by all.

Mr Owen began his career as a surgeon, but soon became a prominent naturalist. After examining the skeletons of the strange *Iguanodon,* armoured *Hylaeosaurus* and colossal *Megalosaurus,* Mr Owen realised that these species belonged to an entire group of extinct reptiles that once dominated the Earth. He named them *Dinosauria* – 'terrible lizard' in ancient Greek – and later helped other naturalists uncover an evolutionary link between the feathered reptile *Archaeopteryx* and modern birds.

Mr Owen is also a firm believer in evolution as a force that has changed life over time into its present-day state. He coined the term 'homology', which refers to the shared characteristics that link different species and help reveal their origins, from the backbones shared by all vertebrates to the similar skeletal structures in human hands and the wings of bats.

But Mr Owen vehemently disagrees with some of Mr Darwin's ideas, most of all that humans have evolved from apes. As a very religious man, Mr Owen believes that humans have some innate quality that differentiates them from animals, and that no other animal could simply 'evolve' into a human.

Mr Owen's new museum of nature is set to astonish visitors for centuries to come. Its thousands of specimens include some of the discoveries of the late Miss Mary Anning, who unearthed and investigated the extraordinary fossils of immense marine animals along the Jurassic coast of Dorset.

American researchers in fossil face off

BY OUR NATURE EDITOR,
New York, 21 January 1890

A DINO WAR has broken out between two fiercely competitive American palaeontologists after a long-standing, simmering rivalry turned into bitter hostility. Not only have Edward Cope and Othniel Marsh viciously attacked one another in newspaper articles but one has even stooped to stealing the other's precious cargo of fossils by diverting a railroad train.

The dispute dissolved into all-out war after an article by Mr Marsh was published earlier this week in which he berates his rival for an error made some twenty years ago, when Mr Cope placed the head on the wrong end of the bones of a long-necked plesiosaur called *Elasmosaurus.*

Mr Cope yesterday responded with the Latin word 'peccavi' ('I have sinned'), but said he had corrected the errors of previous palaeontologists, even though he did admit making this mistake.

Mr Marsh and Mr Cope have used extraordinarily underhand tactics to inflict damage on the other's work and reputation. Mr Marsh has been accused of bribing fossil hunters employed by Mr Cope in a bid to get them to divert their best finds to him. Meanwhile, Mr Cope is said to have had a train full of Mr Marsh's fossil finds diverted for him to study in Philadelphia.

The discovery of abundant fossilised dinosaur bones at Como Bluff in Wyoming by a group of railway workers led to further clashes. This barren landscape has produced more than thirty tons of bones, making it a veritable gold mine for fossil hunters.

When Mr Cope accused Mr Marsh of 'trespassing' on his dig, the latter had the fossils destroyed with dynamite rather than let them fall into his rival's hands. He also sneaked unrelated bone fragments into Mr Cope's fossil pits to try to tarnish his work.

Mr Cope is known to be a supporter of Lamarckism, the theory that living organisms can pass down traits they develop in their lifetime to offspring, while Mr Marsh, who is a Darwinian, strongly disagrees.

In spite of their feuding, Mr Cope and Mr Marsh have made many important contributions to the field of natural history. Together they have unearthed thousands of fossil specimens and identified hundreds of previously unknown species. These have included magnificent dinosaurs, such as the long-necked *Diplodocus,* the *Stegosaurus* with its spiked back, and the three-horned, armour-plated *Triceratops.*

Mule slip leads to big fossil discovery

IT IS BEING HAILED as the most stunning marine fossil discovery of all time. High in the Rocky Mountains in Canada, in an area of shale rocks that five hundred million years ago formed part of the sea floor, new fossil finds are shedding light on some of the earliest forms of animal life, writes our Canada correspondent in 1910.

The Burgess Shale Formation, in British Columbia, was discovered last year by the American palaeontologist Charles Doolittle Walcott after his mule slipped on a rock, exposing an exquisite fossil. Following extensive research, the scientist has announced the discovery of all kinds of marine animals from the Cambrian Period, one of the earliest eras of multicellular life on Earth.

It is thought that the animals died quickly, perhaps buried in an underwater avalanche of mud which has preserved exceptionally fine details of the structure of their soft body parts. Scientists hope to learn more about the origins of today's living creatures by studying these remarkably well-preserved marine fossils.

Walcott's finds include Hallucigenia, *a tube-like creature about an inch long with thorny spines along its back and claws on its many legs, suggesting it lived at the bottom of the sea. Palaeontologists are still debating which is its front end. Other discoveries include* Anomalocaris, *a one-metre-long marine predator with compound eyes on stalks and two large 'arms' near its head. Perhaps the most alien creature found in the Burgess Shale is* Opabinia, *a soft-bodied creature with five stalky eyes, a backwards-facing mouth under its head and a long proboscis, which may have been used for picking up food along the sea floor.*

These creatures represent a major shift in the story of life on Earth and are thought to be the earliest ancestors of many families of vertebrate and invertebrate creatures living today.

Mr Walcott first made his name studying trilobite fossils, a group of widespread marine creatures with sturdy exoskeletons that were amongst the most successful animals on the planet until they disappeared around 250 million years ago.

Palaeontologist puzzles out mystery of pig-like ancestor

Peers rebuke claim that landmasses were once a giant supercontinent

BY OUR PUZZLES EDITOR,
Berlin, 7 January 1912

THE EARTH'S landmasses behave like a giant jigsaw puzzle on the loose! That's the bizarre theory of polar researcher and palaeontologist Alfred Wegener. The German scientist even believes that millions of years ago all the Earth's landmasses collided into a single supercontinent called 'Pangaea' – meaning 'All Earth'.

Mr Wegener spent his early career crossing hundreds of miles of the North Pole, studying weather systems, and he was one of the first people to overwinter on the polar ice sheet. He began investigating his new theory of geological science after noticing the curious shapes of the continents and how they seemed to fit together on a map like a jigsaw: the west coasts of Africa and Europe fitting snugly against the east coasts of South and North America respectively, with India, Madagascar and Antarctica slotting in neatly on the other side.

After studying the rock types on both sides of the Atlantic, Mr Wegener was intrigued by the similarities between the two coasts. It was almost as if they had once been bound together, he thought. However, the greatest evidence for his theory – dubbed 'Continental Drift' – has come from studying the appearance of similar fossils on separate continents. Creatures such as the pig-like reptile *Lystrosaurus* and the seed-fern *Glossopteris* have been found on many continents, suggesting a land connection must have once existed, given the inability of these lifeforms to cross the oceans.

Mr Wegener yesterday proposed in a lecture that this supercontinent – which existed some 250 million years ago – must have split up, with each fragment becoming one of the continents we recognise today. However, his theories have failed to persuade many in the scientific community, largely because he is currently unable to provide enough evidence for the mechanism that might drive the process.

So far Mr Wegener has offered two potential explanations. Firstly, he suggests that the landmasses are moved by forces generated by the rotation of the Earth; and secondly, that hot magma rises up in deep-sea trenches, causing the spreading apart of the sea floor. As yet, neither of these suggestions is backed up by strong enough evidence.

Some experts believe Mr Wegener's theory could provide an explanation of how mountains are formed (when landmasses collide) as well as providing a rationale for earthquakes (when the pressure between landmasses reaches breaking point). His ideas may finally provide a grand unifying theory that underpins all Earth science, in a similar way to Charles Darwin's evolutionary theory for the life sciences.

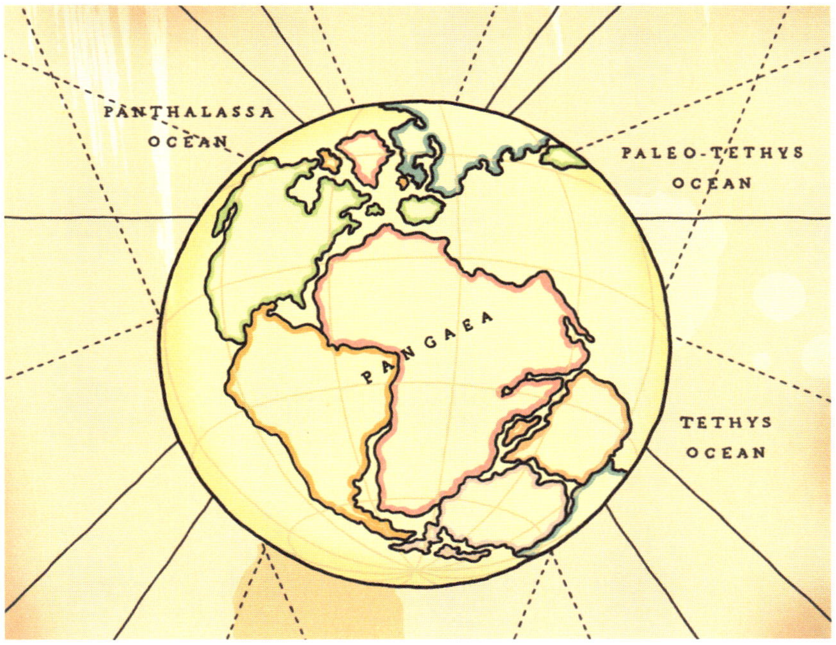

Inheritance theory: a load of flies

EXPERIMENTS in a room full of flies at an American university have shed new light on the physical mechanism of genetic inheritance, *reports our invertebrate correspondent from New York in October 1916.*

Through his research, the biologist Thomas Morgan has concluded that minute biological components called chromosomes are the physical structures that regulate the traits we inherit from our parents, from hair colour to height.

Mr Morgan set up a special 'fly room' at Columbia University to study the common fruit fly, *Drosophila melanogaster*, an ideal specimen for research into genetics due to the speed with which it reproduces.

However, being so small, flies are difficult to examine, so Mr Morgan's research has focused on a few easily observable characteristics, such as eye colour and wing size.

Mr Morgan's findings appear to confirm that chromosomes, tiny biological structures observable in the cells of most organisms, are the carriers of genetic information. When a cell divides (a process known as mitosis), an identical duplicate chromosome is created. But during sexual reproduction chromosomes from each parent combine (a process known as meiosis), leading to offspring with a unique blend of characteristics from both parents.

Eagle-sized dragonfly fossil found

BY OUR COAL CORRESPONDENT,
Bolsover, 1978

A GIGANTIC DRAGONFLY fossil has been unearthed near Bolsover, in Derbyshire, England, revealing a world of huge predatory insects millions of years ago, when higher levels of oxygen in the air allowed invertebrates to grow into giants.

The rare fossil is an example of *Meganeura*, giant predatory dragonflies of the Carboniferous era with wing-spans of up to 75cm – as broad as some eagles. Its size would have made it capable of carrying off small reptiles and amphibians as prey. *Meganeura* is amongst the largest insects ever to have lived on the Earth.

The dragonfly fossil was discovered by miners in a coal seam, which has preserved it for the past three hundred million years or so. The Carboniferous Period saw huge evolutionary changes, including the arrival of the first reptiles, creatures that evolved from the aquatic amphibians.

Reptiles developed hard-shelled eggs, allowing them to reproduce inland, a significant advantage in the age of a single supercontinent, Pangaea. Water-tight skins also helped them live away from water, avoiding dehydration.

Scientists believe *Meganeura* was able to grow to its large size due to increased levels of oxygen in the Earth's atmosphere at the time, making it easier for them to breathe. Since insects absorb oxygen through holes in their exoskeleton, low levels of atmospheric oxygen, as we have today, prevent them from growing so large.

Meganeura would not have been the only giant insect of its time. Other enormous creatures included two-metre-long armoured millipedes and spiders as wide as a metre. Some experts believe this competition of size may explain why *Meganeura* grew to such huge proportions, as predator and prey took part in an evolutionary arms race to outgrow each other. The fossil has been nicknamed the 'Beast of Bolsover' after the coal-mining town close to its place of discovery.

Gigantic asteroid wiped out dinosaurs, say experts

BY OUR SPACE CORRESPONDENT,
Berkeley, California, 1980

WHY DINOSAURS SUDDENLY disappeared sixty-five million years ago has long puzzled scientists, but now father and son researchers Luis and Walter Alvarez have put forward a radical new theory.

The US physicist and his geologist son believe a colossal asteroid impact changed the climate and killed three-quarters of all species across the planet. They say they have found unmistakable proof of their hypothesis – large concentrations of a rare metal from outer space. The super-dense silver-white metal iridium is hardly ever found on the Earth's crust, since its weight means it sinks below other metals towards the molten core. However, a far larger amount of iridium than might be expected can be found at the boundary between layers of Cretaceous and Palaeogene rocks – exactly the period when the dinosaurs vanished and mammals began to take over as the dominant animal lifeform on the planet.

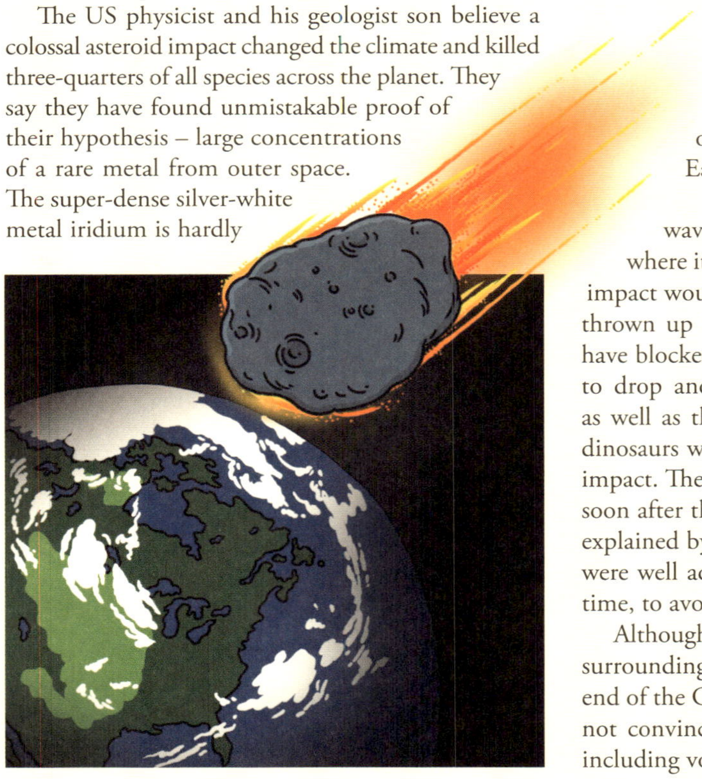

So where did all this iridium come from? The element is found in asteroids, leading the Alvarez team to conclude that one such extraterrestrial object calamitously collided with the Earth, bringing with it the iridium.

The initial blast would have caused giant waves and widespread fires, depending on where it struck. But the most deadly effect of the impact would have been the immense cloud of dust thrown up into the atmosphere. This cloud would have blocked out the sunlight, causing temperatures to drop and killing off plants dependent on light as well as the creatures that grazed on them. Most dinosaurs would have died from starvation after the impact. The sudden increase in varieties of mammals soon after the disappearance of the dinosaurs can be explained by their varied diets and the fact that they were well adapted to hunting in the dark, at night-time, to avoid the threat of dinosaur attack.

Although the theory answers many of the questions surrounding the mysterious mass extinction at the end of the Cretaceous period, some scientists are still not convinced. Many have suggested other causes, including volcanic eruptions and climate change.

Fossils show dinosaurs still flying high

FOSSILS OF REPTILES recently discovered in north-eastern China confirm a long-suspected evolutionary link between birds and dinosaurs, writes our Asia correspondent in August 1996.

Theories that birds and dinosaurs might be related have been circulating amongst scientists for more than 130 years. One of Charles Darwin's supporters, Thomas Huxley, drew up a series of comparisons between them, noting in 1868 the many similarities between the bipedal dinosaur Compsognathus *and the then recently discovered 'first bird',* Archaeopteryx, *meaning 'ancient wing'.*

However, the existence of a bipedal feathered dinosaur, the first of its kind, was revealed after its discovery by Chinese farmer Li Yumin. The 65cm-long feathered reptile has been named Sinosauropteryx, *meaning 'Chinese lizard wing'. The creature is thought to have been smothered in volcanic ash millions of years ago, preserving its delicate feathers.*

For most scientists, the fossil find confirms that birds are part of the same family as theropod dinosaurs (the same family as Tyrannosaurus rex*), sharing not only feathers but other similarities, from bone structure to hard-shelled eggs.*

Experts believe that the dinosaurs' feathers may have first evolved from fish-like scales as a method of body insulation and were only later adapted by some creatures for the purposes of flight in a bid to escape predators.

Climate change: the biggest scientific challenge of all time

BY OUR CLIMATE CHANGE EDITOR,
Geneva, 4 November 2014

DESPITE MANKIND'S knowledge of the Earth being greater than ever, the behaviour of its human inhabitants every day seems to place its health in further jeopardy.

Widespread fears about the future of the planet were yesterday confirmed in the latest report from experts on the Intergovernmental Panel on Climate Change (IPCC). It found that the Earth's climate is getting warmer, posing a major threat to ecosystems around the globe. The report concludes that it is 'extremely likely' that humans are the dominant force behind global temperature rises.

The IPCC report is the fifth in a series of warnings about the Earth's climate. Global warming is causing melting ice caps, rising sea levels and changing weather patterns.

Coastal communities can expect increased flooding and hurricanes, and many species are under threat as their habitats start to change.

The planet Earth has experienced many cycles of warming and cooling before. However, none of the geological and environmental factors which have historically triggered these changes, such as supervolcanic eruptions or violent bouts of mountain-building, are this time present.

It is thought that human populations, which have become addicted to large-scale agriculture and industry, powered by the burning of fossil fuels – coal, oil and natural gas – are to blame for today's global warming.

Such reckless consumption produces large quantities of harmful greenhouse gases, particularly carbon dioxide, which trap the Sun's energy in the atmosphere, warming the planet. Since 1850, carbon dioxide levels have gone up from 280 parts per million (ppm) to more than 400 ppm today.

The IPCC report says that reducing global warming trends will rely on scientists developing cleaner sources of energy such as wind and solar power.

However, climate change is a hard political, social and cultural issue, and progress towards a global solution has repeatedly stalled. Heated discussions often erupt over who should take greater responsibility: the developing nations, who are more inclined to turn to cheap, polluting energy, or the wealthier developed nations, who can more easily afford to develop cleaner alternative sources of energy.

Experts believe that not enough progress has yet been made towards an international solution that can protect future generations from the potentially disastrous effects of climate change.

It is a chilling fact that when all the ice caps have melted, the seas will have risen by at least sixty metres, submerging two-thirds of the iconic British clock tower containing Big Ben, along with other tall buildings in many of the world's most populous cities.

Across

3) T. ___, king of the dinosaurs (3)
4) Aristotle's mentor (5)
6) Heavy metal from outer space (7)
7) Danish geologist (5)
10) Plant used by curious monk (3)
12) Arguably, what made humans into top predator (4)
13) Ancient supercontinent (7)
14) Ship that took Charles Darwin around the world (6)
15) Mary ___, fossil hunter from Lyme Regis (6)
17) Fossilised resin common in Baltic pines (5)

Down

1) Pioneering fish able to do a press-up (9)
2) Cambrian-era, beetle-like sea creature with eyes (9)
5) Famous American fossil treasure trove (4, 5)
6) A type of rock (7)
7) ___ Earth, epoch when the Earth nearly froze over (8)
8) Cambrian creature with five protruding eyes (8)
9) Greek city and home of famous Roman-era medic (8)
11) Original name for microscopic life (11)
16) Wood have been trees, a long time ago (4)

All the correct answers can be found somewhere in this book!

A selection of letters from would-be readers down the ages

DISSECTION – 1543

Calling time on corpse taboos

I WAS SO ENTHRALLED by your article on Mr Andreas Vesalius last week that I immediately booked a place at his next public dissection. The human body is a fascinatingly complex creation and there is still so much to learn about it.

It is such a shame that the dissection of human cadavers is often frowned upon. I do understand that the examination of corpses can be unpleasant, and I dare say it is unacceptable to many on religious grounds. But if we are to learn more about the body and how to protect the living from injury and disease, human dissection is a necessity.

CATHY CUTTER

Keep bodies sacred

MR VESALIUS' dissection of human corpses is completely inexcusable. It is a violation of the sacred nature of the body and should be outlawed. I am distressed to discover that it is not only legal but also available as a twisted form of public entertainment.

Mr Vesalius may claim that it is integral to his medical work, but all he has accomplished is to create a vile spectacle. Physicians across the world still stand by Mr Galen's extensive works, in which he was able to make valuable contributions to his field without resorting to the desecration of the human body.

SIMON SOLEMN

Spectacularly vulgar

WHILE I APPRECIATE the medical importance of dissecting human cadavers, I was surprised to read in your article that Mr Vesalius has been letting members of the public attend his dissections. The scientific rationale for offering these demonstrations to ordinary people truly escapes me.

Not only does Mr Vesalius appear to be transforming his demonstrations into little more than vulgar spectacles, he shows no respect to the previous inhabitants of these bodies by inviting the public to gasp and gawk at them in disgust.

NORA NONPLUSSED

HELIOCENTRICITY – 1633

What on Earth next?

I WAS EXTREMELY upset to read your report yesterday about the plight of Mr Galileo Galilei and the religious and legal quagmire in which he has found himself due to his remarkable scientific work. As an amateur astronomer myself, I have also found many of my observations clash with established opinion.

Scholars investigating the mysteries of the Universe need greater protection from frustrated leaders who find their discoveries 'inconvenient'. We should not be so hasty to lock up those who put forward ideas we are not comfortable with – they may have stumbled across important truths.

Proper scientific debate is the only way to confront new ideas. If Mr Galilei's heliocentric model does prove to be true, no amount of effort from any church or government will be able to suppress it.

HENRIETTA HELIOCENTRIC

TAXONOMY – 1758

What's in a name?

THE INTRIGUING new system of categorisation devised by Mr Carolus Linnaeus raises many new questions for biologists. His work highlights the importance of having a solid definition of species by which to differentiate organisms, a notion already much debated. Above all, it makes us question our own place in nature – or above it.

But I do believe that Mr Linnaeus is wrong to differentiate between humans based on race. Surely our ability to communicate and cooperate with people all over the world shows that the similarities between us are far greater than the differences? We are clearly one people, and we should be moving towards unity rather than separation.

NICK NAMESAKE

Please don't call me an animal!

I WAS SHOCKED by your report of Mr Linnaeus' decision to place man alongside the animals, so I am relieved to hear that he has changed his mind. Revolutionary though his system may be, an obvious division does exist between mankind and the lesser creatures. Our societies, our languages, our religions and technologies – all these differentiate us from other animals.

Animals can't think the way we do, they can't read, write or invent things. In fact, there is simply no sensible comparison between the intellect of a human and any other creature, be it a monkey or a mouse. Mr Linneaus' project to classify living things is fine with me, as long as he respects the special status of humankind.

SIMON SAPIENS

To comment on any issues in this book – visit www.whatonearthbooks.com/nature

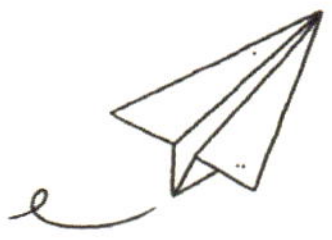

BOTANY - 1789

Plants for progress

YOUR RECENT article on the botanical and agricultural ideas put forward by Sir Joseph Banks offers an exciting vision of the future for Britain and the world. Our ability to harness the riches of the planet is the key not just to improving our own lives, but to lifting other people out of poverty. Humans have been harnessing the environment to make a better world since the dawn of civilisation, when we learned to burn wood, grow crops and raise livestock.

Sir Joseph's direct approach to investigating and cultivating new plants represents natural curiosity at its most authentic. As President of the Royal Society, he is uniquely placed to ensure that here in Britain we gather the widest understanding of the natural world on behalf of all nations. Three cheers, I say, to his remarkable *endeavour*!

BILLY BIOLOGY

It's all exploitation

IT MAY SUIT the British Empire to take plants native to Australia and grow them elsewhere for commercial purposes, but has anyone considered the wider implications of this policy? Eucalyptus trees are not natural in Asia or Europe and their vigorous growth must surely come at the expense of indigenous species that lack experience of defending themselves against this highly aggressive plant.

I think we should proceed with extreme caution when it comes to introducing species into habitats they are not designed for, otherwise we may end up creating an imbalanced, impoverished world.

GEMMA GREEN

THE AGE OF THE WORLD - 1830

Oh, ye of little faith...

THE ENTHUSIASM with which rocks and fossils are being embraced for answers about the Earth's past is worrying. These scientists expect us to believe in a molten core nobody has ever seen, processes that take thousands of years to show any results, and fossilised sea monsters now mysteriously absent from the world's waters.

Meanwhile, solid conclusions found in the Bible itself have been sidelined. Bishop James Ussher created his own history of the Earth from written records and the Bible, the word of God. This to me seems a far more reliable record.

FAITH FAITHFUL

Age of scientific analysis has arrived

IT IS INDEED good news that the scientific community finally seems to agree that the Earth is far older than the few thousand years put forward by outdated scholars such as Bishop Ussher.

The biblical version of the story of the Creation, with its comparatively short timeframe, has always been a barrier to scientific progress, leaving many great scientists totally confused by the ancient rocks and creatures they find. The answer is obvious – the Earth is far older than we have been led to believe. It's great to see so many like-minded scientists now engaged in building such a plausible case for their theories and rejecting these worthless religious timeframes once and for all.

SIMON SCIENCE

CONTINENTAL DRIFT - 1912

Genius idea that may change Earth sciences

I WAS SO PLEASED to see Mr Wegener's exciting new theory reported in your latest issue. While he may not have an answer for all the questions it raises, his ideas offer a starting point for a fascinating discussion that could transform our understanding of the natural world.

Natural scientists surely cannot ignore Mr Wegener's keen observations about the unexpected presence of *Lystrosaurus* and *Glossopteris* on unconnected continents. He is right to suspect some unknown force is at work here; his theories, however unlikely they may seem, may well provide the answer. In my experience, it is always better to create a theory out of unexplained data than search for data to support an unproven theory.

PENNY PANGAEA

Insufficient evidence!

THEORIES SUCH as Mr Alfred Wegener's 'Continental Drift' reflect improper practices that are now all too common in the scientific community. In an effort to make a splash, researchers shamelessly dream up radical theories off the back of maybe only a single observation.

Your article insists that we should take Mr Wegener's theory seriously. Yet he himself is unable to explain it, conjuring up possible causes without the evidence to back them up. This is not how science should be carried out.

EDDIE EVIDENCE

CLIMATE CHANGE - 2014

Science key to avoiding effects of global warming

THE LATEST REPORT from the IPCC confirms what those who have followed the debate have known for years: climate change is real, and humans are the cause. However, it also makes the urgent case for sustained action against climate change from a united global community.

If we act now, together we may yet be able to prevent the worst impacts of climate change. We will not have to drastically alter our way of life, or resign ourselves to destruction through global warming and rising sea levels. However, we may need to make some unpopular changes to the way we produce energy, grow crops and build cities, all of which will need leadership and innovation by scientists and engineers. If we work together as a global community, perhaps we can save the planet before it is too late.

HELEN HOPE

Shocking lack of action

AFTER READING your article about the latest IPCC report on climate change, I was struck by how little progress has been made over the decades that this group has been producing its reports. Climate change and its terrifying implications have been understood for many years, yet governments continue to wilfully ignore what is without doubt the most pressing issue facing the world today.

Soon it will be too late to turn back the clock on the polluting lifestyle that is destroying our planet. If we are to arrest climate change, we need to drastically change society now in very unpopular ways, and make the environment the principal focus of all governmental policy.

ARCHIE ACTIVIST

See how many of our brain-teasing nature questions you can answer...

HADEAN & ARCHEAN

1. About how much of the Earth's water is thought to have arrived with a giant bombardment of comets?
   a) 20%
   b) 40%
   c) 70%
   d) 90%

2. Which of the following gases did not feature in the Earth's early atmosphere?
   a) Oxygen
   b) Nitrogen
   c) Methane
   d) Carbon dioxide

3. What does LUCA stand for?
   a) Largest Underwater Cretaceous Animal
   b) Lower Urinary Causeway & Anterior
   c) Least Uniform Cryogenic Annelid
   d) Last Universal Common Ancestor

4. Chloroplasts are structures in plant cells responsible for photosynthesis. From what lifeforms are they thought to have originated?
   a) Purple bacteria
   b) Spirochaetes
   c) Cyanobacteria
   d) Algae

CAMBRIAN to DEVONIAN

5. How many eyes did the curious arthropod-like sea creature *Opabinia* have?
   a) One
   b) Three
   c) Five
   d) Seven

6. *Vauxia* is an ancient type of:
   a) Branching sponge
   b) Stinging jellyfish
   c) Segmented trilobite
   d) Eel-like fish

7. *Megalograptus* was a:
   a) Gigantic dinosaur
   b) Huge sea scorpion
   c) Towering tree
   d) Terrifying raptor

8. Which of the following continents formed first?
   a) Laurasia
   b) Gondwana
   c) Australia
   d) Pangaea

9. Some of the first arthropods to explore life on land resembled:
   a) Beetles
   b) Scorpions
   c) Lungfish
   d) Worms

10. Which of the following features appeared in primitive land plants?
   a) Stems
   b) Leaves
   c) Roots
   d) Flowers

11. Which of the following plant families did NOT form part of the early terrestrial landscape 400 million year ago?
   a) Mosses
   b) Orchids
   c) Liverworts
   d) *Cooksonia*

12. Which of the following families teamed up with fungi to help them both colonise the land?
   a) Amphibians
   b) Plants
   c) Worms
   d) Reptiles

CARBONIFEROUS to TRIASSIC

13. About when did some terrestrial creatures start laying hard-shelled eggs?
   a) 500 million years ago
   b) 400 million years ago
   c) 300 million years ago
   d) 200 million years ago

14. *Eryops* was a powerful two-metre-long amphibious carnivore that had rudimentary:
   a) Canines
   b) Nostrils
   c) Ears
   d) Eyebrows

15. When limestone is crushed by the collision of tectonic plates it turns into:
   a) Chalk
   b) Alabaster
   c) Slate
   d) Marble

16. *Diplocaulus* was a Carboniferous-era amphibian that had the following curious anatomical feature:
   a) An arrow-shaped head
   b) A heart-shaped tongue
   c) Ears like Mr Spock
   d) Square-shaped feet

17. Deciduous trees lose their leaves for part of the year as a way of:
   a) Protecting against the cold
   b) Conserving water
   c) Saving food
   d) Fertilising the soil

18. *Lystrosaurus* was a mammal-like reptile that survived the Permian Mass Extinction because it was able to:
   a) Tolerate low oxygen environments
   b) Reproduce asexually
   c) See in the dark
   d) Live off a diet of worms

19. The word 'dinosaur' means:
   a) Terrible lizard
   b) Hungry biter
   c) Dangerous reptile
   d) Noisy tooter

20. Birds are directly descended from which animal family:
   a) Saurischian dinosaurs
   b) Ornithischian dinosaurs
   c) Pterodactyls
   d) Bats

JURASSIC & CRETACEOUS

21. Jet is a black mineral that is formed from the fossilised remains of:
   a) Beetles
   b) Termites
   c) Palm trees
   d) Monkey-puzzle trees

22. Which of the following ancient sea creatures had a coiled shell and can often be found as fossils?
   a) Trilobites
   b) Troglodytes
   c) Astomites
   d) Ammonites

23. Diplodocus, the herbivorous dinosaur giant, belonged to which of the following reptile families?
   a) Theropod
   b) Sauropod
   c) Pterosaur
   d) Plesiosaur

24. Termites are close relatives of which of the following insect families?
   a) Ants
   b) Wasps
   c) Maggots
   d) Cockroaches

25. Snakes are directly descended from which of the following animal families?
   a) Worms
   b) Eels
   c) Toads
   d) Lizards

All the correct answers can be found somewhere in this book!

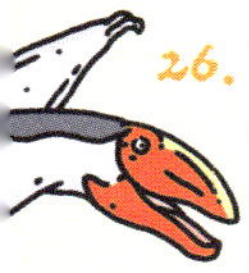

26. Which of the following features were common in ancient birds such as *Archaeopteryx*, but are absent from modern birds?
   a) Teeth
   b) Gizzard
   c) Hollow bones
   d) Feathers

27. Which family of marine reptiles is notorious for having extraordinarily long necks?
   a) Pliosaur
   b) Plesiosaur
   c) Mosasaur
   d) Susisuchus

28. About 90 million years ago India was attached to which continent?
   a) Africa
   b) Europe
   c) Australia
   d) Asia

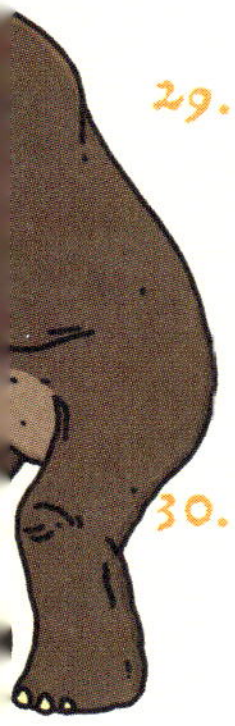

29. Which of the following statements about male mosquitoes is true?
   a) Unlike females they don't suck blood
   b) Unlike females they suck blood
   c) They carry more diseases than females
   d) They are about twice the size as females

30. Songbirds are thought to have originated in which part of the world?
   a) Africa
   b) North America
   c) South America
   d) New Zealand

31. Over millions of years the remains of tiny marine creatures called coccolithophores fall onto the sea floor and gradually turn into:
   a) Limestone
   b) Chalk
   c) Sand
   d) Marble

32. A mosasaur is a type of ancient:
   a) Theropod
   b) Tetrapod
   c) Pterodactyl
   d) Marine lizard

33. Which of the following attributes of flowering plants are NOT designed to attract insects, birds or mammals?
   a) Sugary nectar
   b) Bright flowers
   c) Juicy fruits
   d) Nutritious tubers

PALAEOCENE & EOCENE

34. How are oak trees pollinated?
   a) Wind
   b) Squirrels
   c) Moths
   d) Birds

35. Pigs, goats, sheep, camels, deer, giraffes and cows all belong to which mammal family?
   a) Ungulates
   b) Marsupials
   c) Carnivora
   d) Condylarths

36. What occurred about 49 million years ago that is thought to have dramatically changed the Earth's climate?
   a) Massive meteorite strike
   b) Wobble in the Earth's orbit
   c) Surge in solar activity
   d) Growth of a fern swamp in the Arctic

37. Which of the following types of birds do not belong to the galliform family?
   a) Turkeys
   b) Chickens
   c) Ducks
   d) Pheasants

38. The Antarctic ice sheets began to form in which geological era?
   a) Eocene
   b) Palaeocene
   c) Oligocene
   d) Jurassic

39. Why do pine trees sometimes secrete sticky resin?
   a) To prevent intrusion by infectious microorganisms
   b) To capture insects
   c) To regulate internal fluid levels
   d) To help glue on newly established branches

OLIGOCENE to PLEISTOCENE

40. Which of the following features makes New World monkeys distinctive?
   a) Black fur
   b) A flat nose
   c) Hand gestures
   d) Brightly coloured bottoms

41. Bears first emerged in which part of the world?
   a) North Africa
   b) North America
   c) Southern Asia
   d) Siberia

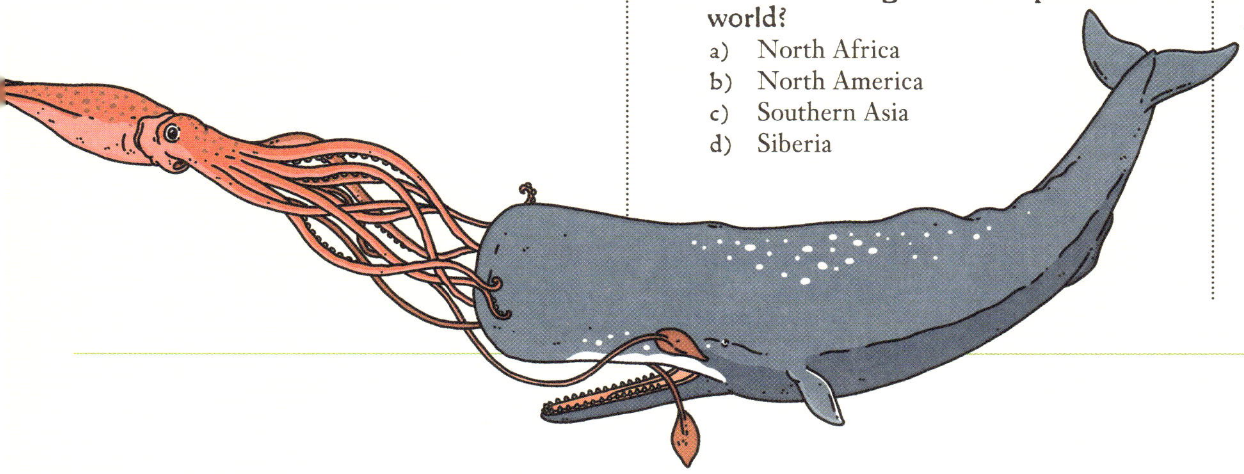

42. Bamboo trees belong to which of the following plant families?
   a) Grass
   b) Palm
   c) Fern
   d) Conifer

43. Camels originally evolved from creatures that once lived in:
   a) Asia
   b) Europe
   c) Africa
   d) America

44. Penguins belong to which of the following animal families:
   a) Birds
   b) Mammals
   c) Amphibians
   d) Fish

HOLOCENE & ANTHROPOCENE

45. A mule is a cross between a:
   a) Horse & zebra
   b) Donkey & ass
   c) Ass & horse
   d) Horse & donkey

46. Coffee berries were first crushed and turned into a beverage in which country:
   a) Ethiopia
   b) Brazil
   c) Kenya
   d) Costa Rica

47. What helped Egyptian farmers leave their land and work as labourers building pyramids for three months a year?
   a) Slave labour
   b) The Aswan Dam
   c) Honeybees
   d) Worms

48. Which Age is the most recent?
   a) Iron Age
   b) Bronze Age
   c) Stone Age
   d) Copper Age

49. Concentrations of carbon dioxide in the atmosphere today are roughly how many parts per million (ppm)?
   a) 200
   b) 300
   c) 400
   d) 500

50. Which of the following does not tend to boost human population levels?
   a) Improvements in agricultural techniques
   b) Artificial fertilisers
   c) Genetic modification
   d) The contraceptive pill

◆ Our Philosophy

WHO ON EARTH ARE WE?

Here at What on Earth Publishing, we think that learning should always be fun.

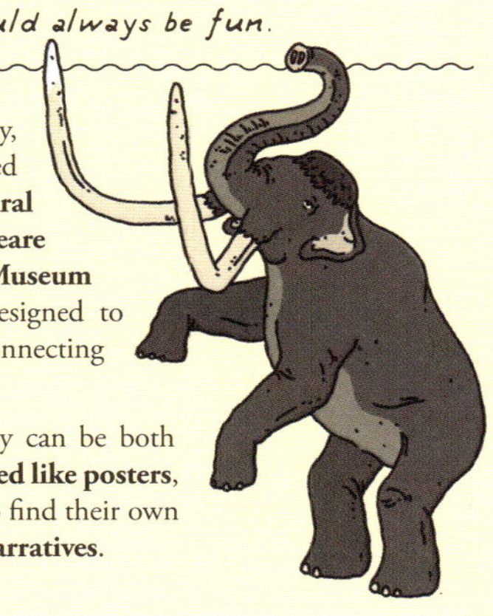

Our **timelines** of nature, history, literature, science and sport, created in partnership with the **Natural History Museum**, the **Shakespeare Birthplace Trust**, the **Science Museum** and the **National Trust**, are designed to stimulate natural curiosity by connecting the dots of the past.

Their unique format means they can be both **browsed like books and displayed like posters**, encouraging readers of all ages to find their own path through **the very biggest narratives**.

◆ Our Formats

WHAT ON EARTH BOOKS COME IN 3 *Fantastic Formats*

◆ Our ***Wallbooks*** feature the original two-metre timeline, plus a newspaper packed with stories, pictures, letters, crossword and quiz. Perfect for everyone.

◆ Our ***Stickerbooks*** each have around a hundred stickers, and a 1.7-metre simplified version of the timeline to fix them on to. Perfect for younger readers.

◆ Our ***Posterbooks*** are a gigantic three-metre version of the timeline, printed on heavy paper and laminated for extra durability. Perfect for schools.

◆ On Tour

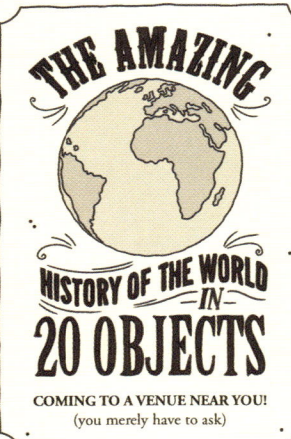

THE AMAZING HISTORY OF THE WORLD IN 20 OBJECTS

COMING TO A VENUE NEAR YOU!
(you merely have to ask)

a BIG BANG of a book!

Find out where it all began. Join **Christopher Lloyd** on the greatest journey of all, the 13.7-billion-year history of the Universe, in his bestselling classic, **What on Earth Happened?**

Now available from Planet Earth's best bookshops.

'Compelling… remarkably far-reaching and even-handed'

THE SUNDAY TIMES

◆ School Visits

The WORLD!! STRANGER THAN FICTION!

We believe that the real world is far more interesting than anything found in fiction. But the fragmented, confined nature of the curriculum can make learning seem all too dry. Our cross-curricular workshops – developed over hundreds of talks at schools, festivals and museums, and available for Year 1 through to Year 13 – are designed to weave narrative threads between different subjects, forge new connections and bring them to life.

'I have been besieged this morning by teachers who have come to say how much their classes had enjoyed the workshops'

Librarian, Hertfordshire

www.whatonearthbooks.com/events

◆ Inset Training

CURIOSITY: antidote to boredom z z z z z

Getting curiosity to flow in the classroom can be a real challenge for teachers working within an established curriculum – yet no-one can learn effectively unless their natural curiosity is engaged. Interweaving neuroscience, memory-based learning techniques and storytelling skills, our **Inset Workshops** are ideal for schools wishing to pursue a more interconnected, curiosity-driven teaching strategy.

'Everyone I spoke to during and after our training yesterday was awe-inspired by the session. It was amazing'

TEACHER, BERKSHIRE

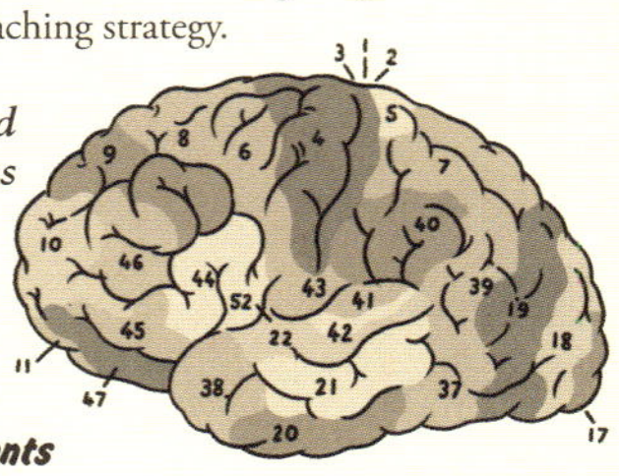

www.whatonearthbooks.com/events

Written by **Christopher Lloyd** and **Patrick Skipworth**. Illustrated by **Andy Forshaw**. Designed by **Will Webb**.
Published by What on Earth Publishing Ltd, The Black Barn, Wickhurst Farm, Leigh, Tonbridge, Kent TN11 8PS, United Kingdom, in association with the Natural History Museum, London.
Printed in China by Waiman. Wallbook is a registered trademark of What on Earth Publishing Ltd.

Contact us at **info@whatonearthbooks.com** or visit our website at **www.whatonearthbooks.com**

HIGHER

HUMAN BIOLOGY

SECOND EDITION

James Torrance

with writing team: James Fullarton, Clare Marsh, James Simms, Caroline Stevenson

DYNAMIC LEARNING

HODDER GIBSON

AN HACHETTE UK COMPANY

The Publishers would like to thank the following for permission to reproduce copyright material:

Photo credits: **p.1** (background) and Section 1 running head image © Alexandr Mitiuc – Fotolia.com, (inset left) © JAMES KING-HOLMES/SCIENCE PHOTO LIBRARY, (inset centre) © Science Photo Library/Alamy Stock Photo, (inset right) © Orlando Florin Rosu/Fotolia.com; **p.4** © Deco Images II/Alamy Stock Photo; **p.7** © CENTRE JEAN PERRIN, ISM/SCIENCE PHOTO LIBRARY; **p.10** JAMES KING-HOLMES/SCIENCE PHOTO LIBRARY; **p.11** (top) © James Torrance, (bottom) © SCIENCE PHOTO LIBRARY; **p.20** © Science History Images/Alamy Stock Photo; **p.47** © Eric Martz, Professor Emeritus, Dept Microbiology, University of Massachusetts; **p.48** © Science Photo Library/Alamy Stock Photo; **p.62** © MAURO FERMARIELLO/SCIENCE PHOTO LIBRARY; **p.109** © Orlando Florin Rosu/Fotolia.com; **p.115** (background) and Section 2 running head image © Imagestate Media (John Foxx)/Patient Care V3063, (inset left) © Armando Babani/EPA/REX/Shutterstock, (inset centre) © DR NAJEEB LAYYOUS/SCIENCE PHOTO LIBRARY, (inset right) © DR P. MARAZZI/SCIENCE PHOTO LIBRARY; **p.127** © Armando Babani/EPA/REX/Shutterstock; **p.137** © DR NAJEEB LAYYOUS/SCIENCE PHOTO LIBRARY; **p.140** © BSIP SA/Alamy Stock Photo; **p.161** © ANDY CRUMP, TDR, WHO/SCIENCE PHOTO LIBRARY; **p.184** © DR P. MARAZZI/SCIENCE PHOTO LIBRARY; **p.201** (background) and Section 3 running head image © Sebastian Kaulitzki – Fotolia.com, (inset left) © BSIP SA/Alamy Stock Photo, (inset centre) © STEVE GSCHMEISSNER/SCIENCE PHOTO LIBRARY, (inset right) © SCIENCE PHOTO LIBRARY; **p.209** © BSIP SA/Alamy Stock Photo; **p.211** © Cindee Madison and Susan Landau, UC Berkeley; **p.212** © PHILIPPE PSAILA/SCIENCE PHOTO LIBRARY; **p.224** MEDICAL BODY SCANS/JESSICA WILSON/SCIENCE PHOTO LIBRARY; **p.230** © Sebastian Kaulitzki – Fotolia.com; **p.232** © STEVE GSCHMEISSNER/SCIENCE PHOTO LIBRARY; **p.233** © DON FAWCETT/SCIENCE PHOTO LIBRARY; **p.241** © Natalie Prinz/stock.adobe.com; **p.245** (top) © MAURO FERMARIELLO/SCIENCE PHOTO LIBRARY, (bottom) © James Torrance; **p.254** © SCIENCE PHOTO LIBRARY; **p.260** © FLPA/Alamy Stock Photo; **p.261** Epipen © Mylan; **p.267** BARBARA RIOS/SCIENCE PHOTO LIBRARY.

Orders: please contact Bookpoint Ltd, 130 Milton Park, Park Drive, Abingdon, Oxon OX14 4SE. Telephone: (+44) 01235 827827. Fax: (+44) 01235 400454. Email education@bookpoint.co.uk Lines are open 9.00–5.00, Monday to Friday, with a 24-hour message answering service. Visit our website at www.hoddereducation.co.uk. If you have queries or questions that aren't about an order, you can contact us at hoddergibson@hodder.co.uk

First published in 2013 © James Torrance, James Fullarton, Clare Marsh, James Simms, Caroline Stevenson
This second edition published in 2019 by
Hodder Gibson, an imprint of Hodder Education,
An Hachette UK Company
211 St Vincent Street
Glasgow G2 5QY

Impression number	5	4	3	2
Year	2022	2021	2020	2019

ISBN: 978 1 5104 5771 3

Cover photo © Fedorov Oleksiy/Shutterstock.com
Illustrations by James Torrance and Integra Software Services Pvt. Ltd., Pondicherry, India
Typeset in Minion Pro 11pt by Integra Software Services Pvt. Ltd., Pondicherry, India
Printed in Italy

A catalogue record for this title is available from the British Library

Contents

Section 1 Human Cells

Section 2 Physiology and Health

Section 3 Neurobiology and Immunology

Appendix 1

Appendix 2

Appendix 3

Appendix 4

Preface

This book has been written to act as a valuable resource for students studying Higher Grade Human Biology. It provides a **core text** which adheres closely to the SQA syllabus for *Higher Human Biology* introduced in 2018. Each section of the book matches a section of the revised syllabus; each chapter corresponds to a content area. In addition to the core text, the book contains a variety of special features:

Learning Activities

Each chapter contains an appropriate selection of learning activities in the form of *Case Studies, Related Topics, Research Topics, Related Information*, *Related Activities* and *Investigations*, as laid down in the SQA Course Support Notes. These non-essential activities are highlighted throughout in yellow for easy identification. They do not form part of the basic mandatory course content needed when preparing for the final exam but are intended to aid understanding and to support research tasks during course work.

Testing Your Knowledge

Key questions incorporated into the text of every chapter and designed to continuously assess *Knowledge and Understanding*. These are especially useful as homework and as instruments of diagnostic assessment to check that full understanding of course content has been achieved.

What You Should Know

Summaries of key facts and concepts as *'Cloze' Tests* accompanied by appropriate word banks. These feature at regular intervals throughout the book and provide an excellent source of material for consolidation and revision prior to the SQA examination.

Applying Your Knowledge and Skills

A variety of questions at the end of each chapter designed to give students practice in exam questions and foster the development of *Skills of Scientific Inquiry and Investigation* (for example, selection of relevant information, presentation of information, processing of information, planning experimental procedure, evaluating, drawing valid conclusions and making predictions and generalisations). These questions are especially useful as extensions to class work and as homework.

Updates and syllabus changes: important note to teachers and students from the publisher

This book covers all course arrangements for Higher Human Biology but does not attempt to give advice on any 'added value assessments' or 'open assignments' that form part of a final grade in Higher Human Biology (2018 onwards).

Please remember that syllabus arrangements change from time to time. We make every effort to update our textbooks as soon as possible when this happens, but – especially if you are using an old copy of this book – it is always advisable to check whether there have been any alterations to the arrangements since this book was printed. You can check the latest arrangements at the SQA website (www.sqa.org.uk), and you can also check for any specific updates to this book at www.hoddereducation.co.uk/scottish-curriculum.

We make every effort to ensure accuracy of content, but if you discover any mistakes please let us know as soon as possible – see our contact details on the back cover.

1 Human Cells

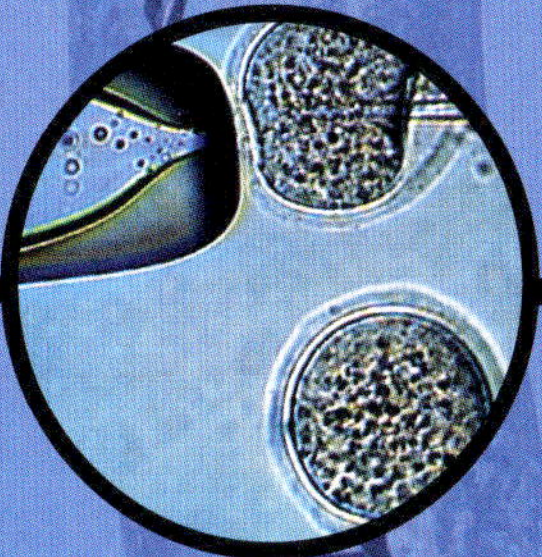
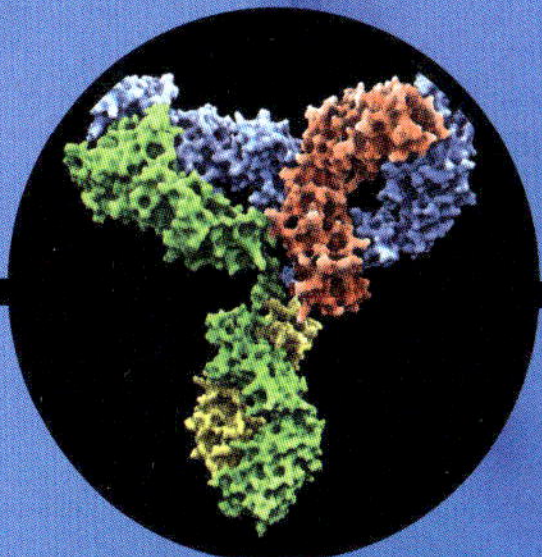

1 Division and differentiation in human cells

Somatic cells

A **somatic** cell is any type of cell in the human body other than those cells that are involved in reproduction.

Division of somatic stem cells

Somatic stem cells divide during growth and tissue repair. In humans, each somatic stem cell contains **46 chromosomes** and is **diploid** (i.e. contains 23 pairs of homologous chromosomes). Prior to nuclear division (**mitosis**), the genetic material undergoes DNA replication (see Chapter 2) and becomes doubled in quantity for a brief time. Nuclear division quickly follows and the genetic material is divided equally between two daughter nuclei. Therefore, each somatic stem cell formed receives an identical copy of the full set of 46 chromosomes and the diploid chromosome number is **maintained**. This process ensures that each somatic stem cell receives a complete set of the genetic information.

Germline cells

Germline cells are the cells involved in reproduction. They include **haploid gametes** (sperm and ova) and the diploid cells that divide to form these gametes.

Division of germline stem cells

Diploid germline stem cells first divide by **mitosis**. The nucleus of each of these cells contains 23 pairs of homologous chromosomes and this genetic material becomes doubled by DNA replication. Following nuclear division, each identical diploid germline stem cell formed receives 23 pairs of homologous chromosomes and the chromosome number is maintained.

Each of these diploid germline stem cells then undergoes a second form of nuclear division called **meiosis**. This involves a further doubling of the genetic material followed by two rounds of nuclear division. The first round separates the homologous chromosomes; the second separates the chromatids. The result is the formation of four haploid gametes, each containing 23 single chromosomes.

The human life cycle alternates between haploid and diploid cells as summarised in Figure 1.1.

Cellular differentiation

A multicellular organism such as a human being consists of a large number of cells. Rather than each cell carrying out every function for the maintenance of life, a **division of labour** occurs and most of the cells become differentiated. **Cellular differentiation** is the process by which an unspecialised cell becomes altered and adapted to perform a specialised function as part of a permanent tissue.

Differentiation in human cells

A human being begins life as a fertilised egg (zygote), as shown in Figure 1.2. The zygote divides repeatedly by mitosis and cell division to form an embryo. Like the cells in an adult, each **embryonic cell** possesses all the genes for constructing the whole organism. However, unlike those in adult cells, all the genes in cells at this early stage are switched on or have the potential to become switched on.

As embryological development proceeds, the unspecialised cells of the early embryo undergo **differentiation** and become **specialised** in structure and biochemical properties, making them perfectly adapted for carrying out a particular function. For example, a motor neuron (see Figure 1.2) is a type of nerve cell that possesses an axon (a long, insulated cytoplasmic extension). This structure is ideally suited to the transmission of nerve impulses. Similarly the cells of the epithelial lining of the windpipe are perfectly suited to their job of sweeping dirty mucus up and away from the lungs.

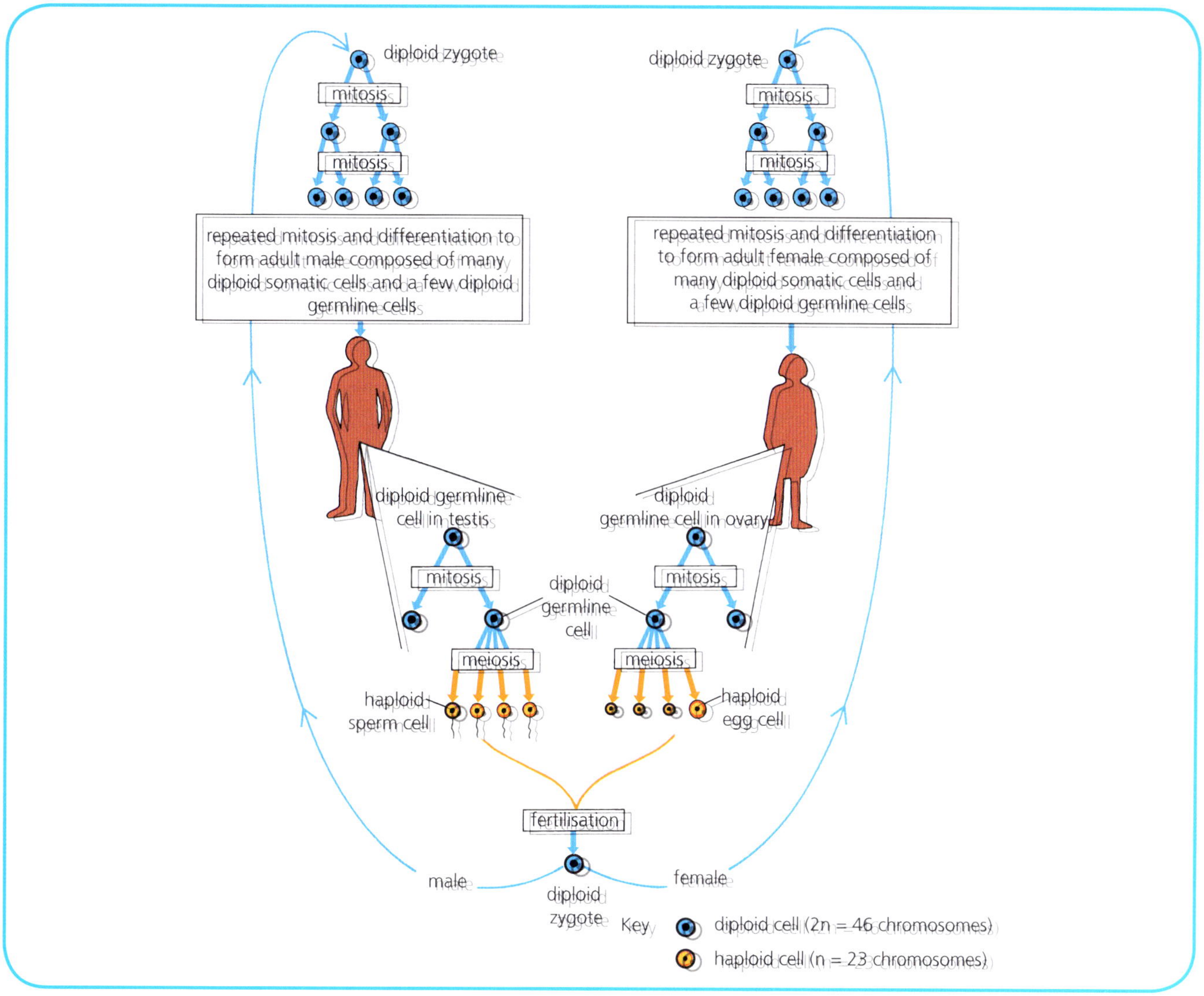

Figure 1.1 Human life cycle

Selective gene expression

Once a cell becomes differentiated, it only expresses the genes that code (see Chapter 3) for the proteins characteristic of that particular type of cell. For example, in a nerve cell, genes that code for the formation of neurotransmitter substances are switched on and continue to operate but those for mucus are switched off. The reverse is true of the genes in a goblet cell in the lining of the windpipe. Only a fraction of the genes in a specialised cell are expressed (e.g. 3–5% in a typical human cell).

Stem cells

Stem cells are unspecialised cells that can:

- **reproduce** ('self-renew') themselves by repeated mitosis and cell division while remaining undifferentiated and unspecialised
- **differentiate** into specialised cells when required to do so by the multicellular organism that possesses them.

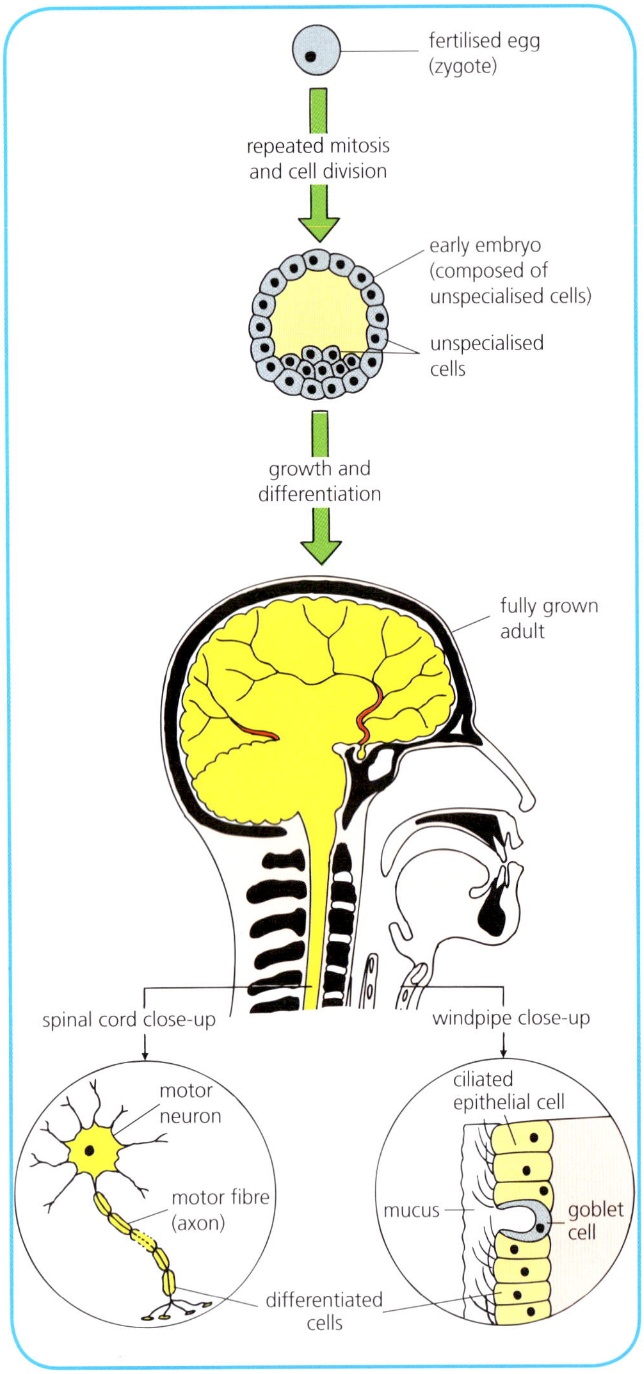

Figure 1.2 Differentiation

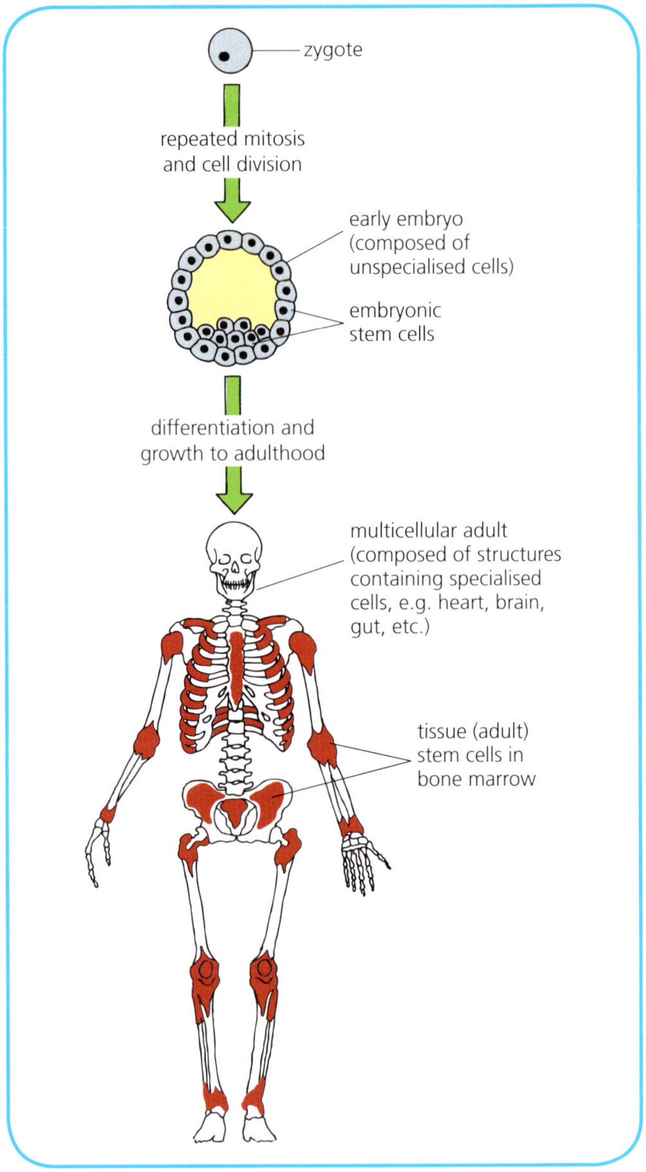

Figure 1.3 Two types of stem cell

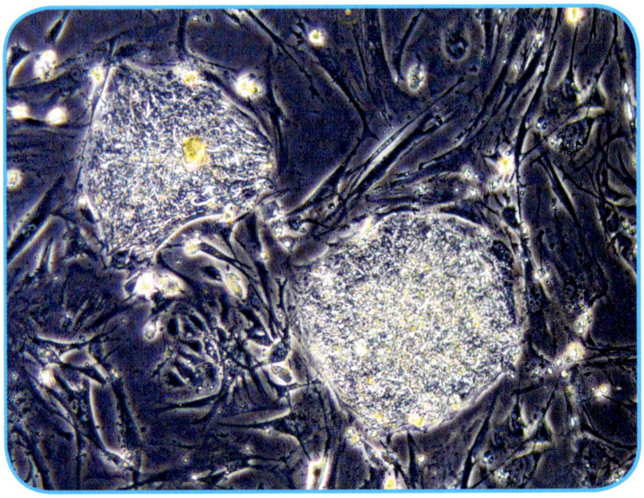

Figure 1.4 Embryonic stem cells

Embryonic stem cells

An early human embryo consists of a ball of **embryonic stem cells** (see Figures 1.3 and 1.4). All of the genes in an embryonic cell have the potential to be switched on, so the cell is capable of differentiating into almost all of the cell types (more than 200) found in the human body. Because of this ability, embryonic stem cells are described as being **pluripotent** (see also page 9).

Tissue stem cells

Tissue stem cells are found in locations such as skin and red bone marrow (see Figure 1.3). They have a much **narrower differentiation potential** than embryonic stem cells because many of their genes are already switched off. However, they are able to replenish continuously the supply of certain differentiated cells needed by the organism such as skin, intestinal lining and blood.

Tissue stem cells can only give rise to a limited range of cell types closely related to the tissue in which they are normally located. However, they are involved in the growth, repair and renewal of all the cell types found in that particular tissue and are therefore described as being **multipotent**. For example, blood stem cells in red bone marrow give rise to red blood cells, white blood cells (various forms of phagocytes and lymphocytes) and platelets. (Also see the Related Topic – Origin of blood cells below.)

Related Topic

Origin of blood cells

Tissue stem cells in red bone marrow (see Figure 1.5) give rise to red blood cells, platelets and specialised white blood cells including phagocytes, natural killer cells and B and T lymphocytes – the cells of the immune system.

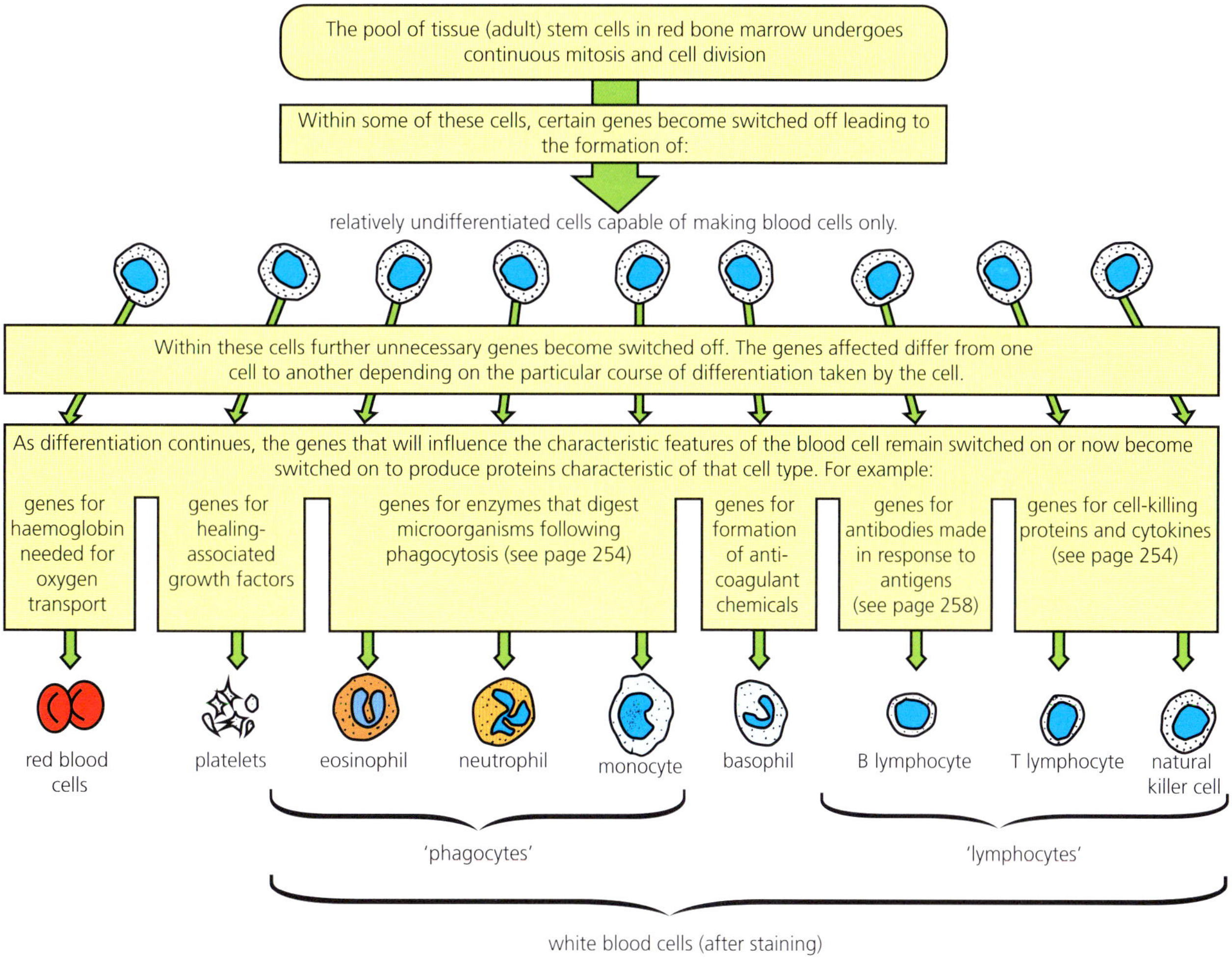

The pool of tissue (adult) stem cells in red bone marrow undergoes continuous mitosis and cell division
Within some of these cells, certain genes become switched off leading to the formation of:
relatively undifferentiated cells capable of making blood cells only.
Within these cells further unnecessary genes become switched off. The genes affected differ from one cell to another depending on the particular course of differentiation taken by the cell.
As differentiation continues, the genes that will influence the characteristic features of the blood cell remain switched on or now become switched on to produce proteins characteristic of that cell type. For example:
genes for haemoglobin needed for oxygen transport
genes for healing-associated growth factors
genes for enzymes that digest microorganisms following phagocytosis (see page 254)
genes for formation of anti-coagulant chemicals
genes for antibodies made in response to antigens (see page 258)
genes for cell-killing proteins and cytokines (see page 254)
red blood cells
platelets
eosinophil
neutrophil
monocyte
basophil
B lymphocyte
T lymphocyte
natural killer cell
'phagocytes'
'lymphocytes'
white blood cells (after staining)

Figure 1.5 Origin of blood cells

Testing Your Knowledge 1

1 a) Briefly describe how chromosome number is maintained in a somatic cell at cell division. (2)
   b) What is the difference between the terms *haploid and diploid?* (2)
   c) What is a *germline* cell? (1)
   d) Briefly describe how a diploid germline cell produces haploid gametes. (2)

2 a) Define the term *cellular differentiation.* (2)
   b) In what way is a ciliated epithelial cell a good example of a specialised cell? (1)
   c) A goblet cell in the lining of the windpipe produces mucus but not insulin. Explain briefly how this specialisation is brought about with reference to genes. (2)

3 a) Give TWO characteristics of stem cells. (2)
   b) i) Name TWO types of stem cell found in humans.
      ii) For each type, identify ONE location where these cells could be found. (4)
   c) Which type of stem cell is capable of differentiating into all the types of cell that make up the organism to which it belongs? (1)

Research value of stem cells

Much of the research to date has been carried out using stem cells from embryos of mice and humans. Human stem cells will renew themselves when grown in optimal culture conditions, provided that certain growth factors are present. In the absence of these growth factors, the stem cells differentiate rapidly.

By investigating why stem cells continue to multiply in the presence of a certain chemical yet undergo differentiation in its absence, scientists are attempting to obtain a fuller understanding of cell processes such as growth and differentiation. It is hoped that this will lead in turn to a better understanding of gene regulation (including the molecular biology of cancer).

Models

A **model organism** is one that is suitable for laboratory research because its biological characteristics are similar to those of a group of related (but often unavailable) organisms. For example, mice are used in research as model organisms for humans since they possess many genes equivalent to the genes in humans that are responsible for certain inherited diseases. Research work on the models helps to provide an understanding of the malfunctioning of these genes and may lead the way to the development of new treatments.

Similarly **stem cells**, which are genetically identical to differentiated somatic cells, can be used in research as **model cells** to investigate:

- the means by which certain diseases and disorders develop
- the responses of cells to new pharmaceutical drugs.

Therapeutic use of stem cells

Cornea repair

In recent years, scientists have shown that **corneal damage** by chemical burning can be successfully treated using stem cell tissue. This can be grown from the patient's own stem cells located at the edge of the cornea. In many cases, the person's eyesight can be restored following grafting of the stem cell tissue from the healthy eye to the surface of the damaged eye.

Skin graft

In a traditional skin graft, a relatively large section of skin is removed from a region of the person's body and grafted to the site of injury. This means that the person has two bodily areas that need careful treatment and time to heal.

A skin graft using stem cells only requires a **small sample** of skin to be taken to obtain stem cells. Therefore the site needs much less healing time and suffers minimum scarring. The sample is normally taken from an area close to and similar in structure to the site of injury. Enzymes are used to isolate and loosen the stem cells which are then cultured. Once a **suspension of new stem cells** has developed, they are sprayed over the damaged area to bring about regeneration of missing skin.

Bone marrow transplant

Tissue stem cells present in bone marrow and blood are routinely used in bone marrow transplantation to treat cancers of the blood.

Case Study: Future potential therapeutic uses of stem cells

Treatment of burns

Recently, human embryonic stem cells grown on synthetic scaffolds have been used to treat burn victims. The stem cell tissue provides a source of **temporary skin** while the patient is waiting for grafts of their own skin to develop. This potential use of stem cells is expected to be developed further in the future.

Treatment of degenerative conditions

Embryonic stem cells are able to differentiate into any type of cell in the body. Therefore, they are believed to have the potential to provide treatments in the future for a wide range of disorders and degenerative conditions such as **diabetes**, **Parkinson's disease** and **Alzheimer's disease** (see Figure 1.6) that traditional medicine has been unable to cure. Already scientists have managed to generate nerve cells from embryonic stem cells in culture. It is hoped that this work will eventually be translated into effective therapies to treat neurological disorders such as multiple sclerosis. However, the use of embryonic stem cells raises questions of **ethics**.

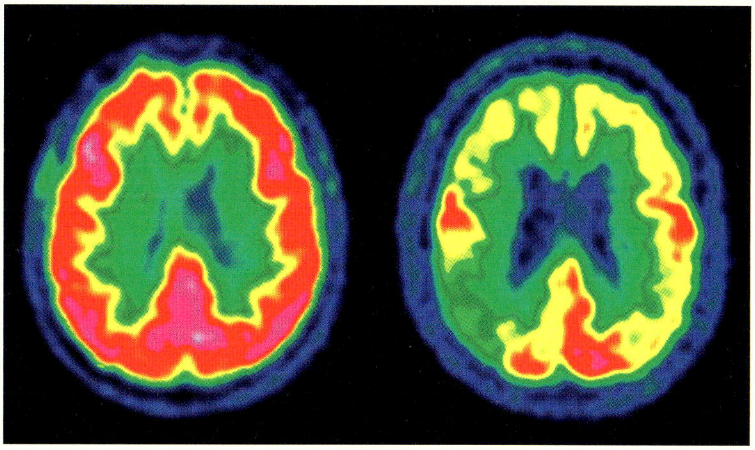

Figure 1.6 Brain scans showing normal brain on the left and brain with Alzheimer's disease on the right

Ethical issues

Ethics refers to the moral values and rules that ought to govern human conduct. The use of stem cells raises several **ethical issues**. For example, the extraction of human embryonic stem cells to create a stem cell line (a continuous culture) for research purposes results in the destruction of the human embryo. Many people believe strongly that this practice is unethical (see Case Study – Embryonic stem cell debate).

Ethical issues are also raised by the use of **induced pluripotent stem cells** (see Case Study – Sources of stem cells) and by the use of **nuclear transfer technique** (see Case Study – Nuclear transfer technique).

Case Study Embryonic stem cell debate

At present the creation of a human embryonic stem cell line using cells from a human embryo (of no more than 14 days) results in the destruction of the embryo. The ethical debate about the use of embryonic stem cells most commonly rests on the controversial question: 'Is a human embryo of less than 2 weeks a human *person*?'

People on one side of the debate believe that the embryo is definitely a human person and argue that fatally extracting stem cells from it constitutes murder. People on the other side of the debate feel certain that the embryo is not yet a person and believe that removing stem cells from it is morally acceptable.

The people who are against stem cell research using human embryos often support their case with the following claims:

- A human life begins when a sperm cell fuses with an egg cell and it is inviolable (i.e. it is sacred and must not be harmed).
- A unique version of human DNA is created at conception.
- A fertilised egg is a human being with a soul.
- Stem cell research violates the sanctity of life.

The people who are in favour of stem cell research using human embryos often support their case with the following arguments:

- An embryo is not a person although it has the potential to develop into a person.
- At 14 days or less an embryo is not sentient (i.e. it does not have a brain, a nervous system, consciousness or powers of sensation).
- The death of a very young embryo is not of serious moral concern when it has the potential to benefit humanity (particularly people whose daily lives are compromised by debilitating medical conditions).
- Abortion is legal in many countries including the UK. Destroying a 14-day-old embryo is far less objectionable to most people than terminating a fetus at 20 weeks.
- Stem cell research uses embryos that were generated for IV fertilisation but were not used and would be destroyed as a matter of course.

Possible solutions to the problem

In the future the ethical issues raised by the use of embryonic stem cells may become less heated if advances in **induced pluripotent stem cell** technology (see page 9) and increased use of stem cells from **amniotic fluid** (see page 9) reduce the need for their use.

Case Study Sources of stem cells

Donated embryos

At present patients undergoing infertility treatment may agree to donate any **extra embryos** that are not required for their treatment to medical science. These very early embryos provide an immediate source of embryonic stem cells for research. In addition **long-term cultures** originally set up using cells isolated from donated embryos and continued for many years provide a further source of embryonic stem cells. However, the number of human embryonic cells available for research remains limited and this restricts the ability of scientists to carry out research work in this important area.

Amniotic fluid

Scientists continue to search for new sources of stem cells. One of these is **amniotic fluid**. The stem cells that it contains can be harvested from the fluid removed from pregnant women for amniocentesis tests (see Figure 1.7). The stem cells obtained are capable of differentiating into many types of specialised cell such as bone, muscle, nerve and liver. One advantage of using stem cells from amniotic fluid is that it does not involve the destruction of a human embryo.

Induced pluripotent stem cells

A **totipotent** stem cell is one that is able to differentiate into any cell type and is capable of giving rise to the complete organism. A **pluripotent** stem cell is a descendent of a totipotent stem cell and is capable of differentiating into many different types of cell.

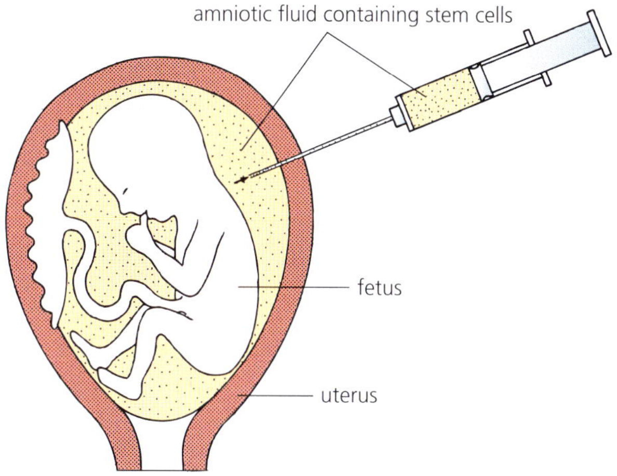

Figure 1.7 Stem cells in amniotic fluid

Induced pluripotent stem cells are, strictly speaking, not true stem cells. They are differentiated cells (e.g. from human skin) that have been genetically reprogrammed using transcription factors (see Chapter 3) to switch some of their turned-off genes back on again. As a result they act as stem cells and can be used for research. However, the viruses used as vectors to deliver the transcription factors have been shown to cause cancers in mouse models. Therefore a significant amount of research is essential in this area before induced pluripotent cells can be considered for use as part of a routine medical procedure.

Case Study Nuclear transfer technique

This technique involves removing the nucleus from an egg (see Figure 1.8) and then replacing it with a nucleus from a donor cell. Some cells constructed in this way divide normally, producing undifferentiated stem cells.

Using this technique, a nucleus from a human cell (e.g. skin) can be introduced into an **enucleated** animal cell (e.g. an egg cell from a cow), as shown in Figure 1.9. The cell formed is called a **cytoplasmic hybrid cell**. Once it begins to divide, stem cells can be extracted after 5 days and used for research. However, they are not 100% human and must not be used for therapeutic procedures.

Some people feel that it is unethical to mix materials from human cells with those of another species even if the hybrid cells formed are used strictly for research purposes only. Other people support the production of cytoplasmic hybrid cells because it helps to relieve the shortage of human embryonic stem cells available for research. In addition, they point out that the practice allows the nucleus from a diseased human cell (e.g. from a patient with a

→

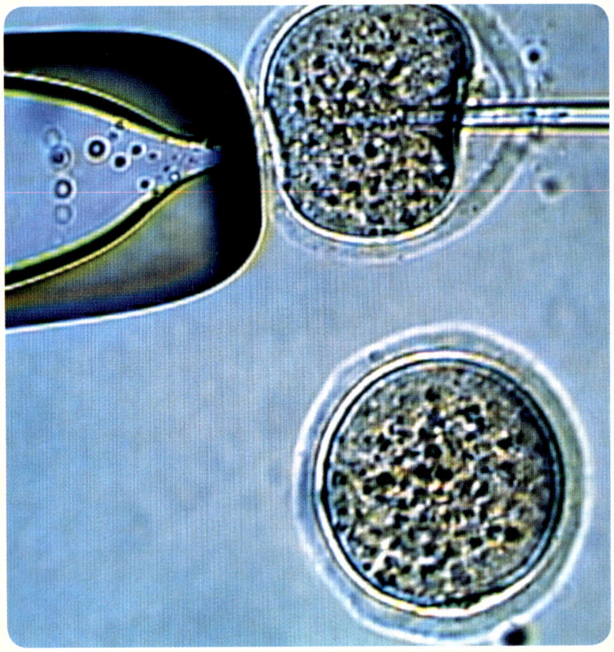

Figure 1.8 Removing the nucleus from an egg

degenerative disease or cancer) to be introduced into the enucleated animal egg. This may allow scientists to study the gene expression in these cells, observe how the disease develops and eventually develop new treatments that disrupt the disease process.

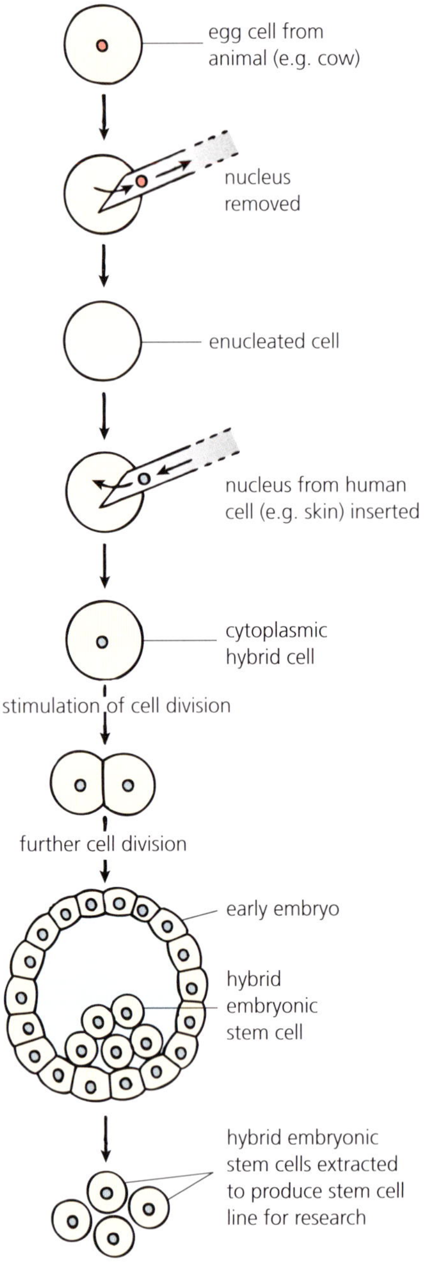

Figure 1.9 Nuclear transfer technique

Cancer cells

A **cancer** is an uncontrolled growth of cells. Cell division in normal healthy cells is controlled by factors such as cell cycle regulators and external chemical signals. Cancerous cells do not respond to these **regulatory signals**.

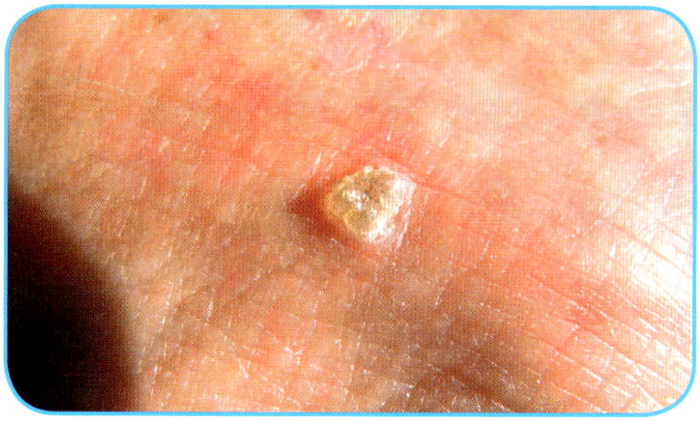

Figure 1.10 Wart

Tumours

Cancer cells divide uncontrollably to produce a mass of abnormal cells called a **tumour**. A tumour is described as **benign** if it remains as a discrete group of abnormal cells in one place within an otherwise normal tissue. Most benign tumours (e.g. warts – see Figure 1.10) do not cause problems and can be successfully removed.

A tumour is said to be **malignant** if some of its cells lose the surface molecules that keep them attached to the original cell group, enter the circulatory system and spread through the body. This enables them to invade other tissues and do harm by 'seeding' new tumours in other parts of the body (see Figure 1.11).

Genetic errors

Most cancers originate from a cell that has undergone a succession of **mutations** to the genes involved in the control of cell division. As these genetic errors accumulate, a point is reached where control of cell division is lost. The cell can now divide excessively, unhindered by any regulatory signal or control mechanism.

Normally it takes a very long time for a cell to accumulate, and be affected by, several different mutations. It is for this reason that the risk of cancer increases with age. However, the risk is also increased by exposure to **agents that cause genetic damage** such as smoking, pollution and excessive exposure of skin to ultraviolet radiation (see Figure 1.12). Cancer is particularly common in skin, lung and bowel tissue because the mutation rate is higher than normal in these cells that have a high frequency of division.

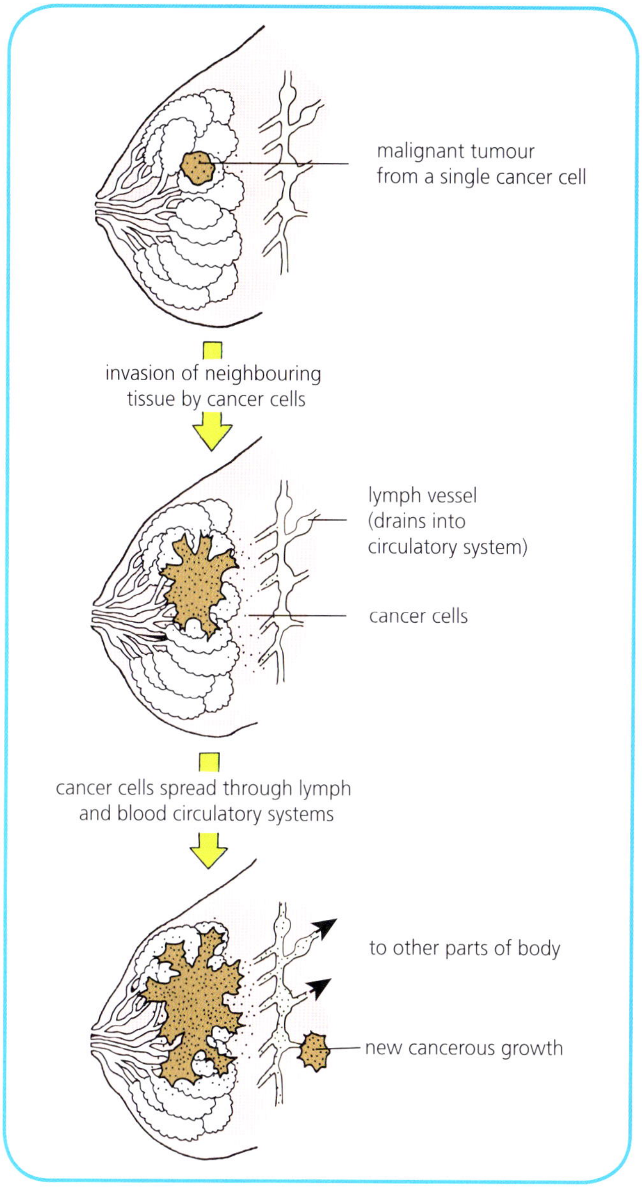

Figure 1.11 Breast cancer

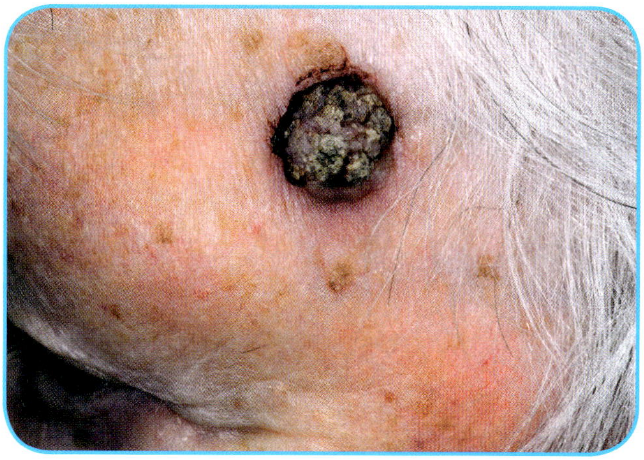

Figure 1.12 Skin cancer

Testing Your Knowledge 2

1 a) i) Name ONE medical condition that is routinely treated using tissue stem cells.
ii) From where in the human body are these cells obtained? (2)
b) Give an example of a medical condition that might be treated in the future using stem cells. (1)
c) Why can the stem cells used to treat the medical condition you gave as your answer to a) not be used to treat patients who have the condition you gave as your answer to b)? (2)

2 One definition of the word *ethical* is 'in accordance with principles that are morally correct'. Briefly explain why stem cell research using human embryos raises ethical issues. (2)

3 Identify TWO characteristics of cancer cells. (2)

Applying Your Knowledge and Skills

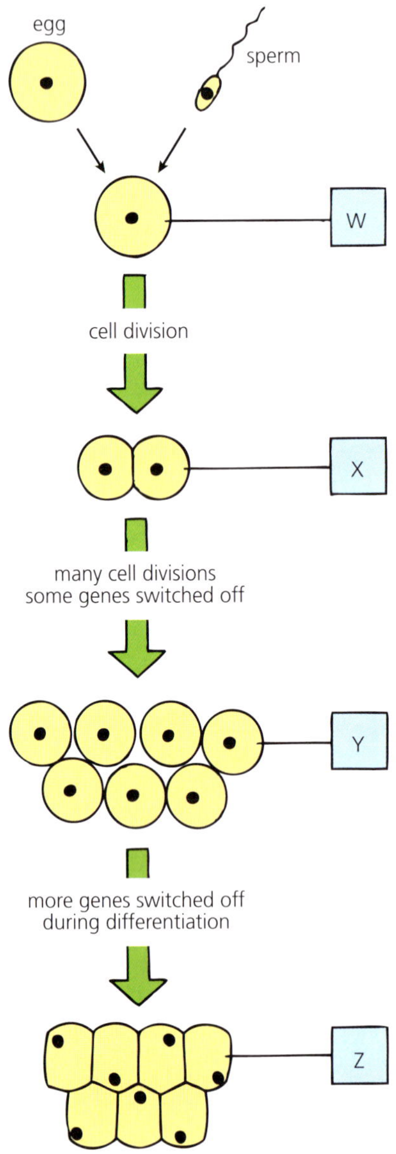

Figure 1.13

1 Figure 1.13 represents the processes of cell division and cellular differentiation in an animal.
Match W, X, Y and Z with the following terms: *specialised cell*, *zygote*, *tissue stem cell* and *embryonic stem cell*. (3)

2 Figure 1.14 shows a possible use of stem cells in the future.

a) Match blank boxes P, Q, R, S, T and U with the following possible answers. (5)

i) stem cells induced to differentiate

ii) nucleus removed and retained

iii) stem cells removed and cultured in laboratory

iv) egg lacking nucleus retained

v) matching tissue transplanted to patient without fear of rejection

vi) nucleus inserted into egg

b) Which of the following is **not** represented in Figure 1.14? (1)

A cytoplasmic hybrid cell

B amniotic stem cell line

C undifferentiated stem cells

D nuclear transfer technique

c) i) Name a source of the donor egg cells used at present in this line of research.

ii) Why does this prevent the series of events shown in the diagram being put into practice? (2)

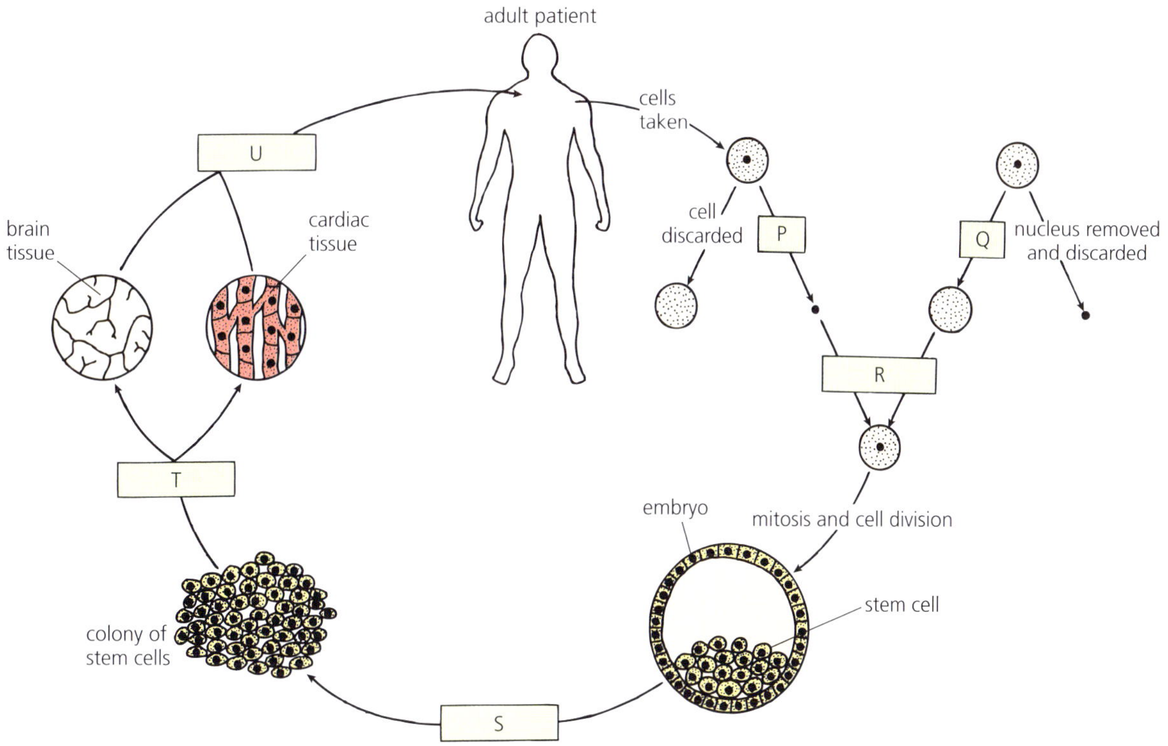

Figure 1.14

3 The procedure that was adopted to produce 'Dolly the sheep' is shown in Figure 1.15.

a) What name is given to the technique employed to create the original cell that gave rise to Dolly? (1)

b) Why is Dolly said to be the result of a *cloning* procedure? (1)

c) i) Did Dolly develop a black face or a white face?

ii) Explain your answer. (2)

d) i) What was the chance of Dolly being a ram?

A 0 B 1 in 1 C 1 in 2

ii) Explain your choice of answer. (2)

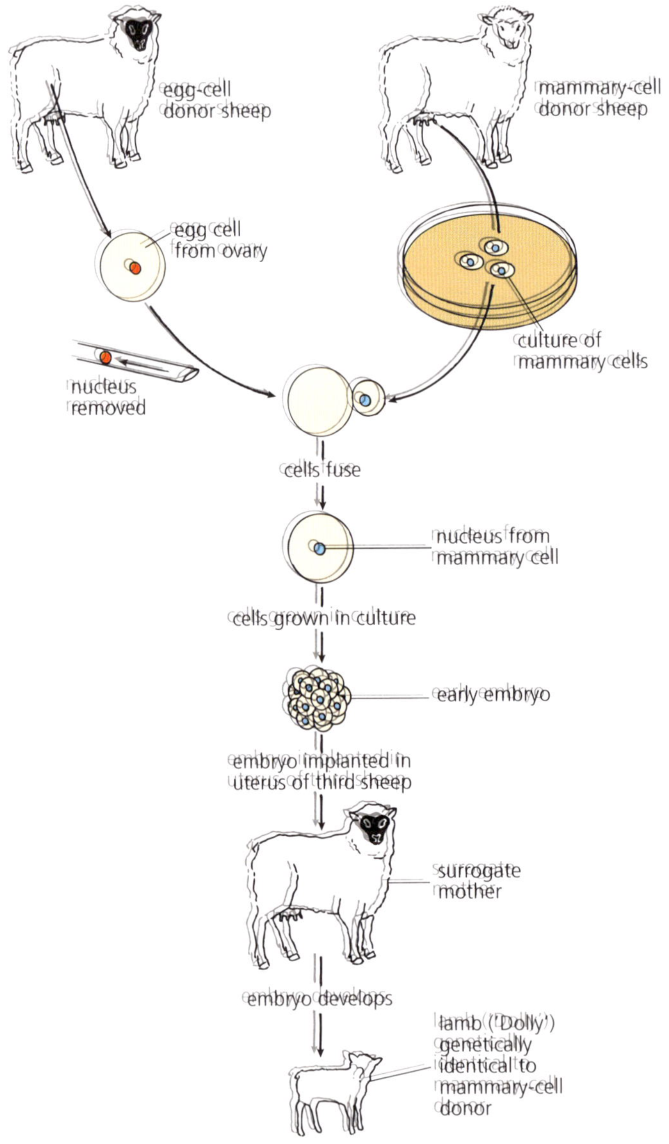

Figure 1.15

→

4 The four people shown in Figure 1.16 all support the use of human embryos in stem cell research.

a) Who is making a statement based on fact rather than expressing an opinion? (1)

b) i) Do you consider this person's statement to be a convincing or an unconvincing argument in support of the use of embryonic stem cells for research?

ii) Justify your answer. (2)

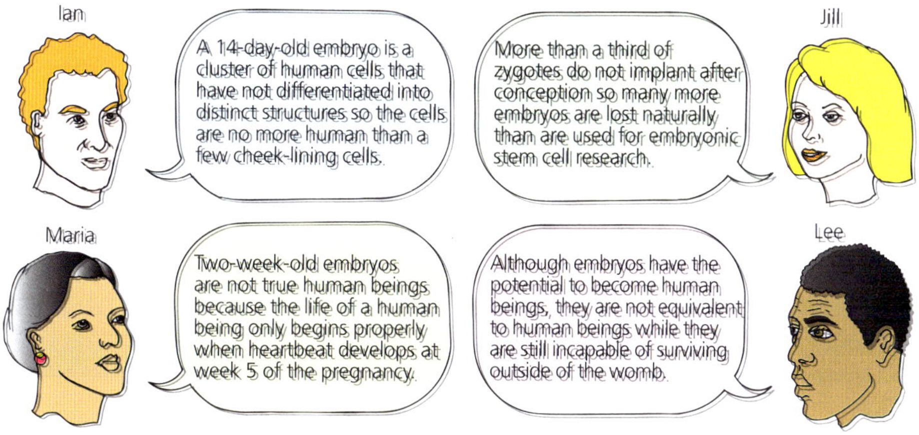
Ian
A 14-day-old embryo is a cluster of human cells that have not differentiated into distinct structures so the cells are no more human than a few cheek-lining cells.
Jill
More than a third of zygotes do not implant after conception so many more embryos are lost naturally than are used for embryonic stem cell research.
Maria
Two-week-old embryos are not true human beings because the life of a human being only begins properly when heartbeat develops at week 5 of the pregnancy.
Lee
Although embryos have the potential to become human beings, they are not equivalent to human beings while they are still incapable of surviving outside of the womb.

Figure 1.16

5 Table 1.1 refers to a country's lung cancer death rates.

	Lung cancer deaths per 100 000 population									
Year	**2000**	**2001**	**2002**	**2003**	**2004**	**2005**	**2006**	**2007**	**2008**	**2009**
Region A	51.2	48.3	52.8	49.3	47.7	47.5	48.4	47.4	47.4	47.2
Region B	60.1	57.8	61.1	60.2	62.5	57.7	53.6	53.6	52.3	51.4
Whole country	55.3	55.1	55.6	54.8	53.9	53.1	52.8	52.3	52.3	52.0

Table 1.1

a) By how many deaths per 100 000 was the lung cancer death rate for region B greater than that for region A in i) 2002? ii) 2007? (2)

b) i) How many people per million died of lung cancer in region A during 2004?

ii) What percentage of people in the whole country died of lung cancer in 2009? (2)

c) i) Which region's data reflect more closely the trend shown by the country as a whole? Explain how you arrived at your answer.

ii) In what way does the **overall** trend for the other region differ from that of the country as a whole? (3)

→

6 The data in Table 1.2 show the results of a survey carried out on people aged 45–64 years in a northern European country who died of melanoma skin cancer.

a) Draw a line graph of the data for the northern European country. (3)

b) Identify the **dependent** and the **independent** variables from your graph. (1)

c) What overall trend does the graph show? (1)

d) i) Which reading in the table is most likely to be a source of error?

ii) Justify your answer with reference to the data in the table. (3)

e) How many northern European people of this age group per million died of melanoma cancer in 1998? (1)

f) i) Calculate the percentage increase in deaths per 100 000 for the northern European country between 1990 and 1992.

ii) Calculate the percentage decrease in deaths per 100 000 for all Europe between 1996 and 1997. (2)

g) i) Which of the following would be the most likely value of deaths per 100 000 for the northern European country for the year 2000?

A 7.8 **B** 5.2 **C** 1.9

ii) Explain your choice of answer. (2)

h) Suggest TWO reasons why death due to melanoma cancer is now less common among the people of this northern European country than it was in the 1990s. (2)

Year	Deaths per 100 000 population (northern European country)	Deaths per 100 000 population (all Europe)
1990	3.2	1.5
1991	3.7	1.9
1992	4.4	2.3
1993	3.6	1.8
1994	7.2	2.2
1995	4.7	2.2
1996	5.3	2.5
1997	4.9	2.3
1998	5.5	2.6
1999	5.5	2.7

Table 1.2

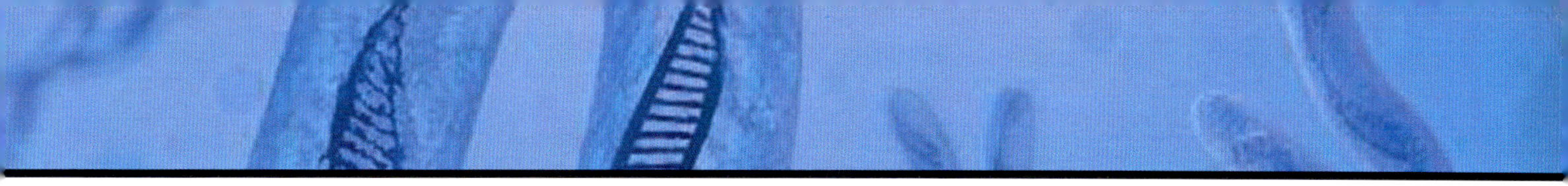

2 Structure and replication of DNA

DNA (deoxyribonucleic acid) is a complex molecule present in all living cells. It is the molecule of inheritance and it stores genetic information in its sequence of bases. This sequence determines the organism's genotype and the structure of its proteins.

Structure of DNA

A molecule of DNA consists of two strands each composed of repeating units called **nucleotides**. Each DNA nucleotide consists of a molecule of **deoxyribose** sugar joined to a **phosphate** group and an organic **base**. Figure 2.1 shows the carbon skeleton of a molecule of deoxyribose. Figure 2.2 shows the four types of base present in DNA.

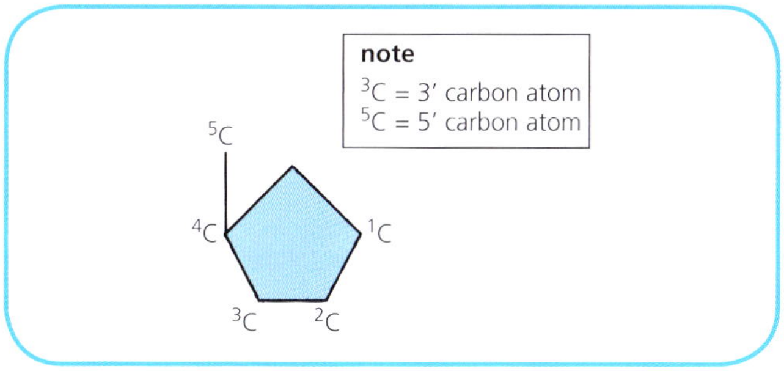

Figure 2.1 Deoxyribose

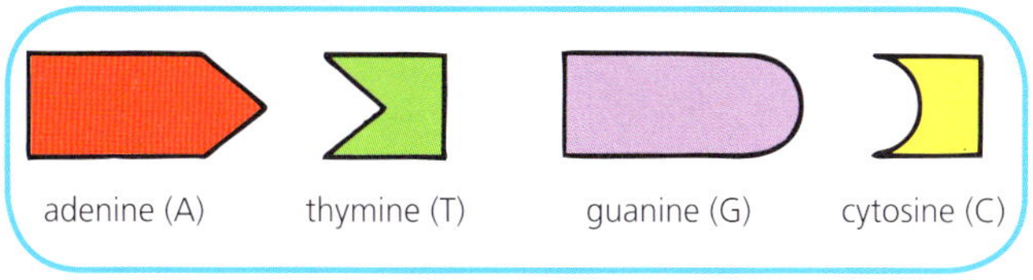

Figure 2.2 Four types of organic base

Figure 2.3 shows how the deoxyribose molecule in a nucleotide has a base attached to its carbon 1 and a phosphate attached to its carbon 5. Since there are four types of base, there are four types of nucleotide.

Sugar–phosphate backbone

A strong **chemical bond** forms between the phosphate group of one nucleotide and the carbon 3 of the deoxyribose on another nucleotide (see Figure 2.4). By this means neighbouring nucleotides become joined together into a long, permanent strand in which sugar molecules alternate with phosphate groups, forming the DNA molecule's **sugar–phosphate backbone**.

Base-pairing

Two of these strands of nucleotides become joined together by weak **hydrogen bonds** forming between their bases (see Figure 2.5). However, the hydrogen bonds can be broken when it becomes necessary for the two strands to separate.

Each base can only join up with one other type of base: adenine (A) always bonds with thymine (T) and guanine (G) always bonds with cytosine (C). A–T and G–C are called **base pairs**.

Antiparallel strands

A DNA strand's **3′ end** on deoxyribose is distinct from its **5′ end** at a phosphate group. The chain is only able to grow by adding nucleotides to its 3′ end. In Figure 2.6 the DNA strand on the left has its 3′ growing end at the bottom of the diagram and its 5′ end at the top. The reverse is true of its complementary strand on the right. This arrangement of the two strands with their sugar–phosphate backbones running in **opposite directions** is

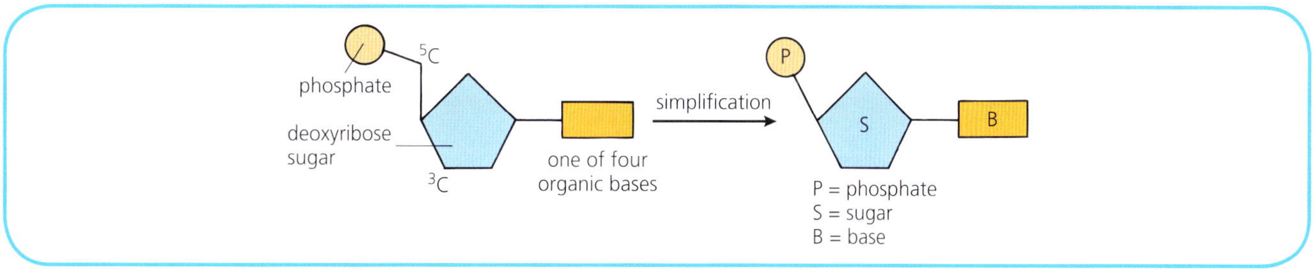

Figure 2.3 Structure of a DNA molecule

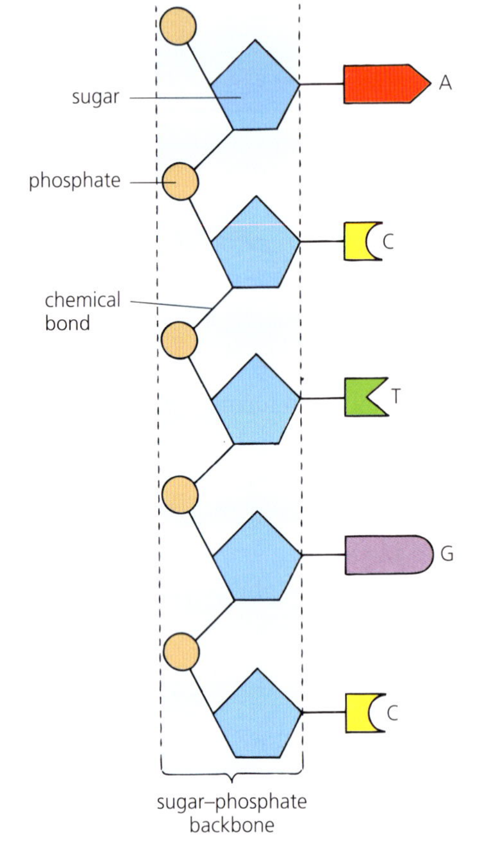

Figure 2.4 Sugar–phosphate backbone

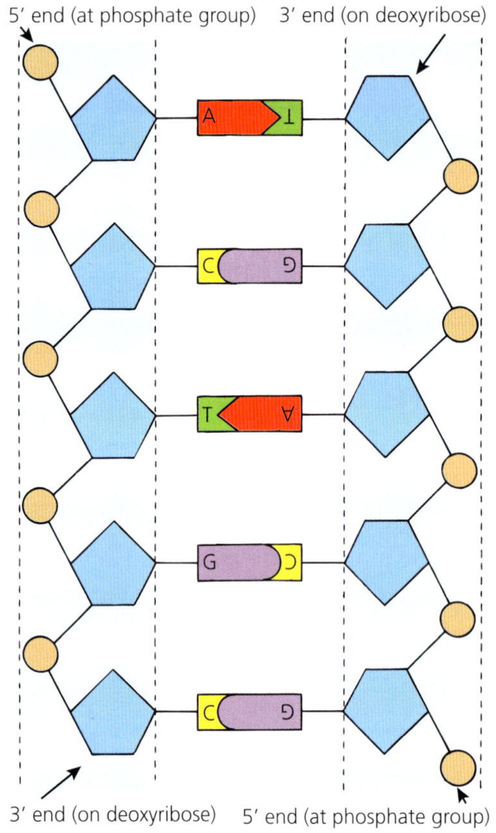

Figure 2.6 Antiparallel strands

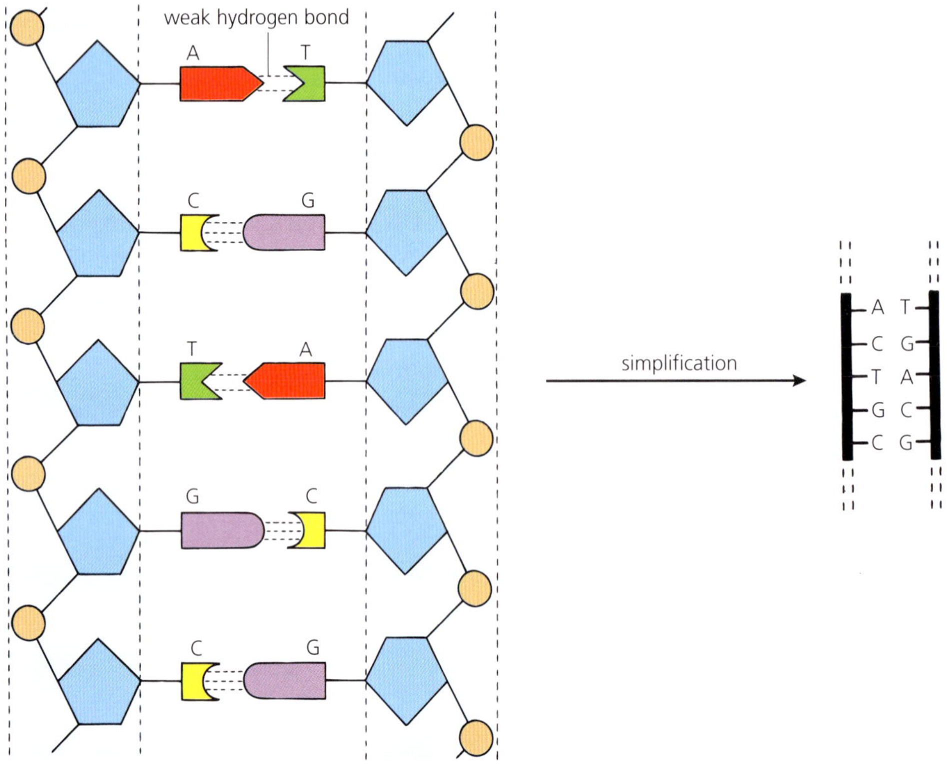

Figure 2.5 Base-pairing

described as **antiparallel**. (For the sake of simplicity the letters in a diagram are normally all written the same way up.)

Double helix

In order for the base pairs to align with each other, the two strands in a DNA molecule take the form of a twisted coil called a **double helix** (see Figure 2.7) with the sugar–phosphate backbones on the outside and the base pairs on the inside. As a result, a DNA molecule is like a spiral ladder in which the sugar–phosphate backbones form the uprights and the base pairs form the rungs.

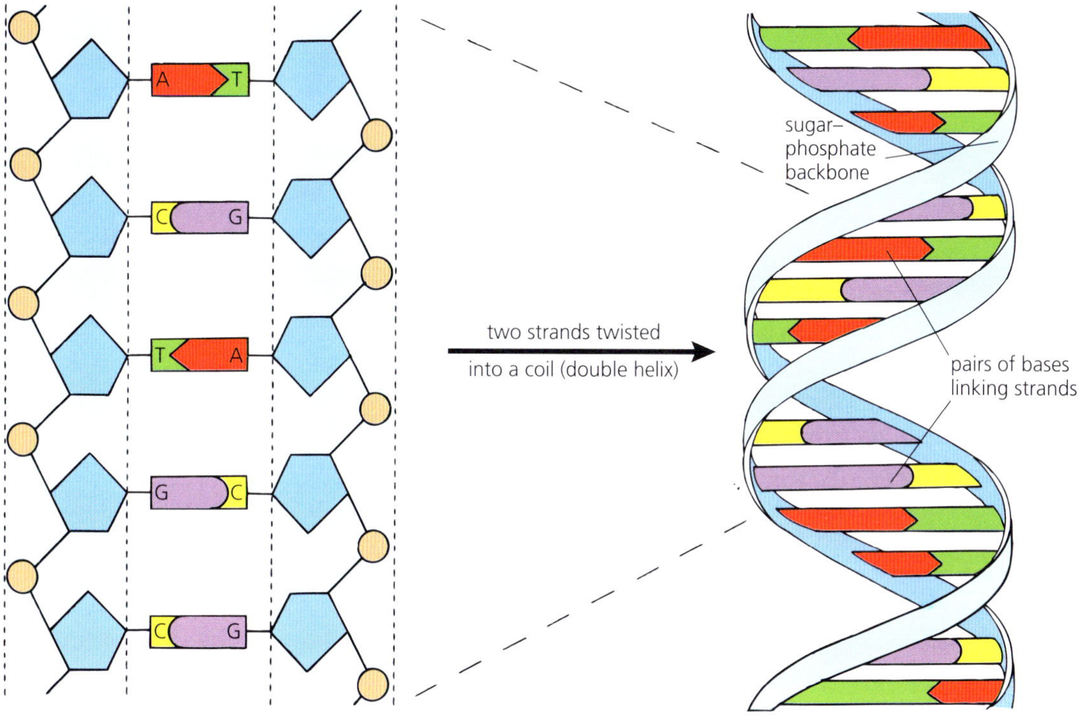

Figure 2.7 Double helix

Case Study — Establishing the structure of DNA

During the first half of the twentieth century, the results from a series of experiments demonstrated conclusively that **DNA** was the genetic material present in cells. Next, scientists became keen to establish the three-dimensional structure of DNA.

Chemical analysis

In the late 1940s, Chargaff analysed the base composition of DNA extracted from a number of different species. He found that the quantities of the four bases were not all equal but that they always occurred in a **characteristic** ratio regardless of the source of the DNA. These findings, called Chargaff's rules, are summarised as follows:

- The number of adenine bases = the number of thymine bases (i.e. A:T = 1:1).
- The number of guanine bases = the number of cytosine bases (i.e. G:C = 1:1).

However, Chargaff's rules remained unexplained until the double helix was discovered.

X-ray crystallography

At around the time that Chargaff was carrying out chemical analysis of DNA, Wilkins and Franklin were employing **X-ray crystallography**. When X-rays are passed through a crystal of DNA, they become deflected (diffracted) into a **scatter pattern**, which is

→

determined by the arrangement of the atoms in the DNA molecule (see Figure 2.8).

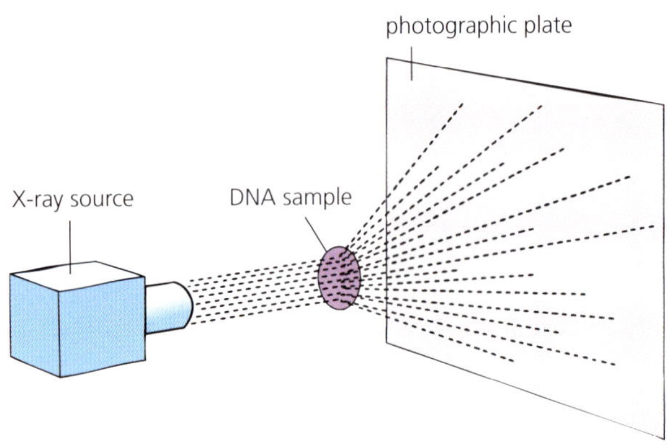

Figure 2.8 X-ray crystallography

When the scatter pattern of X-rays is recorded using a photographic plate, a **diffraction pattern** of spots is produced (see Figure 2.9). This reveals information that can be used to build up a **three-dimensional picture** of the molecules in the crystal. Wilkins and Franklin found that the X-ray diffraction patterns of DNA from different species (e.g. bull, trout and bacteria) were identical.

Formation of an evidence-based conclusion

From the X-ray diffraction patterns of DNA (produced by Wilkins and Franklin) Watson and Crick figured out that the DNA must be a long, thin molecule of constant diameter coiled in the form of a **helix**. In addition, the density of the arrangement of the atoms indicated to them that the DNA must be composed of **two strands**.

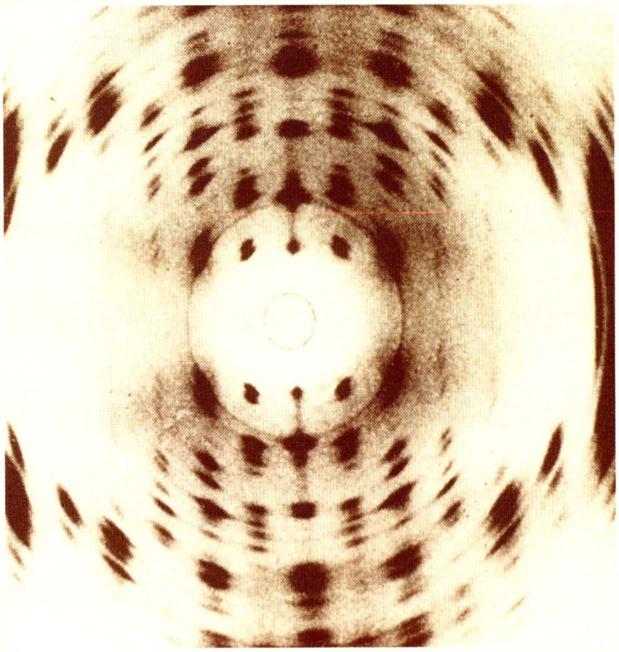

Figure 2.9 X-ray diffraction pattern of DNA

From Chargaff's rules they deduced that base A must be paired with T and base G with C. They figured that this could only be possible if DNA consisted of two strands held together by specific **pairing of bases**. Taking into account further information about distances between atoms and angles of bonds, Watson and Crick set about building a wire model of DNA and in 1953 were first to establish the three-dimensional **double helix** structure of DNA.

Testing Your Knowledge 1

1 a) i) How many different types of base molecule are found in DNA?
   ii) Name each type. (3)
  b) Which type of bond forms between the bases of adjacent strands of a DNA molecule? (1)
  c) Describe the base-pairing rule. (1)

→

2 a) Figure 2.10 shows part of one strand of a DNA molecule.

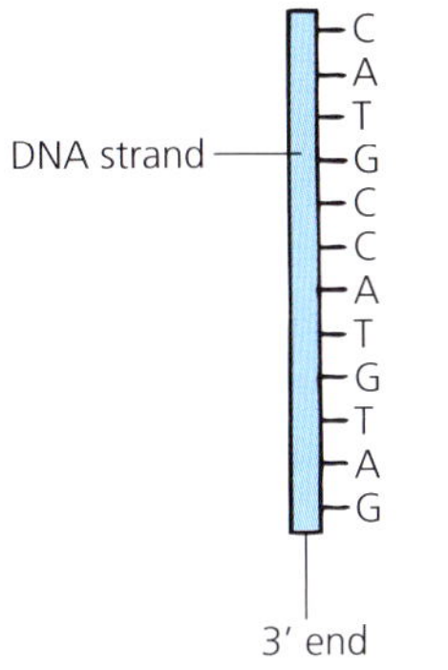

Figure 2.10

i) Redraw the strand and then draw the complementary strand alongside it.

ii) Label the 3′ end and the 5′ end on each strand. (2)

b) DNA consists of two strands whose backbones run in opposite directions. What term is used to describe this arrangement? (1)

3 a) What name is given to the twisted coil arrangement typical of a DNA molecule? (1)

b) If DNA is like a spiral ladder, which part of it corresponds to the ladder's:

i) rungs

ii) uprights? (2)

Replication of DNA

DNA is a unique molecule because it is able to direct its own **replication** and reproduce itself exactly. The replication process is shown in a simple way in Figure 2.11.

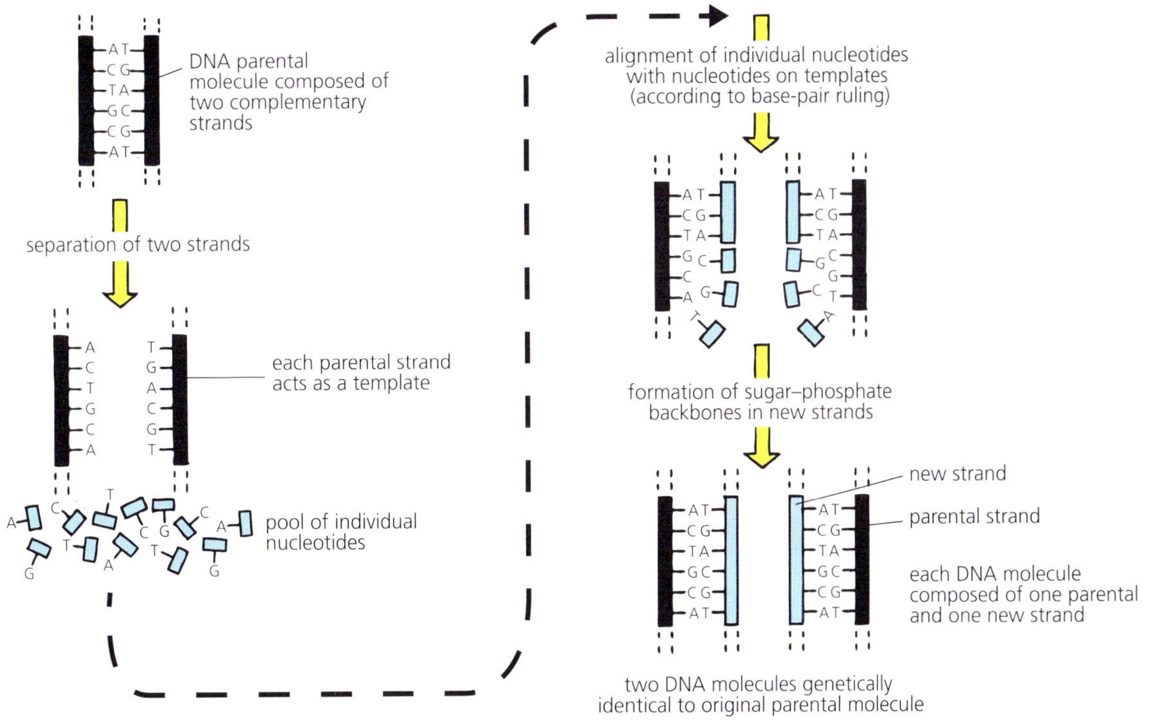

Figure 2.11 DNA replication

Case Study Establishing which theory of DNA replication is correct

Watson and Crick accompanied their model of DNA with a theory for the way in which it could replicate. They predicted that the two strands would unwind and each act as a template for the new complementary strand. This would produce two identical DNA molecules each containing one 'parental' strand and one newly synthesised strand. This so-called **semi-conservative** replication remained a theory until put to the test by Meselson and Stahl.

Hypotheses

Figure 2.12 shows three different hypotheses, each of which could explain DNA replication.

Testing the hypotheses

Background

When *E. coli* bacteria are cultured, they take up nitrogen from the surrounding medium and build it into DNA. They can be cultured for several generations in medium containing the common isotope of nitrogen (^{14}N) or the heavy isotope (^{15}N) as their only source of nitrogen. When DNA is extracted from each type of culture and centrifuged, the results shown in Figure 2.13 are obtained.

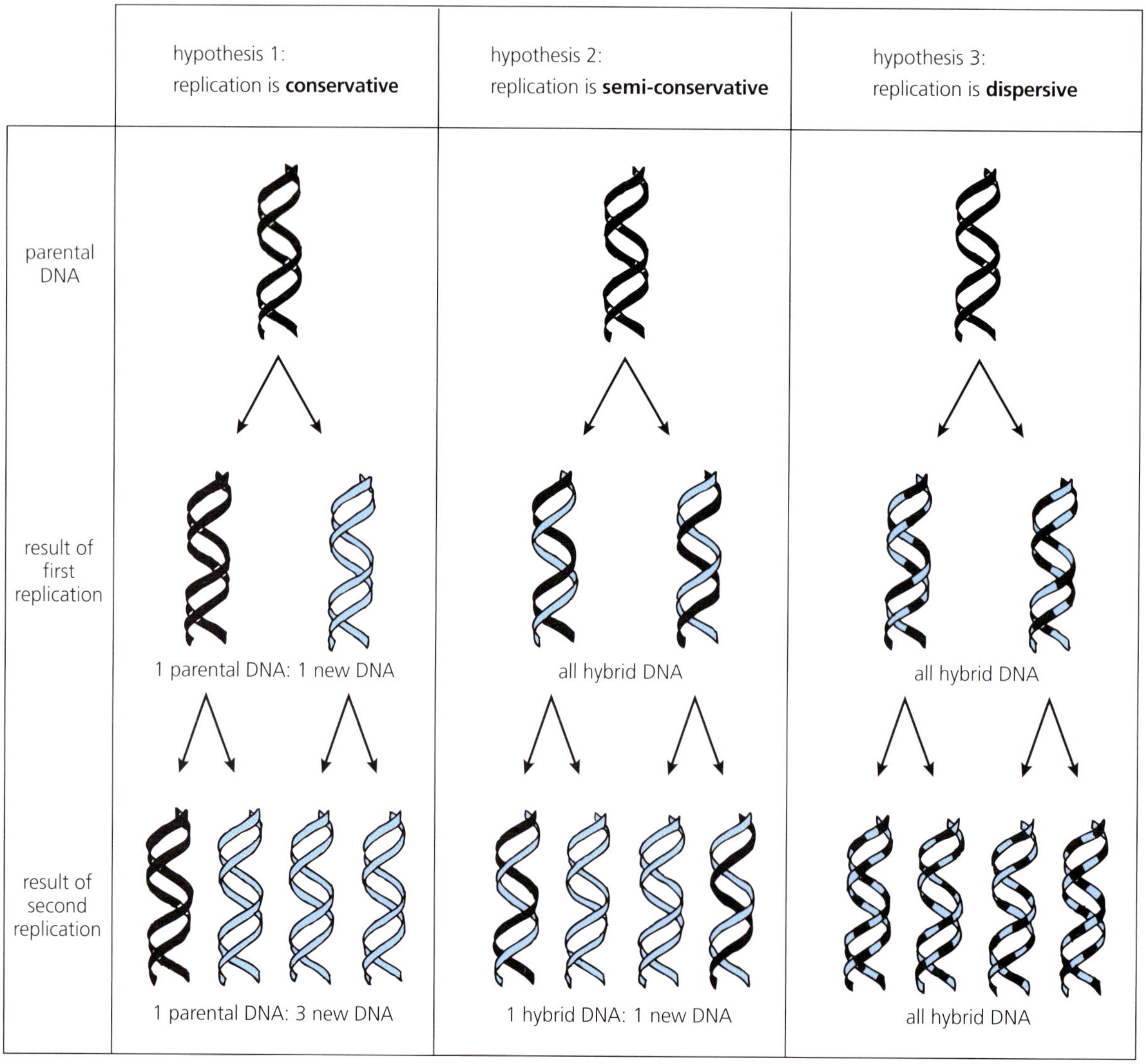

Figure 2.12 DNA replication hypotheses

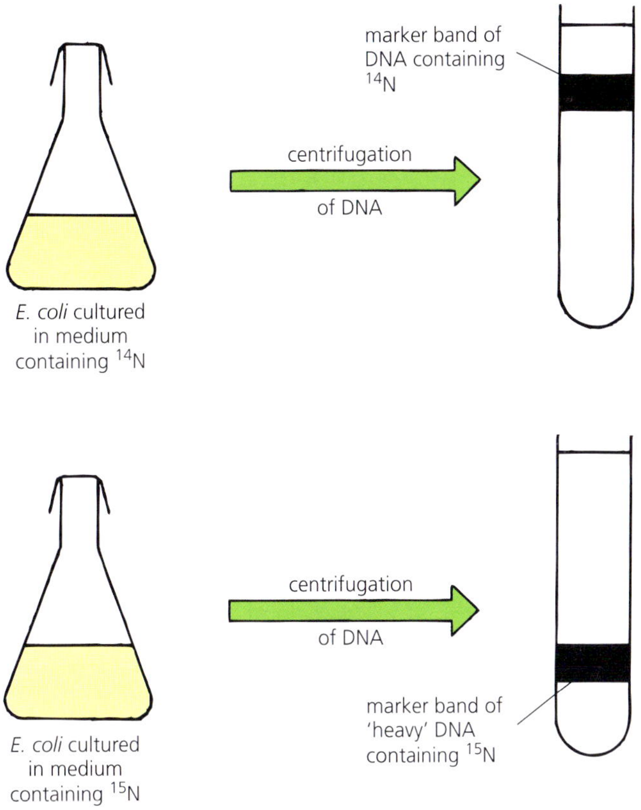

Figure 2.13 Labelling DNA with ^{14}N or ^{15}N

Putting the hypotheses to the test

Meselson and Stahl began with *E. coli* that had been grown for many generations in medium containing ^{15}N. They then cultured these bacteria in medium containing ^{14}N and sampled the culture after 20 minutes (the time needed by the bacteria to replicate DNA once). Figure 2.14 predicts the outcome of the experiment for each of the three hypotheses. Figure 2.15 shows the actual results of the experiment. From these results it is concluded that hypothesis 2 is supported and that the replication of DNA is **semi-conservative**.

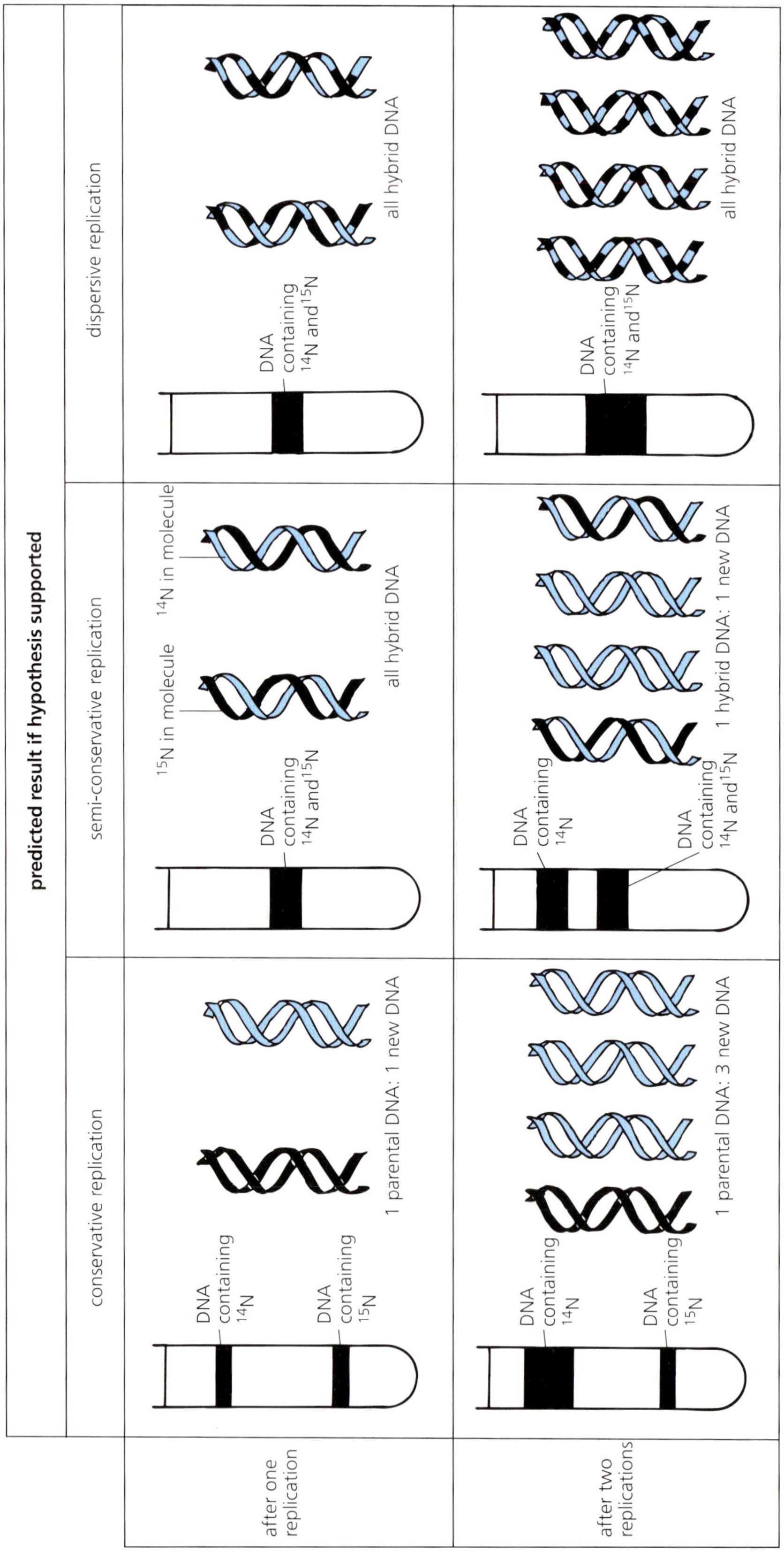

Figure 2.14 Predictions

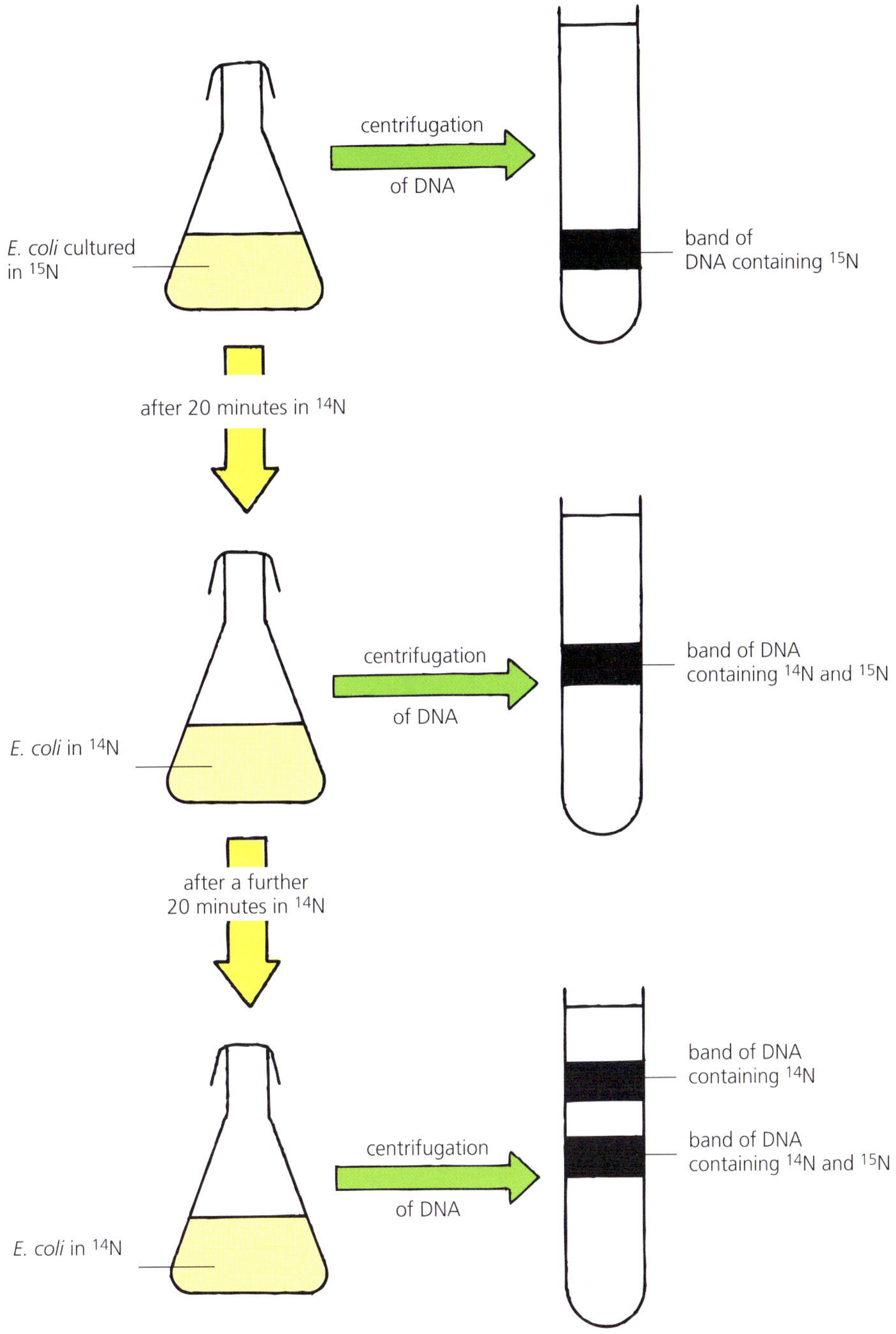

Figure 2.15 Meselson and Stahl's experiment

Enzyme control of DNA replication

DNA replication is a complex process involving many enzymes. It begins when a starting point on DNA is recognised. The DNA molecule unwinds and weak hydrogen bonds between base pairs break, allowing the two strands to separate. These template strands become stabilised and expose their bases at a Y-shaped **replication fork** (see Figure 2.16).

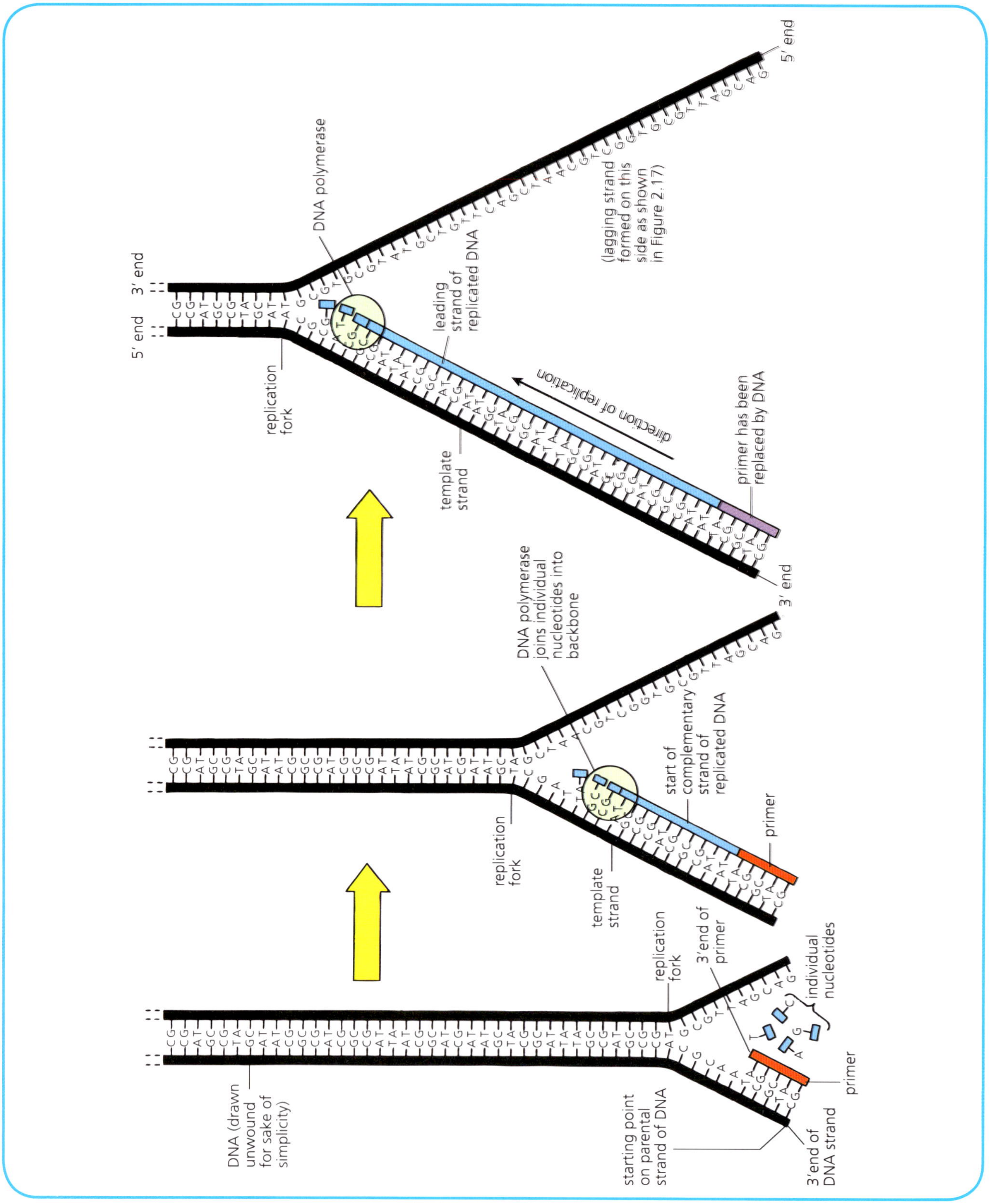

Figure 2.16 Formation of leading strand of replicated DNA

Formation of the leading DNA strand

The enzyme that controls the sugar–phosphate bonding of individual nucleotides into the new DNA strand is called **DNA polymerase**. This enzyme can only add nucleotides to a pre-existing chain. For it to begin to function, a **primer** must be present. This is a short sequence of nucleotides formed at the 3′ end of the parental DNA strand about to be replicated, as shown in Figure 2.16.

Once individual nucleotides have become aligned with their complementary partners on the template strand (by their bases following the base-pairing rules), they become bound to the 3′ end of the primer and formation of the complementary DNA strand begins. Formation of sugar–phosphate bonding between the primer and an individual nucleotide and between the individual nucleotides themselves is brought about by DNA polymerase. Replication of the parental DNA strand that has the 3′ end is **continuous** and forms the **leading** strand of the replicated DNA.

Formation of the lagging DNA strand

DNA polymerase is only able to add nucleotides to the free 3′ end of a growing strand. Therefore the DNA parental template strand that has the 5′ end has to be replicated in fragments, each starting at the 3′ end of a primer, as shown in Figure 2.17.

Each fragment must be primed as before to enable the DNA polymerase to bind individual nucleotides together. Once replication of a fragment is complete, its primer is replaced by DNA. Finally an enzyme called

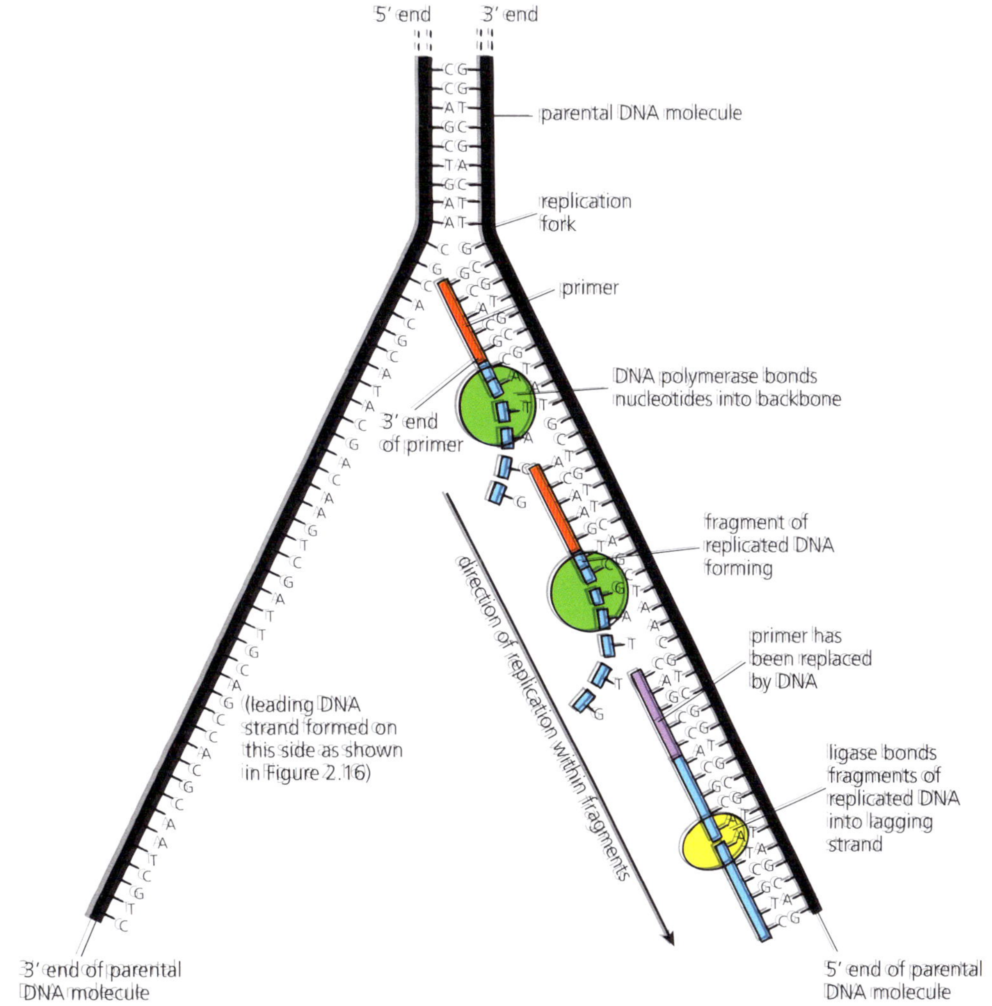

Figure 2.17 Formation of lagging strand of replicated DNA

ligase joins the fragments together. The strand formed is called the lagging strand of replicated DNA and its formation is described as discontinuous.

Many replication forks

When a long chromosome (e.g. one from a mammalian cell) is being replicated, many replication forks operate simultaneously to ensure speedy copying of the lengthy DNA molecule (see Figure 2.18).

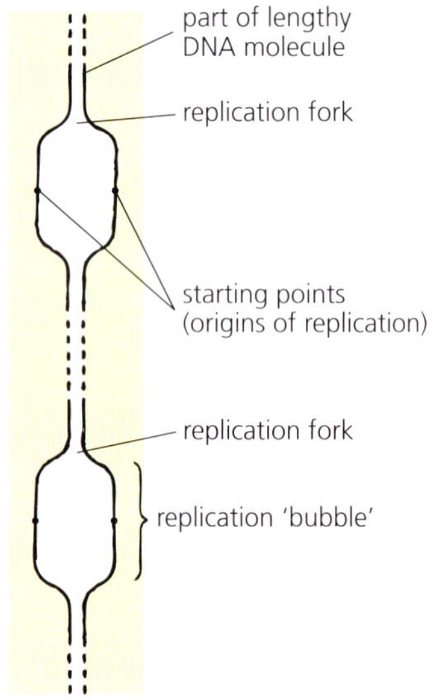

Figure 2.18 Replication forks

Requirements for DNA replication

For DNA replication to occur, the nucleus must contain:

- DNA (to act as a template)
- primers
- a supply of the four types of DNA nucleotide
- the appropriate enzymes (e.g. DNA polymerase and ligase)
- a supply of ATP (for energy – see page 104).

Importance of DNA

DNA is the molecule of inheritance and it encodes the hereditary information in a chemical language. This takes the form of a sequence of organic bases, unique to each species, which makes up its genotype. DNA replication ensures that an exact copy of a species' genetic information is passed on from cell to cell during growth and from generation to generation during reproduction. Therefore, DNA is essential for the continuation of life.

Polymerase chain reaction

The polymerase chain reaction (PCR) is a technique (see Figure 2.19) that can be used to create many copies of a piece of DNA in vitro (i.e. outside the body of an organism). This amplification of DNA involves the use of primers. In this case, each primer is a short length of single-stranded DNA complementary to a specific target sequence at the 3′ end of the DNA strand to be replicated and amplified.

During a cycle of PCR, the DNA is heated to between 92 and 98°C to break the hydrogen bonds between the base pairs and separate the two strands. The DNA is then cooled to between 50 and 65°C to allow each primer to bind to its target sequence. Lastly, the DNA is heated to between 70 and 80°C to allow heat-tolerant DNA polymerase to replicate each strand of DNA by adding nucleotides to the primer at its 3′ end.

The first cycle of replication produces two identical molecules of DNA, the second cycle four identical molecules and so on, giving an exponentially growing population of DNA molecules. By this means a tiny quantity of DNA can be greatly amplified and provide sufficient material for forensic and medical purposes.

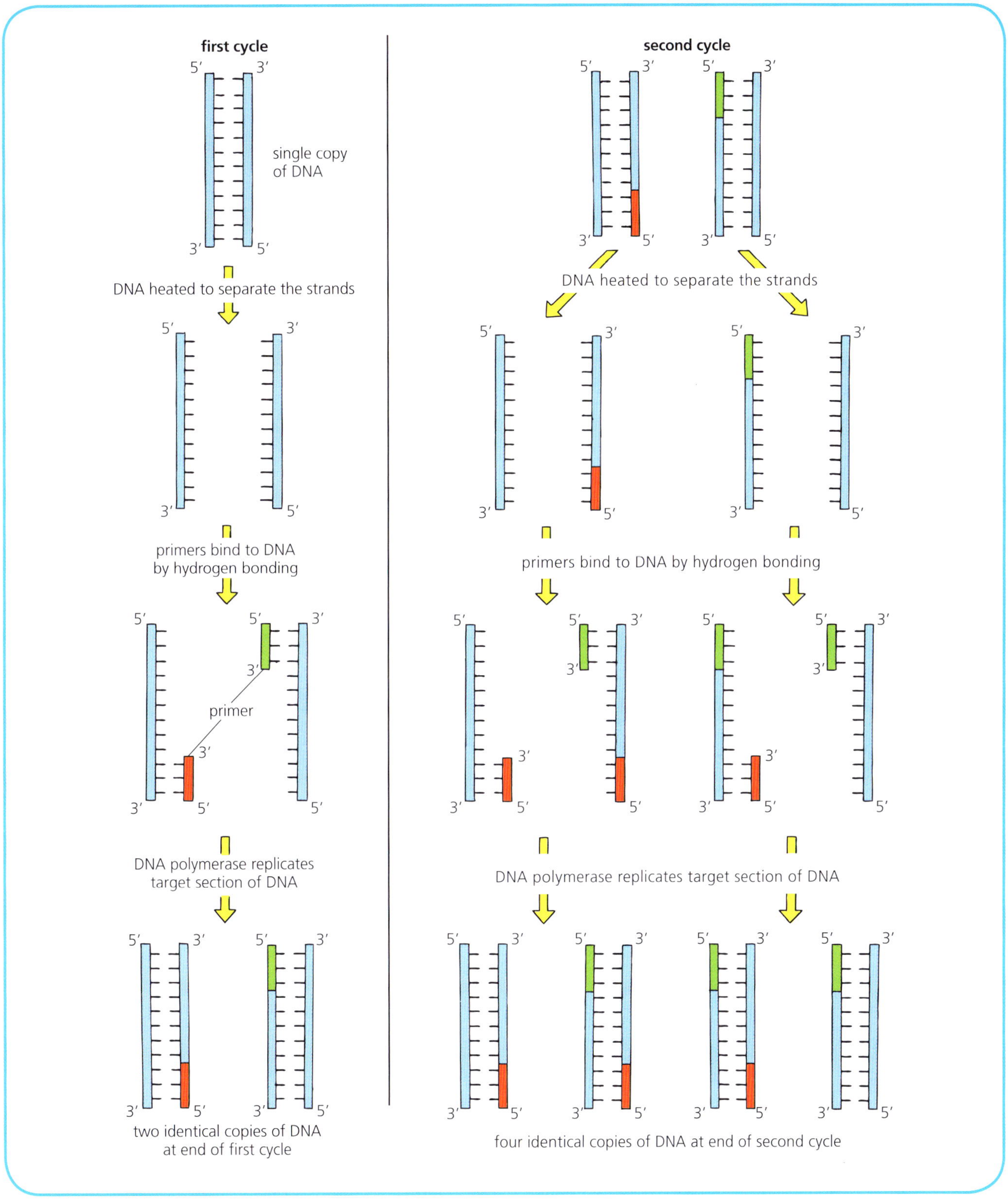

Figure 2.19 Polymerase chain reaction

Case Study Thermal cycling

PCR depends on a process called **thermal cycling**. A cycle consists of three steps each carried out at a different temperature. The earliest designs of this technique used three water baths and normal DNA polymerase. The latter was destroyed during the heating step in the cycle and had to be replaced for use in the next cycle.

The following two important innovations enabled PCR to become automated:

- the isolation of **heat-tolerant** DNA polymerase from a species of bacterium native to hot springs
- the invention of the **thermal cycler**, a computerised heating machine able to control the repetitive temperature changes needed for PCR.

Figure 2.20 shows a simplified version of the steps carried out during thermal cycling in order to amplify DNA.

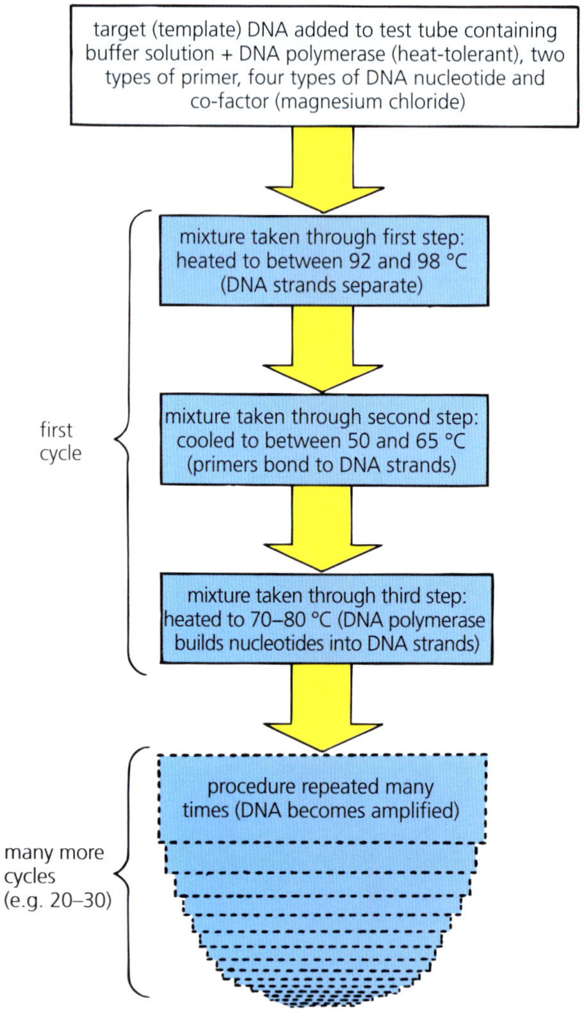
target (template) DNA added to test tube containing buffer solution + DNA polymerase (heat-tolerant), two types of primer, four types of DNA nucleotide and co-factor (magnesium chloride)
mixture taken through first step: heated to between 92 and 98 °C (DNA strands separate)
mixture taken through second step: cooled to between 50 and 65 °C (primers bond to DNA strands)
mixture taken through third step: heated to 70–80 °C (DNA polymerase builds nucleotides into DNA strands)
first cycle
procedure repeated many times (DNA becomes amplified)
many more cycles (e.g. 20–30)

Figure 2.20 Amplification of DNA by thermal cycling

Related Topic

'Needles and haystacks'

Equally as impressive as the amplification of DNA by PCR is the **specificity** of the reaction. Each primer is a piece of single-stranded DNA synthesised as the exact complement of a short length of the DNA strand to which it is to become attached. This enables the primer to find 'the needle in the haystack'. In other words it is able to locate, among many different sites, the specific target DNA sequence that is to be amplified. The process then goes on to produce millions or even billions of copies of the DNA. Therefore this amplification of DNA by PCR is sometimes described as being like 'a haystack from the needle'.

Medical and forensic applications of amplified DNA

Medical

PCR can be used to amplify the genomic DNA from a cell sample taken from a patient. By this means sufficient DNA is generated to allow it to be **screened** for the presence or absence of a specific sequence known to be characteristic of a genetic disease or disorder. This enables medical experts to confirm a **diagnosis** of the genetic disorder if the condition is suspected (based on the patient's family history and/or the fact that the patient is showing early symptoms).

Forensic

DNA profile

The human genome possesses many short, **non-coding regions of DNA** composed of a number of **repetitive sequences**. These regions are found to be randomly distributed throughout the genome and to differ in length and number of repeats of the DNA sequences from person to person. Each region of repetitive sequences is **unique** to the individual who possesses it. Therefore these regions of genetic material can be used to construct a **DNA profile** for that person.

Crime scene

Forensic scientists make use of the PCR reaction to amplify DNA samples from a **crime scene**. DNA samples taken from the victim and the suspects are also amplified. Next the components of the samples are separated using gel electrophoresis and then compared. In the example shown in Figure 2.21, it is concluded that the DNA in sample 1 from the crime scene matches that of the victim and that the DNA in sample 2 from the crime scene matches that of suspect Q.

Paternity dispute

PCR followed by gel electrophoresis can also be employed to generate genetic profiles from DNA samples and **confirm genetic relationships** between individuals. Each person inherits 50% of their DNA from each parent therefore every band in their DNA profile ('genetic fingerprint') must match one in that of their father or their mother. The fact that each person has 50% of their bands in common with each of their parents (see Figure 2.22) allows **paternity disputes** to be settled.

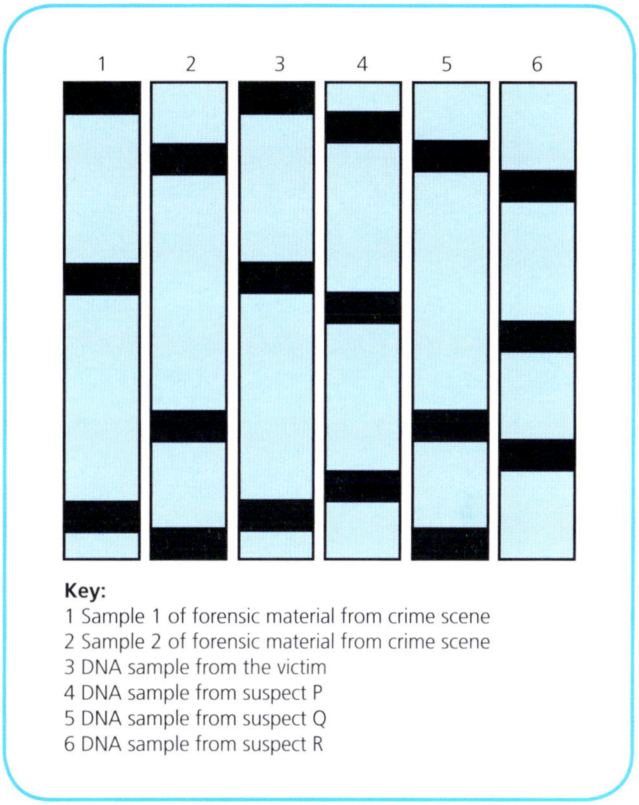

Figure 2.21 Forensic application

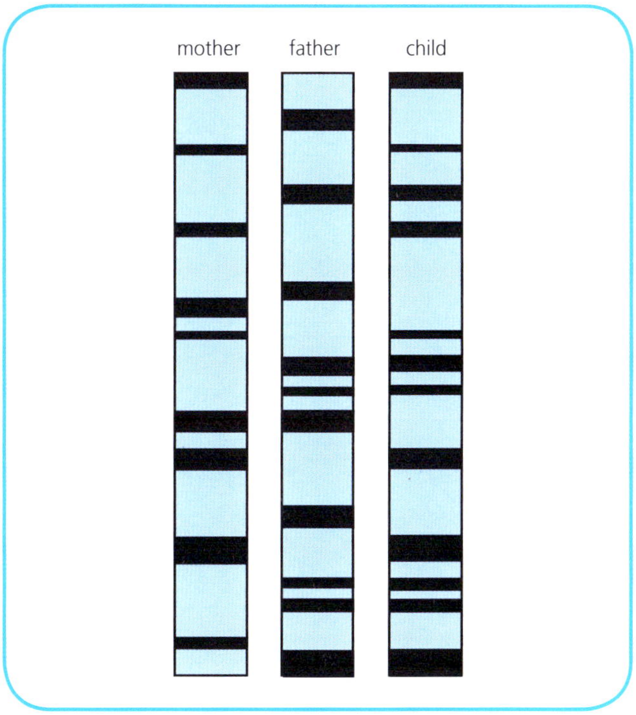

Figure 2.22 Genetic 'fingerprints'

Related Activity

Analysis of DNA by gel electrophoresis

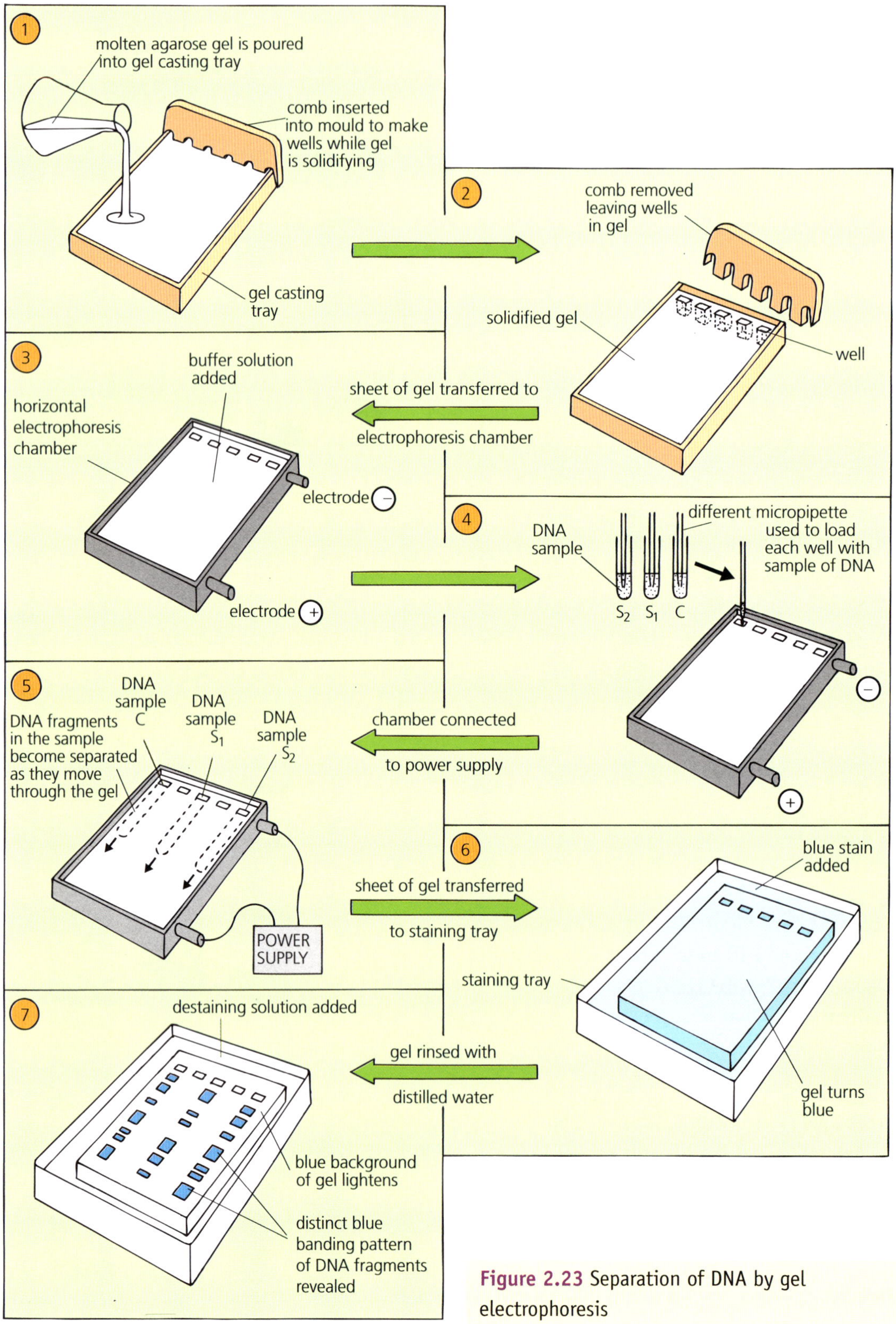

Figure 2.23 Separation of DNA by gel electrophoresis

Gel electrophoresis is a technique used to separate electrically charged molecules that vary in size by subjecting them to an electric current which forces them to move through a sheet of gel. When the molecules are negatively charged, they move towards the positively charged end of the gel. However, they do not all move at the same rate. Smaller molecules move at a faster rate and are therefore found to have **moved further** than larger molecules in a given period of time.

A **restriction enzyme** is used to prepare each DNA sample by cutting it at specific sites into smaller pieces of varying lengths characteristic of that type of DNA. Figure 2.23 illustrates the separation of three sample of DNA: sample C (from the crime scene), sample S1 (from suspect 1) and sample S2 (from suspect 2) using gel electrophoresis. From the results it is concluded that the DNA from suspect 2 matches the DNA from the crime scene.

Evidence based on DNA amplified by PCR has also been used to identify missing people from human remains left at the site of a disaster and to secure the release of innocent people who have been wrongly imprisoned.

Testing Your Knowledge 2

1 Decide whether each of the following statements is true or false and then use T or F to indicate your choice. Where a statement is false, give the word that should have been used in place of the word in bold print. (5)

a) During DNA replication, each DNA parental strand acts as a **template**.

b) A guanine base can only pair up with a **thymine** base.

c) An adenine base can only pair with a **cytosine** base.

d) Complementary base pairs are held together by weak **antiparallel** bonds.

e) Each new DNA molecule formed by replication contains one **parental** and one new strand.

2 Figure 2.24 shows part of a DNA molecule undergoing replication. Match numbers 1–6 with the following statements. (5)

a) DNA polymerase promotes formation of a fragment of the lagging strand of replicating DNA.

b) The parental double helix unwinds.

c) DNA polymerase bonds nucleotide to primer.

d) Ligase joins fragments onto the lagging strand of replicating DNA.

e) DNA polymerase promotes formation of the leading strand of replicating DNA.

f) The DNA molecule becomes stabilised as two template strands.

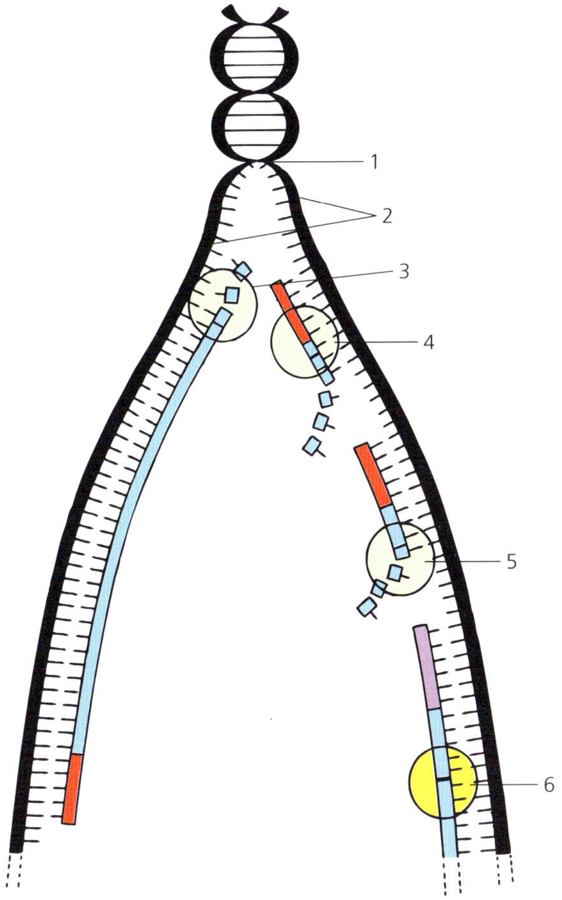

Figure 2.24

3 a) Name FOUR substances that must be present in a nucleus for DNA replication to occur. (4)
b) Briefly explain why DNA replication is important. (2)

4 a) What can be produced *in vitro* by employing the polymerase chain reaction (PCR)? (1)
b) In PCR, what is a *primer*? (2)
c) Why is the DNA heated to between 92 and 98°C during the PCR process? (1)
d) What is the purpose of cooling the DNA sample? (1)
e) What characteristic of the DNA polymerase used in PCR prevents it from becoming denatured during the process? (1)

Applying Your Knowledge and Skills

1 Table 2.1 shows a sample of Chargaff's data following the analysis of DNA extracted from several species.

Species	%A	%C	%G	%T	A/T	G/C
Chicken	28.0	21.6	**Box X**	28.4	0.99	1.02
Grasshopper	29.3	20.7	20.7	29.3	1.00	1.00
Human	29.3	20.0	20.7	30.0	0.98	1.04
Maize	26.8	23.2	22.8	27.2	0.99	**Box Y**
Wheat	27.3	22.8	22.7	27.2	1.00	1.00

Table 2.1

a) Study the data and calculate the figures that should have been entered in boxes X and Y. (2)
b) i) State Chargaff's rules (see core text page 19 for help).
ii) Do the data in the table support these rules?
iii) Explain your answer. (3)
c) With respect to the number of the different bases in a DNA sample, which of the following is correct? (1)
A C = T B A = G C A+G = C+T D A+T = G+C

2 a) Calculate the percentage of thymine bases present in a DNA molecule containing 1000 bases of which 200 are guanine. (1)
b) State the number of cytosine bases present in a DNA molecule that contains 10 000 base molecules of which 18% are adenine. (1)

3 Figure 2.25 (on next page) shows a cell's genetic material.
a) i) Name the parts enclosed in boxes 1, 2 and 3.
ii) Which of these boxed structures contains nucleic acid and consists of many different genes?
iii) Which of these structures is one of four basic units whose order determines the information held in a gene? (5)
b) The DNA helix of one of these chromosomes is found to be 5 cm long when fully uncoiled and 5 µm long when tightly coiled.
i) Express these data as a packing ratio of fully extended DNA:tightly coiled DNA.
ii) Suggest why scientists normally express the length of a chromosome in number of base pairs. (2)

4 Figure 2.26 (on next page) shows a replication 'bubble' on a strand of DNA.
a) i) Redraw the diagram including the given labels and then mark '3' end' and '5' end' on the parental DNA strand for a second time.
ii) Draw in and label a starting point (origin of replication).
iii) Label one of the primer molecules.
iv) Label the leading DNA strand and a fragment of the lagging strand.
v) Use the letter P four times to indicate all the locations where DNA polymerase would be active. (6)

➜

Figure 2.25

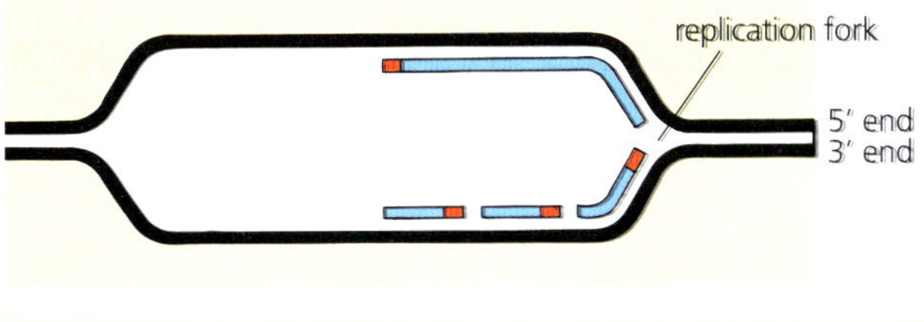

Figure 2.26

b) i) In this chromosome the replication fork moves at a rate of 2500 base pairs per minute. If this chromosome is 5×10^7 base pairs in length, how many minutes would one replication fork take to replicate the entire chromosome?

ii) However, in reality, replication of this chromosome's DNA only takes 3 minutes. Explain how this is achieved. (2)

5 Refer back to Figure 2.14 on page 24 and then draw a labelled diagram to show both the DNA strands and the test tube contents that would result after three DNA replications involving semi-conservative replication only. (4)

6 The graph in Figure 2.27 shows the expected number of copies of DNA that would be generated by the polymerase chain reaction (PCR) under ideal conditions.

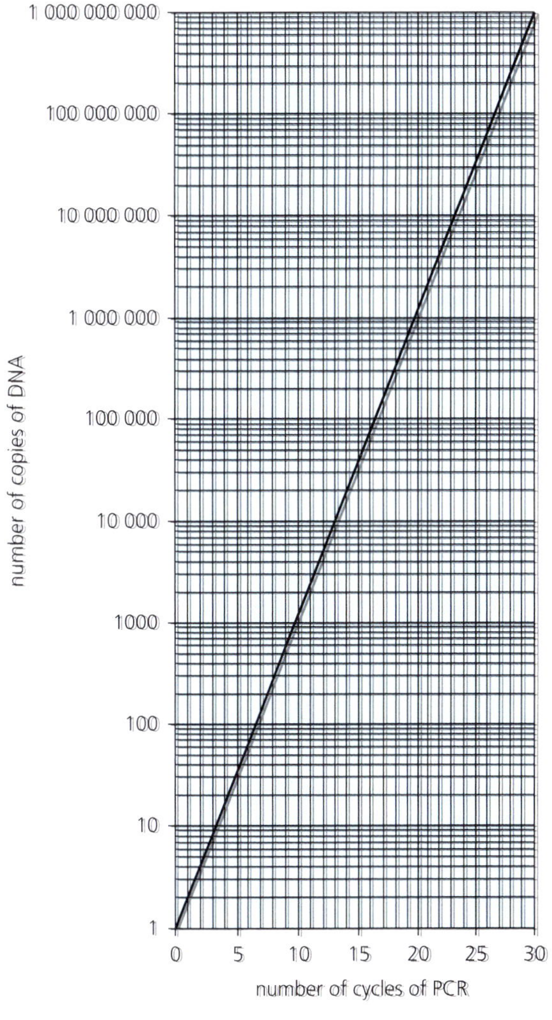

Figure 2.27

a) **i)** What name is given to the type of graph paper used here to present the data?

ii) Why has this type of graph paper been used? (2)

b) How many cycles of PCR are required to produce 10 000 000 copies of the DNA? (1)

c) How many cycles are required to increase the number of copies of DNA already present at ten cycles by a factor of 10^3? (1)

d) **i)** How many copies of the DNA were present after 30 cycles?

ii) Now state your answer in words. (2)

e) Refer back to Figure 2.19 on page 29 and, with the aid of coloured pencils, draw a diagram of the DNA that would be present at the end of the third cycle of PCR. (4)

7 Figure 2.28 shows the DNA profiles (genetic fingerprints) of seven people.

a) Identify the parents of person P. (1)

b) Identify the monozygotic (identical) twins. (1)

c) **i)** Could person P be the twins' brother?

ii) Explain your answer. (2)

d) **i)** Could the remaining two people in the diagram have the same parents as P?

ii) Explain your answer. (2)

8 Describe the main processes that occur during the replication of a molecule of DNA. (9)

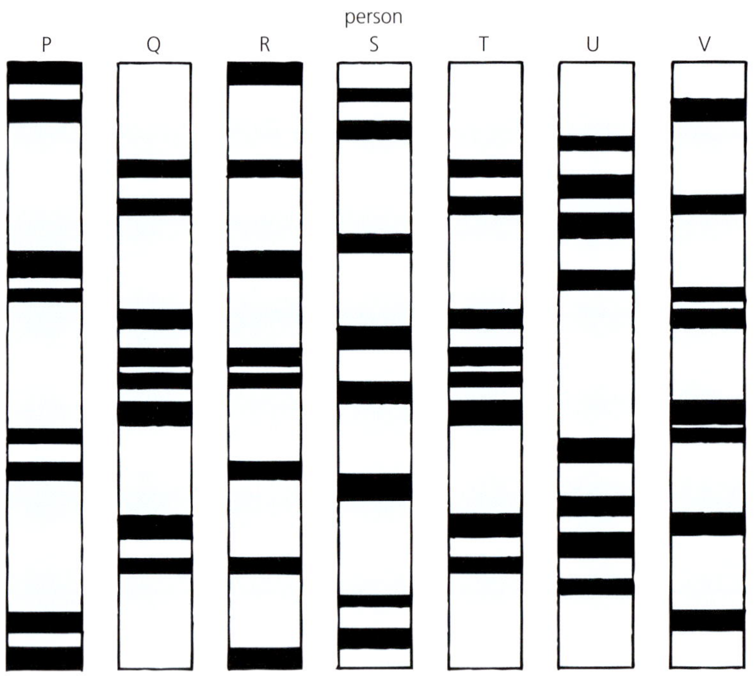

Figure 2.28

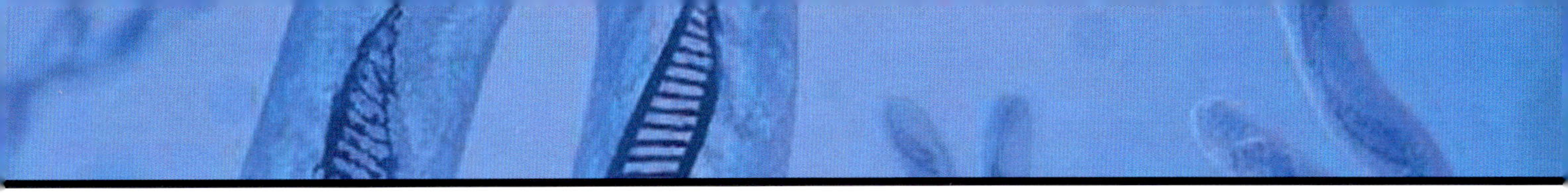

3 Gene expression

A cell's **genotype** (its genetic constitution) is determined by the sequence of the DNA bases in its genes (the **genetic code**). A cell's **phenotype** (its physical and chemical state) is determined by the proteins that are synthesised when the genes are expressed. Gene expression involves the processes of **transcription** and **translation** (discussed in this chapter). Only a fraction of the genes in a cell are expressed.

Structure of RNA

The second type of nucleic acid is called **RNA** (ribonucleic acid). Each nucleotide in an RNA molecule is composed of a molecule of **ribose** sugar, an organic base and a phosphate group (see Figure 3.1). In RNA, the base **uracil** (**U**) replaces thymine found in DNA.

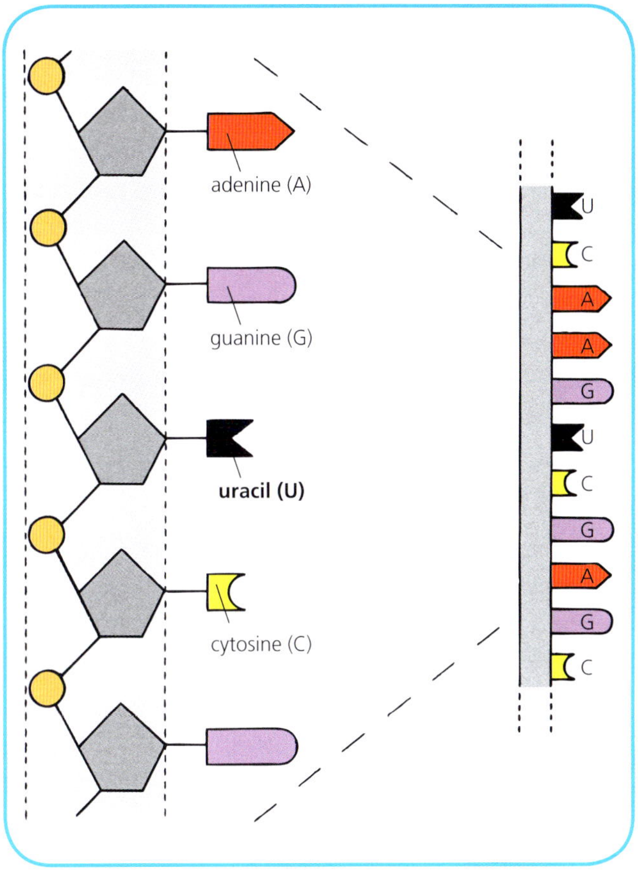

Figure 3.2 Structure of RNA

Unlike DNA, which consists of two strands, a molecule of RNA is a **single strand**, as shown in Figure 3.2. The differences between RNA and DNA are summarised in Table 3.1.

Characteristic	RNA	DNA
Number of nucleotide strands present in one molecule	One	Two
Complementary base partner of adenine	Uracil	Thymine
Sugar present in a nucleotide	Ribose	Deoxyribose

Table 3.1 Differences between RNA and DNA

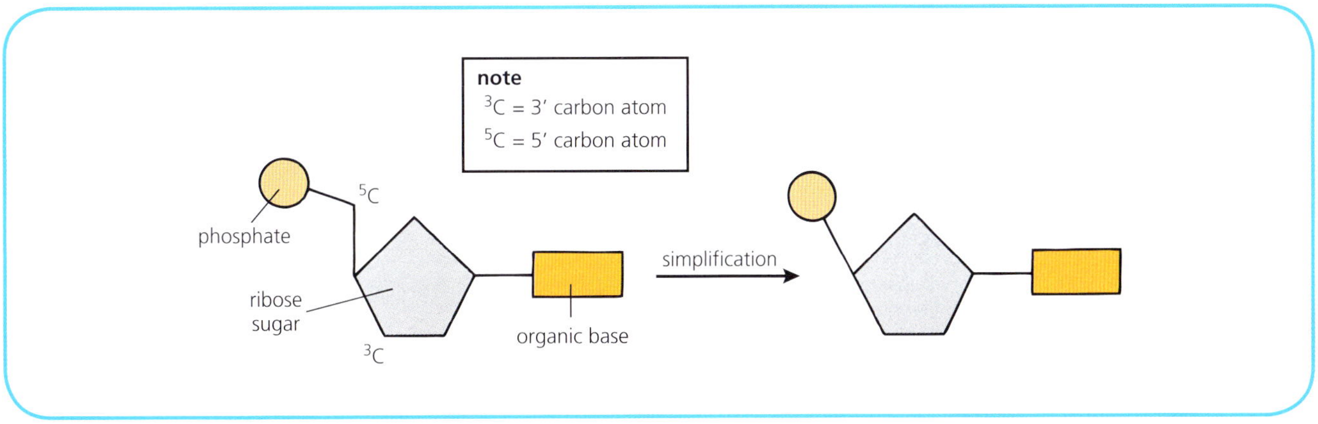

Figure 3.1 Structure of an RNA molecule

Control of inherited characteristics

The sequence of bases along the DNA strands contains the **genetic instructions** that control an organism's inherited characteristics. These characteristics are the result of many biochemical processes controlled by enzymes, which are made of **protein** Each protein is made of one or more **polypeptide** chains composed of subunits called **amino acids**. A protein's exact molecular structure, shape and ability to carry out its function all depend on the **sequence** of its amino acids. This critical order is determined by the order of the bases in the organism's DNA. By this means DNA controls the structure of enzymes and, in doing so, determines the organism's inherited characteristics.

Genetic code

The information present in DNA takes the form of a molecular language called the **genetic code**. The sequence of bases along a DNA strand represents a sequence of 'codewords'. DNA possesses four different types of base. Proteins contain 20 different types of amino acid. If the bases are taken in groups of three then this gives 64 (4^3) different combinations (see Appendix 1). It is now known that each amino acid is coded for by one or more of these 64 **triplets** of bases. Thus an individual's genetic information is encoded in its DNA with each strand bearing a series of base triplets arranged in a specific order for coding the particular proteins needed by that individual.

Gene expression through protein synthesis

The genetic information for a particular polypeptide is carried on a section of DNA in the nucleus. However, assembly of amino acids into a genetically determined sequence takes place in the cell's cytoplasm in tiny structures called **ribosomes**. Figure 3.3 gives an overview of gene expression through protein synthesis. A molecule of **mRNA** (messenger RNA) is formed (**transcribed**) from the appropriate section of the DNA strand and carries that information to ribosomes. There the mRNA meets **tRNA** (transfer RNA) and the genetic information is **translated** into protein.

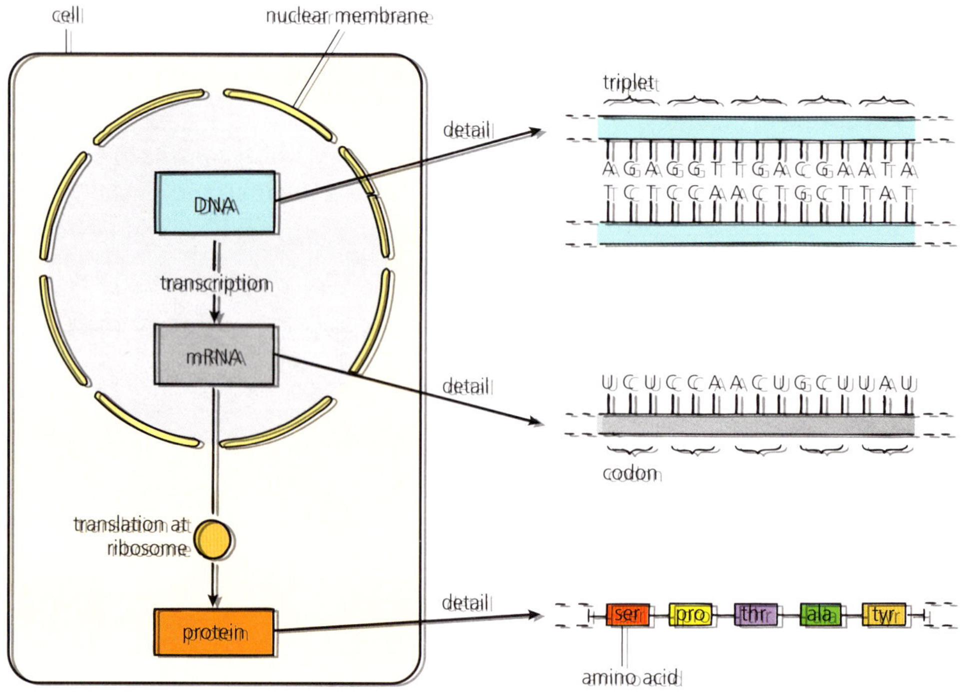

Figure 3.3 Overview of gene expression

Transcription

Transcription is the synthesis of mRNA from a section of DNA. A promoter is a region of DNA in a gene where transcription is initiated, as shown in Figure 3.4 (where the DNA strand has been drawn uncoiled for the sake of simplicity).

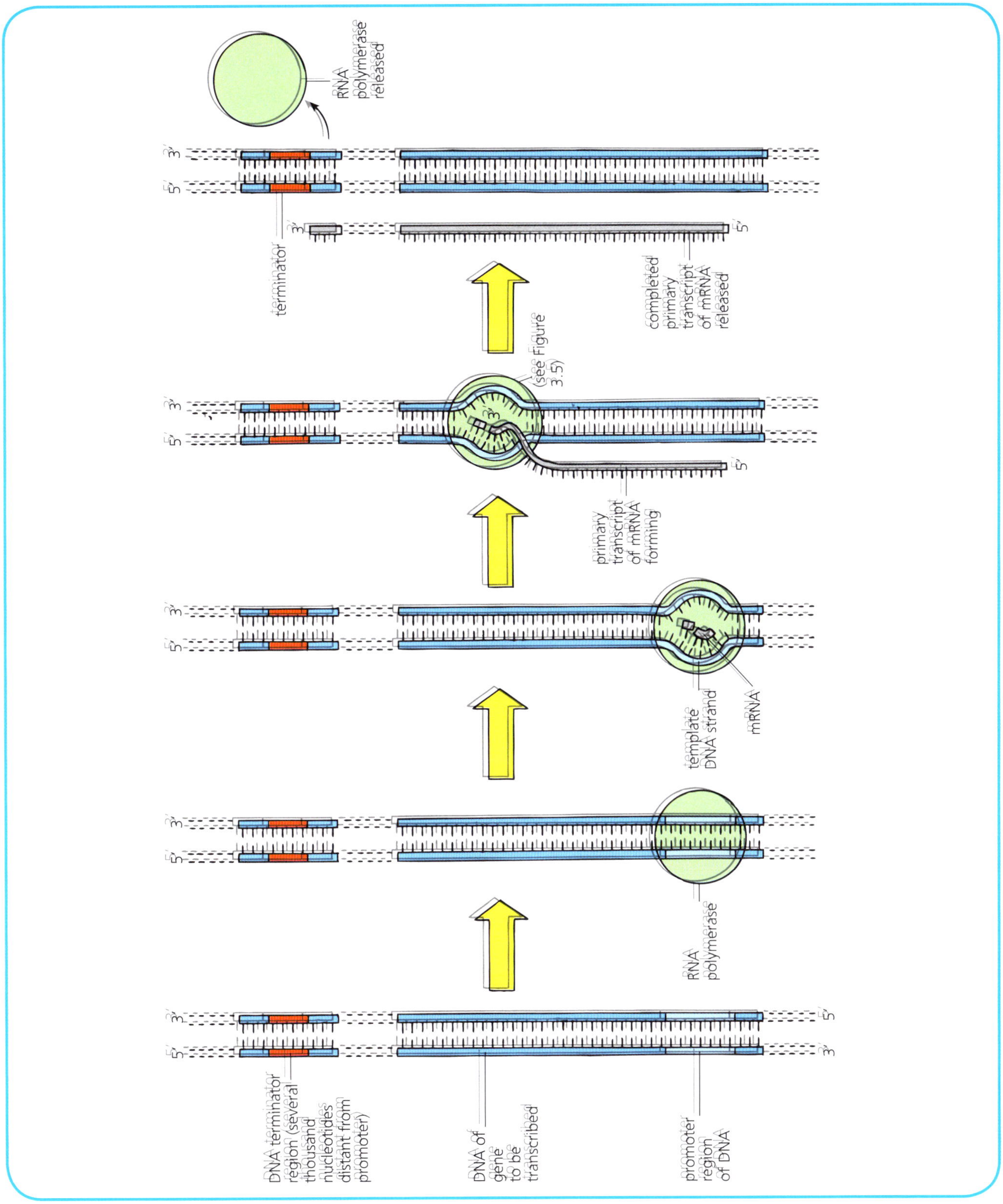

Figure 3.4 Transcription of mRNA

RNA polymerase is the enzyme responsible for transcription. As it moves along the gene from the promoter, unwinding and opening up the DNA strand by breaking the hydrogen bonds between its base pairs, it brings about the synthesis of an **mRNA** molecule. As a result of the base-pairing rule, the mRNA gets a nucleotide sequence complementary to one of the two DNA strands (the template strand), as shown in Figure 3.5.

RNA polymerase can only add nucleotides to the 3′ end of the growing mRNA molecule. The molecule elongates until a terminator sequence of nucleotides is reached on the DNA strand. The resultant mRNA strand that becomes separated from its DNA template is called a **primary transcript** of mRNA.

Modification of primary transcript

Normally the region of DNA transcribed to mRNA is about 8000 nucleotides long yet only about 1200 nucleotides are needed to code for an average-sized polypeptide chain. This is explained by the fact that long stretches of DNA that exist within a gene do not play a part in the coding of the polypeptide. These non-coding regions, called **introns**, are interspersed between the coding regions, called **exons**. Therefore the region in the primary transcript of mRNA responsible for coding the polypeptide is fragmented.

Splicing

Figure 3.6 shows how the introns are cut out and removed from the primary transcript of mRNA and the exons are **spliced** together to form mRNA with a continuous sequence of nucleotides. The order of exons remain unchanged during splicing. The modified mRNA called the **mature transcript** of mRNA passes out of the nucleus into the cytoplasm (see Figure 3.7) and moves on to the next stage of protein synthesis where it becomes translated into a sequence of amino acids.

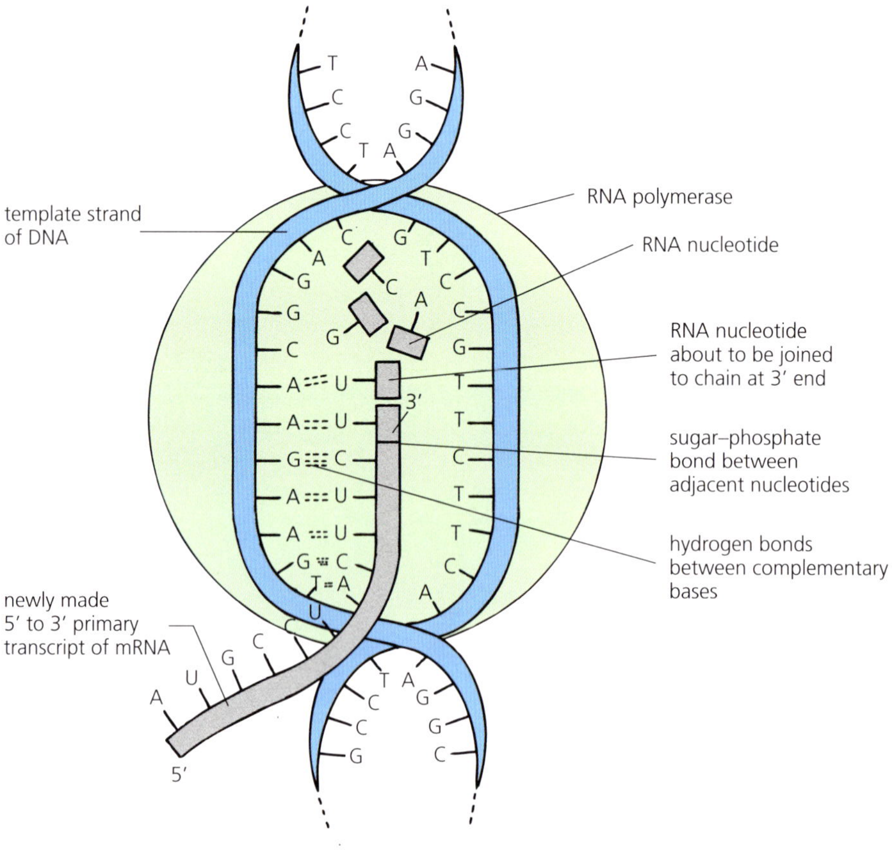

Figure 3.5 Detail of transcription

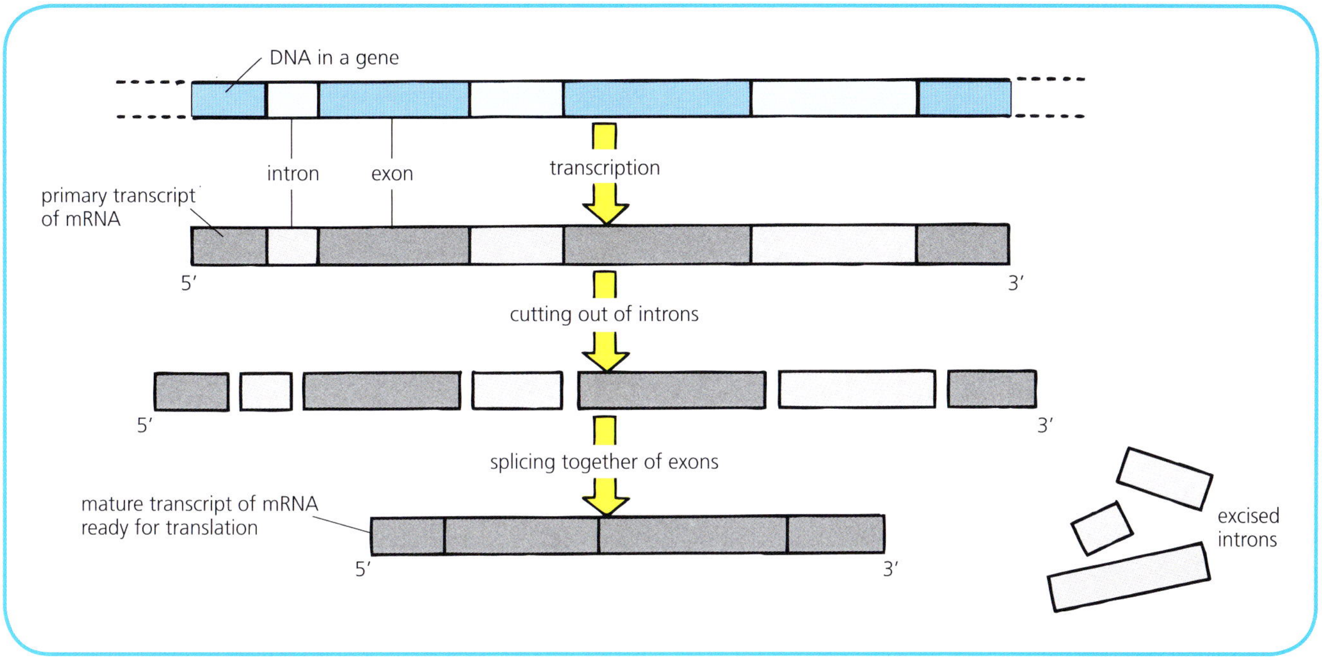

Figure 3.6 Modification of primary mRNA transcript

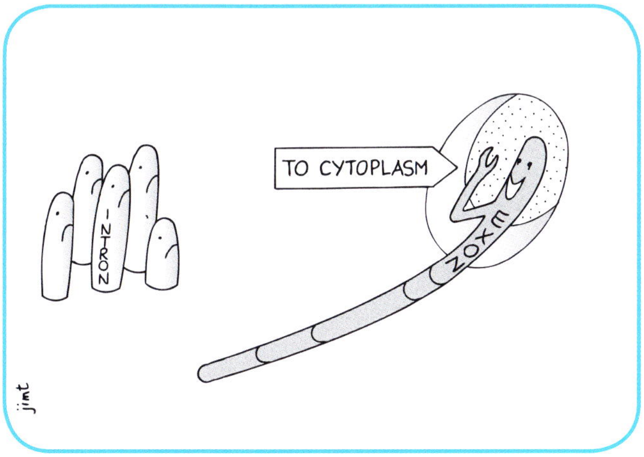

Figure 3.7 'Better luck next time, guys!'

Testing Your Knowledge 1

1 State THREE ways in which RNA and DNA differ in structure and chemical composition. (3)

2 **a)** In what way does the DNA of one species differ from that of another, making each species unique? (1)

b) How many bases in the genetic code correspond to one amino acid? (1)

3 **a)** Draw a diagram of the mRNA strand that would be transcribed from section X of the DNA molecule shown in Figure 3.8. (2)

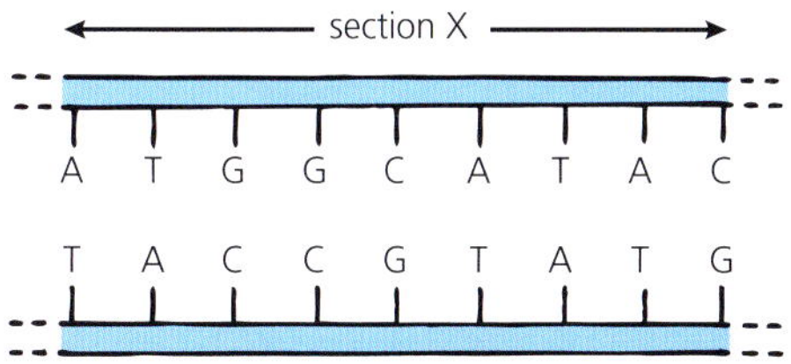

Figure 3.8

b) Name the enzyme that would direct this process. (1)

4 **a)** What is the difference between an *exon* and an *intron*? (1)

b) Which of these must be removed from the primary transcript of mRNA? (1)

c) By what process are they removed? (1)

Translation

Translation is the synthesis of protein as a polypeptide chain under the direction of mRNA. The genetic message carried by a molecule of mRNA is made up of a series of base triplets called codons. The codon is the basic unit of the genetic code. Each codon is complementary to a triplet of bases on the original template DNA strand.

Transfer RNA

A further type of RNA is found in the cell's cytoplasm. This is called tRNA (transfer RNA) and it is composed of a single strand of nucleotides. However, a molecule of tRNA has a three-dimensional structure because it is folded back on itself in such a way that hydrogen bonds form between many of its nucleotide bases, as shown in Figure 3.9. Each molecule of tRNA has only one particular triplet of bases exposed. This triplet is called an anticodon. It is complementary to an mRNA codon and corresponds to a specific amino acid carried by that tRNA at its attachment site.

Table 3.2 shows the relationship between mRNA's codons, tRNA's anticodons and the amino acids coded. Many different types of tRNA are present in a cell – one or more for each type of amino acid. Each tRNA picks up its appropriate amino acid molecule from the cytoplasm's amino acid pool at its site of attachment. The amino acid is then carried by the tRNA to a ribosome and added to the growing end of a polypeptide chain. By this means, the genetic code is translated into a sequence of amino acids.

The mRNA codon AUG (complementary to tRNA anticodon UAC) is unusual in that it codes for methionine (met) *and* acts as the start codon. mRNA codons UAA, UAG and UGA do not code for amino acids but instead act as stop codons.

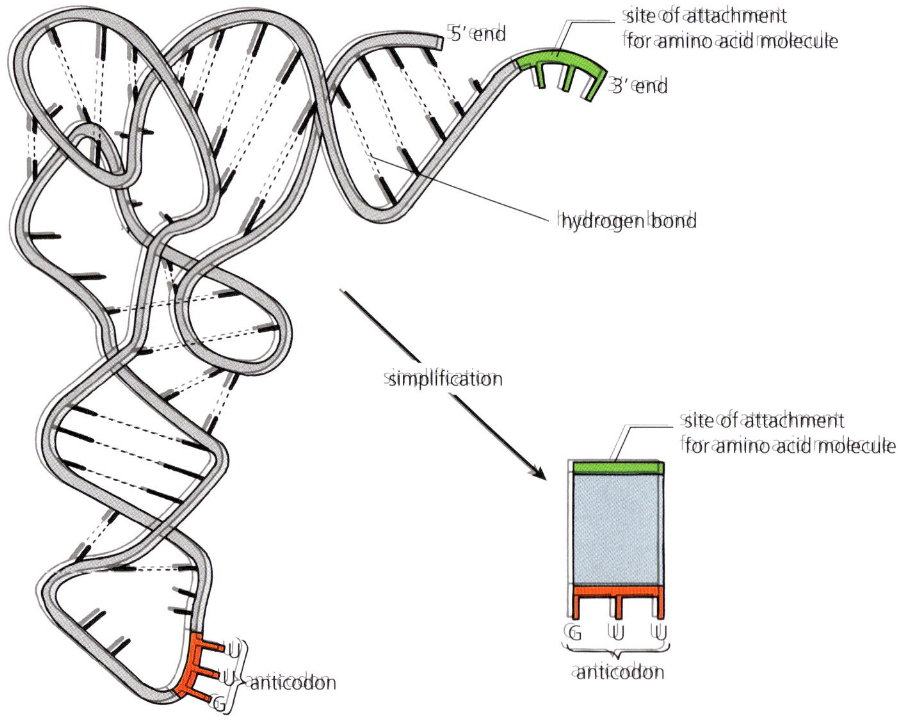

Figure 3.9 Structure of transfer RNA (tRNA)

Related Information

Codons and anticodons

Codon (mRNA)	Anticodon (tRNA)	Amino acid	Codon (mRNA)	Anticodon (tRNA)	Amino acid	Codon (mRNA)	Anticodon (tRNA)	Amino acid	Codon (mRNA)	Anticodon (tRNA)	Amino acid
UUU	AAA	phe	UCU	AGA	ser	UAU	AUA	tyr	UGU	ACA	cys
UUC	AAG	phe	UCC	AGG	ser	UAC	AUG	tyr	UGC	ACG	cys
UUA	AAU	leu	UCA	AGU	ser	UAA	AUU	STOP	UGA	ACU	STOP
UUG	AAC	leu	UCG	AGC	ser	UAG	AUC	STOP	UGG	ACC	trp
CUU	GAA	leu	CCU	GGA	pro	CAU	GUA	his	CGU	GCA	arg
CUC	GAG	leu	CCC	GGG	pro	CAC	GUG	his	CGC	GCG	arg
CUA	GAU	leu	CCA	GGU	pro	CAA	GUU	gln	CGA	GCU	arg
CUG	GAC	leu	CCG	GGC	pro	CAG	GUC	gln	CGG	GCC	arg
AUU	UAA	ile	ACU	UGA	thr	AAU	UUA	asn	AGU	UCA	ser
AUC	UAG	ile	ACC	UGG	thr	AAC	UUG	asn	AGC	UCG	ser
AUA	UAU	ile	ACA	UGU	thr	AAA	UUU	lys	AGA	UCU	arg
AUG	UAC	met or START	ACG	UGC	thr	AAG	UUC	lys	AGG	UCC	arg
GUU	CAA	val	GCU	CGA	ala	GAU	CUA	asp	GGU	CCA	gly
GUC	CAG	val	GCC	CGG	ala	GAC	CUG	asp	GGC	CCG	gly
GUA	CAU	val	GCA	CGU	ala	GAA	CUU	glu	GGA	CCU	gly
GUG	CAC	val	GCG	CGC	ala	GAG	CUC	glu	GGG	CCC	gly

Table 3.2 mRNA codons, tRNA anticodons and the amino acids coded
(See Appendix 1 for full names of amino acids.)

Ribosomes

Ribosomes are small, roughly spherical structures found in all cells. They contain ribosome RNA (rRNA) and enzymes essential for protein synthesis. Many ribosomes are present in growing cells which need to produce large quantities of protein.

Binding sites

A ribosome's function is to bring tRNA molecules (bearing amino acids) into contact with mRNA. A ribosome has one binding site for mRNA and three binding sites for tRNA, as shown in Figure 3.10.

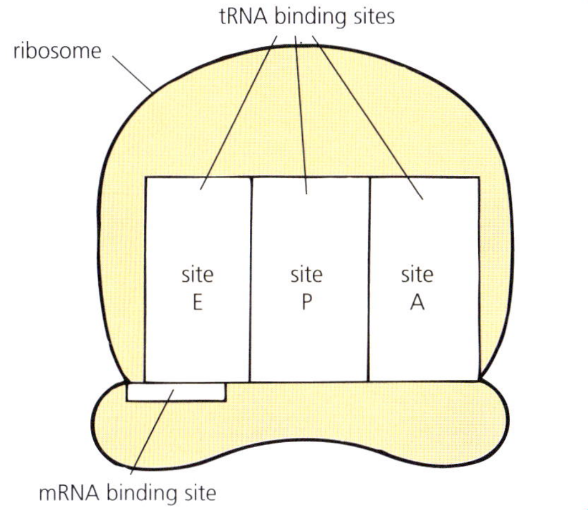

Figure 3.10 Binding sites on a ribosome

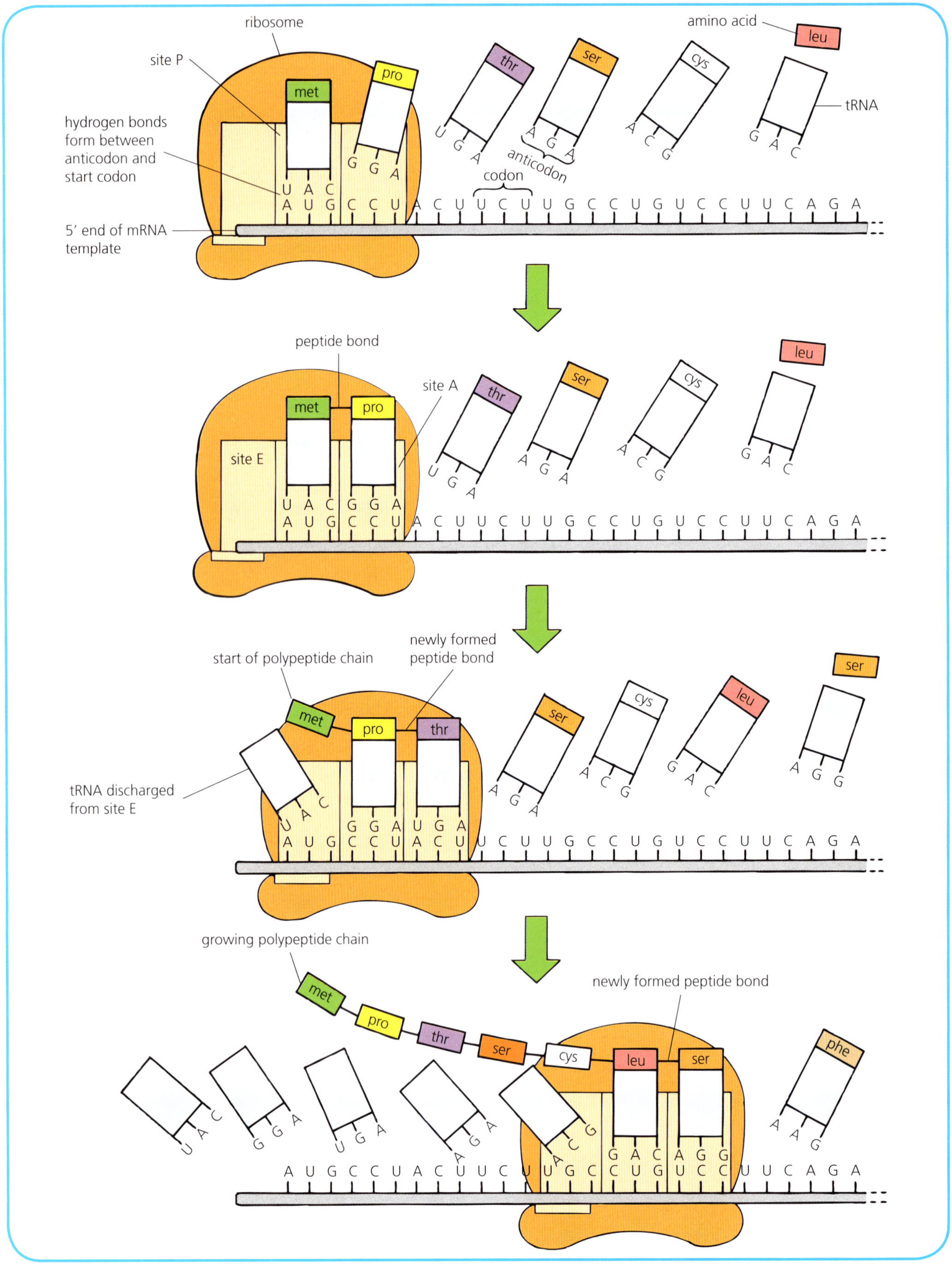

Figure 3.11 Translation of mRNA into polypeptide

Of the tRNA binding sites:

- site P holds the tRNA carrying the growing polypeptide chain
- site A holds the tRNA carrying the next amino acid to be joined to the growing chain by a peptide bond
- site E discharges a tRNA from the ribosome once its amino acid has become part of the polypeptide chain.

Start and stop codons in action

Before translation can begin, a ribosome must bind to the 5′ end of the mRNA template so that the mRNA's **start codon** (AUG) is in position at binding site P. Next a molecule of tRNA carrying its amino acid (methionine) becomes attached at site P by hydrogen bonds between its anticodon (UAC) and the start codon (see Figure 3.11).

The mRNA codon at site A recognises and then forms hydrogen bonds with the complementary anticodon on an appropriate tRNA molecule bearing its amino acid. When the first two amino acid molecules are adjacent to one another, they become joined by a **peptide bond**.

As the ribosome moves along one codon, the tRNA that was at site P is moved to site E and discharges from the ribosome to be reused. At the same time the tRNA that was at site A is moved to site P. The vacated site A becomes occupied by the next tRNA bearing its amino acid, which becomes bonded to the growing peptide chain. The process is repeated many times allowing the mRNA to be translated into a complete **polypeptide chain**.

Eventually a **stop codon** (see Table 3.2) on the mRNA is reached. At this point, site A on the ribosome becomes occupied by a release factor, which frees the polypeptide from the ribosome. The whole process needs energy from ATP (see Chapter 7).

One gene, many proteins

Alternative RNA splicing

Figure 3.6 on page 41 shows a primary transcript of mRNA being cut up and its exons being spliced together to form a molecule of mRNA ready for translation. This mature transcript of mRNA is not the only one that can be produced from that primary transcript. Depending on circumstances, **alternative segments of RNA** may be treated as the exons and introns. Therefore the same primary transcript has the potential to produce several mature mRNA transcripts each with a different sequence of base triplets and each coding for a different polypeptide. In other words, one gene can code for several different proteins and a limited number of genes can give rise to a wide variety of proteins.

One gene, two antibodies – an example of alternative splicing

An antibody is a Y-shaped protein molecule. The two antibody molecules (P and Q) shown in Figure 3.12 are coded for by the same gene yet they are different in structure. P possesses a membrane-anchoring unit coded for by an exon present in its mRNA. However, this membrane-anchoring unit is absent from Q because its mRNA lacks the necessary exon (discarded as an intron at the splicing stage). As a result, antibody P functions as a membrane-bound protein on the outer surface of a white blood cell whereas antibody Q operates freely in the bloodstream.

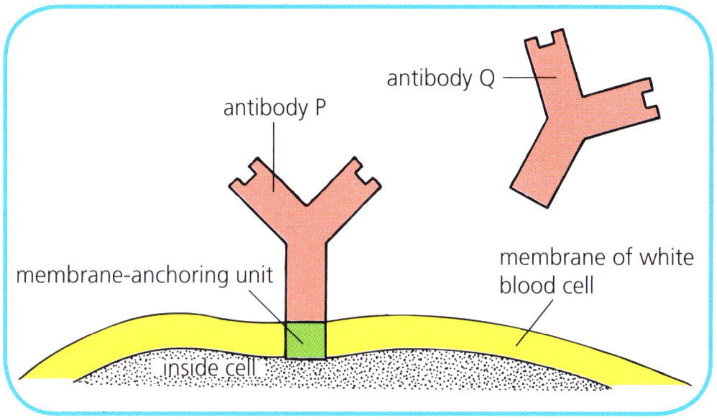

Figure 3.12 Products of alternative RNA splicing

Structure of proteins

All **proteins** contain the chemical elements carbon (C), hydrogen (H), oxygen (O) and nitrogen (N). Often they contain sulphur (S). Each protein is built up from a large number of subunits called **amino acids** of which there are 20 different types. The length of a protein molecule varies from many thousands of amino acids to just a few. Insulin, for example, contains only 51.

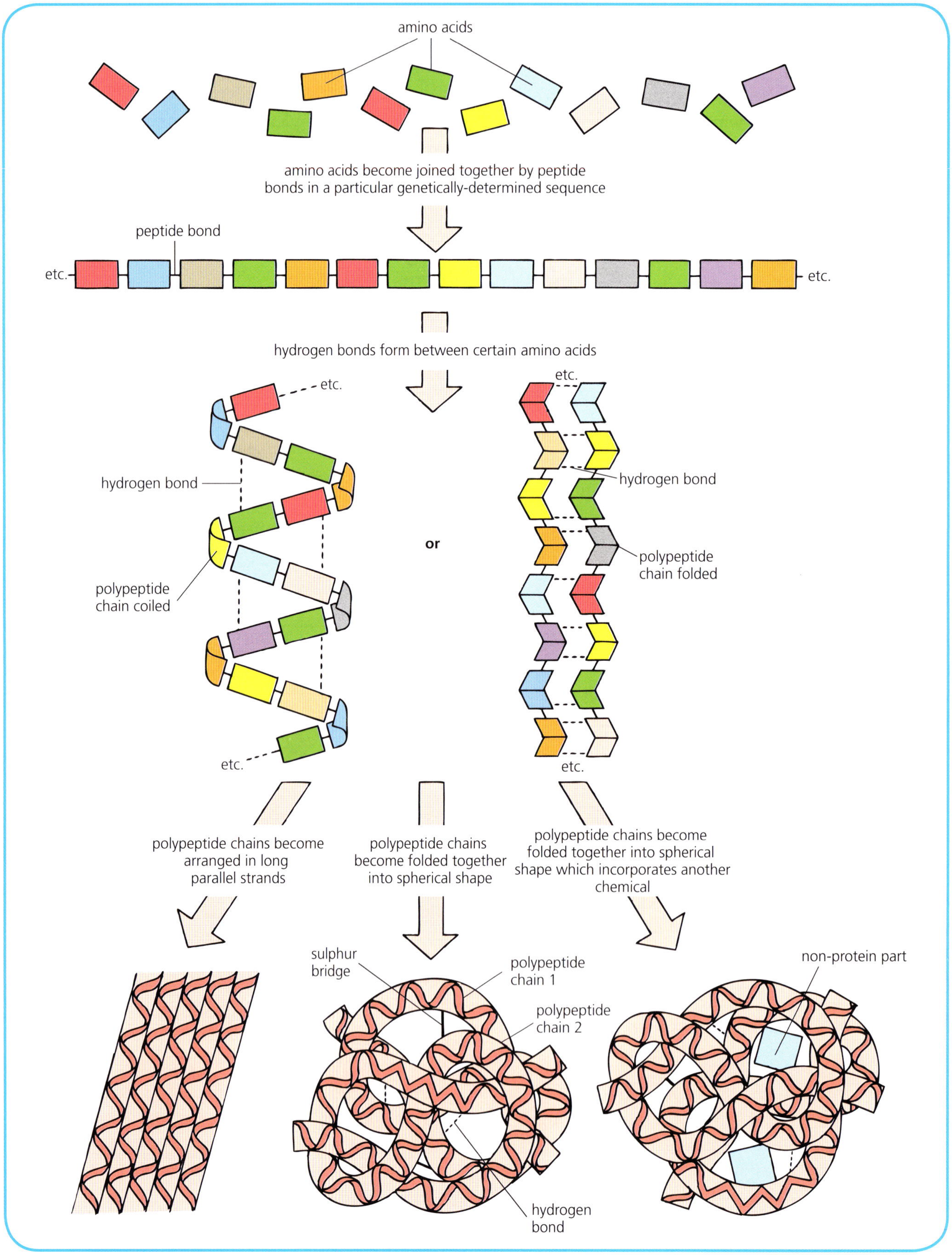

Figure 3.13 Structure of proteins

Polypeptides

Amino acids become joined together into chains by chemical links called **peptide bonds**. Each chain is called a **polypeptide** and it normally consists of hundreds of amino acid molecules linked together. During the process of protein synthesis (see page 38), amino acids are joined together in a **specific order**, which is determined by the sequence of bases on a portion of DNA. This sequence of amino acids determines the protein's ultimate structure and function.

Hydrogen bonds

Chemical links known as **hydrogen bonds** form between certain amino acids in a polypeptide chain, causing the chain to become coiled or folded as shown in Figure 3.13 on page 46.

Further linkages

During the folding process, different regions of the chain(s) come into contact with one another. This allows interaction between individual amino acids in one or more chains. It results in the formation of various types of cross-connection including **bridges** between **sulphur** atoms, attraction between positive and negative charges and further hydrogen bonding. These cross-connections occur between amino acids in the same polypeptide chain and those on adjacent chains. They are important because they cause the molecule to adopt the final **three-dimensional** structure that it needs to carry out its specific function.

Some types of protein molecule are formed by several spiral-shaped polypeptide molecules becoming linked together in parallel when bonds form between them. This gives the protein molecule a rope-like structure (see Figure 3.13). Other types of protein molecule consist of one or more polypeptide chains folded together into a roughly spherical shape like a tangled ball of string (see Figure 3.13). The exact form that the folding takes depends on the types of further linkage that form between amino acids on the same and adjacent chains.

A computer-generated representation of a protein molecule's three-dimensional structure is shown in Figure 3.14.

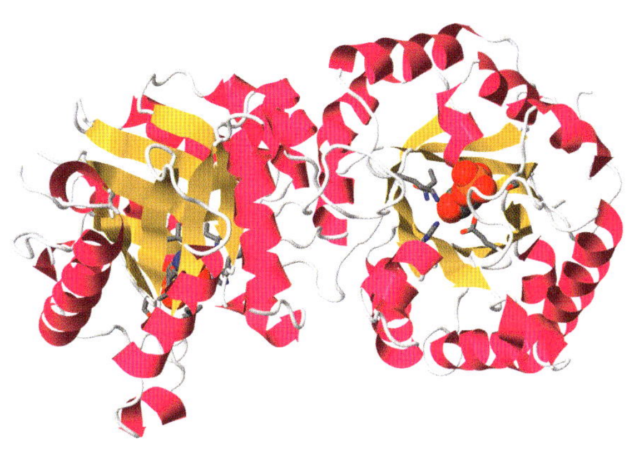

Figure 3.14 Protein molecule as visualised by a molecular graphics viewer

Functions of proteins

A vast variety of structures and shapes exists among proteins and as a result they are able to perform a wider range of functions than any other type of molecule in the body. Some are found in bone and muscle, where their strong fibres provide support and allow movement. Others are vital components of all living cells and play a variety of roles, as follows.

Enzymes

Each molecule of **enzyme** is made of protein and is folded in a particular way to expose an active surface that readily combines with a specific substrate (see Chapter 6). Since intracellular enzymes speed up the rate of biochemical processes such as respiration and protein synthesis, they are essential for the maintenance of life.

Structural proteins

Protein is one of two main components that make up the **membrane** surrounding a living cell. Similarly it forms an essential part of all membranes possessed by a cell's organelles. Therefore this type of protein plays a vital structural role in every living cell.

Hormones

These are **chemical messengers** transported in an animal's blood to 'target' tissues where they exert a specific effect. Some hormones are made of protein and exert a regulatory effect on the animal's growth and metabolism.

Antibodies

Antibodies are also made of protein. They have a characteristic Y-shape (see Figure 3.15). They are produced by white blood cells to defend the body against antigens (see Chapter 22).

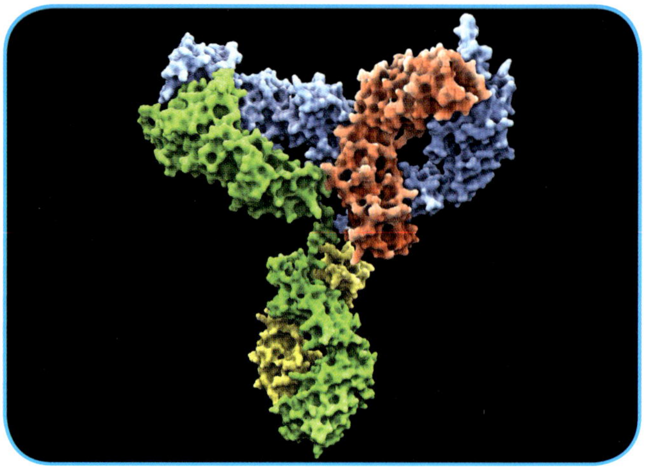

Figure 3.15 Antibody molecule

Proteins and phenotype

An organism's phenotype is the sum of all its physical and physiological characteristics. These features are determined by proteins which have been produced as a result of the organism's genes being expressed.

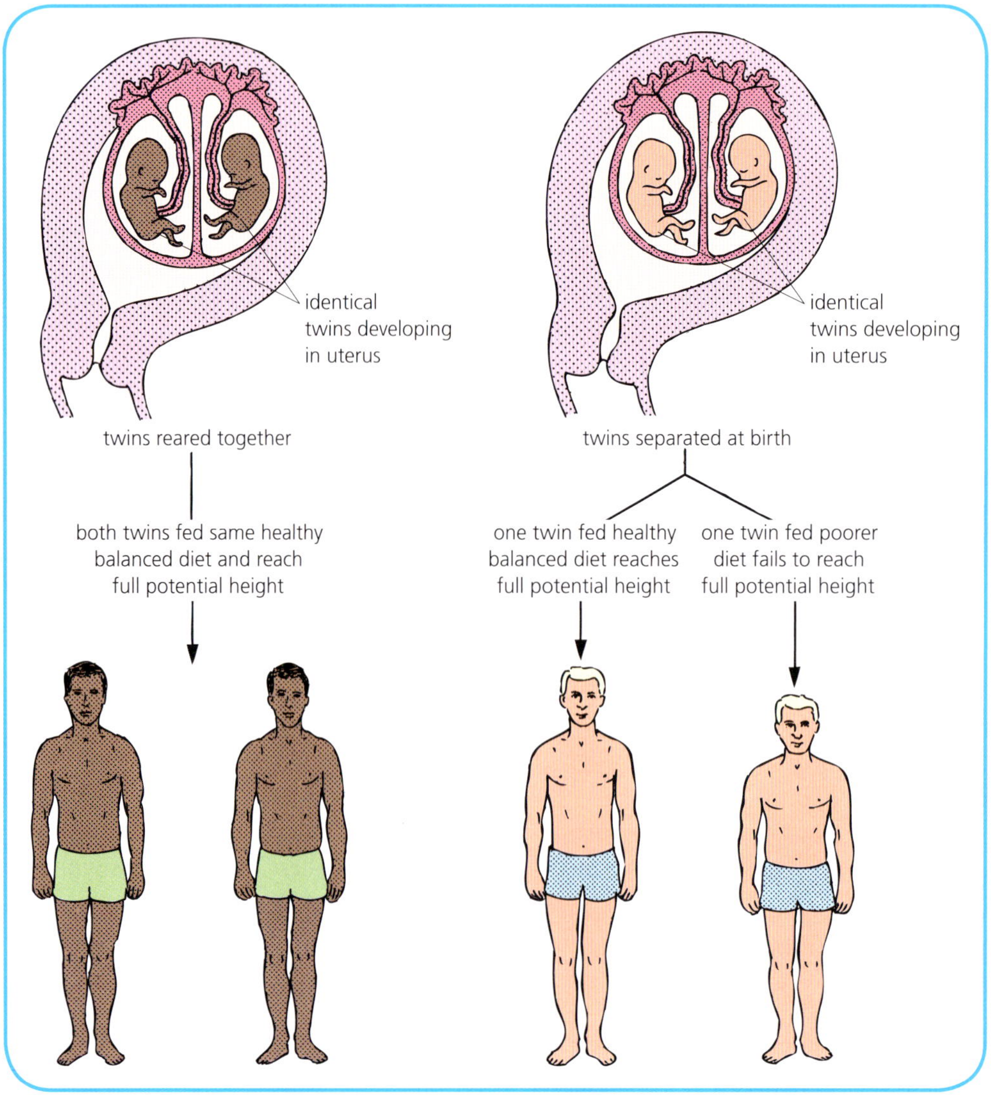

Figure 3.16 Twin study

Environmental factors

An organism's final phenotypic state is the result of the interaction between the information held in its genotype and the effect of environmental factors acting on it during growth and development. This relationship is summarised in the following equation:

$$\text{genotype} + \text{environment} \rightarrow \text{phenotype}$$

The phenotypic expression of some inherited traits remains unaffected by environmental factors. Tongue-rolling and blood group in humans, for example, are determined solely by genotype.

The phenotype of some other characteristics is influenced in part by environmental factors. If, for example, a person inherits the genetic information to become tall but consumes a poor diet during childhood then they will not reach their full potential height. Therefore it is possible for individuals such as identical twins to have the same genotype but to have different phenotypes. For example, one could become tall and the other one remain of medium height because they have been raised separately in different environments (see Figure 3.16).

Testing Your Knowledge 2

1 a) How many anticodons in a molecule of tRNA are exposed? (1)
   b) Each molecule of tRNA has a site of attachment at one end. What becomes attached to this site? (1)

2 a) What is a *ribosome*? (1)
   b) i) How many tRNA binding sites are present on a ribosome?
      ii) To what does a tRNA's anticodon become bound at one of these sites? (2)
   c) What type of bond forms between adjacent amino acids attached to tRNA molecules? (1)
   d) What is the fate of a tRNA molecule once its amino acid has been joined to the polypeptide chain? (2)

3 a) Copy and complete Table 3.3. (2)

Stage of synthesis	Site in cell
Formation of primary transcript of mRNA	
Modification of primary transcript of mRNA	
Collection of amino acid by tRNA	
Formation of codon–anticodon links	

Table 3.3

   b) Name the third type of RNA. (1)

4 Choose the correct answer from the underlined choice for each of the following statements. (6)
   a) The basic units of the genetic code present on mRNA are called <u>anticodons/codons</u>.
   b) The synthesis of mRNA from DNA is called <u>transcription/translation</u>.
   c) A non-coding region of mRNA is called an <u>intron/exon</u>.
   d) The basic units of the genetic code present on molecules of tRNA are called <u>anticodons/codons</u>.
   e) Protein synthesis occurs at a <u>nucleus/ribosome</u>.

5 a) How many different types of amino acid are known to occur in proteins? (1)
   b) What name is given to the chain formed when several amino acids become linked together? (1)
   c) What determines the order in which amino acids are joined together into a chain? (1)
   d) Describe TWO ways in which chains of amino acids can become arranged to form a protein. (2)

Applying Your Knowledge and Skills

1 Figure 3.17 shows the method by which the genetic code is transmitted during protein synthesis. Table 3.4 gives some of the triplets that correspond to certain amino acids.

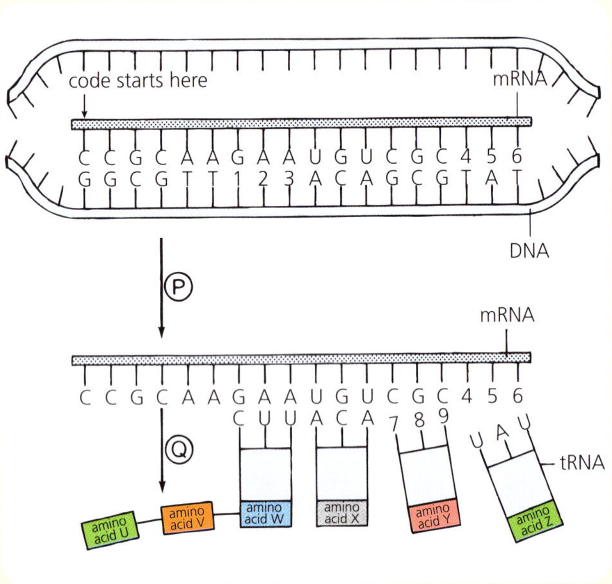

Figure 3.17

Amino acid	Codon	Anticodon
Alanine		CGC
Arginine	CGC	
Cysteine		ACA
Glutamic acid	GAA	
Glutamine		GUU
Glycine	GGC	
Isoleucine		UAU
Leucine	CUU	
Proline		GGC
Threonine	ACA	
Tyrosine		AUA
Valine	GUU	

Table 3.4

a) Identify bases 1–9. (2)
b) Name processes P and Q. (1)
c) Copy and complete Table 3.4. (2)
d) Give the triplet of bases that would be exposed on a molecule of tRNA to which valine would become attached. (1)
e) Use your table to identify amino acids U, V, W, X, Y and Z. (2)
f) i) Work out the mRNA code for part of a polypeptide chain with the amino acid sequence: threonine-leucine-alanine-glycine.
   ii) State the genetic code on the DNA strand from which this mRNA would be formed. (2)

2 Figure 3.18 shows mRNA's codons and the amino acids that they code for.
a) Which letters should have been inserted at positions **X** and **Y** in the wheel? (2)
b) How many codons are able to trigger the process of translation? (1)
c) Identify the codons that can bring translation to a halt. (3)
d) Which amino acid is coded for by codon:
   i) UUU; ii) ACC; iii) GGU? (3)
e) Name all the codons that code for leucine. (2)
f) Refer back to Figure 3.9 on page 42 and then state which amino acid would become attached to this tRNA's site of attachment. (Remember that tRNA has an anticodon and that the wheel shows mRNA codons.) (1)

3 Give an account of translation of mRNA into a polypeptide. (9)

4 A particular polypeptide chain was known to be 10 amino acids in length. When enzymes were used to break down several molecules of it at three different places along its length, the fragments shown in Figure 3.19 were obtained. (Note: AA = amino acid; N = one end of the polypeptide chain.) Draw a diagram of the complete polypeptide chain. (1)

5 Some amino acids can be synthesised by the body from simple compounds; others cannot be synthesised and must be supplied in the diet. The latter type are called the **essential amino acids**. The graph in Figure 3.20 shows the results of an experiment using rats where group 1 was fed zein (maize protein), group 2 was fed casein (milk protein) and group 3 was fed a diet that was changed at day 6.
a) One of the proteins contains all of the essential amino acids, whereas the other lacks two of them.
   i) Identify each protein.
   ii) Explain how you arrived at your answer. (4)

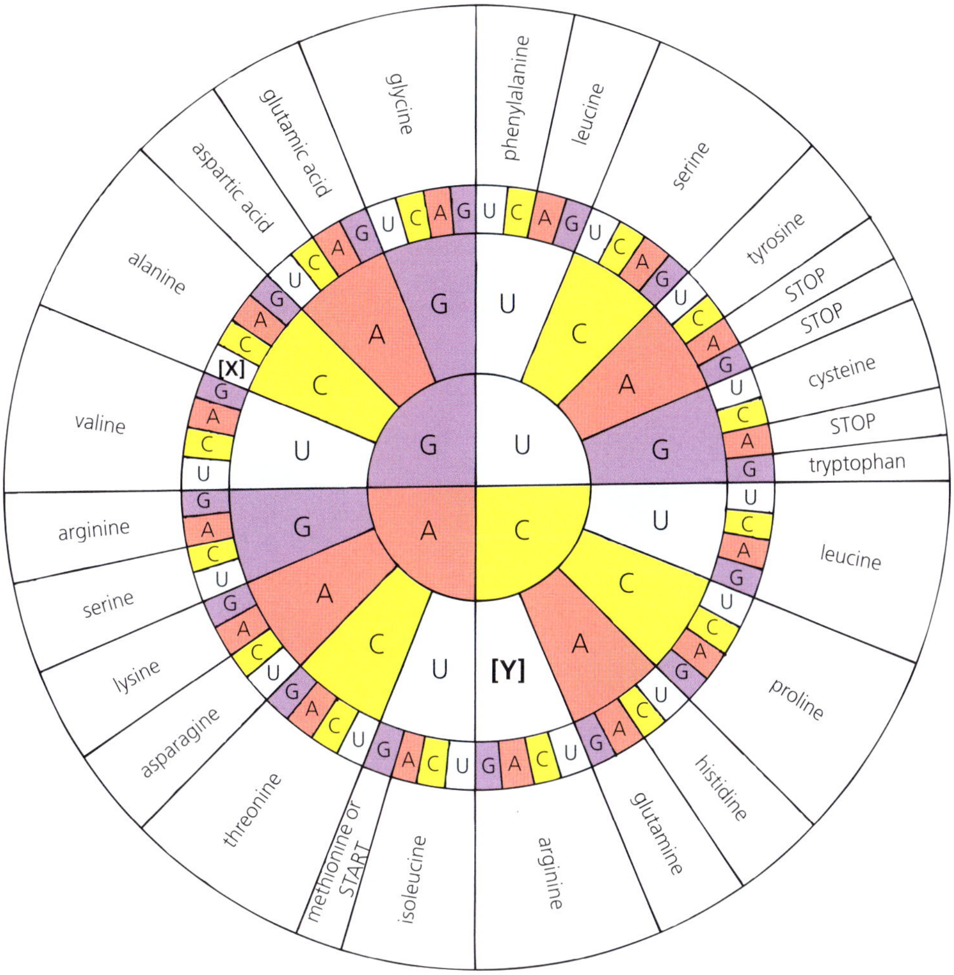

Figure 3.18

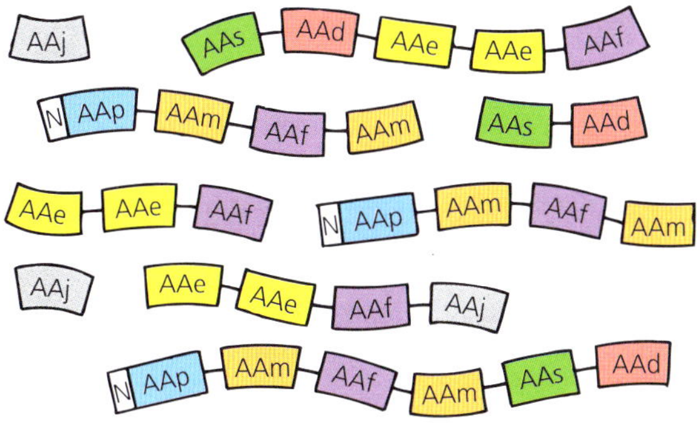

Figure 3.19

b) i) State which protein was given to the rats in group 3 during the first 6 days of the experiment.

ii) Suggest TWO different ways in which their diet could have been altered from day 6 onwards to account for the results shown in the graph. (3)

c) By how many grams did the mean body weight of the rats in group 2 increase over the 20-day period? (1)

d) Calculate the percentage decrease in mean body weight shown by the rats in group 1 over the 20-day period. (1)

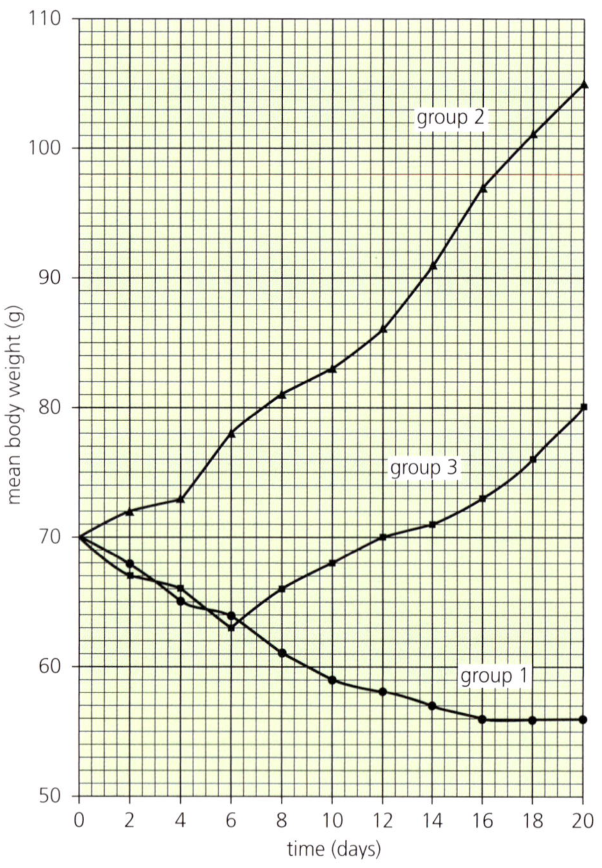

Figure 3.20

6 Human blood serum contains two major groups of protein: albumin and globulins. Some examples of these proteins are given in Table 3.5. Figure 3.21 shows a separation of serum proteins by electrophoresis and the results presented as a graph.

a) i) Compared with the globulins as a group, do albumin proteins have a higher or a lower molecular weight?

ii) Explain how you arrived at your answer. (2)

b) i) Based only on the information given in Table 3.5, identify the specific group of blood proteins that could indicate liver disease if its concentration increased greatly.

ii) What condition might a person have if the concentration of beta-globulins in her bloodstream increased to an abnormal level? (2)

c) i) The graph in Figure 3.22 shows a patient's results from a serum protein electrophoresis test. From which of the following could this person be suffering? (Your answer should be based only on the information in Table 3.5.)

A leakage of blood from vessels
B cirrhosis of the liver
C iron-deficiency anaemia
D cancer of cells in bone marrow

ii) Why is this diagnosis *not* conclusive? (2)

Blood protein group		Details
Albumin		It makes up more than half of the protein in blood serum and prevents blood from leaking out of vessels.
Globulins	Alpha-1-globulins (α1)	They include a high-density lipoprotein that contains 'good' cholesterol *not* taken into the artery wall.
	Alpha-2-globulins (α2)	They include a protein that binds with haemoglobin. Some of the proteins in this group are increased in concentration in conditions such as diabetes and cirrhosis of the liver.
	Beta-globulins (β)	They include a protein called transferrin that carries iron through the bloodstream and increases in concentration during iron- deficiency anaemia.
	Gamma-globulins (γ)	Many are antibodies whose numbers increase in response to viral invasion and some cancers such as myeloma (which affects bone marrow) and lymphatic leukaemia.

Table 3.5

➜

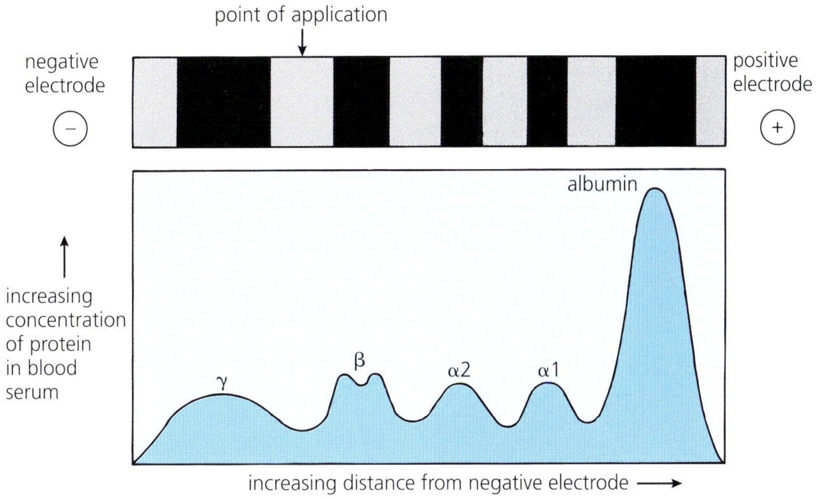

Figure 3.21

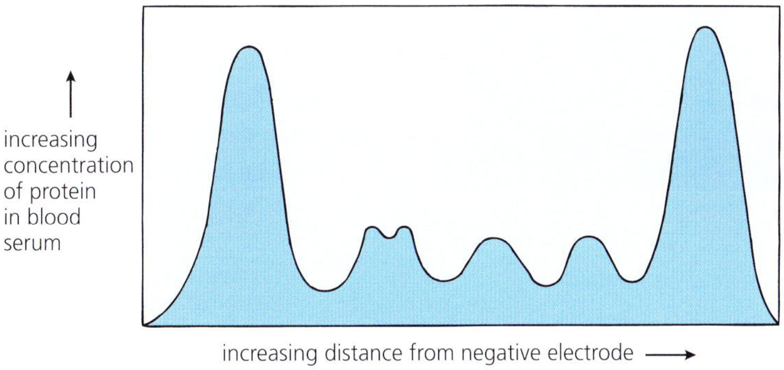

Figure 3.22

What You Should Know Chapters 1–3

adenine	exons	research
amino	folded	ribose
amplified	fragments	ribosomes
anticodons	genetic	RNA polymerase
antiparallel	guanine	splicing
backbone	heat-tolerant	therapy
bonds	helix	three-dimensional
chain	introns	thymine
characteristic	ligase	tissue
codons	nucleotides	transcript
complementary	peptide	transcription
cytosine	polypeptide	translation
deoxyribose	primary	tumour
differentiate	primer	twenty
DNA polymerase	protein	unspecialised
embryonic	regulators	uracil
environmental	replication	

Table 3.6 Word bank for Chapters 1–3

1 Stem cells are ______ cells that can reproduce themselves and can ______ into specialised cells.

2 ______ stem cells are able to differentiate into all the cell types that make up the human body. ______ stem cells are only able to regenerate a limited range of cell types.

3 A differentiated cell only expresses the genes for the proteins ______ of that cell type.

4 Stem cells are used in ______ to gain a better understanding of cell growth and gene regulation. In the future, several debilitating conditions may be treated successfully using stem cell ______.

5 Cancerous cells fail to respond to cell cycle ______ and divide excessively to form a ______.

6 DNA consists of two strands twisted into a double ______. Each strand is composed of ______. Each nucleotide consists of ______ sugar, phosphate and one of four types of base (______, thymine, ______ and cytosine).

7 Adenine always pairs with ______; guanine always pairs with ______.

8 Within each DNA strand neighbouring nucleotides are joined by chemical ______ into a sugar–phosphate ______. The backbones of complementary strands are ______ because they run in opposite directions.

9 DNA is unique because it can direct its own ______. This begins by DNA unwinding and its two strands separating at a starting point. A ______ forms beside the DNA strand with the 3′ end. Individual nucleotides aligned with ______ nucleotides on the DNA strand become joined into a new DNA strand by the enzyme ______.

10 The DNA strand with the 5′ end is replicated in ______ that are joined together by the enzyme ______.

11 DNA can be ______ by the polymerase ______ reaction using primers, ______ DNA polymerase and repeated thermal cycling.

12 RNA differs from DNA in that it is single-stranded, contains ______ (not deoxyribose) and the base ______ in place of thymine.

13 DNA contains an individual's ______ information as a coded language determined by the sequence of its bases arranged in triplets called ______. Expression of this information through ______ synthesis occurs in two stages when a gene is switched on.

14 The first stage, ______, begins when the enzyme ______ becomes attached to, and moves along, the DNA, bringing about the synthesis of a ______ transcript of mRNA from individual RNA nucleotides. Primary RNA is cut and spliced to remove non-coding regions called ______ and to bind together coding regions called ______.

15 The second stage, ______, occurs at ______ where codons on the mRNA strand match up with the ______ on tRNA molecules carrying amino acids. These become joined together by peptide bonds to form a ______ chain whose amino acid sequence reflects the code on the mRNA.

16 Alternative ______ of a primary mRNA ______ enables a gene to be expressed as several proteins.

17 Proteins consist of subunits called ______ acids of which there are ______ different types.

18 Amino acid molecules are joined together by ______ bonds to form polypeptides. Polypeptides are coiled and ______ to form protein molecules whose ______ structure is directly related to their function.

19 An organism's phenotype is affected by both its genotype and ______ factors.

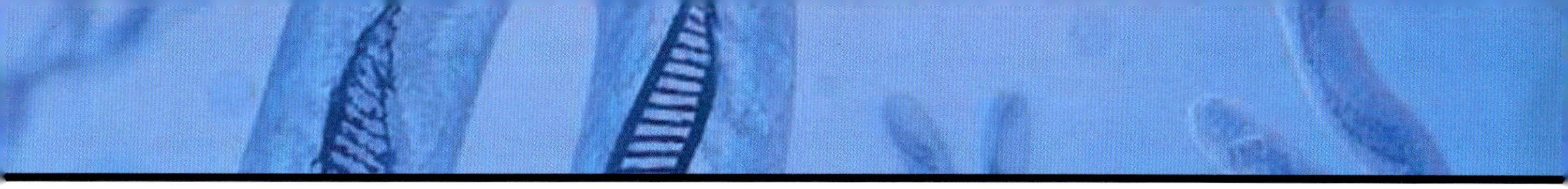

4 Mutations

Mutation

A **mutation** is a change in the structure or composition of an organism's genome. It varies in form from a tiny change in the DNA structure of a gene to a large-scale alteration in chromosome structure or number. When such a change in genotype produces a change in phenotype, the individual affected is called a **mutant**.

Frequency of mutation

In the absence of outside influences, gene mutations arise **spontaneously** and at **random** but only occur **rarely**. The mutation frequency of a gene is expressed as the number of mutations that occur at that gene site per million gametes. Mutation frequency varies from gene to gene and species to species.

Mutagenic agents

Mutation rate can be artificially increased by **mutagenic agents**. These include certain chemicals (e.g. mustard gas) and various types of radiation (e.g. gamma rays, X-rays and UV light). The resultant mutations are described as **induced**.

Genetic disorder

A condition or disease that can be shown to be directly related to an individual's genotype is called a **genetic disorder**. For a protein to function properly it must possess the correct sequence of amino acids determined by the order of the nucleotide bases on a particular region of DNA in a gene. A change to the gene (or chromosome) caused by a mutation may result in the gene expressing a faulty version of the protein that does not function correctly. The mutated gene may even fail to express the protein at all.

Most proteins are indispensible to the organism. For example, an enzyme that controls a key step in a metabolic pathway is essential for the normal functioning of the body. Therefore the presence of an altered version of the protein (or its total absence) may result in disruption of the pathway and result in a genetic disorder. Many genetic disorders are **disabling** and some are **lethal**.

Related Activity

Investigating the effect of UV radiation on UV-sensitive yeast cells

Normal yeast cells have genes that code for enzymes that repair damage done to their DNA by UV radiation. **UV-sensitive yeast** is a strain that has had these genes 'knocked out' by genetic engineering. Therefore it is unable to repair damaged DNA resulting from exposure to UV radiation.

The experiment is carried out as shown in Figure 4.1. After 2 days of incubation, plate X is found to lack yeast colonies whereas plate Y, the control, has many colonies. Therefore it is concluded that exposure to UV radiation has had a lethal effect on UV-sensitive yeast.

Investigating the effect of UV radiation on 'protected' UV-sensitive yeast

The above experiment is repeated and extended to include two further Petri dishes, V and W, wrapped in Clingfilm. Their top surfaces are smeared each with a different sun barrier cream (e.g. protection factors 6 and 20) and then exposed to the UV light source as before. If more yeast colonies grow on the plate with the higher protection factor then this result suggests that the higher factor has given them more protection from the harmful UV rays than the lower factor.

→

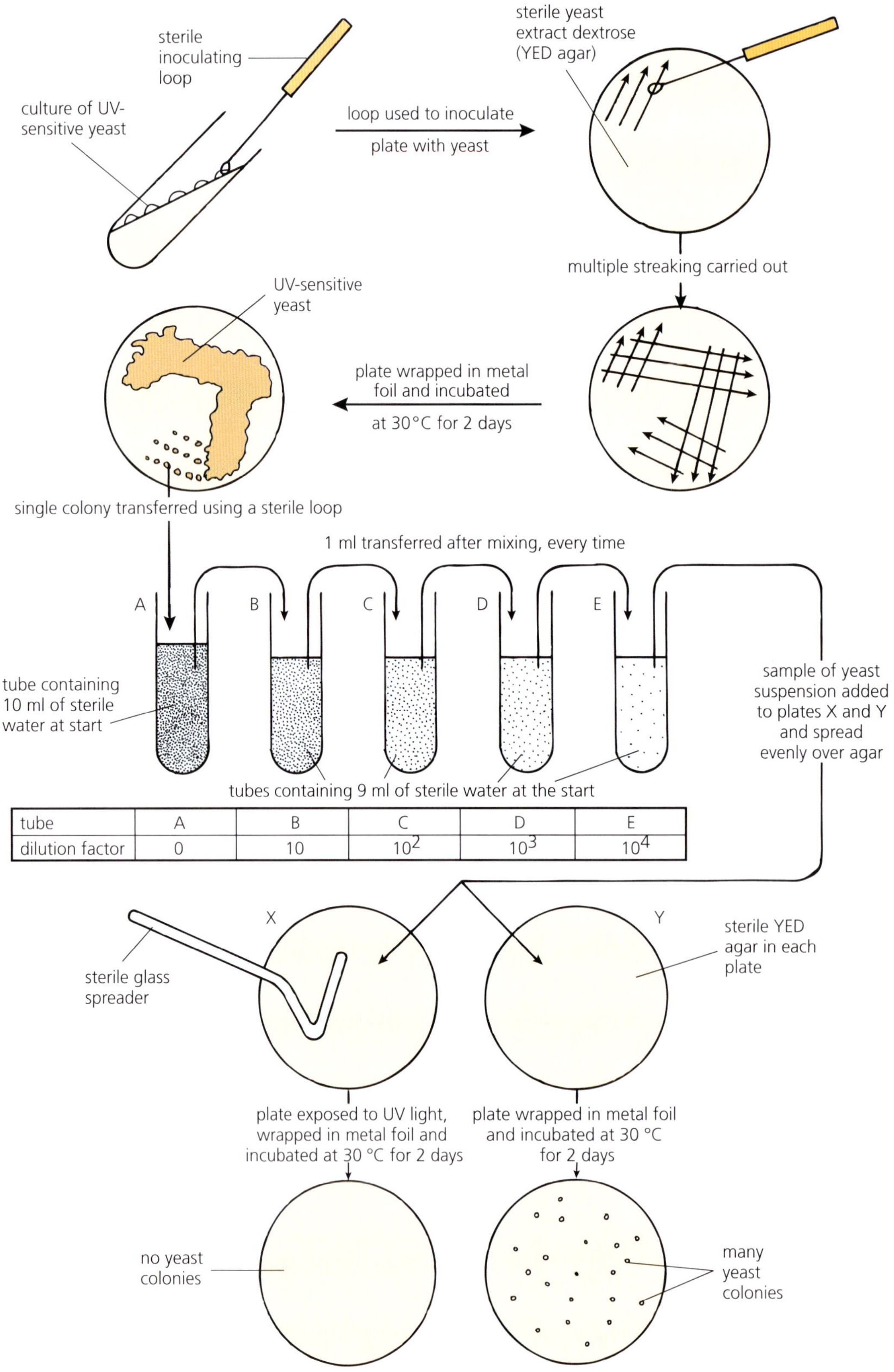

tube	A	B	C	D	E
dilution factor	0	10	10^2	10^3	10^4

Figure 4.1 Effect of UV radiation on UV-sensitive yeast

Single-gene mutation

This type of mutation involves an **alteration of a nucleotide sequence** in the gene's DNA.

Point mutation

A point mutation is a type of single-gene mutation that involves a **change in one nucleotide** in the DNA sequence of the gene. Three types of point mutation are shown in Figure 4.2. A single nucleotide is either **substituted**, **inserted** or **deleted**. In each case this results in one or more codons for one or more amino acids becoming altered.

Splice-site mutation

Before mRNA leaves the nucleus, introns (non-coding regions) are removed and exons (coding regions) are joined together. This process of post-transcriptional processing of mRNA is called **splicing** (see Figure 3.6

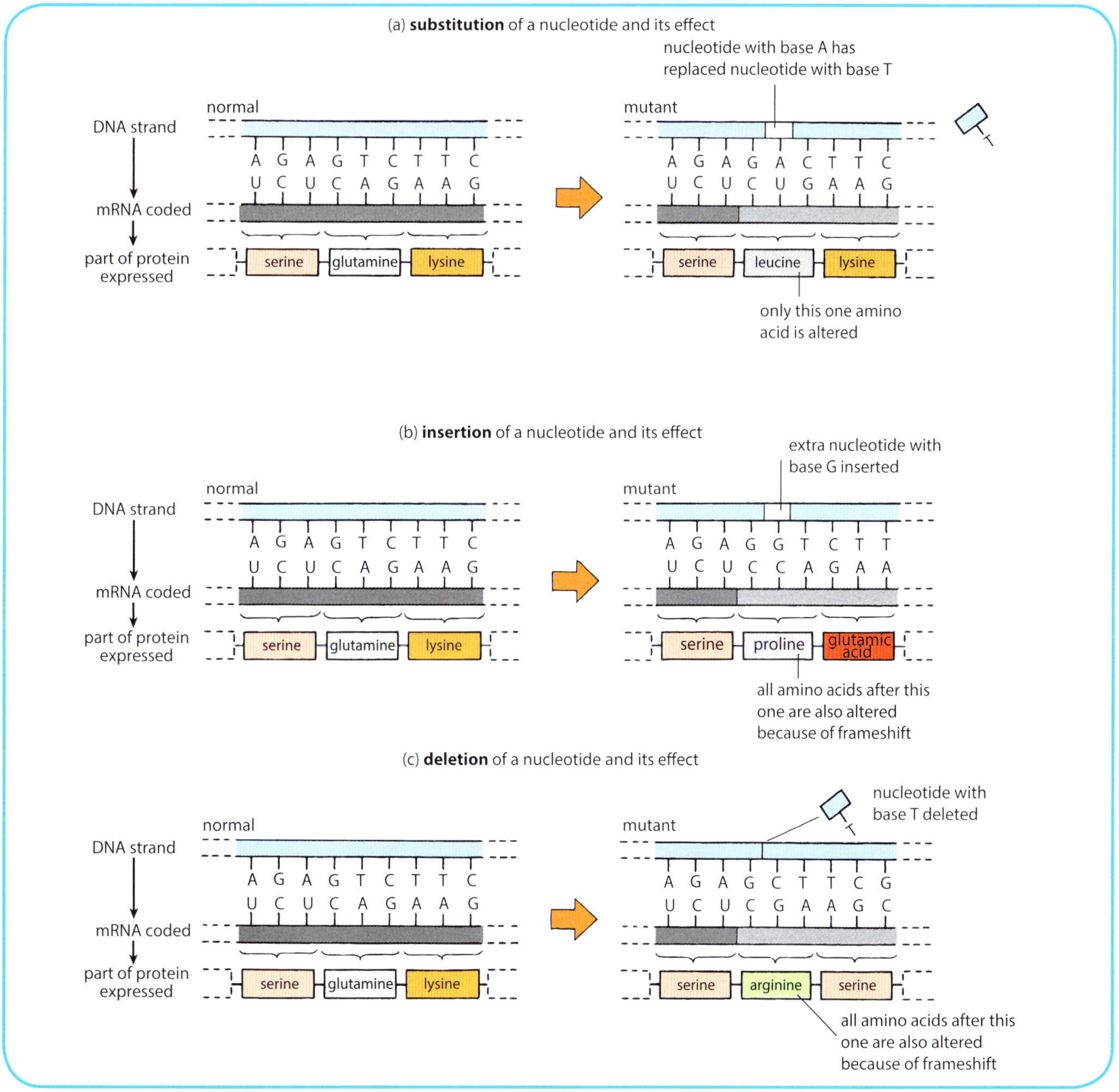

Figure 4.2 Types of point mutation

on page 41). Splicing is controlled by specific nucleotide sequences at **splice sites** on those parts of introns that flank exons. If a mutation occurs at one of these splice sites, the codon for an intron–exon splice may be affected. This could result in an essential exon *not* being retained by the mature transcript of mRNA or an intron being retained in error (see Figure 4.3).

Impact on protein structure

Missense

Following a **substitution**, the altered codon codes for an amino acid that still makes sense but not the original sense (see Figure 4.4). This change in genome is called a **missense** mutation. (See the Case Studies on sickle-cell disease and phenylketonuria.)

Nonsense

As a result of a **substitution**, a codon that used to code for an amino acid is exchanged for one that acts as a premature **stop codon** (UAG, UAA or UGA). It causes protein synthesis to be halted prematurely (see Figure 4.4) and results in the formation of a polypeptide chain that is shorter than the normal one and unable to function. This change in genome is called a **nonsense** mutation. (See the Case Study on Duchenne muscular dystrophy.)

Splice-site mutation

If one or more introns have been retained by the mature transcript of mRNA, they may in turn be translated into an altered protein that does not function properly. (See the Case Study on beta (β) thalassemia.)

Frameshift

mRNA is read as a series of triplets (codons) during translation. Therefore, if one base pair is **inserted** or **deleted** (see Figure 4.2) this affects the reading frame (triplet grouping) of the genetic code. It becomes shifted in a way that alters every subsequent codon and amino acid coded all along the remaining length of the gene. The protein formed is almost certain to be non-functional. This change in genome is called a **frameshift** mutation. (See the Case Studies on Tay-Sachs syndrome and cystic fibrosis.)

Effects on those with genetic disorders

The effects of single gene mutations on the people who develop the resultant genetic disorders are exemplified in the accompanying case studies. Almost without exception, a genetic disorder has an **adverse effect** on the individual affected.

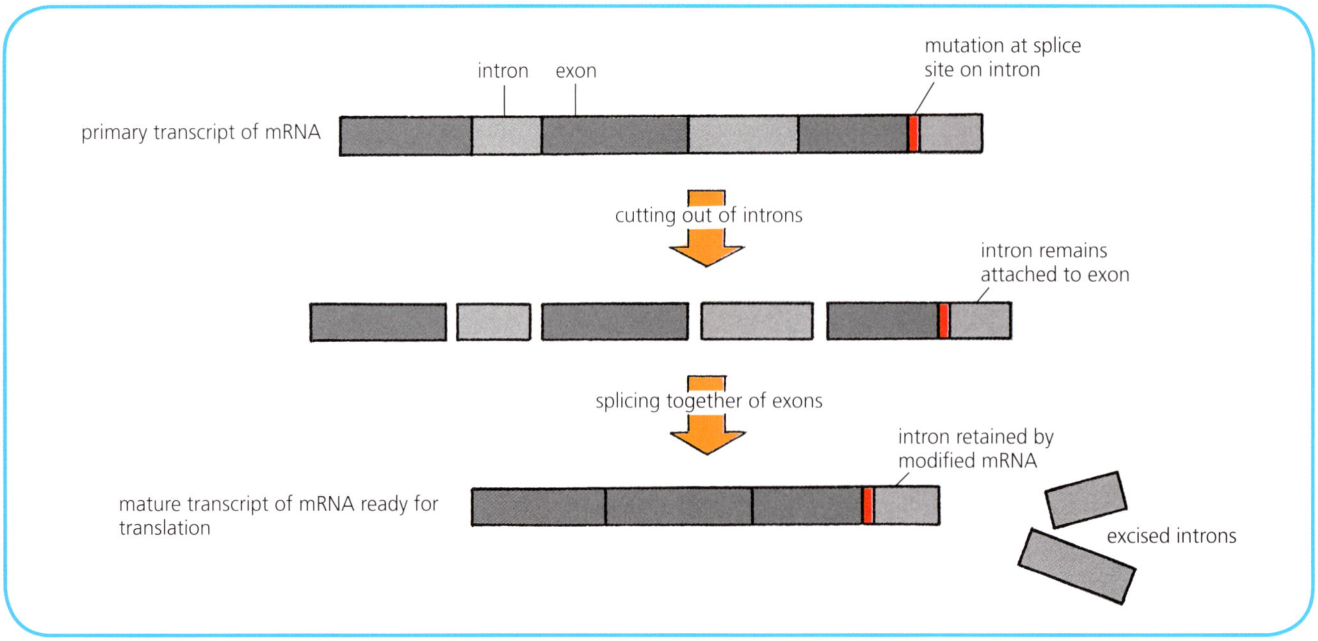

Figure 4.3 Effect of splice-site mutation

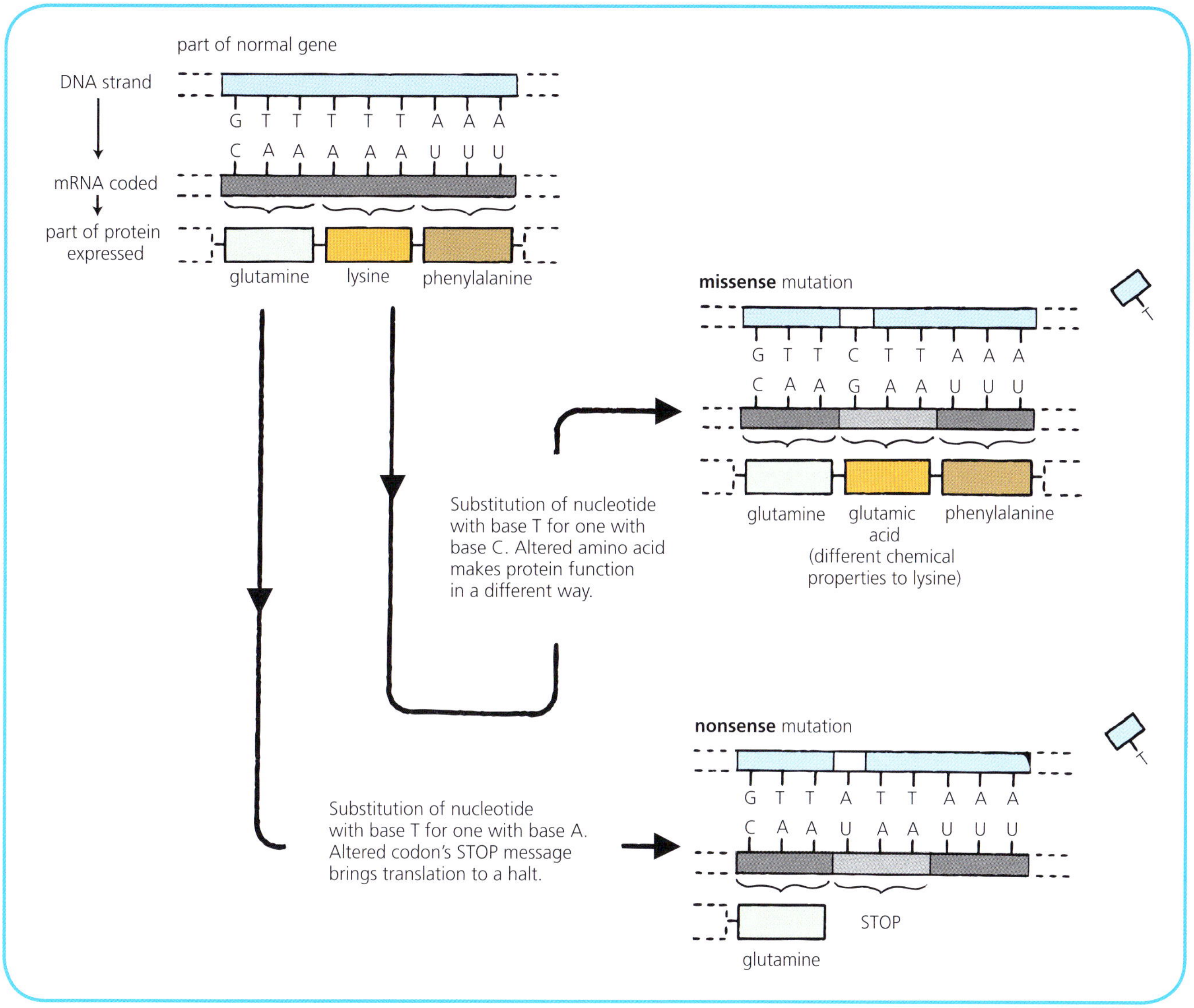

Figure 4.4 Possible effects of a base-pair substitution on sequence of amino acids

Case Study Sickle-cell disease

When one of the genes on chromosome 11 that codes for haemoglobin undergoes a **substitution** (see Figure 4.5), it becomes expressed as an unusual form of haemoglobin called **haemoglobin S**. This is an example of **missense**. Although haemoglobin S differs from normal haemoglobin by only one amino acid, that one tiny alteration leads to profound changes in the folding and ultimate shape of the haemoglobin S molecule, making it a very inefficient carrier of oxygen.

People who are homozygous for the mutant allele experience drastic consequences. In addition to all of their haemoglobin being type S, which fails to perform the normal function properly, they also possess distorted, sickle-shaped red blood cells (see Figure 4.6). These are less flexible than the normal type and tend to stick together and interfere with blood circulation. The result of these problems is severe shortage of oxygen followed by damage to vital organs and, in many cases, death. This potentially lethal genetic disorder is called **sickle-cell anaemia**.

➜

Sickle-cell trait

People who are heterozygous for the mutant allele do not have sickle-cell anaemia. Instead they are found to have a milder condition called **sickle-cell trait**. Their red blood cells contain both forms of haemoglobin but do not show 'sickling'. The slight anaemia that they tend to experience does not prevent moderate activity.

Resistance to malaria

The sickle-cell mutant allele is rare in most populations. However, in some parts of Africa up to 40% of the population have the heterozygous genotype. This is because people with sickle-cell trait are **resistant to malaria**. The parasite cannot make use of the red blood cells containing haemoglobin S. This situation, where a genetic disorder confers an advantage on people with the condition, is very unusual.

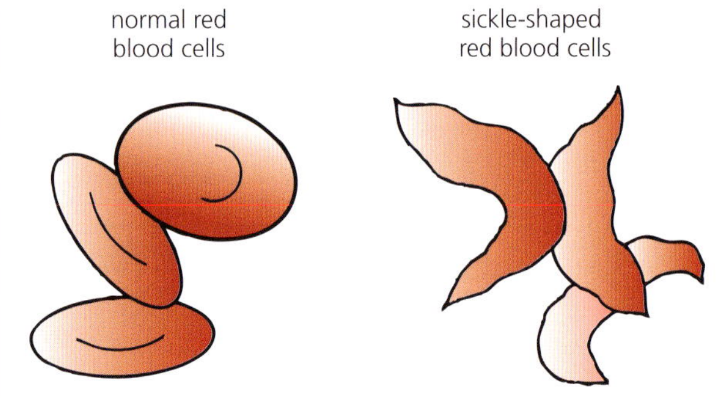

Figure 4.6 Two types of red blood cell

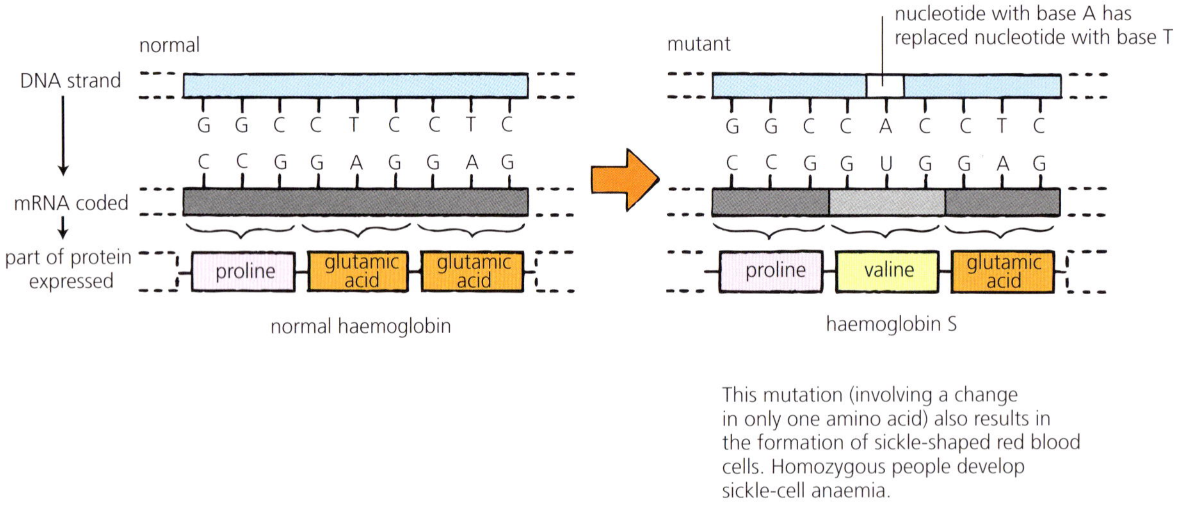

Figure 4.5 Mutation causing sickle-cell disease

Case Study Phenylketonuria (PKU)

Phenylalanine and tyrosine are two amino acids that human beings obtain from protein in their diet. During normal metabolism, excess phenylalanine is acted on by an enzyme (enzyme 1 in the pathway shown in Figure 4.7).

Phenylketonuria is a genetic disorder caused by a mutation to a gene on chromosome 12 that normally codes for enzyme 1 in the pathway. Most commonly, the mutated gene has undergone a **substitution** of a nucleotide and **missense** occurs. The altered form of the protein expressed contains a copy of tryptophan in place of arginine and is non-functional. As a result of this **inborn error of metabolism**, phenylalanine is no longer converted to tyrosine. Instead it accumulates and some of it is converted to **toxins**.

These poisonous metabolites inhibit one or more of the enzymes that control biochemical pathways in brain cells. The brain fails to develop properly, resulting in the person having severe learning difficulties. In Britain, newborn babies are screened for PKU and any found to be affected are put on a diet containing minimum phenylalanine. By this means, the worst effects of PKU are reduced to a minimum.

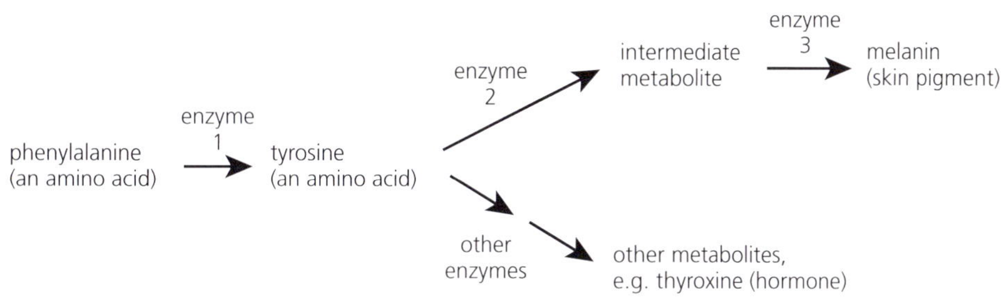

Figure 4.7 Normal fate of phenylalanine

Case Study Duchenne muscular dystrophy (DMD)

Duchenne muscular dystrophy (DMD) is caused by any one of several types of mutation to a particular gene on chromosome X, such as a **deletion** or a **nonsense** mutation. The affected gene fails to code for a protein called dystrophin, which is essential for the normal functioning of muscles. In skeletal and cardiac muscle, for example, dystrophin is part of a group of proteins that strengthen muscle fibres and protect them from injury during contraction and relaxation.

Duchenne muscular dystrophy is the most common form of muscular dystrophy (muscle-wasting disease). In the absence of dystrophin, skeletal muscles become weak and lose their normal structure. This condition is accompanied by progressive loss of coordination. People with this condition are severely disabled from an early age and normally die young without passing the mutant allele on to the next generation. DMD is sex-linked and is almost entirely restricted to males, being passed on by carrier mothers to their sons.

Case Study Beta (β) thalassemia

A molecule of haemoglobin is composed of two alpha-globin and two beta-globin polypeptide chains. These polypeptides are encoded by genes.

Beta (β) thalassemia is a genetic disorder caused by any one of several types of mutation that affect a gene on chromosome 11 that codes for beta-globin. One of the most common of these mutations is a **substitution** that occurs at a **splice site** on an intron and causes base G to be replaced by base A.

There are several forms of β-thalassemia, some more severe than others. One type, for example, is characterised by the complete lack of production of beta-globin; another by the production of an altered version of the protein. In either case, the person has a relative excess of alpha-globin in their bloodstream, which tends to bind to, and damage, red blood cells. Patients with severe β-thalassemia require medical treatment such as blood transfusions.

Case Study Tay-Sachs disease

Tay-Sachs disease is a genetic disorder resulting from a mutation to a gene on chromosome 15. Under normal circumstances the gene is responsible for encoding an enzyme that controls an essential biochemical reaction in nerve cells.

Changes to the gene take the form of point mutations such as **insertions** and **deletions**, which result in the **frameshift** effect. The protein expressed is so different from the normal one that it is non-functional. As a result, the enzyme's unprocessed substrate accumulates in brain cells. This leads to neurological degeneration, generalised paralysis and death at about 4 years of age.

Case Study Cystic fibrosis

Cystic fibrosis is a genetic disorder caused by a three-base-pair **deletion** to a gene on chromosome 7. This type of mutation removes a codon for phenylalanine and causes the coded message to be seriously altered by the **frameshift** effect and produce a non-functional protein.

The normal allele for the gene codes for a **membrane protein** that assists in the transport of chloride ions into and out of cells. In the absence of this protein an abnormally high concentration of chloride gathers outside cells. Those regions of the body that coat their cells with mucus become affected because the high concentration of chloride causes mucus to become **thicker** and **stickier**. Organs such as the lungs, pancreas and alimentary canal become congested and blocked. Regular pounding on the chest to clear thick mucus (see Figure 4.8) and daily use of antibiotics can extend the person's life into their thirties and beyond. Untreated, they normally die at age 4–5 years.

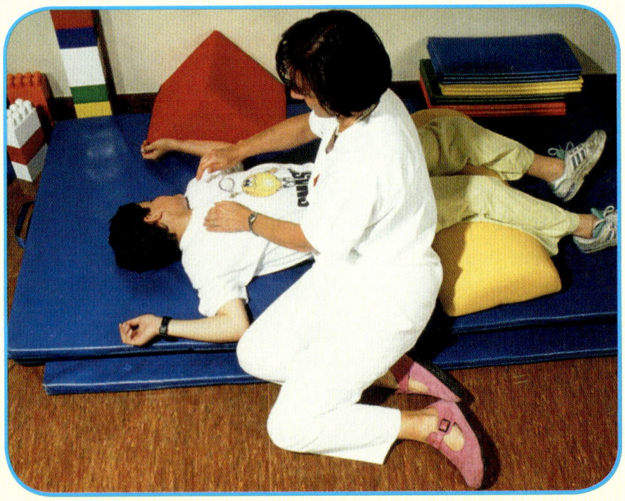

Figure 4.8 Easing symptoms of cystic fibrosis

Chromosome structure mutations

This type of mutation involves the breakage of one or more **chromosomes**. A broken end of a chromosome is 'sticky' and it can join to another broken end. Three of the different ways in which this can occur are discussed below. Each brings about a change in the number or sequence of the genes in a chromosome.

Deletion

A **deletion** occurs when a chromosome breaks in two places and the segment in between becomes detached (see Figures 4.9 and 4.10). The two ends then join up giving a shorter chromosome, which **lacks** certain genes. As a result, deletion normally has a drastic effect on the organism involved. (See the Case Study on Cri-du-chat syndrome.)

Figure 4.10 'Look! Nessie's had a deletion!'

Duplication

A chromosome undergoes **duplication** when a segment of genes (e.g. deleted genes from its homologous partner) becomes attached to one end of the first chromosome or becomes inserted somewhere along its length, as shown in Figure 4.11. This results in a set of genes being **repeated**. Some duplications of genes may have a detrimental effect on the organism. For example, the duplication of certain genes is a common cause of cancer.

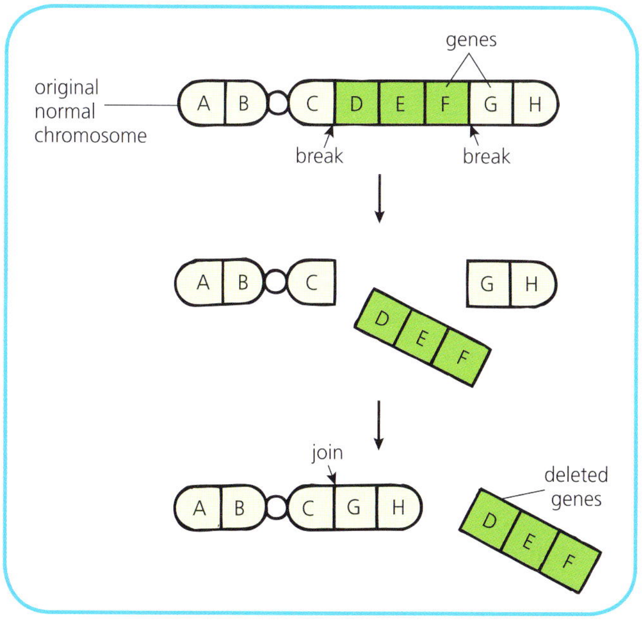

Figure 4.9 Deletion

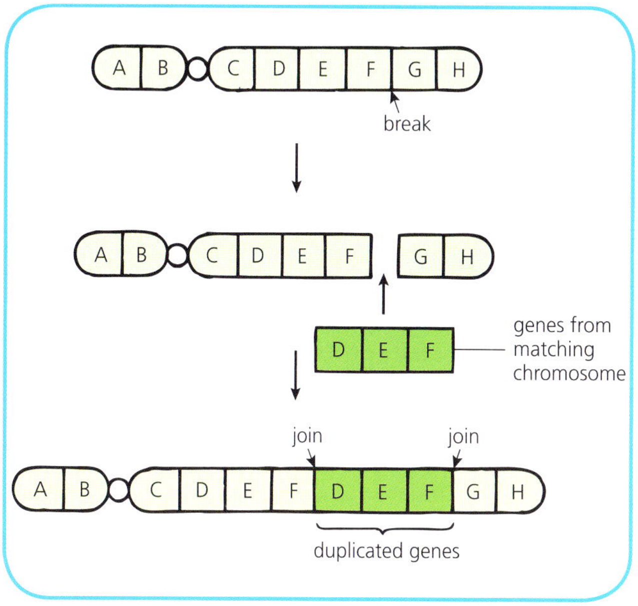

Figure 4.11 Duplication

Translocation

Translocation involves a section of one chromosome breaking off and becoming attached to another chromosome that is *not* its homologous partner. Figure 4.12 shows two ways in which this can occur. Translocation is the most common type of mutation associated with cancer. (See the Case Study on chronic

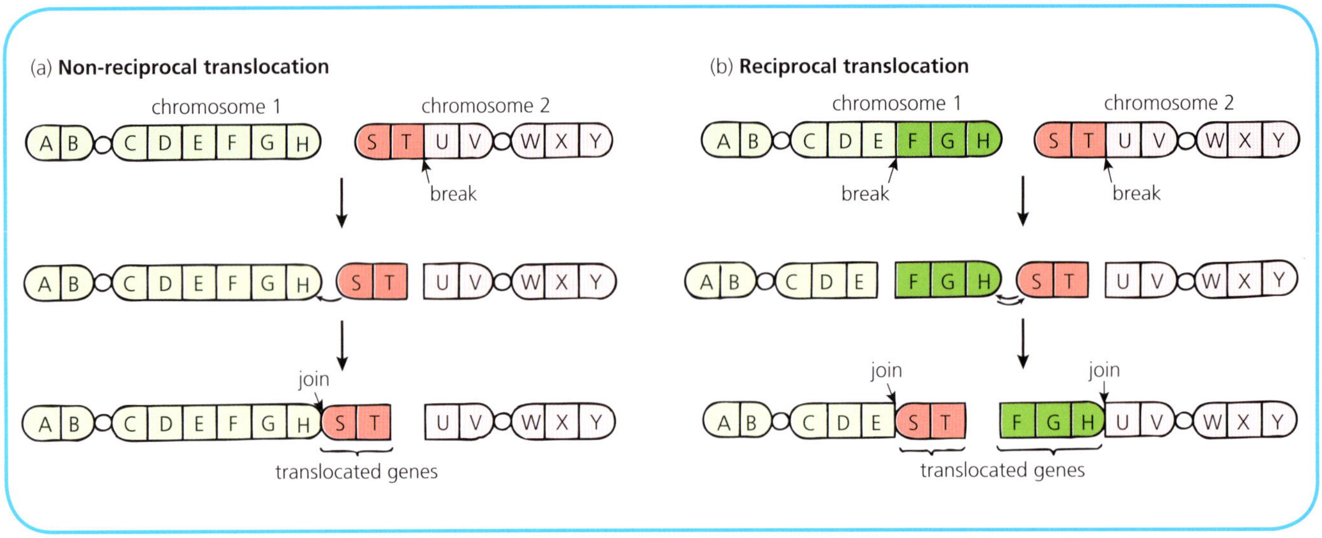

Figure 4.12 Translocation

myeloid leukaemia.) A translocation can bring about a major change in an individual's phenotype.

Lethal effect

A mutation to a chromosome often involves such a substantial change to the chromosome's structure (e.g. loss of several functional genes) that the mutation is **lethal**.

Inversion

A chromosome undergoing **inversion** breaks in two places as shown in Figure 4.13. The segment between the two breaks turns round before joining up again. This brings about a reversal of the normal sequence of genes in the affected area. (See Case Study on Haemophilia A.)

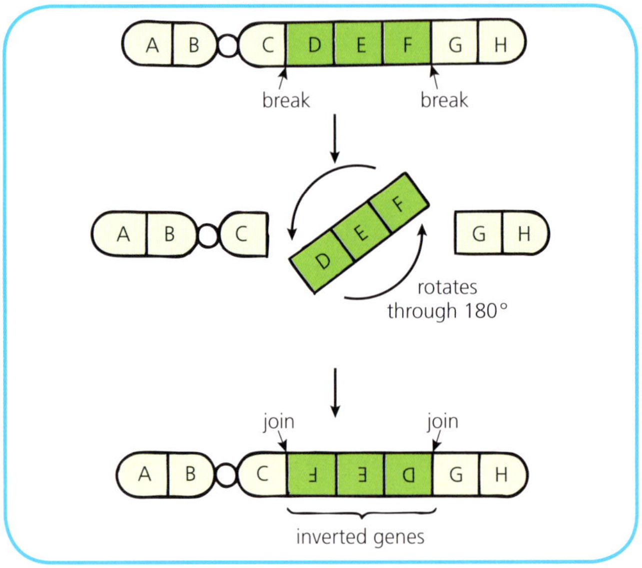

Figure 4.13 Inversion

Case Study Cri-du-chat syndrome

Cri-du-chat syndrome is caused by a **deletion** of part of chromosome 5. Children born with this genetic disorder have severe learning difficulties. They develop a small head with unusual facial features and widely spaced eyes. The condition is so-called because the infant's crying resembles that of a distressed cat. Affected individuals usually die early in childhood.

Case Study Haemophilia A

Haemophilia A is a genetic disorder caused by several types of mutation. One of the most common of these is an **inversion** within the gene that produces **blood-clotting factor VIII**.

People with this condition fail to make normal factor VIII. In the absence of this protein, an untreated person experiences prolonged external bleeding following injury and prolonged internal bleeding both post-operatively and spontaneously into soft tissues and joints. The condition is successfully treated with regular intravenous infusions. Since haemophilia A is a sex-linked recessive trait, it occurs in males and homozygous females.

Case Study Chronic myeloid leukaemia (CML)

Chronic myeloid leukaemia is a form of cancer that affects some of the stem cells that give rise to white blood cells. These stem cells are affected by a **reciprocal translocation** involving genetic material on chromosomes 9 and 22, as shown in Figure 4.14. This translocation results in the formation of an **oncogene**. An oncogene encodes a protein that promotes uncontrolled cell growth (i.e. cancer). In CML the encoded protein is called tyrosine kinase.

CML is treated by using drugs that inhibit the effect of tyrosine kinase and reduce the number of white blood cells produced in the bone marrow. CML occurs most commonly in middle-aged and elderly people. Its incidence is increased by exposure to ionising radiation. The atomic bombing of Hiroshima and Nagasaki in Japan at the end of the Second World War resulted in greatly increased rates of CML among the population. The condition is lethal if left untreated.

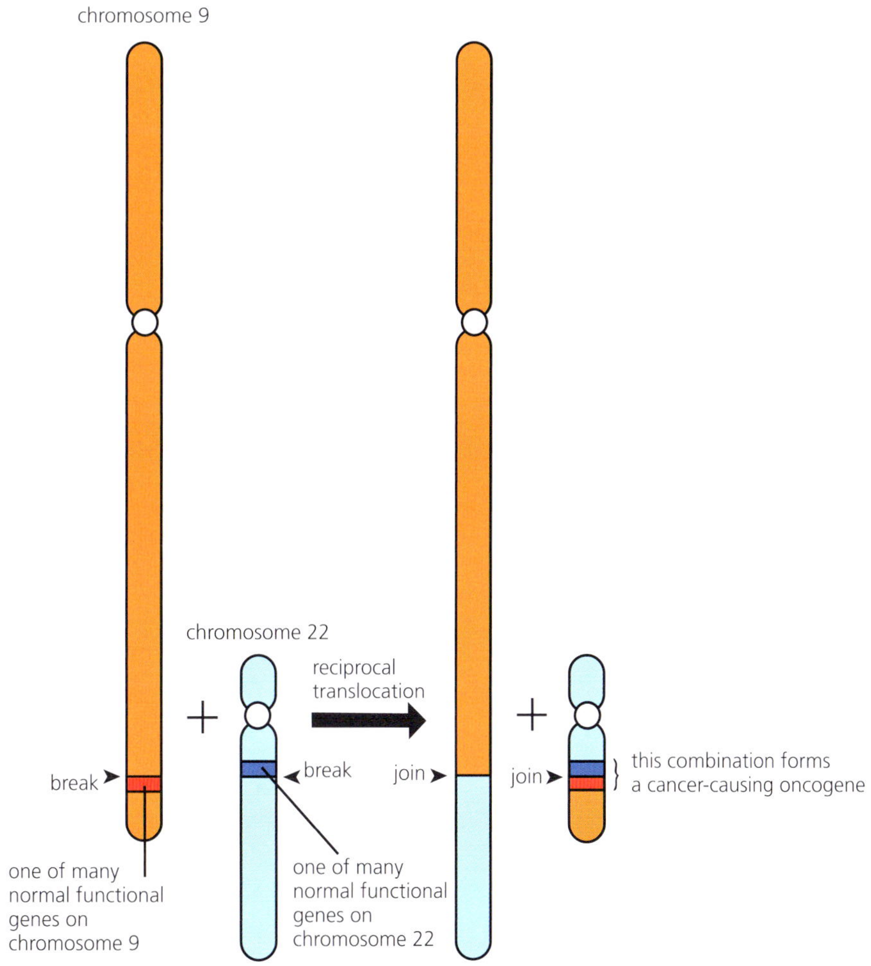

Figure 4.14 Mutation causing chronic myeloid leukaemia

Testing Your Knowledge

1 Distinguish between the terms *mutation* and *mutant*. (2)

2 **a)** Name THREE types of point mutation that involve a change in one nucleotide in the DNA sequence of a gene. (3)

b) Which of your answers to **a)** could result in:

i) a frameshift mutation?

ii) a missense mutation? (2)

3 Rewrite the following sentences using only the correct answer from each choice. (4)

a) An alteration in a chromosome's structure that involves a segment of genes being lost is called *deletion/translocation*.

b) When a section of one chromosome breaks off and joins onto another non-homologous chromosome, this type of mutation is called *duplication/translocation*.

c) The type of chromosomal change involving a segment of genes from one chromosome becoming inserted somewhere along the length of its matching partner is called *deletion/duplication*.

d) A substantial change to a chromosome's structure most often has an *adverse/beneficial* effect on the individual involved.

Applying Your Knowledge and Skills

1 The graph in Figure 4.15 shows the results and the line of best fit for three versions of the same experiment on bacteria carried out by three different scientific teams A, B and C.

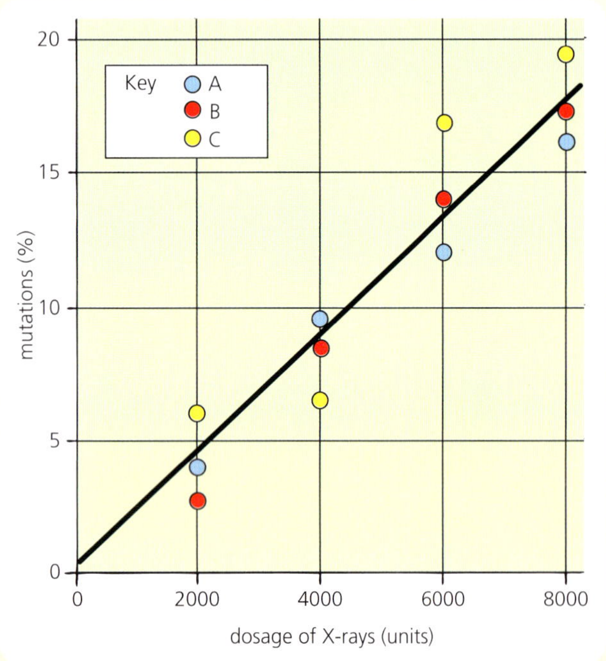

Figure 4.15

a) Identify the **i)** dependent variable, **ii)** independent variable. (2)

b) What conclusion can be drawn from the results? (1)

c) Which team's set of data:

i) deviates to the greatest extent from the line of best fit?

ii) deviates to the least extent from the line of best fit? (2)

d) The mutation frequency of a bacterium can be expressed as the number of mutations that occur at a genetic site per million cells. In the pneumonia bacterium, it is estimated that the gene for resistance to penicillin arises spontaneously in 1 in 10^7 cells. Express this as a mutation frequency. (1)

2 In the following three sentences, a small error alters the sense of the message. To which type of single-gene point mutation is each of these equivalent?

a) Intended: She ordered boiled rice.
Actual: She ordered boiled ice. (1)

b) Intended: He walked to the pillar box.
Actual: He talked to the pillar box. (1)

c) Intended: He put a quid in his pocket.
Actual: He put a squid in his pocket. (1)

→

3 Figure 4.16 shows the base sequence on a region of DNA undergoing a type of point mutation.

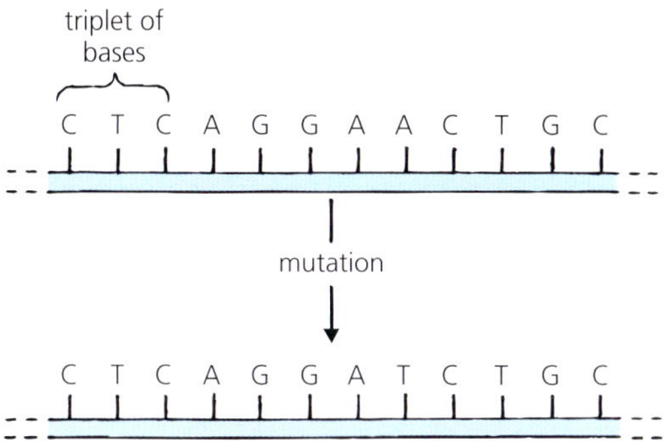

Figure 4.16

a) i) Identify the type of point mutation that occurred.

ii) Describe the way in which the DNA has been altered. (2)

b) Refer to Table 3.2 on page 43 and Appendix 1 and work out the amino acid sequence for:

i) the original DNA

ii) the mutant DNA. (2)

c) i) State whether this mutation would be missensical or nonsensical.

ii) Explain your choice. (2)

4 Beta (β) thalassemia is caused by one of many different types of mutation that affect the HBB gene on chromosome 11. The HBB gene encodes beta-globin protein. Figure 4.17 shows the pattern of inheritance

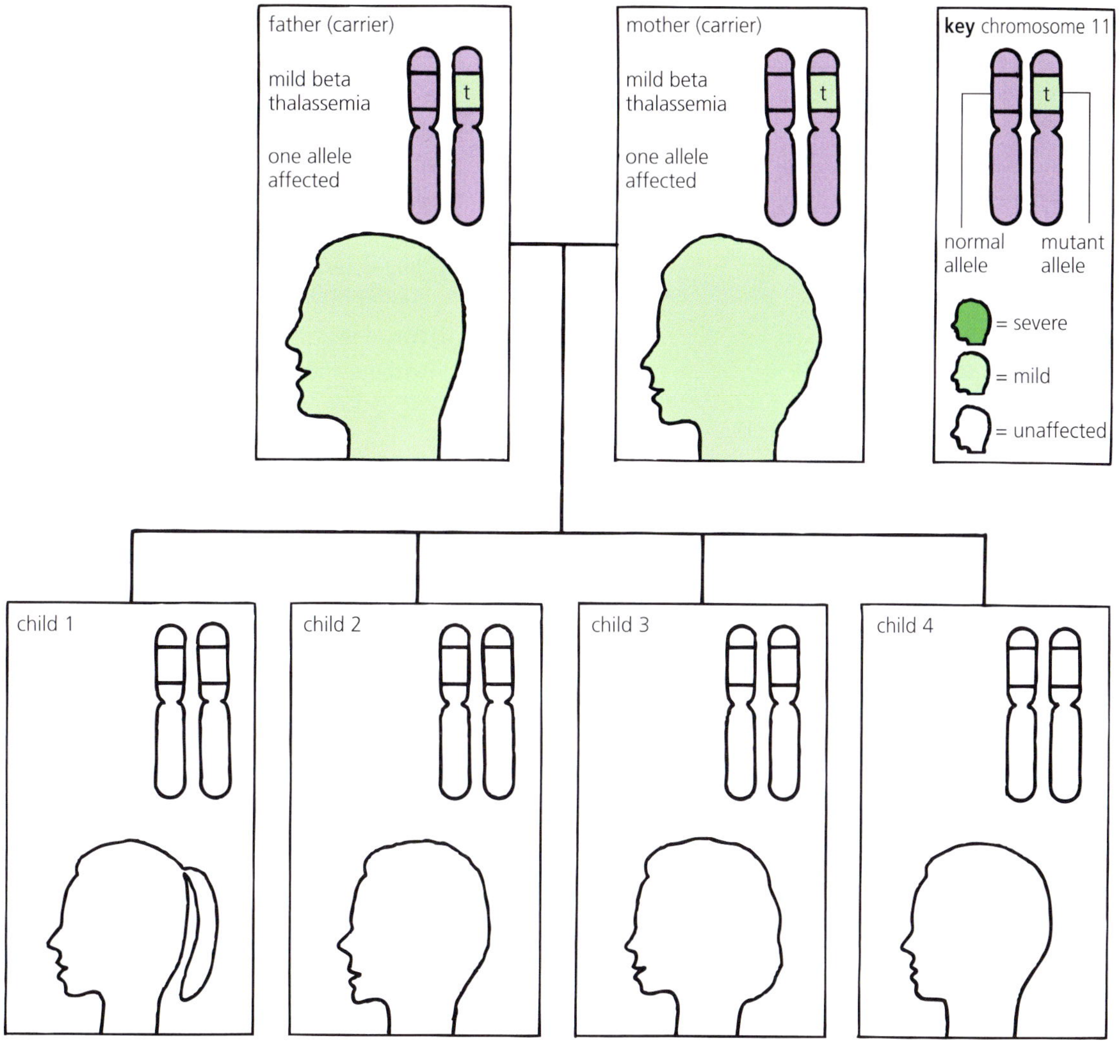

Figure 4.17

Genetic disorder	Type of single-gene mutation responsible	Effect of mutation on structure of protein expressed	Effect of mutation on functioning of protein	Effect of mutation on phenotype of untreated, affected individual
Phenylketonuria (PKU)				
Cystic fibrosis				

Table 4.1

of one form of the genetic disorder where heterozygous carriers are mildly affected and individuals with a genotype homozygous for the mutant allele are severely affected.

Copy and complete the lower half of the diagram to show what would result, on average, in this cross. (4)

5 Copy and complete Table 4.1 which refers to two genetic disorders described in case studies in Chapter 4 (pages 61–2). (8)

6 Figure 4.18 shows part of a metabolic pathway. Each stage is controlled by an enzyme. Some of the stages have been given a letter.

a) Explain how a gene mutation can lead to a blockage in such a pathway. (2)

b) Identify the letter that represents the point of blockage that leads to each of the following genetic disorders:

i) phenylketonuria

ii) albinism (characterised by lack of brown melanin pigment in the skin)

iii) alcaptonuria (characterised by an accumulation of homogentisic acid which is excreted in urine and turns black in light). (3)

c) The graph in Figure 4.19 shows the effect of a phenylalanine meal on a person with phenylketonuria (PKU) and a person without phenylketonuria.

i) Explain the initial rise in level of tyrosine in the person without PKU.

ii) Why does the person with PKU not show a similar increase?

iii) Why does the level of tyrosine in the person without PKU fall after 2 hours? (3)

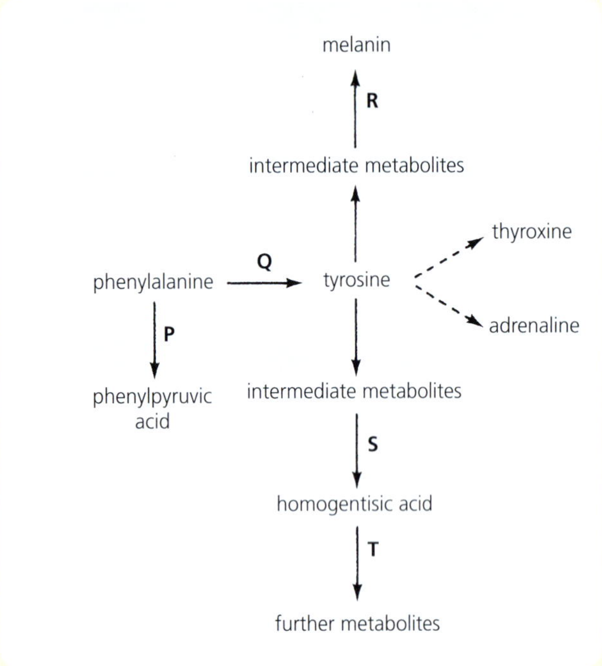

Figure 4.18

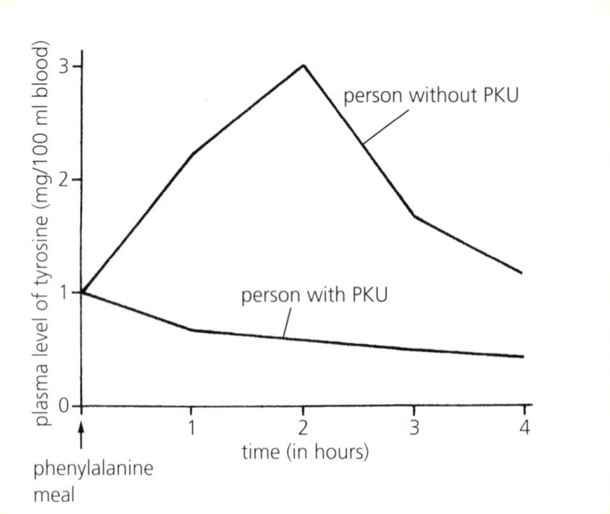

Figure 4.19

7 During gamete formation, homologous chromosomes normally form pairs that match one another, gene for gene, all along their length. The members of each pair of chromosomes shown in Figure 4.20 do not match properly because of a mutation.

a) Which type of mutation has occurred in each case? (2)

b) i) Which of these would be more likely to prove lethal to the organism?

ii) Explain your choice. (2)

8 Describe THREE types of single-gene point mutation and their effects on amino acid sequences. (9)

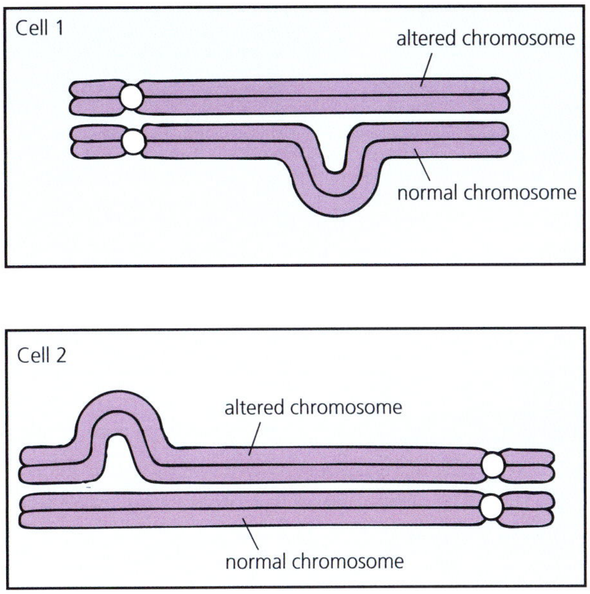

Figure 4.20

5 Human genomics

Genome

An organism's **genome** consists of all of its hereditary information encoded in its DNA. This DNA is composed of a combination of genes that code for proteins and other regions that do not code for proteins.

Sequencing DNA

Human **genomics** is the study of the human genome. It involves the use of **genomic sequencing**. This process (see Case Study – Human genome project) enables scientists to determine the sequence of the nucleotide base molecules all the way along individual

Case Study Human genome project (HGP)

A milestone in human history was reached in 2003 when the DNA sequence of the **human genome** was completed. It is based on the combined genome of a small number of donors and is regarded as the reference genome. This remarkable achievement was accomplished by adopting several procedures, including the following one.

Sequencing DNA

A portion of DNA with an unknown base sequence is chosen to be sequenced. Many copies of one of this DNA's strands (the template) are synthesised. Then, in order to make DNA strands that are complementary to these template strands, all the ingredients needed for synthesis are added to the preparation. These include DNA polymerase, primer and the four types of DNA nucleotide, as shown in Figure 5.1 on page 71. In addition the preparation receives a supply of **modified nucleotides** (ddA, ddT, ddG and ddC), each tagged with a different **fluorescent dye**.

Every so often during the synthesis process, a molecule of modified nucleotide just happens to be taken up instead of a normal one. However, when a modified nucleotide is incorporated into the new DNA strand, it brings the synthesis of that strand to a halt because a modified nucleotide does not allow any subsequent nucleotide to become bonded to it. Provided that the process is carried out on a large enough scale, the synthesis of a complementary strand will have been **stopped at every possible nucleotide position** along the DNA template.

The resultant mixture of DNA fragments of various lengths (each with its modified nucleotide and its unique fluorescent tag) are separated using **electrophoresis**. In this process the smallest (shortest) fragments travel the furthest distance. The identity and sequence of nucleotides (as indicated by their fluorescent dyes) is then read for the complementary DNA using this separation. From this information the sequence of the bases in the original DNA can be deduced.

This process has been automated and links the detection of the four fluorescent dyes to a computer. As these are monitored, the computer, working as an **automated sequence analyser**, processes the information and rapidly displays the sequence of bases in the DNA sample as a series of peaks (see Figure 5.2).

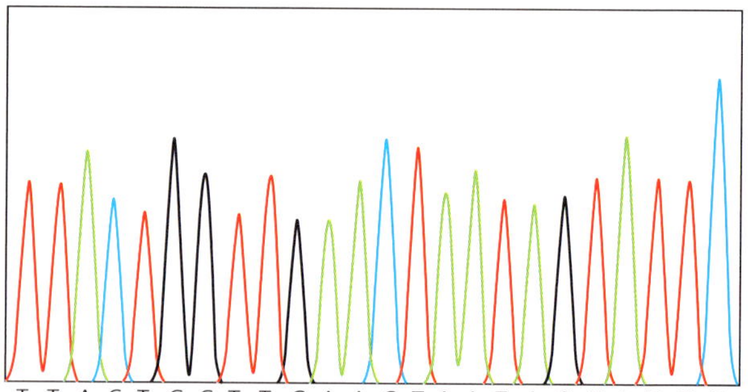

Figure 5.2 Printout from a DNA sequence analyser

Results

After 13 years of work (principally by biologists in the USA and the UK) the sequence of the **three billion** nucleotide bases that make up the human genome was finally unravelled. However, this was by no means the end of the story. Having unravelled the molecular message, the challenge becomes understanding what the message means. One of the many goals of the HGP was to identify the molecular cause of diseases such as cancer in the hope that

→

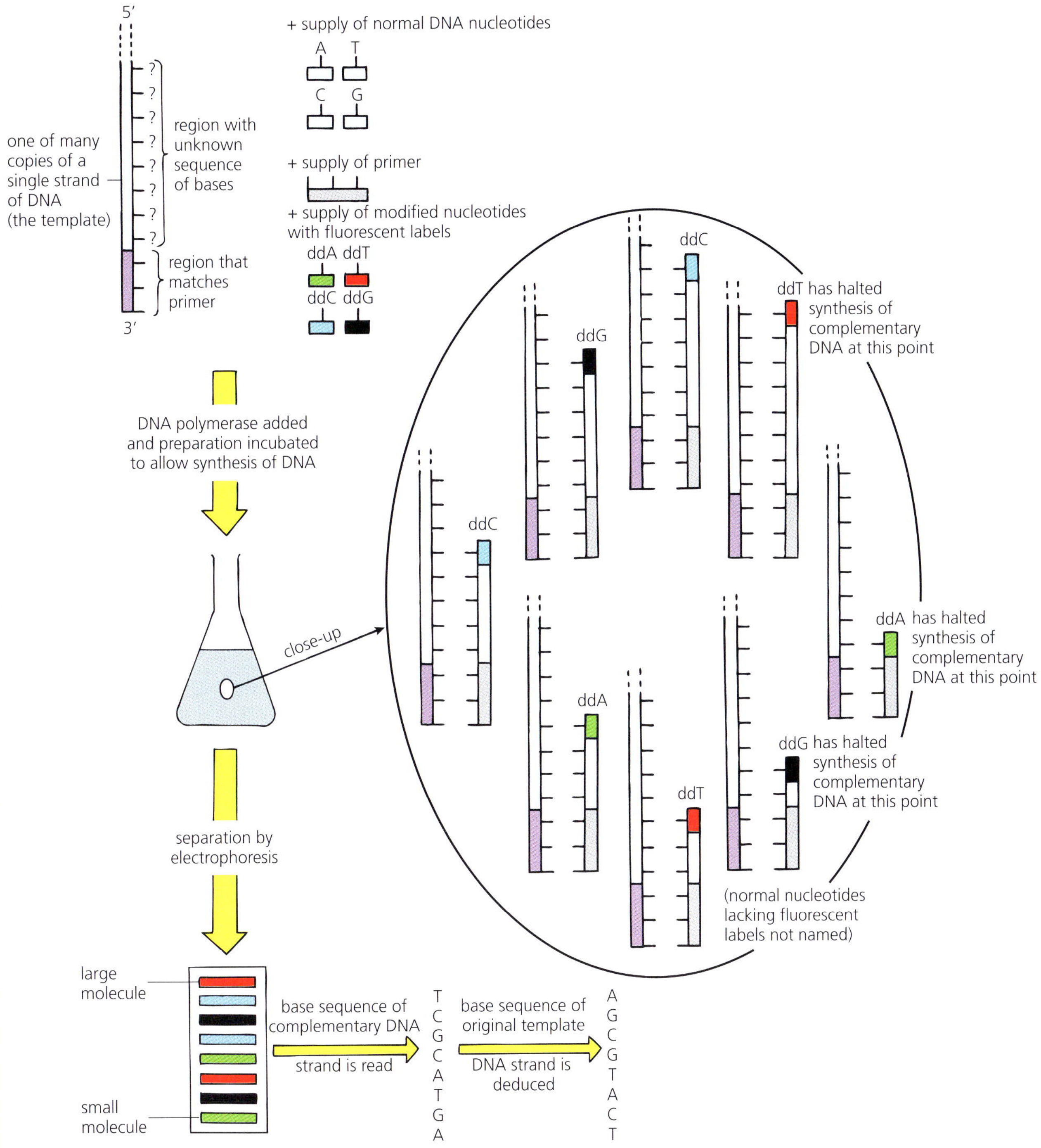

Figure 5.1 Sequencing DNA

this knowledge would enable scientists to generate effective treatments. Some progress has already been made in this area.

It is now known that more than **300 disease-causing genes** exist and that over 4000 genes each express several different forms of the protein that they encode. However, much work remains to be done to accurately relate variation in **genomic structure** to variation in **phenotypic expression** and then to find cures for the genes that cause disorders.

genes and ultimately along the entire genome. This information about genes can then be related to their functions. Progress in this area has been accelerated by **bioinformatics**, making genomics one of the major scientific advances of recent years.

Bioinformatics

The sequencing of the bases in DNA and the amino acids in proteins generates an enormous quantity of data. This information is analysed using computers and the results shared among the members of the molecular biology community over the internet.

Bioinformatics is the name given to the fusion of molecular biology, statistical analysis and computer technology (see Figure 5.3). It is an ever-advancing area that enables scientists to carry out rapid mapping and analysis of DNA sequences on a huge scale and then compare them. Individual **gene sequences** (and their roles) can be identified by searching the complete DNA sequence of the target genome using a computer for:

- **protein-coding sequences** the same as, or very similar to, those present in known genes
- **start sequences** (because there is a good chance that each of these will be followed by a coding sequence)
- long sequences that lack **stop codons** (because a protein-coding sequence is normally a very long chain of base triplets containing no stop codons except the one at its end).

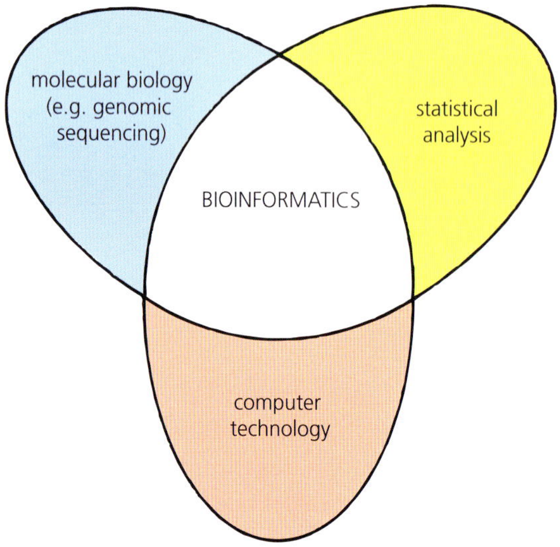

Figure 5.3 Bioinformatics

Similarly, a search for the identity (and role) of a **base sequence** can be mounted using a computer programme. This enables the scientist to find out if the base sequence matches a specific amino acid sequence already known to be typical of a certain protein.

Information about genetic sequences that used to take years to unravel is now obtained in days or even hours. Bioinformatics can be used to investigate evolutionary biology, inheritance and personalised medicine.

Personalised medicine

Personal genome sequence

A complete sequencing of a person's DNA bases is called a **personal genome sequence**. The branch of genomics involved in sequencing the genomes of individuals and analysing them using bioinformatics tools is called **personal genomics**. As a result of advances in computer technology, the process of sequencing DNA is rapidly becoming **faster** and **cheaper**. Routine sequencing of an individual's DNA for medical reasons will soon become a real possibility. In years to come, a person's entire genome may be sequenced early in life and stored as an electronic medical record available for future consultation by doctors when required.

Harmful and neutral mutations

Having located the mutant variants present in the genome, it is important to distinguish between those altered genetic sequences that are genuinely **harmful** (e.g. fail to code for an essential protein) and those that are **neutral** (i.e. have no negative effect).

Genetic disorders

A **genetic disorder** or **disease** is the result of a variation in genomic DNA sequence. The challenge for scientists is to establish a **causal link** between a particular mutant variant in a genomic sequence and a specific genetic disease or disorder.

The causal genetic sequence has been identified, at least in part, for around 2200 genetic disorders and diseases in humans. However, this does not mean that it is a simple matter to produce treatments for these disorders. The nature of disease is highly complex. Most medical disorders depend on both **genetic** and **environmental** factors for their expression, though the specific effects of these are not fully understood.

Pharmacogenetics

Pharmacogenetics is the name given to the use of genome information in the choice of pharmaceutical drugs on the genetically diverse members of the human population. It also includes the study of the drugs' effects (therapeutic, neutral or adverse) on the recipients. Already it is known that one in ten drugs (e.g. the blood thinner warfarin) varies in effect depending on differences in the person's DNA profile.

In the future it may be possible to use genomic information and customise medical treatment to suit an individual's exact metabolic requirements. The most **suitable drug** and the **correct dosage** would be prescribed as indicated by personal genomic sequencing (and *not* as shown in Figure 5.4!). Ideally, this advance would increase drug effectiveness while reducing side effects and the 'one-size-fits-all' approach would be consigned to history.

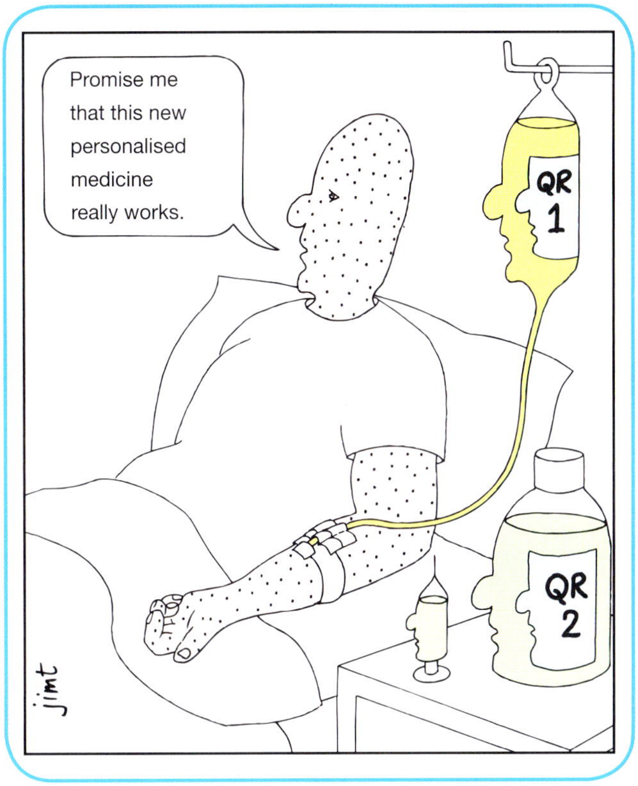

Figure 5.4 'Personalised' medicine

Risk prediction

Already variations in DNA have been linked to conditions such as diabetes, heart disease, schizophrenia and cancer. In the future, when the locations in the human genome of many more markers for common diseases and disorders have been established, it should become possible to scan an individual's genome for **predisposition** to a disease and **predict risk** early enough to allow suitable action to be taken. Eventually reduction of risk may be achieved through appropriate drug treatment combined with a healthy lifestyle.

Testing Your Knowledge

1 a) What information is obtained from the process of genomic sequencing? (1)
b) Give ONE example of a use to which this information can be put. (1)

2 a) What is meant by the term *bioinformatics*? (1)
b) Give TWO examples of the type of sequence that bioinformaticists would look for in a long chain of bases to identify gene sequences present. (2)

3 a) What is meant by *personal genomics*? (2)
b) Give TWO possible benefits of personalised medicine to patients of the future. (2)

Applying Your Knowledge and Skills

1 Figure 5.5 shows the DNA fragments that resulted from two copies of part of a genome, each cut by a different enzyme. The computer works out the sequence of the bases by looking for overlaps between the fragments. It found that the four larger fragments possessed overlaps. Draw a copy of these four larger fragments on squared paper, cut them out and use them to construct this part of the person's genome. (1)

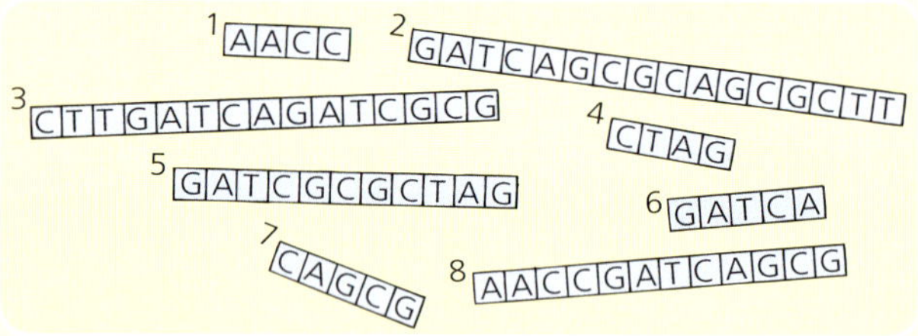

Figure 5.5

2 A single nucleotide polymorphism (SNP) is a variation in DNA sequence that affects a single base pair in a DNA chain. Genetic material from a sample of volunteers of differing ethnic origin was collected and analysed. Table 5.1 summarises the results and shows the SNPs that occur at six closely located sites on the genomes of these people. The results refer to a single strand of DNA.

a) Which site in the table appears to have been least affected by SNPs? (1)

b) By how many bases at sites 1–6 do the genomes of groups 7 and 10 differ? (1)

c) Which group(s) has the same set of bases at these six sites in its genome as: i) group 1; ii) group 2; iii) group 3? (3)

d) How many people of ethnic origin W have the same genotype as people in group 9? (1)

e) i) Which set of six bases occurs most frequently among the total sample group?

ii) What percentage of the total sample group possesses this set of bases in its genome? (2)

f) Which group has the least common set of bases in its genome? (1)

g) If the set of bases in the genome possessed by group 6 is strongly associated with a fatal disease, which other groups are at equal risk? (1)

h) What TWO things could be done to increase the reliability of the results? (2)

Group	Ethnic origin	Number of individuals in group	Set of bases at six sites in the genome as a result of SNPs					
			Site 1	Site 2	Site 3	Site 4	Site 5	Site 6
1	W	1	C	C	T	A	T	G
2	W	17	T	C	C	A	C	A
3	W	63	T	T	C	A	C	A
4	W	21	C	T	T	A	T	G
5	X	44	T	C	C	A	C	A
6	X	36	C	T	T	A	T	G
7	X	1	C	C	T	A	T	G
8	X	1	T	T	C	A	C	A
9	Y	47	T	C	C	A	C	A
10	Y	1	T	C	C	G	C	A
11	Y	87	C	T	T	A	T	G
12	Y	1	C	C	T	A	T	G

Table 5.1

→

3 a) i) Figure 5.6 shows a tiny part of the human genome. Imagine that the 30 base pairs shown are printed on a strip of paper that is 100 mm in length. How many metres of paper strip would be required to print out the entire human genome if it is three billion base pairs in length?

ii) Convert your answer to i) into kilometres and express it as words. (2)

b) i) Is the human genome that was completed in 2003 likely to be an exact match for any one individual?

ii) Explain your answer. (2)

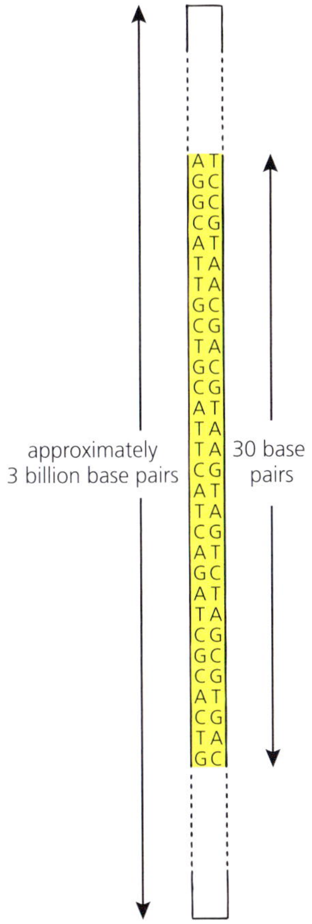

Figure 5.6

4 The DNA fragments shown in Figure 5.7 were formed during the type of sequencing technique illustrated in Figure 5.1 on page 71. Each fluorescent tag indicates the point on the strand where replication of complementary DNA was brought to a halt by a modified nucleotide.

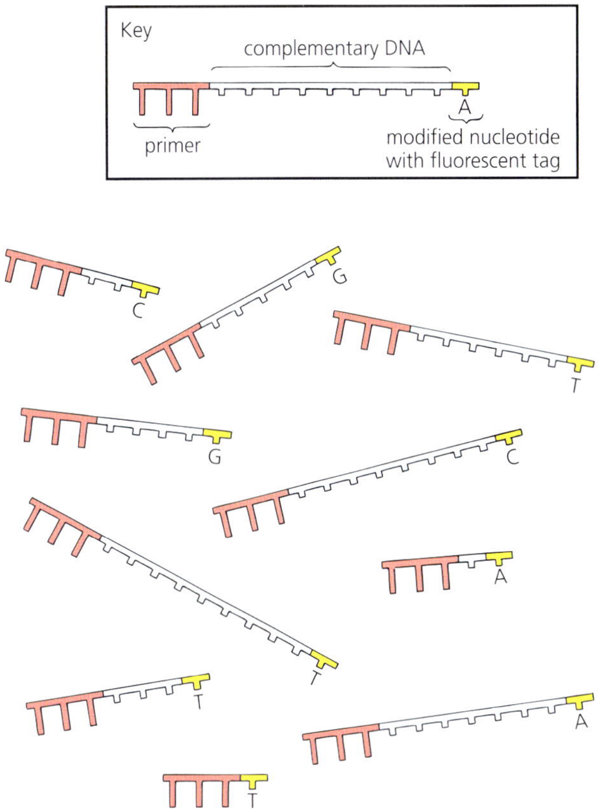

Figure 5.7

a) Work out the sequence of the bases in the complementary DNA strand. (1)

b) Deduce the sequence of bases in the original DNA strand. (1)

5 Read the passage and answer the questions that follow it.

Debrisoquine hydroxylase is an enzyme made by cells in the liver. It is responsible for the breakdown of drugs used to treat a variety of disorders such as nausea, depression and heart disorders once the drugs have brought about their desired effect.

Several alleles of the gene that codes for this enzyme occur among the members of the human population. These alleles code for different versions of the enzyme, which, in turn, vary in their ability to metabolise drugs. Depending on their particular genotype, a person may produce no functional enzyme and be a poor metaboliser because both of their alleles are null and void.

If the person has one null allele and one inferior allele that codes for a partly functional version of debrisoquine hydroxylase, they are said to be an intermediate metaboliser. An extensive metaboliser has one or two normal alleles that code for the fully functional form of the enzyme. Some people possess more than two copies of the normal allele and their metabolic profile is described as ultra-rapid.

a) Copy and complete Table 5.2 which summarises the passage. (4)

Alleles of gene present in genome	State of enzyme	Person's metabolic profile
	Non-functional	
One null allele and one inferior allele		
		Extensive
	Highly functional	

Table 5.2

b) What type of mutation could account for an ultra-rapid metaboliser having more than two copies of the allele of the gene that codes for debrisoquine hydroxylase? (1)

c) i) Which group of people are most likely to be at risk of harmful side effects if given a standard dose of a drug normally broken down by debrisoquine hydroxylase?
ii) Explain your answer. (2)

d) i) For which group of people would a standard dose of such a drug probably be ineffective?
ii) Explain your answer. (2)

e) In what way might personalised medicine (pharmacogenetics) solve the problems referred to in questions c) and d)? (2)

What You Should Know Chapters 4–5

altered	disorder	lethal
bioinformatics	dosages	missense
chromosome	environmental	mutation
coding	frameshift	personalised
customised	genomic	risk
deletion	insertions	translocated

Table 5.3 Word bank for Chapters 4–5

1 A single-gene mutation involves the substitution, insertion or _____ of nucleotides in the DNA chain. Substitutions can result in _____ or nonsense mutations. _____ or deletions lead to _____ mutations.

2 A mutation can result in the production of an _____ protein that does not function properly, or in the failure of the gene to express the protein, thereby causing a genetic _____.

3 A _____ may undergo a structural mutation if one or more of its genes becomes deleted, duplicated, inverted or _____. A _____ to a chromosome involves a major change to the individual's genome and is often _____.

4 Determining the sequence of nucleotide bases for individual genes or for a person's entire genome is called _____ sequencing. Use is made of _____, involving computing and statistics, to compare sequence data.

5 Gene sequences can be identified by comparing them with those of known genes and looking for similar _____ sequences.

6 In the future, routine sequencing of an individual's genome may lead to _____ medicine. This could involve predicting _____ of disease through knowledge of a person's genome and administering _____ drugs in appropriate _____. Diseases are complex and often affected by both genetic and _____ factors.

6 Metabolic pathways

Cell metabolism

Cell metabolism is the collective term for the thousands of biochemical reactions that occur within a living cell. The vast majority of these are steps in a complex network of connected and integrated pathways that are catalysed by enzymes.

Metabolic rate

The quantity of energy consumed by an organism per unit of time is called its **metabolic rate**. Normally this energy is generated by cells respiring aerobically as summarised in the following equation:

glucose + oxygen → carbon dioxide + water + energy

Therefore, metabolic rate can be measured as:

- oxygen consumption per unit time
- carbon dioxide production per unit time
- energy production (as heat) per unit time.

Respirometer

An organism's metabolic rate can be measured by placing it in a **respirometer**. This is a chamber through which a continuous stream of air is pumped. Differences in oxygen concentration, carbon dioxide concentration and temperature between the air entering and leaving the respirometer are detected by **probes** (see Investigation – Measuring metabolic rate using probes).

Investigation

Measuring metabolic rate using probes (sensors)

The experiment is shown in Figure 6.1. Table 6.1 gives the purpose of each piece of equipment. The three probes (sensors) are calibrated in advance. The animal is inserted into the chamber and the experiment run for a set length of time (such as 30 minutes). The computer software monitors the data from the three sensors simultaneously and displays the information on the screen. From these data the animal's **metabolic rate** (as volume of oxygen consumed per unit time) can be determined.

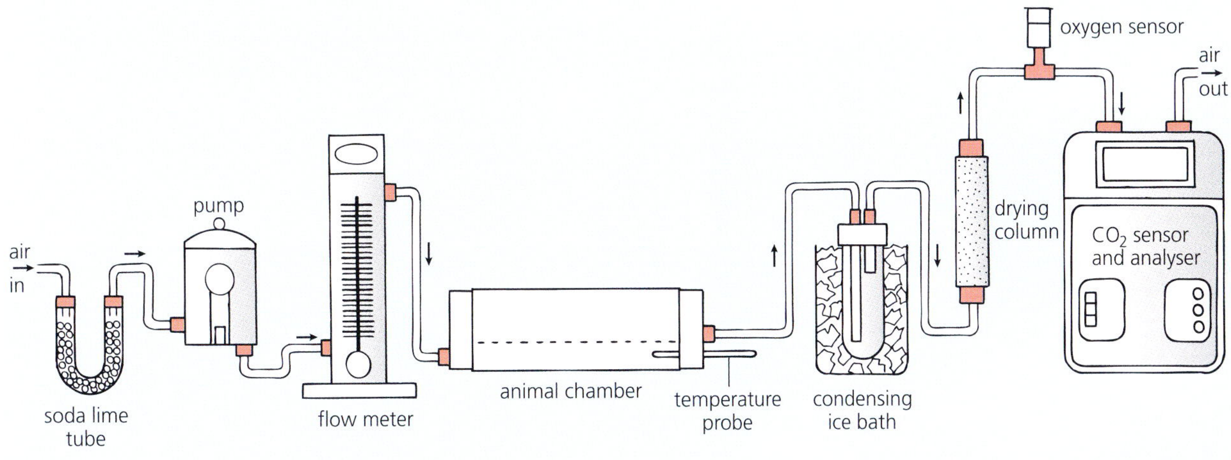

Figure 6.1 Investigating metabolic rate (connections to computer not shown)

Equipment	Purpose
Soda lime tube (containing sodium hydroxide)	To absorb all carbon dioxide from incoming air so that its initial concentration is not a variable factor
Air pump	To pump a continuous flow of air through the system
Flow meter	To maintain the flow of air at a steady rate that is low enough for the carbon dioxide sensor to work
Animal chamber	To accommodate the animal whose metabolic rate is to be measured
Temperature probe (sensor)	To measure changes of temperature in the animal chamber and send data to computer
Condensing bath and drying column	To remove water vapour from passing air since the sensors need air to be dry
Oxygen probe (sensor)	To measure percentage oxygen concentration and send data to computer
Carbon dioxide probe (sensor) and analyser	To measure carbon dioxide in parts per million and send data to computer

Table 6.1 Purposes of respirometer equipment

Metabolic pathways

The biochemical processes upon which life depends take the form of **metabolic pathways**, which fall into two categories:

- **Catabolic** pathways bring about the breakdown of complex molecules to simpler ones, usually releasing energy and often providing building blocks.
- **Anabolic** pathways bring about the biosynthesis of complex molecules from simpler building blocks and require energy to do so.

Such pathways are closely integrated and one often depends upon the other. For example, aerobic respiration in living cells is an example of **catabolism**, which releases the energy needed for the synthesis of protein from amino acids (an example of **anabolism**). This close relationship is shown in Figure 6.2. An important chemical called ATP (see Chapter 7) plays a key role in the transfer of energy between catabolic and anabolic reactions.

Reversible and irreversible steps

Metabolic pathways are regulated by enzymes that catalyse specific reactions. A pathway often contains both **reversible** and **irreversible** steps, which allow the process to be kept under precise control. **Glycolysis** (see page 99) is the metabolic pathway that converts **glucose** to an intermediate metabolite called **pyruvate** at the start of respiration. Figure 6.3 shows the first three enzyme-controlled steps in a long pathway.

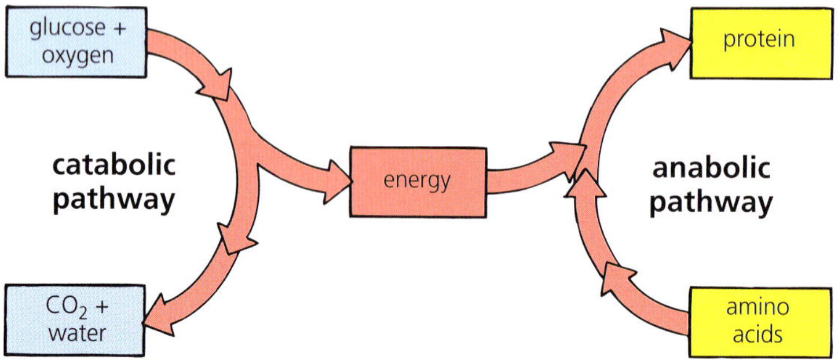

Figure 6.2 Two types of metabolic pathway

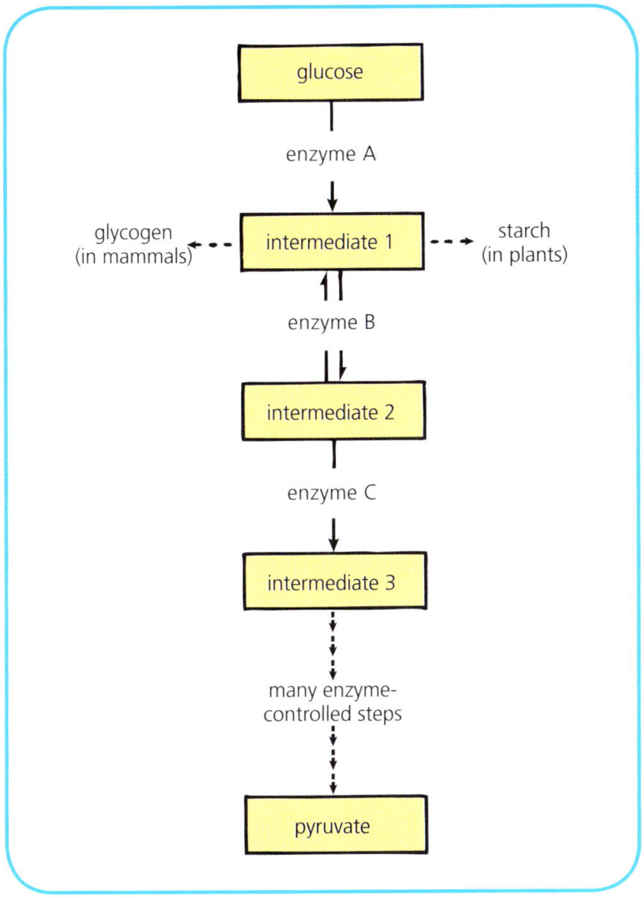

Figure 6.3 Example of a metabolic pathway

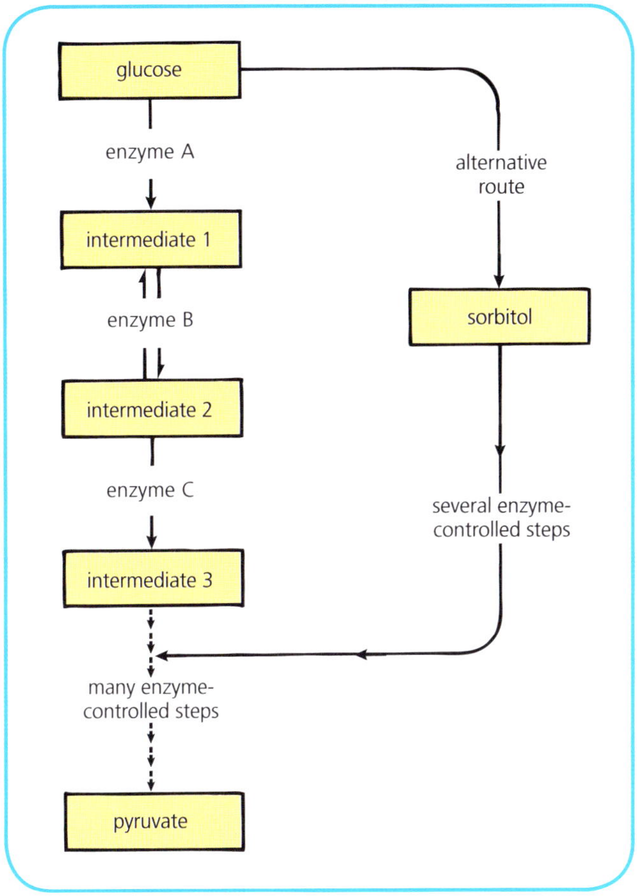

Figure 6.4 Alternative route

Glucose diffusing into a cell from a high concentration outside to a low concentration inside is irreversibly converted to intermediate 1 by enzyme A. This process is of advantage to the cell because it maintains a low concentration of glucose inside the cell and therefore promotes continuous diffusion of glucose into the cell from the high concentration outside.

The conversion of intermediate 1 to intermediate 2 by enzyme B is **reversible**. If more intermediate 2 is formed than the cell requires for the next step then some can be converted back to intermediate 1 and used in an alternative pathway (for example, to build glycogen in animal cells or starch in plant cells). The conversion of intermediate 2 to intermediate 3 by enzyme C is **irreversible** and is a **key regulatory point** in the pathway. There is no going back for the substrate now. It is committed to following glycolysis through all the steps to pyruvate.

Alternative routes

Metabolic pathways can also contain **alternative routes** that allow steps in the pathway to be bypassed. Figure 6.4 shows a pathway from glucose via an intermediate (called sorbitol) that bypasses the steps controlled by enzymes A, B and C but returns to glycolysis later in the pathway. This bypass is used when the cell has a plentiful supply of sugar.

Activation energy and enzyme action

The rate of a chemical reaction is indicated by the amount of chemical change that occurs per unit time. Such a change may involve the joining together of simple molecules into more complex ones or the splitting of complex molecules into simpler ones.

In either case the energy needed to break chemical bonds in the reactant chemicals is called the **activation energy**.

The bonds break when the molecules of reactant have absorbed enough energy to make them unstable. They are now in the **transition state** and the reaction can occur. This energy input often takes the form of heat energy and the reaction only proceeds at a high rate if the chemicals are raised to a high temperature (see Figure 6.5).

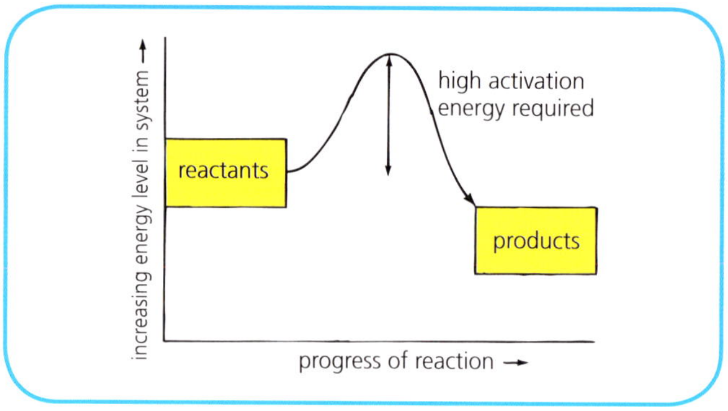

Figure 6.5 Uncatalysed reaction

Related Activity

Investigating the effect of heat on the breakdown of hydrogen peroxide

Hydrogen peroxide is a chemical that breaks down into water and oxygen as shown in the following equation:

hydrogen peroxide → water + oxygen

$$2H_2O_2 \rightarrow 2H_2O + O_2$$

In the experiment shown in Figure 6.6, test tubes containing hydrogen peroxide and drops of detergent are placed in five water baths at different temperatures. The detergent is used to sustain any oxygen bubbles that are released as a froth.

After 30 minutes the tubes are inspected for the presence of a froth of oxygen bubbles which indicates the breakdown of hydrogen peroxide. The diagram shows a typical set of results where the volume of froth is found to increase with increase in temperature.

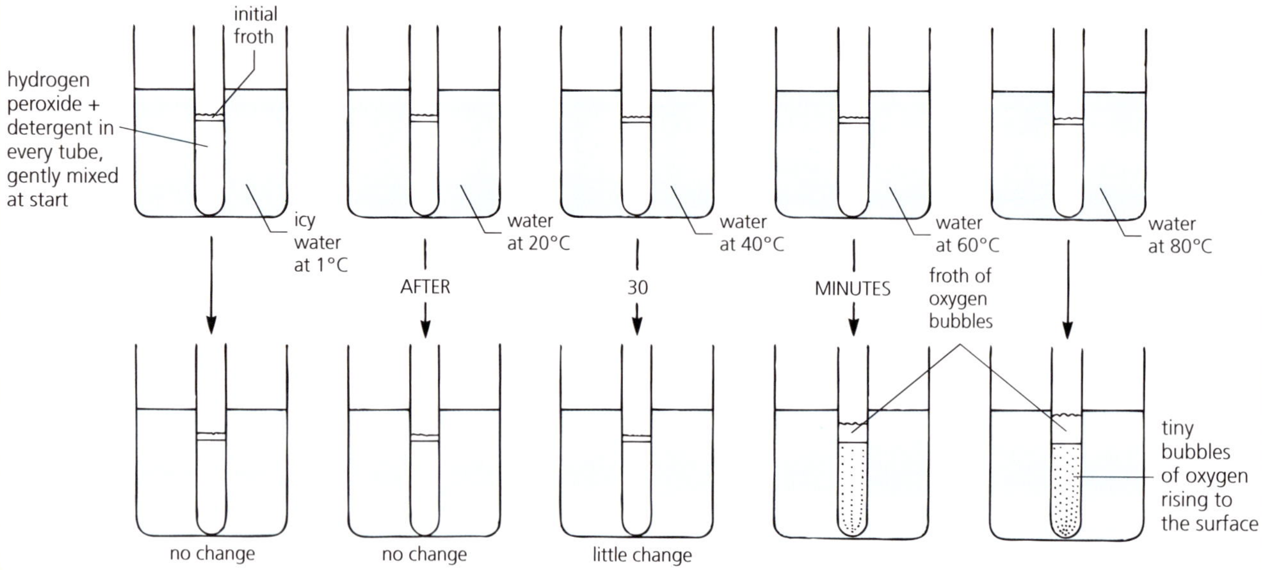

Figure 6.6 Investigating the effect of heat on the breakdown of hydrogen peroxide

Related Activity

Investigating the effect of manganese dioxide on the breakdown of hydrogen peroxide

In the experiment shown in Figure 6.7, the bubbles forming the froth in tube A are found to relight a glowing splint. This shows that oxygen is being released during the breakdown of hydrogen peroxide. In tube B, the control, the breakdown process is so slow that no oxygen can be detected.

It is concluded therefore that manganese dioxide (which remains chemically unaltered at the end of the reaction) has increased the rate of this chemical reaction which would otherwise have only proceeded very slowly. A substance that has this effect on a chemical reaction is called a **catalyst**.

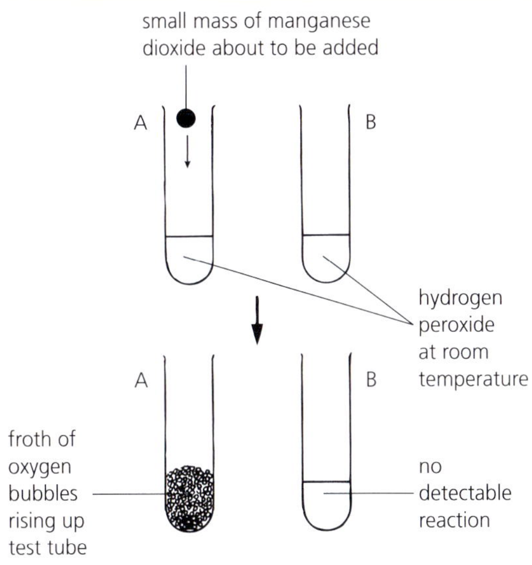

Figure 6.7 Effect of a catalyst

Properties and functions of a catalyst

A **catalyst** is a substance that:

- lowers the activation energy required for a chemical reaction to proceed (see Figure 6.8)
- speeds up the rate of a chemical reaction
- takes part in the reaction but remains unchanged at the end of it.

Importance of enzymes

Living cells cannot tolerate the high temperatures needed to make chemical reactions proceed at a rapid rate. Therefore, they make use of **biological catalysts** called **enzymes**.

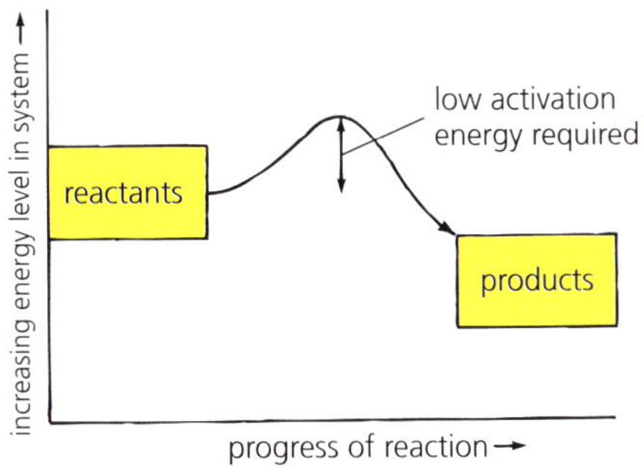

Figure 6.8 Catalysed reaction

Enzymes speed up the rate of the reactions in a metabolic pathway by **lowering the activation energy** needed by the reactant(s) to form the transition state. It is from this unstable state that the end products of the reaction are produced.

By this means biochemical reactions are able to proceed rapidly at the relatively low temperatures (e.g. 5–40°C) needed by living cells to function properly. In the absence of enzymes, biochemical pathways such as respiration and photosynthesis would proceed so slowly that life as we know it would cease to exist.

Enzyme action

Enzyme molecules are made of **protein**. Somewhere on an enzyme's surface there is a groove or hollow where its **active site** is located. This site has a particular shape that is determined by the chemical structure of, and bonding between, the amino acids in the polypeptide chains that make up the enzyme molecule.

Specificity

An enzyme acts on one type of substance (its **substrate**) whose molecules exactly fit the enzyme's active site. The

Related Activity

Investigating the effect of catalase on the breakdown of hydrogen peroxide

Catalase is an enzyme made by living cells. It is especially abundant in fresh liver cells. In the experiment shown in Figure 6.9, the bubbles produced in tube C are found to relight a glowing splint. This shows that oxygen is being released during the breakdown of hydrogen peroxide as follows:

	catalase			
hydrogen peroxide	→	water	+	oxygen
(substrate)	(enzyme)			(end products)

In tube D, the control, the breakdown process is so slow that no oxygen can be detected. It is concluded that the enzyme catalase has increased the rate of this chemical reaction, which would otherwise have proceeded only very slowly.

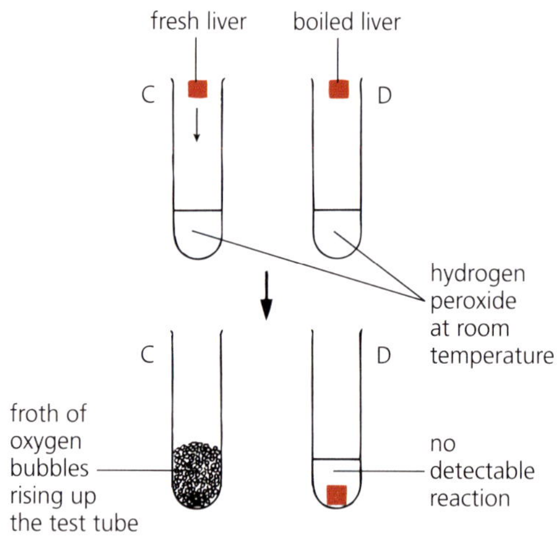

Figure 6.9 Effect of catalase

enzyme is **specific** to its substrate and the molecules of substrate are complementary to the enzyme's active site for which they show an high **affinity** (chemical attraction).

Induced fit

The active site is not a rigid structure. It is **flexible** and **dynamic**. When a molecule of substrate enters the active site, the shape of the enzyme molecule and the active site change slightly, making the active site fit very closely round the substrate molecule. This is called **induced fit** (see Figure 6.10). The process is like a rubber glove, slightly too small, exerting a very tight fit round a hand. Induced fit ensures that the active site comes into very close contact with the molecules of substrate and increases the chance of the reaction taking place.

Orientation of reactants

When the reaction involves two (or more) substrates (see Figure 6.11), the shape of the active site determines the **orientation** of the reactants. This ensures that they are held together in such a way that the reaction between them can take place.

First the active site holds the two reactants closely together in an induced fit. Then it acts on them to weaken chemical bonds that must be broken during the reaction. This process **reduces the activation energy** needed by the reactants to reach the **transition state** that allows the reaction to take place.

Once the reaction has occurred, the products have a **low affinity** for the active site and are released. This leaves the enzyme free to repeat the process with new molecules of substrate.

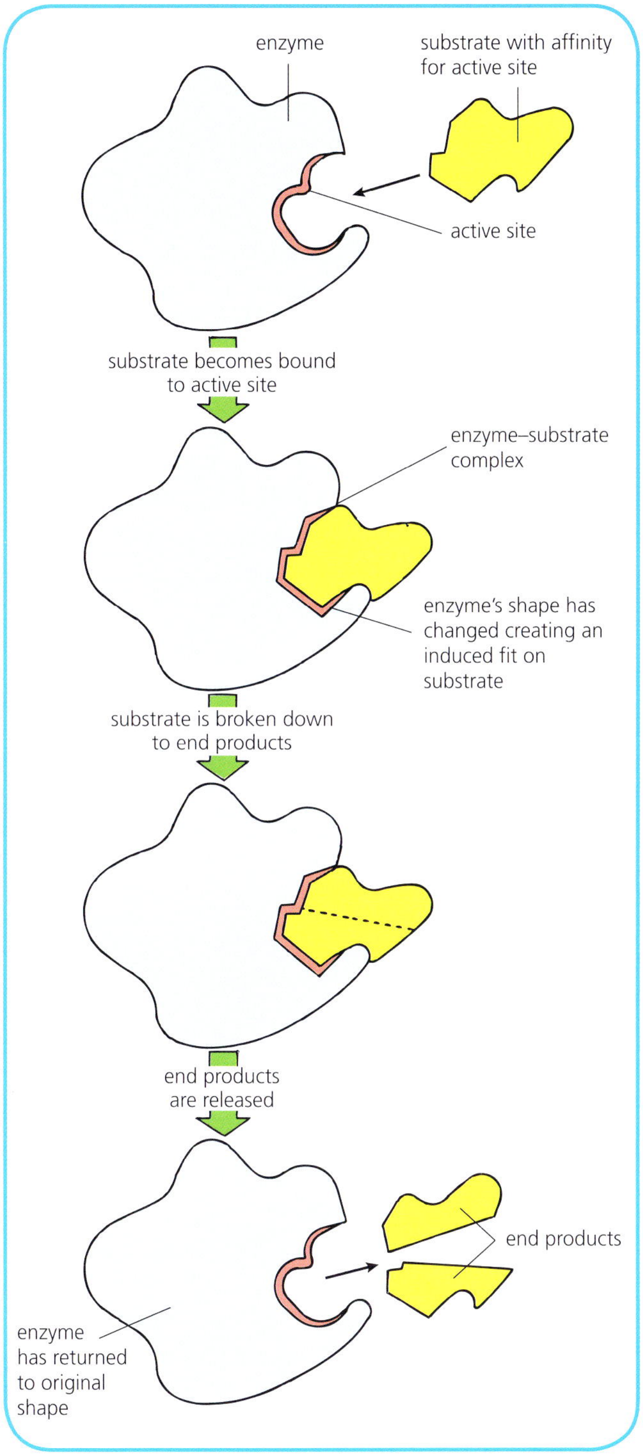

Figure 6.10 Induced fit during an enzyme-catalysed reaction

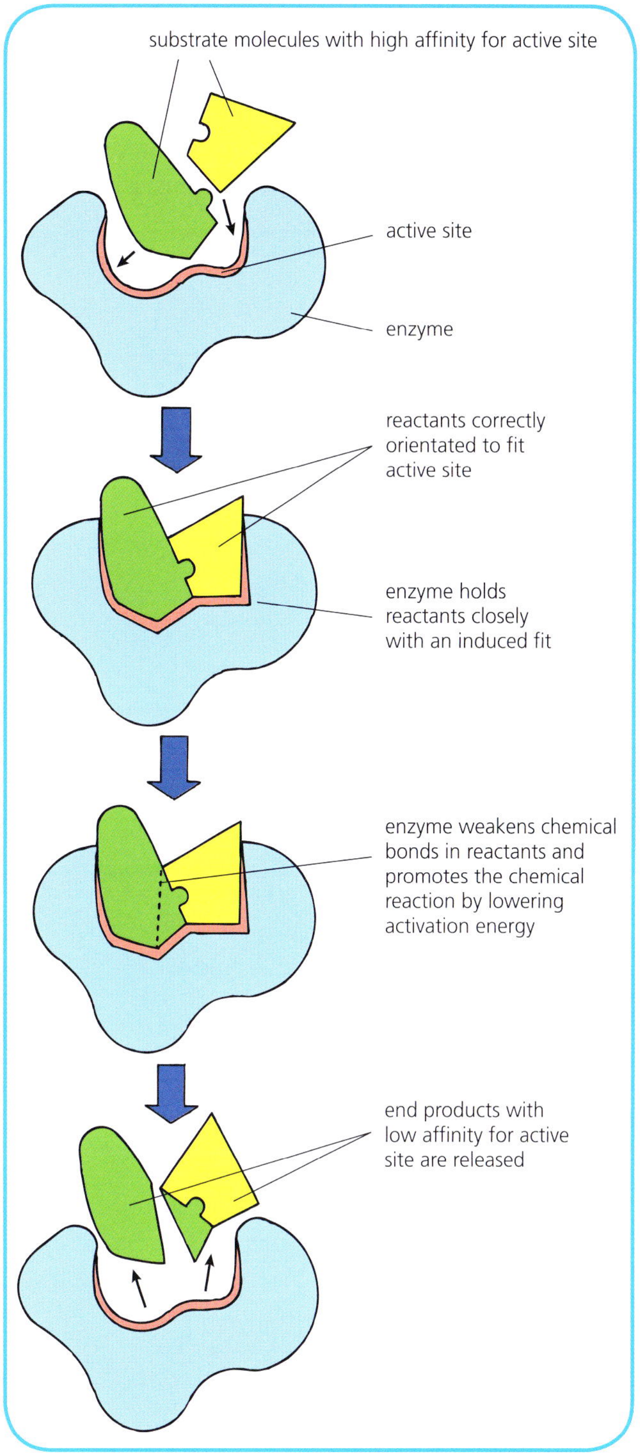

Figure 6.11 Orientation of reactants during an enzyme-catalysed reaction

Factors affecting enzyme action

To function efficiently, an enzyme requires a suitable temperature, an appropriate pH and an adequate supply of substrate. Inhibitors (see page 87) may slow down the rate of an enzyme-controlled reaction or bring it to a halt.

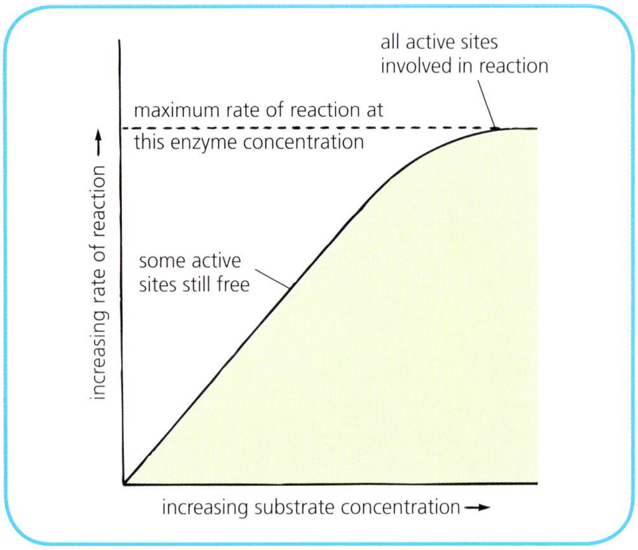

Figure 6.12 Effect of increasing substrate concentration

Effect of substrate concentration on enzyme activity

The graph in Figure 6.12 shows the effect of increasing substrate concentration on the rate of an enzyme-controlled reaction for a limited concentration of enzyme. At low concentrations of substrate, the reaction rate is low since there are too few substrate molecules present to make maximum use of all the active sites on the enzyme molecules. An increase in substrate concentration results in an increase in reaction rate since more and more active sites become involved.

This upward trend in the graph continues as a straight line until a point is reached where further increase in substrate concentration fails to make the reaction go any faster. At this point all the active sites are occupied (the enzyme concentration has become the limiting factor). The graph levels off since there are now more substrate molecules present than there are free active sites with which to combine. The effect of increasing substrate concentration is summarised at molecular level in a simplified way in Figure 6.13.

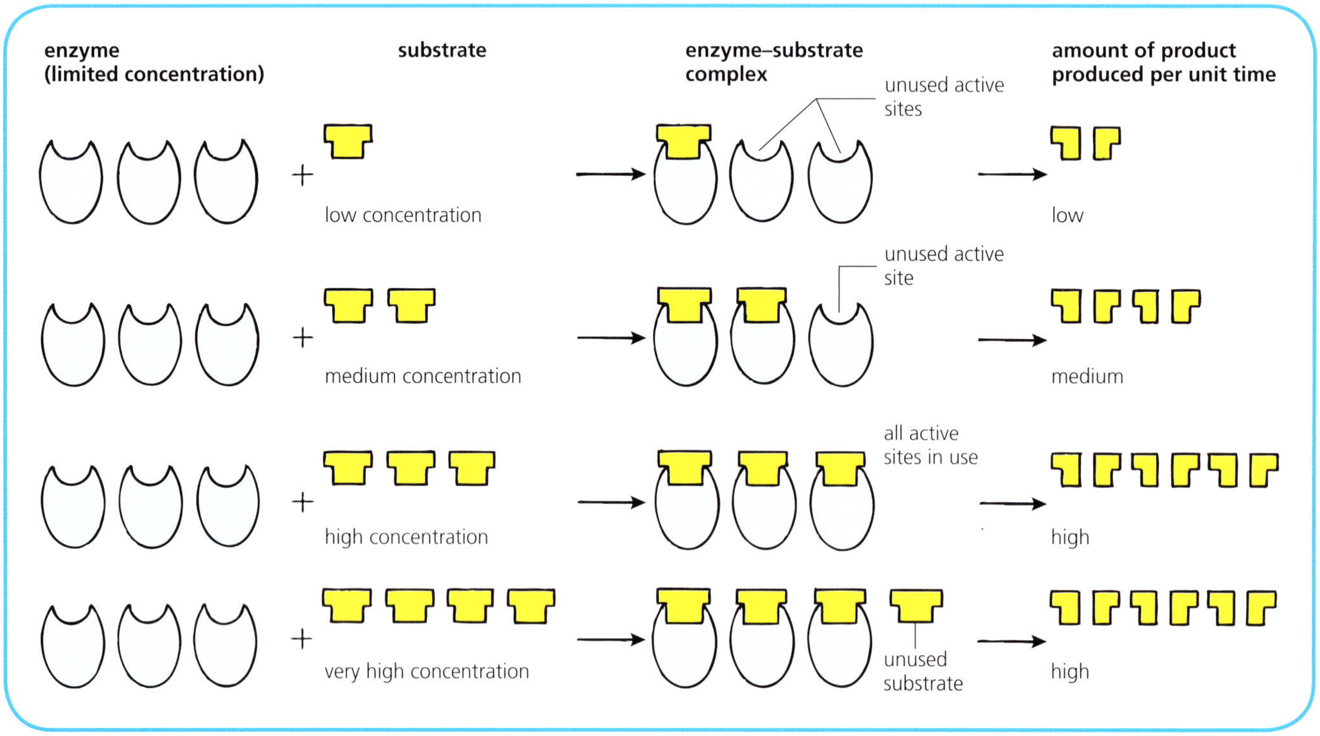

Figure 6.13 Effect of increasing substrate concentration at a molecular level

Related Activity

Investigating the effect of increasing substrate concentration

Liver cells contain the enzyme catalase which catalyses the breakdown of hydrogen peroxide to water and oxygen. In the experiment shown in Figure 6.14, the one variable factor is the concentration of the substrate (hydrogen peroxide). When an equal mass of fresh liver is added to each cylinder, the results shown in the diagram are produced. The height of the froth of oxygen bubbles indicates the activity of the enzyme at each concentration of substrate.

From the experiment it is concluded that increase in substrate concentration results in increased enzyme activity until a point is reached (in cylinder G) where some factor other than substrate concentration has become the limiting factor.

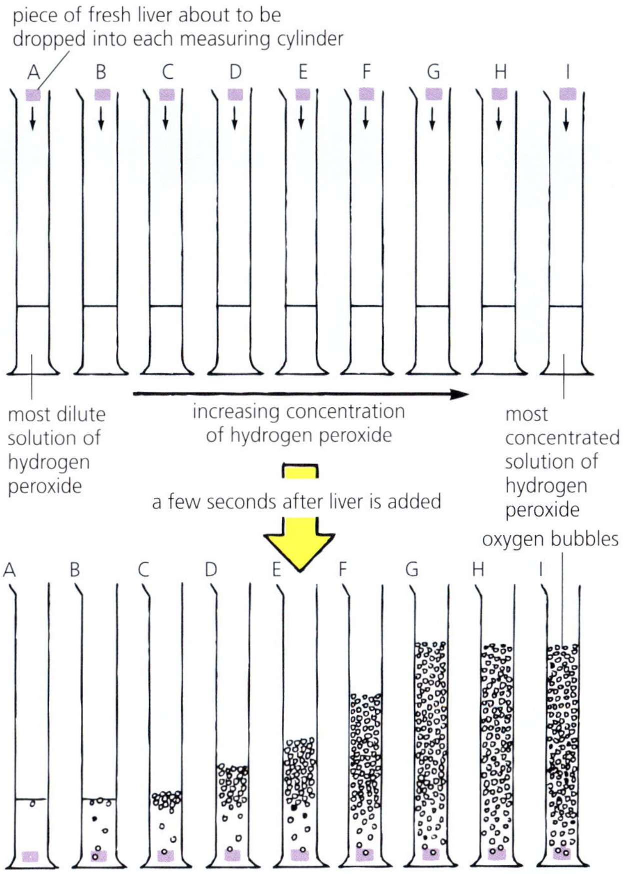

Figure 6.14 Effect of substrate concentration on enzyme activity

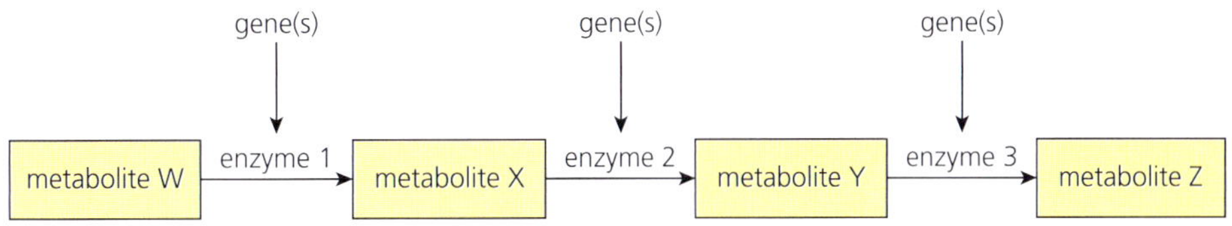

Figure 6.15 Action of a group of enzymes

Direction of enzyme action

A **metabolic pathway** normally consists of several stages, each of which involves the conversion of one metabolite to another. Each stage in a metabolic pathway is driven by a specific enzyme as shown in Figure 6.15. Each enzyme is coded for by one or more genes. As substrate W becomes available, enzyme 1 becomes active and converts W to X. In the presence of metabolite X, enzyme 2 becomes active and converts X to Y and so on. A continuous supply of W entering the system drives the sequence of reactions in the direction W to Z with the product of one reaction acting as the substrate of the next.

Reversibility

Most metabolic reactions are **reversible**. Often an enzyme can catalyse a reaction in both a forward and a reverse direction. The actual direction taken depends on the relative concentrations of the reactant(s) and product(s).

A metabolic pathway rarely occurs in isolation. If, as a result of related biochemical pathways, the concentration of metabolite Y in Figure 6.15 were to increase to an unusually high level and that of X were to decrease, then enzyme 2 could go into reverse and convert some of Y back to X until a balanced state (equilibrium) was restored once more.

Testing Your Knowledge 1

1 a) Define the term *metabolism*. (2)
b) Describe TWO ways in which the two types of metabolic pathway differ from one another. (2)

2 Give THREE reasons why enzymes are referred to as *biological catalysts*. (3)

3 a) What determines the structure of an enzyme's active site? (1)
b) What is meant by the *affinity* of substrate molecules for an enzyme's active site? (1)
c) What term means 'the change in shape of an active site to enable it to bind more snugly to the substrate'? (1)
d) Rewrite the following sentences, choosing the correct answer from each underlined choice.
The shape of the active site ensures that the reactants are correctly orientated/denatured so that the reaction can take place. This is made possible by the fact that the enzyme increases/decreases the activation energy needed by the reactants to reach the transitory/transition state. (3)

4 a) What is meant by the term *rate of reaction*? (See page 87 for help.) (1)
b) i) What effect does an increase in concentration of substrate have on reaction rate when a limited amount of enzyme is present?
ii) Explain why. (4)

Control of metabolic pathways

Regulation by switching genes on or off

Some metabolic pathways are only required to operate under certain circumstances. To prevent resources being wasted, the genes that code for the enzymes controlling certain stages in the pathway can be switched on (by an **inducer**) or off (by a **repressor**) as required. (Also see Related Activity – Investigating enzyme induction.)

Regulation by inhibition of enzyme action

Some metabolic pathways (for example, glycolysis) are required to operate continuously. The genes that code for their enzymes are always switched on and the enzymes which they code for are always present in the cell. Control of these metabolic pathways can be achieved by means of inhibitors. An **inhibitor** is a substance that decreases the rate of an enzyme-controlled reaction.

Related Activity

Investigating enzyme induction

ONPG is a colourless synthetic chemical that can be broken down by the enzyme β-galactosidase as follows:

$$\text{ONPG} \xrightarrow{\beta\text{-galactosidase}} \text{galactose + yellow compound}$$

The presence of the yellow colour indicates activity by β-galactosidase. The experiment is set up as shown in Figure 6.16.

From the results it is concluded that:

- in tube 1, lactose has acted as an inducer and switched on the gene in *E. coli* that codes for β-galactosidase; this enzyme has acted on the ONPG, forming the yellow colour
- in tubes 2 and 4, no yellow colour was produced because ONPG was absent
- in tube 3, β-galactosidase has acted on ONPG, forming the yellow compound.

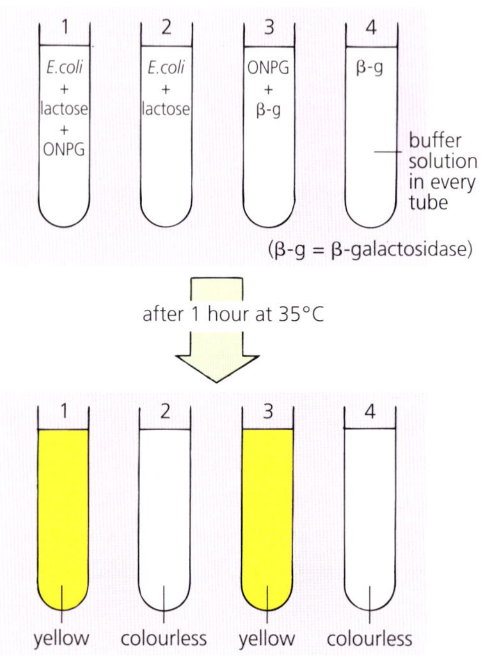

Figure 6.16 Investigating the *lac* operon

Regulation of the action of an enzyme controlling a stage in a metabolic pathway can be brought about by one of the following processes:

- competitive inhibition
- non-competitive inhibition
- feedback inhibition.

Competitive inhibitors

Molecules of a **competitive inhibitor** compete with molecules of the substrate for the active sites on the enzyme. The inhibitor is able to do this because its molecular structure is **similar** to that of the substrate and it can attach itself to the enzyme's active site as shown in Figure 6.17. Since active sites **blocked** by competitive inhibitor molecules cannot become occupied by substrate molecules, the rate of the reaction is reduced.

Effect of increasing substrate concentration

The graph in Figure 6.18 shows the effect of increasing substrate concentration on rate of reaction for a limited amount of enzyme affected by a limited amount of inhibitor. In graph line 1 (the control), increase in substrate concentration brings about an increase in reaction rate until a point is reached where all active

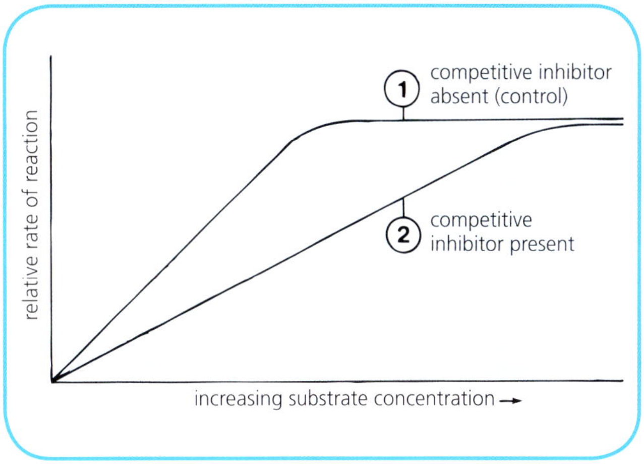

Figure 6.18 Effect of increasing substrate concentration on competitive inhibition

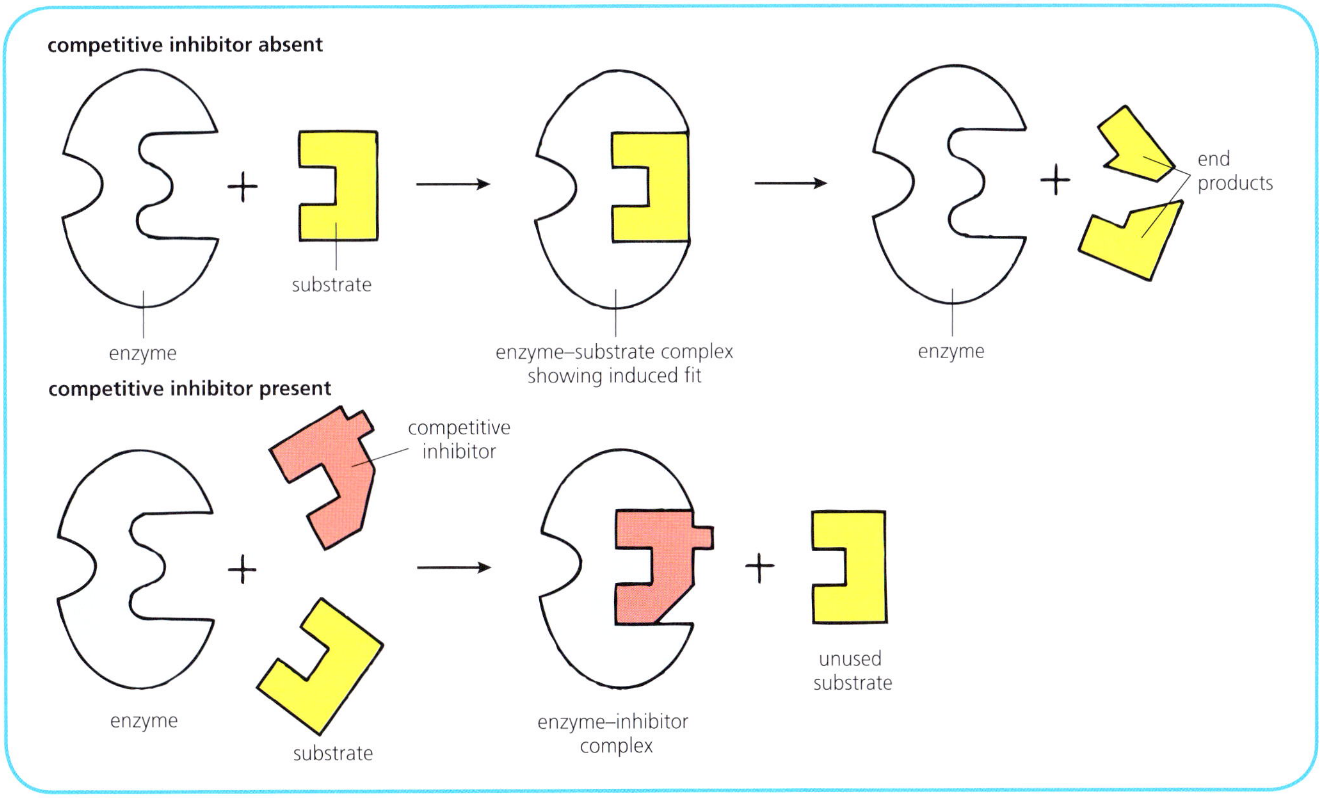

Figure 6.17 Effect of a competitive inhibitor

sites on the enzyme molecules are occupied and then the graph levels off.

In graph line 2, increase in substrate concentration brings about a gradual increase in reaction rate. Although the competitive inhibitor is competing for and occupying some of the enzyme's active sites, the true substrate is also occupying some of the sites. As substrate molecules increase in concentration and outnumber those of the competitive inhibitor, more and more active sites become occupied by true substrate rather than inhibitor molecules. The reaction rate continues to increase until all the active sites are occupied (almost all of them by substrate).

This experiment shows that competitive inhibition is reversed by increasing substrate concentration.

Investigation

Inhibition of β-galactosidase by galactose

Normally the enzyme β-galactosidase catalyses the reaction:

$$\text{lactose} \xrightarrow{\beta\text{-galactosidase}} \text{glucose} + \text{galactose}$$

However, it is also able to break down a colourless, synthetic compound called ONPG, as follows:

$$\text{ONPG} \xrightarrow{\beta\text{-galactosidase}} \text{galactose} + \text{yellow compound}$$

The experiment shown in Figure 6.19 is set up to investigate the inhibitory effect of galactose on the action of β-galactosidase as the concentration of the substrate, ONPG, is increased. The **independent variable** in this experiment is substrate concentration.

At the end of the experiment, an increasing intensity of yellow colour (indicating products of enzyme activity) is found to be present in the tubes, with tube 1 the least yellow and tube 4 the most yellow. The intensity of colour can be measured quantitatively using a **colorimeter**. This allows the results to be displayed as a graph.

A possible explanation for these results is that galactose acts as a **competitive inhibitor**, having most effect at low concentrations of substrate. As the concentration of substrate increases, more and more active sites on the enzyme become occupied by substrate, not inhibitor, and reaction rate increases.

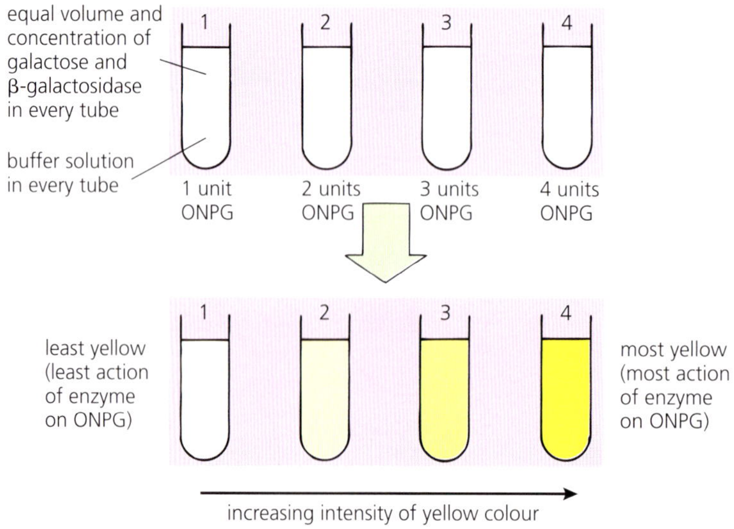

Figure 6.19 Investigating the inhibitory effect of galactose

Non-competitive inhibitors

A **non-competitive inhibitor** does not combine directly with an enzyme's active site. Instead it becomes attached to a non-active site and **changes the shape** of the enzyme molecule. This results in the active site becoming **altered indirectly** and being unable to combine with the substrate as shown in Figure 6.20. The larger the number of enzyme molecules affected in this way, the slower the enzyme-controlled reaction. Therefore, the non-competitive inhibitor acts as a type of regulator. Non-competitive inhibition is not reversed by increasing substrate concentration.

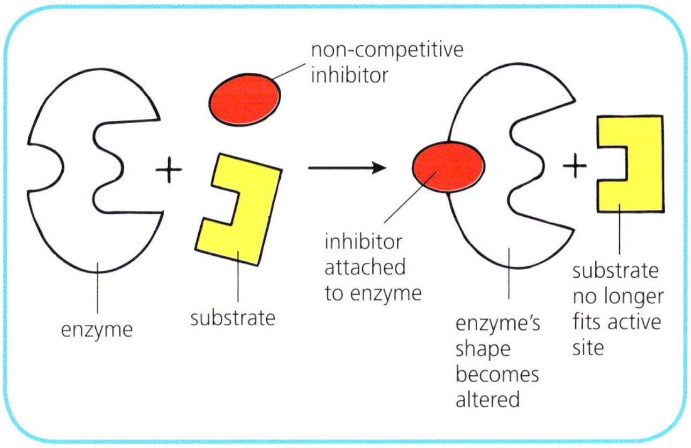

Figure 6.20 Effect of a non-competitive inhibitor

Feedback inhibition by an end product

End-product inhibition (see Figure 6.21) is a further way in which a metabolic pathway can be regulated. As the concentration of end product (metabolite Z) builds up and reaches a critical concentration, some of it binds to and inhibits molecules of enzyme 1 in the pathway. This slows down the conversion of metabolite W to X and in turn regulates the whole pathway.

As the concentration of Z drops, fewer molecules of enzyme 1 are affected and more of W is converted to X and so on. The pathway is kept under **finely tuned control** by this means (called **negative feedback control**) and wasteful conversion and accumulation of intermediates and final products are avoided.

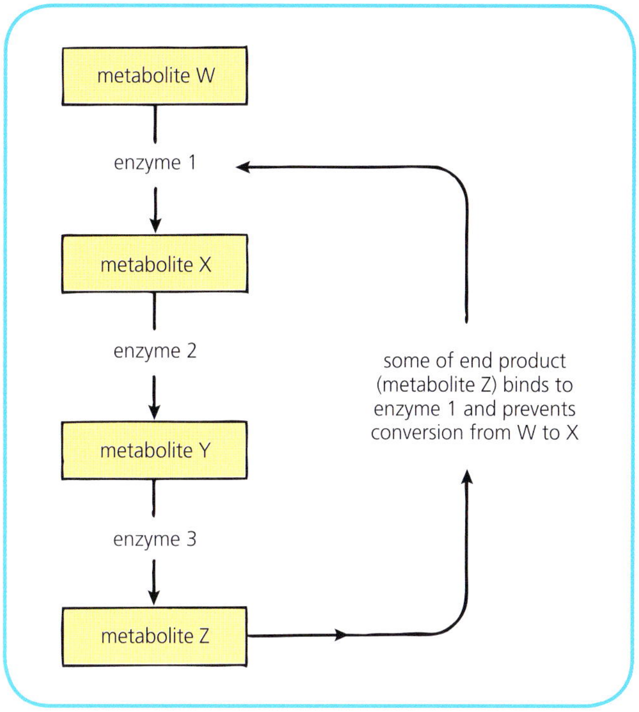

Figure 6.21 Regulation by feedback inhibition

Related Activity

Investigating the effect of phosphate on phosphatase

Phosphatase is an enzyme that releases the phosphate group from its substrate for use in cell metabolism.

Phosphatase is present in the extract obtained from ground-up mung bean sprouts. **Phenolphthalein phosphate** is a chemical that can be broken down by phosphatase as follows:

$$\text{phenolphthalein phosphate} \xrightarrow{\text{phosphatase}} \text{phenolphthalein} + \text{phosphate}$$

(pink in alkaline conditions)

The experiment is set up as shown in Figure 6.22. At the end of the experiment a decreasing intensity of pink colour is found to be present in the tubes. Tube 1 is the most pink and tube 5 is the least pink. From these results it is concluded that tube 1 contains most free phenolphthalein as a result of most enzyme activity and that tube 5 contains least free phenolphthalein as a result of least enzyme activity. In other words as phosphate concentration increases, the activity of the enzyme phosphatase decreases. A possible explanation for this effect is that phosphate acts as an **end-product inhibitor** of the enzyme phosphatase.

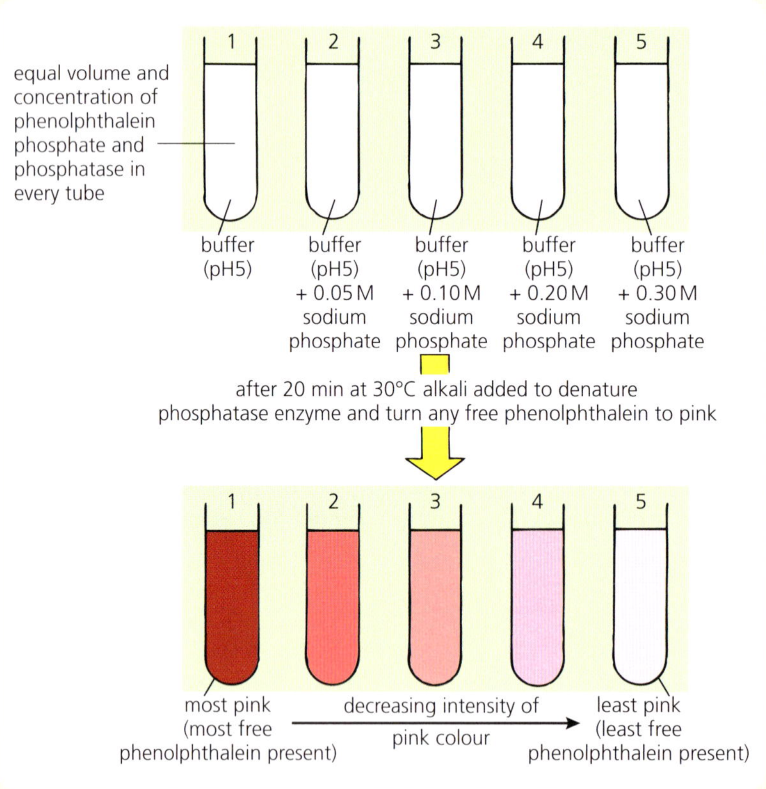

Figure 6.22 Investigating the effect of phosphate on phosphatase

Testing Your Knowledge 2

1 a) What property of a competitive inhibitor enables it to compete with the substrate? (1)

b) i) What effect does an increase in concentration of substrate have on rate of reaction when a limited amount of competitive inhibitor and enzyme are present?

ii) Explain why. (3)

2 Which form of enzyme inhibition cannot be reversed by increasing substrate concentration? (1)

3 Figure 6.23 shows a metabolic pathway where metabolites P, Q and R are present in equal quantities at the start.

a) Name enzyme X's i) substrate, ii) product. (2)

b) Name enzyme Y's i) substrate, ii) product. (2)

c) In which direction will the pathway proceed if more of metabolite P is added to the system? (1)

d) i) Metabolite R can act as an end-product inhibitor. Describe how this would work.

ii) What is the benefit of end-product inhibition? (3)

Figure 6.23

Applying Your Knowledge and Skills

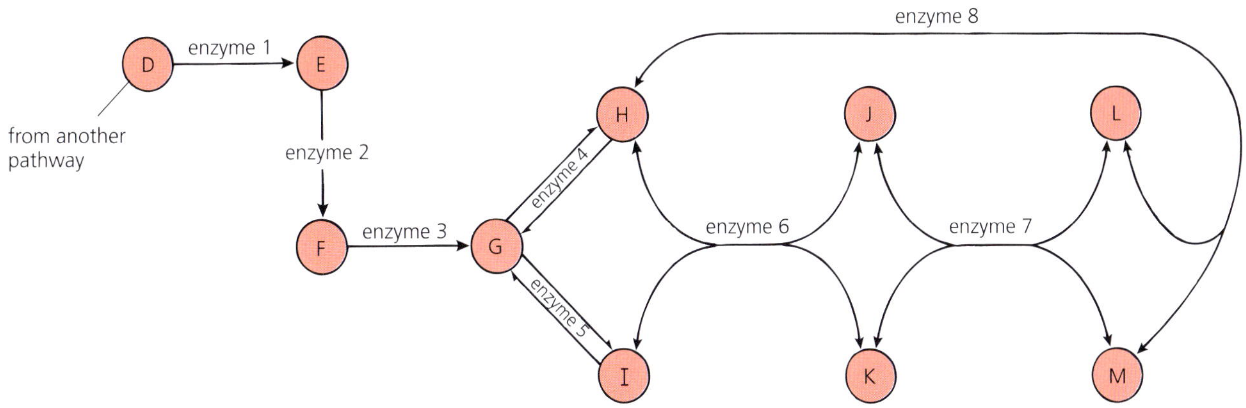

Figure 6.24

1 Figure 6.24 shows a metabolic pathway where each encircled letter represents a metabolite.

a) How many of the reactions under enzyme control in this pathway are i) reversible, ii) irreversible? (2)

b) Predict what would happen if metabolite I built up to a concentration far in excess of that of metabolite H. (2)

c) i) By what alternative route could a supply of intermediates J and K be obtained if enzyme 6 becomes inactive?

ii) By what alternative route could a supply of intermediates L and M be obtained if enzyme 8 becomes inactive?

iii) By what alternative route could a supply of metabolite I be obtained if enzyme 5 becomes inactive? (3)

d) Suggest a benefit to a living organism of its metabolic pathways possessing alternative routes. (1)

2 Figure 6.25 (on page 92) shows the stages that occur during an enzyme-controlled reaction.

a) Which of these stages illustrate induced fit? (1)

➜

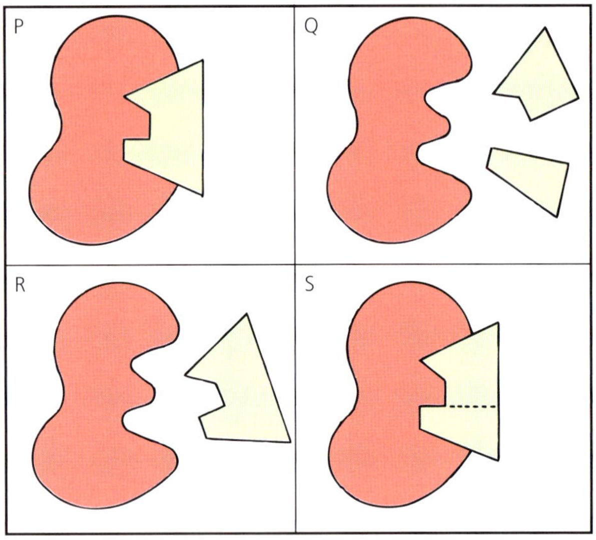

Figure 6.25

b) Using the letters given, indicate the correct sequence in which the four stages would occur if the enzyme were promoting:
   i) the build-up of a molecule from smaller components
   ii) the breakdown of a molecule into smaller constituents. (2)

c) Which of the molecules shown in Figure 6.26 could act as a competitive inhibitor to this enzyme? (1)

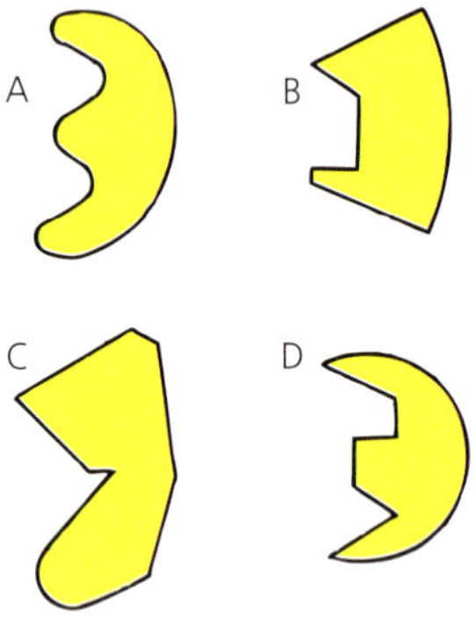

Figure 6.26

3 The graph shown in Figure 6.27 summarises the results from an experiment involving an enzyme-controlled reaction.
   a) i) In this experiment, the enzyme concentration was kept constant. From the graph, identify the factor that was varied by the experimenter.
   ii) Is this factor called the dependent or the independent variable?

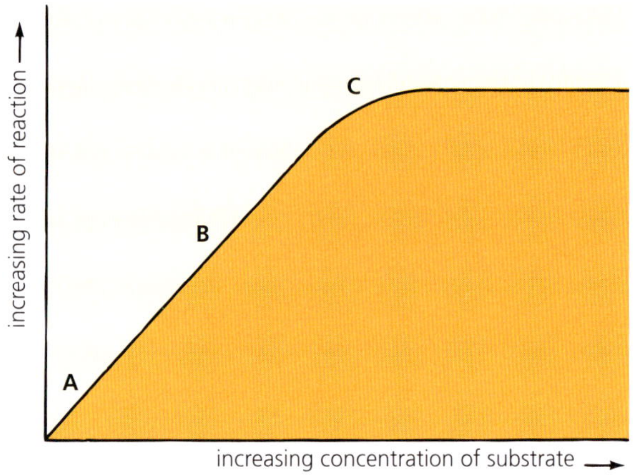

Figure 6.27

   iii) What effect did an increase in this factor have over region AB of the graph? (3)
   b) Suggest which factor became limiting at point C on the graph. (1)
   c) Which letter on the graph represents the situation where i) almost all of the active sites, ii) none of the active sites, iii) about half of the active sites on enzyme molecules are freely available for attachment to substrate molecules? (3)
   d) Suggest what could be done to increase the rate of the reaction beyond the level it has reached at C. (1)

4 Tables 6.2 and 6.3 give the results from an experiment set up to compare the activity of an enzyme (alkaline phosphatase) with its substrate (para-nitrophenol phosphate) in the presence and absence of a competitive inhibitor.

Concentration of substrate (nmol/l)	Enzyme activity (units)
0	0.0
10	1.8
20	2.6
30	3.3
40	3.6
50	3.8
60	4.0
70	4.0

Table 6.2

Concentration of substrate (nmol/l) + inhibitor	Enzyme activity (units)
0	0.0
10	0.6
20	1.0
30	1.5
40	2.1
50	2.7
60	3.0
70	3.6

Table 6.3

a) i) Draw a curve of best fit for the results in Table 6.2.
ii) On the same graph, draw a line of best fit for the results in Table 6.3.
iii) Mark 'presence of inhibitor' and 'absence of inhibitor' on your graph to identify the lines. (4)

b) At which of the following ranges of substrate concentration (in nmol/l) did the enzyme activity increase at the fastest rate in the absence of inhibitor? (1)
A 0–19 **B** 20–39 **C** 40–59

c) By how many times was enzyme activity at substrate concentration of 10 nmol/l greater when the inhibitor was absent? (1)

d) Calculate the percentage decrease in enzyme activity caused by the inhibitor at a substrate concentration of i) 20 nmol/l, ii) 70 nmol/l. (2)

e) Why would the two lines on the graph fail to meet even if higher concentrations of substrate were used? (1)

5 The experiment shown in Figure 6.28 was set up to investigate the inhibitory effect of iodine solution on the action of β-galactosidase as the concentration of the substrate ONPG was increased.

a) In which tubes did the enzyme act on its substrate? (1)

b) Identify the independent variable in this experiment. (1)

c) In which tubes was the enzyme's activity inhibited? (1)

d) Which tubes made up the experiment and which tubes were the controls? (2)

e) i) Identify the inhibitor.
ii) Did it act competitively or non-competitively?
iii) Explain your choice of answer. (4)

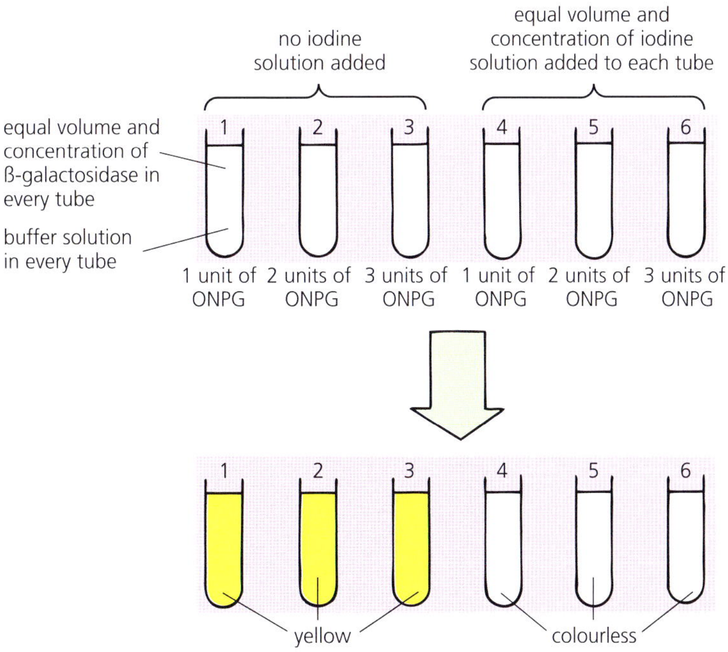

Figure 6.28

6 Figure 6.29 shows a metabolic pathway that occurs in cells of *E. coli*.

a) Identify enzyme P's i) substrates, ii) products, iii) end product inhibitor. (3)

b) i) If there is little or no demand for cytidylic acid for use in other metabolic pathways, what effect will this have on the concentration of carbamyl phosphate?

ii) Explain your answer. (2)

c) i) If there is a high demand for cytidylic acid in other metabolic pathways, will the negative feedback process be increased or decreased?

ii) Explain your answer. (2)

d) Which of the following statements is/are true? (1)

A The end product inhibits an early step in its own synthesis.

B The negative feedback mechanism regulates the rate of synthesis of metabolic intermediates.

C End product inhibition prevents the build-up of intermediates, which would be wasteful to the cell.

7 Give an account of enzyme activity under the headings:

a) induced fit (3)

b) activation energy (3)

c) effect of substrate concentration. (3)

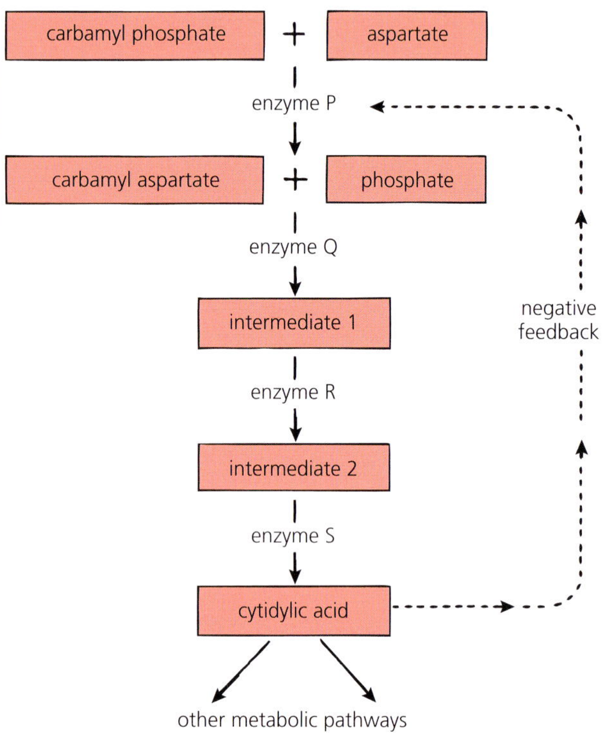

Figure 6.29

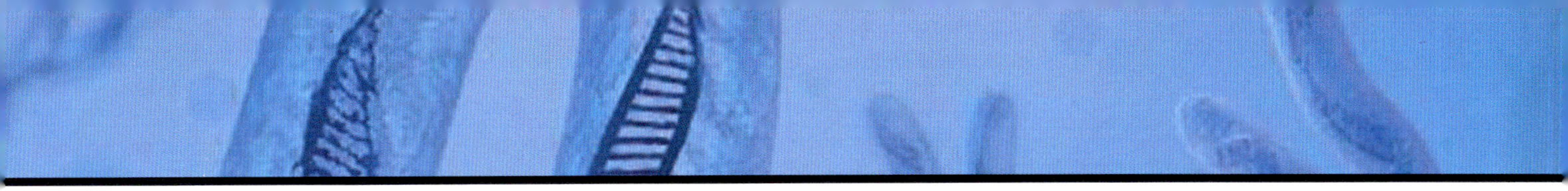

7 Cellular respiration

Cellular respiration is a series of metabolic pathways that brings about the release of energy from a foodstuff and the regeneration of the high-energy compound **adenosine triphosphate (ATP)**.

Investigation and Report

Investigating the use of three different sugars as respiratory substrates for yeast

Underlying biology

- Figure 7.1 shows, in a simple way, the molecular structure of three types of sugar and the digestive enzymes needed to break down maltose and sucrose.
- Strictly speaking, this activity is really three investigations being carried out simultaneously.
- In each case the independent variable is time.
- The dependent variable that you are going to measure is the volume of carbon dioxide released as a result of yeast using a particular type of sugar as its respiratory substrate.

You need

- 3 graduated tubes
- 3 large beakers (e.g. 500 ml) of coloured tap water
- 3 clamp stands
- 1 container of glucose solution (10 g in 90 ml water)
- 1 container of maltose solution (10 g in 90 ml water)
- 1 container of sucrose solution (10 g in 90 ml water)
- 3 conical flasks (250 ml) each with rubber stopper and delivery tube
- 3 labels
- 3 portions of dried yeast, each 1 g
- clock

What to do

1. Read all of the instructions in this section and prepare your results table before carrying out the experiment.
2. Fill each graduated tube with coloured tap water and clamp it in an inverted position in a beaker of coloured water, as shown in Figure 7.2.
3. Label the conical flasks 'glucose', 'maltose' and 'sucrose' respectively and add your initials.
4. Pour the appropriate sugar solution into each conical flask and add a portion of dried yeast.
5. Assemble the stoppers and delivery tubes as shown in Figure 7.2.
6. Start the clock and record, at 5-minute intervals, the total volume of carbon dioxide that has been released for each flask over a period of 2 hours.
7. If other students have carried out the same experiment, pool the results.

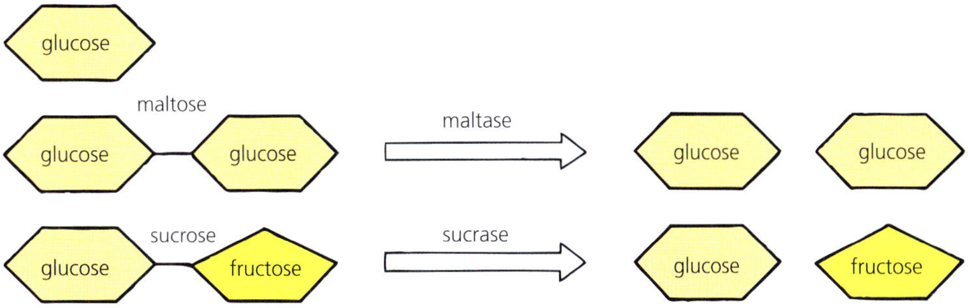

Figure 7.1 Relationship between three sugars

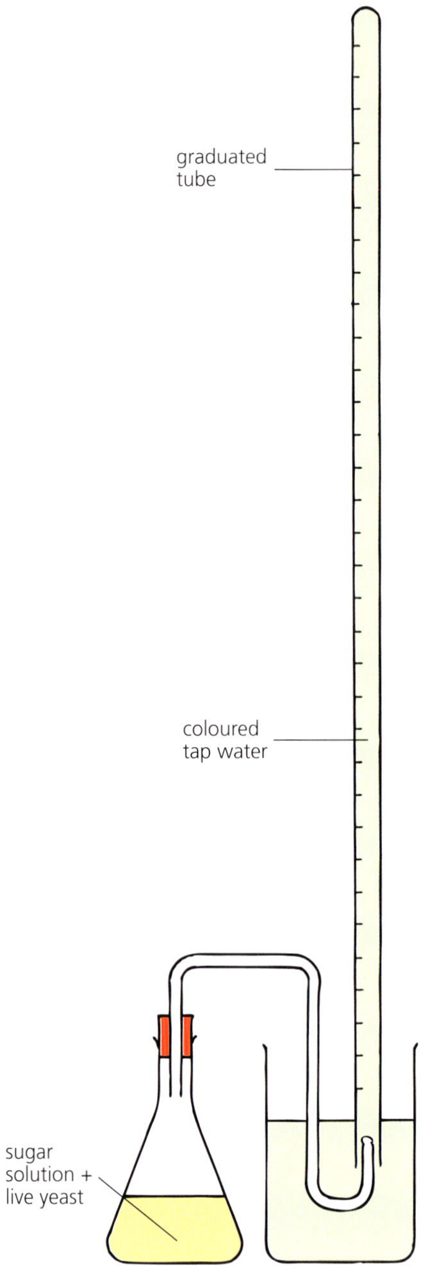

Figure 7.2 Yeast investigation set-up

Reporting

Write up your report by doing the following:

1 Rewrite the title given at the start of this activity.

2 Write the subheading **'Aim'** and state the aim of your experiment.

3 **a)** Write the subheading **'Method'**.

b) Draw a diagram of your apparatus set-up at the start of the experiment after the yeast has been added and bubbles of carbon dioxide are being released.

c) Briefly describe the experimental procedure that you followed using the impersonal passive tense. *Note: The impersonal passive tense avoids the use of 'I' and 'we'. Instead it makes the apparatus the subject of the sentence. In this experiment, for example, you could begin your report by saying 'Three graduated tubes were filled with coloured water . . .' (not 'I filled three graduated tubes with coloured water . . .').*

d) Continuing in the impersonal passive tense, state how your results were obtained.

4 Write the subheading **'Results'** and draw a final version of your table of results.

5 Write the subheading **'Analysis and Presentation of Results'**. Present your results as three line graphs with shared axes on the same sheet of graph paper.

6 Write the subheading **'Conclusion'** and a short paragraph to state what you have found out from a study of your results. This should include answers to the following questions:

a) Which respiratory substrate(s) was yeast able to use effectively?

b) Which enzyme (see Figure 7.1) is probably produced by yeast cells in adequate quantities to digest its substrate before its use in cellular respiration?

c) Which respiratory substrate(s) was yeast not able to use effectively?

d) Which enzyme is probably not produced by yeast in adequate quantities within the 2-hour timescale to digest its substrate and make it suitable for use in cellular respiration?

7 Write the final subheading **'Evaluation of Experimental Procedure'**. Give an evaluation of your experiment (keeping in mind that you may comment on any stage of the experiment that you wish). Try to incorporate answers to the following questions in your evaluation, making sure that at least one of your answers includes a supporting statement.

a) Why is the same mass of yeast and the same mass of sugar used in every flask?

b) Why is the same genetic strain of yeast used in each flask?

c) Why must the rubber stoppers be tightly fitting?

d) Why should a control flask containing distilled water and yeast have been included in this investigation?

e) What is the purpose of pooling results with other groups?

Adenosine triphosphate

A molecule of **ATP** is composed of adenosine and three inorganic phosphate (P_i) groups, as shown in Figure 7.3. Energy held in an ATP molecule is released when the bond attaching the terminal phosphate is broken by enzyme action. This results in the formation of **adenosine diphosphate** (**ADP**) and inorganic **phosphate** (**P_i**). On the other hand, energy is required to regenerate ATP from ADP and inorganic phosphate. This relationship is summarised in Figure 7.4.

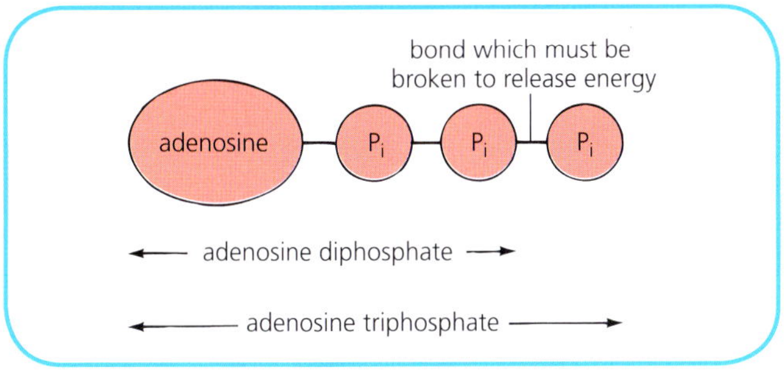

Figure 7.3 Structure of ATP

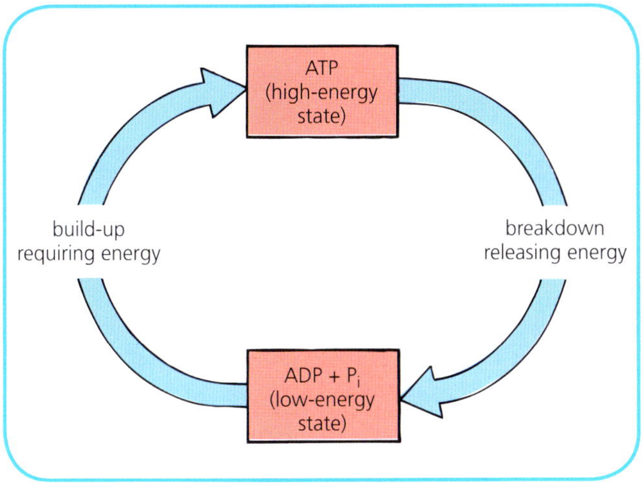

Figure 7.4 Relationship between ATP and ADP + P_i

Phosphorylation

Phosphorylation is an enzyme-controlled process by which a phosphate group is added to a molecule. Phosphorylation occurs, for example, when the reaction shown in Figure 7.4 goes from bottom to top and inorganic phosphate (P_i) combines with low-energy ADP to form high-energy ATP.

Phosphorylation of a reactant in a pathway

Phosphorylation also occurs when phosphate (P_i) and energy are transferred from ATP to the molecules of a reactant in a metabolic pathway, making them **more reactive**. Often a step in a pathway can proceed only if a reactant becomes **phosphorylated** and energised. In the early stages of cellular respiration, for example, some reactants must undergo phosphorylation during what is called the energy investment phase. One of these steps is shown in Figure 7.5.

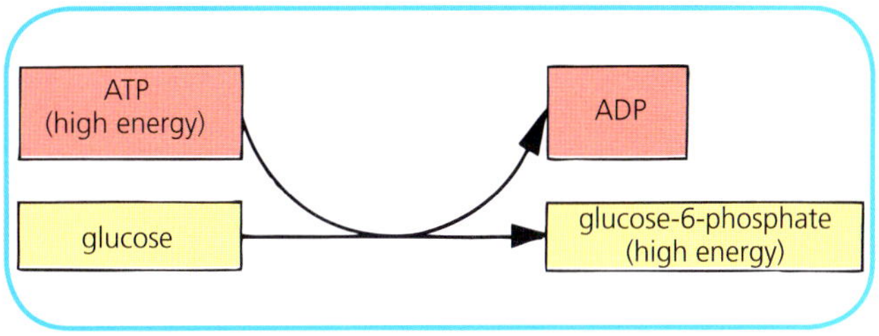

Figure 7.5 Phosphorylation of glucose

Investigation

Effect of phosphorylase on a phosphorylated substrate

Background

- **Glucose-1-phosphate** is a phosphorylated form of glucose.
- A molecule of starch is composed of many glucose molecules linked together in a long chain.
- Potato tuber cells contain **phosphorylase**, an enzyme that promotes the synthesis of starch.
- Potato extract containing phosphorylase is prepared by liquidising a mixture of potato tuber and water and then centrifuging the mixture until the potato extract (see Figure 7.6) is **starch-free**.

The experiment is set up at room temperature on a spotting tile, as shown in Figure 7.7.

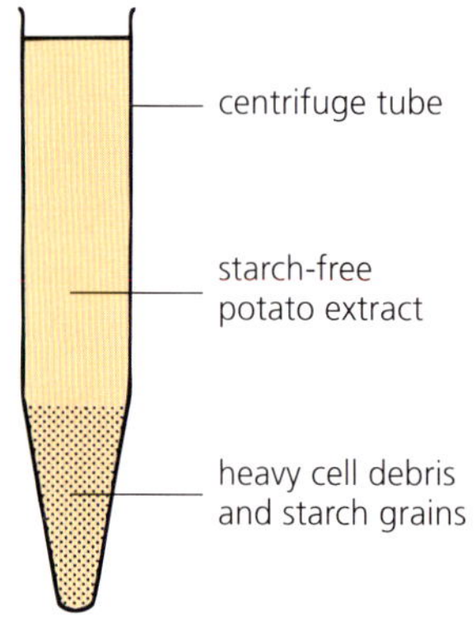

Figure 7.6 Preparation of potato extract

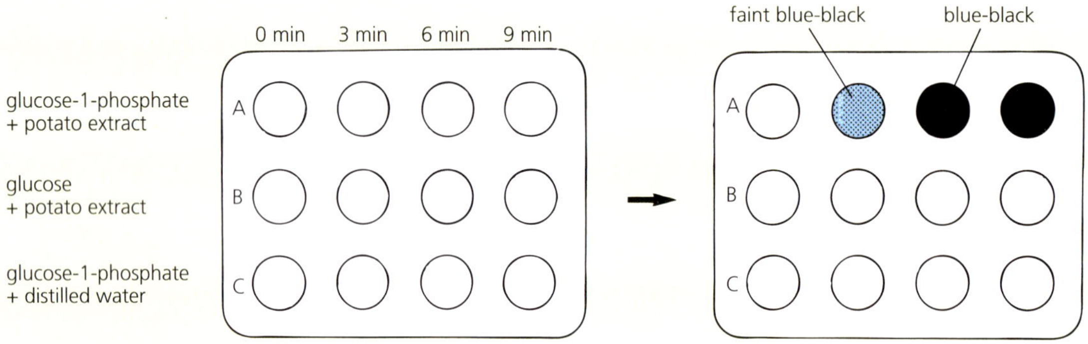

Figure 7.7 Investigating a phosphorylated substrate

One dimple from each row is tested at 3-minute intervals with iodine solution. Starch is found to be formed in row A only. It is concluded that in row A phosphorylase has promoted the conversion of the **phosphorylated** (and more reactive) form of the substrate, glucose-1-phosphate, to starch, as in the following equation:

$$\underset{\text{(phosphorylated substrate)}}{\text{glucose-1-phosphate}} \xrightarrow[\text{(enzyme)}]{\text{phosphorylase}} \underset{\text{(end product)}}{\text{starch}}$$

In row B (a control), phosphorylase has failed to convert the more stable (and less reactive) form of the substrate, glucose, to starch.

In row C (a control), the molecules of glucose-1-phosphate have failed to become bonded together into starch without the aid of phosphorylase.

Positive and negative controls

A **positive control** is set up to assess the validity of a testing procedure or design and ensure that the equipment and materials being used are in working order and appropriate for use in the experiment being carried out.

For example, a positive control for the above experiment could be set up as row D, which would contain starch in every dimple. If the addition of iodine solution at each 3-minute interval gave a blue-black colour, this would confirm that:

- the iodine solution being used was working properly as a testing reagent for starch
- the experiment was not adversely affected in some way, for example, by the contamination of the spotting tile or by changes in room temperature.

If a positive control does not produce the expected result, then this indicates that there is something wrong with the design of the testing procedure or with the materials being used.

A **negative control** is one that should not work. It is a copy of the experiment in which all factors are kept exactly the same except the one being investigated. When the results are compared, any difference found between the experiment and a negative control must be due to the factor being investigated.

In the above investigation, starch is not synthesised in row B, showing that the glucose must be in a phosphorylated state to become converted to starch. If row B had not been set up, it would be valid to suggest that starch would have been formed whether or not the glucose was phosphorylated. Similarly, starch was not formed in row C showing that phosphorylase (in potato extract) must be present for phosphorylated glucose to be converted to starch. If row C had not been included, it would be valid to suggest that phosphorylated glucose would have become starch whether or not phosphorylase was present. Therefore rows B and C in this investigation are negative controls.

Metabolic pathways of cellular respiration

Glycolysis

The process of cellular respiration begins in the cytoplasm of a living cell with a molecule of **glucose** being broken down to form **pyruvate**. This process of 'glucose-splitting' is called **glycolysis**. It consists of a series of enzyme-controlled steps. Those in the first half of the chain make up the **energy investment phase** (where 2ATP are used up per molecule of glucose); those in the second half of the chain make up an **energy payoff phase** (where 4ATP are produced per molecule of glucose), as shown in Figure 7.8.

Phosphorylation of intermediates occurs twice during the first phase:

- in step 1, where an intermediate is formed that can connect with other metabolic pathways
- in step 3, which is an irreversible reaction leading only to the rest of the glycolytic pathway.

The generation of 4ATP that occurs during the second half of the pathway gives a **net gain of 2ATP** per molecule of glucose during glycolysis. In addition, during the energy payoff phase, H^+ ions are released from the substrate by a dehydrogenase enzyme. These H^+ ions are passed to a coenzyme molecule called **NAD** resulting in the formation of **NADH**.

The process of glycolysis does not require oxygen. However, NADH only leads to the production of further molecules of ATP at a later stage in the respiratory process if oxygen is present. In the absence of oxygen, fermentation occurs (see page 109).

Citric acid cycle

If oxygen is present, aerobic respiration proceeds and pyruvate is broken down into carbon dioxide and an **acetyl group**. Each acetyl group combines with **coenzyme A** to form **acetyl coenzyme A**. During this process, further H^+ ions are released and become bound to NAD, forming NADH. A simplified version of the metabolic pathway is shown in Figure 7.9.

The acetyl group of acetyl coenzyme A combines with **oxaloacetate** to form **citrate** and enter the **citric acid cycle**. This cycle consists of several enzyme-mediated stages, which occur in the central matrix of mitochondria and result finally in the regeneration of oxaloacetate.

In three steps in the cycle, dehydrogenase enzymes remove **H^+ ions** and electrons from the respiratory substrate and pass them to the coenzyme NAD to form NADH. In addition, ATP is produced in one of the steps and carbon dioxide is released in two of the steps.

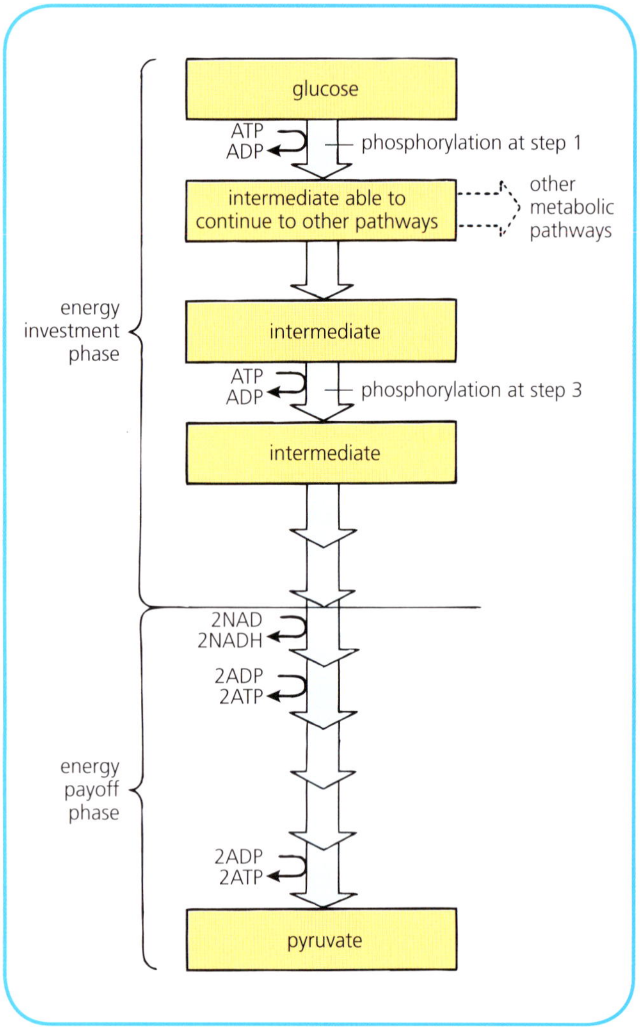

Figure 7.8 Glycolysis

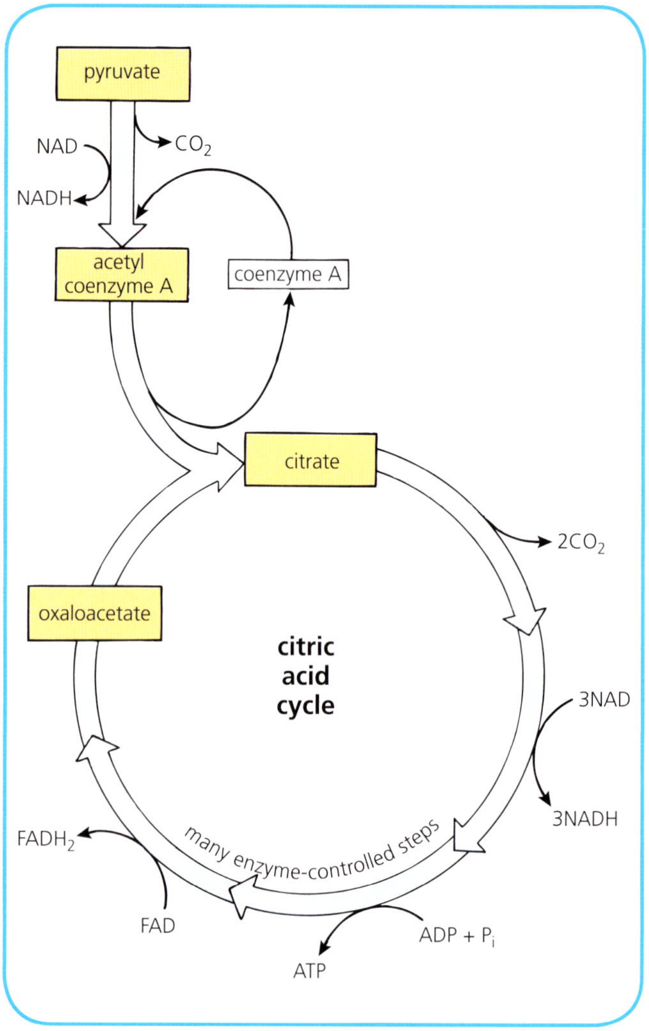

Figure 7.9 Citric acid cycle

Related Activity

Demonstrating the effect of malonic acid

Background

- Succinate and fumarate are two of the intermediates in the citric acid cycle.
- When succinate is converted to fumarate during respiration in a living cell, hydrogen is released and passed to the coenzyme FAD. The reaction is catalysed by the enzyme **succinic dehydrogenase** as follows:

$$\text{succinate} + \text{FAD} \xrightarrow{\text{succinic dehydrogenase}} \text{fumarate} + \text{FADH}_2$$

- **Malonic acid** is a chemical that inhibits the action of succinic dehydrogenase.
- In this investigation a chemical called DCPIP is used as the hydrogen acceptor. DCPIP changes colour upon gaining hydrogen as follows:

dark blue (lacks hydrogen) ⟶ colourless (has gained hydrogen)

→

The experiment is carried out as shown in Figure 7.10. From the results it is concluded that in tube A succinic dehydrogenase in respiring mung bean cells has converted succinate to fumarate and that the hydrogen released has been accepted by DCPIP, turning it colourless. It is concluded that in tube B, the respiratory pathway has been blocked and no hydrogen has been released for DCPIP to accept because malonic acid has inhibited the action of succinic dehydrogenase.

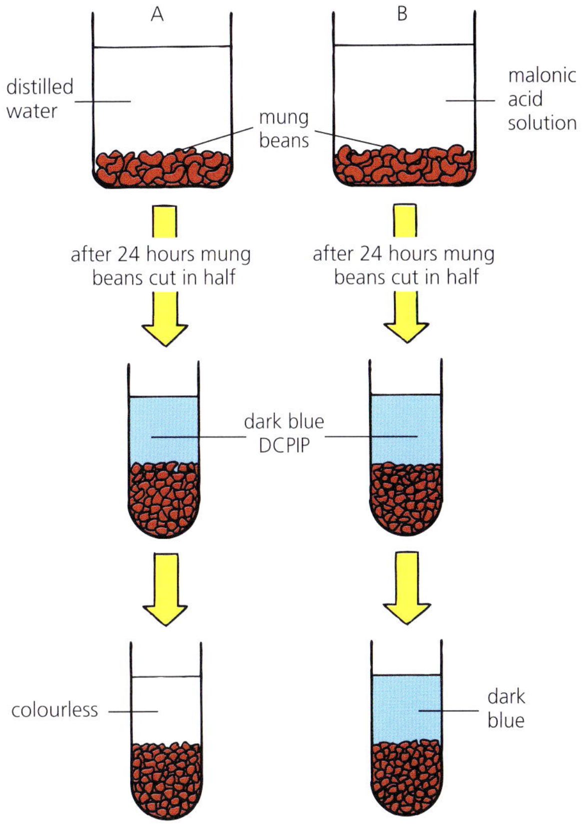

Figure 7.10 Effect of malonic acid

Electron transport chain

An **electron transport chain** consists of a group of carrier protein molecules. There are many of these chains in a cell. They are found attached to the **inner membrane** of mitochondria. NADH from the glycolytic and citric acid pathways releases **electrons** and passes them to the electron transport chains (see Figure 7.11).

Synthesis of ATP

As the electrons flow along a chain of electron acceptors, they release energy. This is used to pump **hydrogen ions** across the membrane from the inner cavity (matrix) side to the intermembrane space, where a higher concentration of hydrogen ions is maintained. The return flow of hydrogen ions to the matrix (the region of lower H^+ concentration) via molecules of **ATP synthase** drives this enzyme to synthesise ATP from ADP and P_i. Most of the ATP generated by cellular respiration is produced in mitochondria in this way.

When the electrons come to the end of the electron transport chain, they combine with **oxygen**, the final electron acceptor. At the same time, the oxygen combines with a pair of hydrogen ions to form **water**. In the absence of oxygen, the electron transport chains do not operate and this major source of ATP becomes unavailable to the cell.

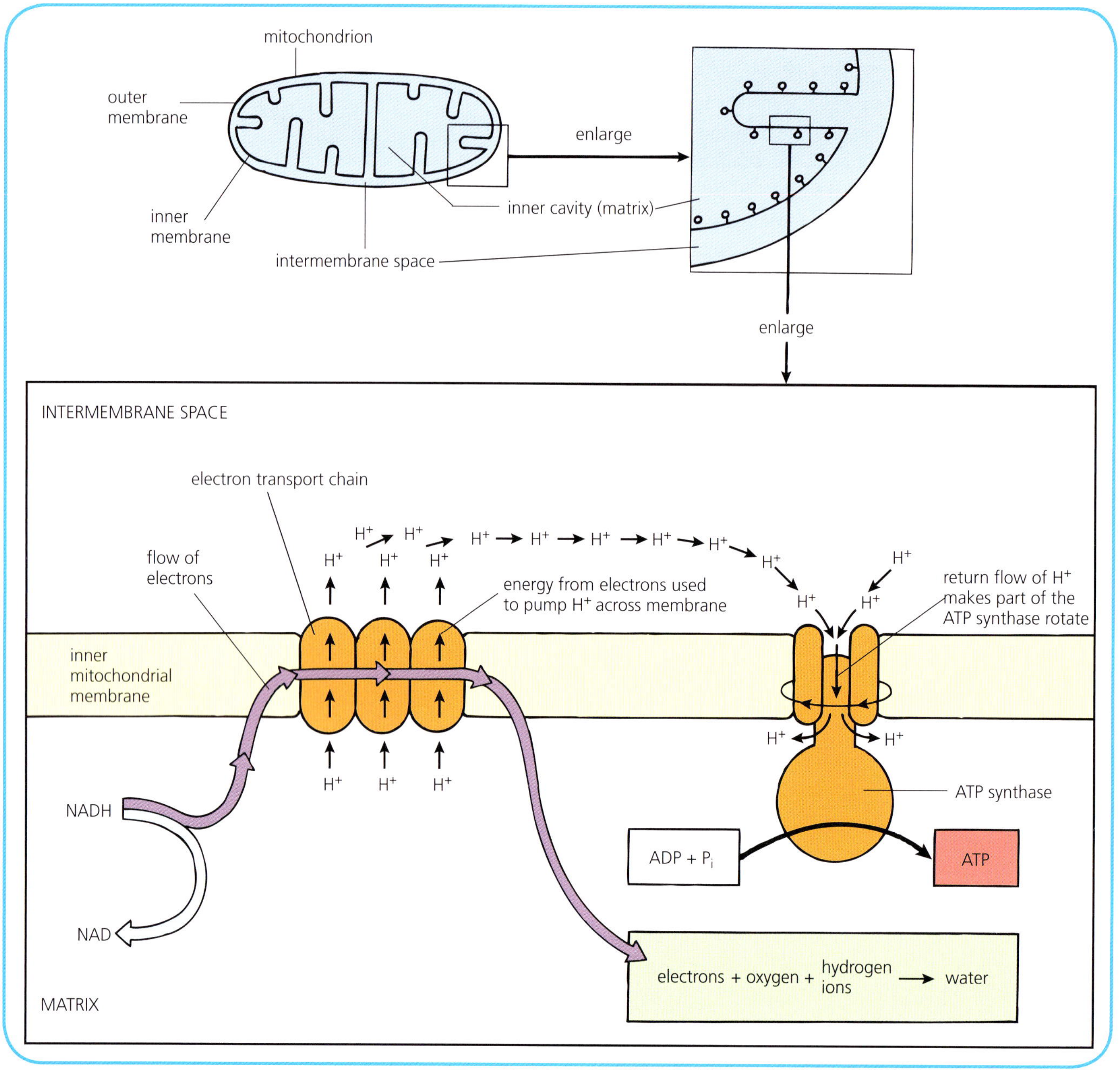

Figure 7.11 Electron transport chain

Related Activity

Investigating the activity of dehydrogenase enzyme in yeast

Background

- During respiration, glucose is gradually broken down and hydrogen released at various stages along the pathway. Each of these stages is controlled by an enzyme called a **dehydrogenase**.
- Yeast cells contain small quantities of stored food that can be used as a respiratory substrate.
- Resazurin dye is a chemical that changes colour upon gaining hydrogen, as follows:

blue (lacks hydrogen) ⟶ pink (some hydrogen gained) ⟶ colourless (much hydrogen gained)

→

- Before setting up the experiment shown in Figure 7.12, dried yeast is added to water and aerated for an hour at 35°C to ensure that the yeast is in an active state.

Once the experiment has been set up, the contents of tube A are found to change from blue via pink to colourless much faster than those of tube B. Tube C, the control, remains unchanged.

It is concluded that in tube A, hydrogen has been rapidly released and has acted on and changed the colour of the resazurin dye. For this to be possible, dehydrogenase enzymes present in the yeast cells must have acted on glucose, the respiratory substrate.

In tube B, the reaction was slower because no glucose was added and the dehydrogenase enzymes could only act on any small amount of respiratory substrate already present in the yeast cells.

In tube C, boiling has killed the cells and denatured the dehydrogenase enzymes.

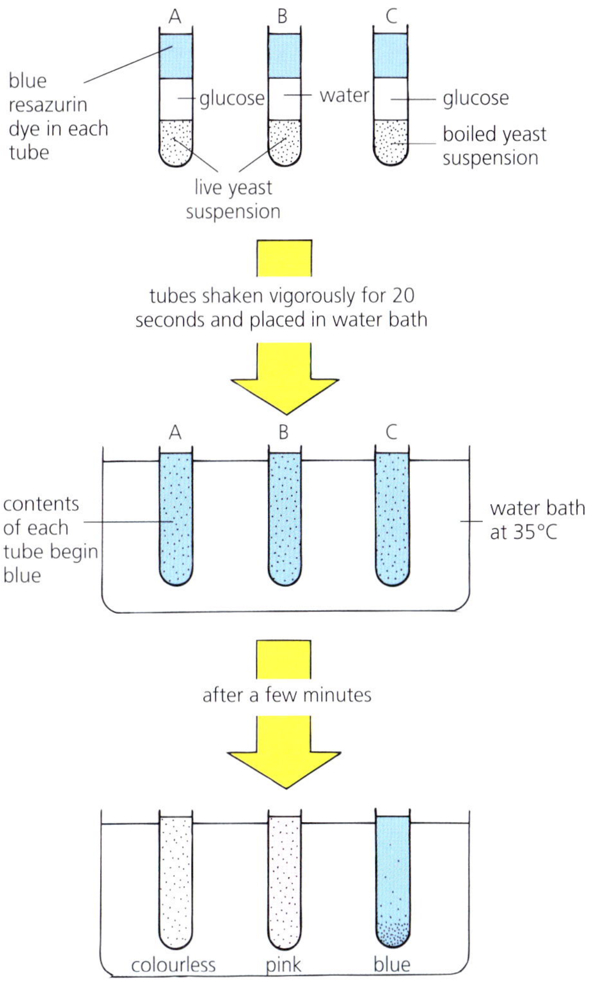

Figure 7.12 Dehydrogenase activity

Testing Your Knowledge

1 a) What compound is represented by the letters ATP? (1)
  b) What is the structural difference between ATP and ADP? (1)
  c) Give a simple equation to indicate how ATP is regenerated in a cell. (2)

2 Explain each of the following:
  a) During the glycolysis of one molecule of glucose, the net gain is two and not four molecules of ATP. (1)
  b) Living organisms have only small quantities of oxaloacetate in their cells. (1)

3 Using the letters G, C and E, indicate whether each of the following statements refers to glycolysis (G), citric acid cycle (C) or electron transport chain (E). (Some statements may need more than one letter.) (8)
  a) It brings about the breakdown of glucose to pyruvate.
  b) It ends with the production of water.
  c) It begins with acetyl from acetyl coenzyme A combining with oxaloacetate.
  d) It involves a cascade of electrons, which are finally accepted by oxygen.
  e) It has an energy investment and energy payoff phase.
  f) It results in the production of NADH.
  g) It involves the release of carbon dioxide.
  h) It results in the production of ATP.

Role of ATP

Transfer of energy via ATP

ATP is important because it acts as the **link** between catabolic energy-releasing reactions (e.g. respiration) and anabolic energy-consuming reactions (e.g. synthesis of proteins, transmission of nerve impulses and replication of DNA). It provides the means by which chemical energy is transferred from one type of reaction to the other in a living cell (see Figures 7.13 and 7.14).

Turnover of ATP molecules

It has been estimated that an active cell (e.g. a bacterium undergoing cell division) requires approximately two million molecules of ATP per second to satisfy its energy requirements. This is made possible by the fact that a **rapid turnover** of ATP molecules occurs continuously in a cell. At any given moment some ATP molecules are undergoing breakdown and releasing the energy needed for cellular processes while others are being regenerated from ADP and P_i using energy released during cell respiration.

Figure 7.14 'What do you mean, I need **ATP**? I thought you said **a teepee**!'

Fixed quantity of ATP

Since ATP is manufactured at the same time as it is used up, there is no need for a living organism to possess a vast store of ATP. The quantity of ATP present in the human body, for example, is found to remain fairly **constant** at around 50 g despite the fact that the body may be using up *and* regenerating ATP at a rate of about 400 g/h.

Further Testing Your Knowledge questions for Chapter 7 are to be found on page 111.

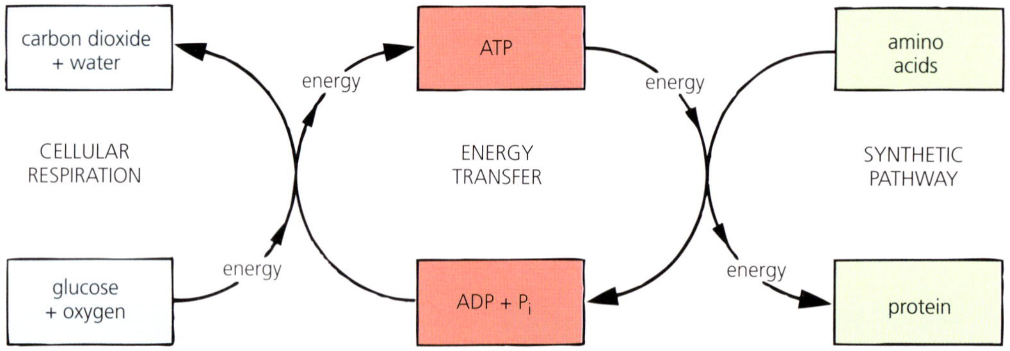

Figure 7.13 Transfer of chemical energy by ATP

Related Activity

Measuring ATP using luciferase

Background

- **Luciferase** is an enzyme present in the cells of fireflies. It is involved in the process of bioluminescence (the production of light by a living organism).
- Luciferase catalyses the following reaction:

$$\text{luciferin} + \text{ATP} \xrightarrow{\text{luciferase}} \text{end products} + \text{light energy}$$

- The presence of **ATP** is essential for the production of light energy and the reaction does not proceed in its absence.
- When luciferin and luciferase are plentiful and ATP is the limiting factor, the intensity of light emitted is proportional to the concentration of ATP present.

The experiment is carried out as shown in Figure 7.15 and the results used to draw a graph of known values of ATP concentration (see Figure 7.16). When the experiment is repeated using material of unknown ATP content, the ATP concentration can be determined from the graph. For example, the sample shown in Figure 7.17 would contain 7.5 units of ATP.

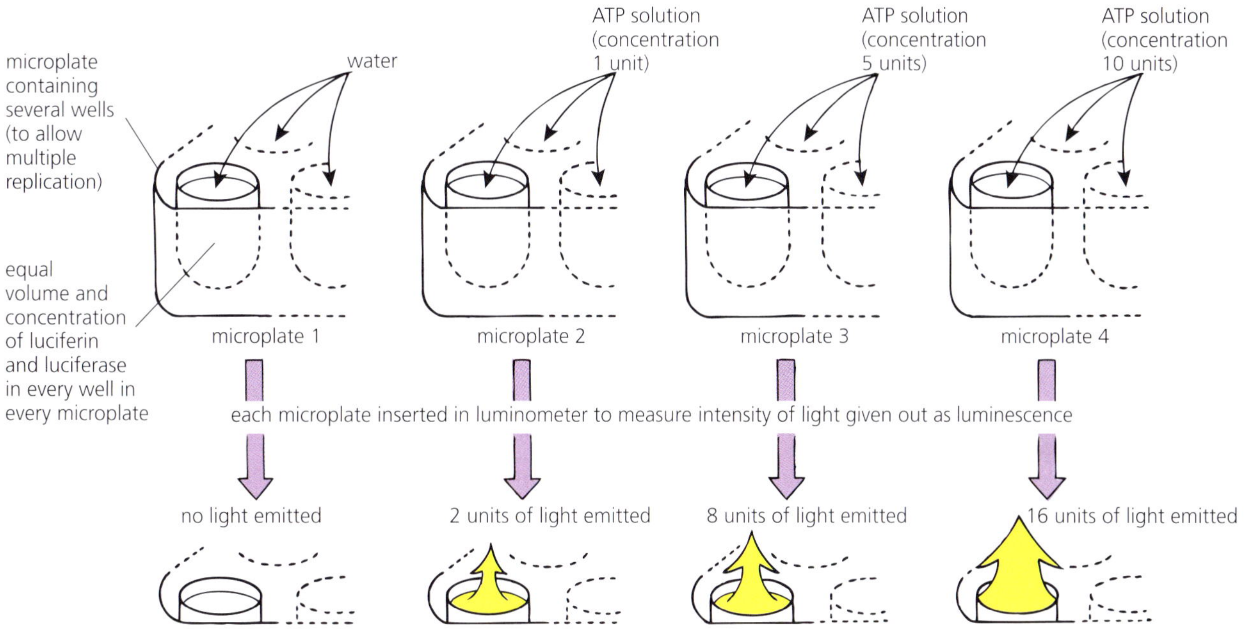

Figure 7.15 Measuring light emitted from known concentrations of ATP

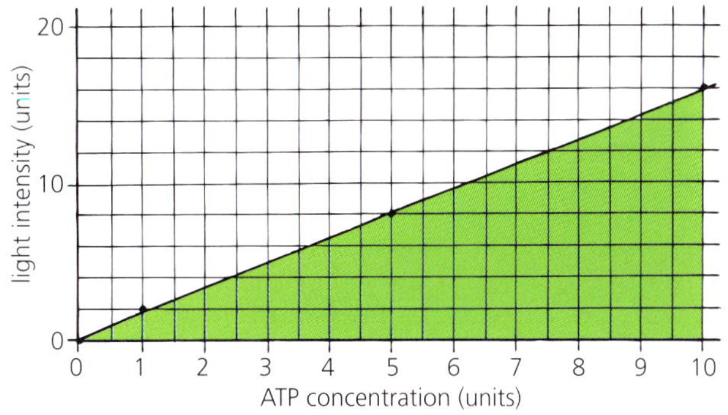

Figure 7.16 Graph of luciferase results

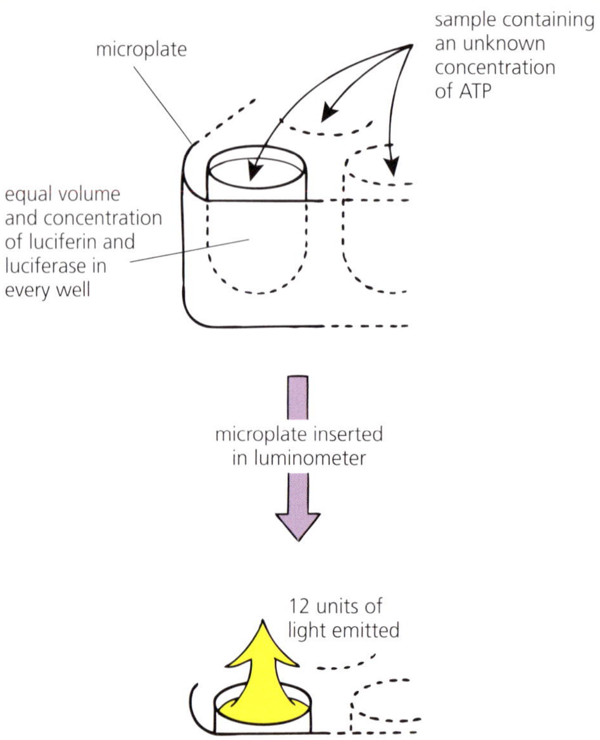

Figure 7.17 Measuring light emitted from unknown concentrations of ATP

Applying Your Knowledge and Skills

1 Figure 7.18 shows, in a simple way, the molecular structure of three types of sugar. Table 7.1 shows the results of an investigation into the use by yeast of each of these sugars as its respiratory substrate.

a) Draw a line graph of the results on the same sheet of graph paper using three different colours. (4)

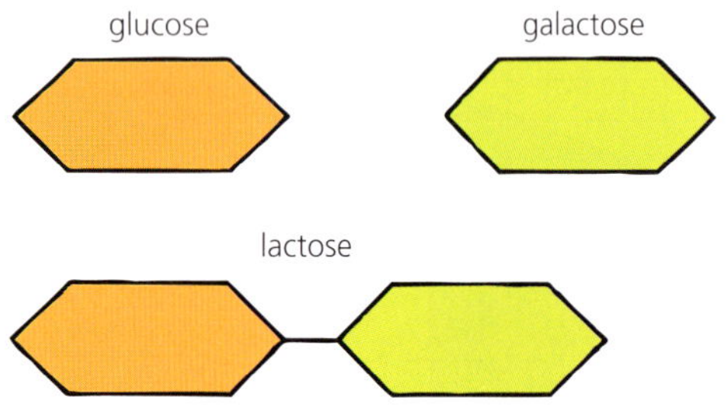

Figure 7.18

b) i) Identify the glucose result that was least reliable.

ii) Justify your choice. (2)

c) What percentage increase in total volume of carbon dioxide released occurred for glucose between 20 minutes and 80 minutes? (1)

d) What conclusion can be drawn about yeast's ability to make use of each of the sugars as its respiratory substrate? (1)

e) i) What conclusion can be drawn about yeast's ability to break lactose down into its component sugars within the given time span?

ii) Explain your answer. (2)

f) What could be done to improve the reliability of the results. (1)

➜

Time (min)	Total volume of carbon dioxide released (ml)		
	Glucose	Galactose	Lactose
0	0.0	0.0	0.0
10	0.0	0.0	0.0
20	0.5	0.0	0.0
30	3.0	0.5	0.5
40	6.0	1.0	0.5
50	11.0	1.5	1.5
60	16.0	1.5	1.5
70	18.0	2.0	2.0
80	32.5	2.0	2.5
90	39.5	2.0	3.0

Table 7.1

2 Metabolism falls into two parts:

- **anabolism**, consisting of energy-requiring reactions that involve synthesis of complex molecules
- **catabolism**, consisting of energy-yielding reactions in which complex molecules are broken down.

Transfer of energy from catabolic reactions to anabolic reactions is brought about by **ATP**. Figure 7.19 is a summary of the above information.

a) Copy the diagram and add four arrowheads to show the directions in which the two coupled reactions occur. (2)

b) Complete boxes 1–4 using each of the terms given in bold print in the passage above. (2)

c) State whether each of the following is an anabolic (A) or a catabolic (C) reaction:

i) destruction of a microbe by enzymes in lysosomes

ii) formation of the hormone thyroxin in the thyroid gland

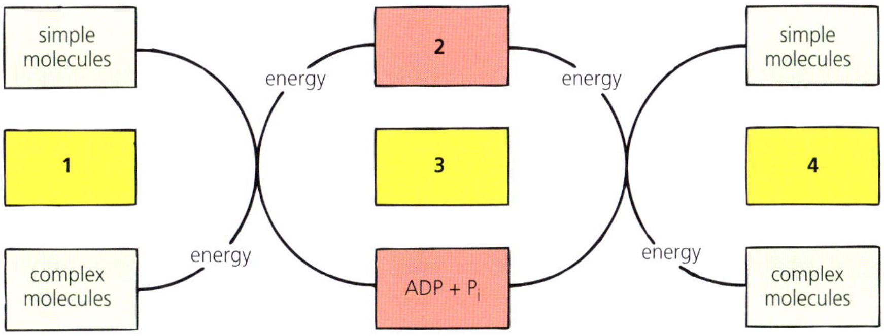

Figure 7.19

iii) conversion of glycogen to glucose in muscle tissue
iv) synthesis of nucleic acids. (4)

3 Table 7.2 refers to the process of cellular respiration in the presence of oxygen.
a) Copy the table and complete the blanks indicated by brackets. (5)
b) Which stage consists of an energy investment phase followed by an energy payoff phase? (1)
c) At which stage is *most* ATP produced per molecule of glucose? (1)
d) Which TWO stages would fail to occur in the absence of oxygen? (2)

4 Figure 7.20 shows a small region of an inner mitochondrial membrane.
a) i) Which side of the membrane has the higher concentration of H^+ ions?
ii) Explain how this higher concentration of H^+ ions is maintained. (3)
b) i) Name molecule X.
ii) Briefly describe how it works. (3)
c) Cyanide is a chemical that binds with the electron transport chains and brings the flow of electrons to a halt. Explain why cyanide is poisonous? (2)

5 Refer back to the investigation shown in Figure 7.10 on page 101. Based only on these results, it could be argued that malonic acid has simply killed the cells.
a) How could the experiment be adapted to investigate if malonic acid really does act as a competitive inhibitor? (1) (Hint: see Chapter 6, pages 87–88.)
b) Explain how you would know from the results of your redesigned experiment whether or not malonic acid had acted as a competitive inhibitor. (2)

6 One mole of glucose releases 2880 kJ of energy. During aerobic respiration in living organisms, 44% of this is used to generate ATP. The rest is lost as heat.
a) What percentage of the energy generated during aerobic respiration is lost as heat? (1)
b) Out of a mole of glucose, how many kilojoules are used to generate ATP? (1)
c) Name TWO forms of cellular work that the energy held by ATP could be used to carry out. (2)

7 Give an account of the production of NADH and the role played by the electron transport chain during cellular respiration. (9)

Stage of respiratory pathway	Principal reaction or process that occurs	Products
Glycolysis	Splitting of glucose into [_____]	[_____], NADH and pyruvate
[_____] acid cycle	Removal of [_____] ions from molecules of respiratory [_____]	[_____], [_____] and ATP
[_____] transport chain	Release of [_____] to form ATP	ATP and [_____]

Table 7.2

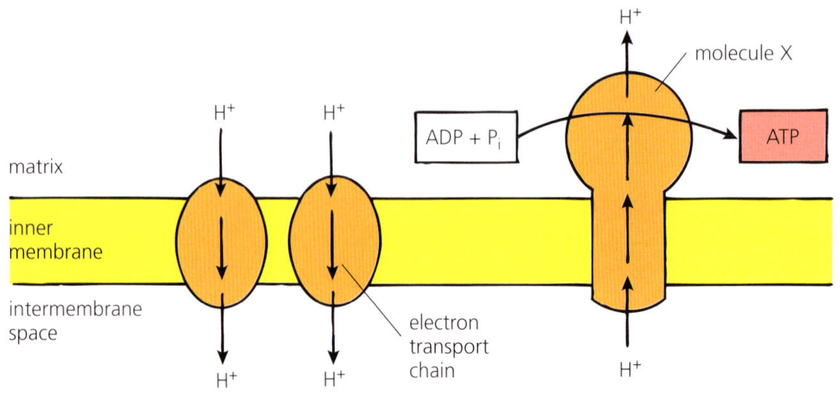

Figure 7.20

8 Energy systems in muscle cells

Lactate metabolism

During strenuous exercise, the tiny quantity of ATP present in muscle cells lasts for a few seconds. As the intensive exercise continues, the cells respire by **fermentation** because they do not receive an adequate supply of oxygen from the bloodstream to support an increased level of **aerobic** respiration.

Neither the citric acid cycle nor the electron transport chain can generate the additional ATP required; only glycolysis is able to provide more ATP. It generates **2NADH** and **2ATP** from each molecule of glucose as it is broken down to pyruvate (see Figure 8.1).

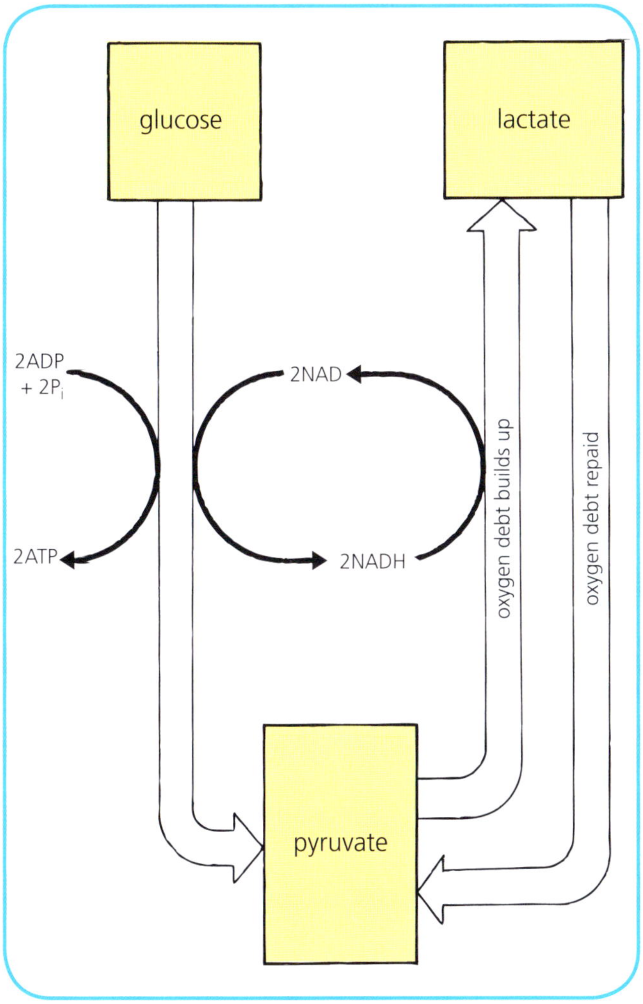

Figure 8.1 Lactic acid metabolism

This process is followed by the conversion of pyruvic acid (pyruvate) to **lactate** (lactic acid) accompanied by the transfer of hydrogen from the NADH and the regeneration of **NAD**. NAD must be present to enable glycolysis to continue and produce more ATP.

However, as lactate gathers in muscle cells, **muscle fatigue** occurs and an **oxygen debt** builds up. This is repaid when exercise comes to a halt (see Figure 8.2). Energy generated by aerobic respiration is now used to convert lactate (transported in the bloodstream to the liver) back to pyruvate and glucose.

Figure 8.2 Repayment of oxygen debt

ATP totals

Compared with aerobic respiration, fermentation is a less efficient process. It produces only 2 ATP per molecule of glucose whereas respiration in the presence of oxygen produces many ATP per molecule of glucose.

Types of skeletal muscle fibre

All physical activities require parts of the body to move. These movements are brought about by the action of skeletal muscle fibres, which fall into two categories based on the duration of their twitches:

- type 1 – **slow**-twitch muscle fibres
- type 2 – **fast**-twitch muscle fibres.

The two types differ in many ways, as shown in Table 8.1.

Feature	Type of skeletal muscle fibre	
	1 (slow-twitch)	2 (fast-twitch)
Speed of contraction	Slow	Fast
Length of time for which contraction is sustained	Long	Short
Speed at which fibre becomes fatigued	Slow	Fast
Respiratory pathway(s) normally used to generate ATP	Glycolysis and aerobic pathways	Glycolysis only
Number of mitochondria present	Large	Small
Density of blood capillaries associated with fibre	High	Low
Concentration of myoglobin in cells	High	Low
Major storage fuels used	Fats	Glycogen

Table 8.1 Comparison of slow- and fast-twitch muscle fibres

Myoglobin

Myoglobin is an oxygen-storing protein present in muscle cells. It has a stronger affinity for oxygen than haemoglobin. (Affinity means tendency to combine with a substance.) Therefore, myoglobin is able to **extract oxygen** from blood for use by muscle cells, especially those in slow-twitch muscle fibres.

Different fibres for different events

Slow-twitch muscle fibres depend on aerobic respiration to generate most of their ATP and are especially effective when put to use during **endurance** events such as rowing, cycling and long-distance running. Fast-twitch muscle fibres depend on glycolysis to generate ATP and are especially effective when put to use during **power** events such as weight-lifting and sprinting.

Skeletal muscles contain a **genetically determined** mixture of slow-twitch and fast-twitch fibres. In most muscles, a fairly even balance exists between the two but in some muscles, one type predominates over the other. For example, the muscles in the back responsible for maintaining posture contain mostly slow-twitch fibres, whereas the muscles that move the eyeballs are made up mainly of fast-twitch fibres.

Athletes

Athletes are found to possess distinct patterns of muscle fibres that reflect their chosen sports (also see Case Study – Muscle fibre types in elite athletes).

Case Study: Muscle fibre types in elite athletes

Skeletal muscles normally contain a balanced mixture of slow- and fast-twitch fibres. The actual composition of an individual's muscles is genetically determined. Some people inherit a higher than average percentage of type 1; others a higher than average percentage of type 2. It is thought therefore that the former are more suited to endurance sports whereas the latter have an edge in power sports.

It is certainly the case that a correlation exists between the type of sporting event performed by athletes who eventually excel in their field at a world-class level and the genetically determined ratio of their slow to fast muscle fibres. Olympic sprinters, for example, have been shown to possess up to **80% fast-twitch** fibres in their leg muscles whereas elite athletes who excel in marathons often have around **80% slow-twitch** fibres in the same muscles. It must also be kept in mind that athletic success is also closely related to the quantity and quality of intensive practice undertaken by the athlete during training.

Testing Your Knowledge Chapters 7 and 8

1 Rewrite the following sentence to include the correct answer at each underlined choice.
ADP/ATP is used to transfer energy to cellular processes (such as protein synthesis/digestion and transmission of nerve impulses/responses) that release/require energy. (4)

2 Explain the following: Despite the fact that the human body is able to produce ATP at a rate of around 400 g/h, at any given moment there are only about 50 g of ATP present in the body. (2)

3 Draw up a table to compare fast- and slow-twitch muscle fibres with reference to major storage fuels used, relative number of mitochondria and relative concentration of myoglobin. (3)

Applying Your Knowledge and Skills

1 The information in Table 8.2 is a set of mean values based on data obtained from many elite athletes.
   a) Present the data in the two columns referring to percentage of energy as a bar chart using two different colours. (3)
   b) Draw THREE conclusions from the data. (3)
   c) i) Calculate the energy expended per metre by athletes performing in events 1 and 5.
      ii) By how many times is the energy expenditure greater in event 1 compared with event 5? (3)

2 The graph in Figure 8.3 shows the concentration of lactate in the blood of an athlete over a period of time.
   a) i) What was the concentration of lactate at 12.28?
      ii) At which TWO times was the concentration of lactate found to be 0.56 mg/cm^3? (2)
   b) i) Between which of the following four times did the athlete undergo 9 minutes of intensive exercise?
      A 12.00 and 12.10
      B 12.10 and 12.20
      C 12.20 and 12.30
      D 12.30 and 12.40
      ii) Explain your choice of answer. (2)
   c) i) By how many times was the concentration of lactate at 12.22 greater than that at 12.10?
      ii) Between which of the following times did the concentration of lactate decrease at the fastest rate?
      A 12.38 and 12.43
      B 12.48 and 12.53
      C 12.58 and 13.03
      D 13.08 and 13.13
      iii) Calculate the percentage decrease in lactate concentration that occurred between 12.32 and 12.55. (Make your answer correct to two decimal places.) (3)

Event	Length of race (m)	Total energy expended (kJ)	Volume of oxygen taken in (dm^3)	Energy from aerobic respiration (%)	Energy in anaerobic conditions (glycolysis) (%)
1	100	200	0	0	100
2	800	520	9	35	65
3	1500	720	19	55	45
4	10000	3000	133	90	10
5	42186	14000	685	98	2

Table 8.2

→

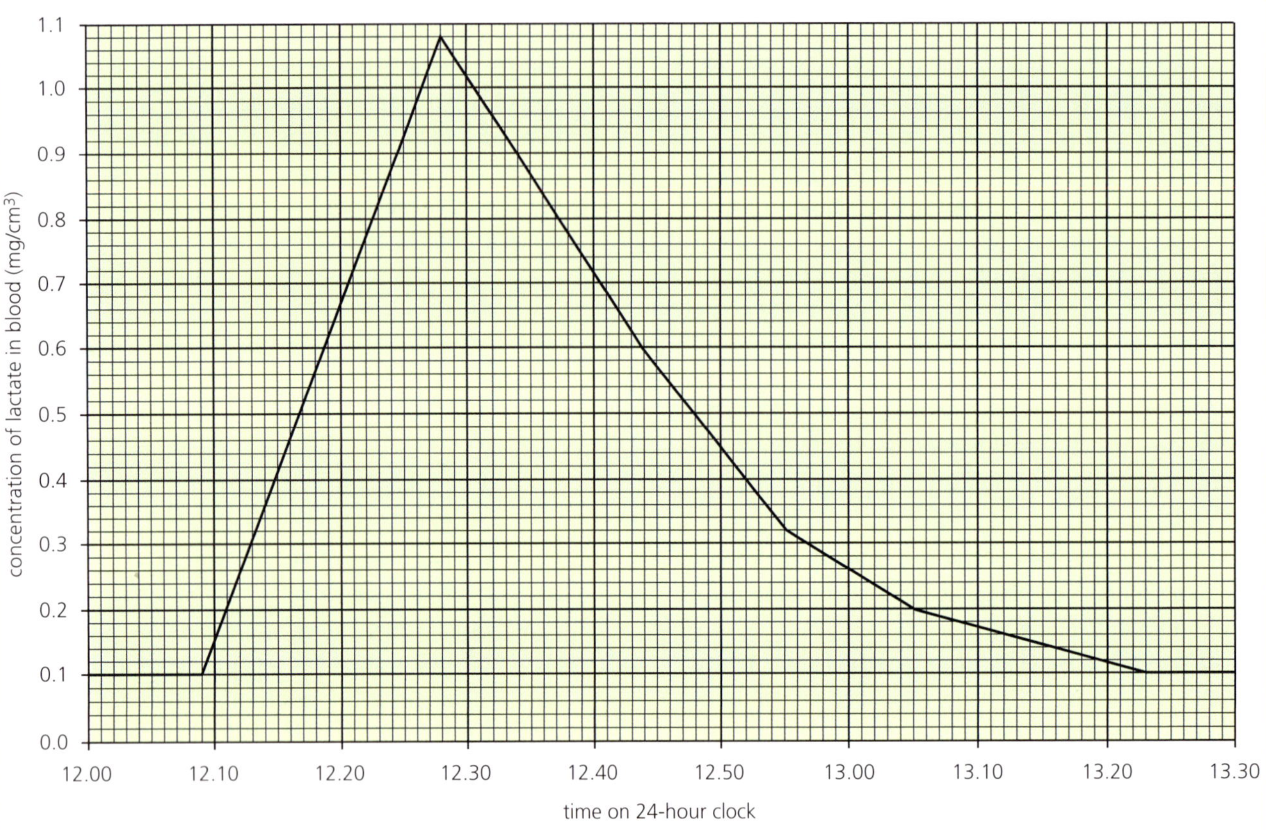

Figure 8.3

What You Should Know Chapters 6–8

acetyl	catabolism	endurance	inhibit	NADH	shape
activation	cellular	energy	inhibition	negative	structure
ADP	citrate	enzymes	inhibitors	orientation	substrate
affinity	competitive	fatigue	investment	oxygen	transferred
anabolism	complex	fibres	irreversible	phosphorylation	transition
ATP	concentration	glycolysis	lactate	product	transport
ATP synthase	debt	hydrogen	lowering	pyruvate	twitch
break	electron	induced	metabolism	regulated	water

Table 8.3 Word bank for Chapters 6–8

→

1 Cell ______ encompasses all the enzyme-catalysed reactions that occur in a cell.

2 ______ consists of biosynthetic metabolic pathways that build up ______ molecules from simpler constituents and need a supply of energy; ______ consists of metabolic pathways that ______ down larger molecules into smaller ones and usually release ______.

3 For a metabolic reaction to occur, ______ energy is needed to form a ______ state from which end products are produced. ______ catalyse biochemical reactions by ______ the activation energy needed by the reactants to form their transition state.

4 Substrate molecules have an ______ for the active site on an enzyme. The active site's shape determines the ______ of the reactants on it and it binds to them closely with an ______ fit.

5 The enzymes controlling a metabolic pathway usually work as a group. Although some steps are ______, most metabolic reactions are reversible. The direction in which the reaction occurs depends on factors such as concentration of the ______ and removal of a ______ as it becomes converted to another metabolite.

6 Each step in a metabolic pathway is ______ by an enzyme that catalyses a specific reaction. Regulatory control of enzyme action can be brought about by ______.

7 Molecules of a ______ inhibitor resemble the substrate in ______. They become attached to the active site and slow down the reaction. Their effect is reversed by increasing the ______ of substrate.

8 Some regulatory molecules stimulate enzyme activity or ______ it non-competitively by changing the ______ of the enzyme molecule and its active site(s).

9 Some metabolic pathways are controlled by end product ______, a form of ______ feedback control.

10 ______ is a high-energy compound. It is regenerated from ______ and P_i by phosphorylation using energy released during cellular respiration. ______ also occurs when P_i and energy are ______ from ATP to a reactant in a pathway.

11 Cellular respiration begins with ______, the breakdown of glucose to ______. This consists of an energy ______ phase and an energy payoff phase with a net gain of two molecules of ATP.

12 In the presence of oxygen, pyruvate is broken down into carbon dioxide and an ______ group. With the help of coenzyme A, the acetyl group enters the citric acid cycle by combining with oxaloacetate to become ______.

13 As one respiratory substrate is converted to another in the citric acid cycle, carbon dioxide is released, ATP is formed and pairs of ______ ions and electrons are removed and passed to coenzyme NAD, forming NADH.

14 ______ passes its electrons to ______ transport chains where the energy released is used to pump hydrogen ions across inner mitochondrial membranes. The return flow of these hydrogen ions makes part of each ______ molecule rotate and catalyse the synthesis of ATP. ______, the final electron acceptor, combines with hydrogen ions and electrons to form ______.

15 ATP generated during respiration is used to transfer energy to ______ processes that need energy.

16 During a period of vigorous exercise, muscle cells do not receive the adequate supply of oxygen needed for the electron ______ chain to operate. Instead of entering the citric acid cycle, pyruvate is converted to ______ and ______ of muscles occurs. Any oxygen ______ that develops is repaid when the vigorous exercise comes to a halt.

17 Skeletal muscle contains fast-twitch ______, good for short-lived power events, and slow-______ fibres, good for ______ activities.

2 Physiology and Health

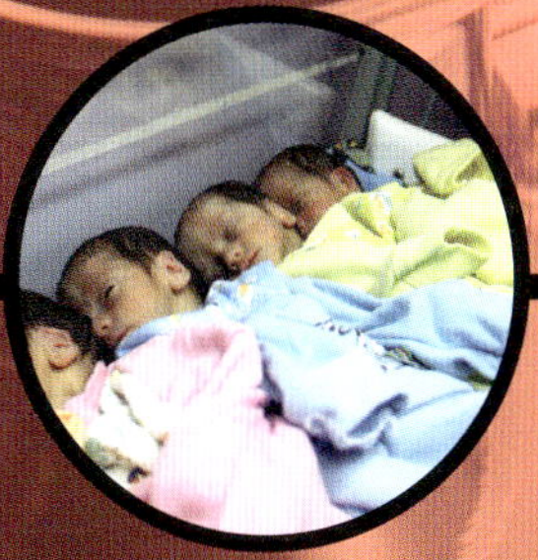

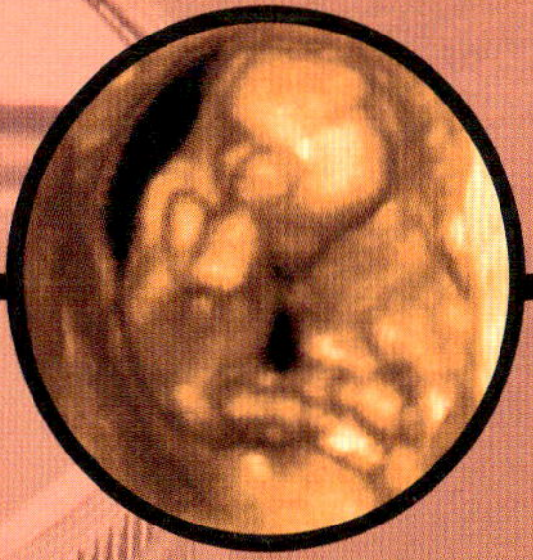

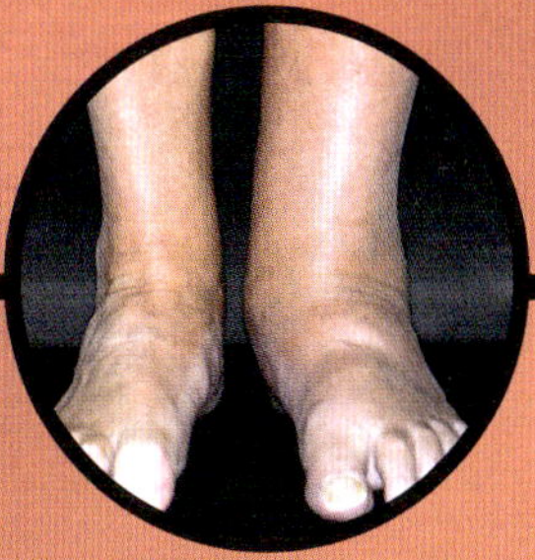

9 Gamete production and fertilisation

Testes

The reproductive system of the human male is shown in Figure 9.1. The testes are the site of **sperm** production and the manufacture of the male sex hormone **testosterone**. Sperm (full name spermatozoa) are male gametes formed from germline cells in tiny tubes called **seminiferous tubules**. These tubules unite to form coiled tubes that connect to the **sperm duct**. It is by the sperm duct that free-swimming sperm leave the testis. Testosterone is produced by **interstitial cells** located in the tissue between the seminiferous tubules. Testosterone passes directly into the bloodstream.

Sperm are **mobile**. On being released during sexual intercourse inside the female body, they move actively through the uterus and along the oviducts where they may meet an egg.

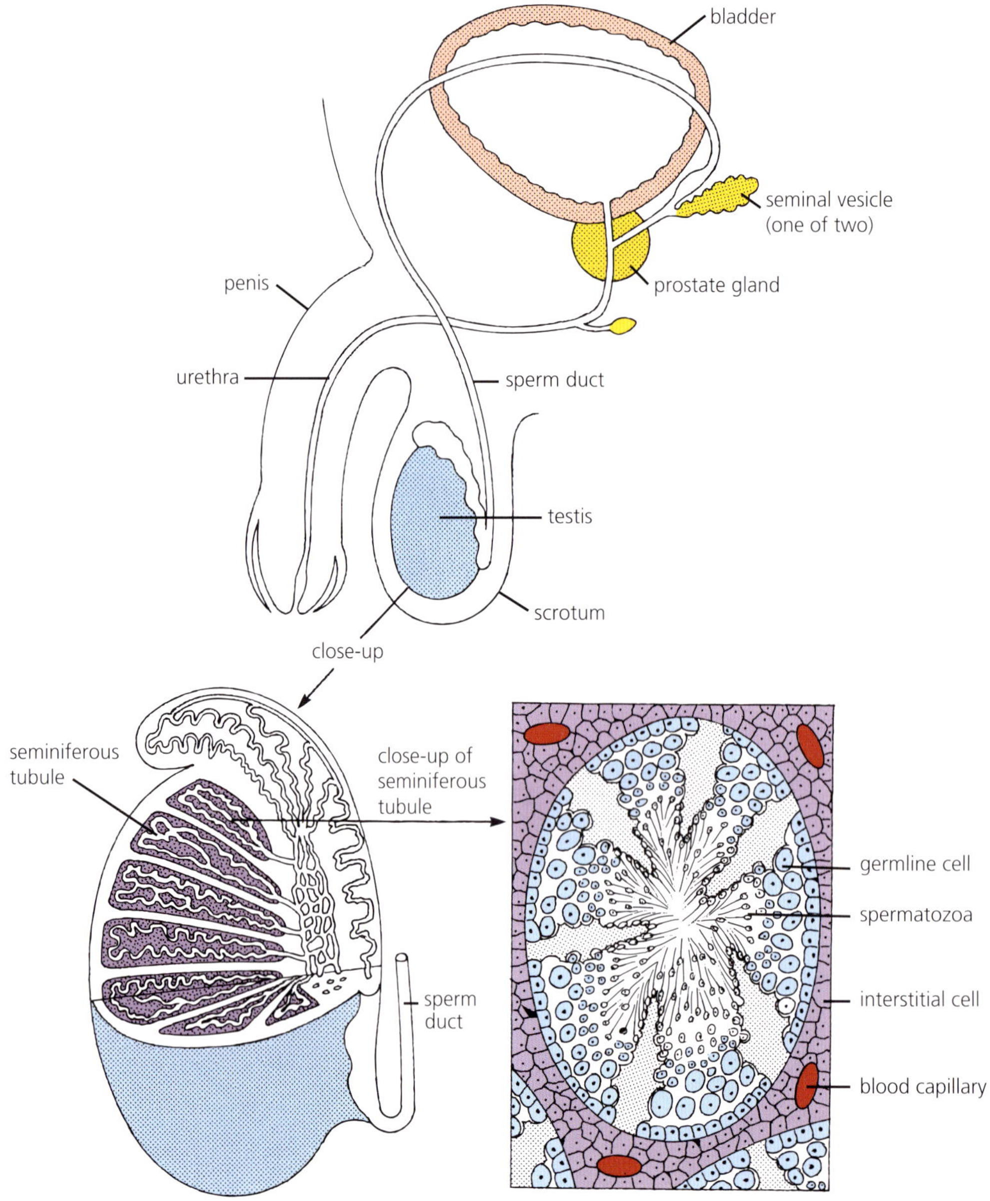

Figure 9.1 Male reproductive system

Accessory glands

The **seminal vesicles** (see Figure 9.1) secrete a liquid rich in fructose. This sugar provides sperm with the **energy** needed for mobility following their release by the male at ejaculation. The liquid secreted by the seminal vesicles also contains hormone-like compounds that stimulate contractions of the female reproductive tract. These movements help the sperm to reach the oviduct at a much faster rate than could be achieved by swimming alone.

The **prostate gland** (see Figure 9.1) secretes a thin, lubricating liquid containing **enzymes** whose action maintains the fluid medium at the **optimum viscosity** for sperm mobility. **Semen** is the collective name given to the milky liquid released by the male. It contains sperm from the testes and the fluid secretions from the seminal vesicles and prostate gland that maintain the **mobility** and **viability** of sperm.

Ovaries

The reproductive system of the human female is shown in Figure 9.2. **Eggs (ova)** are formed from germline cells in the **ovaries**. The ovaries contain immature eggs at various stages of development. Each egg (ovum) is surrounded by a **follicle**, which secretes the hormone **oestrogen** and protects the developing egg. Following

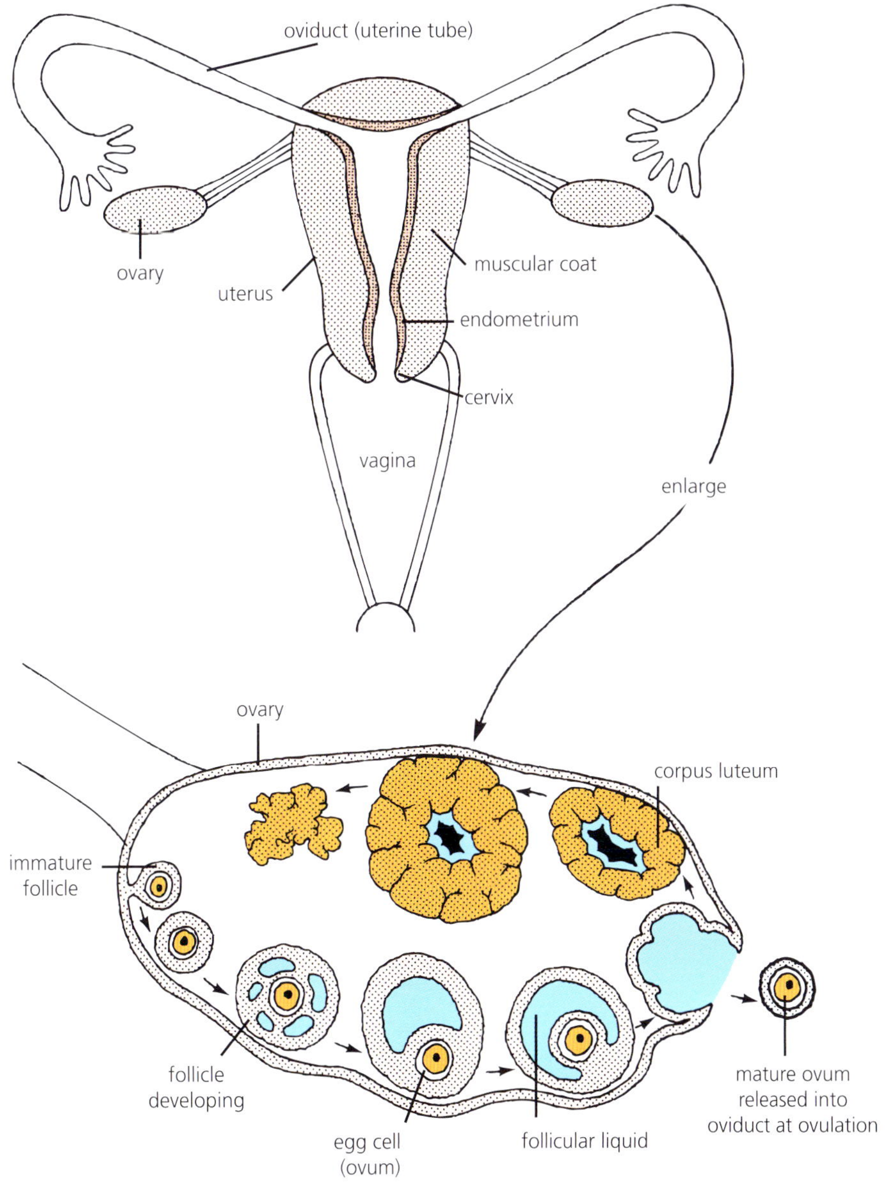

Figure 9.2 Female reproductive system

ovulation (release of an egg), the follicle develops into a **corpus luteum** (see Figure 9.2), which secretes the hormone **progesterone** (see Chapter 10).

Fertilisation

Mature ova are released into the oviduct at ovulation. Each ovum is passively moved along the oviduct by the sweeping action of cilia. The process of **fertilisation** takes place in the **oviduct**. It is dependent upon the mobility of sperm to bring the two gametes together, enabling them to fuse and form a **zygote**.

Testing Your Knowledge and Applying Your Knowledge and Skills questions for Chapter 9 are to be found on pages 123–5.

10 Hormonal control of reproduction

Hormonal control

Hormones are chemical messengers produced by an animal's **endocrine** (ductless) glands and secreted directly into the bloodstream. When a hormone reaches a certain **target tissue**, it brings about a specific effect. Hormones control the onset of puberty, sperm production and the menstrual cycle.

Hormonal onset of puberty

At puberty, the **hypothalamus** (see Figure 10.1) secretes a releaser hormone whose target is the **pituitary gland**. On being stimulated the pituitary responds by producing two hormones. The first of these is called **FSH** (follicle-stimulating hormone); the second is known in men as **ICSH** (interstitial cell-stimulating hormone) and in women as **LH** (luteinising hormone). The release of these hormones at puberty triggers the onset of sperm production in men and the menstrual cycle in women.

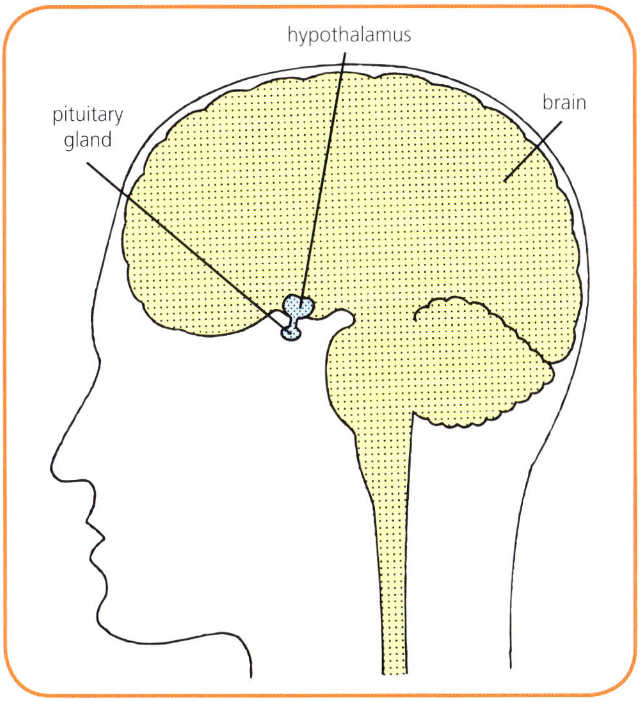

Figure 10.1 Location of hypothalamus and pituitary gland

Hormonal control of sperm production

Influence of pituitary hormones on testes

The two functions of the testes are regulated by the pituitary hormones. When FSH arrives in the bloodstream, it promotes **sperm production** in the seminiferous tubules. When ICSH arrives, it stimulates interstitial cells to produce the male sex hormone **testosterone**.

Influence of testosterone

Testosterone stimulates **sperm production** in the seminiferous tubules. It also activates the prostate gland and seminal vesicles to produce their secretions.

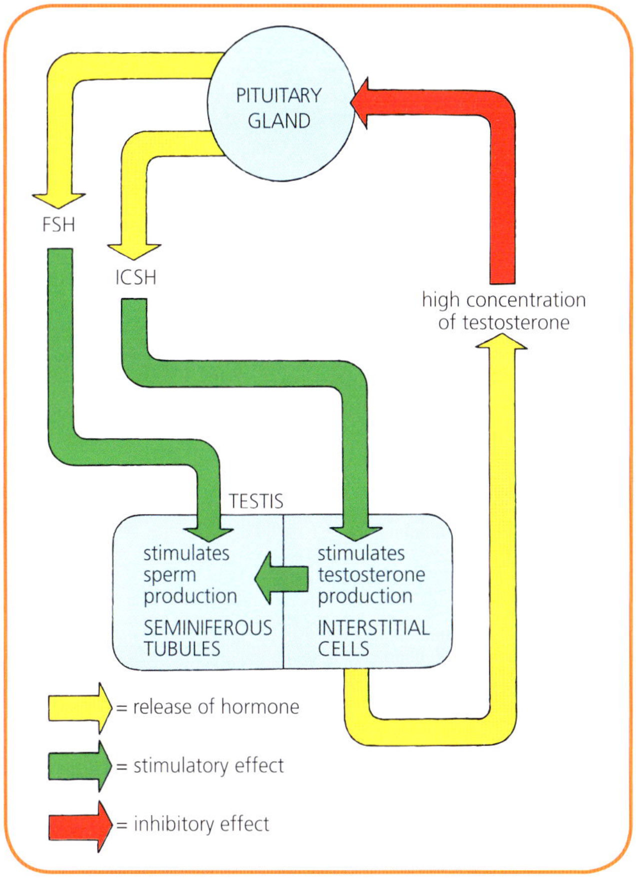

Figure 10.2 Self-regulation of testosterone production

Self-regulation of testosterone production

As the concentration of testosterone builds up in the bloodstream, it reaches a level where it **inhibits** the secretion of FSH and ICSH by the pituitary gland (see Figure 10.2). Since this leads in turn to a decrease in testosterone concentration, it is soon followed by a resumption of activity by the pituitary gland, which makes FSH and ICSH again, and so on. This type of self-regulating mechanism is called **negative feedback control**.

Hormonal control of the menstrual cycle

Influence of pituitary hormones on ovaries

FSH and LH from the pituitary gland affect the ovaries in several ways. FSH stimulates the development and maturation of each **follicle** (see Figure 10.3). It also stimulates ovary tissue to secrete the sex hormone **oestrogen**.

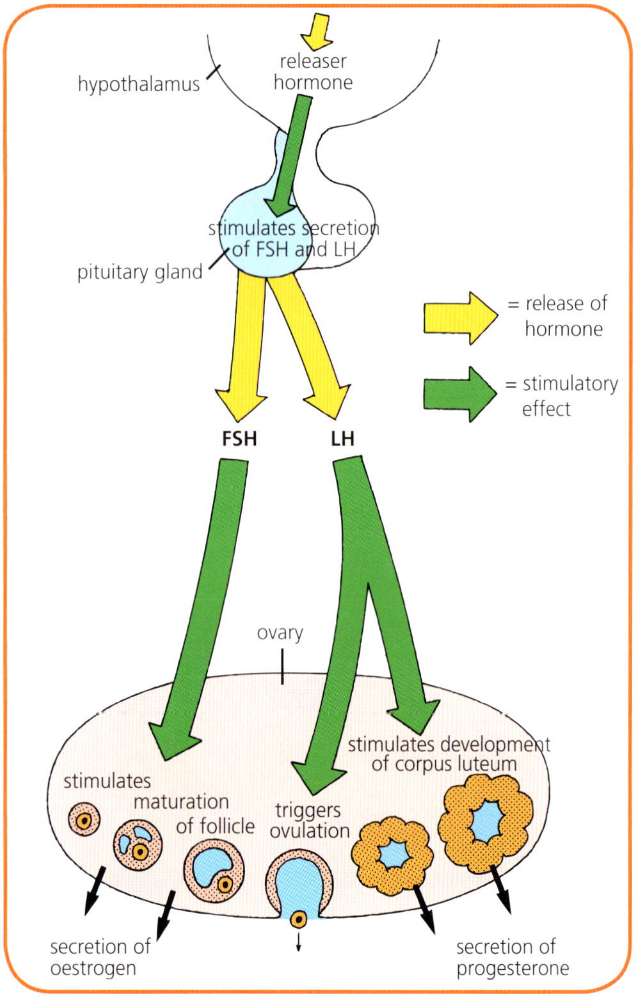

Figure 10.3 Effect of pituitary hormones on ovary

LH triggers **ovulation** (the release of an ovum from a follicle). It also brings about the development of the **corpus luteum** from the follicle and then stimulates the corpus luteum to secrete the sex hormone **progesterone**. Oestrogen and progesterone are known as the **ovarian** hormones.

Influence of ovarian hormones on uterus and pituitary gland

Oestrogen

Oestrogen stimulates **proliferation** (cell division) of the inner layer of the uterus, called the **endometrium**, thereby effecting its repair following menstruation and preparing it for implantation. This ovarian hormone also stimulates the secretion of LH by the pituitary gland (see Figure 10.4).

Progesterone

Progesterone promotes the **further development** and **vascularisation** of the endometrium into a spongy layer rich in blood vessels, making it ready to receive a blastocyst (embryo) if fertilisation occurs. Progesterone also **inhibits** the secretion of FSH and LH by the pituitary gland (see Figure 10.5).

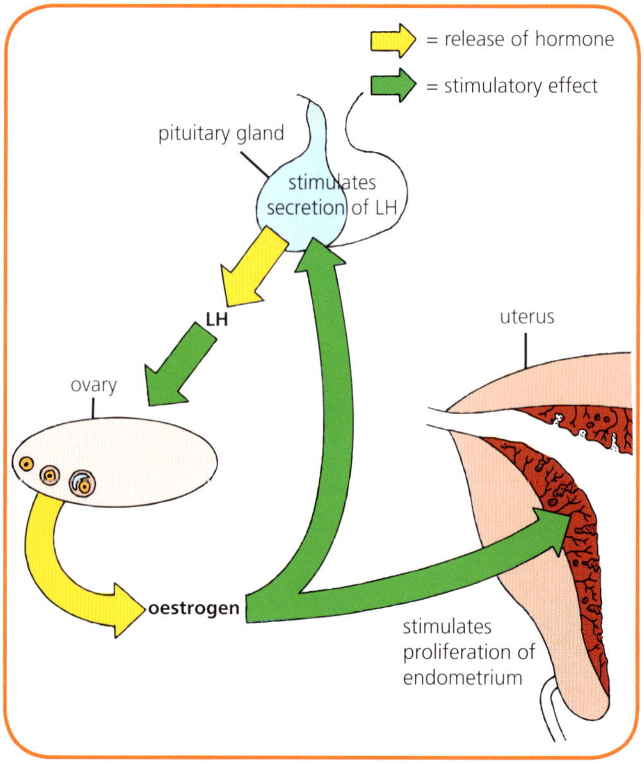

Figure 10.4 Effect of oestrogen on uterus and pituitary

The menstrual cycle

The events described above that are under hormonal control in the human female fit together as interacting parts of a synchronised system – the **menstrual cycle**.

A cycle takes about 28 days though this can vary from woman to woman. Each cycle is continuous with the one that went before and the one about to follow. For convenience the first day of menstruation (as indicated by menstrual blood flow) is regarded as 'day one' of the cycle. The menstrual cycle is summarised in Figure 10.6. It is made up of two phases.

Follicular phase

During this first half of the cycle, FSH from the pituitary gland stimulates:

- the development and maturation of a follicle
- the production of oestrogen by the ovarian tissues.

As the concentration of the oestrogen builds up, it brings about the repair and proliferation of the endometrium. Eventually the high concentration of oestrogen triggers a surge in the production of LH (and FSH) by the pituitary gland at about day 14. This **surge of LH** is the direct cause of **ovulation** since it makes the blister-like wall of the follicle rupture and release the egg. Ovulation usually occurs around the midpoint of the menstrual cycle. The egg is then moved slowly along the oviduct. During a short period of about 3–4 days, fertilisation may occur if the egg meets a sperm.

Luteal phase

During this second half of the cycle (following ovulation), LH stimulates the follicle to become the corpus luteum. This gland-like structure secretes progesterone and oestrogen. The subsequent rise in progesterone concentration stimulates further development of the endometrium. It becomes thick

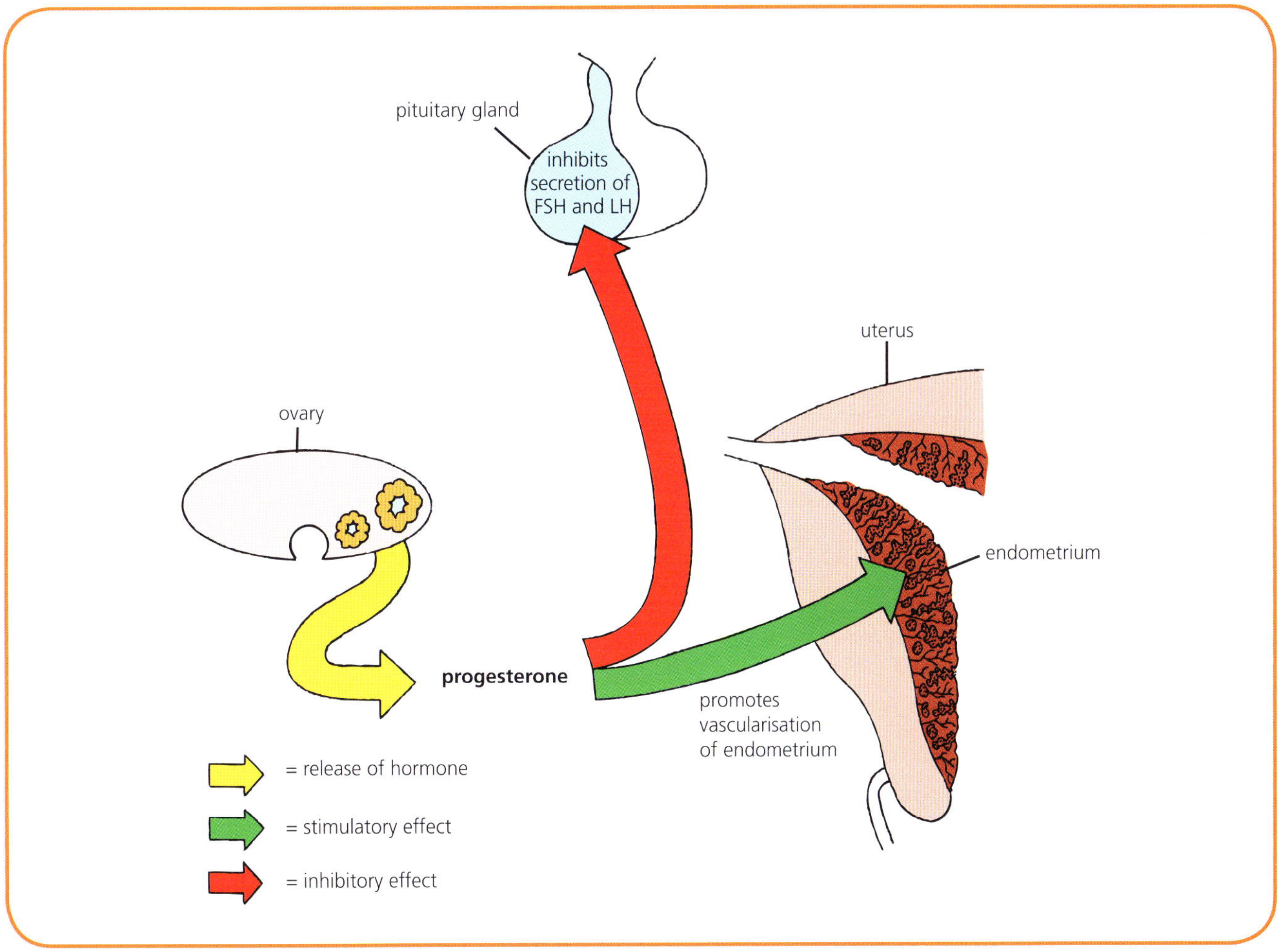

Figure 10.5 Effect of progesterone on uterus and pituitary

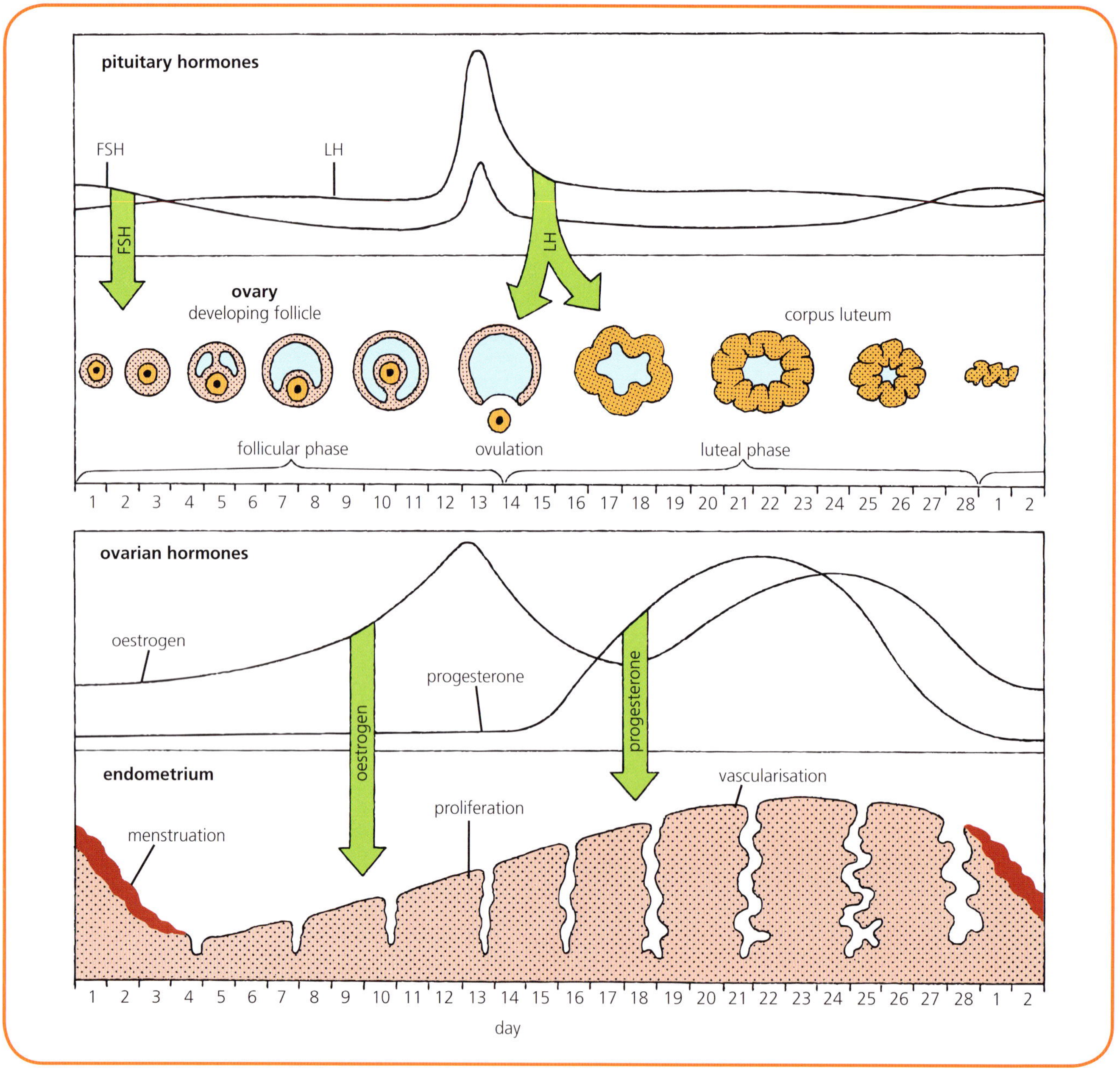

Figure 10.6 Menstrual cycle

(with an increase in vascular blood vessels) and spongy, ready to accept and nourish the early embryo, if fertilisation, cell division and implantation occur.

During this luteal phase the combined high levels of oestrogen and progesterone also trigger an **inhibitory effect** on the pituitary gland. Concentrations of FSH and LH drop as a result and no new follicles develop at this time. This is a further example of negative feedback control.

No fertilisation

If fertilisation does not occur, **lack of LH** leads, in turn, to the **degeneration** of the corpus luteum by about day 22 in the cycle. This is followed by a **rapid drop** in progesterone (and oestrogen). By day 28 in the cycle, these ovarian hormones are at such a low level that the endometrium can no longer be maintained and **menstruation** begins. This involves the loss of the inner layer of the endometrium accompanied by a small volume of blood. This stage continues for a few days.

Fertilisation

If fertilisation does occur, the embryo secretes a hormone that maintains the corpus luteum. It continues to secrete progesterone which prevents menstruation from taking place. After about six weeks the placenta takes on the job of secreting progesterone.

Testing Your Knowledge Chapters 9 and 10

1 a) i) Where in a testis are sperm produced?
ii) Which hormone is produced by interstitial cells? (2)
b) i) Which accessory glands secrete a liquid rich in fructose?
ii) Describe the contribution to fertilisation made by this chemical. (2)

2 a) Name the structure that surrounds an egg in an ovary. (1)
b) What does this structure develop into, following ovulation? (1)

3 Copy and complete Table 10.1, which refers to four hormones in the female body. (8)

4 Decide whether each of the following statements is true or false and then use T or F to indicate your choice. Where a statement is false, give the word that should have been used in place of the word in bold print. (6)
a) The menstrual cycle consists of the **endometrial** phase and the luteal phase.
b) FSH stimulates ovary tissue to secrete **oestrogen**.
c) Oestrogen stimulates the **proliferation** of the endometrium.
d) LH triggers the process of **menstruation**.
e) Progesterone inhibits secretion of FSH and LH by the **ovaries**.
f) Lack of LH leads to **degeneration** of the corpus luteum.

Hormone	Site of production	One function of the hormone
		Stimulates the development and maturation of each follicle
		Brings about development of the corpus luteum
		Stimulates secretion of LH by the pituitary gland
		Promotes vascularisation of the endometrium

Table 10.1

Applying Your Knowledge and Skills Chapters 9–10

1 The male reproductive system is shown in Figure 10.7.

a) Using only the appropriate letters, indicate the route taken by sperm from site of production to point of exit from the male body. (1)

b) Copy and complete Table 10.2. (8)

c) i) Name structure B.

ii) Name the hormones that it produces.

iii) State ONE effect of these hormones on the pituitary gland. (4)

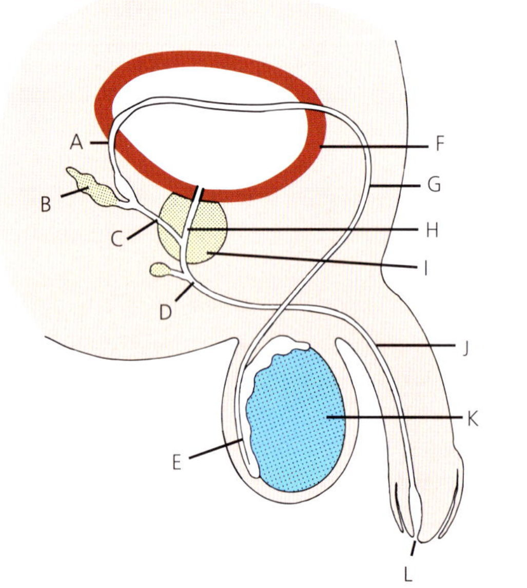

Figure 10.7

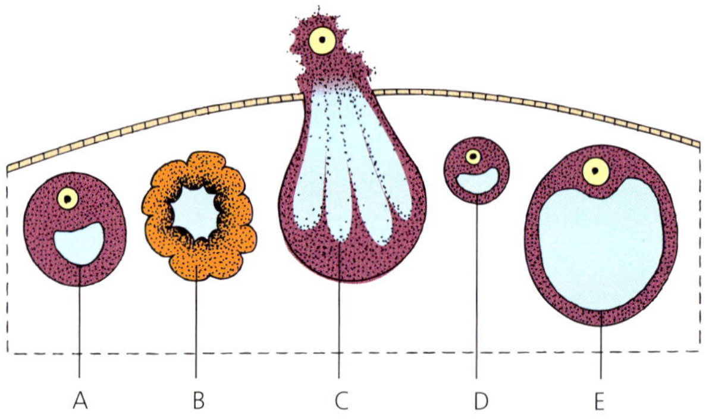

Figure 10.8

2 Figure 10.8 shows a small part of an ovary and some of the stages that occur during maturation of a follicle.

a) Arrange stages A–E into the correct order starting with D. (1)

b) i) Which of these stages are controlled by FSH?

ii) What name is given to the process that occurs at C?

iii) Which hormone triggers this process?

iv) Which endocrine gland secretes the hormone that you gave as your answer to **iii)**? (4)

3 **a)** Use the data in Table 10.3 to construct a chart to illustrate the change in the thickness of the endometrium that occurred during a menstrual cycle. (3)

b) Identify a 3-day period in April during which menstruation was occurring. (1)

c) Predict the date in April when ovulation occurred. (1)

d) Answer HIGH or LOW in each of the following statements:

i) The relative concentration of oestrogen on 7 April would be ______.

ii) The relative concentration of FSH on 16 April would be ______.

iii) The relative concentration of progesterone on 16 April would be ______.

iv) The relative concentration of LH on 23 April would be ______. (4)

Letter in Figure 10.7 indicating accessory gland	Name of this accessory gland	Example of substance secreted by accessory gland that contributes to fertilisation	Way in which named substance contributes to fertilisation

Table 10.2

→

Date		Thickness of endometrium (mm)
Month	Day	
March	26	4.2
	27	2.6
	28	1.8
	29	1.2
	30	1.6
	31	2.0
April	1	2.2
	2	2.4
	3	2.7
	4	3.0
	5	3.4
	6	3.7
	7	4.0
	8	4.4
	9	4.7
	10	5.0
	11	5.4
	12	5.7
	13	5.9
	14	6.0
	15	6.1
	16	6.2
	17	6.2
	18	6.2
	19	6.1
	20	6.0
	21	5.8
	22	5.4
	23	4.2
	24	2.6
	25	1.8

Table 10.3

4 A tiny part of the human testis is shown in microscopic detail in Figure 10.9.

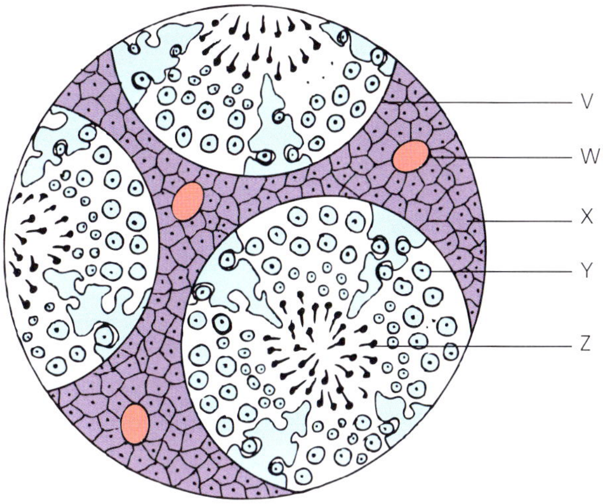

Figure 10.9

a) Name the parts labelled V, W, X, Y and Z. (5)
b) Which of these secretes testosterone? (1)
c) Which hormone from the pituitary stimulates these structures to produce testosterone? (1)
d) Briefly describe the means by which excessive production of testosterone is prevented? (3)

5 Give an account of the hormonal control of a menstrual cycle that does not involve fertilisation under the headings:

a) follicular phase (4)
b) luteal phase. (5)

11 Biology of controlling fertility

Knowledge of the biology of fertilisation is put to effective use when designing treatments for infertility and devising methods of contraception.

Fertile periods

Continuous versus cyclical fertility

The negative feedback effect of testosterone (see Figure 10.2, page 119) maintains a relatively constant level of the pituitary hormones (FSH and ICSH) in the bloodstream of men. This results in a fairly steady quantity of testosterone being secreted and sperm being produced. Therefore men are **continuously** fertile.

This contrasts markedly with the **cyclical** fertility of women. The delicate interplay of pituitary and ovarian hormones that occurs in their body normally results in the **period of fertility** being restricted to the 1–2 days immediately following ovulation.

Calculation of the fertile period

Temperature

Within the menstrual cycle, the alternating processes of menstruation and ovulation are separated by intervals of about 2 weeks. Approximately 1 day after the LH surge that triggers ovulation, the woman's **body temperature** rises by about 0.5°C under the action of progesterone. It remains at this elevated level for the duration of the luteal phase of the cycle (see Figure 11.1).

The period of fertility lasts for about 1–2 days. The infertile phase is resumed, on average, after the third daily recording of the higher temperature by which time the unfertilised egg has disintegrated.

Mucus

The **cervical mucus** secreted into the vagina during the fertile period is thin and watery to allow sperm easy access to the female reproductive system. However, after ovulation, the mucus gradually increases in viscosity under the action of progesterone, showing that the system has returned to the infertile phase.

Use of indicators

The above indicators can be used by a woman to calculate her fertile period. This knowledge is useful to a couple who wish to have a child and want to know when sexual intercourse is most likely to achieve fertilisation.

Treatments for infertility

Stimulating ovulation

A woman may fail to ovulate because of an underlying factor, such as failure of the pituitary gland to secrete adequate FSH or LH. In such cases, ovulation can be successfully stimulated by:

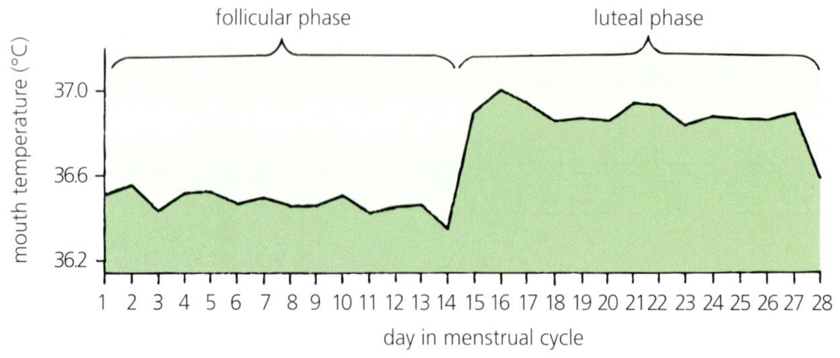

Figure 11.1 Rise in temperature during the luteal phase

- drugs that mimic the normal action of FSH and LH
- drugs that prevent the negative feedback effect of oestrogen on FSH secretion during the luteal phase of the menstrual cycle.

On some occasions these drugs are so effective that they bring about 'super-ovulation' and this can lead to a multiple birth such as quintuplets (see Figures 11.2 and 11.3). Drugs that cause super-ovulation are also used to promote the release of eggs to be used for IVF (see below).

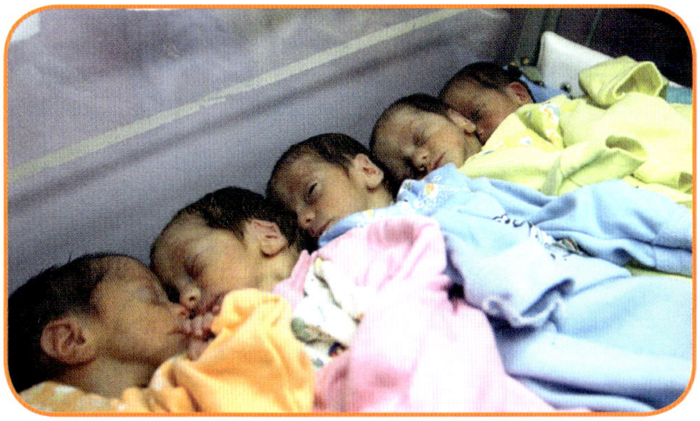

Figure 11.2 Quintuplets

Figure 11.3 Effect of 'super-ovulation'

Artificial insemination

Insemination is the introduction of semen into the female reproductive tract. It occurs naturally as a result of sexual intercourse.

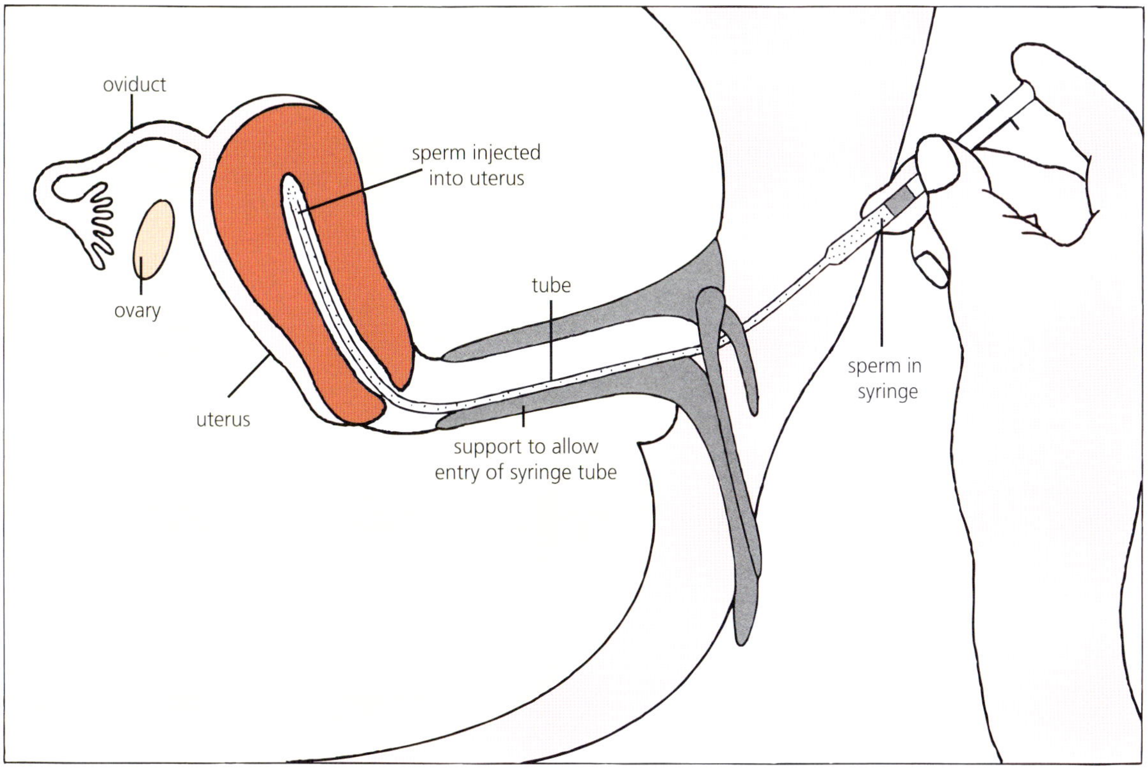

Figure 11.4 Artificial insemination

Artificial insemination is the insertion of semen into the female tract by some means other than sexual intercourse. Artificial insemination may be employed as a method of treating infertility. If a man has a **low sperm count**, several samples of his semen can be collected over a period of time and each preserved by freezing until required. They are then defrosted and released together into his partner's cervical region at the time when she is most likely to be fertile (see Figure 11.4).

Artificial insemination can also be used to insert semen of a **donor** who has a normal sperm count into the cervical region of a woman whose partner is sterile.

In vitro fertilisation (IVF)

This method of treatment attempts to solve the problem of infertility caused by a blockage of the oviducts (uterine tubes). It enables fertilisation to occur outside the bodies of the would-be parents in a culture dish. Figure 11.5 shows some of the stages involved in the procedure.

- At stage 1, the woman is given hormonal treatment to stimulate multiple ovulation.
- At stage 2, a surgical procedure is employed to remove several of these eggs from around her ovary using a piece of equipment similar to a syringe.
- At stage 3, the eggs are mixed with sperm in a culture dish of nutrient medium to allow fertilisation to occur. Alternatively a sperm may be injected directly into an egg at this stage (see ICSI on page 129).
- At stage 4, the fertilised eggs are incubated in the nutrient medium for 2–3 days to allow cell division to occur and form embryos each composed of eight (or more) cells.
- At stage 5, two (or three) of the embryos are chosen and then inserted via the vagina into the mother's uterus (which is now ready for implantation).
- At stage 6, the remaining embryos are frozen and stored in case a second attempt at implantation is required.

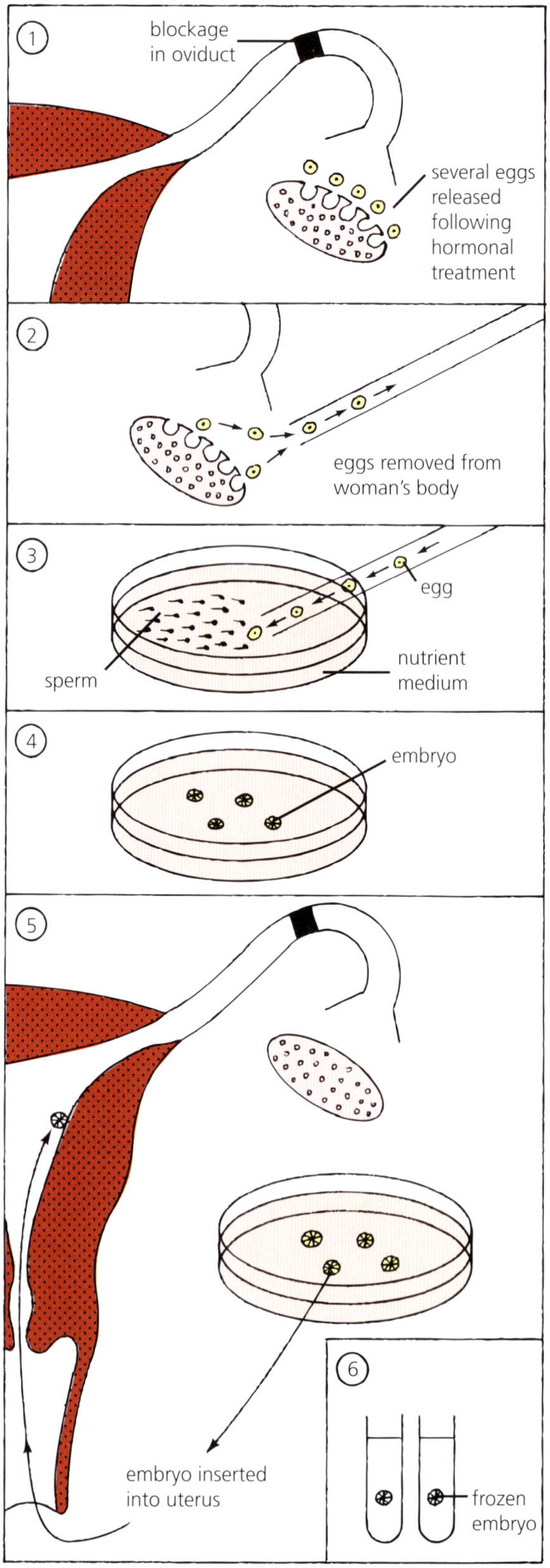

Figure 11.5 *In vitro* fertilisation (IVF)

Pre-implantation genetic screening and diagnosis

Before stage 5 is carried out, one or two cells may be removed and tested for genetic abnormalities. The test may take one of two forms:

- **pre-implantation genetic screening (PGS)** – a non-specific approach that checks the embryo for single gene disorders and common chromosomal abnormalities in general

- **pre-implantation genetic diagnosis (PGD)** – a specific approach that is used to check for a *known* chromosomal or gene defect.

These tests enable experts to select which embryos should and which should not be allowed to become implanted in the mother's endometrium.

Related Topic

Ethics of PGS and PGD

Some people strongly support the practices of PGS and PGD because they offer **reassurance** to couples who would otherwise be at high risk of producing children with serious genetic disorders. In the absence of these techniques, many of these couples would probably choose to remain childless. The supporters also claim that in addition to helping the individual families affected, a reduced frequency of genetic diseases and disorders is of **great benefit** to society as a whole.

Other people are opposed to PGS and PGD. They insist that it is morally wrong to interfere with the process of conception by making it **selective**. They argue that these procedures are the start of **eugenics**, whereby the human race would be subjected to selective breeding in order to 'improve its quality'. They speculate that this route could lead to a world of 'designer' children in which genetic engineering of offspring would become routine practice.

Intracytoplasmic sperm injection

During IVF, eggs and sperm are mixed together in a culture dish. There is only a good chance of fertilisation occurring if a large number of active sperm are present. In those cases where the man's sperm count is low or many of his mature sperm are defective in some way, **intracytoplasmic sperm injection (ICSI)** can be employed.

This procedure involves drawing a healthy sperm into a syringe needle and then injecting it directly into an egg to bring about fertilisation (see Figure 11.6). During the procedure the egg is held in place by a holding tool. ICSI is commonly used as part of IVF treatment.

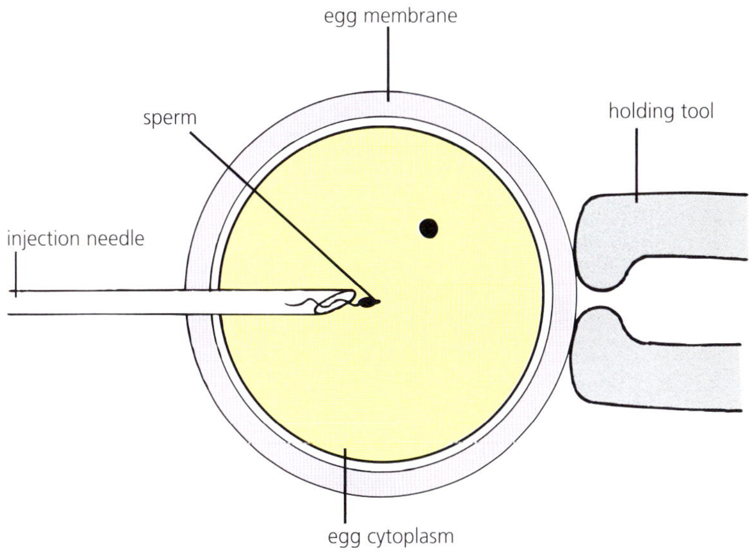

Figure 11.6 Intracytoplasmic sperm injection

Related Activity

Examining data on success rate for IVF and its effect on long-term health

Success rate

Tables 11.1, 11.2 and 11.3 show data that refer to IVF success rates for the UK.

From Table 11.1 it can be concluded that the number of patients receiving IVF treatment and the number of babies born as a result of it increased significantly over the period of time considered. (It should be noted that the number of successful births is smaller than the number of babies born because some births are multiple.)

	Year			
	2006	2007	2008	2014
Number of patients	34 855	36 861	39 879	52 288
Number of cycles	44 275	46 829	50 687	67 708
Number of births as a result of IVF	10 242	11 091	12 211	14 206
Number of babies born	12 596	13 672	15 082	16 380

Table 11.1 Success rate for IVF over 3 years

Age of patient (years)	IVF success rate as live birth rate per cycle (%)			
	Year 2007	Year 2008	Year 2012	Year 2013
Under 35	32.3	33.1	32.9	32.8
35–37	27.7	27.2	27.3	29.5
38–39	19.2	19.3	20.7	21.8
40–42	11.9	12.5	13.2	13.7
43–44	3.4	4.9	5.4	4.9
Over 44	3.1	2.5	1.1	2.0

Table 11.2 Effect of age on IVF success rate

		State of embryo used in IVF	
		Fresh	Frozen
Number of patients		33 520	7 792
Number of cycles		39 334	8 959
Number of births as a result of IVF		10 010	1 618
Number of babies born		12 480	1 855
IVF success rates as percentage of live birth rates by age	Under 35 years	33.1	22.2
	35–37	27.2	17.8
	38–39	19.3	15.8
	Over 39 years	10.7	11.9

Table 11.3 Effect of freezing on success rate for IVF

→

From Table 11.2 it can be concluded that the chance of successfully giving birth following IVF treatment is highest for women under the age of 35 and decreases steadily with increasing age of patient.

From Table 11.3 it can be concluded that during the period studied more fresh than frozen embryos were used. In addition the success rate for IVF using fresh embryos was much higher for women of 39 and under but slightly lower for women over the age of 39.

Long-term health issues of IVF

Mother

Many thousands of children are born annually using IVF treatment involving drugs that stimulate the mother's ovaries to release a large number of eggs. About 6% of patients undergoing this form of IVF are found to experience hyperstimulation of their ovaries. In addition, medical experts are concerned that stimulated-cycle IVF may be exposing many women to an increased risk of uterine cancer in later life and urge that research be carried out in this area. They also recommend that patients consider **natural-cycle** IVF in place of stimulated-cycle IVF despite the fact that the former's success rate is only 7–10% compared with 25–30% for the latter.

Child

Most children conceived through IVF tend to have a body mass at birth that is **significantly lower** than the average for full-term babies conceived naturally, and often closer to that of premature babies.

In general, children born with a low body mass are more likely to develop long-term **health problems** such as obesity, diabetes, heart conditions and hypertension in later life at around 50 or more years of age. Experts are concerned that children conceived through IVF will also be more prone to these conditions. However, the first successful IVF treatment was not carried out until 1978. Therefore no IVF-born people are old enough yet to allow a survey to be conducted and tentative conclusions to be drawn.

Contraception

Contraception is the intentional prevention of conception or pregnancy by natural or artificial means.

Physical methods of contraception

Barrier methods

A **barrier method** makes use of a device that physically blocks the ability of sperm to reach an ovum. These devices include:

- the **condom** – a rubber sheath that fits over the man's penis
- the **diaphragm** – a dome-shaped rubber cap that is inserted into the woman's vagina to block the cervix before each act of sexual intercourse
- the **cervical cap** – a rubber structure that fits tightly round the cervix and can be left in position for a few days.

These methods are very effective but they are not as successful as chemical methods (see page 132).

Intra-uterine devices

An **intra-uterine device (IUD)** is a T-shaped structure (see Case Study – Example of a physical contraceptive) that is fitted into the uterus for many months or even years to prevent the implantation of an embryo into the endometrium.

Sterilisation procedures

In men, **vasectomy** involves the cutting and tying of the two sperm ducts, thereby preventing sperm being released during sexual activity. (Sperm produced after this sterilisation procedure normally undergo phagocytosis and are destroyed.)

In women, **tubal ligation** involves the cutting and tying of the two oviducts (see Figure 11.7) to prevent eggs meeting sperm and reaching the uterus. Sterilisation is a highly effective means of contraception but it is normally irreversible.

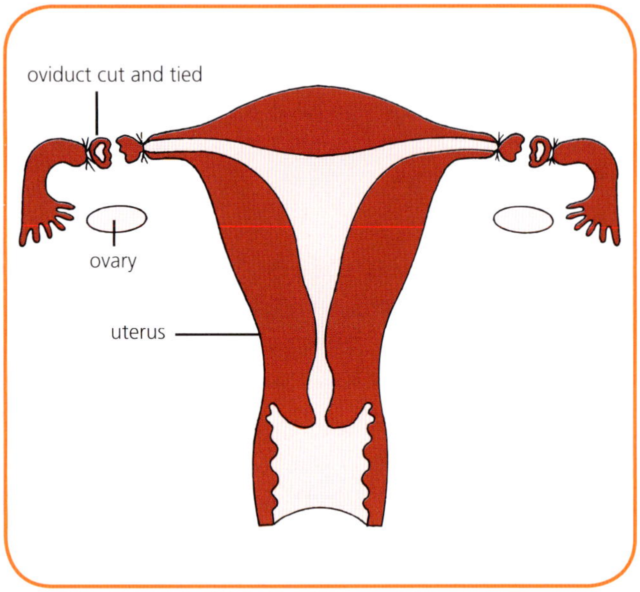

Figure 11.7 Sterilisation by tubal ligation

Chemical methods of contraception

Pills containing a combination of hormones

These **oral contraceptive pills** normally contain **synthetic progesterone** combined with **synthetic oestrogen**. One common method requires the woman to take a pill every day without fail for 3 weeks from the final day of the previous menstrual period. This procedure makes the concentration of progesterone and oestrogen in her bloodstream increase and exert negative feedback control.

Therefore, secretion of FSH and LH by the pituitary gland is inhibited. Since little or no FSH is present, follicle maturation remains inhibited and ovulation fails to occur. Dummy (placebo) pills are usually taken during the fourth week to allow the levels of oestrogen and progesterone to drop and menstruation to occur.

'Morning-after' pills

These are also known as **emergency hormonal contraception pills**. They often contain higher doses of the hormones (progesterone and oestrogen) found in standard oral contraceptive pills. They are taken by the woman after unprotected sexual intercourse to prevent implantation from occurring if fertilisation has taken place unintentionally. Ideally these pills should be taken as soon after unprotected sex as possible but may be effective up to about 72 hours. This form of contraception also inhibits ovulation.

'Mini pills'

These are also known as **progesterone-only pills** because they contain synthetic progesterone but not oestrogen. They work by causing thickening of cervical mucus, which reduces the viability of sperm and their access to the uterus.

Case Study: Example of a physical contraceptive

Although widely used to mean any system of birth control that prevents pregnancy, strictly speaking the word *contraception* means prevention of conception. If this definition is adhered to strictly, then an intra-uterine device (IUD) has to be described as a contragestic device since it prevents the *gestation* of an already conceived embryo.

In the UK, the term **intra-uterine device (IUD)** refers to a T-shaped plastic structure with copper wound around its outside (see Figure 11.8). It also has threads attached to it that can be used by a medical expert to gently remove the device when required. An IUD works in several ways:

- Its presence in the uterus stimulates the release of white blood cells and various substances that are hostile to sperm (and perhaps to the very early embryo).
- It impairs the mobility of sperm and prevents them reaching the egg.
- It irritates the lining of the uterus making it unreceptive to an embryo, which therefore fails to become implanted in the endometrium.

There is no denying that the IUD is an effective contraceptive device but it has tended to be less popular than other forms of contraception. This is probably due to the fact that it has had a history of causing **complications**, including inflammation of the uterus and oviducts and also ectopic pregnancies (those that result from the implantation of an embryo at a site other than the uterus).

→

In addition, many people feel uneasy about the **ethics** involved in preventing an already conceived embryo from becoming implanted in the endometrium. They prefer to use a method of contraception that stops sperm reaching an egg in the first place and therefore prevents any chance of conception taking place.

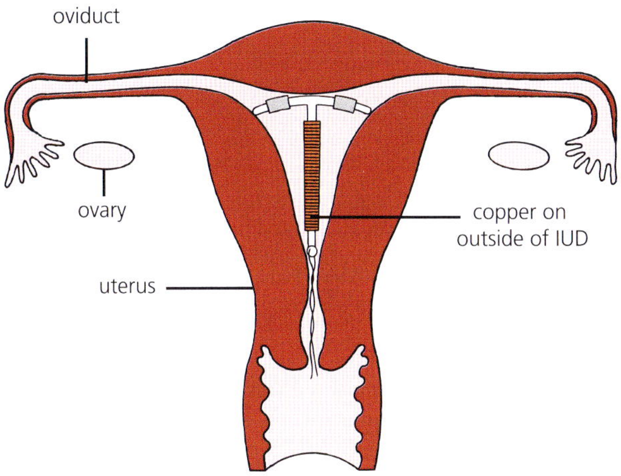

Figure 11.8 Intra-uterine device

Related Information

Comparison of success rate of different methods of contraception

Table 11.4 shows the result from a recent UK survey.

Method of contraception		Effectiveness based on typical use (%)
Physical	Condom (female internal)	79
	Condom (male external)	82
	Diaphragm	88
	Cervical cap	88
	Intra-uterine device	99
	Vasectomy (male sterilisation)	99
	Tubal ligation (female sterilisation)	99
Chemical	Oral contraceptive pill	91
	Contraceptive patch	91
	Contraceptive injection	94
Fertility awareness method (natural family planning by monitoring cervical secretions and basal body temperature)		76

Table 11.4 Effectiveness of different methods of contraception

Testing Your Knowledge

1 a) Distinguish clearly between the terms *continuous fertility* and *cyclical fertility* with reference to human beings. (2)

b) i) For how long does a woman's period of fertility last during each menstrual cycle, on average?

ii) Describe TWO signs that give an approximate indication of when this time occurs. (3)

2 a) What is *artificial insemination*? (1)

b) Under what TWO sets of circumstances might artificial insemination be used as a means of treating infertility? (2)

3 a) The following list gives the steps in the procedure employed during *in vitro* fertilisation. Arrange them into the correct order. (1)

A Incubation of fertilised eggs in nutrient medium.

B Deep-freezing of unused fertilised eggs.

C Stimulation of ovaries to bring about multiple ovulation.

D Mixing of eggs with sperm in a dish.

E Insertion of two or three fertilised eggs into the uterus.

F Removal of eggs from the mother's body.

b) What treatment is used in step **C**? (1)

c) What is the purpose of carrying out steps **A** and **B**? (2)

4 Rewrite the following sentences about contraception using the correct answer from each underlined choice. (5)

a) The use of a cervical cap is a barrier/cyclical method of contraception.

b) The 'morning after' pill is a physical/chemical means of preventing pregnancy.

c) An intra-uterine device prevents implantation of an embryo in the oviduct/endometrium.

d) The 'mini pill' contains synthetic oestrogen/progesterone, which works by making cervical mucus thicker.

e) Sterilisation in a woman involves a procedure called tubal ligation/vasectomy.

Applying Your Knowledge and Skills

1 The data in Table 11.5 refer to four patients attending a fertility clinic.

	Patient			
	A	B	C	D
Total number of sperm (millions/cm^3)	25	30	35	40
Number of active sperm (millions/cm^3)	10	11	15	18
Number of normal sperm (millions/cm^3)	15	16	22	24

Table 11.5

a) Present all of the data in Table 11.5 as a multicoloured bar chart. (3)

b) The clinic considers a man to be fertile if:

- over 20 million sperm are present in 1 cm^3 of his semen
- at least 40% of his sperm are active
- at least 60% of his sperm are normal.

Which patient in the table fails to meet these criteria fully? (1)

2 Figure 11.9 shows a simplified version of the male reproductive system following a vasectomy.

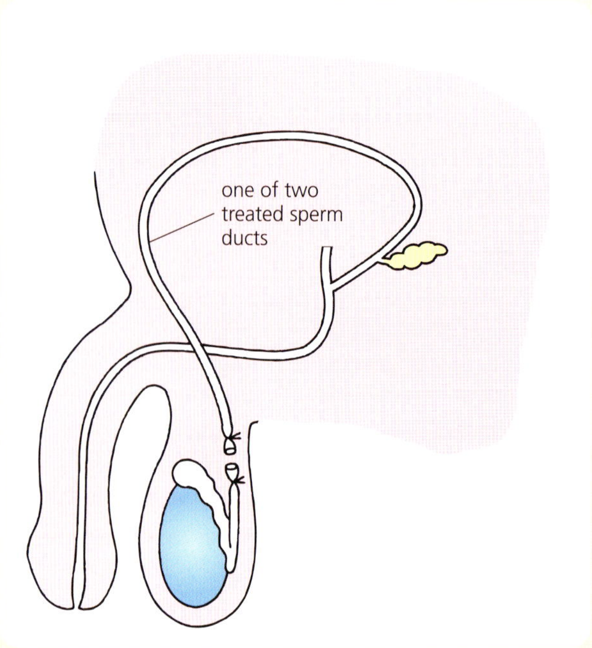

Figure 11.9

a) Explain how this works as a method of contraception. (1)
b) Suggest why vasectomy is more popular among middle-aged men than among men in their twenties. (1)

3 *In vitro* fertilisation often results in extra, unused fertilised eggs being kept in frozen storage. The very existence of these eggs raises many controversial issues. Briefly give your opinion of the following:
a) Should the extra eggs be destroyed after the mother has successfully given birth to a healthy baby?

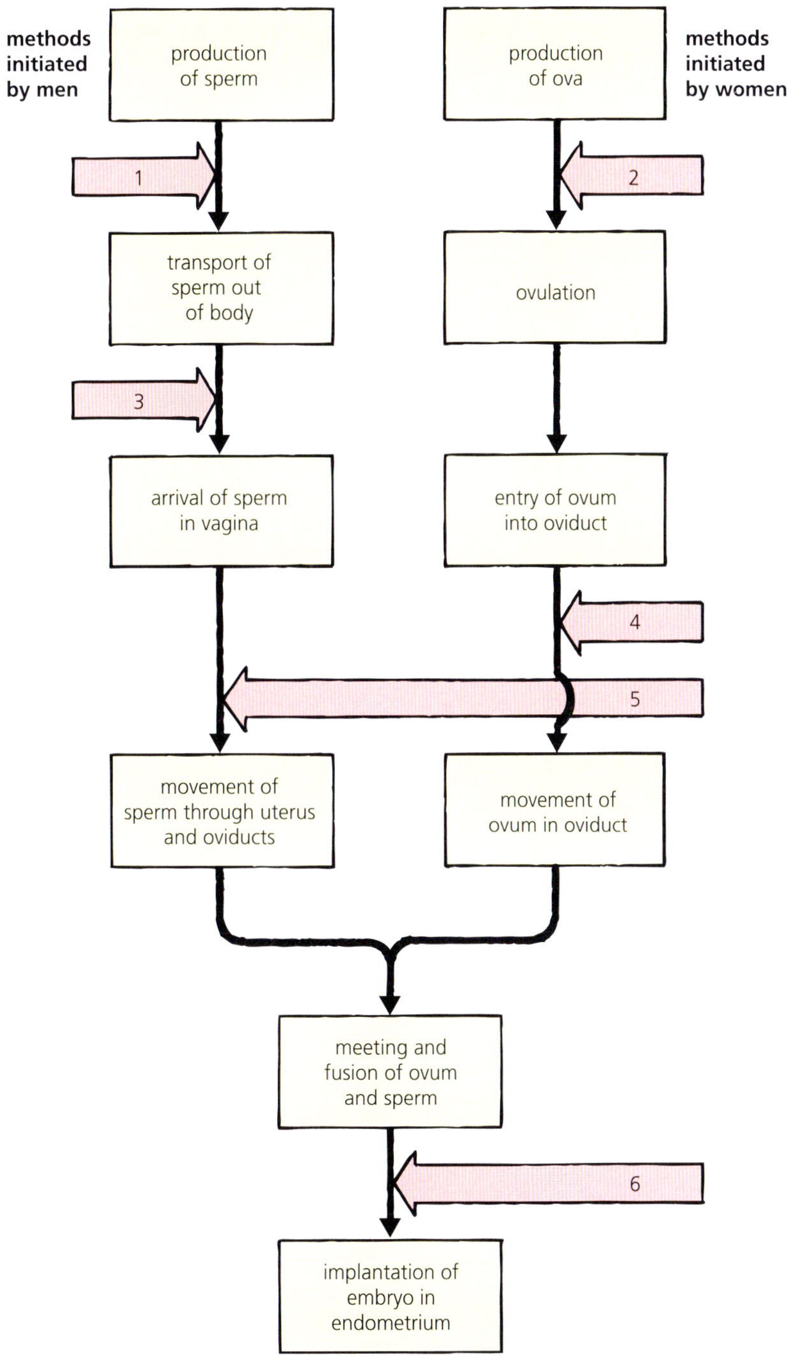

Figure 11.10

b) Should the extra fertilised eggs be kept in storage in case the woman wishes to have more children?

c) i) Should the extra fertilised eggs be offered (with permission) to other women who are experiencing fertility problems?

ii) If so, who in your opinion are the legal parents of the children produced?

d) Should the extra fertilised eggs be made available to scientists to obtain stem cells for research?

4 Each pink arrow in Figure 11.10 indicates the point at which a certain method of contraception may act and prevent the sequence of events that leads to implantation from occurring. Match arrows 1–6 with the following methods of contraception. (5)

A condom

B contraceptive pill containing progesterone and oestrogen

C diaphragm

D intra-uterine device

E ligation of oviducts

F vasectomy

5 Give an account of the different ways in which infertility in humans may be treated. (9)

6 Figure 11.11 represents some of the events that occurred during a complete menstrual cycle in a woman.

a) i) On which dates would sexual intercourse have been most likely to result in fertilisation in this woman?

ii) Give TWO reasons to explain how you arrived at your answer. (3)

b) Give a further physical sign unrelated to the graph that might have helped the woman to identify her most fertile time. (1)

c) What evidence from the graph tells you that fertilisation did not occur during the cycle shown? (1)

d) i) Assuming that the cycle remains the same length, on which dates in October will sexual intercourse be most likely to lead to conception in this woman?

ii) If fertilisation were to occur, in what way would the progesterone curve differ from the one in Figure 11.11? (2)

e) i) Instead of trying to avoid the fertile phase, the woman decided to use a hormonal method of contraception containing progesterone. Explain how this prevents fertilisation.

ii) Why do women 'on the pill' take pills lacking sex hormones 1 week in every four?

iii) Suggest why women are recommended to take the placebo pills rather than no pills at all during that week. (4)

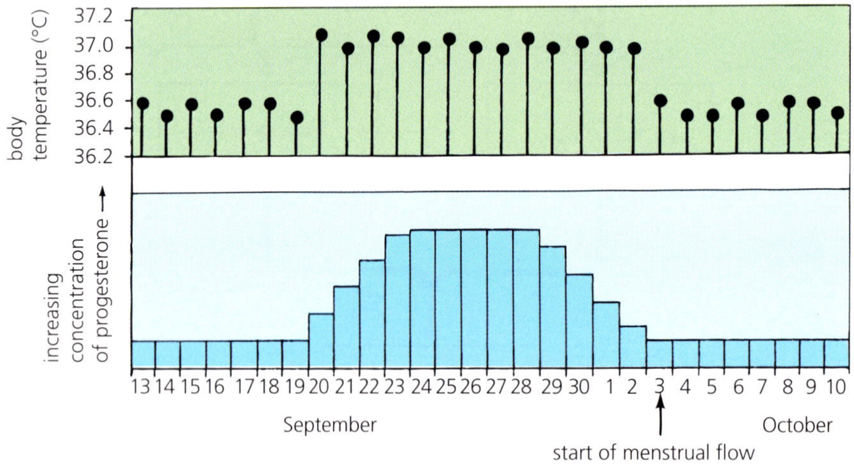

Figure 11.11

12 Ante- and postnatal screening

The health of a pregnant woman and her developing fetus can be monitored using a variety of techniques and tests. Several methods of **antenatal (prenatal) screening** can be employed to identify the risk of the fetus inheriting a genetic disorder or chromosomal abnormality. Further tests can then be carried out if necessary.

Antenatal care

With her consent, the mother's blood pressure is monitored, her blood type identified and general health checks such as blood and urine tests carried out.

Ultrasound imaging

When an **ultrasound scanner** is held against a pregnant woman's abdomen, it picks up high-frequency sounds that have bounced off the fetus. These are converted to an ultrasound image on a computer screen. A pregnant woman is given two ultrasound scans as follows.

Figure 12.2 The bad old days before ultrasound scanning

Dating scan

Ultrasound imaging is carried out at 8–14 weeks to produce a **dating scan** (see Figures 12.1 and 12.2). This scan is used to determine the stage of the pregnancy (gestational age assessment) and to calculate the date when the baby is due to be born. Dating scans are used in conjunction with biochemical tests for marker chemicals (see below).

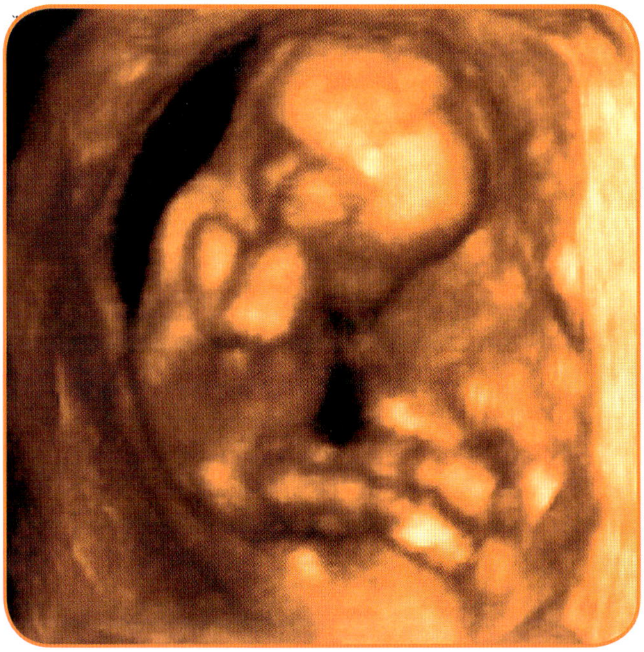

Figure 12.1 Ultrasound image at 14 weeks

Anomaly scan

Further ultrasound imaging is performed at 18–20 weeks to produce an **anomaly scan**. This allows a check to be made for the presence of any serious physical abnormalities in the fetus.

Blood and urine tests

A woman's body undergoes many physiological changes during pregnancy. This is the normal course of events. Many of these changes, such as the concentration of human chorionic gonadotrophin (HCG), can be monitored by **biochemical tests**. (The detection of HCG in blood and urine following implantation of an embryo is also the basis of early pregnancy tests.)

At 16–18 weeks, the pregnant woman is offered a series of biochemical tests that check for three **markers**.

(One of these markers is AFP. See Related Topic – Assessing the probability of Down's syndrome using screening tests on page 140.) The results of these tests, used in conjunction with the mother's age, enable medical experts to assess the likelihood of chromosomal abnormalities being present in the fetus.

Normally other routine tests are also carried out to check the health of the pregnant woman and the developing fetus by monitoring altered renal, liver and thyroid functions and other biochemical changes. (See Related Activity – Examining data on altered biochemistry during pre-eclampsia.)

False positives and false negatives

Some medical conditions are indicated by the presence of certain **marker chemicals** in blood and urine. However, these marker chemicals vary during pregnancy. At one stage the presence of a high (or low) concentration of a certain marker may indicate the presence of a genetic disorder in the fetus, whereas at another stage in the pregnancy, a high (or low) level of the marker may be of no significance. For example, in a normal pregnancy, the level of human chorionic gonadotrophin (HCG) increases during weeks 6–10 and then decreases to a steady low level later in gestation, as shown in Figure 12.3. However, it remains at a high level if the fetus has Down's syndrome. Risk assessment based on a result at 10 weeks would be meaningless since both a normal pregnancy and a Down's syndrome one would show an elevated result.

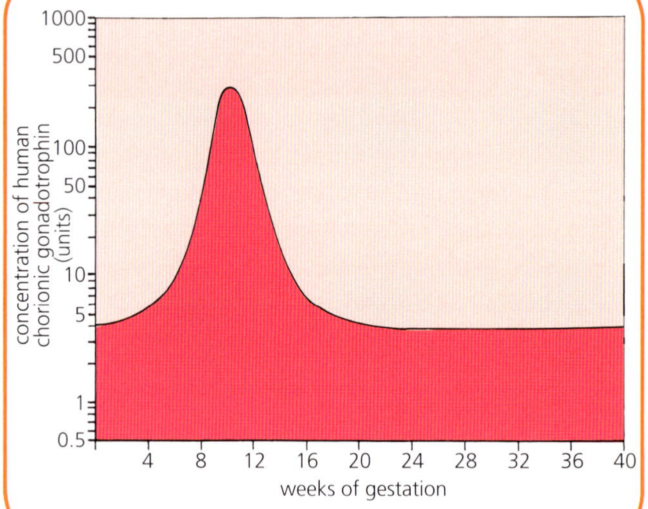

Figure 12.3 HCG levels during normal pregnancy

If a marker chemical was measured at an inappropriate point in the timescale and found to be high, significance could be attributed to it mistakenly. This would lead to a **false positive** result where the test would show the fetus to have the condition when, in fact, it does not have it. Similarly, if the test for the marker was carried out and found to be low at a time when the normal value is also low, this could give a **false negative** result. It would suggest that the fetus does not have the condition when in fact it might really have it (see Appendix 4). It is for this reason that the times chosen for biochemical tests are closely synchronised with information deduced from ultrasound dating scans.

Related Activity

Examining data on altered biochemistry during pre-eclampsia

Pre-eclampsia is a medical condition that affects a minority of pregnant women. It is regarded as the most common cause of several dangerous complications that can arise during pregnancy. A woman who has pre-eclampsia displays some or all of the following symptoms:

- high blood pressure (hypertension)
- excess protein in blood plasma
- changes to blood biochemistry caused by factors such as altered liver or renal function.

The data in Table 12.1 refer to a series of studies carried out on a large population of women. Some were non-pregnant (NP), some were pregnant but did not have pre-eclampsia (P) and some were pregnant and did have pre-eclampsia (PE).

From the table it is concluded that the concentration of **urea** in blood plasma is significantly **higher** for the PE women than for the NP and P women. Also, the concentration of **calcium** in urine is significantly **lower** for the PE women than for the NP and P women. This latter difference becomes even more apparent when the data are presented as the bar chart shown in Figure 12.4 and drawn to include **error bars** (see Appendix 3).

→

Group	Urea in blood plasma ($mg\ l^{-1}$)	Calcium in urine ($mg\ l^{-1}$)
NP	189.3 ± 13.7	163.4 ± 24.8
P	187.0 ± 14.1	177.5 ± 39.1
PE	228.7 ± 20.2	91.8 ± 21.2

Table 12.1 Results of biochemical tests

The differences are thought to be the result of a decrease in renal blood flow and glomerular filtrate rate in PE women causing them to retain higher concentrations of urea and calcium in their blood. Altered levels of these chemicals are just two of many possible indicators of pre-eclampsia. At present there is no cure for the condition and in serious cases the baby may be induced early or be delivered by Caesarean section to avoid the mother's life being put in danger and the baby suffering long-term adverse effects.

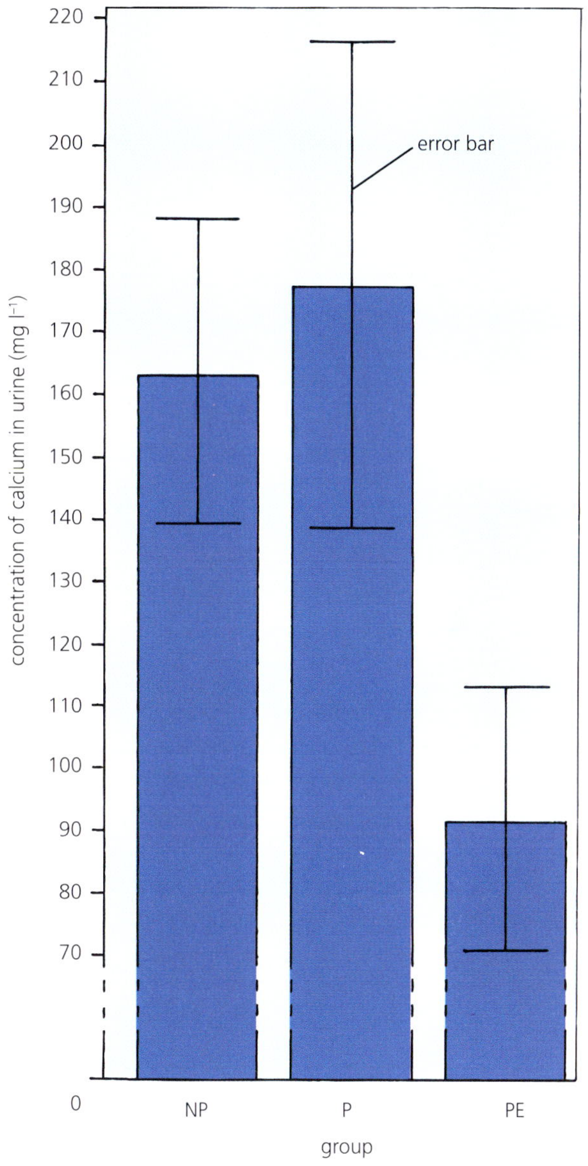

Figure 12.4 Effect of pre-eclampsia on renal function

Diagnostic testing

A **screening test** is one that is used to detect signs and symptoms associated with a certain condition or disorder. If the signs are found, the probability that the individual has the condition can be assessed as a **degree of risk**. (See Related Topic – Assessing the probability of Down's syndrome using screening tests.)

A **diagnostic test**, on the other hand, is a definitive test that produces results that can be used to establish without doubt whether or not the person has a specific condition or disorder. Certain diagnostic tests may be offered to a pregnant woman if:

- evidence of a potential problem has already emerged from the results of earlier routine screening tests
- there is a history of a harmful genetic disorder in her family
- she is already known to belong to a high-risk category (e.g. women over the age of 35). (See Related Information – Down's syndrome probability and associated test risks.)

Related Topic

Assessing the probability of Down's syndrome using screening tests

Blood test for alpha-fetoprotein

During pregnancy **alpha-fetoprotein (AFP)** is produced by the fetus and its concentration in the mother's blood increases. The level in the mother's blood decreases sharply soon after the baby is born. Low levels of AFP (lower than 0.4 where 0.5–2.49 is the normal range of values during pregnancy) are found in cases of Down's syndrome (trisomy 21) and Edwards syndrome (trisomy 18). However, this test marker is part of a **biochemical screening test** and not a diagnostic one. Therefore, even if a result shows a low level of AFP to be present and indicates *high likelihood*, it does not mean that a chromosomal abnormality has been **diagnosed**.

Multiple gestation

The predictive power of biochemical tests for a **multiple gestation** such as twins is much lower than for a single fetus. This is because the tests depend on analysis of the mother's blood and may still give normal results even if one of the fetuses is abnormal. The nuchal translucency ultrasound test (see below) is much more reliable since it examines each fetus individually.

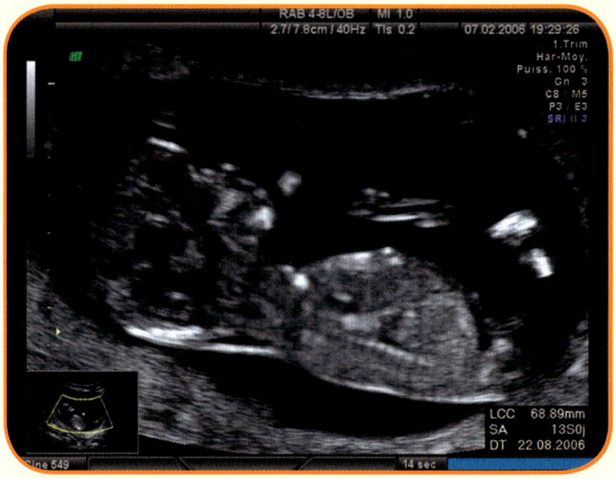

Figure 12.5 Nuchal translucency scan

Nuchal translucency scan (NT)

A **nuchal translucency scan** helps experts to estimate more accurately the probability of a woman having a baby with Down's syndrome than by considering her age alone (as shown in Table 12.2 on page 141). The test is carried out at 11–14 weeks (the time found to give the most reliable results). It enables an assessment to be made of the thickness of the fluid in the tissue at the nape of the fetus's neck by viewing it as a **nuchal translucency** (see Figure 12.5). If the nuchal translucency exceeds the normal value, there is a possibility of a chromosomal abnormality in the fetus. However, as before, this is not a diagnostic test.

Related Information

Down's syndrome probability and associated test risks

There are two different aspects of risk associated with Down's syndrome. The first line of assessment associated with Down's syndrome relates to the **mother's age** and the increased likelihood of her having a baby with this condition. In older women the germline cells that produce eggs are found to be more prone to a type of mutation that leads to eggs being formed that contain an extra copy of chromosome 21. Therefore, the older the woman, the higher the probability that she will have a baby with Down's syndrome, as shown in Table 12.2. When a combination of maternal age, biochemical tests and thickness of nuchal translucency all indicate a high likelihood of Down's syndrome, the woman may be advised to have an **amniocentesis** or a **chorionic villus sampling** test, both of which are **diagnostic** but invasive.

The second aspect of risk relates to the **tests themselves**. Amniocentesis (carried out at a later stage in gestation) slightly increases the risk of miscarriage, whereas chorionic villus sampling (carried out at an earlier stage in gestation) runs a much higher risk of losing the baby. Therefore when making a choice, the pregnant woman has to weigh up the risk of a miscarriage against the risk of wanting to seek a termination fairly late in the pregnancy. →

Maternal age at full term of gestation period (years)	Probability of Down's syndrome
20	1:1450
22	1:1450
24	1:1400
26	1:1300
28	1:1150
30	1:940
32	1:700
34	1:460
36	1:270
38	1:150
40	1:85
42	1:55
44	1:40
46	1:30

Table 12.2 Probability of Down's syndrome with increasing maternal age

Use of karyotype

A person's **karyotype** is a visual display of their complete chromosome complement, with the chromosomes arranged as pairs showing their size, form and number. The two diagnostic tests described below depend on fetal material being obtained to allow a karyotype to be prepared for examination.

Amniocentesis

Amniocentesis is carried out at about 14–16 weeks. It involves the withdrawal of a little amniotic fluid containing fetal cells (see Figure 1.7 on page 9). These are cultured, stained and examined under the microscope. A full chromosome complement is photographed and the chromosomes arranged into pairs to form the karyotype, as shown in Figure 12.6. This technique, which takes about 2 weeks, allows chromosomal abnormalities to be detected. A karyotype containing an extra copy of chromosome 21, for example, indicates Down's syndrome. The parents may then elect to have the pregnancy terminated.

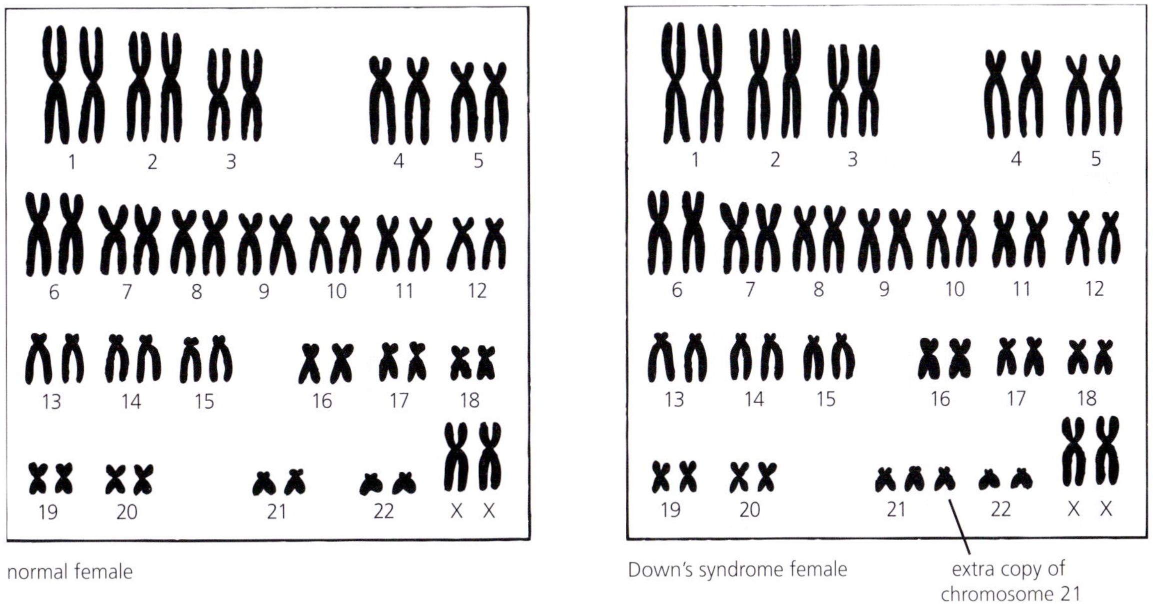

Figure 12.6 Normal and Down's syndrome karyotypes

Chorionic villus sampling

Chorionic villus sampling (CVS) involves taking a tiny sample of placental cells using a fine tube inserted into the mother's reproductive tract (see Figure 12.7). The cells are then cultured and used for karyotyping as before. One benefit of CVS is that it can be carried out as early as 8 weeks into the pregnancy. The prospect of a termination at this stage is much less traumatic for many would-be parents than at 16 or more weeks following amniocentesis. However, CVS causes a higher incidence of miscarriages than amniocentesis.

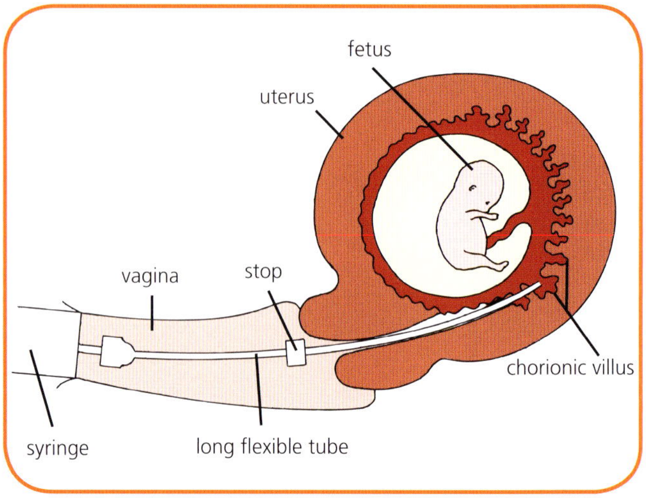

Figure 12.7 Chorionic villus sampling

Related Topic

Karyotypes indicating genetic disorders

Figure 12.6 on page 141 compares the karyotypes of a normal female with a female with **Down's syndrome** (**trisomy 21**). This condition, caused by the presence of an extra copy of chromosome 21, is characterised by learning difficulties and distinctive physical features. It occurs in 1 in 800 live births.

Figure 12.8 shows the karyotype of a person with **Turner's syndrome**, caused by the lack of one of the two X chromosomes. It occurs with a frequency of about 1 in 2500 female live births. Individuals affected in this way are always female and short in stature. Since their ovaries do not develop, they are infertile and fail to develop secondary sexual characteristics at puberty.

Figure 12.9 shows the karyotype of a person with **Klinefelter's syndrome**, caused by the presence of an extra sex chromosome to give the grouping XXY. It occurs with a frequency of about 1 in 1000 male live births. An individual with this unusual chromosome complement is always male and possesses male sex organs. However, people affected in this way are infertile because their testes are very small and fail to produce sperm.

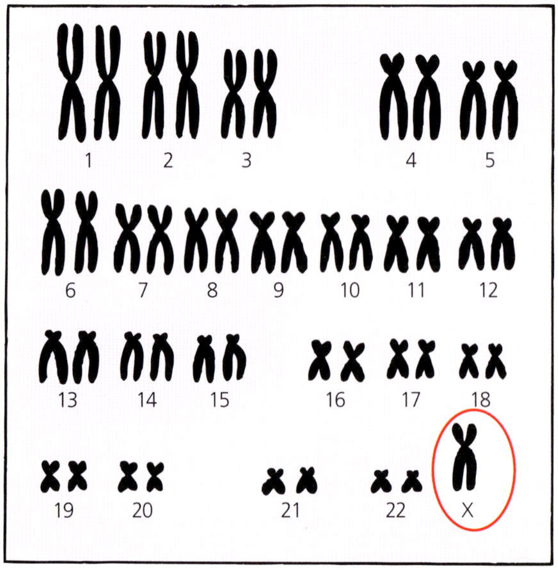

Figure 12.8 Turner's syndrome karyotype

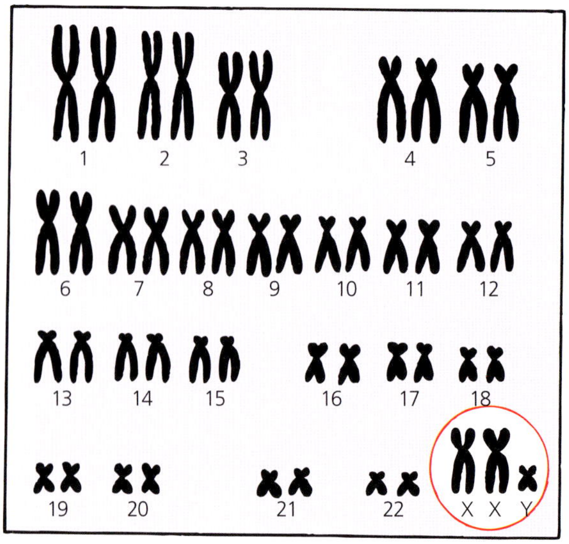

Figure 12.9 Klinefelter's syndrome karyotype

Testing Your Knowledge 1

1 What is meant by the term *antenatal screening*? (1)

2 a) At approximately what stage in pregnancy is i) a *dating* scan, ii) an *anomaly* scan performed? (2)

b) What is the purpose of each of these scans? (2)

c) What name is given to the technique used to obtain these scans? (1)

3 Distinguish clearly between the terms *screening test* and *diagnostic test.* (2)

4 Give TWO differences between *amniocentesis* and *chorionic villus sampling.* (2)

Genetic screening and counselling

Standardised human pedigree nomenclature and symbols

In humans, the X and Y chromosomes are the **sex chromosomes**. All the other chromosomes in the genotype are called **autosomes**. The most commonly used forms of the nomenclature and symbols used for human pedigrees are shown in Figures 12.10, 12.11 and 12.12. Further information about sex-linked inheritance is given in the Related Topic on pages 148–9.

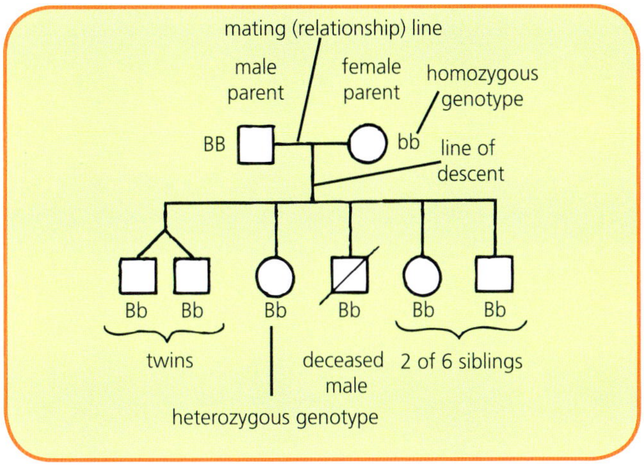

Figure 12.10 Human pedigree nomenclature and symbols

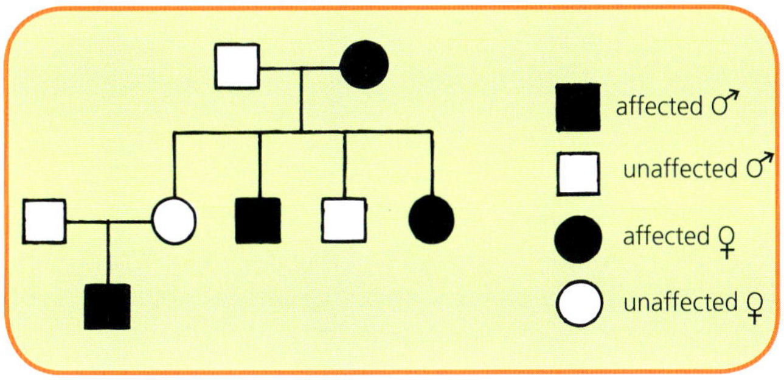

Figure 12.11 Symbols in an autosomal recessive pedigree

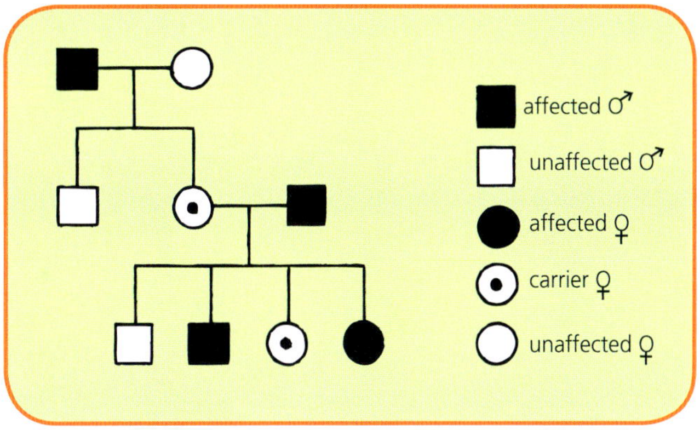

Figure 12.12 Symbols in a sex-linked pedigree

Pedigree charts

A pattern of inheritance can be revealed by collecting information about a particular characteristic from the members of a family and then using it to construct a **family tree (pedigree chart)**. Once the phenotypes are known, most of the genotypes can be deduced.

Such construction of a family tree is carried out by a genetic counsellor when information and advice are required by a couple who are worried about the possibility of passing a genetic disorder (known to exist in their family) on to their children.

Different patterns of inheritance

Autosomal recessive inheritance

Figure 12.13 shows a family history of cystic fibrosis.

The geneticist recognises that such a trait shows a typical **autosomal recessive** pattern of inheritance because:

- the trait is expressed relatively rarely
- the trait may skip generations
- the trait is expressed in some of the offspring of a consanguineous marriage (in this case cousins)

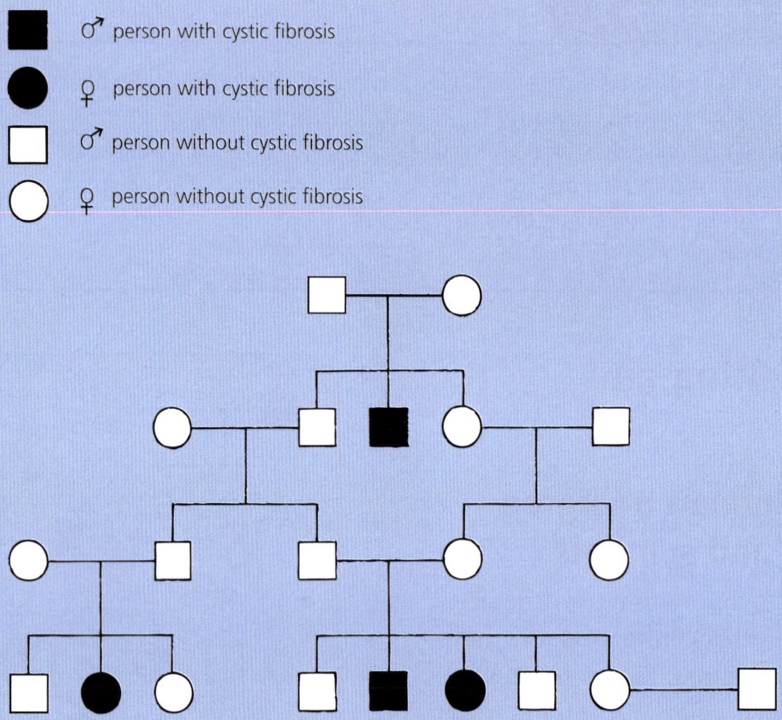

Figure 12.13 Autosomal recessive inheritance

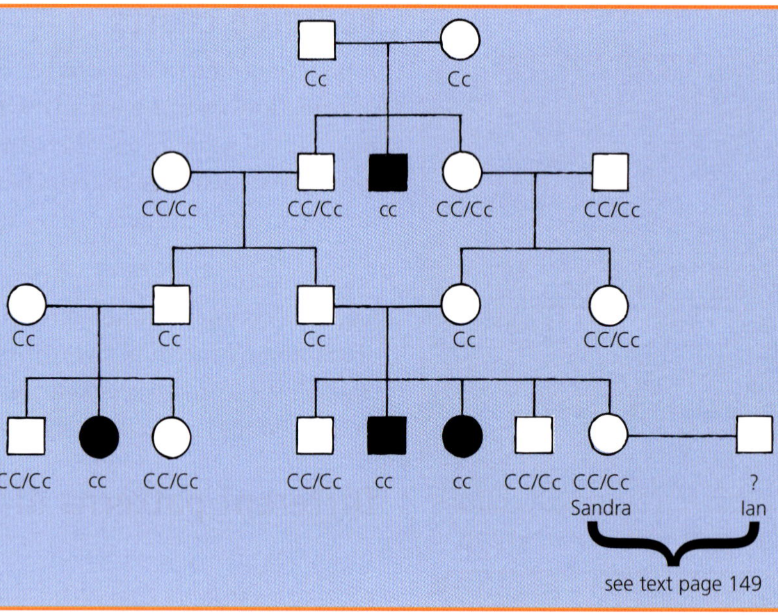

Figure 12.14 Genotypes for autosomal recessive example

- males and females are affected in approximately equal numbers.

The geneticist can therefore add genotypes to the family tree by applying the following rules governing any characteristic showing autosomal recessive inheritance:

- All persons with the trait are homozygous recessive (e.g. cc).
- All persons without the trait are homozygous dominant (e.g. CC) or heterozygous (e.g. Cc) and most of these genotypes can be deduced by referring to other closely related members of the tree.

The outcome of the cystic fibrosis example is shown in Figure 12.14.

Autosomal dominant inheritance

Figure 12.15 shows a family history of Huntington's disease.

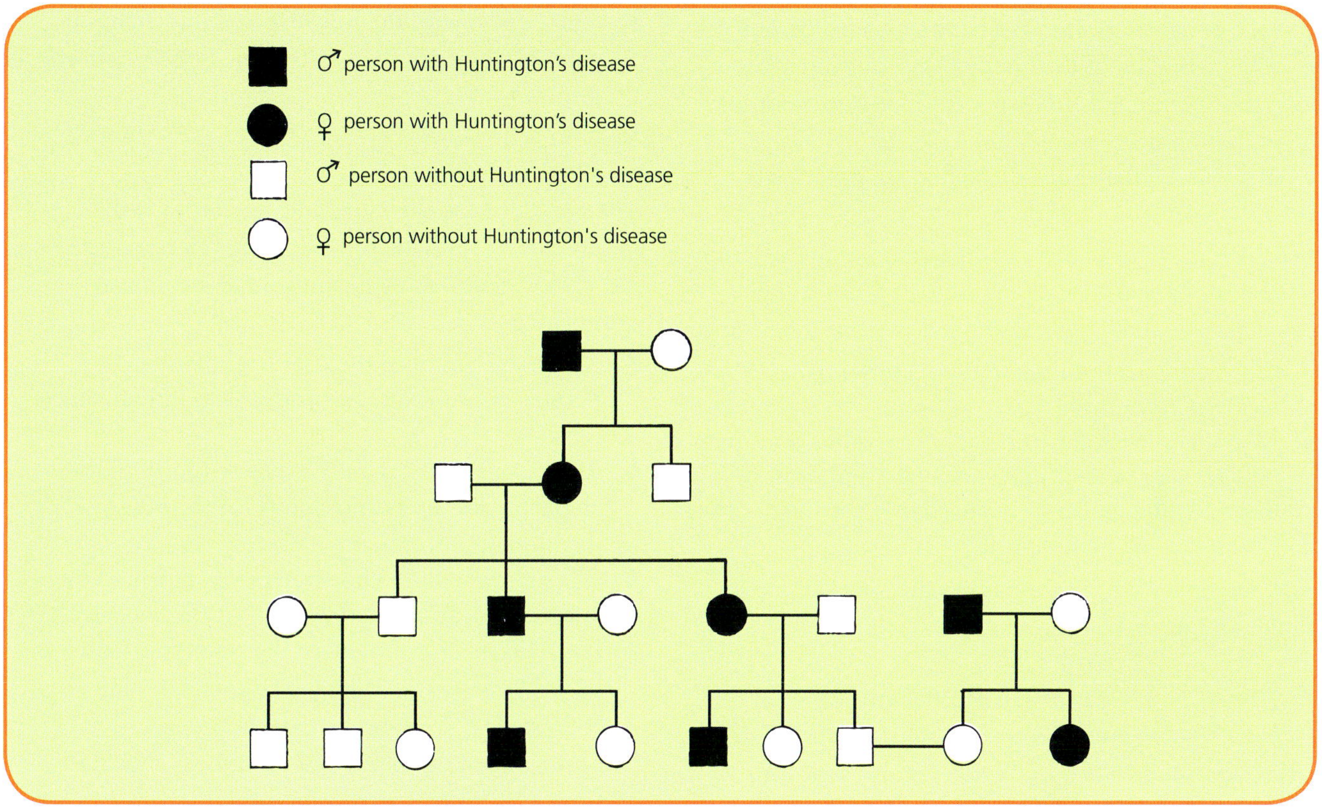

Figure 12.15 Autosomal dominant inheritance

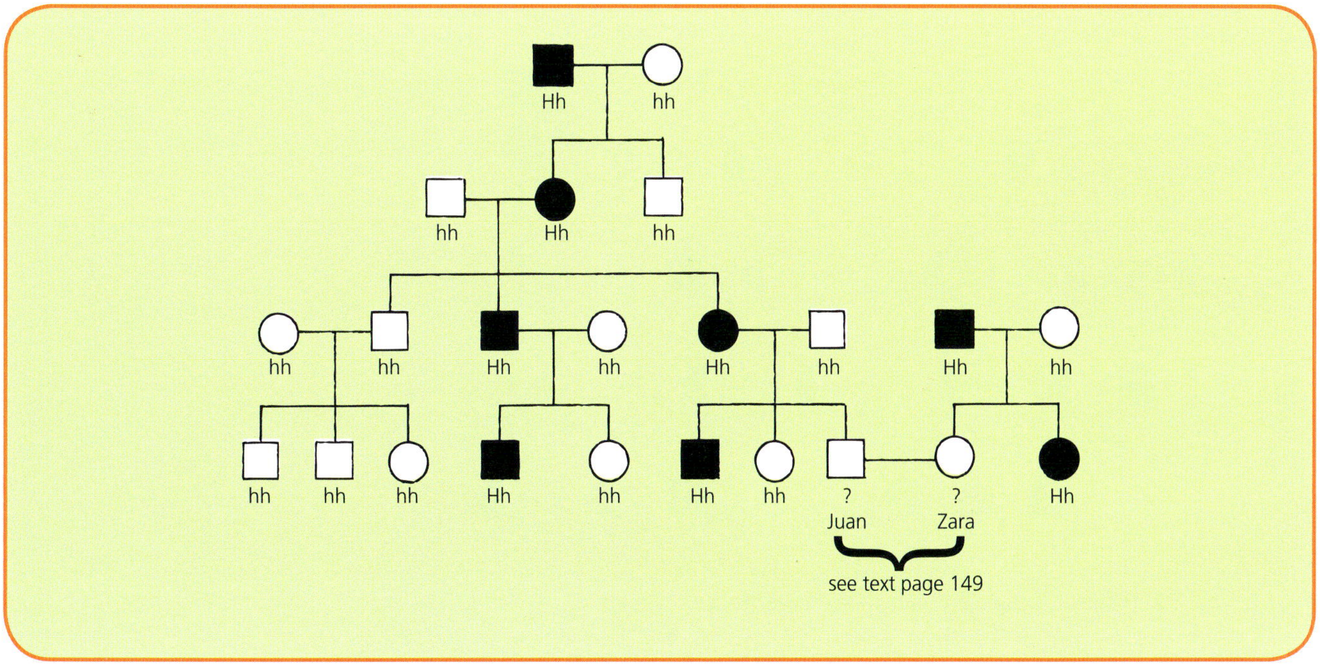

Figure 12.16 Genotypes for autosomal dominant example

The geneticist recognises that such a trait shows a typical **autosomal dominant** pattern of inheritance because:

- the trait appears in every generation
- each person with the trait has an affected parent
- when a branch of the family does not express the trait, the trait fails to reappear in future generations of that branch
- males and females are affected in approximately equal numbers.

The geneticist can therefore add genotypes to the family tree by applying the following rules governing any characteristic showing autosomal dominant inheritance:

- All persons without the trait are homozygous recessive (e.g. hh).
- All persons with the trait are homozygous dominant (e.g. HH) or heterozygous (e.g. Hh) and most of these genotypes can be deduced by referring to other closely related members of the tree.

The outcome of the Huntington's disease example is shown in Figure 12.16.

Autosomal incomplete dominance

Figure 12.17 shows a family tree with a history of sickle-cell anaemia and sickle-cell trait (see also page 60).

The geneticist recognises that such a disorder shows a typical **autosomal incompletely dominant** pattern of inheritance because:

- the fully expressed form of the characteristic occurs relatively rarely
- the partly expressed form occurs much more frequently
- each person with the fully expressed form has two parents who have the partly expressed form of the disorder
- males and females are affected in approximately equal numbers.

The geneticist can therefore add genotypes to the family tree by applying the following rules governing any characteristic showing autosomal incomplete dominance:

- All persons without the characteristic are homozygous for one incompletely dominant allele (e.g. HH).
- All persons with the fully expressed form of the characteristic are homozygous for the other incompletely dominant allele (e.g. SS).
- All persons with the partly expressed form of the characteristic are heterozygous for the two alleles (e.g. HS) and most or all of the genotypes can be deduced by referring to other closely related members of the tree.

The outcome of the sickle-cell example is shown in Figure 12.18.

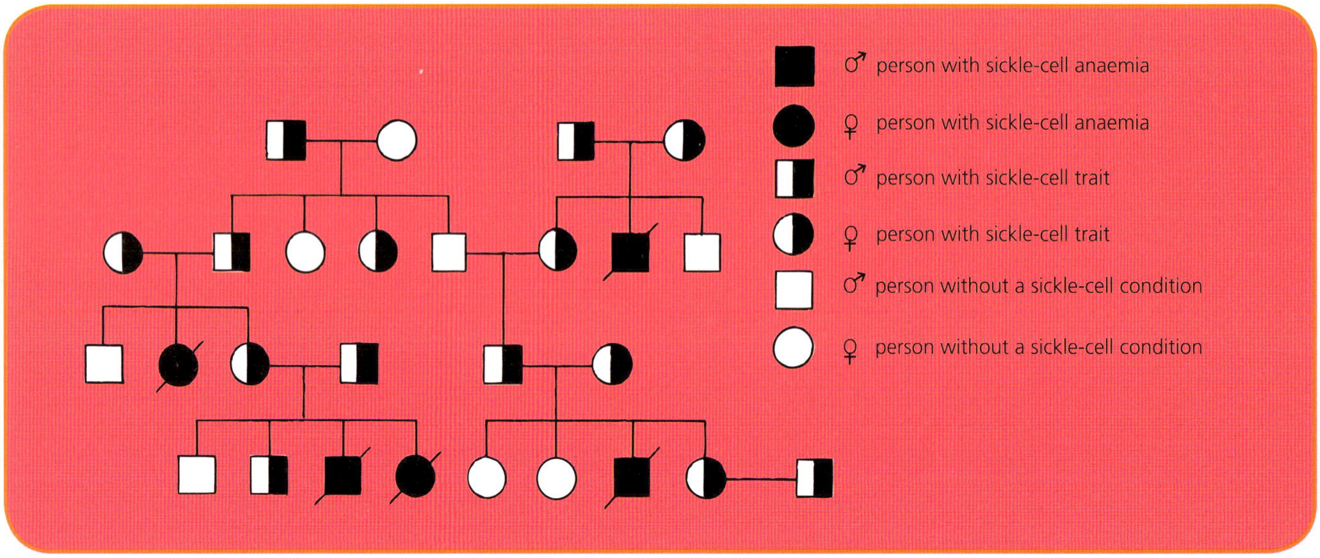

Figure 12.17 Autosomal incomplete dominance inheritance

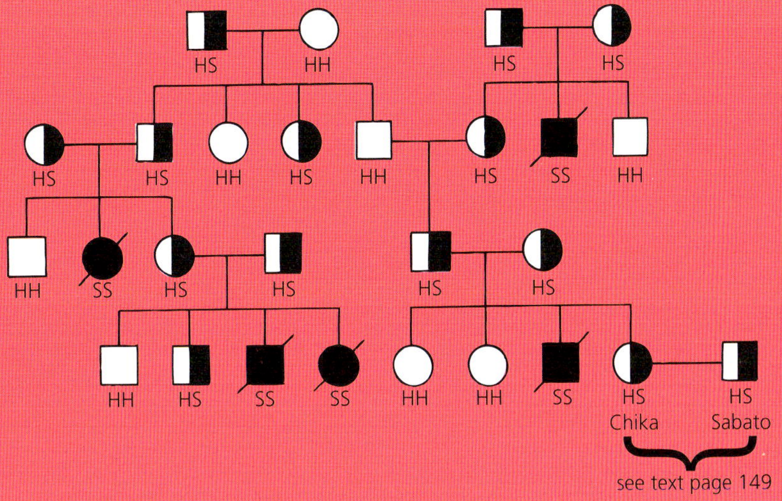

Figure 12.18 Genotypes for autosomal incomplete dominance example

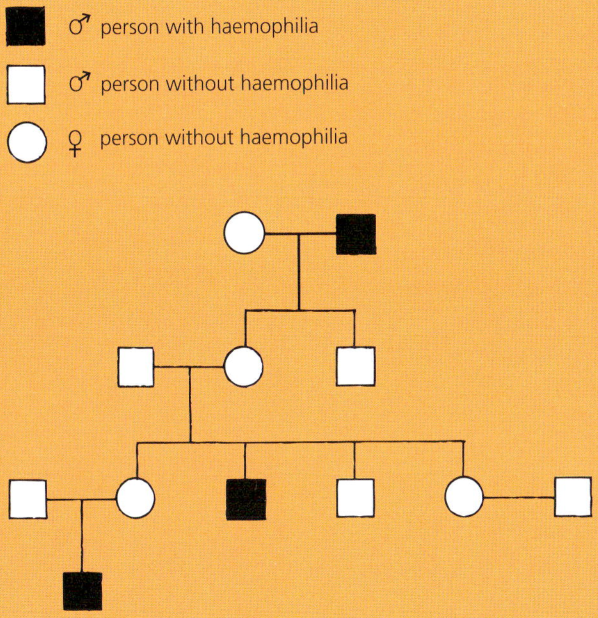

Figure 12.19 Sex-linked recessive inheritance

Sex-linked recessive trait

Figure 12.19 shows a family with a history of haemophilia. (Further information about sex-linked inheritance is given in the Related Topic on pages 148–9.)

The geneticist recognises that such a trait shows a typical **sex-linked recessive** pattern of inheritance because:

- many more males have the trait than females (if any)
- none of the sons of a male with the trait show the trait
- some grandsons of a male with the trait do show the trait.

The geneticist can therefore add genotypes to the family tree by applying the following rules governing any characteristic showing sex-linked recessive inheritance:

- All persons with the trait are 'homozygous' recessive (normally male X^hY, and very rarely female X^hX^h).
- Persons without the trait are 'homozygous' dominant (X^HY or X^HX^H) or heterozygous carrier females (X^HX^h) and most or all of these genotypes can be deduced by referring to other closely related members of the tree.

The outcome of the haemophilia example is shown in Figure 12.20, where symbols for the female carriers can now be added.

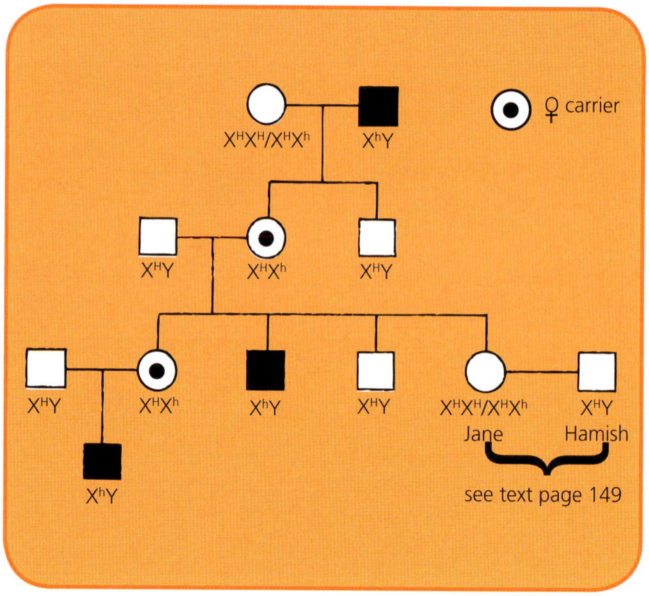

Figure 12.20 Genotypes of sex-linked recessive example

Related Topic

Sex-linked inheritance

Although the X and Y sex chromosomes make up a pair, an X chromosome differs from a Y in that the X has many genes that are absent from the Y. These genes are said to be **sex-linked** (see Figure 12.21). When an X chromosome meets a Y chromosome at fertilisation, each sex-linked gene on the X chromosome becomes expressed in the phenotype of the human male produced. This is because the Y chromosome does not possess alleles of any of these sex-linked genes and cannot offer dominance to them.

Haemophilia

Clotting of blood is the result of a complex series of biochemical reactions involving many essential chemicals.

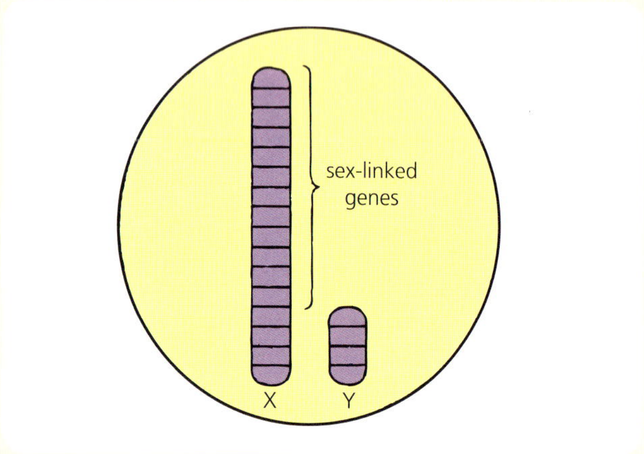

Figure 12.21 Sex-linked genes

One of these blood-clotting agents is a protein called **factor VIII**. In humans the genetic information for factor VIII is carried on the X chromosome. However, a defective version of the factor VIII protein is formed if the gene is changed by a mutation. A person who inherits the altered genetic material develops a condition called **haemophilia A** (see page 64). Their blood takes a very

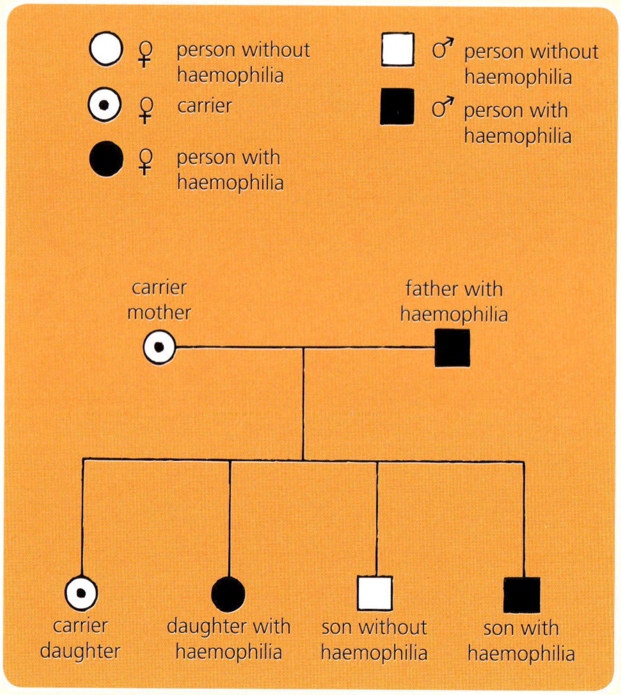

Figure 12.22 Haemophilia A cross using alternative symbols

→

long time (or even fails) to clot, resulting in prolonged bleeding from even the tiniest wound. Internal bleeding may occur and continue unchecked, leading to serious consequences.

Since haemophilia A is caused by a recessive allele carried on the X but not the Y chromosome, it is a **sex-linked** condition. The genotypes of individuals in crosses involving haemophilia A are normally represented by the following symbols: X^H (normal blood-clotting allele), X^h (haemophilia) and Y (no allele for this gene). Figure 12.22 shows the outcome of a cross between a carrier woman and a man with haemophilia using standardised human pedigree symbols. Figure 12.23 shows the same cross using symbols where the sex chromosomes are represented by X and Y and the alleles of the sex-linked gene by appropriate superscripts.

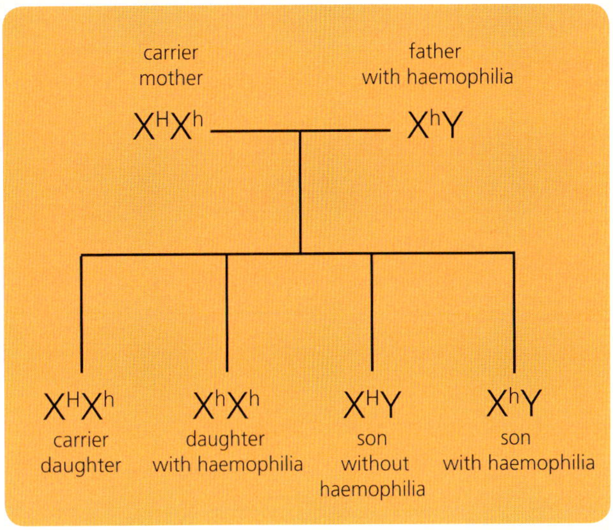

Figure 12.23 Haemophilia A cross using superscript symbols

Related Activity

Assessing the risk

Once the genetic counsellor has constructed the pedigree chart and established as many genotypes as possible, they are in a position to assess risk and state probabilities.

Autosomal recessive

Returning to the **cystic fibrosis** example shown in Figure 12.14, consider the situation that Sandra and Ian find themselves in. Cystic fibrosis is known to exist in Sandra's family but not that of Ian. The genetic counsellor would work out from the family tree that Sandra has a 2 in 3 chance of being a carrier. The counsellor would already know that the frequency among the British population of an individual being heterozygous for the cystic fibrosis allele is 1 in 25, and would therefore regard this as the risk of Ian being a carrier. Combining all these probabilities, they would conclude that the risk of Sandra and Ian having a child with cystic fibrosis is fairly low.

Autosomal dominant

Returning to the **Huntington's disease** example shown in Figure 12.16, consider the situation that Juan and Zara find themselves in. Unlike their siblings, both are still too young to know whether or not they have received the harmful allele from an affected parent. At present it is a 1 in 2 chance that each is heterozygous for the condition and destined to develop it later in life. From the information available, the genetic counsellor would conclude that there is a high risk that each of their children would inherit this debilitating disease. For example, if both Juan and Zara turn out to be Hh then 3 in 4 of their children on average would inherit Huntington's disease.

Autosomal incompletely dominant

Returning to the **sickle-cell disease** example shown in Figure 12.18, consider the situation that Chika and Sabato find themselves in. The genetic counsellor would explain to them that each of their children would have a 1 in 4 chance of inheriting the fully expressed condition of the disease, a 1 in 2 chance of inheriting the milder condition and a 1 in 4 chance of being unaffected.

Sex-linked recessive

Returning to the **haemophilia** example shown in Figure 12.20, consider the position that Jane and Hamish find themselves in. Jane is anxious to know if she could pass the trait on to her sons. There is no history of the condition in Hamish's family. From the information in the family tree, the genetic counsellor would note that Jane's brother and nephew have developed this sex-linked trait. This shows that Jane's mother and sister are carriers. They would conclude therefore that there is a 1 in 2 chance of Jane being a carrier. If she does turn out to be a carrier, then each of her sons (but none of her daughters) would stand a 1 in 2 chance of developing haemophilia. However, from the information presently available, the counsellor would assess the risk of each son being a haemophiliac as a 1 in 4 chance.

Postnatal (after birth) screening

Diagnostic testing for phenylketonuria (PKU)

At present almost none of the inherited disorders can be successfully treated. An exception is **phenylketonuria** (PKU). This inborn error of metabolism is caused by a substitution mutation. The protein expressed is an enzyme which should convert the amino acid phenylalanine to tyrosine but is non-functional. This results in a build-up of phenylalanine (also see page 61). PKU occurs with a frequency of about 1 in 10 000 in the UK. If it is not detected soon after birth, the baby's mental development is affected adversely.

In the UK, all newborn babies are routinely **screened** for PKU by having their blood tested for the presence of **excess phenylalanine** within the first few days of life. Babies with PKU are then placed on a **restricted diet** containing the minimum quantity of phenylalanine needed for normal growth. Provided that a person with PKU continues to consume this diet low in phenylalanine (especially during childhood when the brain is still developing), mental impairment is prevented and other adverse effects are kept to a minimum.

Testing Your Knowledge 2

1 a) Name TWO characteristics of a family's pedigree chart that would enable a geneticist to recognise that it showed a pattern of autosomal recessive inheritance. (2)
b) Give ONE rule that the geneticist would apply when adding genotypes to a family tree showing a pattern of autosomal recessive inheritance. (1)

2 a) Name TWO characteristics of a family's pedigree chart that would enable a geneticist to recognise that it showed a pattern of sex-linked recessive inheritance. (2)
b) Give ONE rule that the geneticist would apply when adding genotypes to a family tree showing a pattern of sex-linked recessive inheritance. (1)

3 a) By what means is postnatal screening for phenylketonuria (PKU) carried out? (1)
b) Why is PKU described as an inborn error of metabolism? (Hint: see Chapter 4, page 61.) (2)
c) What treatment is given to people with PKU? (1)

Applying Your Knowledge and Skills

Chemical tested	Pregnancy trimester (3-month period)		
	First	Second	Third
Bilirubin	↓	↓	↓
AST (aspartate aminotransferase)	–	–	–
5′-nucleotidase	–	– or ↑	↑
ALT (alanine aminotransferase)	–	–	–
Albumin	↓	↓	↓
Alkaline phosphatase	–	– or ↑	↑
GGT (gamma-glutamyl transferase)	–	↓	↓
Serum bile acids (fasting state)	–	–	–

Table 12.3

Key: ↑ = increase, ↓ = decrease, – = no change (compared with non-pregnant women)

→

1 Table 12.3 indicates the effect of normal pregnancy on the concentration of several chemicals present in the woman's blood.

a) Which chemicals in the blood of women undergoing a normal pregnancy increase in concentration during the third trimester when compared with non-pregnant women? (1)

b) Which chemicals in the blood of women undergoing a normal pregnancy decrease in concentration during the third trimester when compared with non-pregnant women? (1)

c) Why is detection of elevation of aminotransferase levels regarded as a most useful indicator in the diagnosis of problems during pregnancy? (1)

d) Intrahepatic cholestasis of pregnancy (ICP) is a condition experienced by some pregnant women. It is characterised by intense itching and elevation of alkaline phosphatase and serum bile acid levels.

i) Which of these chemical changes can be used to test for the condition?

ii) Which of these chemical changes cannot be used to test for the condition?

iii) Explain your answer to ii). (3)

e) Suggest why a patient undergoes a period of fasting before a sample of her blood is taken to be tested for serum bile acids. (1)

2 The graph in Figure 12.24 shows the relationship between incidence of Down's syndrome and maternal age.

a) Use the graph to estimate the chance of a woman at each of the following ages having a baby with Down's syndrome: i) 20 years, ii) 30 years, iii) 40 years. (3)

b) Account for the trend shown by the graph. (1)

3 Figure 12.25 shows a frequency distribution of human chorionic gonadotrophin (HCG) concentrations in pregnancies affected by Down's syndrome and unaffected pregnancies. (Note: the concentration of HCG is expressed as MoM. This means a multiple of the median for unaffected pregnancies at that gestational age.)

a) Which frequency distribution covers a greater range of HCG values? (1)

b) What percentage of i) unaffected pregnancies, ii) Down's syndrome pregnancies have an HCG value of 0.7? (2)

c) What percentage of i) unaffected pregnancies, ii) Down's syndrome pregnancies have an HCG value of 4? (2)

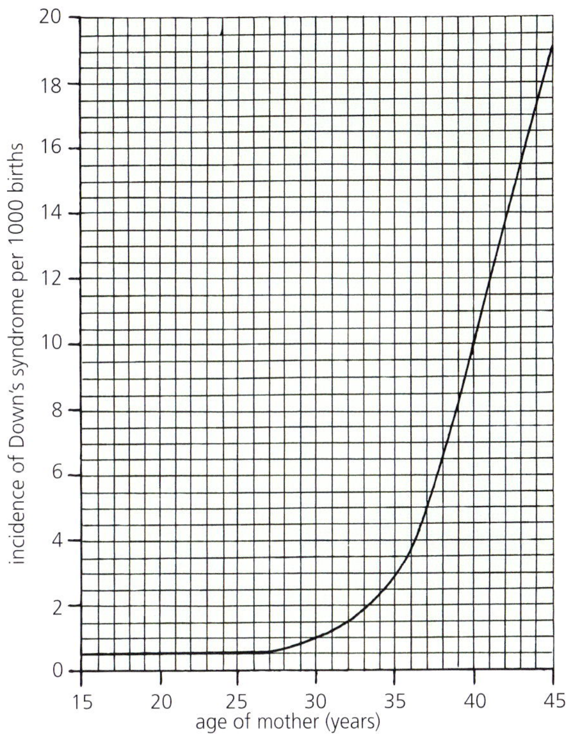

Figure 12.24

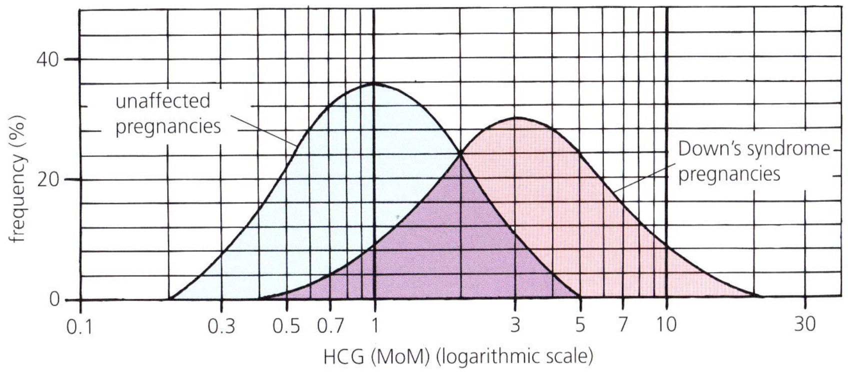

Figure 12.25

d) i) What is the most common HCG value for Down's syndrome pregnancies?

ii) What is the percentage frequency of affected pregnancies for this MoM value? (2)

e) i) Which HCG value occurs with the same frequency in both groups?

ii) State this frequency. (2)

f) i) Does an HCG level of 0.9 MoM exclude the risk of a Down's syndrome pregnancy?

ii) Explain your answer. (2)

4 Following ultrasound scanning, the fetuses listed in Table 12.4 were all found to show a nuchal translucency (NT) of above normal thickness.

a) Some people are under the impression that women must be over the age of 35 to be carrying a fetus with Down's syndrome. What evidence from the table shows this impression to be wrong? (1)

b) Some people think that a thickened nuchal translucency indicates, for certain, that the fetus will develop a chromosomal abnormality. In what way does the data cast doubt on this theory? (1)

c) The mother of which fetus went on to give birth to the live baby knowing that it would have Down's syndrome? (1)

d) Following the results of fetal karyotype analysis, what percentage of women, found to have a fetus with trisomy 21, chose to have the pregnancy terminated? (1)

5 Figure 12.26 shows a pedigree chart for an inherited form of deafness.

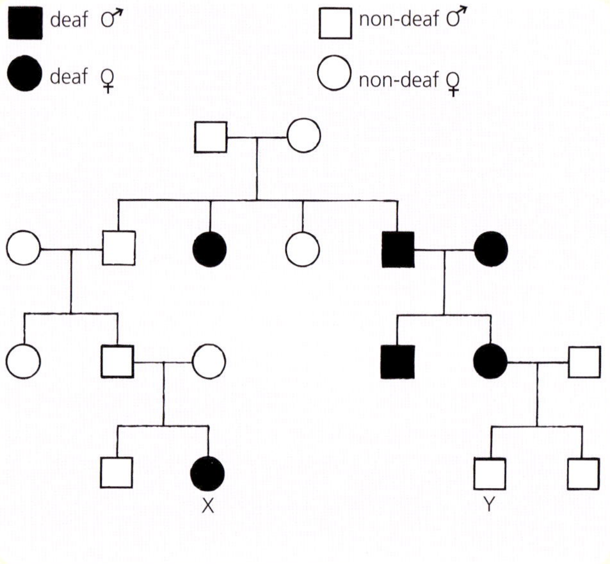

Figure 12.26

Fetus number	Age of mother (years)	NT (mm)	Result of karyotype analysis	Outcome for fetus
1	22	5.4	Normal	Live birth
2	27	3.3	Trisomy 21	Termination of pregnancy at 16 weeks
3	28	3.7	Normal	Live birth
4	33	4.4	Normal	Live birth
5	35	7.4	Trisomy 21	Termination of pregnancy at 17 weeks
6	36	4.3	Trisomy 21	Termination of pregnancy at 16 weeks
7	36	3.9	Trisomy 21	Termination of pregnancy at 18 weeks
8	37	3.5	Normal	Live birth
9	38	8.1	Trisomy 21	Termination of pregnancy at 17 weeks
10	38	4.7	Trisomy 21	Live birth
11	40	5.6	Normal	Live birth
12	42	3.8	Trisomy 21	Termination of pregnancy at 16 weeks
13	43	3.4	Normal	Live birth
14	44	6.6	Trisomy 21	Dead at full term
15	45	5.9	Trisomy 21	Termination of pregnancy at 18 weeks

Table 12.4

a) i) Which of the following patterns of inheritance is shown by this trait?
A autosomal recessive
B autosomal dominant
C sex-linked recessive
ii) Give ONE reason to support your choice.
iii) Give ONE reason for deciding against each of the other choices. (4)

b) Copy the pedigree chart and, using symbols of your choice, attempt to supply the genotype of each person (giving both possibilities in uncertain cases). (9)

c) If X conceives children with a man who is homozygous for the normal allele, what is the percentage chance of each child of this union being:
i) deaf
ii) a carrier of the allele for deafness? (2)

d) If Y conceives children with a woman who is homozygous for the normal allele, what is the chance of each child of this union being:
i) deaf
ii) a carrier of the allele for deafness? (2)

e) If X conceives children with Y, what is the chance of each child being:
i) deaf
ii) a carrier of the allele for deafness? (2)

6 Huntington's disease has a debilitating effect on the nervous system. It is caused by a dominant allele, which normally remains unexpressed until the person is over 30. Figure 12.27 shows two family trees involving this trait.

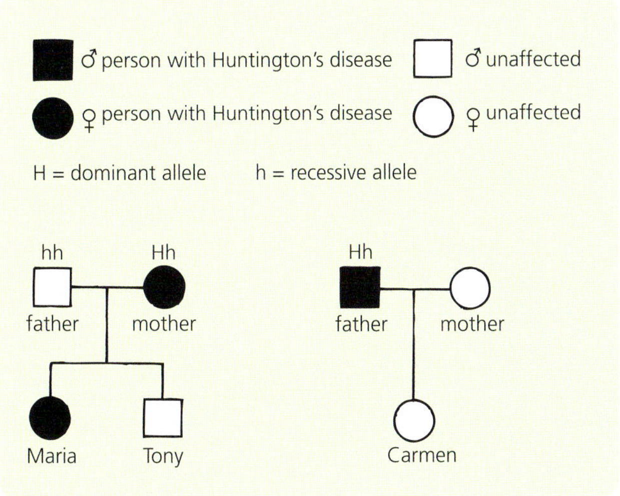

Figure 12.27

a) State the genotype of i) Maria, ii) Carmen's mother (who is aged 45). (2)

b) Carmen and Tony, both aged 21, intend to marry so they seek the advice of a genetic counsellor. He advises them that, depending on their genotypes, their children would be the result of one of the four situations shown in Table 12.5.

Possible situation	Carmen	Tony
A	Hh	Hh
B	Hh	hh
C	hh	Hh
D	hh	hh

Table 12.5

i) Why is the counsellor unable to state which of the four situations would arise?
ii) State the chance of a child from each of the four situations inheriting Huntington's disease. (5)

7 Figure 12.28 shows a pedigree chart for Duchenne muscular dystrophy.

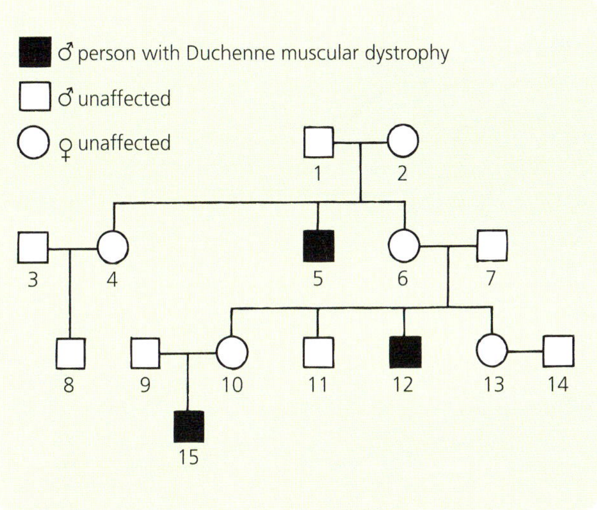

Figure 12.28

a) Which females are definitely carriers of the trait? (1)

b) What is the probability that person 13 is heterozygous for the trait? (1)

c) i) If couple 13 and 14 have a son, what is the chance, going on the information so far available, that he will have Duchenne muscular dystrophy?
ii) If couple 13 and 14 produce a son with Duchenne muscular dystrophy, what is the chance of their next son also being affected? (2)

What You Should Know Chapters 9–12

amniocentesis	genetic	oviducts
anomaly	germline	ovulation
avoidance	implantation	pedigree
barriers	injection	phase
biological	insemination	postnatal
chemical	interstitial	progesterone
chorionic	karyotype	prostate
chromosomal	luteinising	seminal
continuous	luteum	sperm
cyclical	marker	sterilisation
dating	menstrual	stimulate
diagnostic	miscarriage	testes
endometrium	mucus	testosterone
follicle	negative	ultrasound
follicle-stimulating	oestrogen	vascularisation
	ovaries	vitro

Table 12.6 Word bank for Chapters 9–12

1 The ______ of the human male produce sperm from germline cells in seminiferous tubules and make testosterone in ______ cells.

2 The mobility and viability of sperm are maintained by fluids secreted by the ______ gland and ______ vesicles.

3 The ______ of the human female contain ______ cells that produce ova (eggs) each surrounded by a protective ______. Hormones made by the ovary are oestrogen and ______.

4 The pituitary gland releases ______ hormone (FSH) and interstitial-cell-stimulating hormone (ICSH)/______ hormone (LH).

5 In men, FSH stimulates sperm production and ICSH promotes ______ production. The concentration of testosterone is maintained at a steady level by ______ feedback control.

6 In women, FSH stimulates the development of a follicle containing an ovum (egg) and the secretion of ______. LH triggers ______ and brings about the development of the corpus ______ which secretes progesterone.

7 Oestrogen stimulates the proliferation of the ______ and progesterone promotes its further development and ______.

8 The ______ cycle lasts for about 28 days and involves a follicular ______ and a luteal phase.

9 Fertility in men is ______; fertility in women is ______, being restricted to the 1–2 days following ovulation in each monthly cycle.

10 Infertility may be caused by failure to ovulate, blockage of ______ or failure of ______ in women, and low ______ count in men.

11 Methods of treatment of infertility include the use of drugs that ______ ovulation, artificial ______, *in-* ______ fertilisation (IVF) and intracytoplasmic sperm ______ (ICSI). Pre-implantation ______ diagnosis may be used during IVF to check an embryo for chromosomal defects before implantation.

12 Some methods of contraception are based on ______ knowledge of the menstrual cycle and the ______ of fertile periods. Other physical methods depend on ______, intra-uterine devices or ______. Some ______ methods prevent follicles from being stimulated and eggs from being released. Others cause thickening of cervical ______.

13 During antenatal care, a ______ scan is made by ______ imaging to determine the stage the pregnancy has reached. An ______ scan is used to detect physical problems in the fetus.

14 Signs of medical conditions experienced by pregnant women can be detected using screening tests for ______ chemicals. These allow risk of genetic disorders in the fetus to be assessed and may be followed up by ______ tests.

15 A ______ is a display of a complement of chromosomes arranged in pairs to show their form, size and number.

16 During ______, a sample of amniotic fluid is taken to obtain cells for karyotyping to check for ______ abnormalities. During ______ villus sampling, cells for the same purpose are obtained from the placenta. This procedure carries a higher risk of ______ than amniocentesis.

17 ______ screening is carried out on newborn babies to check for metabolic disorders such as PKU. Information about a particular characteristic can be collected from the members of a family and be used to construct a ______ chart. Single gene disorders show different patterns of inheritance, such as autosomal recessive.

13 Structure and function of arteries, capillaries and veins

Cardiovascular system

In the human body, substances need to be exchanged continuously between the different structures that make up the body's internal environment. In addition, exchanges must be made between the organism as a whole and the external environment. These requirements are met by the **cardiovascular system**, which contains a fluid connective tissue (**blood**) confined to tubes (**vessels**). The smallest of these vessels transport materials to within rapid diffusion distance of every living cell. A muscular pump (**heart**) continuously circulates blood round the system.

Related Topic

Circulation of blood

Figure 13.1 shows the route taken by blood as it passes from the heart to a region of the body and then back to the heart. **Arterial** branches of the aorta supply **oxygenated** blood to all parts of the body. **Deoxygenated** blood leaves the organs in **veins**. These unite to form the vena cava, which returns blood to the heart.

Pulmonary system

This is the route by which blood is circulated from the heart to the lungs and back to the heart. It should be noted that as a rule arteries carry oxygenated blood and veins carry deoxygenated blood. However, the pulmonary system is exceptional in that the artery carries deoxygenated blood and the vein carries oxygenated blood.

Hepatic portal vein

Whereas veins normally carry blood from a capillary bed in an organ directly back to the heart, the hepatic portal vein is exceptional in that it carries blood from the capillary bed of one organ (the intestine) to the capillary bed of a second organ (the liver). This means that the liver has *three* blood vessels associated with it.

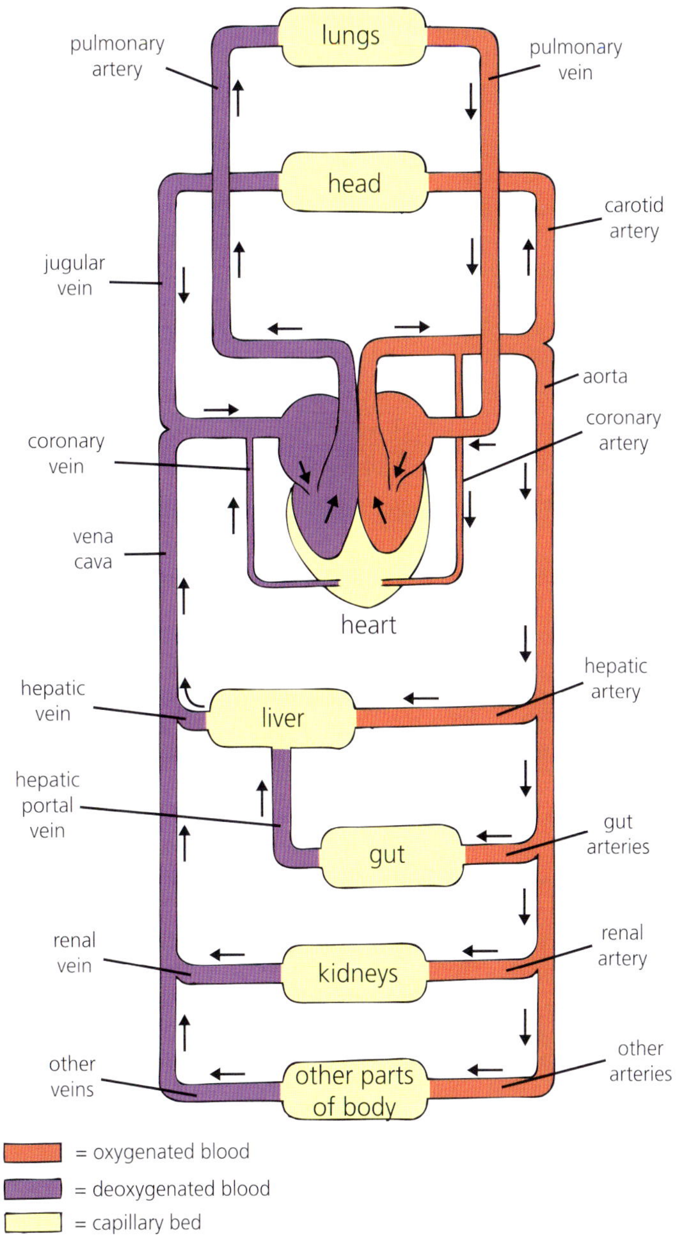

Figure 13.1 Human circulatory system

(Remarkably there are approximately 60 000 miles of vessels in a human adult!)

The distribution of blood is under efficient control at all times, allowing the cardiovascular system to work in close harmony with the digestive, respiratory, excretory, locomotor and endocrine systems. (See Related Topic – Circulation of blood.)

Structure and function of blood vessels

The lumen (central cavity) of a blood vessel is lined with a thin layer of epithelial cells called the **endothelium**. The composition of the vessel wall surrounding the endothelium is found to be different in an artery compared with a vein, as shown in Figure 13.2.

Arteries

Arteries carry blood away from the heart. The wall of an artery possesses a thick middle layer composed of smooth muscle and elastic fibres surrounded by an outer layer of connective tissue containing more elastic fibres. The elastic fibres enable the wall of an artery to **pulsate** (stretch and recoil with a rhythmical beat) thereby accommodating the surge of blood received after each heartbeat.

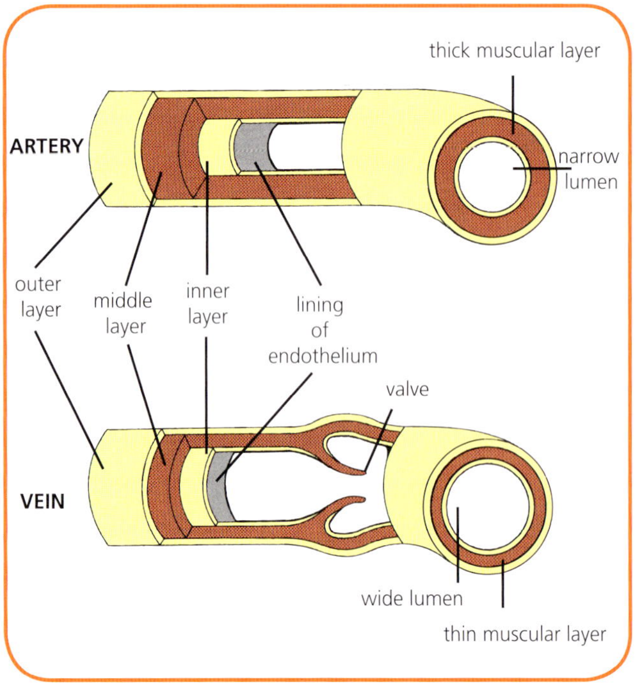

Figure 13.2 Comparison of structure of an artery and a vein

Vasoconstriction and vasodilation

The smooth muscle in the walls of **arterioles** (small arteries) can contract (or become relaxed) depending on the body's requirements. This process allows the changing demands of different tissues to be met by finely tuned adjustments in the local distribution of blood. For example, during strenuous exercise, arterioles leading to working muscles undergo **vasodilation** (see Figure 13.3). This allows an increase in blood flow to the skeletal muscles involved in the strenuous exercise. At the same time the arterioles leading to abdominal organs such as the small intestine undergo **vasoconstriction**, which reduces blood flow to these parts.

Capillaries

Blood is transported from **arterioles** to **venules** (small veins) by passing through a dense network of tiny microscopic vessels called **capillaries** (see Figure 13.4). Capillaries are the most numerous type of blood vessel in the body. They are referred to as the **exchange vessels** since all exchanges of substances between blood and living tissues take place through their thin walls. These are composed of epithelium and are only one cell thick.

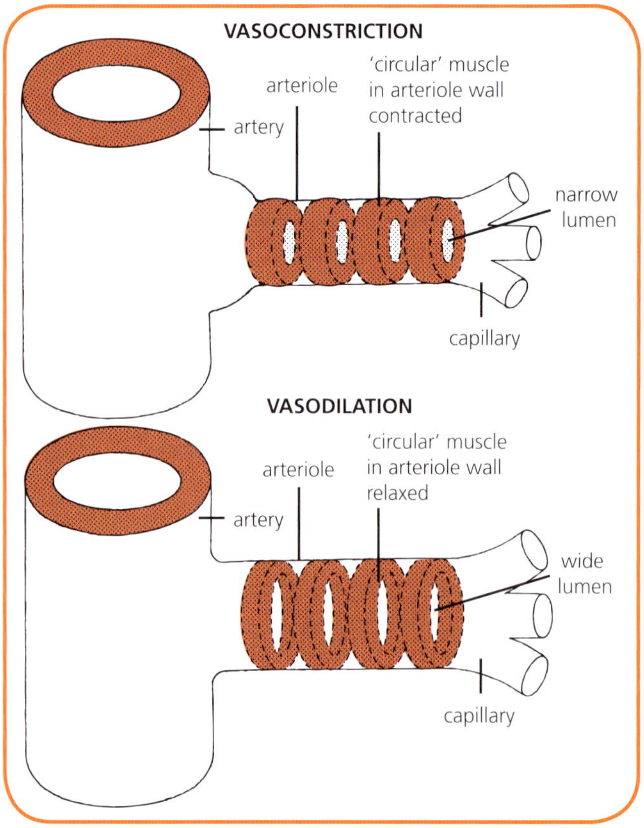

Figure 13.3 Simplified version of vasoconstriction and vasodilation

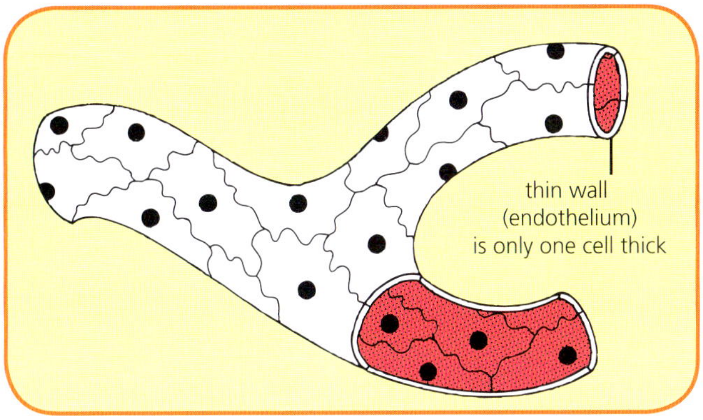

Figure 13.4 Capillary

Veins

Veins carry blood back to the heart. The muscular layer and the layers of elastic fibres in the wall of a vein are thinner than those in an artery because blood flows along a vein at low pressure. Compared with an artery, the lumen of a vein is **wider**. This reduces resistance to flow of blood to a minimum. **Valves** are present in veins (but not in arteries) to prevent backflow of blood. (See Related Activity – Demonstrating the presence of valves in veins.)

Related Activity

Demonstrating the presence of valves in veins

The presence of a valve in a vein in the arm can be demonstrated by the method shown in Figure 13.5.

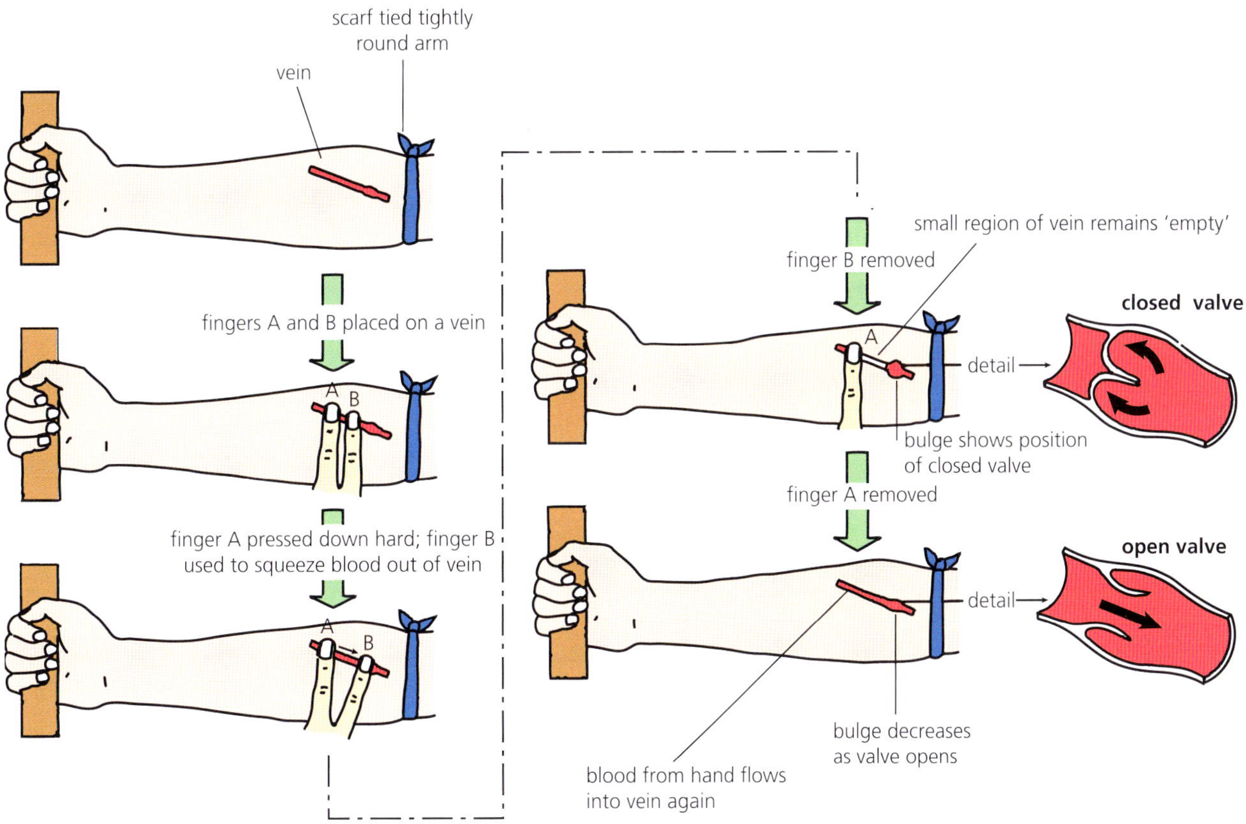

Figure 13.5 Demonstrating the presence of valves in a vein

Related Activity

Measuring the degree of stretching in arteries and veins

Figure 13.6 shows the apparatus set up and ready for use. The rings of artery and vein used in this experiment are cut from the aorta and vena cava of a cow or sheep. The length of a ring of artery with a mass carrier attached to it is measured. This is regarded as the 'original length' for all calculations. A 10 g mass is added to the carrier. The new length of the ring of artery is recorded and the percentage change in length (compared with the original length) calculated. The procedure is continued using additional 10 g masses up to 50 g and then repeated using a ring of vein.

A greater percentage increase in length is obtained for arteries than for veins in response to increasing mass added. This shows that arteries are able to stretch more than veins and it is explained by the fact that arteries contain more elastic fibres in their walls than veins.

When the experiment is extended to measure percentage change in length on *removing* each applied mass, arteries are found to return to their original length more readily than veins, showing that they are capable of more elastic recoil.

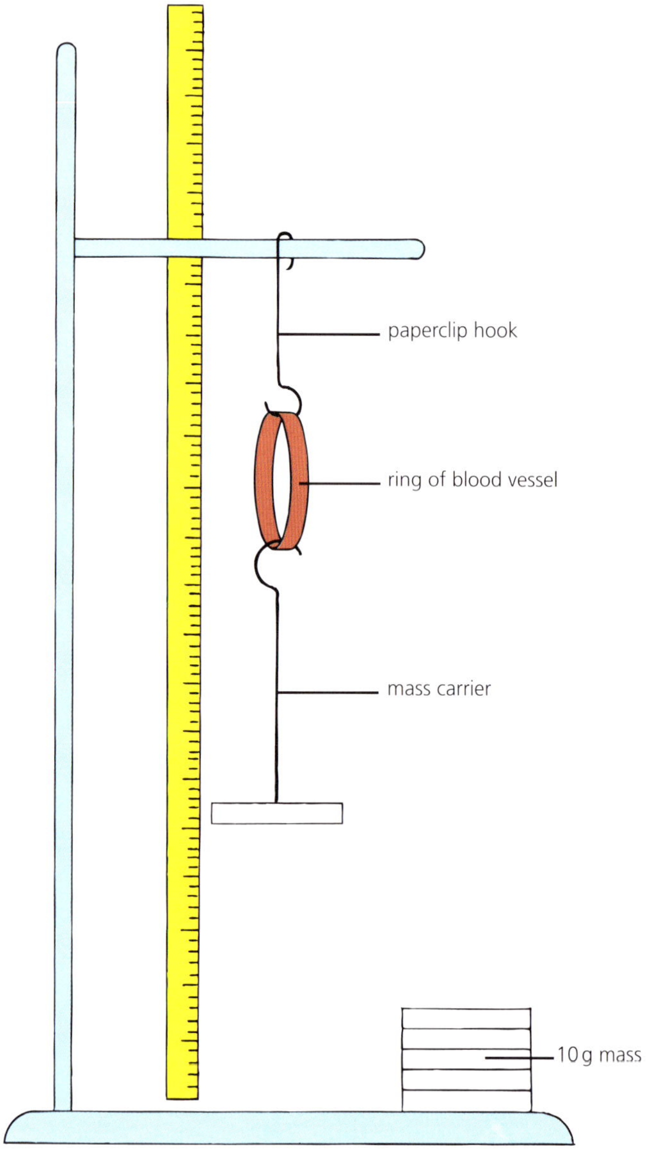

Figure 13.6 Measuring the stretching of a blood vessel

Tissue fluid

Blood consists of red blood cells, white cells and platelets bathed in plasma. **Plasma** is a watery yellow fluid that contains many dissolved substances such as glucose, amino acids, respiratory gases, plasma proteins and useful ions.

Blood arriving at the arteriole side of a capillary bed (see Figure 13.7) is at a higher pressure than blood in the capillaries. As blood is forced into these narrow exchange vessels, it undergoes a form of **pressure filtration** and much of the plasma (containing small dissolved molecules) is squeezed out through the thin walls. This liquid is called **tissue fluid**. It differs from blood plasma in that it does not contain plasma proteins because these molecules are too large to be filtered out through the capillary walls.

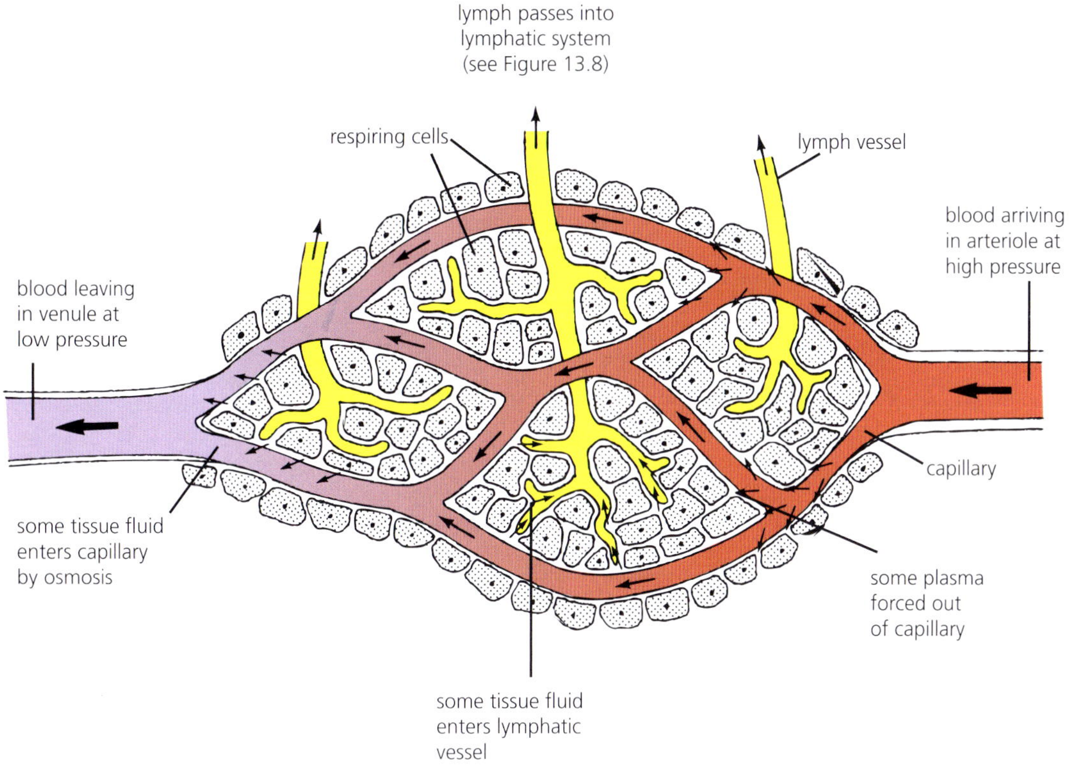

Figure 13.7 Exchange of materials in a capillary bed

Exchange of materials

The network of capillaries in a capillary bed is so dense that every living cell in the body is located close to a blood capillary and is constantly bathed in tissue fluid. Since tissue fluid contains a high concentration of soluble food molecules, dissolved oxygen and useful ions, these diffuse down a concentration gradient into nearby cells, supplying them with their requirements. At the same time, carbon dioxide and other metabolic wastes diffuse out of the cells into the tissue fluid to be excreted.

Osmotic return of tissue fluid

Much of the tissue fluid returns to the blood in the capillaries at the venule side of the capillary bed. This process is brought about by **osmosis**, with water passing from a region of higher water concentration (tissue fluid lacking plasma proteins) to a region of lower water concentration (blood plasma rich in soluble proteins) down a water concentration gradient. Carbon dioxide and metabolic wastes enter the bloodstream by diffusion.

Lymphatic return of tissue fluid

Some of the tissue fluid does not return to the blood in the capillaries. Instead this excess tissue fluid is absorbed by thin-walled lymphatic vessels, which have blind ends and are located in the connective tissue among the living cells (see Figure 13.7). Once in a lymphatic vessel, the tissue fluid is called **lymph**.

Lymphatic system

Lymph is collected by a vast network of tiny lymph vessels, which unite to form larger vessels, a few of which are shown in Figure 13.8. Flow of lymph through the lymphatic system is brought about mainly by the vessels being **periodically compressed** when muscles contract during breathing, locomotion and other body movements. Backflow of lymph is prevented by the presence of **valves** in the larger vessels. These vessels eventually return their contents via two lymphatic **ducts**, which enter the veins coming from the arms (see Figure 13.8).

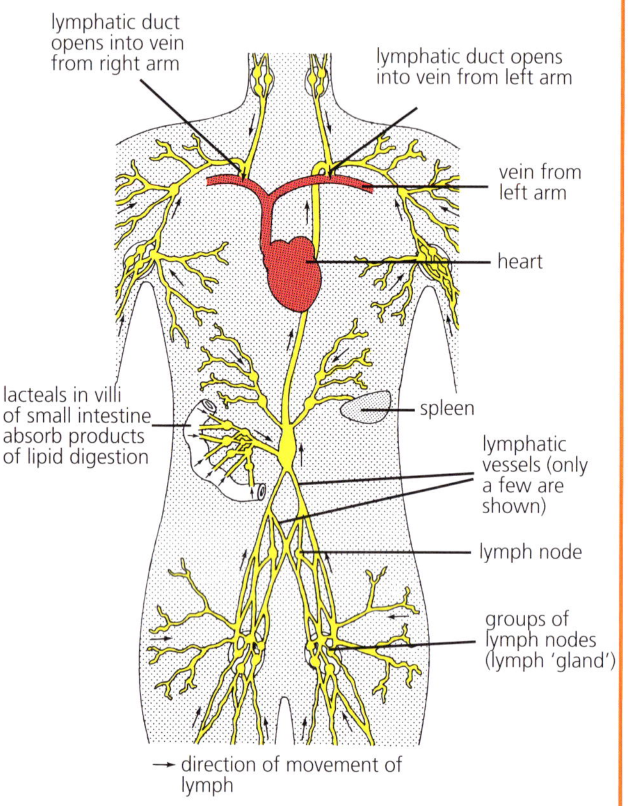

Figure 13.8 Lymphatic system

The lymphatic system is regarded as a specialised part of the cardiovascular system because it consists of:

- lymph fluid that is derived from blood
- a system of vessels that returns lymph to the bloodstream.

Case Study Disorders of the lymphatic system

Oedema

Oedema is the name given to the condition where tissue fluid accumulates in the spaces between cells and blood capillaries, causing tissues to swell up. Oedema can be caused by several factors, including the following.

Blood pressure

High blood pressure can result in tissue fluid being produced at a rate faster than it is drained away by the lymphatic system.

Malnutrition

A prolonged dietary deficiency of protein can result in the plasma protein level in the blood being so low that it is similar in concentration to that of the tissue fluid. Under these circumstances, little or no tissue fluid is returned osmotically to the blood. The lymphatic system is unable to remove the extra volume of fluid, which tends to gather in the abdominal region. An abdomen swollen in this way is a symptom of **kwashiorkor** (see Figure 13.9). This is a severe form of malnutrition experienced by young children (especially infants weaned off breast milk by a mother with a newborn baby to feed).

Parasites

The tiny larvae of one type of parasitic worm are transmitted by mosquitoes. Once inside the body, they invade the lymphatic system. When they mature into adult worms, they take up residence in, and block, lymph vessels, especially those in the legs. This obstruction along with excessive growth of neighbouring tissues in the infected area results in **elephantiasis** (see Figure 13.10), an enormous enlargement of the affected extremity.

→

Figure 13.9 Kwashiorkor

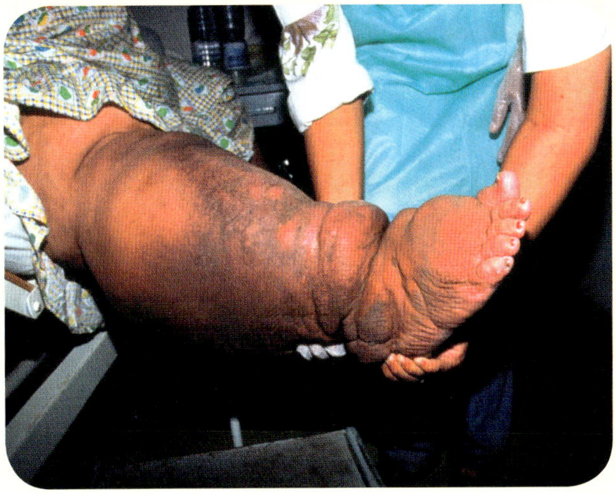

Figure 13.10 Elephantiasis

Testing Your Knowledge

1 Decide whether each of the following statements is true or false and then write T or F to indicate your choice. Where a statement is false, give the word that should have been used in place of the word in bold print. (6)

a) The **carotid** vein returns deoxygenated blood from the head to the vena cava.

b) The **renal** artery carries blood to the kidneys to be purified.

c) The pulmonary **vein** carries deoxygenated blood from the heart to the lungs.

d) The **hepatic portal** vein carries deoxygenated blood from the gut to the liver.

e) The **coronary** vein carries oxygenated blood from the lungs to the heart.

f) The hepatic **artery** carries deoxygenated blood from the liver to the vena cava.

2 **a)** Give TWO structural differences between an artery and a vein. (2)

b) Give ONE functional difference between an artery and a vein. (1)

3 **a)** What is *tissue fluid*? (2)

b) Name a substance that passes from body cells into tissue fluid. (1)

c) Briefly describe TWO methods by which tissue fluid returns to the bloodstream. (2)

4 **a)** Briefly describe the means by which lymph in a lymph vessel is forced along through the lymphatic system. (1)

b) What structures prevent backflow of lymph in the lymphatic system? (1)

c) Which structures enable lymph to return to the blood circulatory system? (1)

Applying Your Knowledge and Skills

1 By naming the heart chambers and the main blood vessels involved, describe the route taken by:

a) an oxygen molecule absorbed into the blood at an alveolus in the lungs and transported to a kidney cell (5)

b) a carbon dioxide molecule formed in a respiring brain cell and transported to an alveolus for removal. (5)

2 Figure 13.11 shows a transverse section of part of a vein and the outline for the equivalent part of an artery.

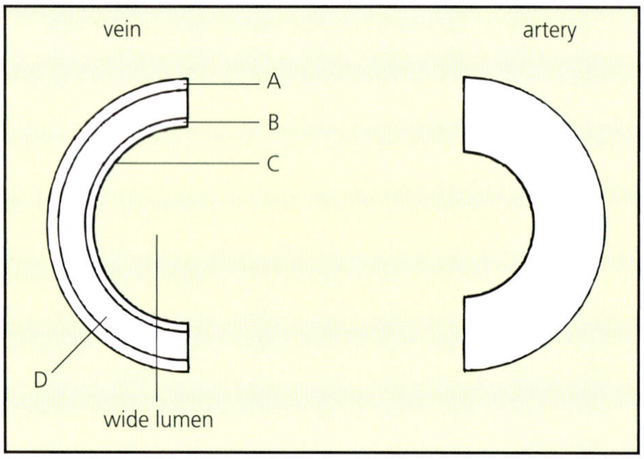

Figure 13.11

a) Copy or trace the diagram and name parts A, B, C and D. (4)

b) Complete the diagram to show the structure of an artery and label the parts. (4)

c) i) State a further structural difference between the two types of vessel that is not shown in this diagram.

ii) With the aid of simple diagrams, describe the role played by these structures. (4)

3 *Arteriole, artery, capillary, vein* and *venule* are five types of blood vessel. Using only these terms (but as often as you require), construct a flow chart to indicate the route taken by a red blood cell as it travels from a capillary bed in the body via the heart, lungs and heart again before returning to a capillary bed in the body. (4)

4 Table 13.1 shows the rate of blood flow in various parts of a person's body under differing conditions of exercise.

a) What effect does increasingly strenuous exercise have on blood flow:

i) in skeletal muscle?

ii) to the gut?

iii) Suggest the reason for the difference in each case. (4)

b) Which other body part(s) shows the same trend in response to an increase in exercise as i) skeletal muscle, ii) gut? (2)

c) i) Which body part's rate of blood flow remains unaffected by exercise?

ii) Suggest why. (2)

d) Briefly describe the mechanism by which blood vessels control distribution of blood to different parts of the body. (2)

5 The eight set-ups in Figure 13.12 show the apparatus used to investigate the elasticity of a ring of blood vessel.

a) Which of the following pairs could be used to compare the effect of type of blood vessel on elasticity? (1)

A 1 and 4 **B** 2 and 5 **C** 3 and 6 **D** 7 and 8

b) Which of the following pairs should be compared to find out the effect of number of weights on the elasticity of a vein? (1)

A 1 and 2 **B** 3 and 7 **C** 5 and 6 **D** 4 and 8

Part of body	Rate of blood flow (cm^3/min)		
	At rest	Light exercise	Strenuous exercise
Skeletal muscle	1200	4500	12500
Gut	1400	1100	600
Skin	500	1500	1900
Kidneys	1100	900	600
Brain	750	750	750
Cardiac muscle	250	350	750

Table 13.1

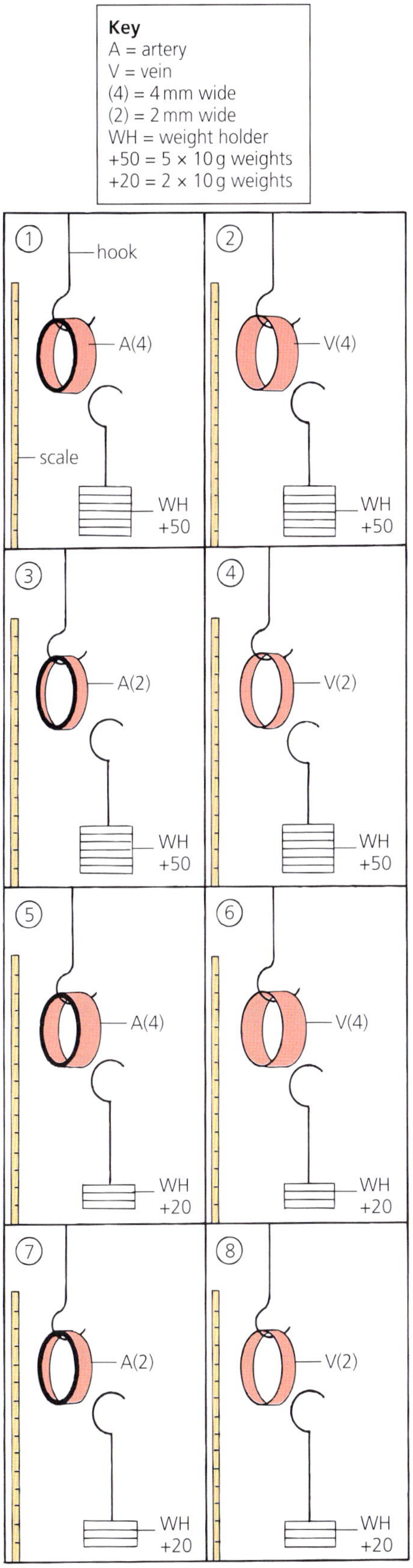

Figure 13.12

c) Which of the following pairs could be used to compare the effect of width of a ring on its elasticity? (1)

A 1 and 3 **B** 2 and 4 **C** 5 and 8 **D** 6 and 7

d) A comparison of 1 and 5 would indicate the effect of which of the following factors on elasticity of a vessel? (1)

A type of blood vessel
B width of ring of vein
C number of weights added
D thickness of vessel wall

6 Figure 13.13 shows part of the human circulatory system and the details of exchange of materials in a capillary bed.

a) Name the different types of blood vessel numbered 1–5. (5)

b) In what way does blood pressure differ between points W and X in the diagram of the close-up? (1)

c) i) Name the liquid present in space Y.

ii) Describe how it is formed.

iii) Explain why the presence of this liquid is of importance to nearby cells.

iv) State ONE way in which the liquid differs from blood plasma. (4)

d) Identify structure Z and state its function. (2)

e) Which of arrows A–D represents the osmotic return of tissue fluid to the bloodstream? (1)

7 Give an account of the structure and function of the lymphatic system. (9)

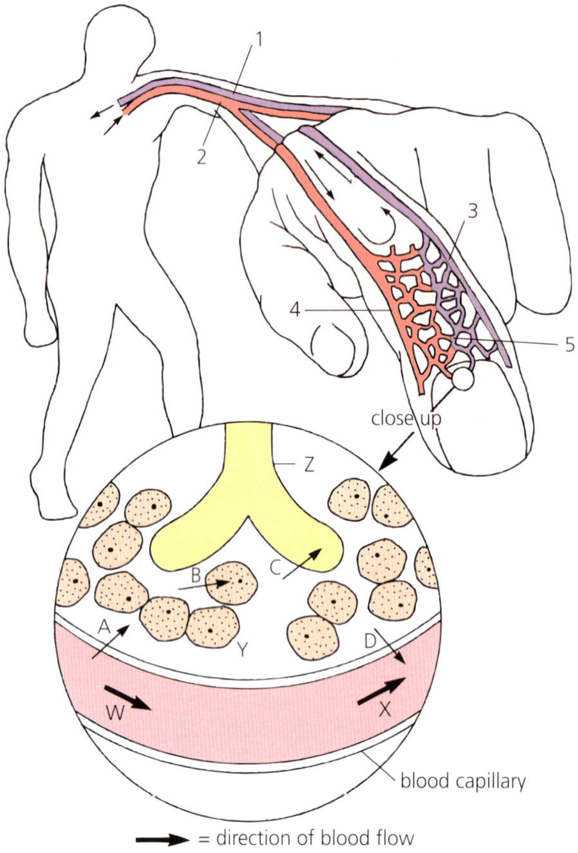

Figure 13.13

14 Structure and function of the heart

Structure of the heart

The continuous circulation of blood round the body is maintained by a powerful muscular pump, the **heart**. This organ is divided into four chambers, two **atria** and two **ventricles** (see Figure 14.1). The right atrium receives deoxygenated blood from all parts of the body via two main veins called the **venae cavae**. This deoxygenated blood passes into the right ventricle and then leaves the heart by the **pulmonary artery** which divides into two branches each leading to a lung.

Following oxygenation in the lungs, blood returns to the heart by the **pulmonary veins** and enters the left atrium. It flows from the left atrium into the left ventricle and leaves the heart by the **aorta**, the largest artery in the body.

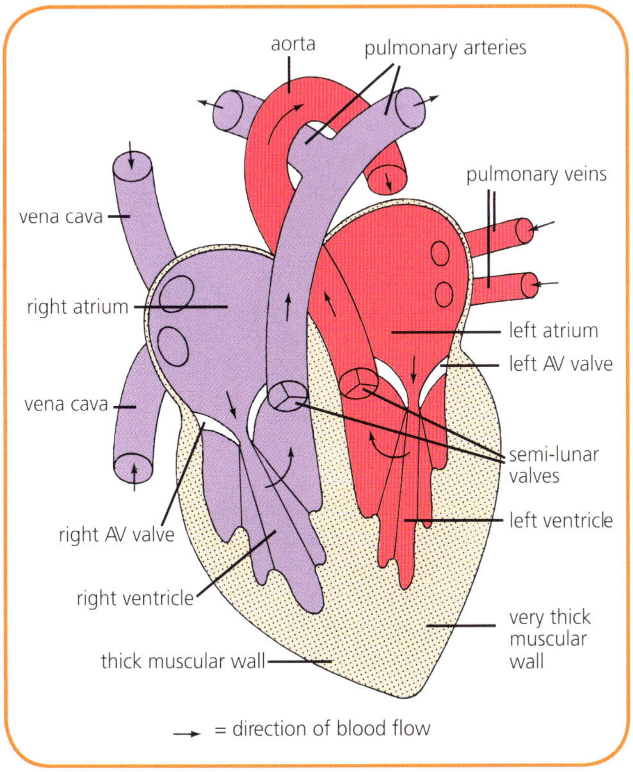

Figure 14.1 Human heart

Thickness of ventricle walls

The wall of the left ventricle is particularly thick and muscular since it is required to pump blood all round the body. The wall of the right ventricle is less thick since it only pumps blood to the lungs.

Valves

Figure 14.1 shows the four heart valves. Two of these, situated between the atria and the ventricles, are called the **atrio-ventricular (AV)** valves. They allow blood to flow from atria to ventricles but prevent backflow from ventricles to atria.

The other two heart valves, situated at the origins of the pulmonary artery and aorta, are called **semi-lunar (SL)** valves. These valves open during ventricular contraction allowing blood to flow into the arteries. When arterial pressure exceeds ventricular pressure, they close, preventing backflow. The presence of the valves ensures that blood is only able to flow in **one direction** through the heart.

Cardiac function

At each contraction of the heart, the right ventricle pumps the same volume of blood through the pulmonary artery (and round to the lungs) as the left ventricle pumps through the aorta (and round the body).

Heart rate (pulse) is the number of heartbeats that occurs per minute. (See Related Activity – Measuring pulse rate using a pulsometer.)

Stroke volume is the volume of blood expelled by each ventricle on contraction. The stronger the contraction, the greater the stroke volume.

Cardiac output is the volume of blood pumped out of a ventricle per minute. Thus cardiac output (CO) = heart rate (HR) × stroke volume (SV).

Table 14.1 shows an example of the effect of exercise on cardiac output for a human adult.

State of body	Heart rate (beats/min)	Stroke volume (ml)	Cardiac output by each ventricle (l/min)
At rest	60	60	3.6
During exercise	120	70	8.4
During strenuous exercise	180	80	14.4

Table 14.1 Effect of exercise on cardiac output

Related Activity

Measuring pulse rate using a pulsometer

Pulse rate can be measured by using a **pulsometer**, as shown in Figure 14.2. **Resting pulse rate** is a measure of pulse rate when the body is at rest and has not been exercising for some time. On average, resting pulse rate for men is approximately 75 beats/minute and slightly higher for women, although any value between 60 and 90 is regarded as being within the normal range.

Pulse as a health indicator

If a person is fit, the relative quantity of cardiac muscle present in their heart wall is greater and more efficient than that of an unfit person. A very fit person tends to have a **lower pulse rate** than an unfit person because the fit person's heart is larger and stronger. Therefore it does not need to contract as often to pump an equal volume of blood round the body. (In other words, the stroke volume is greater.)

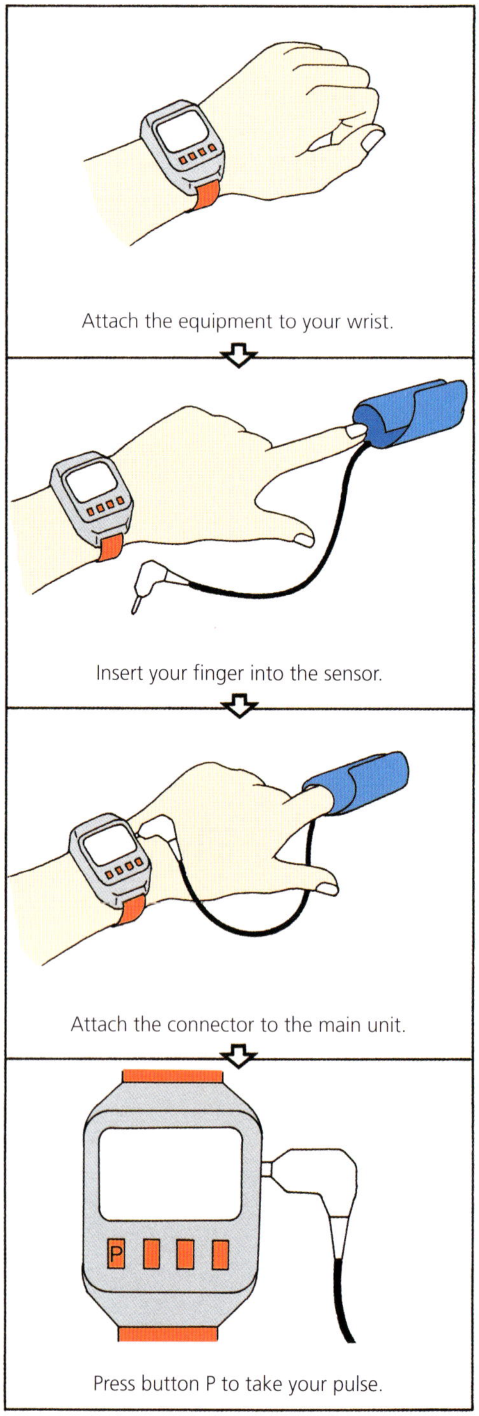
Attach the equipment to your wrist.
Insert your finger into the sensor.
Attach the connector to the main unit.
P
Press button P to take your pulse.

Figure 14.2 Using a pulsometer

Testing Your Knowledge 1

1 Construct a table that names the four chambers of the human heart, the type of blood (oxygenated/deoxygenated) that it contains, where this blood has come from and where this blood is going. (8)

2 Compare the location and function of an AV valve with those of an SL valve. (2)

3 Distinguish clearly between the terms *stroke volume, cardiac output* and *heart rate.* (3)

Cardiac cycle

The term **cardiac cycle** refers to the pattern of contraction (**systole**) and relaxation (**diastole**) shown by the heart during one complete heartbeat. On average, the length of one cardiac cycle is 0.8 seconds, as shown in Figure 14.3 which is based on a heart rate of 75 beats per minute.

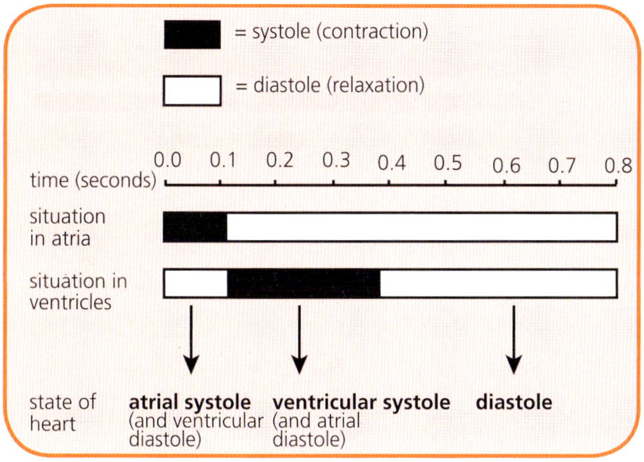

Figure 14.3 One cardiac cycle

During **diastole**, the return of blood via the venae cavae and pulmonary veins to the atria causes the volume of blood in the atria to increase. Eventually atrial pressure exceeds that in the ventricles, the AV valves are pushed open and blood starts to enter the ventricles.

During **atrial systole** (see Figure 14.4) the two atria contract simultaneously and send the remainder of the blood down into the ventricles through the open AV valves. The ventricles (still in the relaxed state of ventricular diastole) fill up with blood and the SL valves remain closed.

Atrial systole is followed about 0.1 seconds later by **ventricular systole**. This stage involves the contraction of the ventricles and the closure of the AV valves. The pressure exerted on the blood in the ventricles (as the cardiac muscle contracts) soon exceeds the blood pressure in the arteries. The SL valves are pushed open and blood is pumped out of the heart and into the aorta and pulmonary arteries.

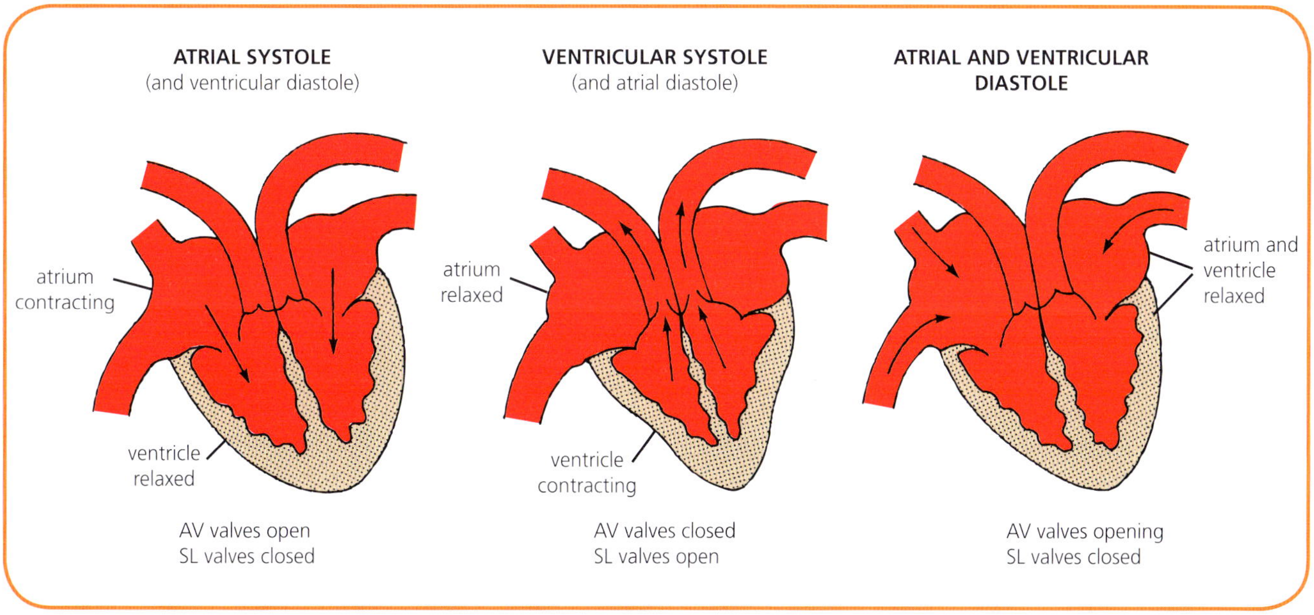

Figure 14.4 Systole and diastole

Related Topic

Valves and heart sounds

Figure 14.5 refers to some of the changes that occur during the cardiac cycle. At point W in the graph (which refers to the left side of the heart only), ventricular pressure exceeds atrial pressure forcing the AV valve to close. This produces the first heart sound ('**lubb**') which can be heard using a **stethoscope**. It can also be detected as a pattern shown on a **phonocardiogram** (see Figure 14.5).

At point X, ventricular pressure exceeds aortic pressure forcing open the SL valve. At point Y, ventricular pressure falls below aortic pressure causing the SL valve to close. This produces the second heart sound ('**dupp**') heard through a stethoscope. At point Z, ventricular pressure falls below atrial pressure and the AV valve opens.

The heart sound 'lubb' is heard at the start of ventricular systole and 'dupp' at the start of ventricular diastole. Abnormal heart sounds produced by abnormal patterns of cardiac blood flow are called **heart murmurs**. These are often caused by defective valves, which fail to open or close fully. This type of condition can be inherited or result from diseases such as rheumatic fever.

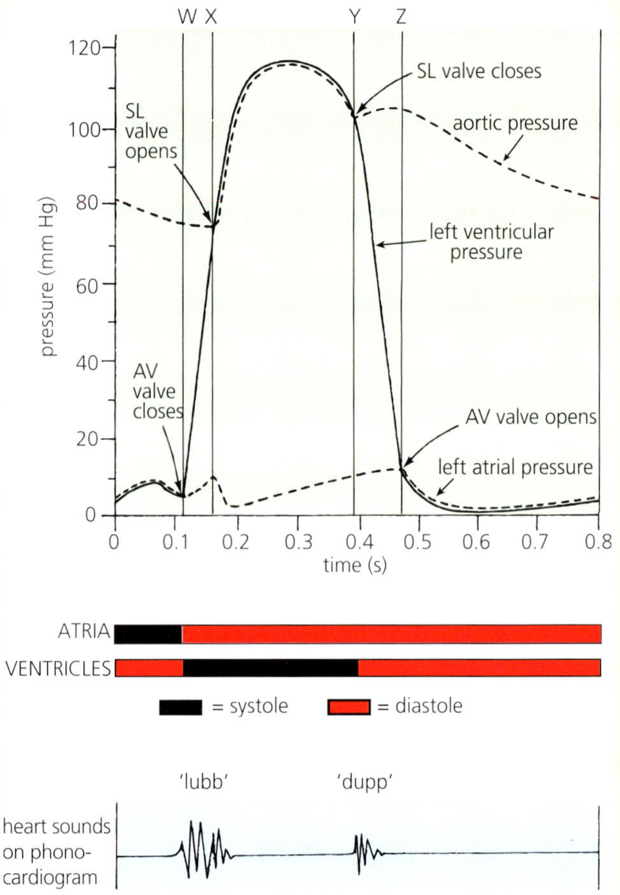

Figure 14.5 Pressure changes and heart sounds

During **diastole** the higher pressure of blood in the arteries closes the SL valves again and the next cardiac cycle begins. The closing of the AV and SL valves are responsible for the sounds that can be heard during each cardiac cycle. (See Related Topic – Valves and heart sounds.)

Cardiac conducting system

The heartbeat originates in the heart itself. The sequence of events that occurs during each heartbeat is brought about by the activity of the **pacemaker** and the **conducting system** of the heart (see Figure 14.6). The pacemaker, also known as the **sino-atrial node (SAN)**, is located in the wall of the right atrium. It is a small region of specialised tissue (composed of autorhythmic cells) that exhibits **spontaneous excitation**. This means that the pacemaker initiates electrical impulses that make cardiac muscle cells contract at a certain rate. This rate can be regulated by other factors to suit the

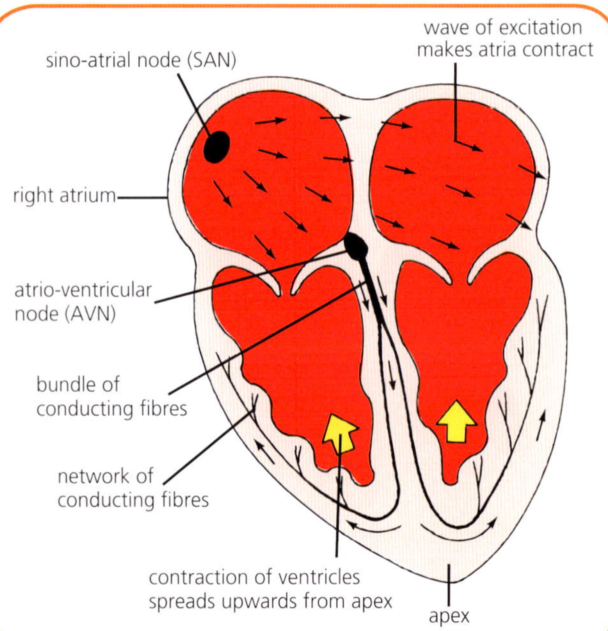

Figure 14.6 Conducting system of the heart

body's requirements (see below). The pacemaker works automatically and would continue to function even in the absence of nerve connections from the rest of the body.

A wave of excitation originating in the SAN spreads through the muscle cells in the wall of the two atria making them contract simultaneously (**atrial systole**). The impulse is then picked up by the **atrio-ventricular node (AVN)** located centrally near the base of the atria.

The impulse passes from the AVN into a bundle of **conducting fibres**, which divides into left and right branches. Each of these branches is continuous with a dense network of tiny conducting fibres in the ventricular walls. Stimulation of these fibres causes simultaneous contraction of the two ventricles (**ventricular systole**) starting from the heart apex and spreading upwards.

Such coordination of heartbeat ensures that:

- each type of systole involves the combined effect of many muscle cells contracting
- ventricular systole occurs slightly later than atrial systole, allowing time for the ventricles to fill completely before they contract.

Regulation

The pacemaker tissue alone initiates each heartbeat. However, heart rate is not fixed as it is altered by **nervous** and **hormonal** activity.

Autonomic nervous control

The heart is supplied with branches of the opposing parts of the **autonomic nervous system** (see page 203). Control centres located in the medulla of the brain regulate heart rate (see Figure 14.7). The **cardio-accelerator centre** sends its nerve impulses via a sympathetic nerve to the heart; the **cardio-inhibitor centre** sends its information via a parasympathetic nerve.

The two pathways are **antagonistic** to one another in that they have opposite effects on heart rate. An increase in the relative number of nerve impulses arriving at the SAN (pacemaker) via the **sympathetic** nerve results in an **increase** in heart rate. An increase in the relative number of impulses arriving at the SAN via the **parasympathetic** nerve results in a **decrease** in heart rate. The actual rate at which the heart beats is determined by which system exerts the greater influence over the heart at any given moment.

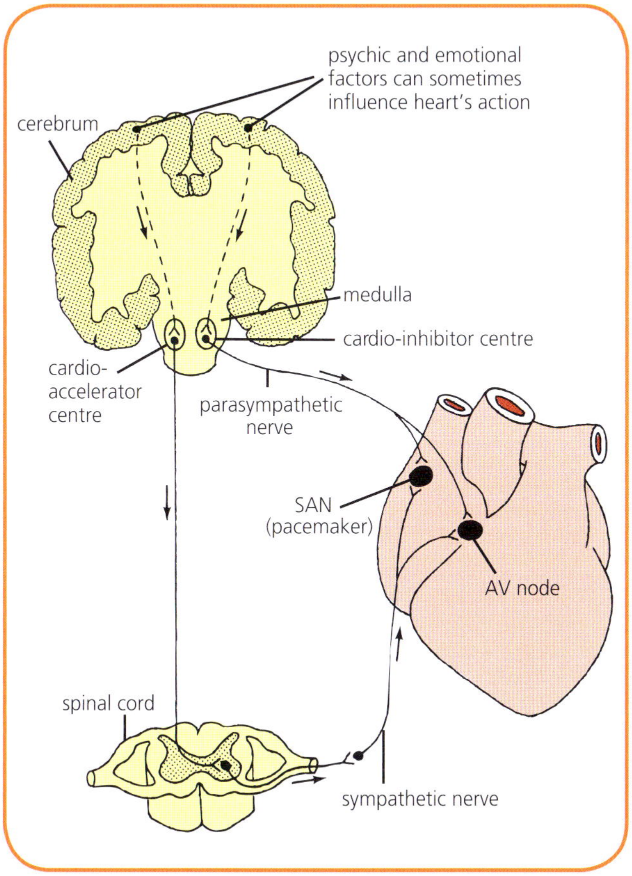

Figure 14.7 Autonomic nervous control of heart rate

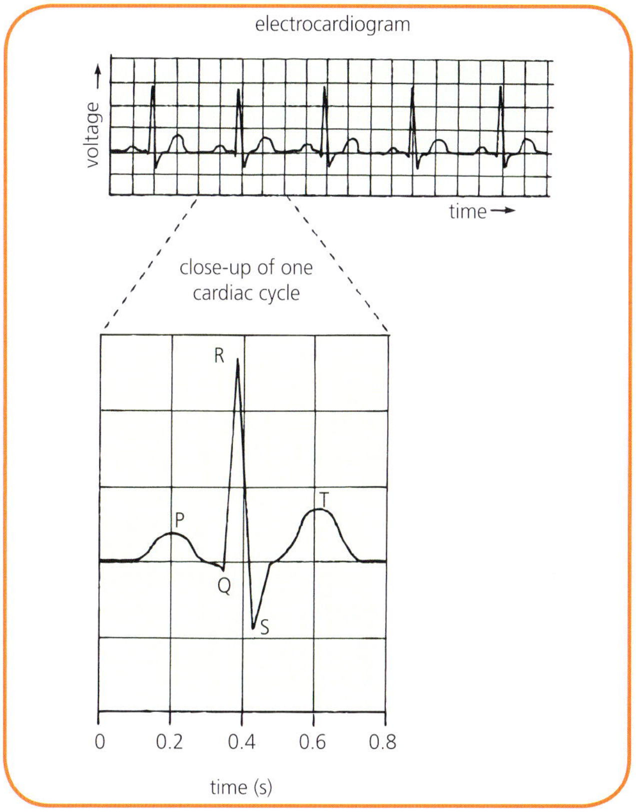

Figure 14.8 Normal electrocardiogram

Neurotransmitter substances released by these nerves influence the SAN. Sympathetic nerves release the neurotransmitter **noradrenaline**, whereas parasympathetic nerves release **acetylcholine** (see page 232).

Hormonal control

Under certain circumstances (such as 'fight or flight' – see page 205), the sympathetic nervous system acts on the adrenal glands, making them release the hormone **adrenaline** into the bloodstream. On reaching the SAN, this hormone makes the pacemaker generate cardiac impulses at a higher rate and bring about an **increase** in heart rate.

Electrocardiogram

The electrical activity of the heart generates tiny currents that can be picked up by electrodes placed on the skin surface. The electrical signals, once amplified and displayed on an oscilloscope screen, produce a pattern called an **electrocardiogram** (**ECG**).

The normal ECG pattern is shown in Figure 14.8. It consists of three distinct waves normally referred to as P, QRS and T. The **P wave** corresponds to the wave of electrical excitation spreading over the atria from the SAN that brings about atrial systole. The **QRS complex** represents the wave of excitation passing through the ventricles that brings about ventricular systole. The **T wave** corresponds to the electrical recovery of the ventricles occurring towards the end of ventricular systole. In the example shown in Figure 14.8, each cardiac cycle lasts for 0.8 seconds. From this reading, heart rate can be calculated. In this case it would be 60/0.8 = 75 beats/min.

Related Activity

Examining abnormal ECGs

Abnormal heart rhythms and some forms of heart disease can be detected and diagnosed using **ECGs** because these produce unusual but identifiable patterns. Some examples are shown in Figure 14.9.

When extremely rapid rates of electrical excitation occur, these lead to an increase in rate of contraction of either atria or ventricles. In an **atrial flutter**, for example, the contractions occur much more rapidly than normal but do remain coordinated. The example in Figure 14.9 shows three P waves for every one QRS complex.

In a **fibrillation**, contractions of different groups of heart muscle cells occur at different times, making it impossible for coordinated pumping of the heart chambers to take place. Ventricular fibrillation, for example, produces an ECG with an irregular pattern. This condition is lethal if it is not corrected.

During **ventricular tachycardia**, abnormal cells in the ventricle walls act like pacemakers and make these chambers beat rapidly and independently of the atria. The P (atrial) waves are absent and the wide QRS waves are abnormal.

Relief for some sufferers of abnormal heart rhythms can be provided by fitting them with an **artificial pacemaker**. This acts as a stimulator and sends out small electric impulses to the heart, making it beat in a normal, regular manner.

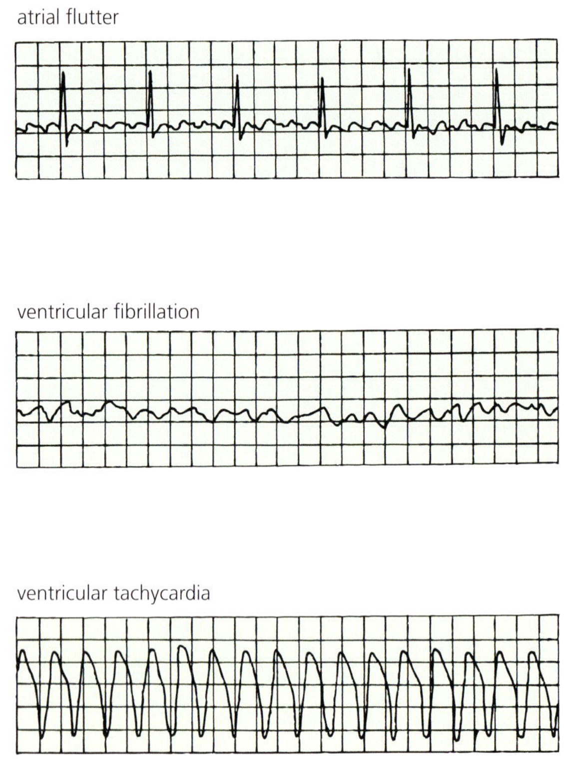

Figure 14.9 Abnormal ECGs

Emergency

CPR (cardiopulmonary resuscitation) is an emergency procedure involving chest compressions administered to a person who has suffered a cardiac arrest. If it is followed soon after by **defibrillation** (the administration of an electric shock to the subject's heart by trained staff), the person's chance of survival is increased by up to 30%. Defibrillation is only effective for certain abnormal heart rhythms such as fibrillation and ventricular tachycardia.

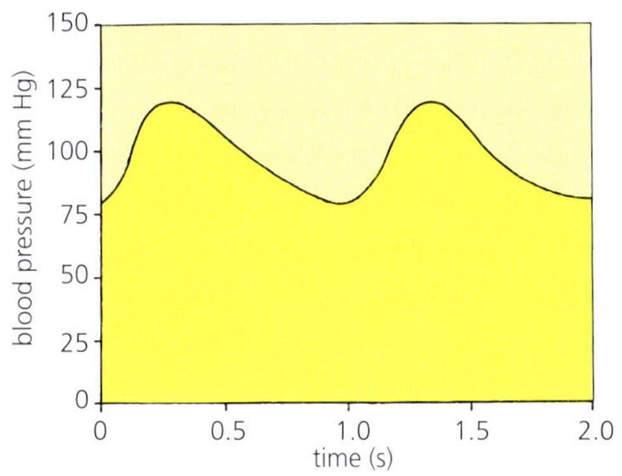

Figure 14.10 Blood pressure trace

Blood pressure

Blood pressure is the force exerted by blood against the walls of the blood vessels. It is measured in millimetres of mercury (mm Hg) as described below.

Blood pressure is generated by the contraction of the ventricles and it is therefore highest in the large elastic arteries (aorta and pulmonary artery). As the heart goes through systole and diastole during each cardiac cycle, the **arterial pressure rises and falls**. For example, during ventricular **systole**, the pressure of blood in the aorta rises to a maximum (for example, 120 mm Hg); during ventricular **diastole**, it drops to a minimum (for example, 80 mm Hg). Figure 14.10 shows the blood pressure trace for a normal 18-year-old at rest.

Decreasing blood pressure during circulation

Although the pumping action of the heart causes fluctuations in aortic blood pressure, the average pressure in the aorta remains fairly constant. Figure 14.11 shows how a progressive **decrease in pressure** occurs as blood travels round the circulatory system dropping to almost zero by the time it reaches the right atrium again.

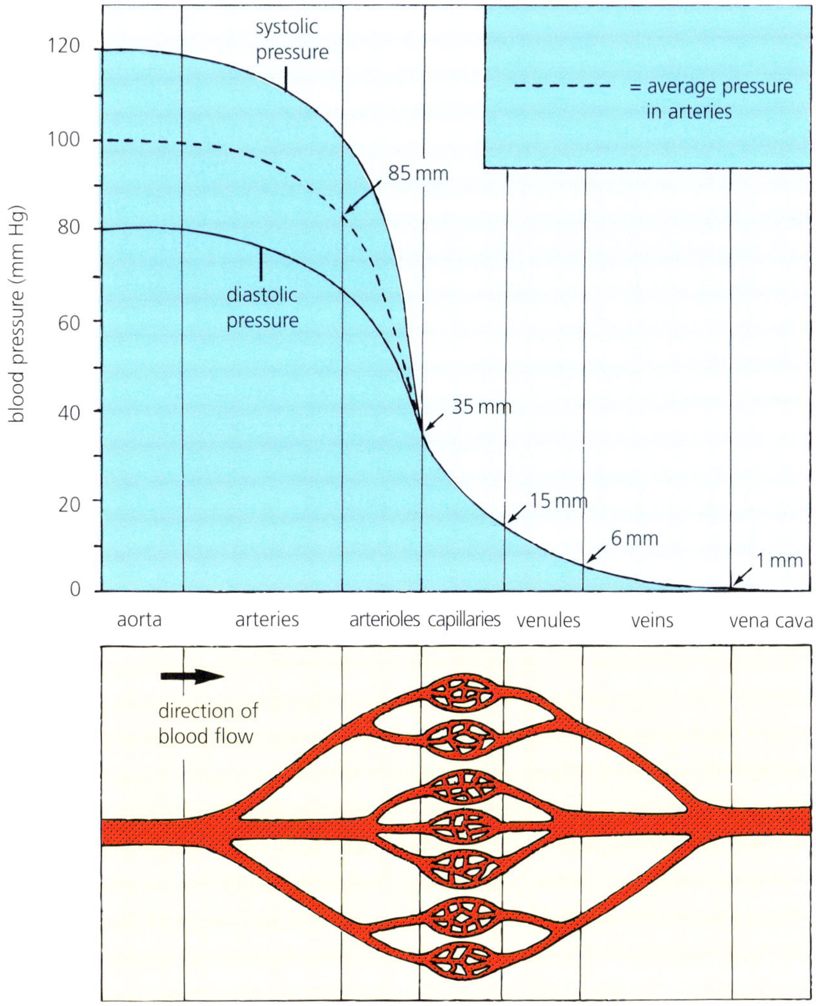

Figure 14.11 Decrease in blood pressure

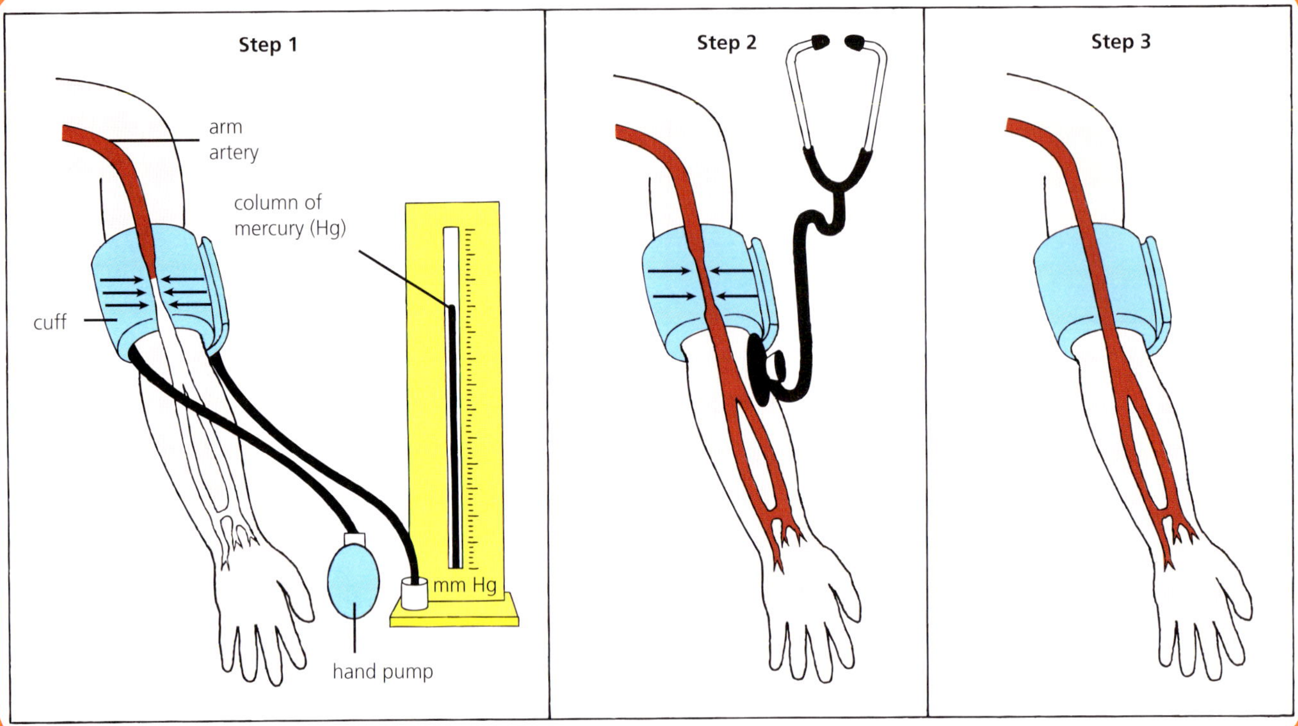

Figure 14.12 Measuring blood pressure

As blood flows through a narrow blood vessel, friction occurs between the blood and the vessel wall making the wall resist blood flow to some extent. It is this resistance by vessel walls to the flow of blood that causes the decrease in its pressure.

Measurement of blood pressure

Systolic and diastolic pressures can be measured using an inflatable **sphygmomanometer**, which makes use of a column of mercury to give the pressure readings as shown in Figure 14.12. (A sphygmomanometer can be digital, as shown in Figure 20.14 on page 240.)

- In step 1, the cuff is inflated until the pressure that it exerts stops blood flowing through the arm artery.
- In step 2, the cuff is allowed to deflate gradually until the pressure of blood in the artery exceeds the pressure in the cuff. A pulse can now be felt and blood can be heard to spurt through the arm artery again using a stethoscope. The pressure at which this first occurs is a measure of **systolic pressure**.
- In step 3, more air is released from the cuff until the sound of spurting blood disappears and a pulse is no longer detected. The pressure at which this first occurs is a measure of **diastolic pressure**.

Blood pressure is found to vary considerably from person to person. A typical set of values for a healthy young adult would be a systolic pressure of 120 mm Hg and a diastolic pressure of 80 mm Hg. These values are normally written as 120/80 mm Hg and referred to as '120 over 80'.

Hypertension

Hypertension (high blood pressure) is the prolonged elevation of blood pressure when at rest. It is normally indicated by values of systolic pressure greater than 140 mm Hg and diastolic pressure greater than 90 mm Hg. It is rare in young people but fairly common in adults over the age of 35. It is a major risk factor for many diseases that have a relatively high incidence later in life such as **coronary heart disease** and **strokes**.

Hypertension is commonly found in people with an unhealthy lifestyle that includes some or all of:

- being overweight
- not taking enough exercise
- eating a diet excessively rich in fatty food especially animal fat
- consuming too much salt
- drinking alcohol to excess regularly
- being under continuous stress.

Testing Your Knowledge 2

1 a) Distinguish between the terms *systole* and *diastole*. (2)
b) Construct a table to compare atrial systole and ventricular systole with reference to state of atrial wall, state of ventricular wall, state of AV valves and state of SL valves. (4)

2 a) i) By what other name is the heart's pacemaker known?
ii) Briefly describe the function performed by the pacemaker. (2)
b) i) What heart structure is represented by the letters AVN?
ii) This structure passes impulses on to the conducting fibres. In which region of the heart are these fibres located?
iii) Which stage of the cardiac cycle occurs as a direct result of the conducting fibres passing on the impulses? (3)

3 a) What is an *electrocardiogram*? (1)
b) i) Of how many waves does a normal ECG consist?
ii) How many of these represent waves of electrical excitation affecting regions of the heart? (2)

4 a) i) Is the pressure of blood in the aorta at its maximum during ventricular systole or ventricular diastole?
ii) Explain your answer. (2)
b) What name is given to an instrument used to measure blood pressure? (1)
c) Give ONE reason why prolonged hypertension is dangerous. (1)

Applying Your Knowledge and Skills

1 a) Show by means of an equation the relationship between heart rate (HR), cardiac output (CO) and stroke volume (SV). (1)
b) Calculate:
i) CO when HR = 72 beats/min and SV = 80 ml
ii) HR when SV = 85 ml and CO = 8.5 l/min
iii) SV when HR = 150 beats/min and CO = 15 l/min
iv) SV when HR = 125 beat/min and CO = 15 l/min. (4)
c) If situations **iii)** and **iv)** in **b)** refer to identical twins doing the same exercise, which one is fitter? Explain your answer. (2)

2 Figure 14.13 represents the repeated series of events that occurs during the human heartbeat.
a) i) Which lasts longer, atrial or ventricular systole?
ii) Explain why this difference is necessary. (2)
b) i) Name the stages of the cardiac cycle represented by X and Y.
ii) In what state is cardiac muscle in the atria during stage X? (3)
c) i) How many complete heartbeats are represented by the diagram?
ii) Express the person's pulse rate in beats per minute. (2)
d) Redraw part of the diagram to represent one complete heartbeat and then add the letters L and D and arrows to indicate when the two heart sounds would be heard. (3)

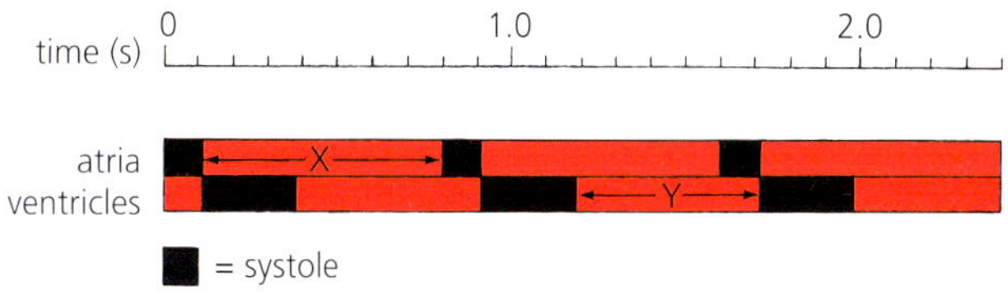

Figure 14.13

3 The graphs in Figure 14.14 show the pressure changes that occur in the heart and associated blood vessels.
a) i) State the highest pressure exerted by each ventricle during the cycle.
ii) With reference to the structure of the heart, explain the marked difference between these two pressures. (2)

→

b) State the pressure at which the following valve movements occurred:
   i) The right AV valve closed.
   ii) The SL valve opened.
   iii) The SL valve closed.
   iv) The left AV valve opened. (4)

c) At what time in the cycle did ventricular systole begin? (1)

d) Between which TWO times in the cycle did ventricular pressure exceed aortic pressure? (1)

e) State the effect of diastole on the pressure of blood in the pulmonary artery. (1)

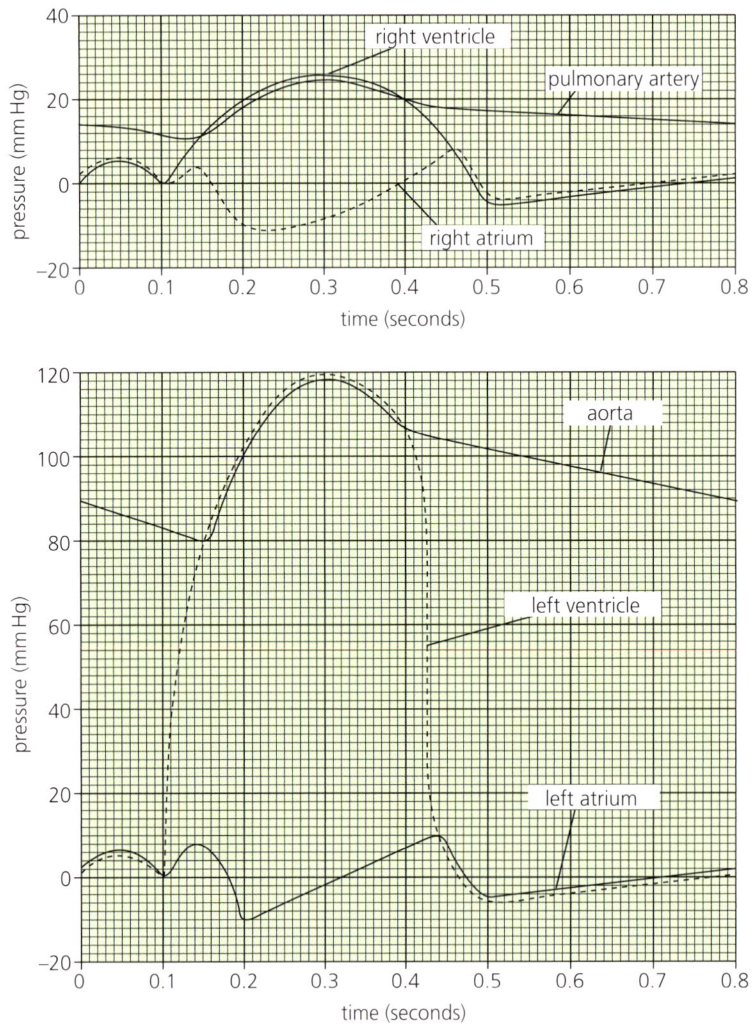

Figure 14.14

4 The data in Table 14.2 refer to normal systolic blood pressures found in humans at different ages.

Age (years)	Systolic blood pressure (mm Hg)	
	Male	Female
0–4	93	93
5–9	97	97
10–14	106	106
15–19	119	116
20–24	123	116
25–29	125	117
30–34	126	120
35–39	127	124
40–44	129	127
45–49	130	131
50–54	135	137
55–59	138	139
60–64	142	144
65–69	143	154
70–74	145	159
75–79	146	158

Table 14.2

a) Present the data as a two-tone bar chart. (4)

b) i) Make a generalisation about the effect of age on blood pressure.

ii) Give a possible explanation (related to lifestyle) to account for this trend. (2)

c) It has been suggested that female sex hormones may in some way offer protection against high blood pressure. What information from the table seems to support this theory? (1)

5 Read the passage and use the information that it contains to help you to match the answers that follow it with the blanks numbered 1–10 in Figure 14.15. (9)

Role of elastic walls

Although the ventricles do not contract during diastole, the blood pressure in the aorta does not drop to a low level. This maintenance of pressure is made possible by the fact that the walls of the aorta (and large conducting arteries near the heart) are **elastic**, enabling them to stretch during ventricular systole. During ventricular diastole (with the SL valve closed), the elastic walls **recoil** and continue to propel blood through the vessels. A similar set of events occurs in the pulmonary artery.

aorta, body, decreases, increases, open, recoil, relax, reservoir, shut, stretched

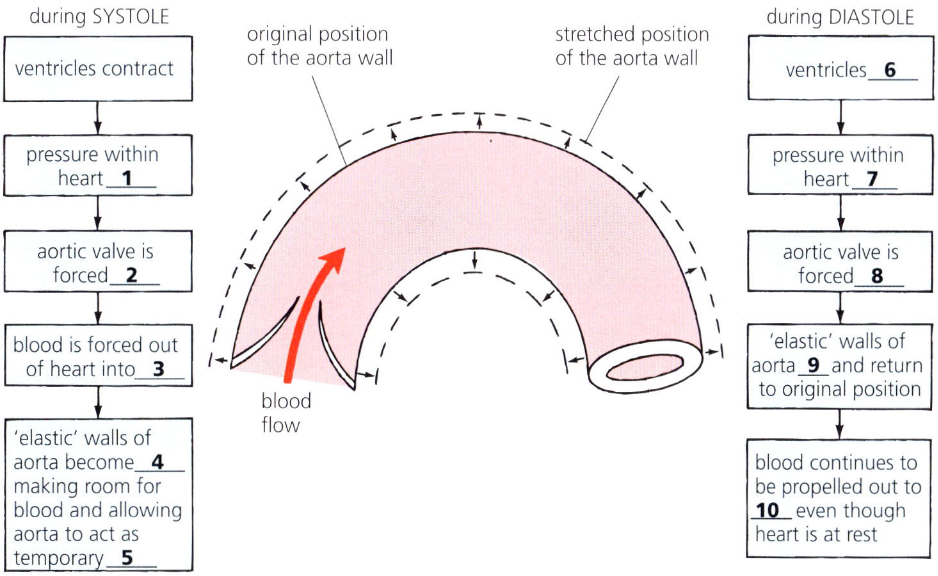

during SYSTOLE
ventricles contract
pressure within heart 1
aortic valve is forced 2
blood is forced out of heart into 3
'elastic' walls of aorta become 4 making room for blood and allowing aorta to act as temporary 5
original position of the aorta wall
stretched position of the aorta wall
blood flow
during DIASTOLE
ventricles 6
pressure within heart 7
aortic valve is forced 8
'elastic' walls of aorta 9 and return to original position
blood continues to be propelled out to 10 even though heart is at rest

Figure 14.15

6 a) Figure 14.16 shows a normal electrocardiogram containing waves X, Y and Z.
Which of these waves is produced during:
i) electrical recovery of the ventricles?
ii) spread of electrical impulses across the atria?
iii) spread of electrical signals through the ventricles? (2)

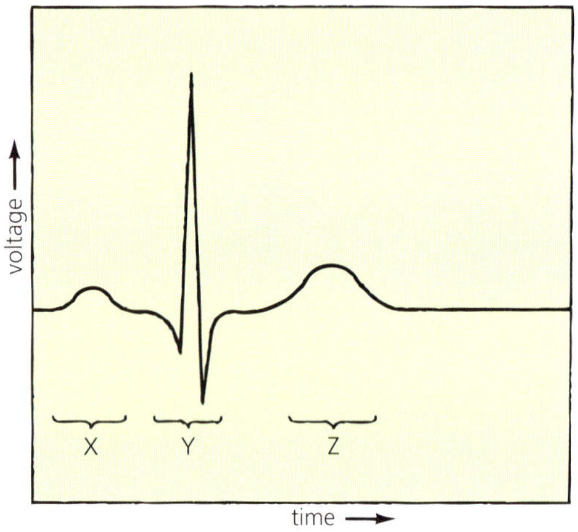

Figure 14.16

b) Figure 14.17 shows two abnormal ECGs.

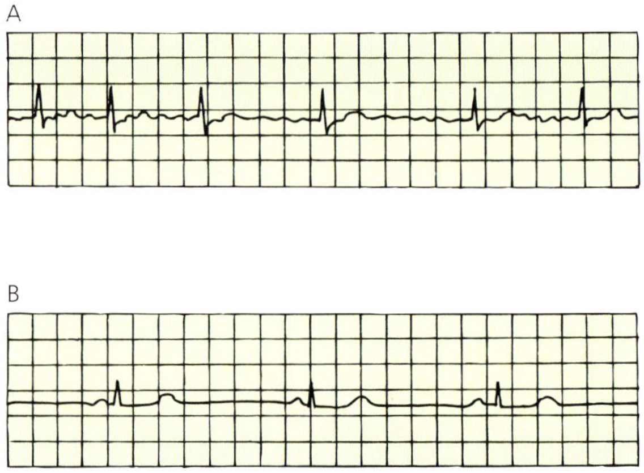

Figure 14.17

Which of these indicates:
i) an abnormally slow heart rate?
ii) atrial fibrillation?
iii) Briefly explain your choice in each case. (4)

Part of circulatory system	Blood pressure (mm Hg)	Drop in pressure in this part of system (mm Hg)
	100	0
Aorta		
	95–100	
	85–95	
Arterioles		
	15–35	
	6–15	
Small veins		
Large veins	1–2	
	0–1	

Table 14.3

7 a) i) Copy Table 14.3 and complete the left column using the terms *capillaries, large arteries, left ventricle, small arteries, venae cavae and venules.*
ii) Complete the other two columns. (6)
b) i) In which TWO parts of the system do the greatest drops in pressure occur?
ii) With reference to these parts only, state the total drop in pressure that occurs.
iii) Account for this drop in pressure. (3)

8 Write notes on each of the following:
a) the cardiac cycle (5)
b) the conducting system of the heart. (4)

What You Should Know Chapters 13–14

aorta	endothelium	semi-lunar
arterioles	fibres	sino-atrial
atria	heartbeats	sounds
atrio-ventricular	high	sphygmomano-meter
autorhythmic	hormonal	stretch
backflow	hypertension	stroke
capillary	low	systole
cardiovascular	lumen	tissue fluid
chambers	lymph	valves
circulatory	nerves	vasoconstriction
closing	osmosis	veins
contraction	output	venae cavae
decrease	protein	ventricles
diastole	pulmonary arteries	
elastic	pulmonary veins	
electro-cardiogram	pulse	

Table 14.2 Word bank for Chapters 13–14

1 The ______ is the inner cellular layer of a blood vessel's wall that lines the central cavity (______).

2 Arteries carry blood away from the heart at ______ pressure and their walls are thicker, more muscular and more ______ than those of ______ which carry blood back to the heart at ______ pressure.

3 The elasticity of arterial walls enables them to ______ and recoil in response to the surge of blood that arrives after each ______ of the heart. Veins have ______ to prevent backflow of blood.

4 Flow of blood to particular body parts can be controlled by ______ and vasodilation of ______.

5 When blood is forced through a ______ bed, some plasma passes out through the vessel walls. This liquid, which bathes the cells, is called ______. It differs from plasma in that it contains little or no plasma ______.

6 Some tissue fluid returns to blood capillaries by ______; the remainder is absorbed by tiny lymphatic vessels and becomes ______.

7 The heart has two upper ______ called atria and two lower chambers called ______. Deoxygenated blood returns to the heart from the body by the ______; it is pumped by the heart to the lungs via the ______. Oxygenated blood returns to the heart from the lungs by the ______; it is pumped by the heart to the body via the ______.

8 The atrio-ventricular (AV) valves in the heart prevent ______ of blood from the ventricles to the ______. The ______ (SL) valves prevent backflow from the large arteries to the ventricles.

9 Heart rate (______) is the number of ______ that occurs per minute. ______ volume is the volume of blood expelled by each ventricle on contraction. Cardiac ______ is the volume of blood pumped out of a ventricle per minute.

10 A cardiac cycle consists of a period of contraction called ______ and a period of relaxation called ______. During a cardiac cycle two separate heart ______ can be heard; each indicates the ______ of a set of valves.

11 Heartbeat is initiated in the heart itself by the ______ cells of the ______ node (pacemaker) which set it at a certain rate. This rate of heartbeat is then regulated by autonomic ______ and ______ control.

12 Impulses from the SAN spread through the atria and are picked up by the ______ node and passed via conducting ______ to the ventricular walls which respond by contracting.

13 The electrical activity of the heart can be displayed on a screen as an ______.

14 Blood pressure shows a progressive ______ as blood travels round the ______ system.

15 Arterial blood pressure can be measured using a ______. High blood pressure (______) is a major risk factor for ______ disease.

15 Pathology of cardiovascular disease

Pathology of cardiovascular disease (CVD)

In the UK, cardiovascular diseases are responsible for a high proportion of deaths annually, as shown in Figure 15.1.

Atherosclerosis

Atherosclerosis is the formation of plaques called atheromas beneath the inner lining (endothelium) in the wall of an artery. Initially plaques are composed largely of fatty material (mainly cholesterol – see page 186), but as the years go by they become enlarged by the addition of fibrous material, calcium and more cholesterol (see Figure 15.2).

The presence of these larger atheromas leads to:

- a significant reduction in the diameter of the affected artery's lumen
- the restriction of blood flow to the capillary bed served by that artery
- an increase in blood pressure.

In addition, large plaques hardened by deposits of calcium cause arterial walls to become thicker and lose their elasticity. This process, which occurs as a direct result of atherosclerosis, is often called hardening of the arteries. Symptoms of atherosclerosis normally remain absent until later in life when problems can arise. Then the condition can lead to the development of various cardiovascular diseases such as coronary heart disease (including angina), strokes and heart attacks (myocardial infarctions). Atherosclerosis is also the root cause of peripheral vascular disease (see page 184).

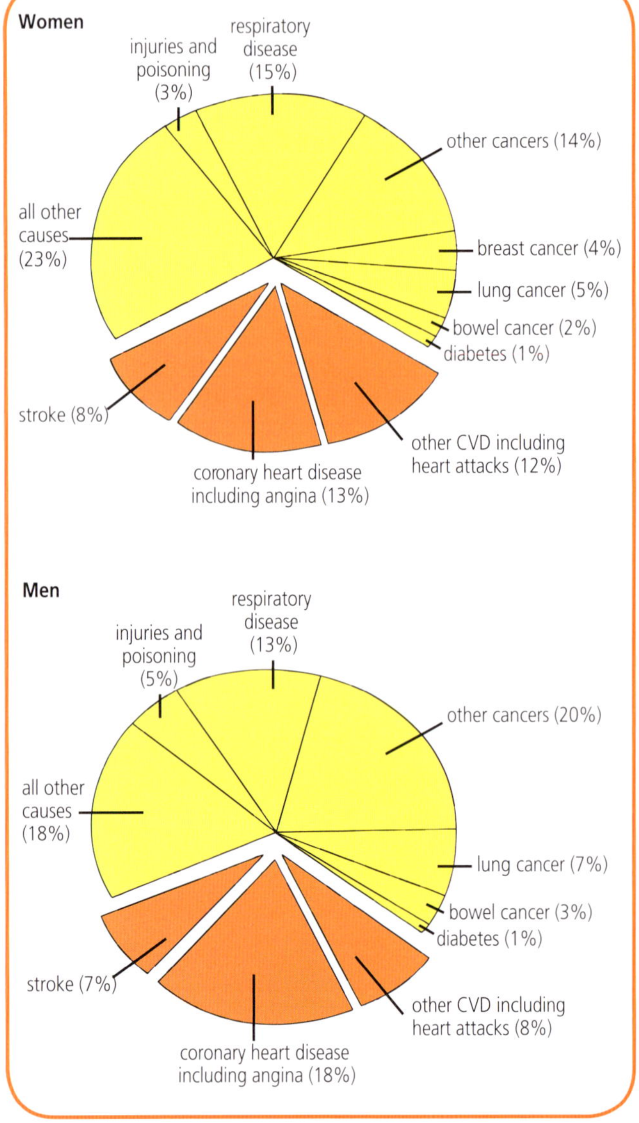

Figure 15.1 Causes of death in the UK

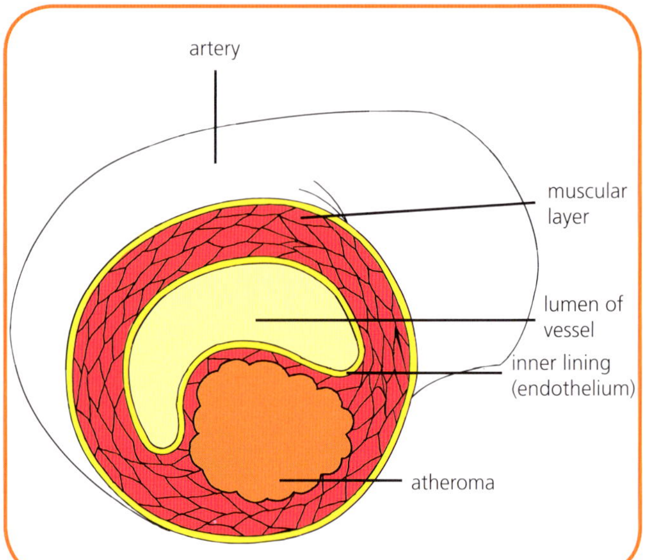

Figure 15.2 Atheroma in an artery

Related Topic

Coronary heart disease

Coronary arteries

The first two branches of the aorta are the left and right **coronary arteries** (see Figure 15.3). These vessels spread out over the surface of the heart and divide into an enormous number of tiny branches leading to a dense network of capillaries among the cardiac muscle cells that make up the wall of the heart.

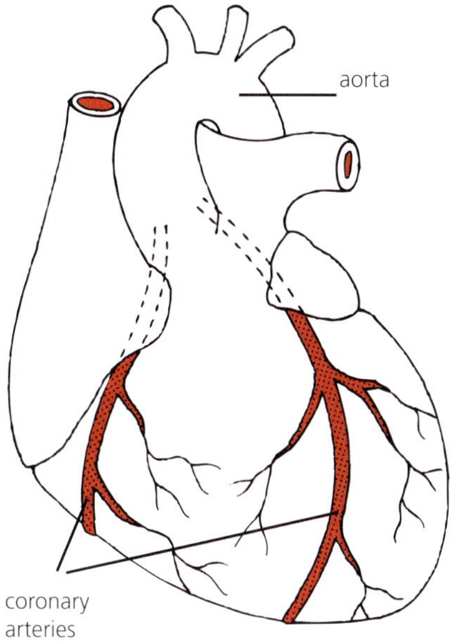

Figure 15.3 Coronary arteries

Each cardiac muscle cell is within 10 μm of a capillary, compared with the average distance of 60–80 μm in other organs. This close proximity to exchange vessels allows very rapid diffusion of oxygen and food into the actively respiring cardiac muscle cells.

Coronary heart disease (CHD)

This general term refers to any disease that results in **restriction** or **blockage** of the coronary blood supply to part of the heart's muscular wall. It often takes the form of **angina**, a condition characterised by a crushing pain in the centre of the chest, which tends to radiate out into the left arm and up to the neck and jaws. It affects people whose coronary arteries have become narrowed by atherosclerosis. Coronary arteries obstructed to such an extent that their diameter is reduced by about 70% allow sufficient blood to flow to the cardiac muscle only when the person is at rest.

However, during exercise or stress, the heart beats faster and the demand for oxygen by cardiac muscle cells increases accordingly. This demand cannot be met because of the reduced blood flow through the narrowed coronary arteries. Therefore a sudden pain occurs in the chest, often accompanied by feelings of suffocation.

Examining league tables

CHD is the most common cause of premature death in many developed countries. Table 15.1 contains data from a European survey. It compares death rates from CHD per 100 000 population in men (all ages) for several European countries for five different years.

From the data it can be seen that almost without exception the countries occupying the five positions at the 'undesirable' top of the 'league table' have tended to show little change in position over the 16-year period with Hungary remaining the undisputed leader. The good news is that they have all shown a decrease in CHD deaths over the years with Bulgaria and Ireland making impressive progress.

The data also shows that the countries occupying the four positions at the 'desirable' bottom end of the table have shown little change in position and all four countries have continued to show a decrease in CVD deaths over the years. The five countries in positions 6-10 in the league have also shown an improvement over the 16-year period and the UK has moved to a significantly better position (though its current position still leaves plenty of room for improvement).

Table 15.2 contains data collected in the UK. It compares death rates from CHD per 100 000 population from the four parts of the UK over a 20-year period. From the data it can be concluded that the number of deaths caused by CHD is decreasing in all parts of the UK with time. It can also be seen that death rate per 100 000 population is always higher for men than for women in any year in any part of the UK. In addition, the **death rate in Scotland** for both men and women is always higher than that in any other part of the UK in any given year.

→

Year									
1998		2002		2006		2010		2014	
Country	Deaths per 100 000 population	Country	Deaths per 100 000 population	Country	Deaths per 100 000 population	Country	Deaths per 100 000 population	Country	Deaths per 100 000 population
Hungary	578	Hungary	520	Hungary	577	Hungary	513	Hungary	479
Bulgaria	536	Bulgaria	452	Czech Republic	425	Czech Republic	412	Czech Republic	388
Finland	493	Czech Republic	447	Finland	385	Finland	344	Finland	269
Czech Republic	487	Finland	445	Bulgaria	350	Bulgaria	271	Bulgaria	251
Ireland	480	Ireland	375	Austria	288	Austria	261	Austria	226
UK	402	Austria	338	Ireland	284	Ireland	252	Ireland	221
Austria	393	UK	332	Poland	279	Poland	231	Germany	189
Sweden	375	Sweden	324	Sweden	269	Sweden	221	Poland	176
Germany	370	Germany	317	Germany	254	Germany	212	Sweden	174
Poland	367	Poland	312	UK	252	UK	203	UK	172
Netherlands	258	Netherlands	202	Italy	172	Italy	150	Italy	145
Italy	220	Italy	194	Netherlands	149	Spain	119	Spain	102
Spain	185	Spain	161	Spain	137	Netherlands	112	Netherlands	87
France	142	France	130	France	106	France	88	France	74

Table 15.1 Deaths from coronary heart disease for European men of all ages

		Year				
		1995	2000	2005	2010	2015
Women under 75 years	UK mean	76	55	36	23	20
	England	74	53	34	21	18
	Wales	80	62	42	27	25
	Scotland	101	74	50	35	26
	N. Ireland	100	59	48	27	21
Men under 75 years	UK mean	207	152	109	78	64
	England	200	148	103	75	62
	Wales	226	165	121	84	75
	Scotland	255	188	137	99	78
	N. Ireland	249	164	125	82	60

Table 15.2 Deaths from coronary heart disease for British men and women per 100 000 population

Clotting of blood

Blood clotting is a protective device triggered by damage to cells. Normally it occurs to prevent loss of blood at a wound. The presence of damaged cells leads to the release of blood **clotting factors** that activate the cascade of reactions shown in Figure 15.4. The enzyme **prothrombin**, which is always present in blood plasma but inactive, now becomes converted to its active form called **thrombin**. Thrombin promotes the conversion of molecules of **fibrinogen** (a soluble plasma protein) into threads of **fibrin** (an insoluble protein). These fibrin threads become interwoven into a framework to which platelets adhere, forming a **blood clot**. By this means the wound is sealed and a scaffold is produced upon which scar tissue can be formed.

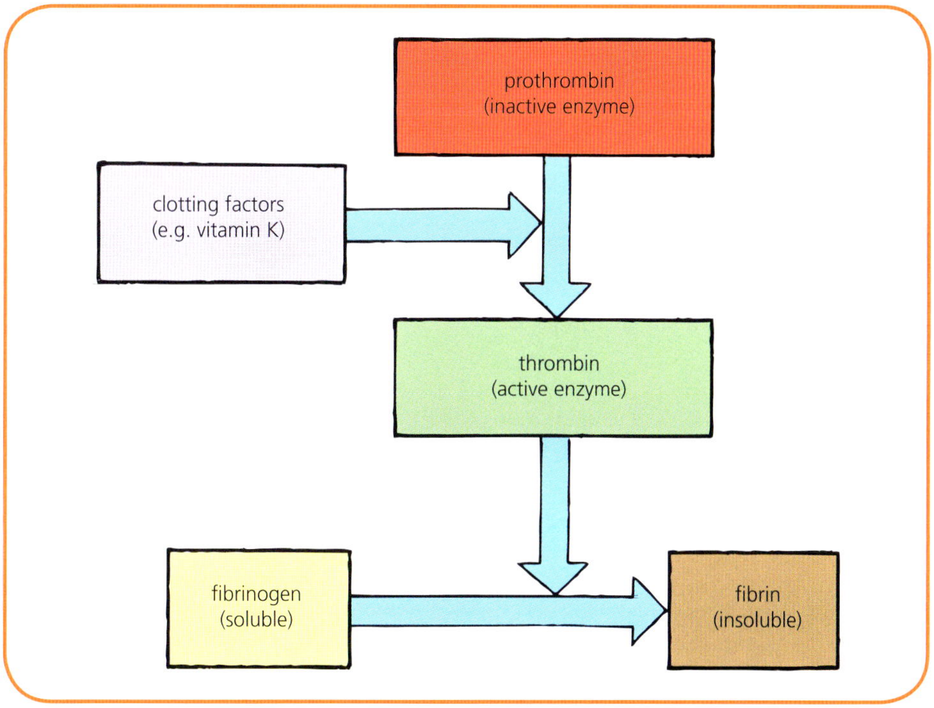

Figure 15.4 Chemical reactions resulting in fibrin formation

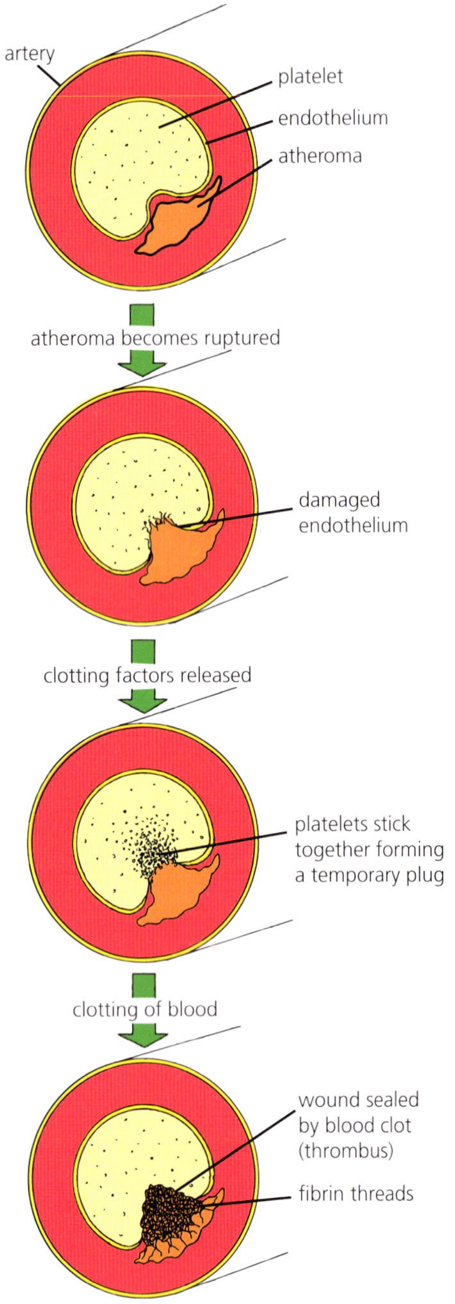

Figure 15.5 Formation of a thrombus in a blood vessel

Thrombosis

Atheromas on the inside lining of an artery make the surface uneven and disturb the smooth flow of blood. As an atheroma gradually becomes enlarged it may eventually burst through the endothelium and damage it (see Figure 15.5). Under these circumstances, **thrombosis** may occur. Thrombosis is the formation of a blood clot (**thrombus**) in a vessel.

Embolus

The presence of a thrombus in an artery causes further blockage in addition to that caused by atheromas. If a thrombus breaks loose, it is known as an **embolus**. An embolus is carried along by the blood until it blocks some narrow vessel and causes blood flow to be severely restricted or even brought to a complete halt. Blockage of a coronary artery by this type of thrombus is called **coronary thrombosis** (see Figure 15.6). It deprives part of the heart muscle of oxygen and may lead to a **myocardial infarction** (heart attack). A thrombus that causes a blockage in an artery in the brain may lead to a **stroke**. This normally results in the death of some of the tissues served by that artery because they are deprived of oxygen.

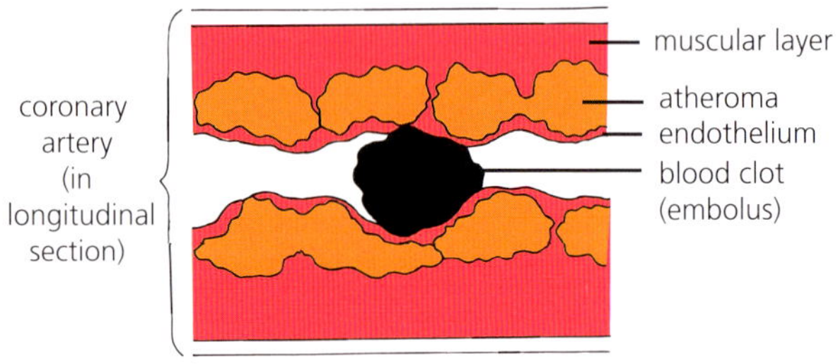

Figure 15.6 Coronary thrombosis

Research Topic — Use of thrombolytic medications

Background

The main constituent of a thrombus is fibrin. Under normal circumstances, once a blood clot has served its purpose, the clot is broken down and removed. For this to happen, **plasminogen**, the inactive form of the necessary enzyme, must first be converted to **plasmin**, the active form. This conversion is brought about by a further enzyme called **tissue plasminogen activator (tPA)** present on the endothelial cells lining blood vessels. The series of reactions involved is shown in Figure 15.7.

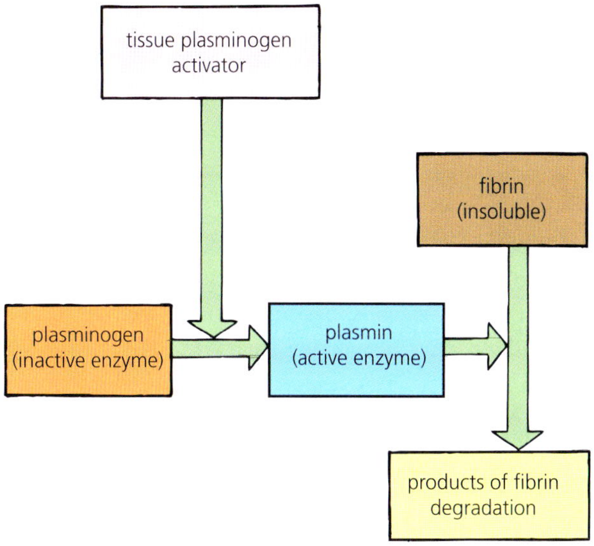

Figure 15.7 Action of tissue plasminogen activator

Thrombolysis

The formation of a blood clot in a blood vessel and its subsequent movement through the circulatory system as an embolus that finally blocks a narrow blood vessel is the root cause of several serious conditions such as myocardial infarction, stroke and deep vein thrombosis (see page 184). **Thrombolysis** is the process by which such a clot is broken down using a special medication in order to limit the damage caused by the blockage. Examples of thrombolytic drugs are **streptokinase** (originally extracted from bacteria) and **tissue plasminogen activator** (produced by recombinant DNA technology).

Both of the above drugs work by converting inactive plasminogen to active plasmin and they are given intravenously as soon as possible after the onset of the heart attack or stroke. However, great care must be taken to ensure that their use is appropriate. For example, they are suitable for treatment of a stroke caused by an embolus (blood clot) but not for a stroke caused by a haemorrhage (bleeding from a ruptured blood vessel).

Related Topic

Comparison of use of antiplatelet and anticoagulant therapies

Both of these forms of medication are used to prevent the formation of clots in the circulatory system.

Antiplatelet drugs

An **antiplatelet** drug is a form of pharmaceutical medication that interferes with the formation of a blood clot by inhibiting the sticking together of platelets. Therefore antiplatelet drugs are used to prevent the formation of a thrombus that could cause a coronary thrombosis or a stroke in people who run a significant risk of developing such a condition.

Aspirin is an example of a relatively mild antiplatelet drug. It inhibits the action of an enzyme essential for the production of a chemical that makes platelets stick together. However, daily use of aspirin, even in low-to-moderate doses, is accompanied by the risk of gastrointestinal bleeding in some individuals. **Glycoprotein inhibitors** are a more potent form of antiplatelet drug. They also cause gastrointestinal bleeding in some patients and their use is restricted to a hospital setting because they can cause complications such as low blood pressure.

Anticoagulants

Anticoagulants are used in the treatment of thrombotic disorders such as deep vein thrombosis (see page 184) and pulmonary embolism (see page 185). An anticoagulant differs from an antiplatelet drug in that it reduces or prevents blood clotting by interfering with a stage in the biochemical pathway that leads to fibrin production (see Figure 15.4).

→

In the UK, **warfarin** is the most commonly used anticoagulant. It works by preventing **vitamin K** from carrying out its function in the pathway. However, excessive depletion of vitamin K increases the risk of calcification (hardening) of the arteries. **Heparin** is another anticoagulant. It works by preventing thrombin from playing its role in the pathway.

Side effects

Like antiplatelet drugs, the most serious side effect of anticoagulants is bleeding. This may take the form of prolonged nosebleeds, gastrointestinal bleeding or increased bleeding during menstruation.

Clinical investigation

Table 15.3 shows the results of a randomised trial comparing the two types of treatment on a large population of patients recovering from the implantation of metallic stents (supports) in their coronary arteries. From these results it was concluded that in this trial, three of the side effects occurred significantly less frequently in antiplatelet therapy compared with anticoagulation therapy. However, there is insufficient evidence available at present to enable experts to favour conclusively one type of therapy over the other.

Side effect	Percentage of patients in sample affected by side effect	
	Antiplatelet therapy	Anticoagulation therapy
Swelling caused by partially clotted blood	25	34
Discoloured 'bruised' areas of skin	16	38
Prolonged bleeding during surgical repair	1	2
All bleeding complications	33	48

Table 15.3 Side effects of two therapies

Peripheral vascular disorders

The **peripheral** arteries are those *other than* the aorta and coronary and carotid arteries. When any of the peripheral arteries are affected by atherosclerosis, their central cavity becomes narrower (see Figure 15.2). This leads to **peripheral vascular disease**, which most commonly affects the leg arteries. When these blood vessels suffer an obstruction of this type, blood flow is restricted and pain is felt in the leg muscles because they are receiving an inadequate supply of oxygen.

Deep vein thrombosis

Deep vein thrombosis is the formation of a thrombus (blood clot) in a vein, most commonly one in the calf of the lower leg. Normally this causes the affected extremity to become painful and swell up (see Figure 15.8). In addition, veins close to the skin surface can become engorged with blood.

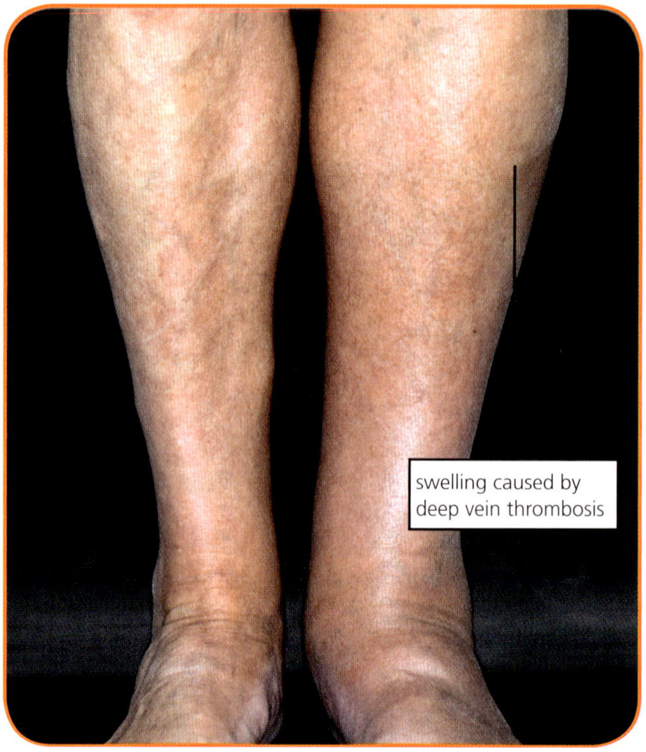

Figure 15.8 Deep vein thrombosis

Pulmonary embolism

If a thrombus in a vein breaks free, a serious complication may arise. The clot (now an embolus) is transported via the vena cava and heart chambers to the pulmonary artery where it may block a small arterial branch. This serious situation which affects a lung is called a **pulmonary embolism** (see Figure 15.9) and is characterised by symptoms such as chest pains, breathing difficulties and palpitations. Treatment takes the form of anticoagulant drugs or, in severe cases, thrombolytic drugs. If untreated, a pulmonary embolism can lead to collapse and sudden death.

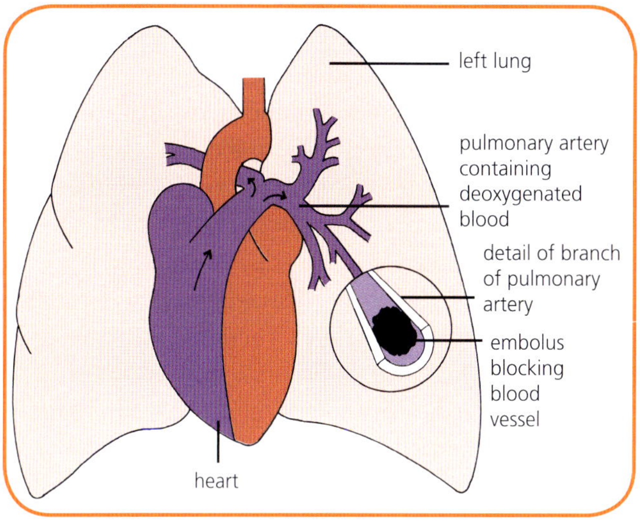

Figure 15.9 Pulmonary embolism

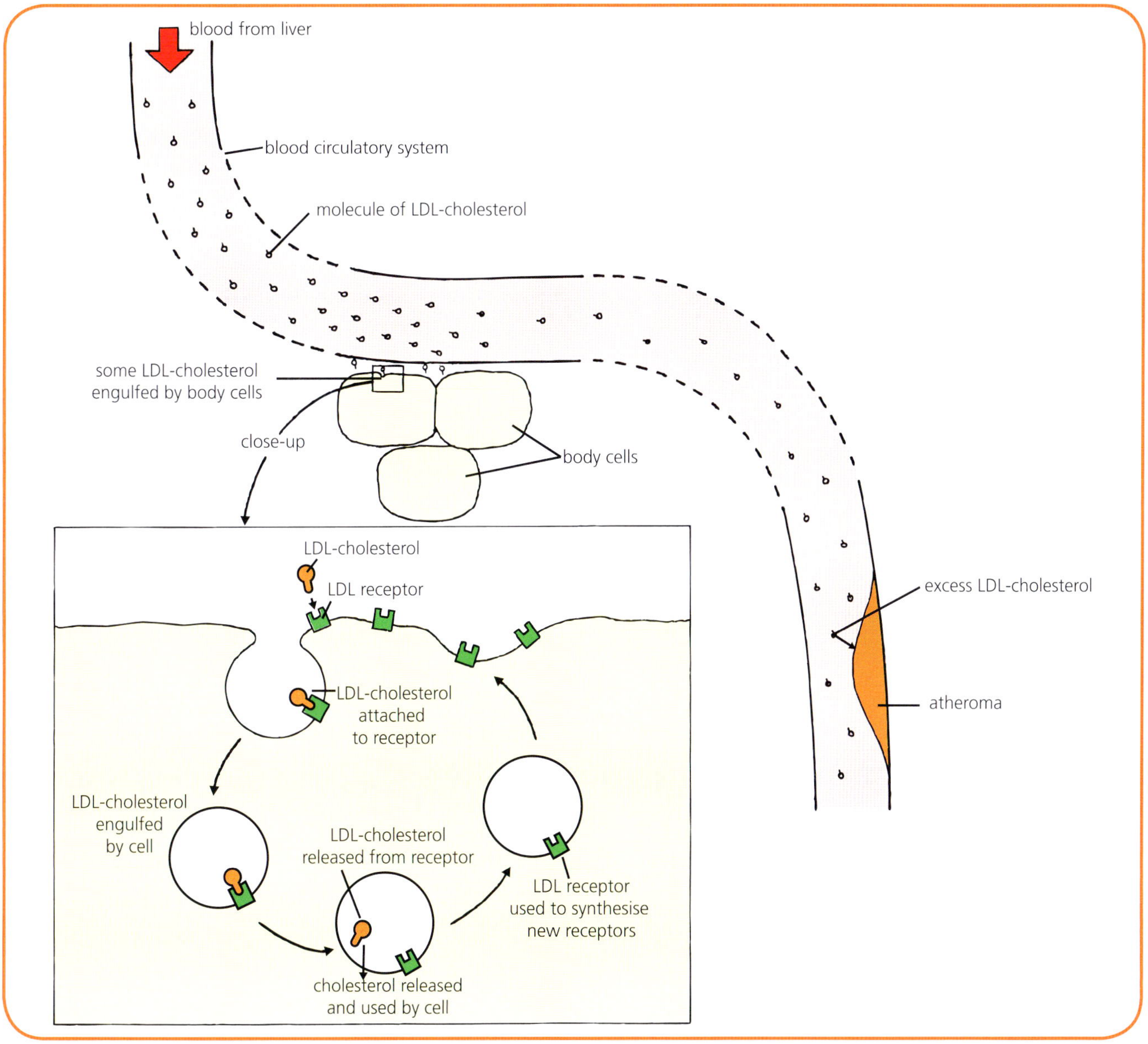

Figure 15.10 Transport of cholesterol by LDL

Cholesterol

The term **lipid** refers to a diverse group of organic compounds which includes simple lipids such as fats (saturated and unsaturated) and more complex substances such as steroids. **Cholesterol** is an important lipid because it is a precursor for the synthesis of steroids (such as the sex hormones, testosterone, oestrogen and progesterone). Cholesterol is also a basic component of cell membranes. Therefore its presence in the bloodstream at an appropriate concentration is *essential* to the health and well-being of the human body. It is synthesised from saturated fats present in a normal balanced diet. It is made by all cells but 25% of total production takes place in the liver.

Transport of cholesterol

Lipoproteins are molecules containing a combination of lipid and protein. They are present in blood plasma and transport lipids from one part of the body to another.

Low-density lipoprotein (LDL)

Cholesterol is transported to body cells by **low-density lipoproteins (LDL)** produced by the liver. Most body cells synthesise LDL **receptors** which then become inserted in their cell membrane. When a molecule of LDL carrying cholesterol (LDL-cholesterol) becomes attached to a receptor, the cell engulfs the LDL-cholesterol and the cholesterol is released for use by the cell (see Figure 15.10).

Atherosclerosis

Once a body cell contains an adequate supply of cholesterol, a negative feedback system is triggered which inhibits the synthesis of new LDL receptors. Therefore less of the LDL-cholesterol circulating in the bloodstream is absorbed by body cells. Instead, some of it is taken up by endothelial cells lining the inside of an artery. The cholesterol is then deposited in an atheroma in the wall of the artery. This process is very likely to occur if the person eats a diet rich in saturated fat throughout their life.

High-density lipoprotein (HDL)

Some excess cholesterol is transported by **high-density lipoproteins (HDL)** from body cells to the liver for elimination. Under normal circumstances, this process prevents a high level of cholesterol accumulating in the bloodstream. In addition, HDL-cholesterol is not taken into artery walls and therefore does not contribute to atherosclerosis. However, these benefits are dependent on a **healthy balance** existing between the HDL-cholesterol molecules (sometimes called 'good cholesterol') and the LDL-cholesterol molecules (sometimes called 'bad cholesterol'). (It should be noted that the cholesterol attached to a molecule of LDL is identical to that attached to HDL.)

Normally HDL molecules carry about 20–30% of blood cholesterol and LDL molecules carry about 60–70%. A higher ratio of HDL to LDL is described as a **good blood lipid profile** because it results in a decrease in blood cholesterol and a reduced chance of atherosclerosis and cardiovascular disease. The reverse is true of a lower ratio of HDL to LDL.

The concentration of HDL-cholesterol in the bloodstream is normally higher and the risk of CVD lower in people who exercise regularly. In addition, evidence suggests that HDL levels may also be raised by the replacement of some saturated fat with unsaturated fat in the diet and the consumption of less total fat.

Statins

The level of cholesterol in the blood can be reduced by medication. Drugs such as **statins** bring about this effect by inhibiting an enzyme essential for the synthesis of cholesterol by liver cells. (See Research Topic – Action of cholesterol-reducing drugs.)

Research Topic Action of cholesterol-reducing drugs

HMG-CoA reductase is an enzyme found in liver cells that promotes the first step in a long chain of biochemical reactions that leads to the production of cholesterol (see Figure 15.11). **Statins** are the most widely used cholesterol-reducing drugs. They act by competing with the enzyme's substrate (**HMG-CoA**) for the active sites on the molecules of the enzyme. This process of **competitive inhibition** reduces the rate at which the enzyme is able to produce intermediate 1 and subsequently reduces the rate at which the cell is able to make cholesterol.

Since more cholesterol originates from internal manufacture in liver cells than from the diet, a drop in cholesterol production by the liver soon results in a drop in the level of cholesterol in the blood. Statins also act by increasing the number of LDL receptors made by liver cells. These receptors bring about a reduction in the level of 'bad cholesterol' by removing some molecules of LDL-cholesterol from the bloodstream.

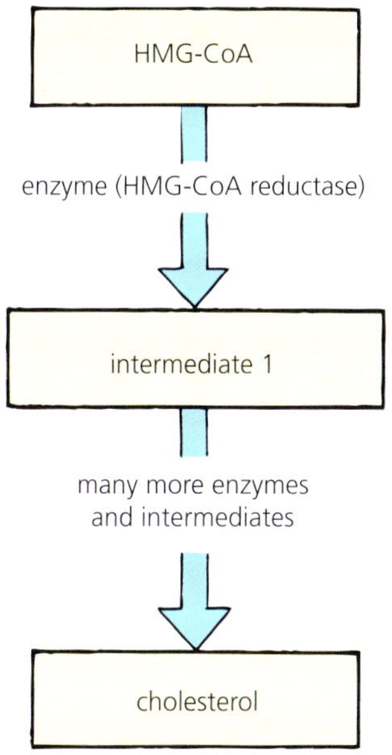

Figure 15.11 Production of cholesterol

Night or day

Normally cholesterol synthesis occurs mainly at night. Therefore statins that only act over a short time span are more effective if taken at bedtime rather than in the morning.

Clinical trials

Several clinical trials have shown the benefits of statins in reducing death rates among patients affected by cardiovascular disease (CVD). In recent years, further clinical trials have been carried out to investigate if statins reduce coronary and cerebrovascular events in people who are **at risk of**, but are not affected by CVD. Table 15.4 shows the results from one of these trials. It was carried out over a period of 4 years on many thousands of participants of average age 63 years. About 25% had diabetes but none of them were affected by CVD at the start of the trial.

The results from this trial and many others have been collated. From the vast quantity of data produced, it has been concluded that statins, by reducing cholesterol levels in patients at risk of CVD, bring about a significant reduction in the risk of major cardiovascular events and a significant decrease in mortality caused by CVD.

Condition	Percentage of group affected after 4 years		Percentage risk reduction
	Control group	Statin group	
Major coronary event	5.4	4.1	24
Major cerebrovascular event	2.3	1.9	17
All-cause mortality	5.7	5.1	11

Table 15.4 Results of clinical trial investigating action of statin

Testing Your Knowledge

1 a) What is meant by the term *atherosclerosis*? (2)
b) Identify TWO ways in which the structure of an artery is altered by atherosclerosis. (2)

2 a) Arrange the following four stages that occur during thrombosis into the correct order. (1)
A clotting factors are released
B soluble fibrinogen changes into threads of insoluble fibrin
C an atheroma bursts and damages the endothelium
D inactive prothrombin becomes active thrombin
b) What might be the result of a thrombus blocking:
i) an artery in the brain
ii) a coronary artery? (2)

3 a) Give ONE reason why all cells need a supply of cholesterol. (1)
b) How is cholesterol transported:
i) from the liver to body cells
ii) from body cells to the liver? (2)
c) By what means do drugs such as statins reduce blood cholesterol level? (1)

4 Decide whether each of the following statements is true or false and then use T or F to indicate your choice. Where a statement is false, give the word that should have been used in place of the word in bold print. (5)
a) Atherosclerosis causes the lumen of an affected artery to become **wider**.
b) A thrombus that has broken loose and is free to travel through the bloodstream is called an **angina**.
c) The development of an atheroma in the wall of an artery results in an **increase** in blood pressure.
d) Peripheral vascular disease is characterised by the narrowing of **capillaries** in body extremities.
e) If a small clot formed by deep vein thrombosis travels through the bloodstream it may cause a **pulmonary** embolism.

Applying Your Knowledge and Skills

Year	Deaths per 100 000 population from cardiovascular disease							
	Men aged 35–44	Women aged 35–44	Men aged 45–54	Women aged 45–54	Men aged 55–64	Women aged 55–64	Men aged 65–74	Women aged 65–74
1999	22	5	97	20	317	94	902	387
2000	19	5	92	20	291	84	823	347
2001	20	4	93	19	271	79	763	328
2002	21	4	89	19	250	72	707	304
2003	19	5	85	18	238	66	660	275
2004	19	4	81	16	219	57	599	250
2005	19	4	73	16	204	54	558	225
2006	18	4	72	15	194	52	500	207
2007	17	4	69	15	188	49	471	187
2008	17	4	67	14	175	47	443	179

Table 15.5

→

1 Table 15.5 shows death rates per 100 000 population from coronary heart disease in the UK. Draw THREE conclusions from the data. (3)

2 Table 15.6 shows part of a lipid profile table from the USA where cholesterol levels are measured in milligrams per decilitre (mg/dl). In the UK, cholesterol levels are measured in millimoles per litre (mmol/l). 1 mmol/l = 386.6 mg/l. 1 litre (l) = 10 decilitres (dl). Convert the following values for Ian, a UK resident, and interpret his cholesterol levels. His HDL-cholesterol level is 1.56 mmol/l and his LDL-cholesterol level is 3.88 mmol/l. Show your working. (4)

3 The graph in Figure 15.12 shows the results of a survey on the effectiveness of four brands of statin (E, F, G and H) at bringing about a decrease in LDL-cholesterol in the bloodstream.

a) What daily dose of E brings about a decrease in LDL-cholesterol of 2.2 mmol/l? (1)

b) What decrease in LDL-cholesterol is brought about by a dose of 10 mg of H? (1)

c) What daily dose of **i)** F, **ii)** H would have the same effect as 40 mg of G? (2)

d) Which brand of statin produces the least overall decrease in LDL-cholesterol compared with the others? (1)

e) Which TWO brands of statin show no overlap in range of values of LDL-cholesterol decrease regardless of daily dose? (1)

f) **i)** Assuming that all four brands are equally priced and equally safe to use, which one is the best value for money?

ii) Explain your answer. (2)

HDL-cholesterol level (mg/dl)	LDL-cholesterol level (mg/dl)	Interpretation by experts
60 or more	60–129	Desirable
40–59	130–159	Borderline
39 or less	160–199	Heightened risk

Table 15.6

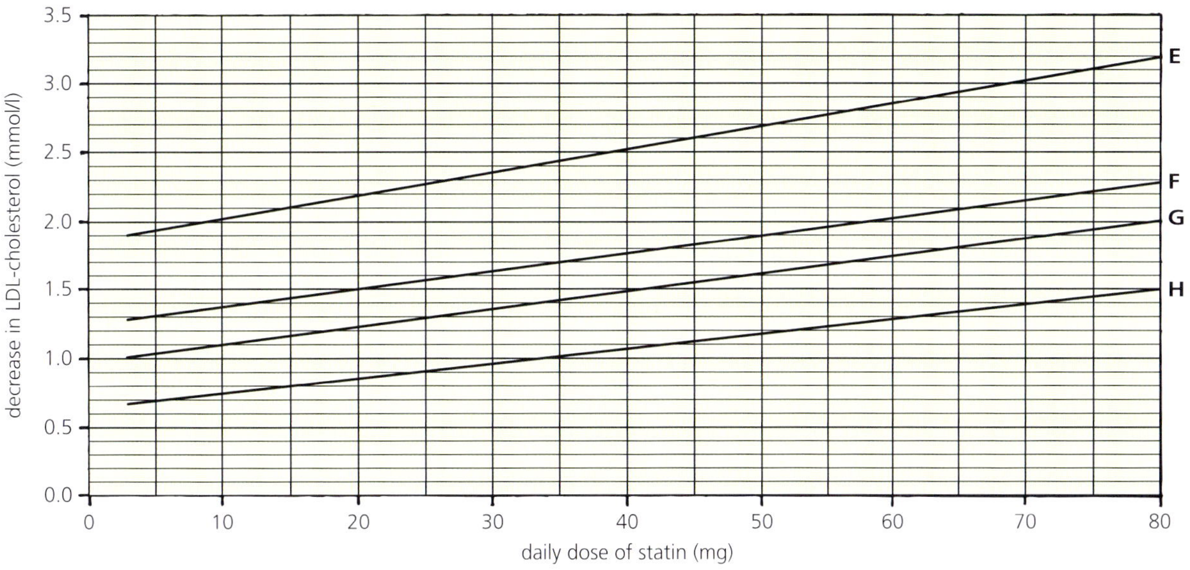

Figure 15.12

Age (years)	Expected percentage decrease in incidence of CVD						
	Projected decrease in LDL-cholesterol (mmol/l) brought about by statins						
	0.6	1.0	1.4	1.8	2.2	2.6	3.0
50	39%	56%	68%	77%	84%	88%	91%
60	27%	41%	52%	61%	68%	74%	79%
70	20%	31%	41%	49%	56%	62%	67%

Table 15.7

4 Table 15.7 shows the varying values of percentage decrease in incidence of CVD (cardiovascular disease) that some medical experts predict will result from decreases in level of LDL-cholesterol brought about by statin treatment. What TWO trends do the data forecast? (2)

5 Figure 15.13 shows a family tree (pedigree) for familial hypercholesterolaemia (FH) where H (the mutant allele for this inherited condition) is dominant to h (the allele for the unaffected state).

a) Identify **i)** a man who does not have FH, **ii)** a woman who does have FH. (2)

b) Give the genotype and phenotype of **i)** person M, **ii)** person X. (2)

c) **i)** Identify the person whose genotype cannot be worked out from the information given.
ii) Explain your answer. (2)

d) If person Y conceives children with a man with the same genotype as her father, what is the chance that each of their children will **i)** have FH, **ii)** not have FH? (2)

e) Identify one piece of evidence from the pedigree that shows that FH is *not* a sex-linked trait. (1)

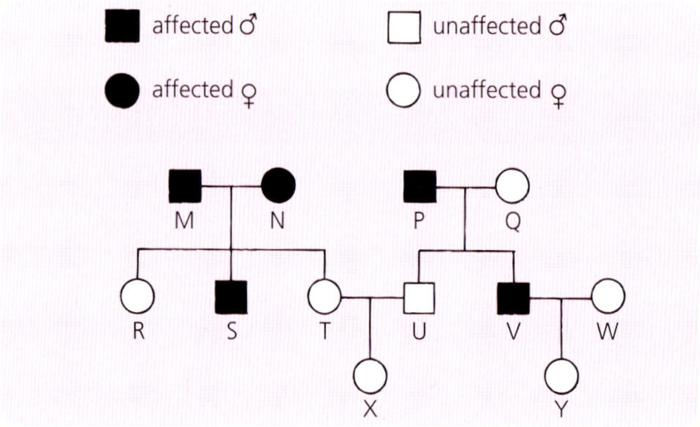

Figure 15.13

6 Give an account of thrombosis following the rupture of an atheroma. (9)

16 Blood glucose levels and obesity

Blood glucose levels concentration

Normally blood plasma contains glucose at a concentration of around 5 millimoles per litre (mmol/l) with this glucose concentration varying slightly depending on demand by respiring tissues. However, if a person is affected by untreated **diabetes** (see page 192) their level of blood glucose may become **elevated** to an abnormal and chronic level such as 30 mmol/l. Under these circumstances endothelial cells lining blood vessels absorb far more glucose than normal. This process causes damage to blood vessels and may lead to peripheral vascular disease, CVD or stroke.

Microvascular (small vessel) disease

When the endothelial cells lining a small blood vessel such as an arteriole (see Figure 16.1) take in more glucose than normal, their basement membrane becomes thicker but weaker. Therefore, as the walls of an affected blood vessel become abnormally thick, they lose their strength and may **burst** and **bleed** (haemorrhage) into the surrounding tissues. This leakage reduces rate of flow of blood through the body. A tissue may be affected either by being flooded with leaked blood or by not receiving an adequate oxygen supply. Microvascular disease can cause damage to the **retina**, affecting vision, and to the **kidneys**, causing renal failure. In addition it affects nerves in the body's extremities, which suffer **peripheral nerve dysfunction**. (See Related Activity – Investigating symptoms associated with microvascular disease.)

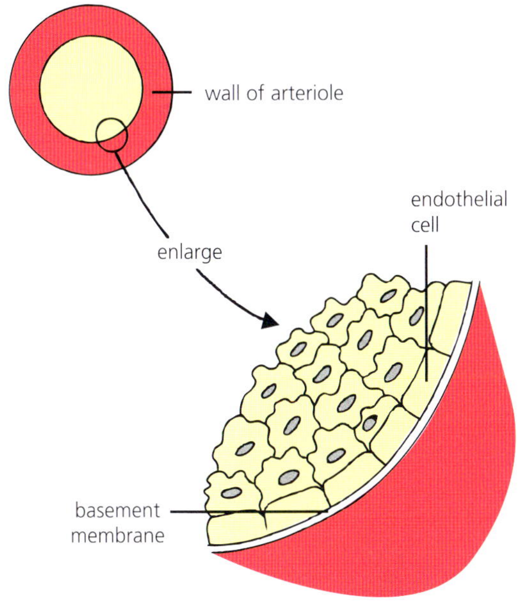

Figure 16.1 Endothelium of an arteriole

Regulation of blood glucose level

All living cells in the human body need a continuous supply of energy released from the breakdown of **glucose** during tissue respiration. However, the body obtains supplies of glucose only on those occasions when food is eaten. To guarantee that a regular supply of glucose is present in the bloodstream and available for use by cells regardless of when and how often food is consumed, the body employs a system of **negative feedback control (homeostasis)**.

Liver as a storehouse

About one hundred grams of glucose are stored as **glycogen** in the liver. Glucose can be added to or removed from this reservoir of stored carbohydrate depending on changes in supply or demand.

Insulin and glucagon

A rise in blood glucose concentration to above its normal level (for example, following a meal) is detected by receptor cells in the **pancreas**. These cells trigger an increase in secretion of **insulin**. This hormone is transported in the bloodstream from the pancreas to the liver where it is picked up by insulin receptors. Excess glucose is absorbed by the liver cells and an enzyme is activated that catalyses the reaction:

$$\text{glucose} \rightarrow \text{glycogen}$$

This process brings about a decrease in blood glucose concentration to around its normal level. If the blood glucose drops below its normal level (for example,

Related Activity

Investigating symptoms associated with microvascular disease

Whereas **macrovascular** (large vessel) disease is caused by an obstruction blocking a main artery, **microvascular** disease results from damage to small blood vessels. Symptoms of a macrovascular problem such as coronary heart disease tend to be readily apparent, severe and often life-threatening. Symptoms of a microvascular problem such as peripheral nerve dysfunction tend to lack specific expression for a long time but to become severe eventually. They tend to be restricted to localised areas and to respond to treatment if an associated condition such as elevated blood glucose level is controlled in time.

Microvascular complications are common among people who have long-term, poorly controlled diabetes. **Diabetic retinopathy** resulting from prolonged high blood glucose levels, for example, causes small vessels in the retina to haemorrhage and leak into the back of the eye. This early sign of diabetes is normally picked up during a routine eye test. In its early stages, diabetic retinopathy can occur without obvious symptoms or pain. As the condition becomes more serious, vision is affected and, if left untreated, it eventually causes blindness.

Microvascular disease that causes damage to kidney arterioles can lead to **renal failure**. This occurs because the kidneys are eventually no longer able to perform their function of filtering and purifying blood. This form of kidney disease is common among people with diabetes who do not control their condition strictly. Its symptoms include:

- swelling of the ankles, feet and lower legs
- production of darker urine, containing traces of blood
- shortage of breath when climbing stairs.

In order to have kidney disease diagnosed and treated before it reaches an extreme stage, people with diabetes are advised to be screened annually for kidney complications.

Peripheral neuropathy (peripheral nerve dysfunction) is a condition resulting from microvascular disease of blood vessels closely associated with nerves that serve the body's extremities such as hands and feet. These nerves are damaged by prolonged exposure to elevated levels of blood glucose. Symptoms can take the form of numbness, tingling or pain in hands, arms, toes, feet or legs. Peripheral neuropathy is common among older, overweight diabetics who continue to exert poor control over their condition. If left untreated, it can lead to the development of ulcers and eventually to the amputation of the affected extremity.

between meals or during the night), different receptor cells in the pancreas detect this change and trigger an increase in secretion of **glucagon**. This second hormone is transported to the liver and activates a different enzyme, which catalyses the reaction:

$$\text{glycogen} \rightarrow \text{glucose}$$

Now glucose is released from liver cells and the blood glucose concentration rises to around its normal value. Figure 16.2 gives a summary of this **homeostatic system** and shows how insulin and glucagon act antagonistically.

Adrenaline

During exercise or 'fight or flight' reactions (see page 205) when the body needs additional supplies of glucose to provide energy quickly, the adrenal glands secrete an increased quantity of the hormone **adrenaline** into the bloodstream. Adrenaline overrides the normal homeostatic control of blood glucose level by inhibiting the secretion of insulin and promoting the breakdown of glycogen to glucose. Once the crisis is over, secretion of adrenaline is reduced to a minimum and blood glucose level is returned to normal by the appropriate corrective mechanism involving insulin or glucagon.

Diabetes

People who have **diabetes** are unable to control their blood glucose level. If untreated, it can rise to 10–30 mmol/l compared with the normal blood glucose concentration of around 5 mmol/l. There are two types of diabetes and they are compared in Table 16.1.

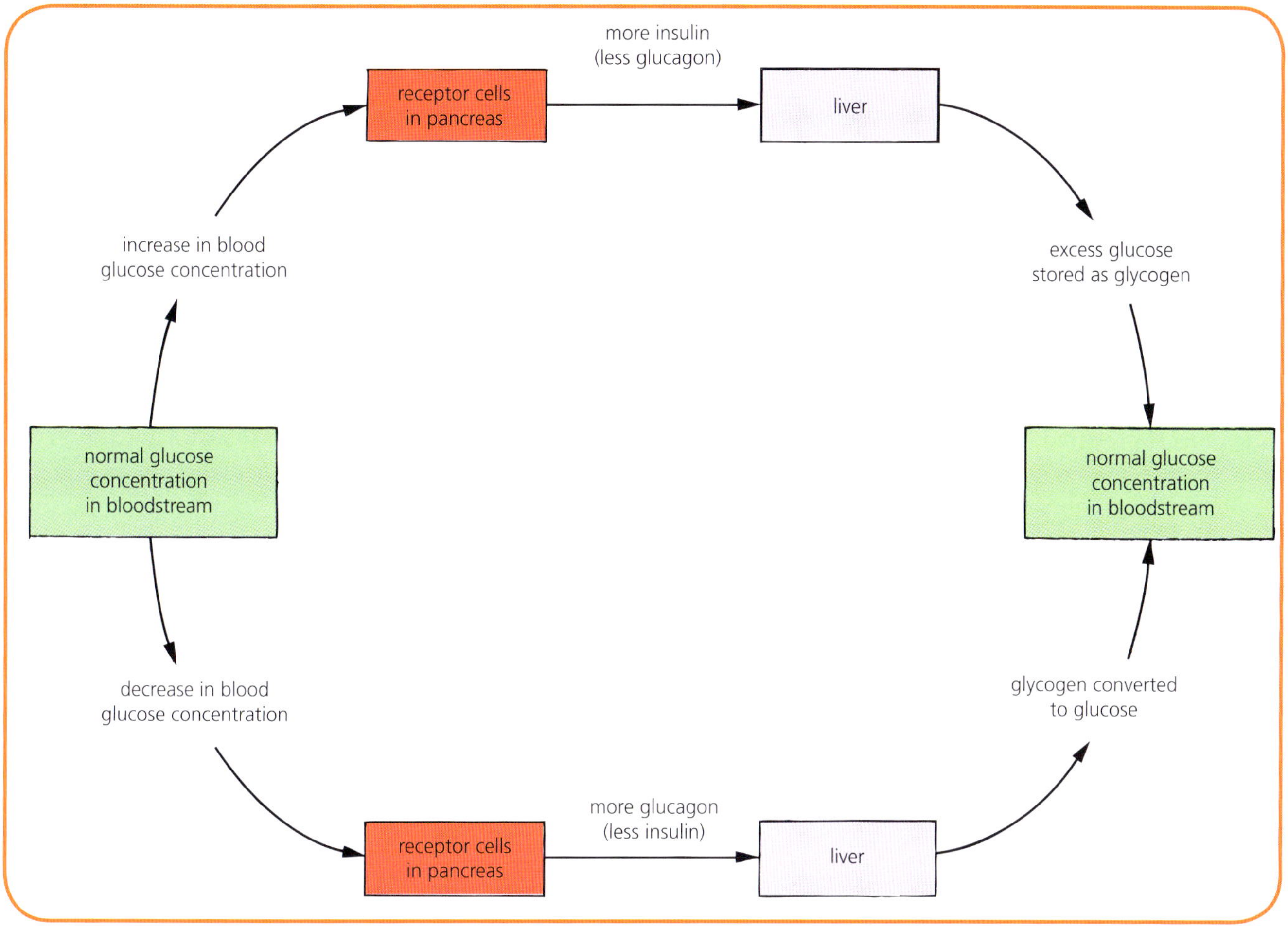

Figure 16.2 Regulation of blood glucose level by negative feedback control

	Type 1 diabetes	Type 2 diabetes
Percentage of all cases	5–10	90–95
Stage of life at which condition normally first occurs	Childhood or early teens (therefore often referred to as 'juvenile onset' diabetes)	Adulthood (therefore often referred to as 'adult onset' diabetes)
Typical body mass of person	Normal or underweight	Overweight or obese
Ability of pancreatic cells to produce insulin	Absent	Present
Sensitivity of cells (e.g. liver and skeletal muscle) to insulin	Cells have the normal number of insulin receptors on their surfaces. They respond to the presence of insulin (if given as treatment) and bring about the opening of glucose channels into the cells.	Cells have a decreased number of insulin receptors on their surfaces, making them less sensitive (or even resistant) to insulin. Therefore few (or no) glucose channels are opened, much glucose fails to enter the cells and normal conversion of glucose to glycogen is prevented.
Treatment	Regular injections of insulin and a careful diet	Exercise, weight loss, diet control (and insulin in some cases)

Table 16.1 Comparison of two types of diabetes

Both types of diabetes, if untreated, result in a rapid increase in blood glucose level following a meal. The filtrate formed in the kidneys of an untreated diabetic is so rich in glucose that much of the glucose is not reabsorbed into the bloodstream but instead excreted in **urine**. Therefore, testing urine for glucose is often used as an **indicator** of diabetes.

Many vascular diseases are closely associated with chronic (long-lasting) complications of diabetes. Whereas it used to be a fatal disorder, diabetes can now be successfully treated provided that the affected individual is prepared to adopt a healthy lifestyle.

Glucose tolerance test

Glucose tolerance is the capacity of the body to deal with ingested glucose. This depends on the body being able to produce adequate quantities of insulin. Measurement of glucose tolerance is a clinical test used to **diagnose** diabetes. It investigates by indirect means whether (or not) insulin production is normal. After fasting for 8 hours, a person has their blood glucose concentration measured and then consumes a known mass of glucose to give a **glucose load**. Their blood glucose concentration is monitored over a period of 2½ hours and the results plotted to give a glucose tolerance curve. During the test, a diabetic person's

Related Activity

Analysing glucose tolerance curves

Figure 16.3 shows three different glucose tolerance curves resulting from glucose tolerance tests.

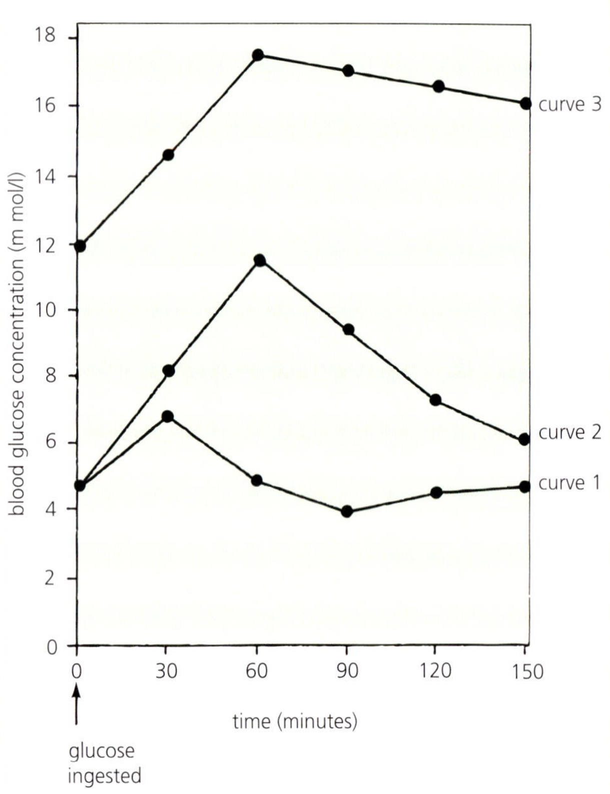

Figure 16.3 Glucose tolerance curves

Curve 1

The person's glucose concentration rises to a maximum at around 30 minutes and then quickly drops to its initial low level well within the 2½ hour period. This indicates that insulin production is normal. The increase in blood glucose concentration has triggered the sequence of events shown in Figure 16.2 and has been brought back to normal by negative feedback control. In this example, the process is so effective that the blood glucose level close to the end of the test dips below the initial fasting level for a short time.

Curve 2

The person's blood glucose concentration begins at the normal fasting level but continues to rise to a maximum at around 60 minutes (or even later) before beginning to decrease. The delay in insulin response to glucose load indicates a mild form of type 2 diabetes. This condition will probably respond to a careful diet and not require treatment with insulin.

Curve 3

After fasting, the person's blood glucose concentration is still at an abnormally high level. After ingestion of glucose, it continues to rise for 60 minutes (or more) and then shows a slight decrease but fails to drop even to its initial high level. This sequence of events indicates severe diabetes (probably type 1). The person is either producing no insulin or their cells are failing to make a normal insulin response to glucose load. Regular injections of insulin and a carefully controlled diet will probably be needed to control this condition.

blood glucose concentration is found to rise to a much higher level than that of a non-diabetic person and take much longer to drop to its starting level. (Also see Related Activity – Analysing glucose tolerance curves.)

Obesity

Obesity is a condition characterised by the accumulation of **excess body fat** in relation to lean tissue such as muscle. Being obese greatly increases the individual's risk of suffering a variety of health problems (see Figure 16.4).

Figure 16.4 Obesity and health problems

Body mass index (BMI)

There is an ideal body mass (weight) for each person. This varies from one individual to another. A person's **body mass index (BMI)** is calculated using the formula:

$$\text{BMI} = \frac{\text{body mass}}{\text{height}^2}$$

(where body mass is measured in kg and height is measured in m). The currently accepted classification of BMI values is shown in Table 16.2.

Limitation of BMI method

Some individuals such as body-builders, who have a relatively low percentage of body fat and an unusually high percentage of muscle bulk, would be wrongly classified as obese by the BMI method.

Causes of obesity

Genetic, psychological, environmental, metabolic and dietary factors are all thought to be possible contributors to obesity. However, the most common cause is the excessive consumption of food rich in fats and free sugars combined with lack of physical activity.

Treatment

A **reduction in energy intake** and **an increase in energy expenditure** are the mainstays of treatment for obesity. Affected individuals are advised to reduce energy intake by limiting their consumption of fat (which has a high calorific value relative to other foods) and free sugars (which do not need any metabolic energy to be expended to digest them). They are also encouraged to take regular exercise in order to expend some of the energy in their body fat while keeping their muscle tissue lean. Increased exercise also helps to bring about:

- a reduction in the risk factors associated with CVD by keeping weight under control
- an increase in the level of HDL-cholesterol ('good cholesterol') in the blood thereby improving blood lipid profile (also see page 186)
- a decrease in hypertension and stress.

BMI value	Opinion of experts	Risk of associated health problems
20–25	Ideal for height	Average
26–30	Overweight	Increased
31–40	Obese (very overweight)	Greatly increased
Over 40	Very obese (grossly overweight)	Very greatly increased

Table 16.2 BMI values

Related Activity

Examining risk factors associated with CVD

Risk factors

The main CVD risk factors are:

- high LDL-cholesterol level
- obesity (Also see Related Topic – Patterns of fat distribution.)
- unhealthy diet high in saturated fat and cholesterol
- physical inactivity
- high blood pressure
- smoking
- diabetes
- drinking alcohol to excess
- very stressful lifestyle.

All of these risk factors can be reduced significantly by adopting a healthy lifestyle supported by medication where necessary.

Related Topic

Patterns of fat distribution

Waist/hip ratio

Although the total quantity of fat in the body is a very important factor when assessing health risk, the **distribution pattern** of the fat is even more important. '**Apple**-shaped' people (see Figure 16.5) with excess abdominal fat are now known to be, on average, at a greater risk of type 2 diabetes and CVD than '**pear**-shaped' people with excess fat round their hips. Women are considered to be at risk when their waist/hip ratio is greater than 0.8 and men are considered to be at risk when their waist/hip ratio is greater than 1.0.

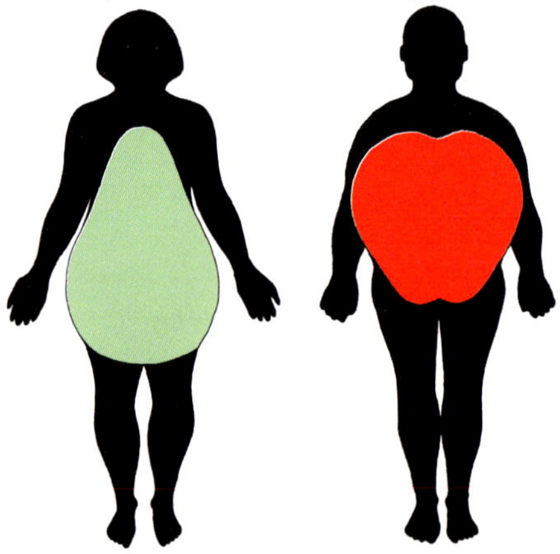

Figure 16.5 Two patterns of fat distribution

Testing Your Knowledge

1 a) i) In what way do the endothelial cells lining an arteriole respond to chronic elevation of blood glucose level?
ii) What effect can this process have on the structure of the arteriole? (2)
b) Identify TWO parts of the body that would be seriously affected if one or more of the small blood vessels supplying them with blood were to burst. (2)

2 a) Which hormone promotes the conversion of:
i) glucose to glycogen
ii) glycogen to glucose?
iii) Where in the body are these hormones produced?
iv) In which organ do the conversions promoted by these hormones occur? (4)
b) Construct a table to show THREE differences between type 1 and type 2 diabetes. (3)
c) i) What is meant by the term *glucose tolerance*?
ii) What is the purpose of a glucose tolerance test? (2)

3 a) What is meant by the term *obesity*? (1)
b) Give the formula used to calculate body mass index (BMI). (1)
c) What are the TWO main ways in which an obese person can reduce the risk factors for CVD? (2)

Applying Your Knowledge and Skills

1 An alternative method of illustrating the regulation of blood glucose level is shown in Figure 16.6.

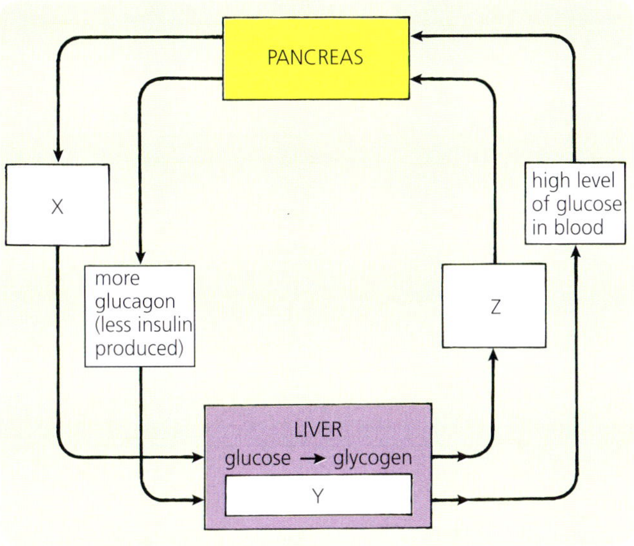

Figure 16.6

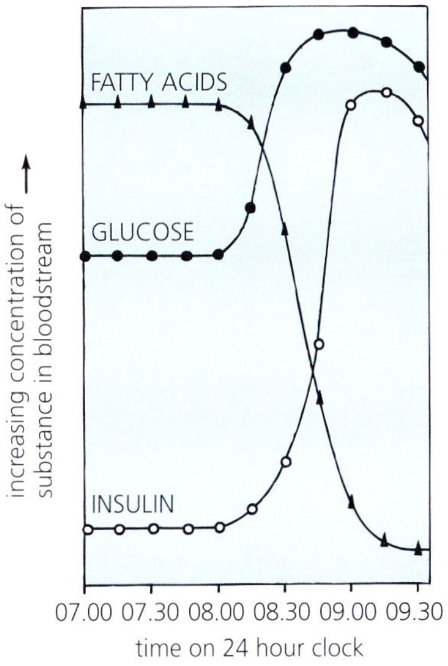

Figure 16.7

a) Redraw the diagram and complete blank boxes X, Y and Z. (3)

b) Copy and complete the following paragraph using the answers that follow it.
The diagram has been drawn as two interrelated circuits to show that a ______ factor under ______ control is constantly wavering on either side of its ______ value. When it ______ from the norm, it is returned to this value by negative ______ control. If it overshoots the mark, a ______ set of mechanisms is triggered that returns the factor to its norm. If it now overshoots the mark in the opposite direction, the opposite set of ______ is made and so on.
deviates, feedback, homeostatic, normal, physiological, responses, reverse (6)

2 Figure 16.7 shows the effect of consuming 50 g of glucose (after a period of fasting) on the concentrations of fatty acids, glucose and insulin in the bloodstream of a person who is not a diabetic.

a) i) During which period of time was the person's blood glucose concentration at a steady level?
ii) By what means is this steady level maintained? (2)

b) i) At what time was the glucose consumed?
ii) What initial effect did this intake have on blood glucose level and concentration of insulin in the blood?
iii) Why was there a short time lag between these two effects? (4)

c) Fatty acids are the breakdown products of fats.
i) Does the information in the graph suggest that insulin promotes or suppresses the breakdown of stored fat?
ii) Explain your answer to i). (2)

d) i) Redraw the axes and extend the time scale to 11.00 hours. Draw the glucose curve to show the concentration from 07.00 to 11.00 hours.
ii) State TWO ways in which the glucose tolerance curve for a person with uncontrolled diabetes would differ from the one that you have drawn. (4)

e) Suggest why the average birth weight of babies born to diabetic mothers is significantly higher than that of non-diabetic mothers. (Do not attempt to give a genetic explanation in your answer.) (1)

3 How many weeks would it take a person to lose 5 kg of body fat if their total energy output exceeded their total energy input by i) 840 kJ/day, ii) 2100 kJ/day? (Note: 1 kg of body fat contains 29.4 MJ of energy. 29.4 MJ = 29 400 kJ.) (2)

→

4 Tables 16.3–16.11 comprise a 10-year risk calculator for coronary heart disease (CHD).

SCORE CARD	
Feature	**Risk points**
Age	
LDL-cholesterol	
HDL-cholesterol	
Blood pressure	
Diabetes	
Smoker	
Total	

Table 16.3

Age (years)	Risk points
30–34	−1
35–39	0
40–44	1
45–49	2
50–54	3
55–59	4
60–64	5
65–69	6
70–74	7

Table 16.4

Concentration of LDL-cholesterol (mmol/l)	Risk points
<2.60	−3
2.60–4.14	0
4.15–4.92	1
>4.92	2

Table 16.5

Concentration of HDL-cholesterol (mmol/l)	Risk points
<0.91	2
0.91–1.16	1
1.17–1.55	0
>1.55	−1

Table 16.6

Risk points associated with blood pressure				
Systolic (mm Hg)	Diastolic (mm Hg)			
	<85	85–89	90–99	>99
<130	0	1	2	3
130–139	1	1	2	3
140–159	2	2	2	3
>159	3	3	3	3

Table 16.7

Diabetes	Risk points
Present	2
Absent	0

Table 16.8

Smoker?	Risk points
Yes	2
No	0

Table 16.9

➜

Total number of risk points	10-year CHD risk (%)
≤−3	1
−2	2
−1	2
0	3
1	4
2	4
3	6
4	7
5	9
6	11
7	14
8	18
9	22
10	27
11	33
12	40
13	47
≥14	≥56

Table 16.10

Age (years)	Average 10-year CHD risk (%)
30–34	3
35–39	5
40–44	7
45–49	11
50–54	14
55–59	16
60–64	21
65–69	25
70–74	30

Table 16.11

Joe is a 49-year-old diabetic whose blood pressure is 129/84. He smokes 20 cigarettes daily and is slightly overweight but takes regular exercise. The last time his cholesterol levels were checked, his LDL-cholesterol was 4.58 mmol/l and his HDL-cholesterol was 1.05 mmol/l.

a) Calculate Joe's 10-year CHD risk using the risk calculator. (1)

b) Compare Joe's 10-year CHD risk with the average value. (1)

c) What advice would you give Joe in the light of these findings? (1)

5 Figure 16.8 shows box plots of body weight for three populations of British men of average height at three different times in recent history.

a) What percentage of data is contained in the box in a box plot? (See Appendix 2 for help.) (1)

b) i) By what means is the median value of the data indicated in a box plot?

ii) State the median value for each of the populations. (2)

c) i) Which box set shows the widest distribution of values between its median and its upper quartile?

ii) Which box set shows the smallest overall distribution of values? (2)

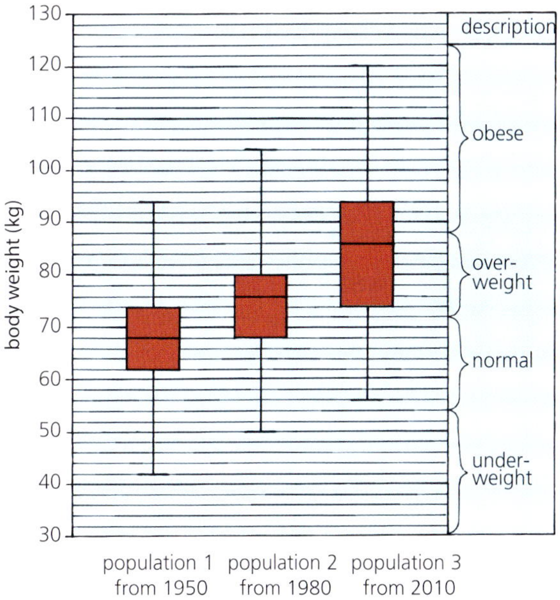

Figure 16.8

d) Does a whisker represent a 95% level of confidence or an actual value? (1)

e) What was the lowest value recorded? (1)

f) If the data were plotted as a graph of number of individuals against body weight, which population would give a symmetrical, bell-shaped curve? (1)

g) i) What trend is shown by the three box plots?

ii) Suggest a reason for this trend that does not refer to food intake. (2)

What You Should Know Chapters 15–16

activity	embolism	liver
arterioles	embolus	low-density
atheromas	endothelium	membranes
atherosclerosis	exercise	negative
attack	fibrin	obesity
burst	glucagon	peripheral
cardiac	glucose	receptors
cardiovascular	glycogen	restricted
cholesterol	high-density	statins
clotting	hormone	stroke
coronary	indicator	thrombosis
deep	insulin	tissues
diabetes	kidneys	tolerance
diagnosed	lean	wound

Table 16.12 Word bank for Chapters 15–16

1 Atherosclerosis is the accumulation of plaques (______) under the ______ in the walls of arteries. The diameter of an affected artery becomes reduced and blood flow is ______. The condition is the root cause of many cardiovascular diseases.

2 ______ is the formation of a blood clot (thrombus). Cells damaged by the rupture of an atheroma release ______ factors that activate a series of chemical reactions. These result in the formation of threads of ______ that clot blood and seal the ______.

3 A thrombus that travels through the bloodstream and eventually blocks a blood vessel is called an ______. If it blocks the ______ artery, it can cause a heart ______. If it blocks an artery to the brain, it can cause a ______.

4 The narrowing of arteries other than those supplying parts of the body core, such as the ______ muscle and brain, causes ______ vascular disease.

5 The formation of a blood clot in a large peripheral vein is called ______ vein thrombosis. If the clot travels to a blood vessel supplying the lungs, it can cause a pulmonary ______.

6 Cholesterol is a fatty substance made in the ______ and needed as a component of cell ______. It is transported to body cells by ______ lipoproteins (LDL) and back to the liver by ______ lipoproteins (HDL).

7 Excess LDL-cholesterol in the blood can result in ______ being deposited in atheromas causing ______. Drugs such as ______ reduce blood cholesterol levels.

8 Very high levels of blood glucose can cause damage to ______ and lead to vascular disease. Damage to small blood vessels can make them ______ and leak their contents into nearby ______.

9 Blood glucose level is regulated by ______ feedback control. When the glucose level is too high, the ______ insulin promotes the conversion of glucose to ______; when it is too low, the hormone ______ promotes the conversion of glycogen to glucose.

10 People with ______ are unable to control their blood glucose level effectively.

11 Those with type 1 diabetes are unable to make ______. Those with type 2 diabetes are able to make insulin but their cells lack an adequate number of insulin ______ and fail to allow enough glucose to enter.

12 The fact that, in both types of diabetes, the ______ cannot cope with the elevated blood glucose level and release ______ in urine, is used as an ______ of the condition.

13 Diabetes is ______ using the glucose ______ test.

14 ______ is characterised by the accumulation of excess body fat relative to ______ body tissue. Obesity is closely associated with lack of physical ______ and a diet rich in fat.

15 Risk factors for ______ disease are reduced by taking ______ and keeping body weight at an optimum level.

3 Neurobiology and Immunology

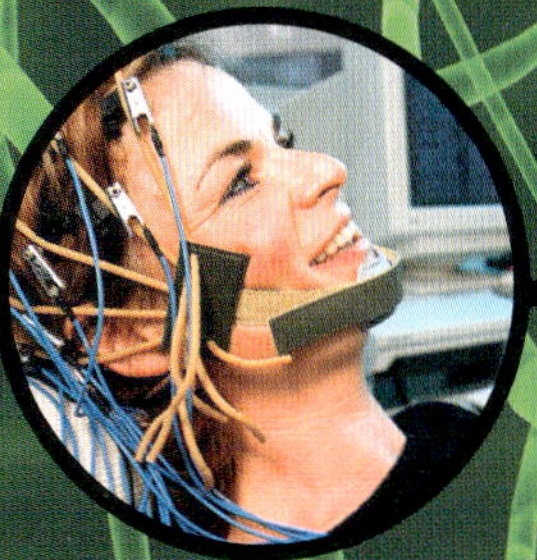
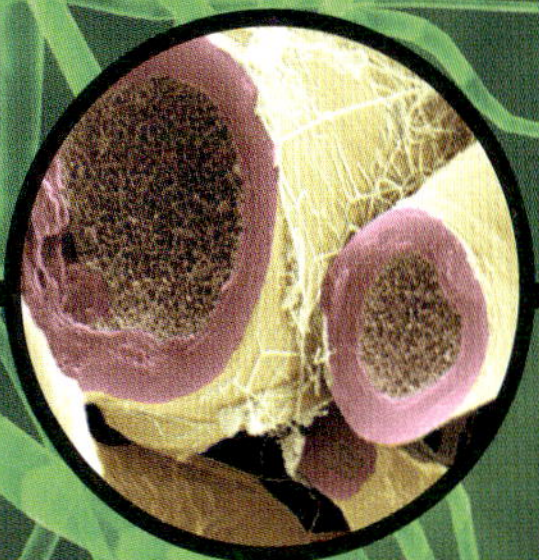
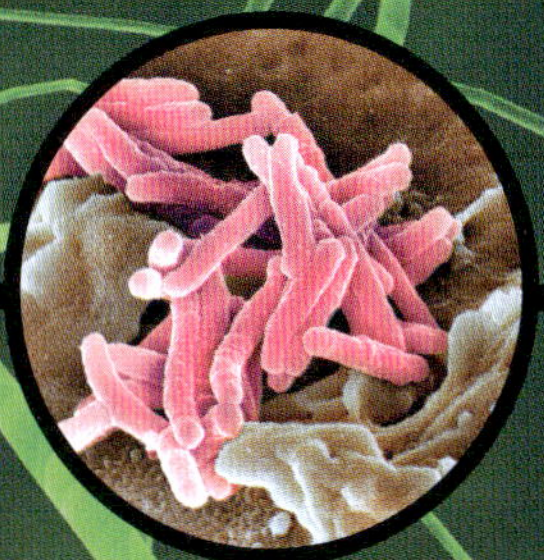

17 Divisions of the nervous system and neural pathways

Sensory information from receptors in contact with the external environment and the internal environment (the inside of the body) is collected by the **nervous system** and analysed. Some of this information is stored for possible future use. Meanwhile, appropriate voluntary and involuntary motor responses are initiated which lead to muscular contractions or glandular secretions.

Divisions of the nervous system

Based on **structure** and **location** of component parts, the nervous system can be divided as shown in Figure 17.1. Figure 17.2 shows, in a simple way, where these parts are located in the human body.

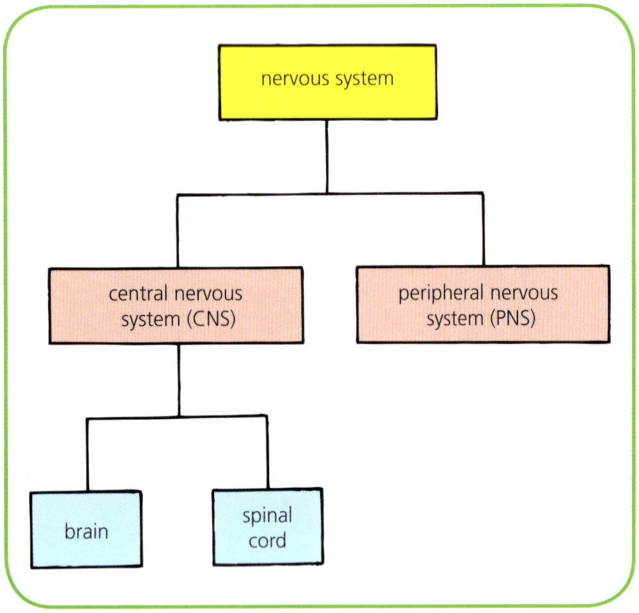

Figure 17.1 Structural division of the nervous system

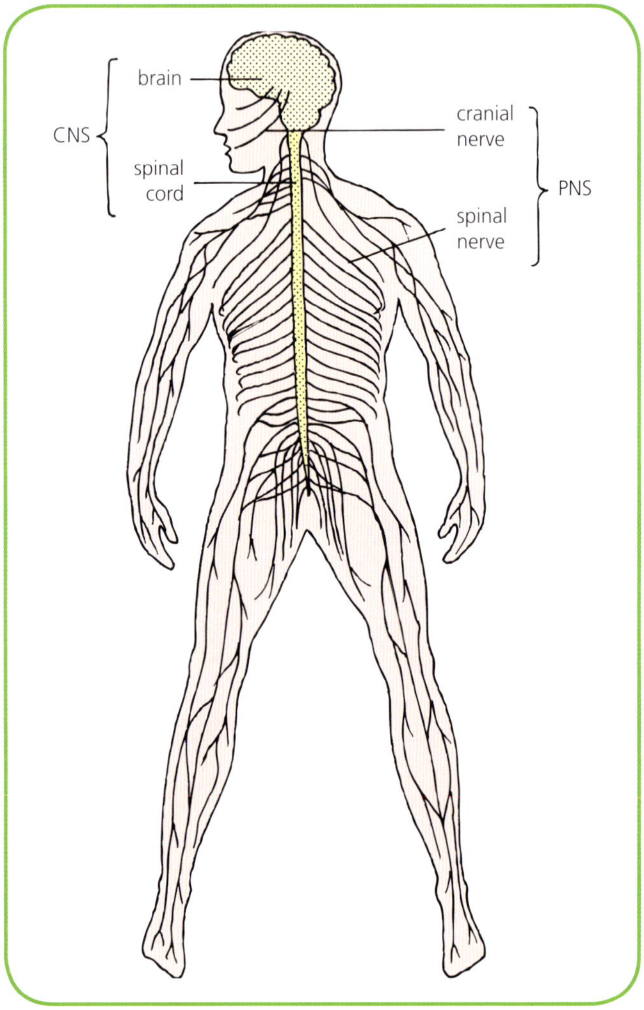

Figure 17.2 Location of CNS and PNS

Sensory and motor pathways

Peripheral nerves contain a **sensory pathway** consisting of sensory nerve cells and/or a **motor pathway** consisting of motor nerve cells. Sensory pathways carry nerve impulses to the CNS from **receptors**. Some receptors are located in external sense organs (such as the skin, eye retina and ear cochlea); others are found in internal sense organs (such as CO_2 receptors in carotid arteries and thermoreceptors in the cerebellum). Sensory pathways keep the brain in touch with what is going on in the body's external and internal environments.

The brain analyses, interprets, processes and stores some of this constant stream of information, which is based on stimuli such as sounds, sights, colours, tastes, temperature of skin and blood and CO_2 concentration and water concentration of blood. The brain's association centres may act on this information by sending nerve impulses via the motor pathways to **effectors** (e.g. muscles and glands). These then bring about the appropriate **response**, such as muscular

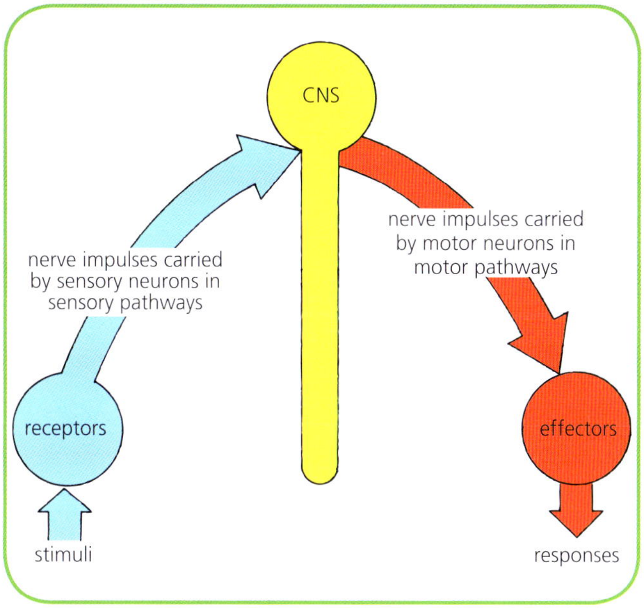

Figure 17.3 Flow of information through the nervous system

contraction or enzyme secretion. This relationship is summarised in Figure 17.3.

Functional division

A further method of dividing up the nervous system is based on the different **functions** performed by the two separate branches of the peripheral nervous system, as shown in Figure 17.4.

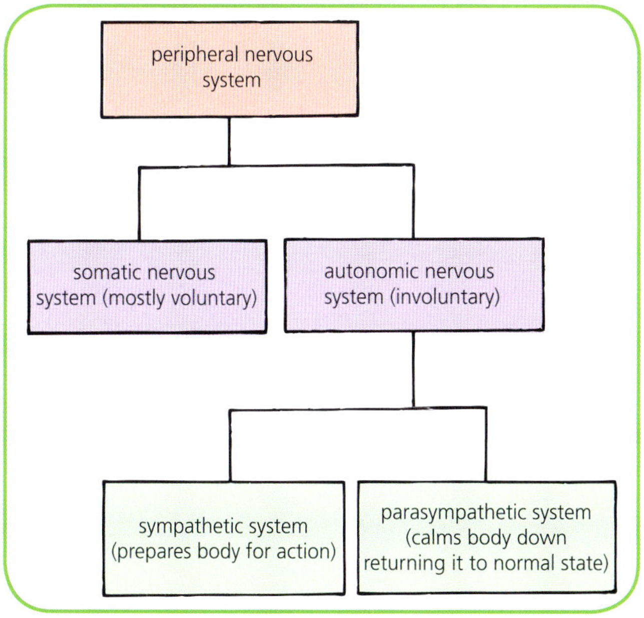

Figure 17.4 Functional divisions of the nervous system

Somatic nervous system

The **somatic nervous system (SNS)**, which includes the spinal nerves, controls the body's skeletal muscles. This involves sensory and motor pathways, as outlined in Figure 17.3. The somatic nervous system is responsible for bringing about certain **involuntary reflex** actions (for example, limb withdrawal), but most of the control that it exerts is over **voluntary movements** of skeletal muscles.

Imagine, for example, that you are invited to select your four favourite chocolates from a large box of a familiar make. The displayed chocolates act as visual stimuli. Nerve impulses pass from each retina via sensory nerve cells in the optic nerve to the brain. There, association centres process the information and compare it with previous experiences. Decisions are taken and nerve impulses pass to the brain's motor area. This in turn sends impulses via motor nerve cells to the appropriate skeletal muscles of the arm and hand allowing the voluntary responses needed to pick out the four sweets. This series of events involves the somatic nervous system.

Autonomic nervous system

The **autonomic nervous system (ANS)** (see Figure 17.5) regulates the **internal** environment by controlling structures and organs such as the heart, blood vessels, bronchioles and alimentary canal. This control is generally **involuntary** because it normally works **automatically** without the person's conscious control being involved (although, under exceptional circumstances, some people are able to heighten or suppress certain autonomic responses intentionally).

The nerves that comprise the autonomic nervous system arise from nerve cells in the brain and emerge at various points down the spinal cord to reach the effectors (cardiac muscle, smooth muscle and glands) that they stimulate with nerve impulses.

Antagonistic nature of autonomic nervous system

The **sympathetic** and **parasympathetic** systems that make up the autonomic nervous system are described as being **antagonistic**. This means that they affect many of the same structures but exert opposite effects on them. Figure 17.5 shows only a few of the many tissues and organs controlled in this way.

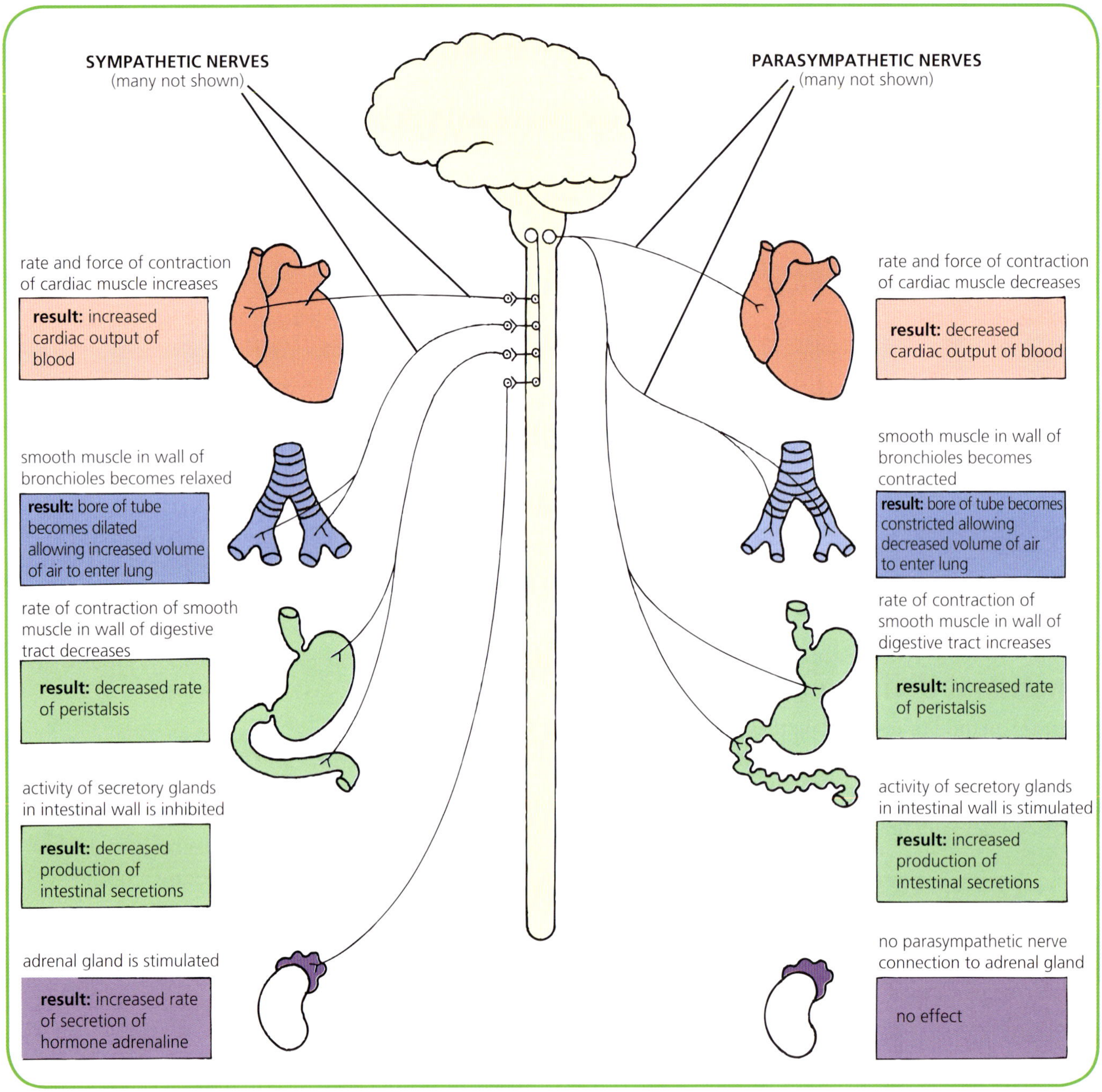

Figure 17.5 Autonomic nervous system

Harmonious balance

The autonomic nervous system is concerned with maintaining a **stable internal environment** by playing its part in the process of **homeostasis** (see Related Topic – Homeostasis). Under normal circumstances the sympathetic and parasympathetic systems are constantly working in an equal but opposite manner, with neither gaining the upper hand. The activity of a tissue or organ under their control is the result of the two **opposing influences**. It is therefore normally in a state somewhere between the extremes of hypo- and hyperactivity.

Finely tuned control

The stimulation of an effector by both sympathetic and parasympathetic nerves provides a **fine degree of control** over the effector. The system works like a vehicle equipped with both an **accelerator** and a **brake**.

If the car had an accelerator but no brake then the process of reducing speed would depend solely on decreasing the pressure on the accelerator. This method would require too much time to elapse before the car responded and slowed down. Use of a brake, which can be applied in addition to decreasing the pressure on the accelerator, allows for a much more rapid and effective means of regulating the car's speed.

There are exceptions to the rule of dual innervation of an effector by both parasympathetic and sympathetic nerves. For example, the adrenal gland, which secretes the hormone **adrenaline**, receives a supply of sympathetic nerves only (see Figure 17.5).

Fight or flight

On being stimulated and briefly gaining the upper hand, the **sympathetic** system arouses the body in preparation for action and the expenditure of energy during '**fight or flight**'. The heart rate and blood pressure increase. Blood supplies are diverted to the skeletal muscles (in great need of an increased supply of oxygen) and away from the gut and skin (which require minimal servicing during the crisis). Rate of nervous perspiration also increases. Hence a thudding heart, a face white with fear and a clammy sensation in localised areas of the body that are in a 'cold sweat' (e.g. armpits and palms of hands) are all characteristic responses to a crisis.

The hormone adrenaline helps to sustain the arousal effects until the emergency is dealt with. This might involve taking a determined and defensive stand, perhaps involving a fight or cutting your losses and running away. In either case the vast amount of energy required by the skeletal muscles is supplied by their increased blood flow.

Rest and digest

When the excitement is over, the **parasympathetic** system takes over for a brief spell, calming the body down and returning it to normal for '**rest and digest**'. Heart rate and blood pressure drop to normal. Rate of peristaltic contractions in the digestive tract increases. Blood is diverted to the intestines where it can resume its job of absorbing the end products of digestion now that the crisis is over. The effects brought about by the parasympathetic nerves help the body to **conserve resources** and **store energy**.

Complex neural pathways

Further details of complex neural pathways such as those that converge or diverge are given on pages 235–7.

Related Topic

Homeostasis

Homeostasis is the maintenance of the body's internal environment within certain tolerable limits despite changes in the body's external environment (or changes in the body's rate of activity).

Principle of negative feedback control

When some factor affecting the body's internal environment deviates from its normal optimum level (called the **norm** or **set point**), this change in the factor is detected by **receptors**. These send out nerve or hormonal messages which are received by **effectors**. The effectors then bring about certain responses that counteract the original deviation from the norm and return the system to its set point. This corrective homeostatic mechanism is called **negative feedback control**. It provides the stable environmental conditions needed by the body's community of living cells to function efficiently and survive. (Also see Figure 16.2 on page 193.)

Testing Your Knowledge

1 a) Name the TWO components of the central nervous system (CNS). (2)
   b) What collective name is given to all the nerves excluding the central nervous system? (1)

2 Differentiate between the following pairs of terms:
   a) *sensory* and *motor* pathways (2)
   b) *receptors* and *effectors*. (2)

3 a) Name the TWO branches of the autonomic nervous system. (2)
   b) State the effect of each branch of the autonomic nervous system on:
      i) cardiac output
      ii) width of bore of the bronchioles. (4)

4 Rewrite the following sentences, choosing the correct word from each underlined choice.
The body becomes aroused ready for 'fight or flight' by the action of the sympathetic/parasympathetic nerves. As a result, rate of blood flow to the heart increases/decreases, rate of peristalsis increases/decreases and rate of breathing increases/decreases. (4)

Applying Your Knowledge and Skills questions for Chapter 17 are to be found on pages 213–5.

18 Cerebral cortex

Cerebral cortex

The **cerebral cortex** is the outer layer of the cerebrum, which forms the largest and most complex part of the brain. It is the centre of conscious thought. In addition, it is able to retrieve memories and alter behaviour in the light of past experience.

The cerebrum is split by a deep cleft into two halves called **cerebral hemispheres**. The left hemisphere processes information from the right visual field and controls the right side of the body. The reverse is true of the right hemisphere.

The two hemispheres are not completely separated but are connected by a large bundle of nerve fibres called the **corpus callosum** (see Figure 18.1). This fibrous link between the two hemispheres is important to allow information to be transferred from one to the other. Whatever happens in one side of the brain is quickly communicated to the other side, thereby coordinating brain functions and enabling the brain to act as an integrated whole.

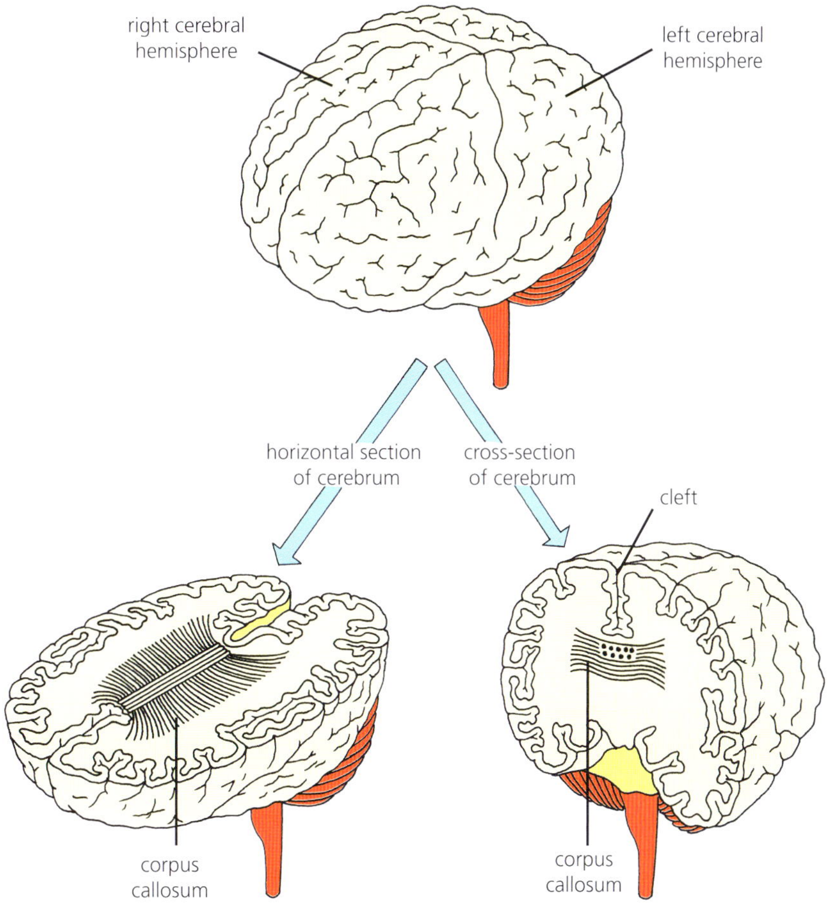

Figure 18.1 Location of the corpus callosum

Localisation of brain function in the cerebral cortex

The cerebral cortex contains three types of functional area: **sensory**, **association** and **motor**. Each area performs its own particular function distinct from the others. The sensory areas **receive information** as sensory impulses from the body's receptors (e.g. touch receptors in the skin and thermoreceptors in the hypothalamus). The association areas **analyse** and **interpret** these impulses, 'make sense' of them and 'take decisions' if necessary. The motor areas receive information from the association areas and 'carry out orders' by **sending motor impulses** to the appropriate effectors (such as muscles). By this means, coordination of voluntary movement is effected.

Interconnections

No part of the cerebral cortex works in complete isolation. **Interconnections** in the form of tiny nerve fibres link up the different areas and messages are constantly passing between them from sensory areas to motor areas via association areas. This allows for sophisticated perception of a situation involving several types of sensory impulse and the ability to make an **integrated response**.

As a simple example, imagine that you are blindfolded and a very large ice cube is placed in your hand. Sensory areas in your cerebral cortex receive information from touch, pressure and cold receptors in your skin. By analysing and interpreting these impulses, association centres in your cerebral cortex gain an impression of the size, shape, weight, texture and temperature of the 'mystery object'. When they put all this information together, it results in you experiencing the sensation of holding a very large ice cube. As the ice cube becomes uncomfortably cold and heavy, you reach a decision to let it go. The appropriate motor centre carries out orders by sending out impulses to the muscles that operate the hand, causing your grip on the ice cube to relax.

Higher mental processes

Specific association areas in the cerebral cortex are responsible for **higher mental processes** such as language processing, intelligence, personality, creativity, imagination and conscience.

Related Topic

Evidence from brain injuries

Some forms of tumour and disease can injure certain areas of the brain. Similarly, specific regions of the brain can be damaged by accidents. Careful study of the effects of such **injuries** sometimes allows experts to infer the role played by a particular part of the brain.

Damaged frontal lobe

In 1848, an accident led to an inch-thick rod being driven into the head of a young American railroad worker. The rod entered beneath his left eye and exited through the top of his head (see Figure 18.2). Amazingly the man survived and was able to speak, think, remember and eventually return to work. However, he had changed. From having been mild-mannered and dependable, he had become ill-tempered, unreliable and no longer able to stick to a plan. This case and others involving damage to the **frontal lobes** of the brain show that they are involved in planning, goal setting and personality.

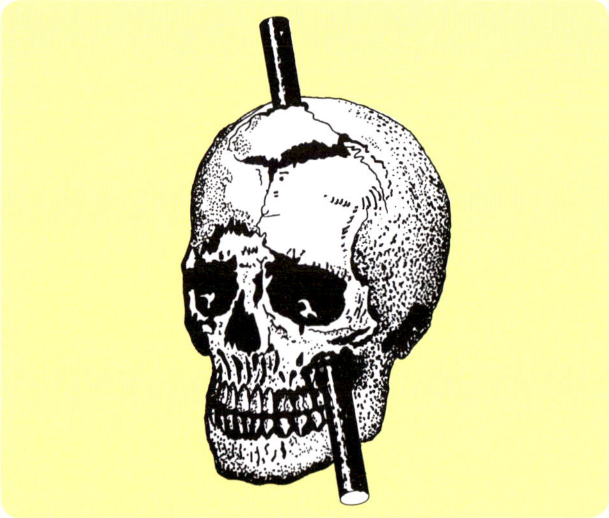

Figure 18.2 This brain damage was not fatal

Wife or hat?

In another case, a musician of great ability developed a problem in later life. He no longer recognised people or objects and failed to remember the past visually. He would chat to pieces of furniture thinking that they were people. On one occasion he reached out, took hold of his wife's head and tried to lift it to put it on, thinking that it was his hat! The problem was due to damage to his **visual association centres**.

Lesions

Lesions are small regions of damage. The location of the brain's **language areas** is verified by the fact that lesions in these regions give rise to speech defects. For example, extensive damage to the speech motor areas results in the person being unable to articulate words despite the fact that they fully understand the words that they hear.

Related Topic

Electroencephalograms (EEGs)

An **EEG** is a record of the cerebrum's **electrical activity** over a short period of time (e.g. 20–30 minutes). It is made using information from impulses picked up by electrodes placed on different regions of the scalp (see Figure 18.3). Different brain wave patterns indicate different levels of mental activity, as shown in Figure 18.4.

Figure 18.3 Preparing for an EEG

Compare the long, rolling wave pattern typical of sleep with the concentrated non-rolling pattern obtained when the subject is awake and concentrating. The more densely packed the 'spikes' in the pattern, the higher the level of electrical activity present in the brain. An extreme version of this is seen in the EEG of the person suffering an epileptic attack. In addition, patients who experience personality problems accompanied by extreme changes of behaviour are often found to produce abnormal EEGs.

EEGs are useful but not very precise since they reflect the simultaneous activity of many cells all over the brain. Although an EEG may show an abnormal pattern indicating a possible problem, it fails to pinpoint the particular region of the brain responsible. However, reliable use can be made of EEGs in the diagnosis of comas and brain death.

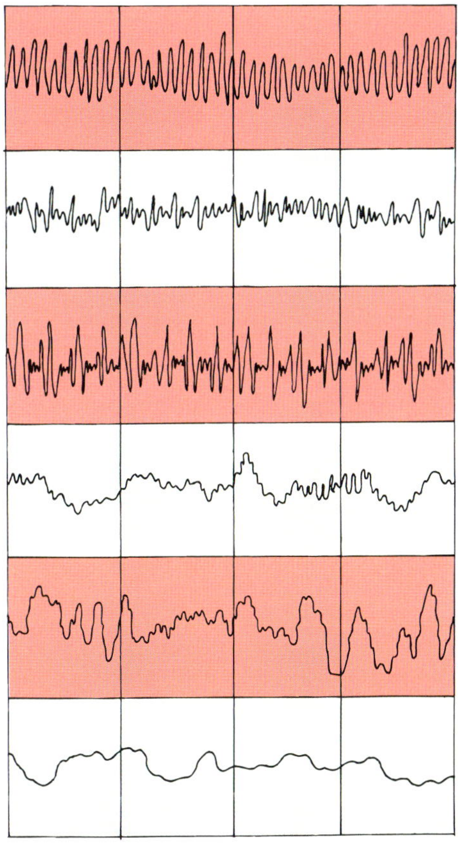

Figure 18.4 EEG wave patterns

Related Topic

Split-brain studies

Visual pathways

Normal situation

Each cerebral hemisphere controls the opposite side of the body. When the two eyes are focused on the centre of a two-tone field of view, each eye receives light from both sides of the field of view, as shown in Figure 18.5. However, each cerebral hemisphere only receives information from about half of this visual field. Everything to the left of the central line (the left field of view – blue in the diagram) is represented in the visual area of the right cerebral hemisphere; everything to the right of the central line (the right field of view – orange in the diagram) is represented in the left cerebral hemisphere.

This occurs because half of the nerve fibres in each optic nerve **cross over** to the opposite side of the brain at the optic chiasma. Normally each side of the cerebrum quickly communicates its share of the information with the other side via the **corpus callosum**. As a result, both hemispheres perceive the whole field of view.

Abnormal situation

A person whose corpus callosum has been cut (for example, during an operation to try to relieve intractable epilepsy) is described as a '**split-brain**' patient. In such a person the exchange of information between the

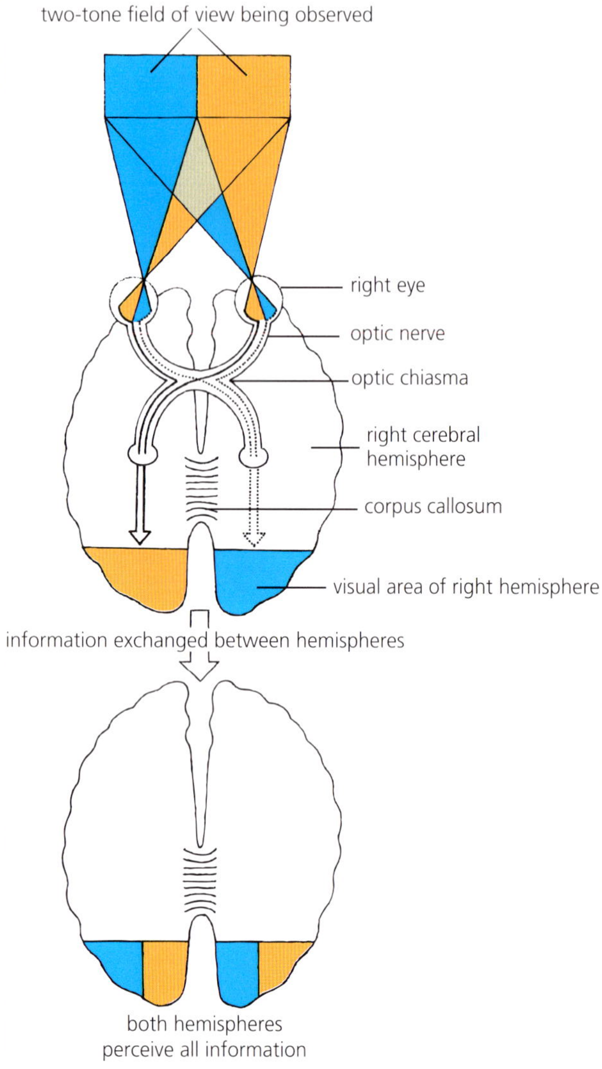

Figure 18.5 Normal visual pathway

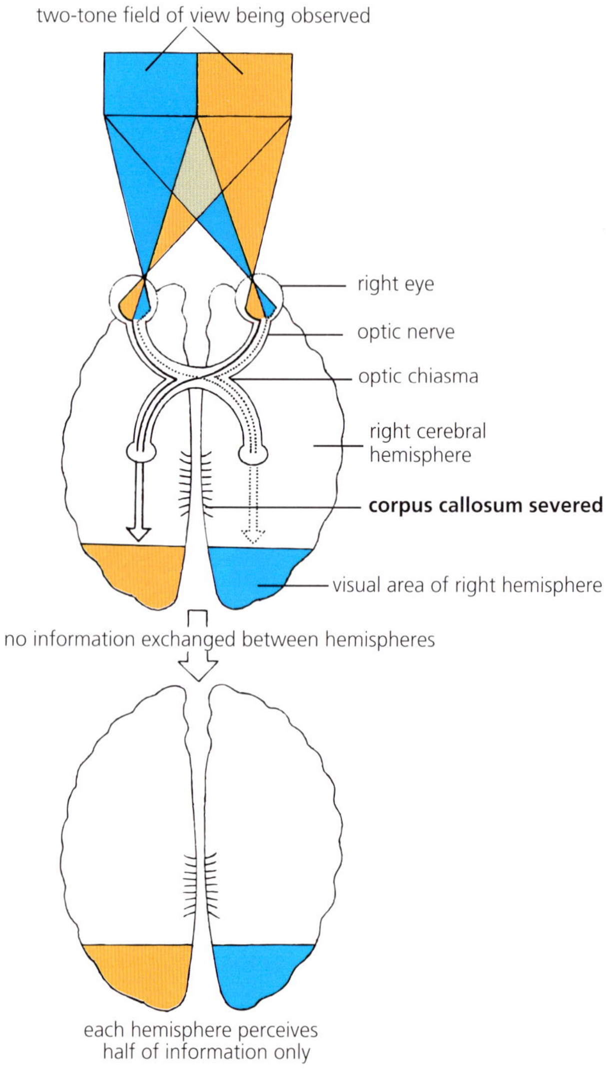

Figure 18.6 Abnormal visual pathway

cerebral hemispheres as described above cannot take place and each hemisphere receives only half of the information about the field of view (see Figure 18.6).

When asked to **say** what they see, the split-brain patient describes a field of view that is completely orange. This is further evidence of the localisation of brain function. It indicates that the motor speech area is in the left cerebral hemisphere only and that this is the left side of the brain 'talking'. However, when asked to **point with the left hand** to what they saw from a selection of possible fields of view, the person chooses a field of view that is completely blue since the left hand is controlled by the right side of the brain, which is now indicating its version of events.

Related Topic

Imaging the brain

Several techniques are now available that enable medical experts to create clear, visual **images of inside the brain** without involving surgery. These are used to study the normal workings of the brain and to diagnose various disorders. Two such techniques are described below.

PET (positron-emission tomography)

This type of **brain scan** reveals the location of active areas of the brain, showing **high metabolic activity** (an increased demand for glucose and oxygen). In preparation for a **PET** scan, the person receives an injection of glucose (or an appropriate alternative) labelled with a harmless isotope that shows up at the most active areas of the brain. These areas are detected by a PET camera and converted to a colourised image by a computer.

PET scans are used to diagnose abnormalities such as brain tumours (areas of high metabolic activity) and areas of neuron damage (low metabolic activity) that may lead to forms of dementia such as Alzheimer's disease (AD). For example, the PET scan in Figure 18.7 shows lower metabolic rates and lower levels of brain activity in a person who is affected by AD.

PET scans can also be used to identify those parts of the brain that show highest metabolic activity during particular **actions** and **emotions**. For example, a scan will show which area of the brain is most active when the person is, say, listening to music or stroking a furry object or suddenly feeling angry. These findings provide convincing evidence for the **localisation** of brain functions.

Language areas

The process of speech is found to involve several specific regions of the brain. These different '**language' areas** also show up on brain scans as regions of high metabolic activity (see Figure 18.8). When the information from several scans is put together, it gives a map of the brain's language areas, as shown in Figure 18.9.

fMRI (functional magnetic resonance imaging)

This technique employs radio waves and magnetic fields to produce images of the brain. It also depends on properties of haemoglobin present in blood that enable

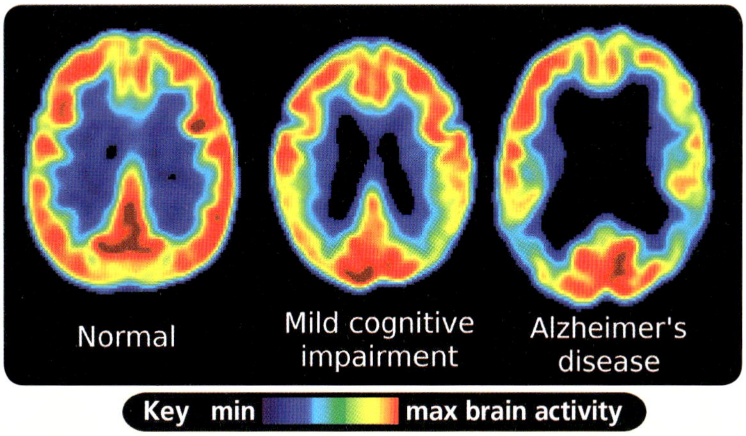

Figure 18.7 PET scans

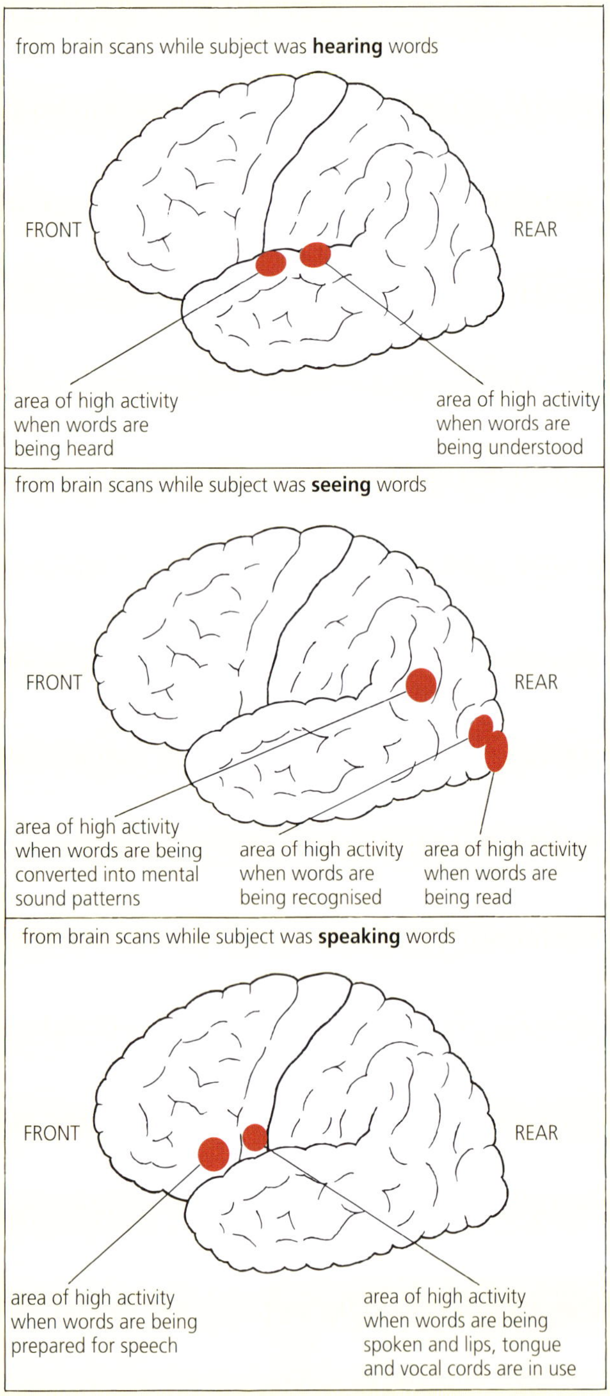

Figure 18.8 Language areas from brain scans

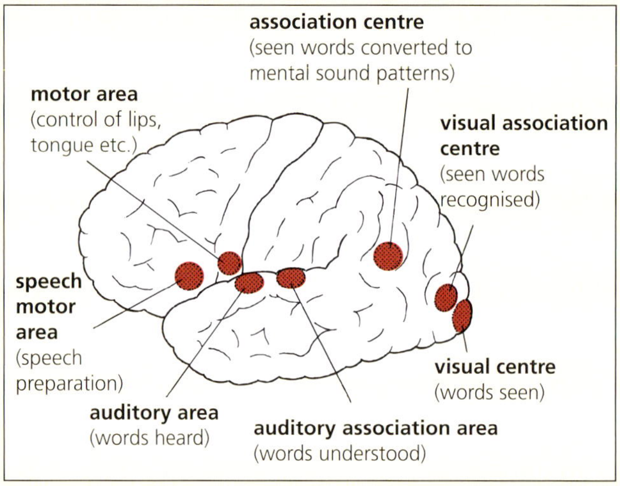

Figure 18.9 Map of the brain's language areas

changes in patterns of blood flow to be followed. These indicate activity of brain cells. By this means, experts are able to create **anatomical and functional images** of the brain.

During an **fMRI scan** (see Figure 18.10), a person might, for example, be subjected to a variety of visual, auditory or tactile stimuli. The scan would then reveal those areas of the brain involved in vision, hearing or touch. In addition to research using healthy volunteers, fMRI is used to diagnose disease and disorders such as brain tumours.

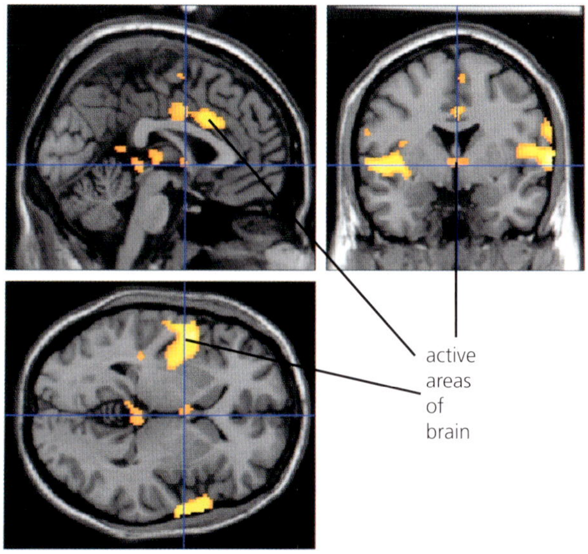

Figure 18.10 fMRI scan

Testing Your Knowledge

1 a) Which cerebral hemisphere controls
   i) the left,
   ii) the right side of the body? (1)
   b) i) What is the *corpus callosum*?
   ii) State its function. (2)

2 a) Name THREE different types of functional area present in the cerebral cortex. (3)
   b) Briefly describe the function carried out by each of these different types of area. (3)

3 Identify THREE higher mental processes for which the cerebral cortex is responsible. (3)

Applying Your Knowledge and Skills Chapters 17–18

1 Copy and complete Figure 18.11, which shows two ways of classifying the parts of the human nervous system. (5)

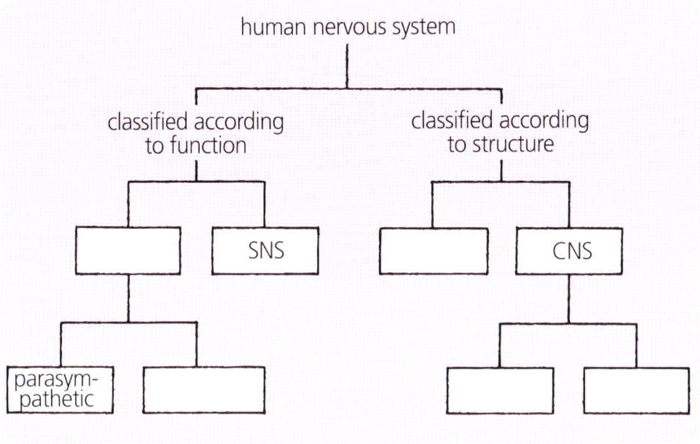

Figure 18.11

2 Imagine a person taking a carefree stroll through a field on a summer's day. Suddenly a bull appears from behind a hedge and charges towards the person. She runs for her life and just manages to escape in time.
   a) With reference to BOTH parts of the autonomic nervous system, briefly describe the events occurring in the person's body during and immediately after this crisis. (4)
   b) Predict the possible outcome to a person if the parasympathetic system took control of the body on a permanent basis. (1)

3 Figure 18.12 shows a simplified version of the sympathetic nerve supply to two parts of the body containing smooth involuntary muscle.
   a) i) Predict the effect of nerve impulses on the smooth muscle of the arteriole supplying blood to the gut.
   ii) What effect will this have on the bore of the tube?
   iii) Why is this response of survival value to the body during a crisis? (3)

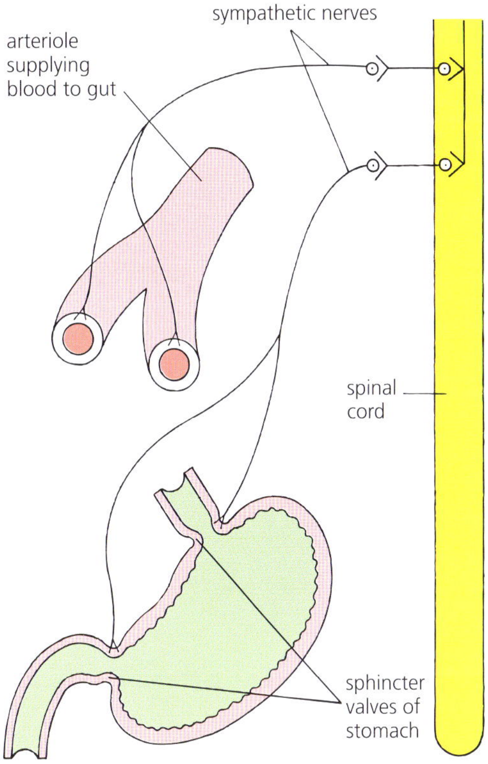

Figure 18.12

   b) i) Predict the effect of sympathetic nerve impulses on the muscle making up the stomach's sphincter valves.
   ii) By what means could the reverse effect be brought about?
   iii) Under what circumstances would this reverse effect be of advantage to the body? Explain why. (4)

4 Figure 18.13 is a composite picture that was shown to several split-brain patients. A little later the patients were asked to study the four pictures shown in Figure 18.14.

Figure 18.13

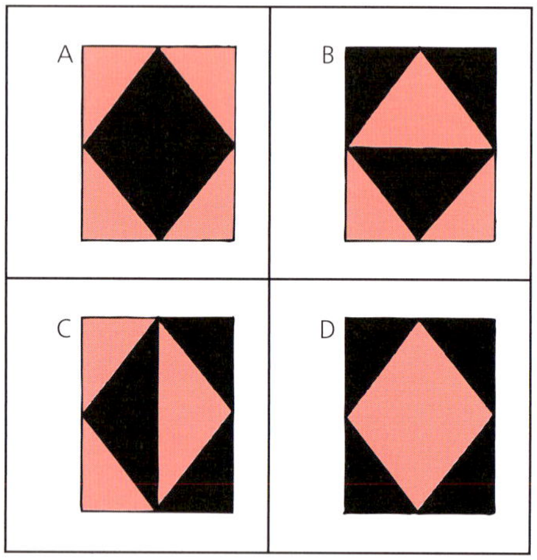

Figure 18.14

State, with reasons, which picture all of the patients chose when asked to:

a) say what they had seen (2)

b) point with their left hand to what they had seen. (2)

5 Figure 18.15 shows a map of the brain's language areas in the left cerebral hemisphere. These numbered areas are identified in Figure 18.9 on page 212.

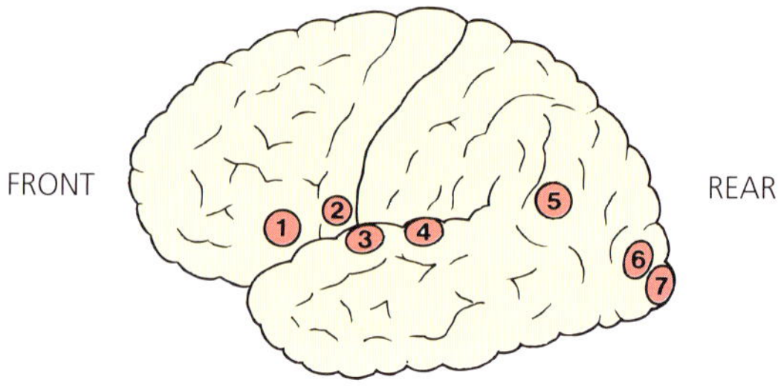

Figure 18.15

a) Which TWO areas would show highest activity while the person was listening to and understanding a conversation on a mobile phone? (2)

b) Suggest what the person is doing when a high level of activity is registered in the following language areas in the order shown:

i) 7, 6, 5, 4

ii) 7, 6, 5, 4, 1, 2. (2)

c) Identify the areas involved and state their correct sequence of involvement when a spoken message is heard and then repeated out loud. (1)

d) Suggest what effect severe damage to region 1 in Figure 18.15 would have on the ability to i) understand language, ii) speak language. (2)

6 Schizophrenia is a condition characterised by personality disorders often involving delusions or hallucinations generated in the cerebral cortex. Table 18.1 shows the results from four surveys investigating the incidence of schizophrenia among twins. The members of each pair of twins were raised together by their natural parents.

Survey	Identical twins		Non-identical twins	
	Number of twin pairs	Percentage of affected twin pairs	Number of twin pairs	Percentage of affected twin pairs
1	21	66.69	60	4.67
2	41	68.32	101	14.91
3	41	76.07	115	14.06
4	268	85.16	685	14.52

Table 18.1

a) Calculate the average percentage (accurate to two decimal places) of twin pairs affected with schizophrenia when the twins are i) identical, ii) non-identical. (2)

b) What conclusion about the part played by inherited factors can be drawn from these findings? (1)

c) Which survey's data do you consider to be:
i) the most reliable
ii) the least reliable?
iii) Explain your choices for i) and ii). (4)

What You Should Know Chapters 17–18

autonomic	experience	parasympathetic
central	external	peripheral
conscious	hemisphere	recalled
contractions	integrated	receptors
corpus	involuntary	somatic
cortex	left	sympathetic
effectors	nervous	voluntary

Table 18.2 Word bank for Chapters 17–18

1 Sensory information from the body's internal and ______ environment is analysed by the ______ system. Appropriate motor responses are then initiated which lead to muscular ______ and glandular secretions.

2 The nervous system can be divided on a structural basis into the ______ nervous system (CNS) and the ______ nervous system (PNS).

3 The nervous system can be divided on a functional basis into the ______ nervous system (SNS) and the ______ nervous system (ANS).

4 The SNS controls ______ movement of the skeletal muscles.

5 The ANS works automatically without involving the person's ______ thought. It regulates the internal environment by exerting ______ control over structures such as the heart and alimentary canal.

6 The ANS is made up of the ______ system which arouses the body in preparation for 'fight or flight' and the ______ system which calms the body and promotes 'rest and digest'.

7 The cerebral ______ is the centre of conscious thought. Its sensory areas receive sensory impulses from ______. Its association areas analyse and interpret information and its motor areas send motor impulses to ______.

8 The right cerebral ______ receives information from the left visual field and controls the ______ side of the body. The reverse is true of the left cerebral hemisphere. Information is transferred from one hemisphere to the other via the ______ callosum, enabling the brain to work as an ______ whole.

9 Nerve cell activity in the cerebral cortex enables decisions to be made, memories to be ______ and behaviour to be altered in the light of ______.

19 Memory

Memory is one of our major mental faculties. It is the capacity of the brain to **store** information, **retain** it and then **retrieve** it when required. The brain is so **versatile** that it can capture images of sights, sounds, smells, tactile sensations and emotions all experienced at the one time and retain them as memories.

The brain is able to store a vast quantity of knowledge, thoughts and detailed information relating to past experiences as **memories**. Memory enables us to deal with future situations in the light of past experience. In the absence of memory we would be helpless, unable to manage even the simplest task without having to first relearn it.

Selective memory

The receptors in the human sense organs are continuously picking up stimuli and transmitting sensory impulses to the brain. However, only a fraction of the sensory images formed become **committed to memory** because the process is highly **selective**. If this were not the case the mind would become cluttered with useless information such as every phone number ever used, every musical note of every tune ever heard whether liked or disliked, and so on.

Encoding, storage and retrieval

To become part of the memory, the selected sensory image must first become **encoded** (converted to a form that the brain can process and store). **Storage** is the retention of information over a period of time. This may last for only a brief spell such as 30 seconds or for a very long period, perhaps a complete lifetime.

Retrieval is the recovery of stored material. This involves the recall of information that has been committed to either the **short-term** or the **long-term** memory. Thus when memory is functioning properly, encoding leads to storage of information that can be retrieved later when required.

Different levels of memory

Memory is thought to involve three separate **interacting levels**, as shown in Figure 19.1. All information that gains access to the brain must first pass through the **sensory memory (SM)** and then, if selected, enter the **short-term memory (STM)**. From there it may be transferred to the **long-term memory (LTM)** or be discarded.

Level 1 – sensory memory (SM)

Stimuli from the outside world are continuously being perceived as sensory images by the brain. These impressions are very **short-lived** (e.g. 0.5 seconds for visual and 2 seconds for auditory) and only a few are selected and transferred to level 2. The SM provides a detailed representation of the person's entire sensory experience from which relevant pieces of information are sent to the STM.

Level 2 – short-term memory (STM)

Most of the information encoded into this second level of the system consists of visual and auditory images. However, the STM holds only a limited amount of information – about seven items at the one time (see Investigation – Length of memory span). Not only does the STM have a limited capacity but, in addition, the items are held for a short time (approximately 30 seconds). During this time, retrieval of items is very accurate. Thereafter they are either transferred to level 3 or lost by **displacement** (the pushing out of 'old' by new incoming information) or by **decay** (the breakdown of a fragile 'memory trace' formed when a group of neurons briefly became activated).

Memory span

A person's **short-term memory span** can be measured by finding out the number of individual 'meaningless' items that the person can reproduce correctly, and in order, immediately after seeing or hearing them once. (Also see Investigation – Length of short-term memory span.)

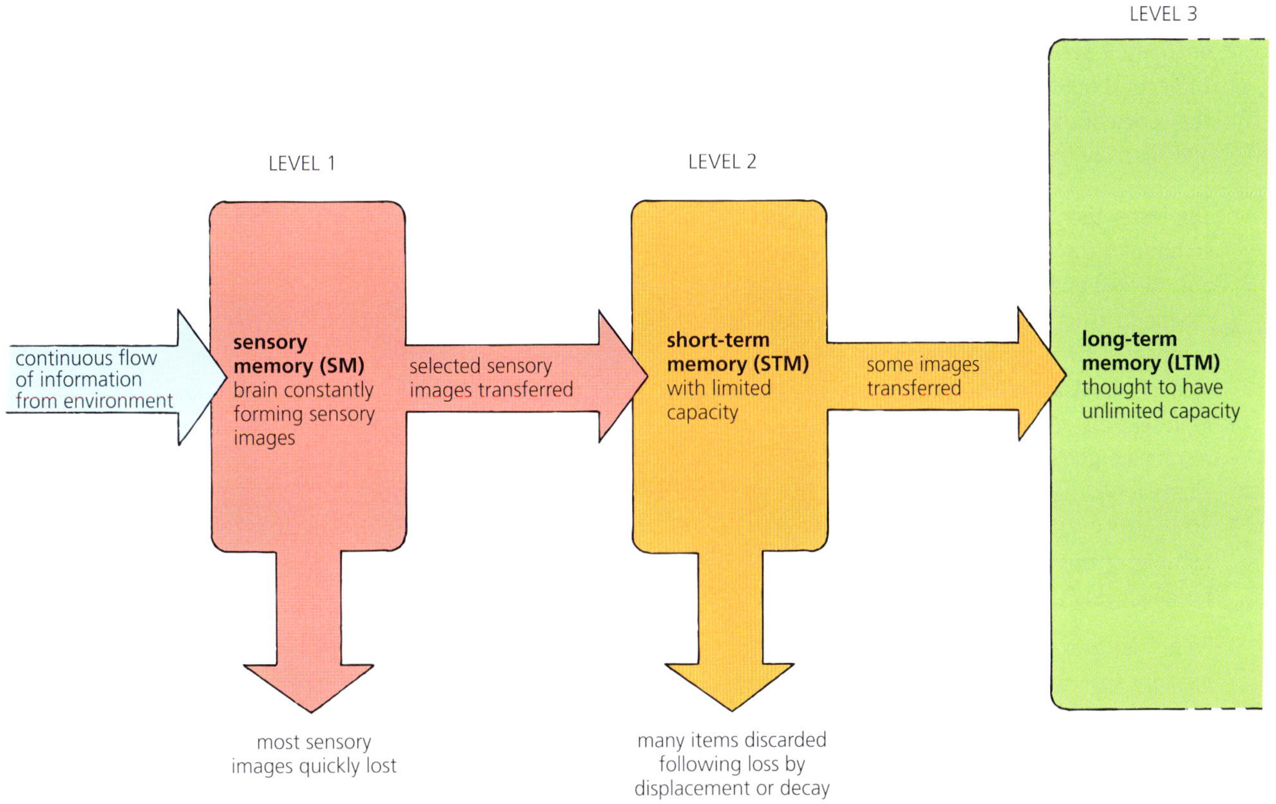

Figure 19.1 Three levels of memory

Investigation

Length of short-term memory span

In the following investigation there is one tester (e.g. the teacher) and many subjects (the members of the class). The tester reads out the first series of digits (see Table 19.1) clearly and at uniform speed.

Series	Number of digits in series
741	3
2835	4
46279	5
584153	6
9082637	7
16136209	8
592403517	9
8076148362	10
78501942493	11
512367509308	12
6821496708754	13

Table 19.1 List of series of digits

Immediately after reading out the last digit of the first series, the tester signals that all subjects should lift their pencils, write down the series of digits that they have just heard and then lay their pencils down again.

The tester then reads out the next series, and so on until the end of the list. The responses are checked and each subject's memory span for the first list is established. The procedure is repeated twice using different lists. Each subject's **best overall score** is taken to represent his or her memory span. The class results are pooled and graphed. Figure 19.2 charts a typical set of results for a class of 20 students. Table 19.2 outlines the design features of this investigation and the reasons for employing them.

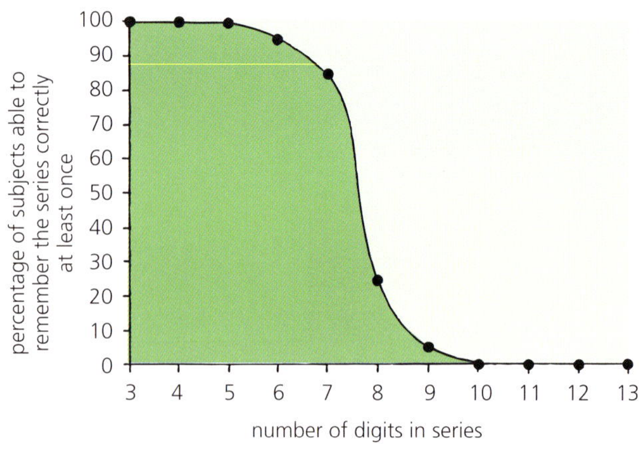

Figure 19.2 Graph of memory span results

From the results in Figure 19.2, it is concluded that for this group of students, the poorest (minimum) memory span was 5 digits (one student), the best (maximum) memory span was 9 digits (one student) and that all of the other subjects had a memory span somewhere in between. On average, the human short-term memory span is found to be 7 ± 2 digits, though some amazing exceptions have been recorded.

Design feature or precaution	Reason
Series of random numbers used	To eliminate easily remembered sequences or groups of numbers
All information read out clearly at uniform speed by the same tester	To ensure that the only variable factor is the number of digits in the series
Pencils laid down between responses	To prevent over-eager subjects starting to write down the series before it has been completely read out
Each subject given three attempts	To obtain a more reliable result for each subject's best score
Many students tested and the results pooled as a graph	To further increase the reliability of the results

Table 19.2 Design features for memory span investigation

Chunking

A **chunk** is a meaningful unit of information made up of several smaller units. To most people familiar with the dates of the Second World War, 1945 is one chunk of information not four chunks. However, to most people 4951 is four chunks of information (unless it happens to be something significant such as the PIN number of their bank account). Since short-term memory is only capable of holding about seven new items at one time, **chunking** is a useful method of increasing its memory span. The compilers of all-digit telephone numbers provide users with means to transfer an 11-digit number from directory to telephone by chunking.

Imagine, for example, that a business woman in Aberdeen wishes to phone an unfamiliar Glasgow number (e.g. 01416293801). If she already knows that Glasgow's national code is 0141 then that chunk reduces her task to remembering 8 items. If in addition she has

Related Activity

Investigating the effect of chunking on memory span

In this investigation, the subjects view list 1 only (in Table 19.3) for 2 minutes and are then allowed 4 minutes to write down as many of the 3-lettered items as they can remember. The procedure is repeated for list 2. The items in list 2 are found to be much more easily remembered than those in list 1. This is because each is an acronym that acts as a meaningful chunk of information.

List 1	List 2
ICL	PIN
TPT	KGB
OML	HIV
MVM	SQA
EZQ	VAT
CPG	FBI
UPR	PTO
DUL	USA
MCA	RAC
SUT	NYC
ATX	UFO
NSE	BBC
RPA	MOT
YAD	RIP
BCU	PLC

Table 19.3 Effect of chunking

cause to phone Glasgow fairly regularly and recognises 629 as a district code then this becomes a second chunk. The job now demands a memory span of 6 items, which many people can manage comfortably.

Rehearsal

Rehearsal involves repeating to yourself over and over again (silently or out loud) a piece of information that you are trying to memorise. This process helps to extend the time for which the information is maintained in the STM.

Serial position effect

From the results in Related Activity – Investigating the serial position effect, it can be seen that recall is best for the objects shown at the end (**recency effect**), closely followed by those shown at the start (**primacy effect**). Those in the middle of the viewing sequence gain a very poor score. This memory pattern is called the **serial position effect**.

Related Activity

Investigating the serial position effect

In this investigation, the tester informs the subjects that they will be required to memorise 20 fairly similar objects. The tester reveals the first object and allows the subjects to view it for 5 seconds. Object 1 is then removed and object 2 revealed for 5 seconds.

This procedure is repeated for the remaining objects. As soon as the last one has been removed, the subjects are invited to pick up their pencils and write down as many of the objects as they can recall in any order. Figure 19.3 shows a graph of a typical set of results for a group of 100 subjects.

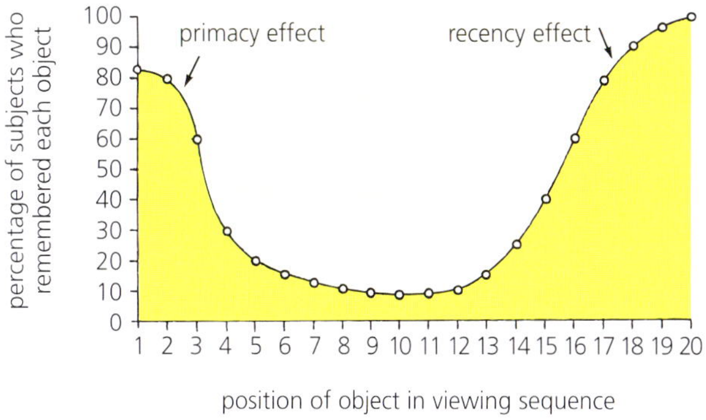

Figure 19.3 Serial position effect

Explanation of serial position effect

Images of the first few objects can be remembered because during the experiment there has been enough time for them to have been well **rehearsed**. In many cases they have therefore become **encoded** and **transferred** to the **LTM** from where they can be retrieved at the end of the experiment.

The last seven or so objects are remembered because images of them are still present in the **STM** and are quickly 'dumped' onto paper by the subjects as soon as they start writing. (If there is a 1 minute delay and rehearsal is prevented before subjects are allowed to write down the objects that they recall, the recency effect vanishes.) Images of the objects in the middle of the sequence are not well retained by the vast majority of subjects because, by the time these images enter the STM, it is already crowded. Therefore many are forgotten before they can be rehearsed, encoded and stored in the LTM.

Working memory model

In addition to briefly storing information, the short-term memory is able to process data to a limited extent. This ability is explained by the '**working memory model**' which proposes that the STM is made up of several components that can work independently of one another. One of these, for example, is thought to be involved in problem-solving and decision-making, thereby enabling the STM to perform simple **cognitive tasks**. (A cognitive task is one that requires processes such as perception, intuition and reasoning.)

Imagine, for example, that you have been asked to think of all the pieces of furniture containing drawers that are present in your home and then calculate the total number of drawers. To do this, you form a mental image of your home and then go for a visuo-spatial tour, room by room. As you come to each relevant piece of furniture, you employ your working memory to count the number of drawers and add this value to the running total in your STM.

Level 3 – long-term memory (LTM)

This third level in the system (see Figure 19.4) is thought to be able to hold an **unlimited** amount of information. During encoding, the items are organised into **categories**

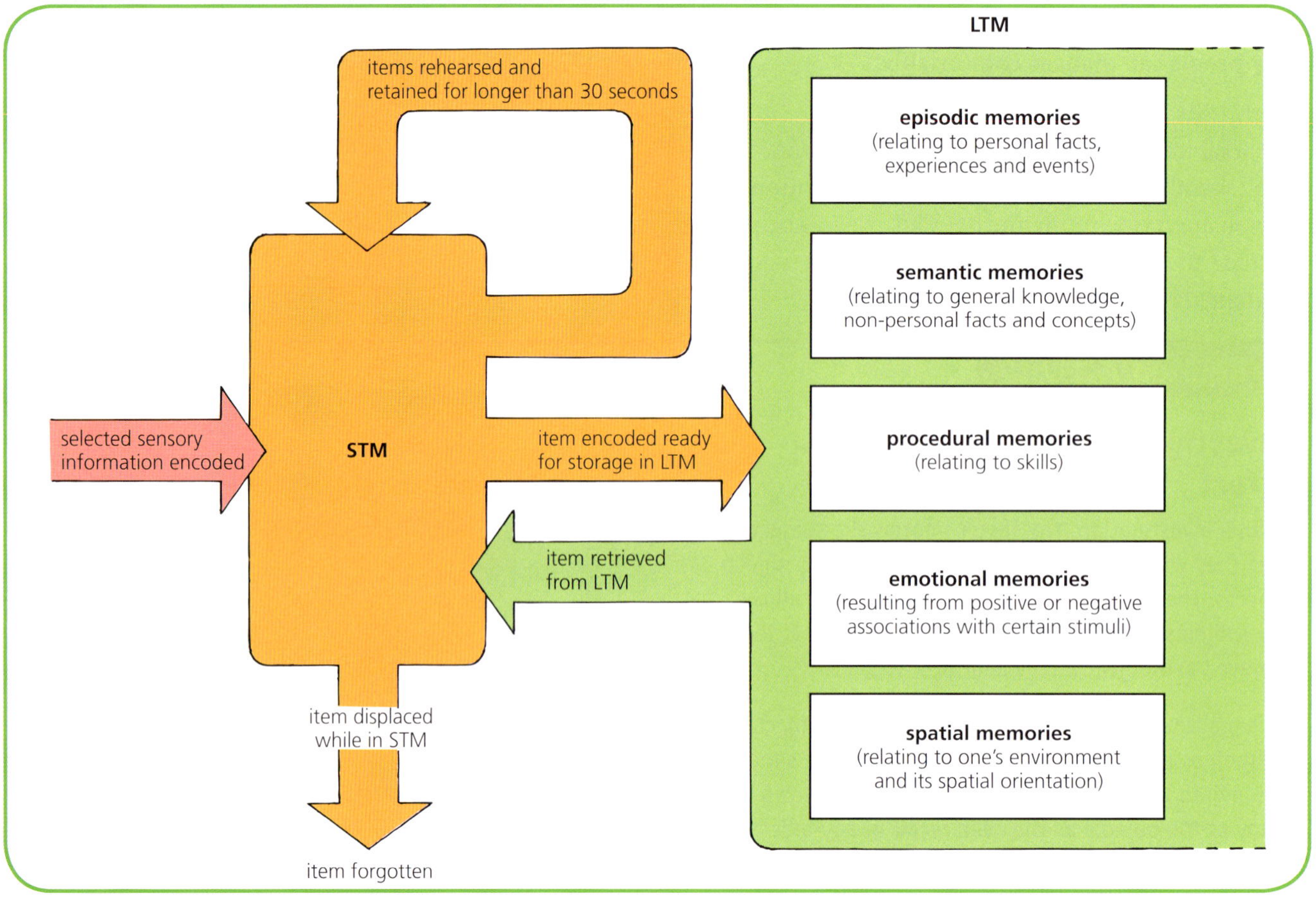

Figure 19.4 Transfer of information

such as personal facts and useful skills. These are then stored for a long time, perhaps even permanently. It must be stressed that this multi-level model of memory and how it works is probably an oversimplification. In addition, the three levels of memory should not be thought of as occupying three distinct regions of the brain.

Transfer of information between STM and LTM

A hypothetical representation of this process is shown in Figure 19.4. Information is constantly being **transferred** between the brain's two storage 'depots' – the **STM** and the **LTM**. If, during its brief stay in the STM, an item is successfully **encoded** (see page 216) then this enables it to be transferred for **storage** in the LTM which has an enormous, perhaps unlimited, capacity. This item may later be **retrieved** from the LTM when required. Successful transfer of information from the STM to the LTM is promoted by the processes of **rehearsal**, **organisation** and **elaboration of meaning**.

Benefit of rehearsal

In addition to extending the length of time for which a piece of information is held in the STM, **rehearsal facilitates its transfer** from STM to LTM. Research shows that students who regularly stop and rehearse what they are reading (and try to learn) are much more successful at committing the information to memory than students who read continuously and resist taking rehearsal breaks. Reciting in your own words what you have just read forces your attention (probably starting to wander) back to the material. Several short rehearsal breaks during the learning process are found to be more effective than one long rehearsal at the end of a marathon learning session.

Organisation

Information that is **organised** into logical categories is more easily transferred from the STM to the LTM (see Investigation – Effect of organisation on retrieval from LTM).

Investigation

Effect of organisation on retrieval from LTM

In this investigation, the subjects are divided into two groups, A and B. The members of group A are given 1 minute to memorise the 20 words in list 1 (in Table 19.4). The members of group B are given 1 minute to memorise list 2. All participants then count backwards from 50 to 0 out loud in unison. Finally, all subjects are given 2 minutes to write down as many words as they can remember from their list.

List 1	List 2
apple	apple
skirt	orange
autumn	banana
father	pear
pear	spring
iron	summer
brother	autumn
summer	winter
jacket	mother
lead	father
trousers	sister
winter	brother
orange	copper
tin	lead
sister	iron
shirt	tin
spring	jacket
copper	shirt
banana	trousers
mother	skirt

Table 19.4 Effect of organisation

→

The members of group B are found to be much more successful. This is because the words in list 2 are much easier to memorise than those in list 1. The reason for this is that the items in list 2 have been organised into **categories**. Grouping items of information in an **organised fashion** increases their chance of being successfully encoded and transferred from STM to LTM. The group headings ('fruit', 'seasons', 'family', etc.) act as **contextual cues** (see page 223), which facilitate the retrieval of the information from LTM to STM at a later stage. Thus **organisation** of material helps to transfer it in both directions.

The experiment is repeated using new lists and giving group A the organised list and group B the disorganised list to memorise. Table 19.5 gives some design features of this investigation and the reasons for employing them.

Design feature or precaution	Reason
Large number of subjects used	To increase the reliability of the results
20 items present on each list	To make the task beyond the scope of the STM
Only 1 minute allowed to memorise list	To reduce the effect of other memory aids such as rehearsal
Subjects count backwards from 50 before writing answers	To prevent the STM contributing answers
Experiment repeated with new lists and groups reversed	To increase the reliability of the results

Table 19.5 Design features for organisation investigation

Elaboration of meaning

Elaboration is a further means of aiding the encoding and transfer of information from STM to LTM. It involves analysing the meaning of the item to be memorised and taking note of its various features and properties. Let us imagine, for example, that you are trying to commit the idea 'cerebral cortex' to your LTM. You could try rehearsing 'cerebral cortex – important part of the brain' a few times and it might become encoded. However, as it stands, this information is sparse and lacking in interest. Therefore it will probably make little impression and is unlikely to be well retained.

Successful **long-term retention** is much more likely if elaboration of meaning is employed, as shown in Figure 19.5. By being **analysed** and **elaborated**, the idea 'cerebral cortex' becomes more interesting and meaningful, enabling it to make a long-lasting impression.

Encoding

Encoding is the conversion of one or more nerve impulses into a form that can be received and held by the brain and retrieved later from the STM or LTM. The quality of the memory is affected by the attention given to the task of encoding the material. Some forms of encoding are shallow; others are deeper. Information encoded by rehearsal is an example of **shallow** encoding. Information encoded by elaboration is regarded as a **deeper** form of encoding.

It is for this reason that rehearsing material (such as a group of words in a foreign language) simply by repetition (shallow encoding) can be a less effective way of memorising the words than by linking them to their meaning and to other related words already known (deeper encoding).

Classification of information in the LTM

The system of storage in the LTM is analogous to a filing cabinet of unlimited capacity, organised into **distinct categories** of information. As items are encoded and transferred to the LTM, they are classified and filed in the appropriate section(s).

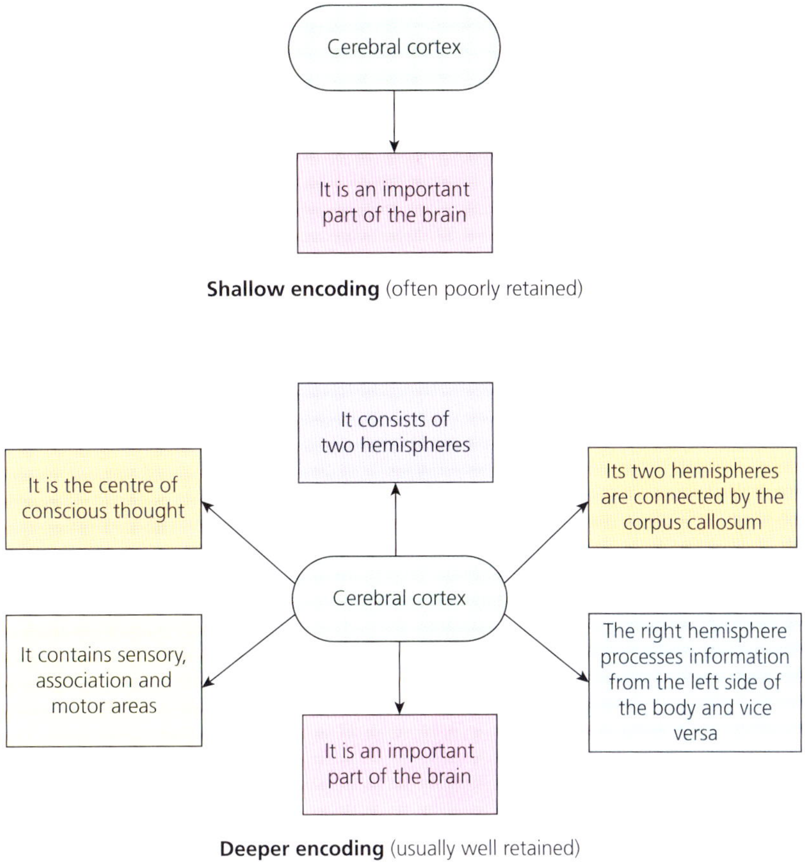
Cerebral cortex
It is an important part of the brain
Shallow encoding (often poorly retained)
It consists of two hemispheres
It is the centre of conscious thought
Its two hemispheres are connected by the corpus callosum
Cerebral cortex
It contains sensory, association and motor areas
The right hemisphere processes information from the left side of the body and vice versa
It is an important part of the brain
Deeper encoding (usually well retained)

Figure 19.5 Elaboration of meaning

Retrieval of items from the LTM

The LTM contains a vast and permanent store of remembered experience which is constantly being revised, reorganised and enlarged as new material flows into it. When a piece of information needs to be called up and **retrieved** from the LTM, a search is mounted (see Figure 19.6). This is aided by **contextual cues**. (A cue is a signal or reminder; contextual means relating to the conditions or circumstances that were present at the time when the information was encoded and committed to the LTM.) It is thought that a contextual cue somehow triggers an impulse through a '**memory circuit**'.

They're trying to retrieve the meaning of the term retrieval but I bet they've only used shallow encoding.
HUMAN BIOLOGY EXAM

Figure 19.6 Attempting retrieval

If a memory has been stored under several different categories (e.g. dandelion might feature under 'plants', 'flowers', 'leaves', 'clocks', 'weeds', etc.) then it can be retrieved in various ways. This is because many contextual cues for it exist and lead to the different files relating to it. These can then be checked out to see if one contains the information being sought (e.g. names of common weeds with yellow flowers).

It is more difficult to retrieve a memory that has been filed under a few categories only, since it will have few contextual cues relating to it. Hence the beneficial effects of organisation and elaboration when trying to memorise information. A memory whose encoding in the LTM is accompanied by unusual, emotional or dramatic events (e.g. the person's wedding day) possesses powerful contextual cues. These enable the experience to be retrieved and recalled clearly throughout life.

Case Study Alzheimer's disease

Alzheimer's disease (AD) is the most common type of dementia (mental deterioration). It is incurable and the person's brain gradually degenerates (see Figure 19.7). It is diagnosed most often among people over the age of 65.

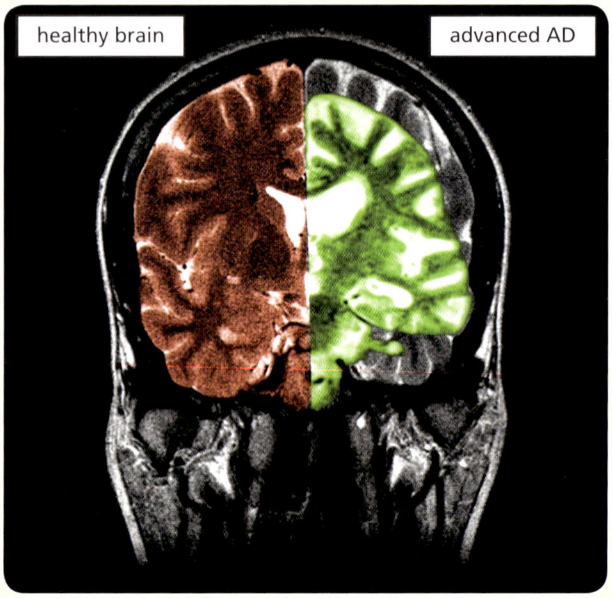

Figure 19.7 Degeneration of the brain

Symptoms

The earliest symptoms often take the form of problems with attentiveness, planning and abstract thought, accompanied by partial memory loss. The latter is observed as an **inability** by the person **to acquire new memories** (for example, they cannot recall recently observed events). This state is often wrongly attributed simply to aging.
As the condition continues to develop, some or all of the following symptoms develop:

- confusion
- mood swings
- irritability
- aggression
- loss of LTM
- loss of speech.

AD is incurable and gradually leads to death as bodily functions are lost.

Diagnosis

AD is normally diagnosed using information based on the patient's medical history and on the results of **behavioural assessments** and **neuropsychological screening tests**. Figure 19.8, for example, shows a diagram that a patient would be asked to copy as part of a test. Many AD patients find the task difficult. When AD is suspected, the diagnosis is often followed by a brain scan such as a PET (see Chapter 18, page 211).

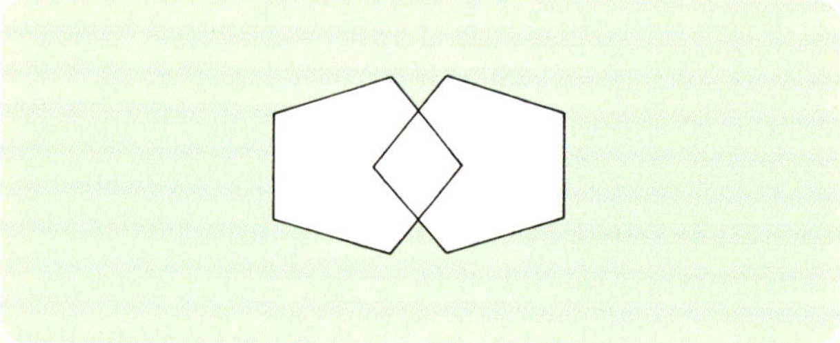

Figure 19.8 Test item

Cause

In AD, cell-to-cell connections in the brain are progressively lost but the cause of this breakdown is not clearly understood. One hypothesis proposes that AD is caused by reduced synthesis of **acetylcholine**, a neurotransmitter substance. But drugs that are used to treat this deficiency are not very effective. A second hypothesis suggests that AD is caused by the accumulation of proteins called β-amyloids as **plaques**. However, a vaccine that was found to

→

clear the plaques in a clinical trial did not have any effect on dementia. Further studies have shown that deposition of the plaques is not closely correlated to loss of neurons. A third hypothesis proposes that the formation of **tangles of tiny fibres** inside the cell bodies of neurons leads to their degeneration and that the resultant breakdown of synapses (neuron connections) in the cerebrum causes AD.

Management

At present no drug that halts or even delays the progression of the disease is available, although some antipsychotic drugs are used to reduce aggression and psychosis in AD patients with behavioural problems. Care for an AD patient is often provided by the person's partner or close relative. However, this places an enormous burden on the carer, especially when the condition progresses and the patient becomes incapable of tending to their own basic needs such as feeding themselves.

Future

Approximately half of new dementia cases each year are AD. Every 5 years after the age of 65, the risk of acquiring AD doubles. As people live longer, the incidence of dementia (including AD) is expected to increase (see Table 19.6).

Year	Estimated percentage of people worldwide with dementia
2005	0.379
2015	0.441
2030	0.556

Table 19.6

Prevention

Some studies suggest that factors such as regular exercise, balanced diet, social interaction and activities that promote mental stimulation may reduce the risk of AD. However, no causal relationship has been established.

Testing Your Knowledge

1 a) Approximately how many items can be held in the STM at any one time? (1)
b) Is the memory capacity of the STM limited or unlimited? (1)
c) For approximately how long are items held in the STM? (1)
d) Identify TWO ways in which items may be lost from the STM. (2)
e) Explain what is meant by the term *chunking* and include an example in your answer. (2)

2 a) The three stages involved in memorising facts are *storage, retrieval* and *encoding*. Arrange these into the order in which they occur. (1)
b) Explain the reasons for the *primacy* and *recency* effects found to occur during an investigation into the serial position effect. (2)

3 a) What is meant by the term *rehearsal* in relation to pieces of information to be memorised? (1)
b) Suggest why rehearsal aids the transfer of information from the STM to the LTM. (1)

4 a) Explain the meaning of the terms *organisation* and *elaboration* in relation to the transfer of information from the STM to the LTM. (4)
b) Why is it easier to retrieve information from the LTM if its components were organised and elaborated prior to their transfer to the LTM? (1)

Applying Your Knowledge and Skills

1 In an investigation into memory span, 40 students were asked to listen to and then attempt to write down each of several series of letters, the first series containing three letters. The results are shown in Figure 19.9.

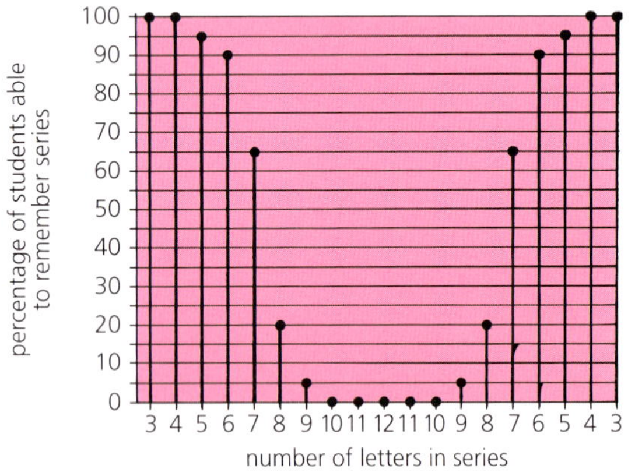

Figure 19.9

a) What relationship exists between the number of letters in a series and the percentage of students able to remember the series? (1)

b) i) What was the best memory span recorded in this experiment?

ii) How many students possessed this memory span? (2)

c) i) What was the poorest memory span recorded in this experiment?

ii) What percentage of students possessed this memory span? (2)

d) i) Does presenting the series of letters in descending order of length produce a different set of results from presenting them in ascending order of length?

ii) Explain how you arrived at your answer to **i)**. (2)

e) Give a reason for the adoption of each of the following design features in this investigation:

i) nonsense groups of letters used to make up the series rather than proper words

ii) each series of letters read out by the same tester at a uniform speed

iii) 40 students invited to take part rather than just a few. (3)

2 The plastic card used to release money from a bank's cash dispensing machine has a PIN (personal identification number) known only to the owner. Suggest why banks decided to give each PIN **four** digits. (2)

3 00349544423317 is the phone number of a hotel in the centre of Seville, Spain, when phoned from Britain. Analysis of this series of numbers shows it to be made up of the parts shown in Table 19.7.

International code	Code for Spain	Code for Seville	District of city	Hotel number
00	34	954	442	3317

Table 19.7

Imagine that this hotel is about to be telephoned from Britain by:

a) a person who has never phoned Spain before

b) a travel agent who regularly phones Seville's city centre hotels.

Predict which person will be faster at placing the call and explain your answer. (2)

4 In an experiment to investigate the effect of lack of rehearsal on memory, some students listened to a group of three unrelated letters being read out. They were asked to try to recall the letters at 3-second intervals but were asked to count backwards in threes from 99 (99, 96, 93, etc.) during each of the intervals between recall attempts. Figure 19.10 shows the results.

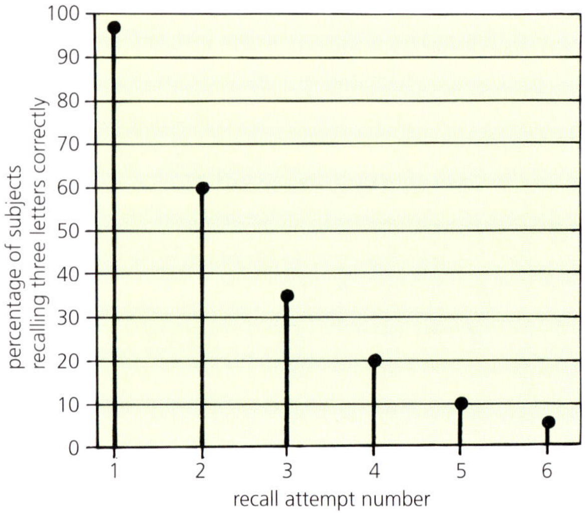

Figure 19.10

a) What was the purpose of asking students to count backwards in threes from 99 between recall attempts? (1)

b) i) What percentage of students were able to correctly recall the three letters 6 seconds after attempt number 1?

ii) At which recall attempt did 80% of the students fail to recall the correct answer? (2)

c) Figure 19.11 shows a graph of the results from the control experiment. In what way would the instructions given to the control subjects differ from those given to the subjects involved in the original experiment? (1)

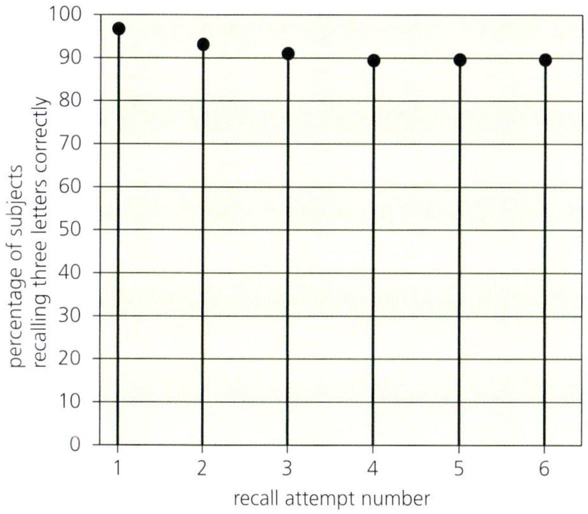

Figure 19.11

d) i) State the factor under investigation in the original investigation.

ii) What conclusion can be drawn about the effect of this factor?

iii) Suggest why this should be the case. (3)

5 Present the information contained in the following paragraph as a flow diagram. (3)

Once an item (e.g. the French words for the request 'Two coffees, please') has been retrieved from the LTM and is back in the STM, it can be recalled into the conscious mind and put to use. In this case nerve impulses would pass to those parts of the cerebrum responsible for language. Once certain mental and motor operations had occurred, the words would be spoken to the French waiter patiently awaiting the person's order.

6 The accompanying list **a)–h)** gives eight instructions that, according to experts, aid the processes of memory and learning if put into practice. Rewrite them and complete the blanks using the following words: *attention, groups, long, meaning, overlearn, recreation, repeating, rest, short, unusual, visual.* (10)

a) Pay close ______ to the information to be memorised.

b) Organise items to be learned into ______.

c) Rehearse items by ______ them over and over to yourself.

d) Elaborate the ______ of a difficult item.

e) Create a ______ image of a group of unrelated items (the more ______ the image, the better).

f) ______ the information well beyond the point of bare recall rather than risk underlearning it.

g) Spread the learning process over several ______ sessions rather than one ______one.

h) Use breaks from study for ______ and ______.

What You Should Know Chapter 19

chunking	memory	sensory
contextual	organisation	seven
displacement	rehearsal	short-term
elaboration	retain	span
long-term	retrieval	working

Table 19.8 Word bank for Chapter 19

1 ______ is the capacity of the brain to store, ______ and then retrieve information when required.

2 Information entering the ______ memory lasts for a few seconds on its way to the ______ memory (STM).

3 The STM has a memory ______ of about ______ items which it holds for about 30 seconds. This time can be increased by ______ and the number of items remembered can be increased by ______.

4 If information is not passed to the ______ memory it is lost by ______ or decay.

5 An extension of the STM used to perform cognitive tasks is called ______ memory.

6 Transfer of information from STM to LTM and its ______ from LTM at a later stage are aided by rehearsal, ______ of meaning and ______ during encoding.

7 ______ cues aid the retrieval of information from LTM.

20 Cells of the nervous system and neurotransmitters at synapses

Cells of the nervous system

The nervous system consists of a complex network of nerve cells called **neurons** which receive and transmit electrical signals (nerve impulses), and **glial cells** which support and maintain the neurons.

Neurons

The efficient working of the human body and all of its parts depends on the coordinated activity of billions of neurons. These cells provide the body with rapid means of communication and control. They are structurally adapted to suit their function of conducting nerve impulses from one part of the body to another. There are three types of neuron – **sensory**, **inter** and **motor** – as shown in Figure 20.1.

Although these appear to be very different, they all share the same basic structures. Each consists of a **cell body** and associated processes: one **axon** and

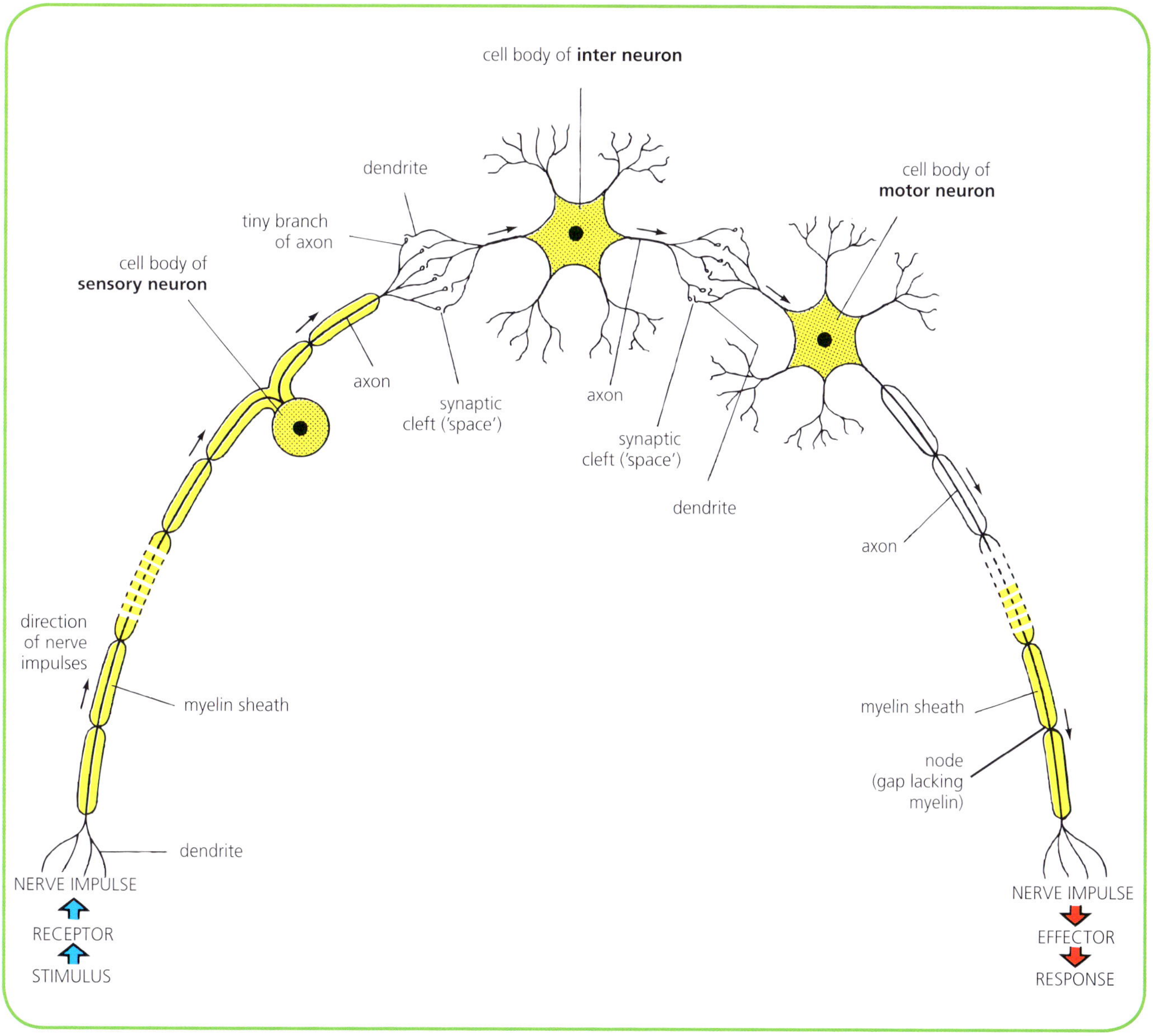

Figure 20.1 Three types of neuron

several **dendrites** (see Figure 20.2). These thread-like extensions of the cytoplasm are often referred to as **nerve fibres**.

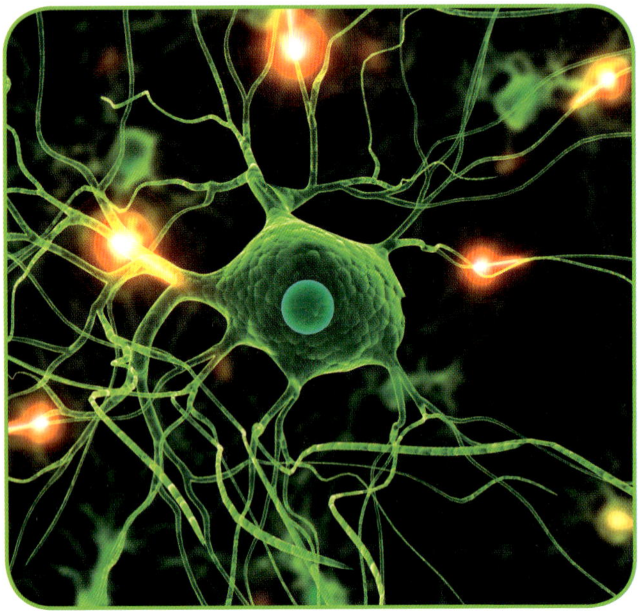

Figure 20.2 Neuron

Dendrites

Dendrites are nerve fibres that receive nerve impulses and pass them **towards** a cell body. A sensory neuron's dendrites gather into one elongated fibre, which transmits information from **receptors** (in contact with the environment) and sends it to the cell body. Inter and motor neurons have several short dendrites that collect messages from other neurons and send them to their respective cell bodies.

Cell body

The cell body of a neuron contains the **nucleus** and most of the **cytoplasm**. It is the **control centre** of the cell's metabolism and contains clusters of ribosomes. These are required to make various proteins including the enzymes needed for the synthesis of neurotransmitters (see page 233). The cell bodies of inter neurons are situated in the central nervous system.

Axon

An axon is a single nerve fibre that carries nerve impulses **away from** a cell body and, in the case of sensory and inter neurons, on to the next neuron in the sequence. The axons of motor neurons are extremely long. For example, those that connect with distant parts of the body (e.g. toes) can be more than a metre in length! Each axon from a motor neuron carries a message from the cell body to an effector.

The direction in which a nerve impulse travels is always:

dendrites → cell body → axon

At the two points in Figure 20.1 where information passes from the axon of one neuron to the dendrites of the next, there is great potential for successful transmission because in reality one neuron ends in many tiny axon 'branches' and the next neuron normally begins as many tiny dendrite 'branches'.

Myelin sheath

The **myelin sheath** is the layer of fatty material that insulates an axon. The small gaps in the myelin sheath along an axon are called nodes. A nerve fibre lacking myelin is described as **unmyelinated**.

Speed of transmission of impulse

The presence of the myelin sheath greatly **increases the speed** at which impulses can be transmitted from node to node along the axon of a neuron. In unmyelinated fibres, the axon is exposed to the surrounding medium and the velocity at which impulses are conducted is greatly reduced.

Myelination

Myelination, the development of myelin round axon fibres of individual neurons (see Figure 19.3), takes time and is not complete at birth but continues during postnatal development until adolescence.

The **hypothalamus** (see page 119) is not fully myelinated until about 6 months. For this reason a very young baby does not have a fully effective 'thermostat' able to bring about finely tuned control of body temperature. Similarly, an infant is unable to control fully the lower body because the neurons in the spinal cord that transmit impulses from the brain to the lower body are not fully myelinated until the child is about 2 years old.

Diseases

In some diseases the myelin sheath around axons becomes damaged or destroyed. This leads to problems such as a loss of muscular coordination. (See Related Topic – Multiple sclerosis.)

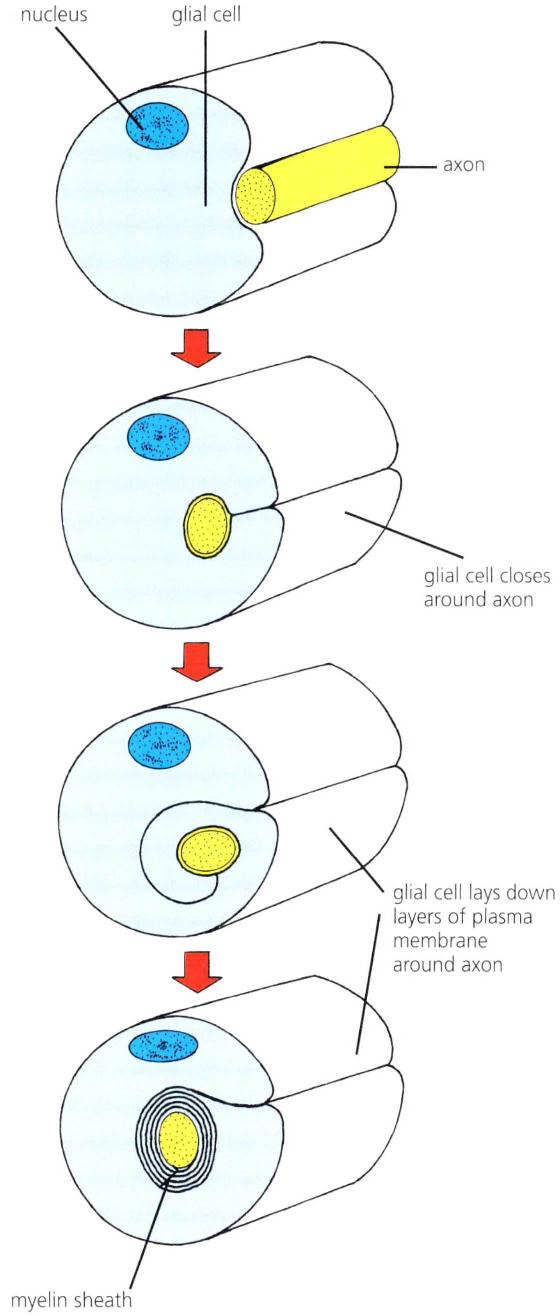

Figure 20.3 Myelination

Glial cells

There are several types of **glial cell**. They do not transmit nerve impulses but are essential to provide neurons with **physical support**. Some are responsible for the process of **myelination**. This production of the myelin sheath occurs when a type of glial cell lays down successive, tightly packed layers of plasma membrane around an axon (see Figures 20.3 and 20.4).

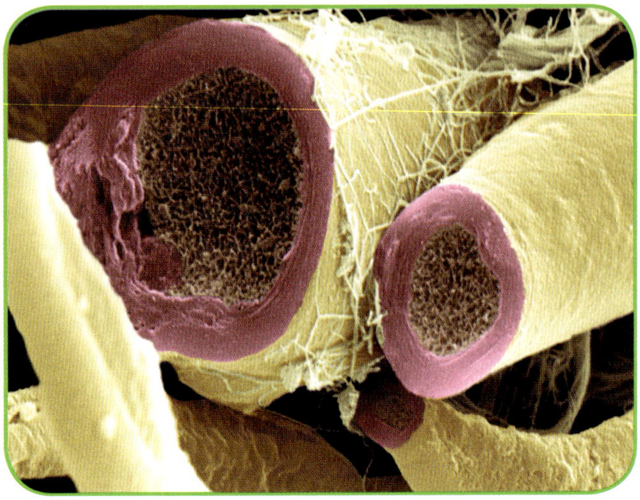

Figure 20.4 Myelin sheath

Synaptic clefts and neurotransmitters

The tiny region of functional contact between an axon ending of one neuron and a dendrite (or sometimes cell body) of the next neuron in a pathway is called a **synapse**. The plasma membranes of the two neurons at a synapse are very close to one another and separated only by a narrow space called a **synaptic cleft** (see Figure 20.5).

The nerve cell before the synaptic cleft is called the **presynaptic** neuron; the one after the synaptic cleft the **postsynaptic** neuron. Neurons also connect with muscle fibres and endocrine gland cells via spaces similar to synaptic clefts. Messages are relayed across synaptic clefts from neuron to neuron by chemicals called **neurotransmitters**. Two examples are acetylcholine and noradrenaline.

Related Topic

Multiple sclerosis

Table 20.1 gives an analysis of this disease which results from problems affecting neurons.

	Multiple sclerosis (MS)
Cause	The cause is unknown. It is thought that a complex interaction between the person's genotype and some unidentified environmental factor or agent results in the person's own immune system damaging the myelin sheaths around axons. This produces demyelinated nerve fibres unable to transmit nerve impulses efficiently (especially between the brain and spinal cord).
Symptoms	The person experiences numbness, walking difficulties, impaired vision and progressive loss of coordination as the ability to control muscles is lost. Some forms of MS involve episodic attacks interspersed with spells when symptoms decrease and may disappear temporarily. In other forms the symptoms persist and slowly accumulate.
Treatment	There is no cure for MS. Treatment involves trying to prevent the person from having new attacks and helping them to regain function when they have suffered an attack. Several types of medication are available that help to decrease the number of attacks but they are often accompanied by adverse side effects. Some people with MS resort to alternative treatments unsupported by clinical evidence, such as medicinal cannabis.

Table 20.1 Analysis of multiple sclerosis

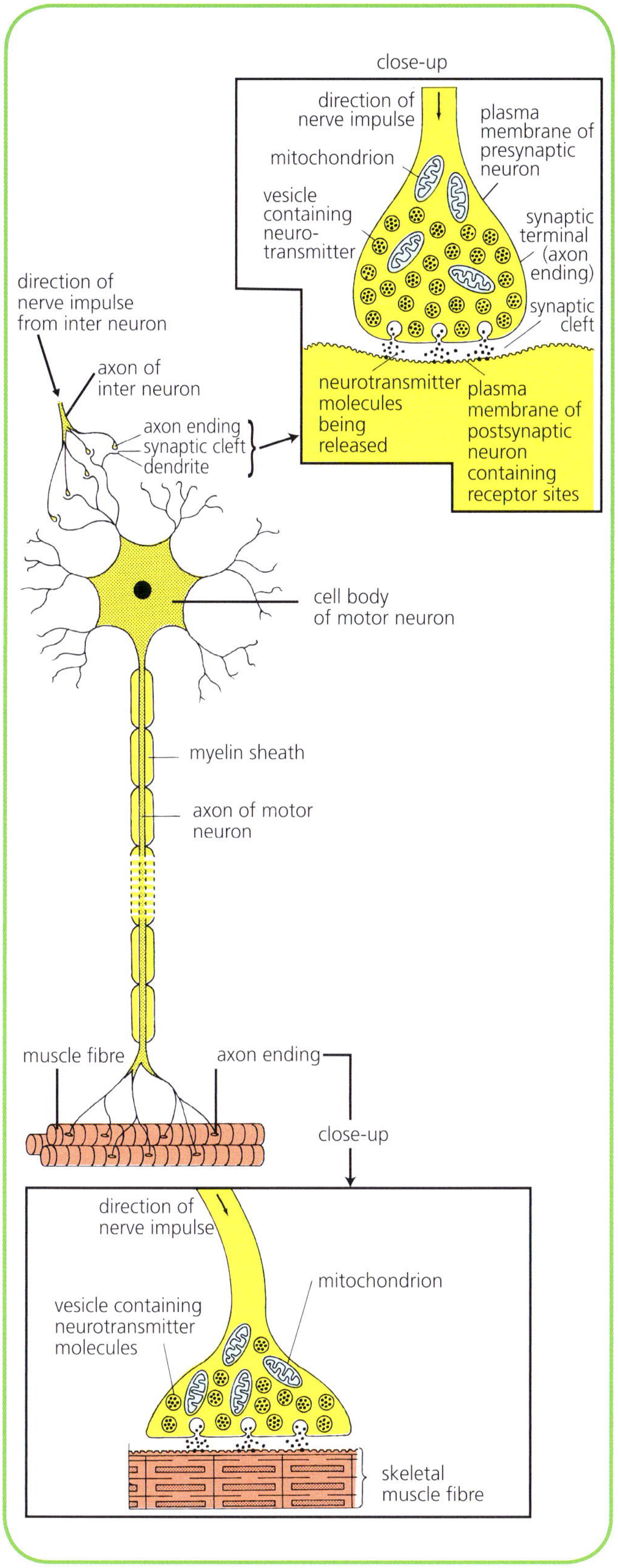

Figure 20.5 Synaptic cleft

Action of neurotransmitter

Each synaptic terminal of an axon holds a rich supply of **vesicles** containing a store of one type of neurotransmitter (see Figures 20.5 and 20.6). When a nerve impulse passes through the presynaptic neuron and reaches the synaptic terminal, it stimulates several vesicles. These simultaneously move to the terminal's surface, fuse with its membrane, form openings and discharge their contents (about 10 000 molecules of neurotransmitter per vesicle) into the synaptic cleft.

Once in the cleft, the neurotransmitter molecules briefly combine with **receptor molecules** at sites on the membrane of the postsynaptic dendrite. This process alters the membrane and its electrical state. For example, the binding of acetylcholine to receptor sites makes 'gates' in the postsynaptic membrane open

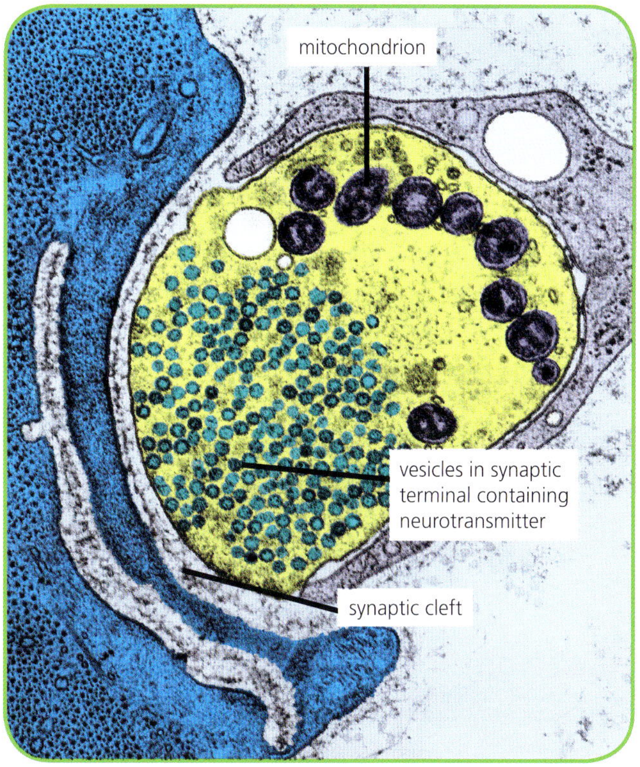

Figure 20.6 Electron micrograph of a synaptic cleft

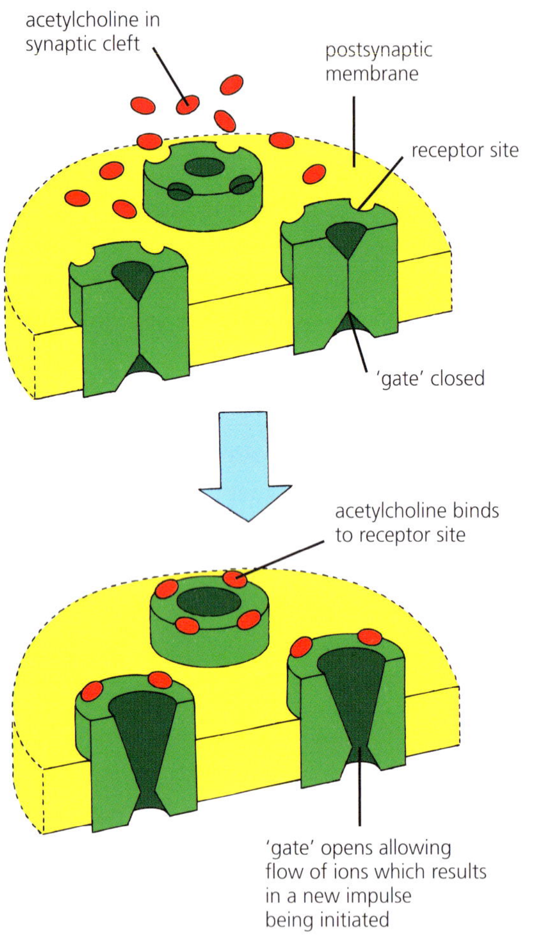

Figure 20.7 Neurotransmitter in action

(see Figure 20.7). This allows increased flow of ions to occur through the membrane, resulting in a nerve impulse being initiated in the postsynaptic membrane.

Excitatory and inhibitory signals

The type of alteration to a postsynaptic membrane that occurs following the binding of a neurotransmitter to its receptors depends on the **type of receptor** present. The signal generated is determined by the receptor and may be **excitatory** or **inhibitory**.

Direction of impulses

Vesicles containing neurotransmitter occur on one side only of a synapse. This ensures that nerve impulses are transmitted in **one direction** only.

Need for removal of neurotransmitter after transmission of impulse

To ensure precise control of the system and allow for the successful transmission of each short-lived impulse, the postsynaptic membrane must remain excited for only the brief moment required to pass on that impulse. This is achieved by the neurotransmitter being **rapidly removed** as soon as the impulse has been transmitted, thereby **preventing continuous stimulation of postsynaptic neurons**.

Removal of neurotransmitters

There are two types of mechanism for the removal of neurotransmitters. These are **enzyme degradation** and **reuptake**.

Acetylcholine, for example, is broken down into non-active products by an enzyme present on the postsynaptic membrane, as in the following equation:

$$\text{acetylcholine} \xrightarrow{\text{enzyme}} \text{non-active products}$$

The non-active products are **reabsorbed** by the presynaptic neuron and **resynthesised** into active neurotransmitter, which is stored in vesicles ready for reuse. The energy required is supplied by the **mitochondria** present in the synaptic terminal. Noradrenaline, on the other hand, undergoes reuptake by being **reabsorbed** directly by the presynaptic membrane that secreted it and is stored in the vesicle ready for reuse.

Filtering out weak stimuli

A nerve impulse is only transmitted across a synapse and on through the postsynaptic neuron if it first brings about the release of a certain **minimum number** of neurotransmitter molecules. This critical number is needed to affect a sufficient number of receptor sites on the membrane of the postsynaptic neuron. Achievement of this is called reaching the membrane's **threshold**.

Weak stimuli that fail to do so are called **subthreshold** stimuli. They are **filtered out** by the synapse acting as an unbridgeable gap. The continuous low-level hum of machinery, for example, fails to evoke a response because the weak 'background' stimuli do not bring about the release of enough neurotransmitter to create an impulse in the postsynaptic membrane. However, a sudden change in the stimulus (such as an increase in volume) brings about the normal response and makes the person aware of the machinery.

Summation

The electrical change in a postsynaptic membrane that results from the binding of a neurotransmitter to its receptors can be too weak to enable threshold to be reached. However, a postsynaptic cell may receive information via synapses from several neighbouring neurons in a converging pathway (see page 236). If many synaptic terminals of many presynaptic neurons discharge their neurotransmitter simultaneously or in rapid succession, then enough of the chemical is released to reach threshold and trigger an impulse. This **cumulative effect** of a series of weak stimuli that together bring about an impulse is called **summation** (see Figure 20.8).

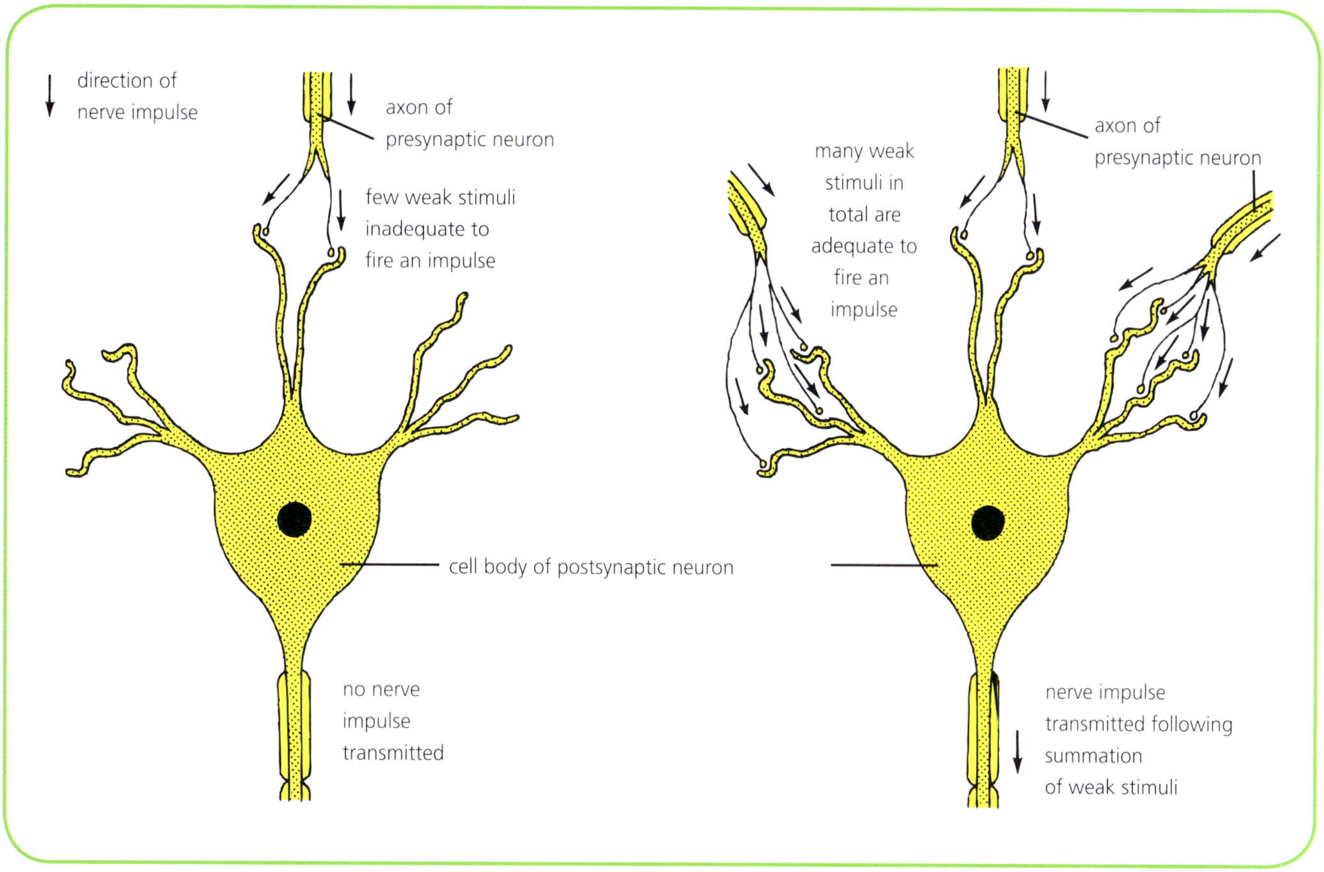

Figure 20.8 Summation

Complex neural pathways

Neurons are found to be connected to one another in many different ways in the CNS. The various combinations allow many types of complicated interaction to occur between neurons. This enables the nervous system to carry out its many complex functions. Examples of neural pathways are as outlined on the next page.

Converging neural pathway

To **converge** means to come together and meet at a common point. In a converging neural pathway, impulses from several sources are channelled towards, and meet at, one neuron as shown in Figure 20.9. This brings about a concentration of (and increased sensitivity to) excitatory or inhibitory signals at the neuron, where release of sufficient neurotransmitter raises the postsynaptic membrane to threshold. (See Related Topic – Convergence of neurons from rods.)

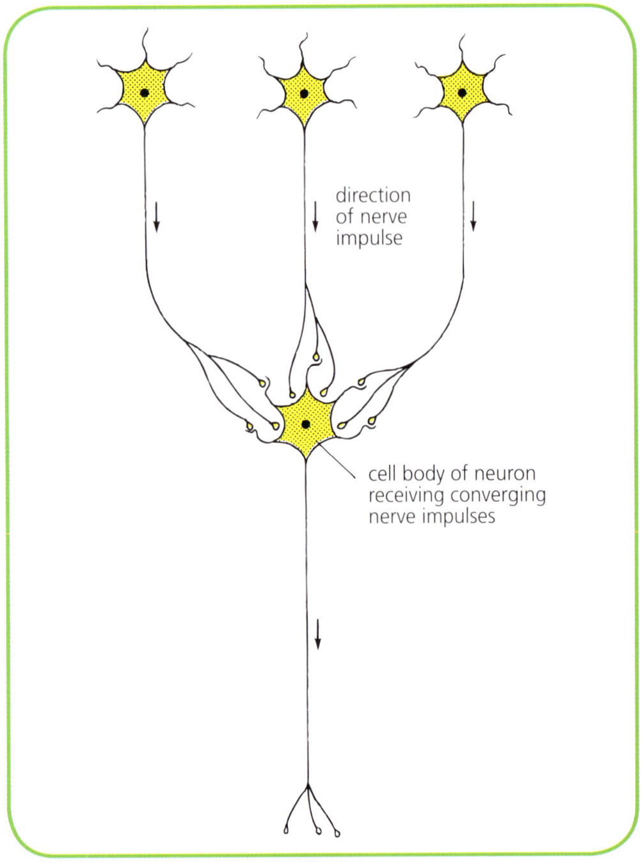

Figure 20.9 Converging neural pathway

Related Topic

Convergence of neurons from rods

Rods and cones

Rods and **cones** are visual receptors present in the retina of the eye. They contain pigments that break down in the presence of light. In each case, this breakdown forms a chemical that triggers nerve impulses along a pathway of neurons. The pigment present in cones is not very sensitive to light. Bright light (e.g. daylight) is needed to break it down and trigger the transmission of nerve impulses. The pigment in rods, on the other hand, is so sensitive to light that it even reacts in very **dim light** and fires off impulses. It is quickly rendered temporarily inactive in bright light.

Convergence of signals from rods

As the intensity of light entering the eye decreases, cones cease to respond and rods take over. Unlike cones, several rods form synapses (connections) with the next neuron in the pathway, as shown in Figure 20.10.

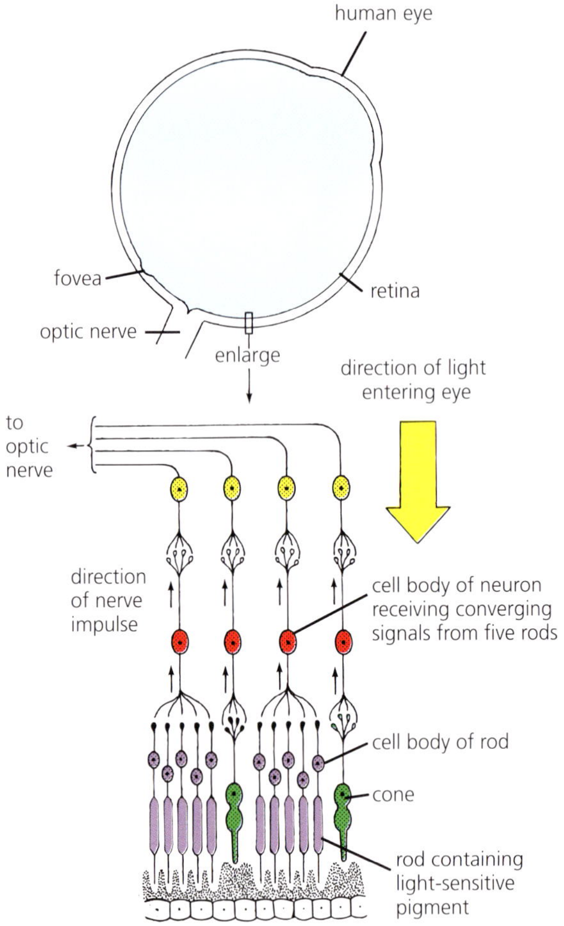

Figure 20.10 Rods and cones

The nerve impulse transmitted by one rod in dim light is weak. On its own it would be unable to bring about the release at the synapse of enough neurotransmitter to raise the postsynaptic membrane to threshold. However, the **convergent arrangement** of several rods allows several impulses to be transmitted simultaneously and these have the combined effect of releasing enough neurotransmitter. The postsynaptic membrane now reaches **threshold** and transmits the nerve impulse on through the neural pathway of the optic nerve to the brain.

This process increases the human eye's **sensitivity** to low levels of illumination and allows vision in conditions of almost total darkness. Furthermore, we gain a reasonably comprehensive view of the surroundings because the rods are thoroughly distributed throughout the retina (except for the fovea).

Diverging neural pathway

To **diverge** means to branch out from a common point. In a diverging neural pathway, the route along which an impulse is travelling divides. This allows information from the original neuron to be transmitted to several neurons and affect several destinations simultaneously. Figure 20.11 shows a simplified version of this principle.

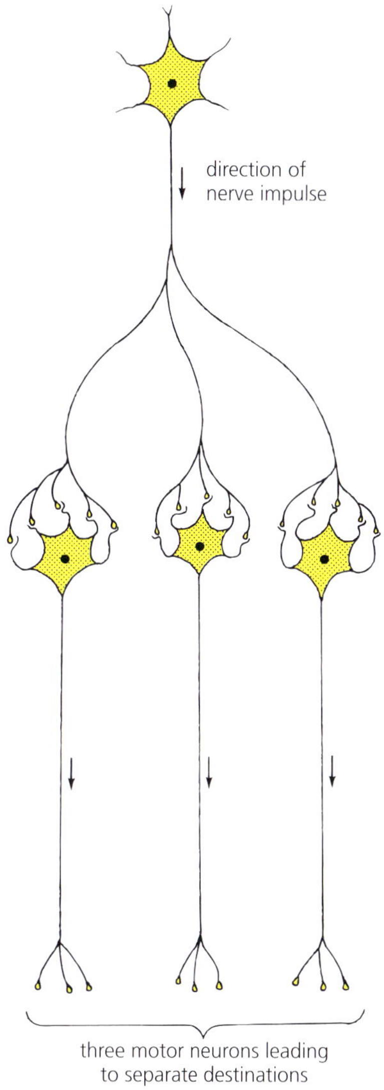

Figure 20.11 Diverging neural pathway

Related Topic

Examples of diverging neural pathways

Fine motor control

Movement of those parts of the body operated by skeletal muscles is controlled by the motor area of the cerebrum. The cerebrum communicates with the muscles by sending impulses via motor neurons in neural pathways. Divergence of these pathways from a common starting point allows impulses to be simultaneously transmitted to different muscles of the hand, for example. This brings about fine motor control of the fingers and thumb by allowing them to operate in unison when required to do so.

Temperature control

Similarly, a neural pathway that begins in the **hypothalamus** is found to diverge into branches that lead to sweat glands, skin arterioles and skeletal muscles. This enables the hypothalamus to exert **coordinated** control over the structures involved in temperature regulation. For example, vasoconstriction, shivering and decreased rate of sweating can all be initiated simultaneously if the body temperature begins to drop.

Reverberating pathway

A **reverberation** means a sound that occurs repeatedly, as in an echo or a vibrating tuning fork. In a reverberating neural pathway, neurons later in the pathway possess axon branches that form synapses with neurons **earlier** in the pathway (see Figure 20.12). This arrangement enables nerve impulses to be recycled and to repeatedly stimulate the presynaptic neurons. Once the circuit is activated and reverberating as a result of this feedback of impulses, it continues to give out signals until the process is brought to a halt when no longer required.

Related Information

Examples of reverberating pathways

Complex reverberating circuits in the brain are involved in the control of rhythmic activities such as breathing. They are also thought to be involved in short-term memory but not long-term memory. Electroconvulsive shock, which brings electrical activity in the nervous system to a temporary halt, affects breathing and STM but not LTM. A pathway can reverberate and transmit impulses for seconds, for hours or, in the case of breathing, for a lifetime.

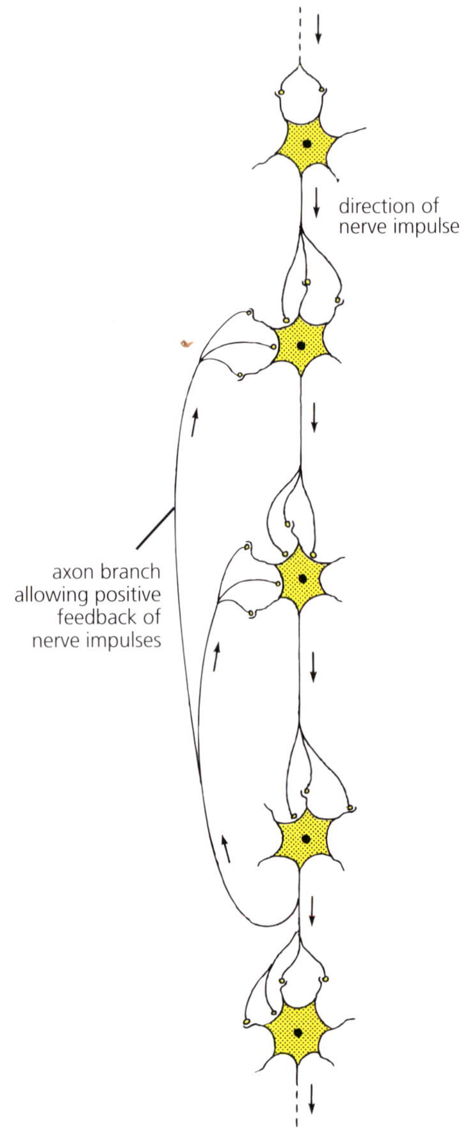

Figure 20.12 Reverberating pathway

Testing Your Knowledge 1

1 **a)** Draw a simple diagram of a motor neuron and label the parts: *cell body, dendrite* and *axon.* (3)
b) State the function of each of the labelled parts in your diagram. (3)

2 **a)** What effect does the presence of a myelin sheath around a nerve fibre have on the speed at which the fibre can transmit a nerve impulse? (1)
b) Why are children unable to exert full control of their lower body before the age of 2 years? (1)

3 Figure 20.13 shows a synapse.
a) Match numbered parts 1–4 with the following terms: *synaptic cleft, axon, synaptic terminal, membrane of dendrite.* (4)
b) **i)** Identify structure P.
ii) Give the name of a neurotransmitter that could be released at Q.
iii) To what structures would these neurotransmitter molecules briefly combine?

→

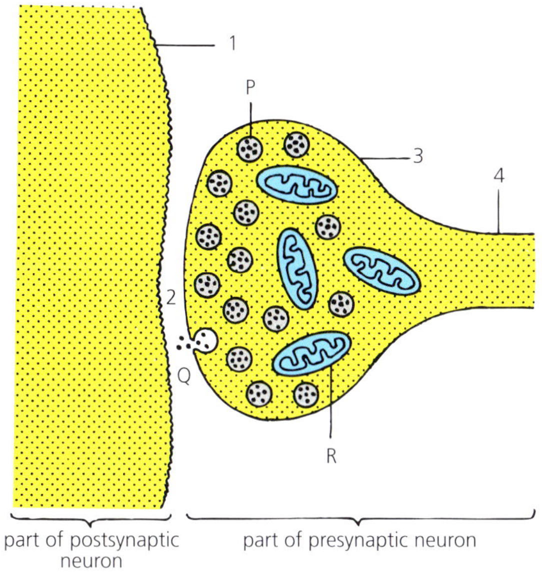

Figure 20.13

iv) In which direction would the nerve impulse pass in this diagram?

v) State the fate of the neurotransmitter that you gave as your answer to part **ii)** once the nerve impulse has been transmitted.

vi) Identify structure R and state its function. (8)

4 What is meant by the term *summation* with reference to nerve impulses? (2)

5 Briefly explain what is meant by the terms *converging* neural pathway, *diverging* neural pathway and *reverberating* neural pathway. (6)

Endorphins

When the body is injured or affected by illness, nerve impulses pass to the brain, resulting in the sensation of pain. **Endorphins** are chemicals that function like neurotransmitters and act as natural painkillers by combining with receptors at synapses and blocking the transmission of pain signals. Endorphins are produced in the hypothalamus and their level of production increases in response to:

- physical and emotional stress
- severe injury
- lengthy periods of vigorous exercise
- certain foodstuffs such as chocolate.

Increased levels of endorphins are also closely associated with the feelings of pleasure that accompany:

- lengthy periods of vigorous exercise
- consumption of favourite foods
- sexual activity.

Dopamine and the reward pathway

Dopamine is a neurotransmitter produced in several regions of the brain. Two of these centres, 'V' and 'N', are shown in a simplified way in Figure 20.15. They are connected by nerve fibres which form a neural circuit. When a survival-related urge such as hunger, thirst or sexual need is being satisfied by current behaviour, neurons in centre 'V' release dopamine which is carried to centre 'N'. Neurons in centre 'N' also release dopamine and induce a pleasurable feeling. It is for this reason that V and N are often referred to as **pleasure centres** and the route from V to N is called the brain's **reward pathway**. It is thought to have evolved because activation of this pathway reinforces forms of beneficial behaviour (such as eating when hungry) that are of survival value. Several other circuits that release dopamine are also present in the brain, although only one of these is shown in Figure 20.15. It leads to the frontal area of the cerebral cortex which is responsible for cognitive appreciation of pleasure.

Related Topic

Endorphins and pain threshold

In an investigation, the endorphin level in the blood plasma of each of the participants was measured. Then each person's **pain threshold** was tested. This was done using a blood-pressure cuff (see Figure 20.14) pumped up until the volunteer indicated that they could not take any more pressure. The participants were split into groups A and B. The members of group A exercised vigorously for 10 minutes whereas those in group B remained at rest.

After exercise, the **endorphin level** of the members of group A was found to have risen in every case and, when the blood-pressure cuff test was repeated, their pain threshold was found to have increased. They were, on average, able to stand the cuff at a higher pressure for a longer time. The endorphin level and pain threshold of group B was found to have remained unchanged. The result of this and many similar experiments support the theory that endorphins act as **natural painkillers**.

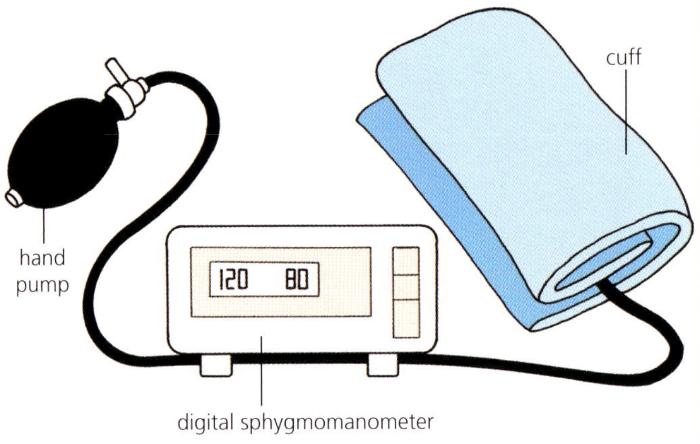

Figure 20.14 Digital sphygmomanometer with manually inflated cuff

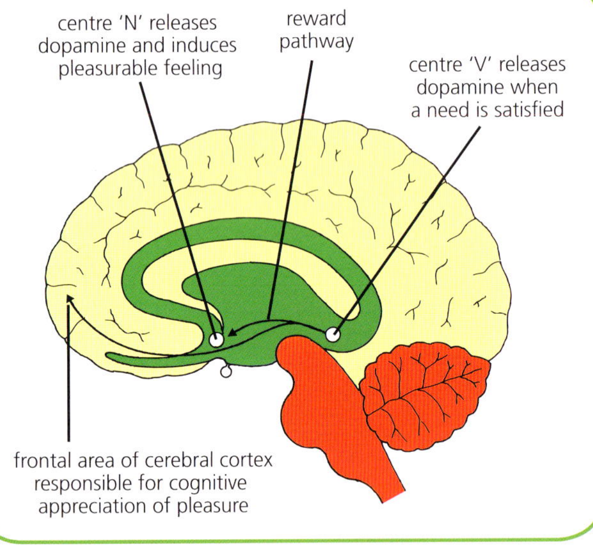

Figure 20.15 Reward pathway

Treatment of neurotransmitter-related disorders

Agonists and antagonists

An **agonist** is a chemical that binds to and stimulates specific receptors on the membrane of postsynaptic neurons in a neural pathway. Since the agonist **mimics the action** of a naturally occurring neurotransmitter at a synapse, it triggers the normal cellular response. Therefore, nerve impulses are transmitted, sometimes at an enhanced level (see Figure 20.16).

An **antagonist** is a chemical that binds to specific receptors on the membrane of postsynaptic neurons in a neural pathway. By **blocking the receptor sites**, an antagonist prevents the normal neurotransmitter from acting on them. Therefore normal transmission of nerve impulses in that neural pathway is greatly reduced or brought to a halt.

Many drugs used to treat neurotransmitter-related disorders are very similar in chemical structure to neurotransmitters. Therefore some are employed to act as agonists where appropriate and others are used as antagonists.

Inhibitors

Other drugs act in a different way by preventing the removal of the neurotransmitter from synaptic clefts. Some of these work by inhibiting the enzyme that would normally degrade the neurotransmitter acetylcholine. Others act by inhibiting the normal reuptake of the neurotransmitter noradrenaline by presynaptic neurons. In each case, persistence of the neurotransmitter causes the effect to continue and be enhanced.

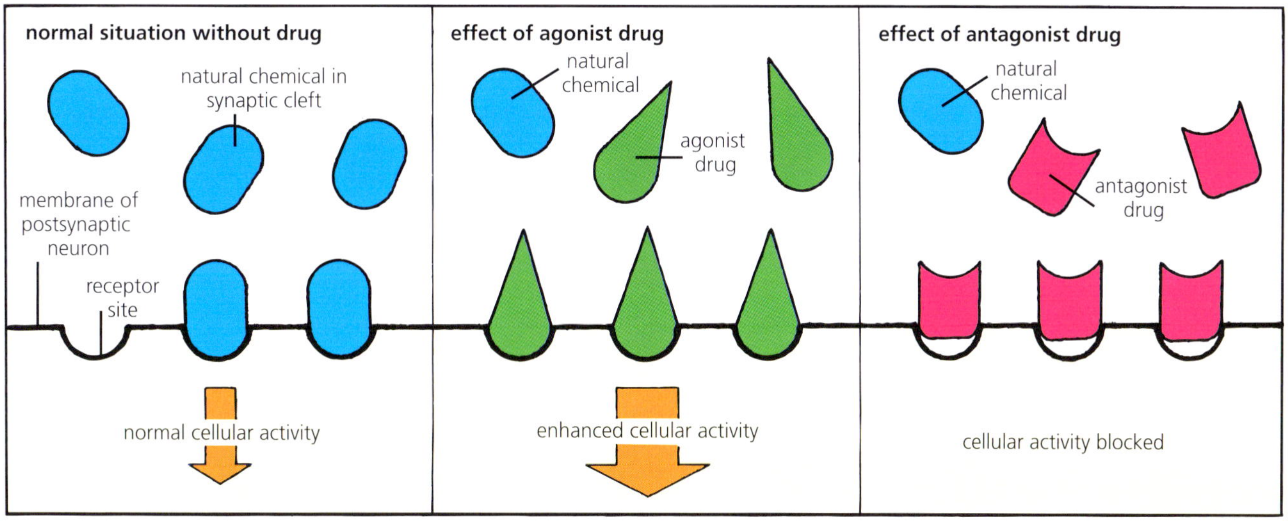

Figure 20.16 Action of agonist and antagonist

Research Topic: Action of morphine and strychnine

Agonistic action of morphine

Opium is extracted from unripe seed capsules of the opium poppy, *Papaver somniferum* (see Figure 20.17). Opium contains a variety of drugs called **opiates**. The most abundant opiate in opium is **morphine**.

Figure 20.17 Opium poppy seed capsule

Morphine is an **agonist** and its principal effect is to bind to and excite opioid receptors on certain neurons in the central nervous system. This excitation results in **analgesia** (pain relief) and **sedation** (state of calm or sleep).

Morphine is effective for use in the treatment of severe pain that is **acute** (arising suddenly) and severe pain that is **chronic** (of long duration). Following intramuscular or subcutaneous administration, morphine can provide analgesia for 3–7 hours. However, patients vary greatly in the concentration of dose required for effective pain relief and in their response to the drug.

Although morphine is widely used in the management of moderate to severe pain, it does have a number of possible side effects, such as:

- nausea and vomiting
- constipation
- depression of respiratory rate
- decrease in blood pressure.

Antagonistic action of strychnine

Strychnine is a highly poisonous chemical made by many members of the plant genus *Strychnos*. It is used to control pests such as rats, which suffer muscular convulsions and eventually die of asphyxiation.

Glycine is a neurotransmitter that occurs naturally in the bodies of many types of animal including mammals. When it binds to its receptors on the postsynaptic membranes of motor neurons in the brain and spinal cord, it has an **inhibitory** effect, which prevents excessive contraction of skeletal muscles. Strychnine acts as an **antagonist**

→

and competes with glycine for the same receptor sites. The higher the concentration of strychnine absorbed into the body, the fewer the number of glycine molecules that manage to combine with their receptors and bring about the normal, natural inhibitory effect.

In the absence of the inhibitory effect, an **excitatory** state results and motor neurons are able to transmit an unchecked flow of nerve impulses to skeletal muscles. Therefore the victim suffers continuous spasms of muscular contraction that can affect the whole body. In addition, skeletal muscles may become fully contracted.

Related Information

Use of inhibitors in treatment of neurotransmitter-related disorders

Alzheimer's disease

Alzheimer's disease (AD) is a form of dementia that is incurable and eventually terminal (see also page 224). The patient's brain gradually degenerates. One theory proposes that AD is caused by the loss, in several parts of the brain, of neurons that make **acetylcholine**. Under normal circumstances this neurotransmitter crosses synaptic clefts, binds to receptors and allows nerve impulses to be transmitted through neural pathways. After transmission of the nerve impulse, acetylcholine in a synaptic cleft is broken down by the enzyme cholinesterase.

Several drugs have been developed to treat AD by acting as **cholinesterase inhibitors**. The intention is that the use of one of these drugs will bring about an increase in concentration of acetylcholine in the patient's synaptic clefts and lead to improved communication between those neurons that use acetylcholine as a neurotransmitter. These treatments do improve symptoms in some patients and may temporarily slow down the progression of the condition, but for the most part they have not been found to be very effective.

Depression

Serotonin is a neurotransmitter with various functions including regulation of mood, appetite and sleep. It is known to contribute to feelings of well-being when it is at its optimum level.

Very low levels of serotonin often cause **depression**. Many prescribed anti-depressant drugs alter serotonin levels. For example, **serotonin reuptake inhibitors** (such as Prozac) decrease the reuptake of serotonin, making it stay longer in the synapses. This prolongs its effect.

Mode of action of recreational drugs

Many people choose to alter their state of consciousness by using **recreational drugs** (some legal, some illegal) that affect the transmission of nerve impulses in the reward circuit of the brain. The subsequent alteration in the person's neurochemistry may lead to changes in:

- **mood** (the person feels happier, more confident or more aggressive)
- **cognitive thinking** (the person becomes poorer at carrying out complex mental tasks such as problem solving and decision making)
- **perception** (the person misinterprets environmental stimuli – sounds, colours, and sense of time seem altered)
- **behaviour** (the person is able to stay awake for longer and talk about him/herself endlessly).

Recreational drugs mimic or interact with neurotransmitters in different ways. For example, they can:

- stimulate the release of a natural neurotransmitter
- act as an agonist by initiating the action of a neurotransmitter
- act as an antagonist by binding with receptors and blocking the action of a neurotransmitter
- inhibit the reuptake of a neurotransmitter
- inhibit the breakdown of a neurotransmitter by an enzyme.

Related Information

Examples of mode of action of recreational drugs

Cocaine

This drug, extracted from the coca plant, acts as a **psychostimulant**. It produces feelings of well-being in the user and gives the person the impression that they have untapped reserves of energy available to tackle any task with confidence (usually *over*confidence – see Figure 20.18). **Cocaine** can induce hallucinations, such as the sensation that there is sand under the skin surface or that thousands of bugs are crawling over it. Continued use of cocaine leads to social withdrawal, depression and dependence on ever higher dosages. People intoxicated with cocaine, especially 'crack' (the form that is smoked), readily become aggressive and violent. They also risk taking a life-threatening overdose.

Cocaine works by **inhibiting the dopamine reuptake channels** (see Figure 20.19). This creates an over-abundance of dopamine in neural pathways such as the reward circuit and causes them to become **overstimulated**. Drugs such as cocaine that can increase normal dopamine levels by more than 10 times can cause severe mental disorders such as **paranoia**.

Figure 20.18 Cocaine-fuelled delusions of self-importance

Cannabis

This drug, obtained from the Indian hemp plant (see Figure 20.20), acts first as a pleasurable **stimulant** and then as a **sedative**.

The user may feel excited, restless and uninhibited at first but later feels drowsy and normally falls into a deep sleep. The nature and intensity of the effects of **cannabis** depend on:

- the dose
- the strain of the source plant
- the method of consumption
- the physical and mental state of the user.

Like cigarette smoke, cannabis smoke contains chemicals that cause lung diseases. Heavy use of cannabis may trigger schizophrenia in some susceptible individuals.

Cannabis contains chemicals called **cannabinoids**, which work by binding to **cannabinoid receptors**. Under normal conditions, these receptors become occupied by a natural neurotransmitter during the transmission of nerve impulses that bring about control of muscles and regulation of pain sensitivity. Since cannabis mimics these effects, its use in a **medical context** (for example, in the treatment of multiple sclerosis and arthritis) is approved of in many countries.

MDMA

MDMA ('ecstasy') is a synthetic drug sold illegally in tablet form (see Figure 20.21). It makes the users feel more alert, energetic and in tune with their surroundings and the people around them. Dancing for long periods while under the influence of MDMA increases the chance of **overheating** and serious **dehydration**. Other adverse effects include anxiety, panic attacks and feelings of paranoia and depression during the days that follow use of the drug.

Serotonin is a natural neurotransmitter whose effects include a contribution towards feelings of well-being. Under normal circumstances reuptake of serotonin occurs in synapses following the transmission of nerve impulses. MDMA works by **inhibiting serotonin's reuptake**, thereby causing an increase in its level in synaptic clefts and promoting temporarily heightened sensations of well-being.

Nicotine

This drug is the active ingredient of tobacco plant products. Cigarette smokers report that nicotine has

→

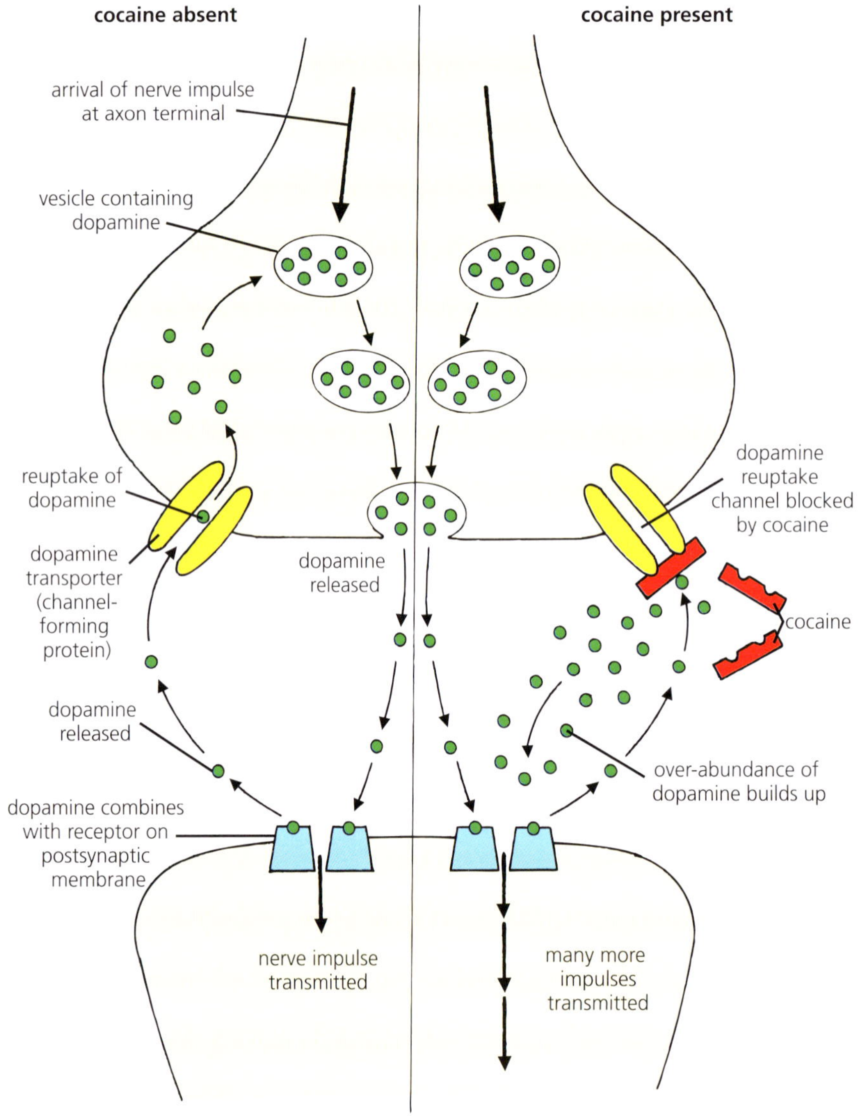

Figure 20.19 Effect of cocaine on dopamine reuptake

a soothing effect and helps them to concentrate. However, **nicotine** is highly addictive and cigarette smoke (see Figure 20.22) is responsible for many diseases, including **lung cancer**.

Under normal circumstances nicotinic acetylcholine receptors on brain neurons become occupied by the neurotransmitter acetylcholine causing transmission of nerve impulses. Such transmission leads to an increase in the level of dopamine, serotonin and noradrenaline. Since nicotine mimics this effect and **increases the activity of these nicotinic acetylcholine receptors**, one of its effects is to increase the level of dopamine in the reward circuit of the brain, resulting in euphoria, relaxation and eventual addiction.

Alcohol

Alcohol, which is a **depressant**, is one of the most widely used recreational drugs in the world. Although its use is almost universally legal, it is not safer than many other drugs that remain illegal. The effect of alcohol on the brain varies from feelings of relaxation and good humour after a drink or two, to complete loss of consciousness following excessive consumption (see Figure 20.23). Short-term effects of drinking alcohol include decreased

➜

Figure 20.20 Indian hemp plant

inhibitions, motor impairment, confusion and drowsiness. Long-term effects include **liver and brain damage**.

GABA receptors normally have an inhibitory effect on neural pathways when the neurotransmitter GABA binds to them. Alcohol **mimics the effect of GABA** and reduces feelings of anxiety. Alcohol can also lead to **activation of dopamine-synthesising neurons** thereby elevating dopamine levels and making the person feel good temporarily while the reward system in the brain continues to be over-stimulated.

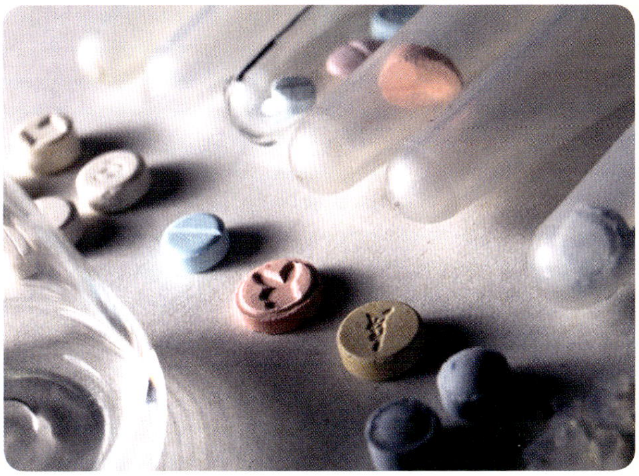

Figure 20.21 MDMA tablets

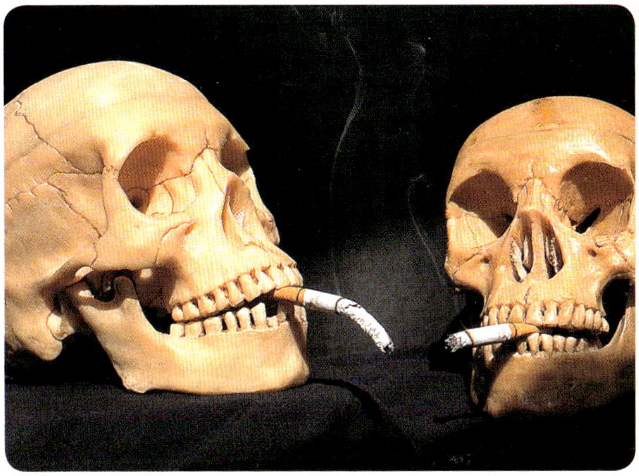

Figure 20.22 Not long to go!

Figure 20.23 Stages of drunkenness

Drug addiction

Drug addiction can be defined as a chronic disease that causes a person to compulsively seek out and use the drug regardless of the consequences. Although the initial decision to take the drug is voluntary, subsequent changes that take place in the person's brain soon override their self-control. This makes the person incapable of resisting the overpowering urge to take more of the drug.

Repeated use of antagonist

Repeated use of a drug that acts as an **antagonist** (see page 240) by blocking certain neuroreceptors prevents the normal neurotransmitter from acting on them. The nervous system compensates for the reduced stimulation of the receptors by increasing their number. In addition, the receptors themselves become sensitive to the antagonist drug.

This process involving an increase in number and sensitivity of receptors as a result of repeated exposure to a drug acting as an antagonist is called **sensitisation**. It appears that sensitisation results in other psychological changes which transform ordinary sensations of 'wanting' into excessive drug-craving and addiction.

Drug tolerance

A drug user is said to have built up a **drug tolerance** when their reaction to an addictive drug is found to have decreased in intensity compared with previous times, even though the concentration of the drug has remained unaltered. A larger dose is now required to bring about the original effect.

Repeated use of agonist

Repeated use of a drug that acts as an **agonist** (see page 240) results in certain neuroreceptors (e.g. those that promote the release of dopamine) being repeatedly stimulated, causing increased feelings of well-being or euphoria. The nervous system compensates for the overstimulation of these receptors by reducing their number. In addition, the remaining receptors become less sensitive to the agonist drug. This leads to drug tolerance because a larger dose of the drug is now required to stimulate the reduced number of less sensitive receptors. This process involving a decrease in number and sensitivity of receptors as a result of repeated exposure to a drug acting as an agonist is called **desensitisation** (and is also referred to as drug tolerance).

Testing Your Knowledge 2

1 a) Identify the chemical substances made in the hypothalamus that function like neurotransmitters and act as natural painkillers. (1)
   b) Give TWO examples of situations to which the body would respond by increasing the level of production of these chemicals. (2)

2 Choose the correct answer from the underlined choice given in each of the following statements. (7)
   a) Acetylcholine/dopamine is a neurotransmitter that activates the reward pathway and induces feelings of pleasure.
   b) Endorphin production is increased/decreased in response to physical and emotional stress.
   c) A drug that mimics a neuroreceptor by binding to and stimulating certain receptors is called an agonist/antagonist.
   d) A chemical that binds to specific receptors and blocks the action of the neurotransmitter is called an agonist/antagonist.
   e) Some drugs work by promoting/inhibiting the action of enzymes that degrade neurotransmitters.
   f) The euphoric effect of recreational drugs is the result of altered neurotransmission in the brain's cognitive/reward pathway.
   g) An increase in the number and sensitivity of neurotransmitter receptors as a result of exposure to a drug acting as an agonist is called sensitisation/desensitisation.

Applying Your Knowledge and Skills

1 Figure 20.24 shows the reflex arc involved in the withdrawal of the arm when the hand touches a naked flame.

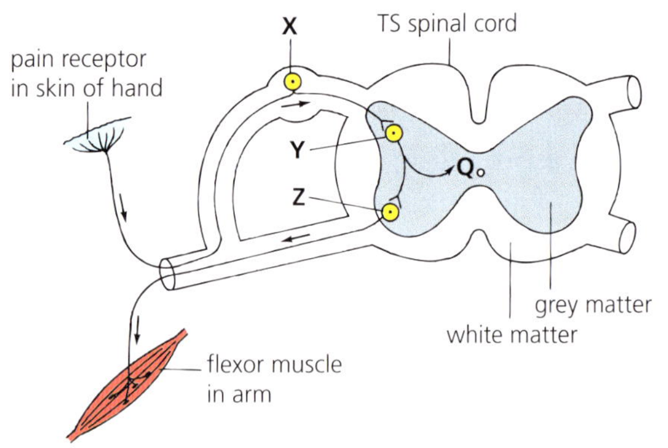

Figure 20.24

a) Identify neuron types X, Y and Z. (3)

b) Rewrite the following sentence to include only the correct word from each underlined choice. When the reflex action of limb withdrawal occurs, this involves the <u>somatic/autonomic</u> nervous system and the type of response is described as <u>voluntary/involuntary</u>. (2)

c) Suggest where the impulse passing along route Q could be going to. (1)

2 Copy and complete Figure 20.25, which shows a simplified version of a reflex arc involving three neurons. (5)

3 Figure 20.26 shows the events involving a neurotransmitter that occur at a synapse during the transmission of a nerve impulse. Arrange them into the correct order, starting with stage E. (1)

4 The graphs in Figure 20.27 represent four types of multiple sclerosis (MS). Match them with the following descriptions. (3)

a) A primary, progressive form of MS involving steady increase in disability without attacks.

b) A 'benign' form of MS which lacks increasing disability and returns to normal between attacks.

c) A relapsing-remitting form of MS where increasing disability occurs during but not between attacks.

d) A secondary, progressive form of MS where increasing disability occurs initially during attacks and is followed later by a steady increase in disability.

5 Figure 20.28 shows a small portion of the retina of the human eye.

a) Identify the receptors X and Y. (2)

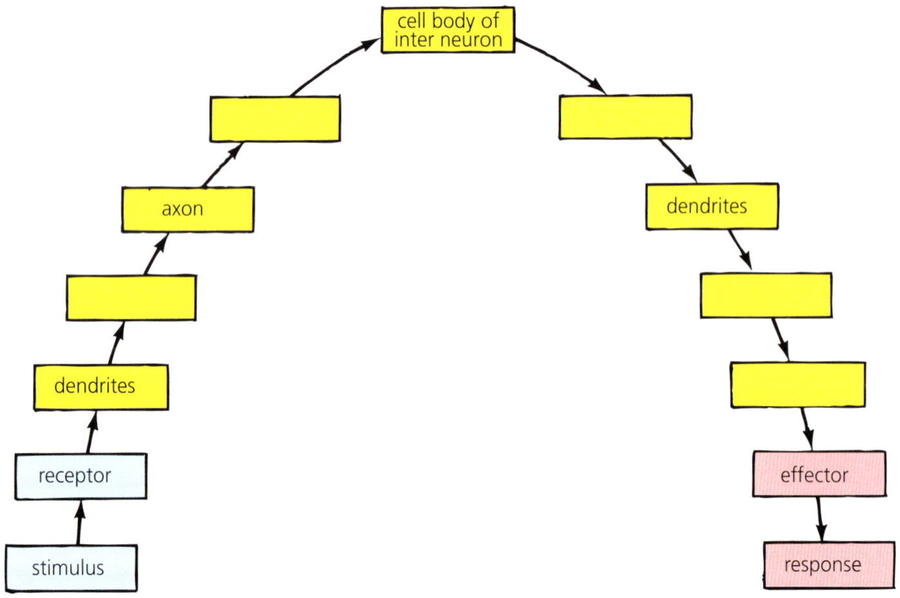

Figure 20.25

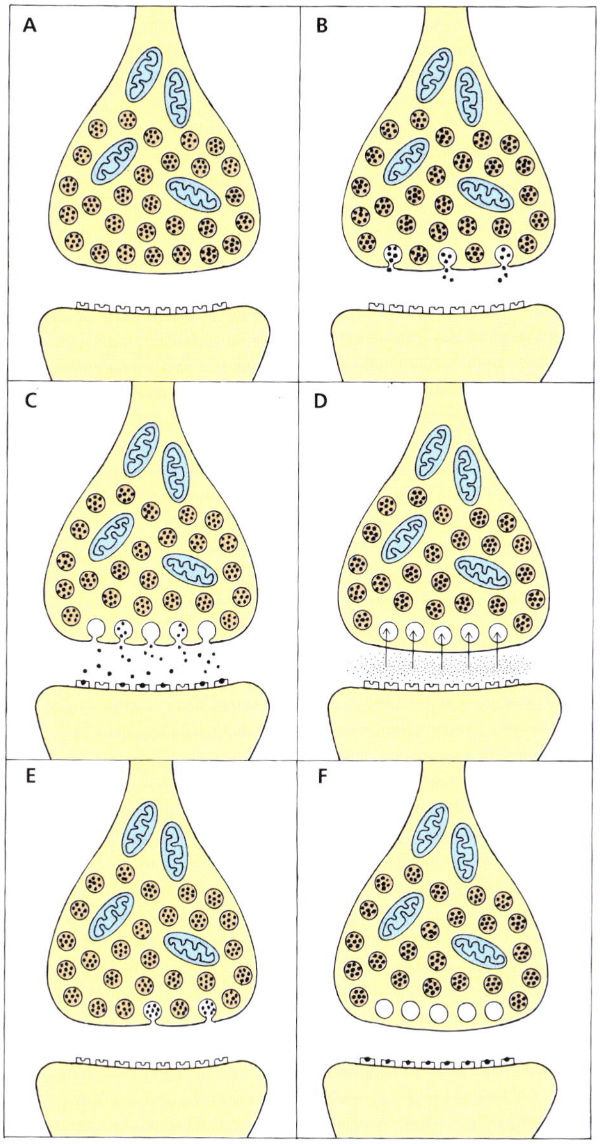

Figure 20.26

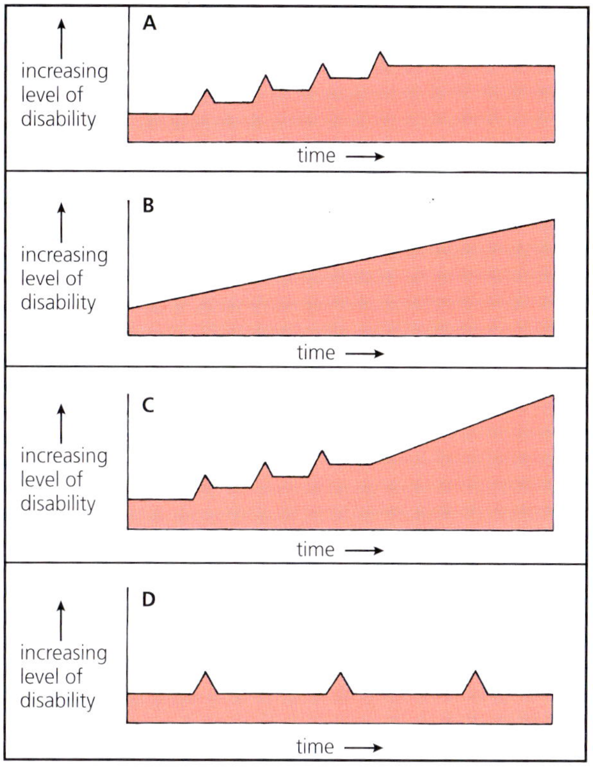

Figure 20.27

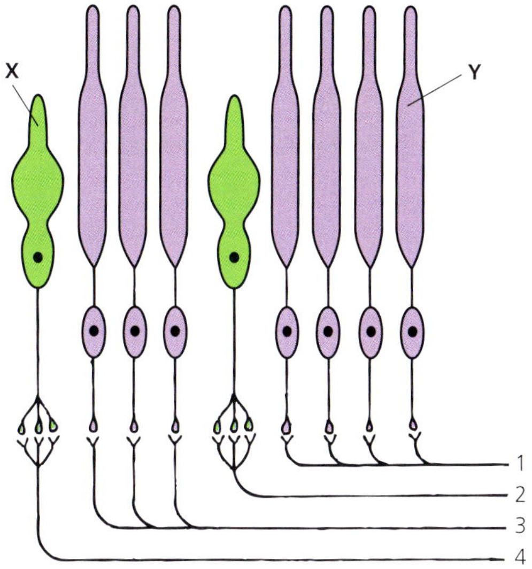

Figure 20.28

b) Which TWO of the numbered nerve fibres will transmit an impulse when light of very low intensity reaches the retina? (1)

c) Explain fully your answer to question **b)**. (3)

6 Write notes on the transmission of nerve impulses under the following headings:

a) the synapse (5)

b) diverging pathways (2)

c) converging pathways. (2)

7 An investigation was carried out to see if elevation of pain threshold could be related directly to laughter. A large group of volunteers (male and female) were tested for pain threshold using frozen vacuum wine cooler sleeves. Each subject indicated when they could no longer stand the pain and then the sleeve was removed. The group was divided into two smaller groups, X and Y. Members of X were shown a documentary video, those of Y, a comedy video. The members of group Y →

were found to spend much more time laughing than those of group X. The pain threshold of all subjects was then measured again using wine cooler sleeves as before. The results are shown in Figure 20.29.

a) i) By how many units did the mean pain threshold for people shown the documentary video decrease?
ii) Was this value significantly different from the original value?
iii) Explain your answer to ii). (3)

b) i) By how many units did the mean pain threshold for people shown the comedy video increase?
ii) Was this value significantly different from the original value?
iii) Explain your answer to ii). (3)

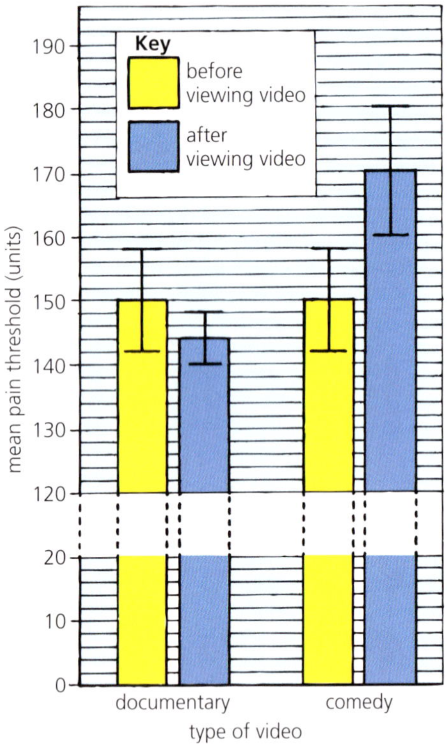

Figure 20.29

c) What conclusion can be drawn from the results of this investigation? (1)

d) Since high levels of endorphins are known to be associated with elevated pain thresholds, it is possible that the physical act of laughing results in release of endorphins. By what means could this hypothesis be tested? (2)

e) In this investigation, it could be argued that changes in pain threshold might be caused by some type of group effect rather than by comedy. How could this possible source of error be overcome? (1)

8 a) Which lettered curve in the graph in Figure 20.30 represents the activity of a drug that acts as i) an agonist, ii) an antagonist during neurotransmission? (1)

b) Explain your choice of answer to a). (2)

c) i) What concentration of drug X in nanomoles per litre (nmol/l) brings about 80% activity?
ii) Express this concentration in moles per litre (mol/l). (2)

d) Suggest why drug Y never fully reaches 0% activity. (2)

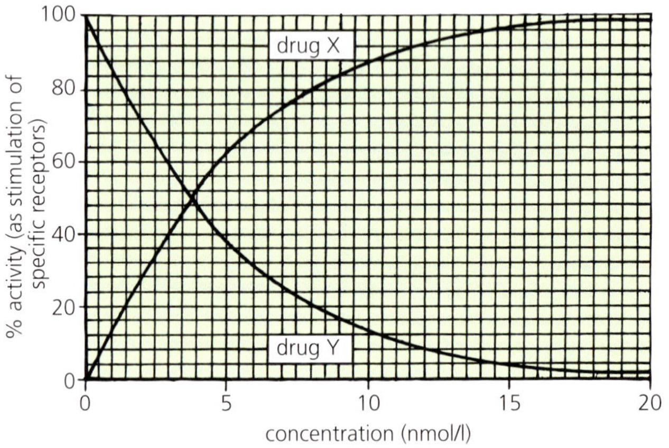

Figure 20.30

What You Should Know Chapter 20

addiction	enzyme	receptor
agonist	excitatory	recreational
antagonist	glial	removed
back	inhibiting	reuptake
behaviour	mimics	reverberating
body	mood	reward
converging	myelin	sensitisation
dendrites	myelination	sheath
desensitisation	neurons	speed
diseases	neurotransmitter	summation
diverging	painkillers	support
dopamine	postsynaptic	tolerance
endorphins	presynaptic	weak

Table 20.2 Word bank for Chapter 20

1 The nervous system is composed of sensory, inter and motor ______ which transmit electrical signals, and ______ cells.

2 Each neuron consists of a cell ______ and associated nerve fibres: one axon and several ______.

3 An axon is surrounded by a ______ sheath of insulating material whose presence greatly increases the ______ at which nerve impulses can be transmitted through the fibre.

4 Glial cells ______ neurons and produce the myelin ______.

5 ______ continues until adolescence. The myelin sheath is destroyed by certain ______ causing loss of coordination.

6 A synaptic cleft is a tiny space between two neurons. Information is transmitted at a synapse by a chemical called a ______ being released from vesicles in the ______ neuron. The neurotransmitter combines with ______ sites on the postsynaptic membrane.

7 The receptor determines whether the signal generated is ______ or inhibitory.

8 To prevent continuous stimulation of ______ neurons, neurotransmitters are ______ from the synaptic cleft by ______ action or reuptake.

9 The cumulative effect of a series of ______ stimuli that together bring about an impulse is called ______.

10 In a ______ neural pathway, nerve impulses from several sources meet at a common destination.

11 In a ______ neural pathway, the route along which a nerve impulse travels divides, allowing information to pass to several destinations.

12 In a ______ pathway, later neurons form synapses with earlier ones, allowing the nerve impulse to be sent ______ through the circuit.

13 ______ are chemicals that function like neurotransmitters and act as natural ______.

14 ______ is a neurotransmitter secreted by neurons in the brain's ______ pathway which is activated by certain types of beneficial behaviour.

15 Chemicals that act like neurotransmitters are used in the treatment of some disorders. An ______ is a chemical that stimulates specific receptors on postsynaptic neurons and ______ the action of the naturally occurring neurotransmitter. An ______ blocks receptors and prevents the neurotransmitter from acting on them.

16 Some drugs act by ______ the enzyme that degrades the natural neurotransmitter or by inhibiting its ______.

17 Many ______ drugs bring about their effect by affecting the brain's reward circuit thereby altering the person's ______, perception and ______. The drugs may act as agonists, antagonists or inhibitors.

18 An increase in the number and sensitivity of neurotransmitter receptors following repeated exposure to a drug that is an antagonist is called ______ and leads to ______.

19 A decrease in the number and sensitivity of neurotransmitter receptors following repeated exposure to a drug that is an agonist is called ______ and leads to drug ______.

21 Non-specific body defences

A **pathogen** is an organism such as a bacterium or virus that causes disease. The body defends itself against pathogens, some toxins (poisons produced by living things) and cancer cells by means of its **immune system**. **Immunity** is the ability of the body to resist infection by a pathogen or to destroy the organism if it succeeds in invading and infecting the body.

Line of defence	Specific or non-specific	Mechanisms employed	Location in Figure 21.1
First	Non-specific	Use of skin as a physical barrier to keep pathogens out Secretion of acid by internal lining of stomach to kill microbes Secretion of mucus by epithelial lining of trachea to trap microbes	1 2 3
Second	Non-specific	Inflammatory response Cellular response – phagocytosis Cellular response – action of natural killer cells	4 4 4
Third	Specific	Response by T lymphocytes from thymus gland (see page 258) Production of antibodies by B lymphocytes from bone marrow (see page 258)	5 6

Table 21.1 Three lines of defence

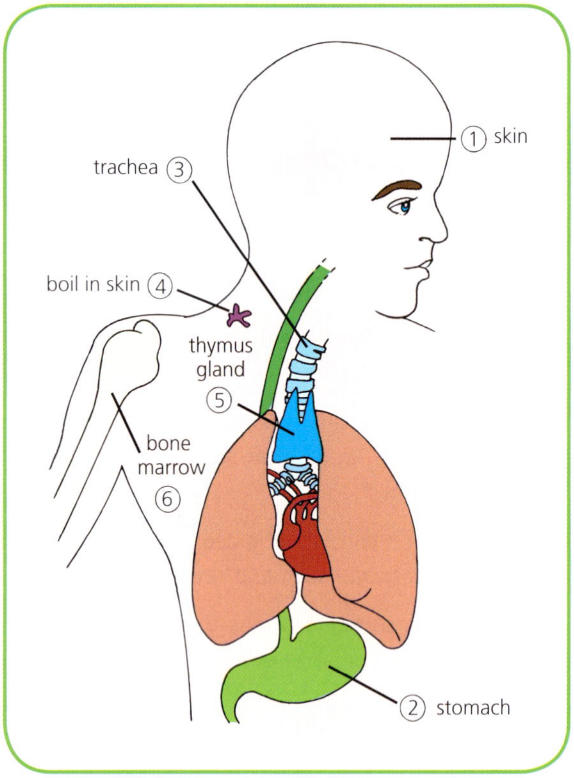

Figure 21.1 Lines of defence in the human body

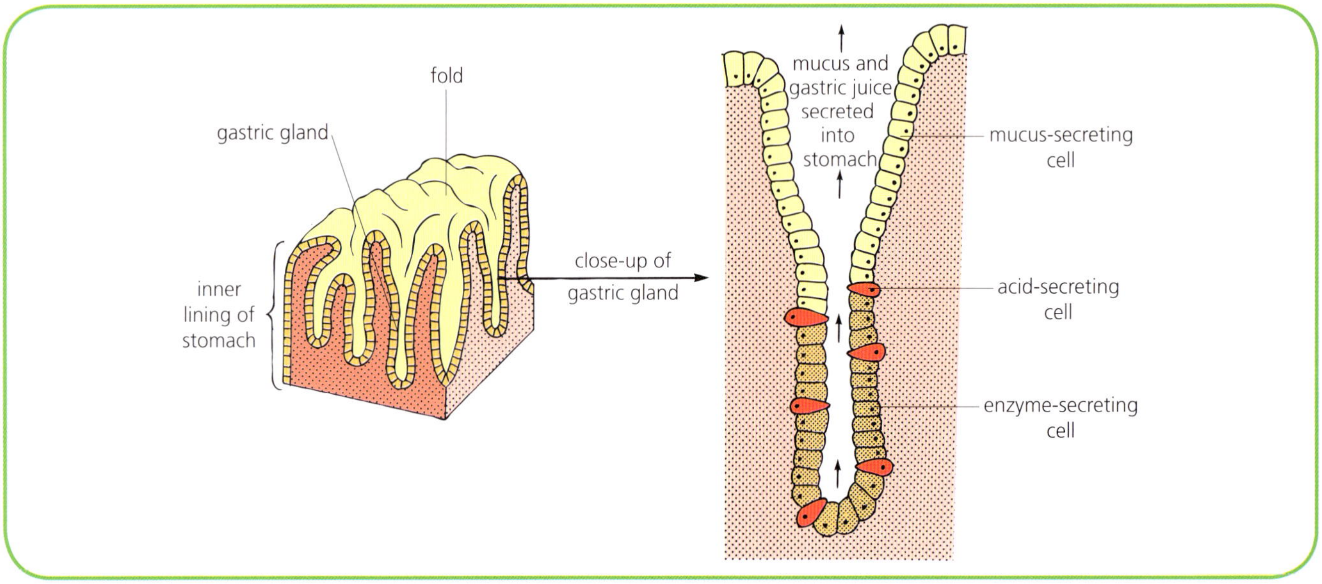

Figure 21.2 Epithelial lining of the stomach

Three lines of defence employed by the body are shown in Table 21.1 and Figure 21.1. The first two are **non-specific**. This means that they work against any type of disease-causing agent. The third line of defence is **specific**, meaning that its components each work against a particular pathogen.

Non-specific defences

Physical and chemical defences by skin and mucous membranes

The surface of the **skin** is composed of layers of closely packed **epithelial cells**, which offer physical protection against bacteria and viruses provided that the skin remains intact. In addition, **mucous membranes** that line the body's digestive and respiratory tracts are composed of epithelial cells that form a protective physical barrier.

The skin and mucous membranes also provide chemical defences against potential pathogenic microorganisms. Secretions from the skin's sweat glands and sebaceous glands keep the skin at a pH that is too low for most microbes to thrive. Secretions such as tears and saliva contain the enzyme **lysozyme**, which digests the cell walls of bacteria and destroys them.

Cells in the mucous membranes secrete sticky **mucus**, which traps microorganisms. The epithelial cells lining the trachea are ciliated and sweep the mucus and trapped microbes up and away from the lungs. **Acid** secreted by cells in the epithelial lining of the stomach (see Figure 21.2) destroys many of the microbes that have been swallowed. However, some do survive the acid conditions and may gain further access to the body.

Inflammatory response

When the body suffers a physical injury such as a cut and/or invasion by microorganisms, it responds with a localised defence mechanism called the **inflammatory response** at the affected site (see Figure 21.3).

Mast cells and histamine

Mast cells are present in connective tissue throughout the body. They are closely related to (and arise from the same stem cells as) white blood cells. Mast cells possess many granules containing histamine. **Histamine** is a chemical that causes blood vessels to **dilate** (become wider) and capillaries to become **more permeable**.

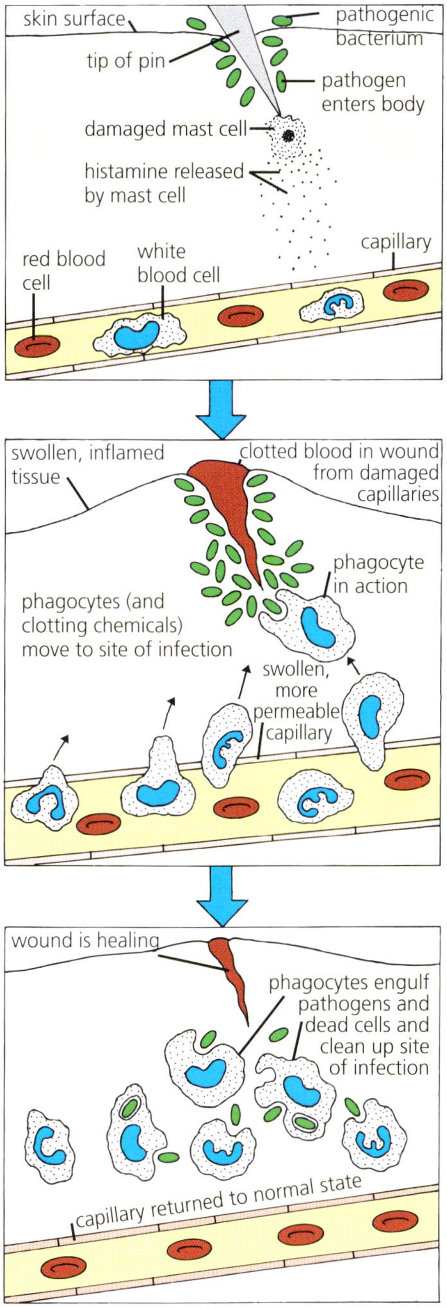

Figure 21.3 Inflammatory response

Following injury, mast cells become activated and release large quantities of histamine. This results in blood vessels in the injured area undergoing **vasodilation** and capillaries becoming swollen with blood. The additional supply of blood makes the injured area **red** and **inflamed**. It swells up because the stretched capillary walls become more permeable and leak fluid into neighbouring tissues.

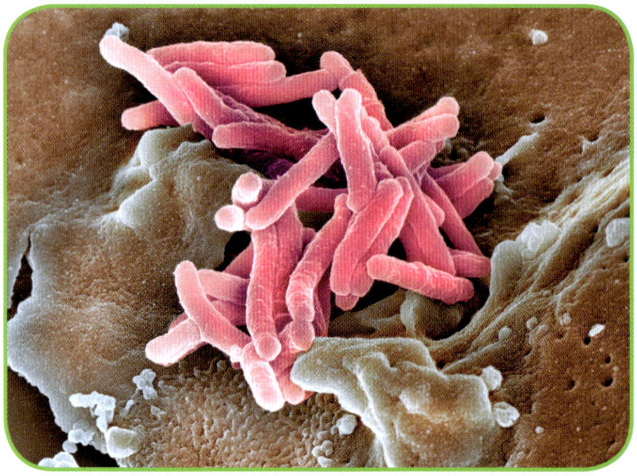

Figure 21.4 Phagocyte engulfing bacteria

Cytokines

Cytokines are cell-signalling protein molecules secreted by white blood cells that have arrived at a site of injury or infection. They attract other white blood cells to accumulate at the site.

During the inflammatory response, increased flow of blood and permeability of capillary walls at the site of injury bring about the following beneficial effects:

- **Enhanced migration of phagocytes to the damaged tissue (attracted by cytokines).** Within a short time, a variety of phagocytes have arrived at the scene and are engaged in engulfing pathogens by **phagocytosis** (see Figure 21.4). Some also clean up the injured site.
- **Rapid delivery of blood-clotting chemicals (clotting elements) to the injured area.** Coagulation of blood stops loss of blood, helps to prevent further infection of the wound and marks the start of the tissue repair process.

Phagocytosis

The process of **phagocytosis** is illustrated in Figure 21.5. A phagocyte is **mobile**. When it detects chemicals released by a pathogen such as a bacterium, or antigens present on the surface of a pathogen (also see Chapter 22), it moves towards the pathogen. It then engulfs the invader in an infolding of the cell membrane which becomes pinched off to form a **vacuole** (sometimes called a phagocytic vesicle).

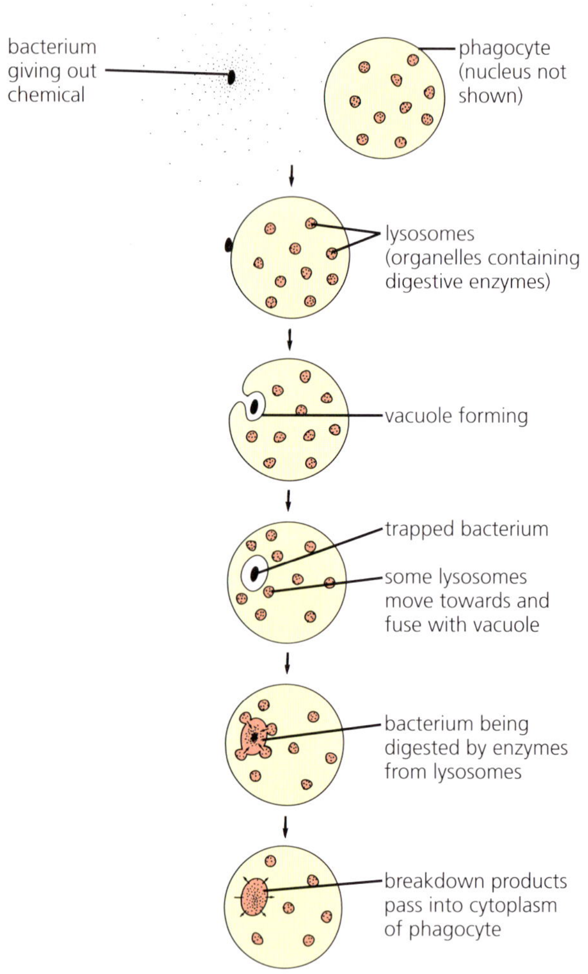

Figure 21.5 Phagocytosis

A phagocyte's cytoplasm contains a rich supply of **lysosomes** which contain digestive enzymes (such as lysozyme). Some lysosomes fuse with the vacuole and release their enzymes into it. The bacterium becomes digested and the breakdown products are absorbed by the phagocyte.

Following digestion of the microorganism by phagocytosis, the phagocyte releases **cytokines** which attract more phagocytes to the infected area to continue the battle against the pathogenic invasion. Dead bacteria and phagocytes may accumulate at an infected site as **pus**.

Testing Your Knowledge

1 a) i) Identify the protective secretion produced by the epithelial lining of the trachea.
ii) Name a different protective secretion made by the stomach lining.
iii) Briefly describe how each of these secretions defends the body against attack by pathogens. (4)
b) Against which other type of unwanted cell does the body defend itself? (1)

2 a) What are *mast* cells? (1)
b) i) Why does injured tissue at a cut quickly become red and swollen?
ii) What name is given to this response to injury?
iii) Briefly explain why it is of benefit to the body. (5)

3 a) Phagocytosis and antibody production are cellular responses to invasion by pathogens. Which of these is i) specific, ii) non-specific? (1)
b) Briefly explain what is meant by the term *phagocytosis*. (2)

4 Decide whether each of the following statements is true or false and then use T or F to indicate your choice. Where a statement is false, give the word that should have been used in place of the word in bold print. (4)
a) Following injury, mast cells in connective tissue release **histamine** which causes vasodilation.
b) **Decreased** capillary permeability occurs at an infected site showing inflammation.
c) A phagocyte's cytoplasm contains **ribosomes** full of digestive enzymes.
d) Following phagocytosis, phagocytes release **cytokines** which attract other phagocytes to the infected area.

Applying Your Knowledge and Skills

1 Figure 21.6 shows a small part of a phagocyte that is approaching a bacterium. Figure 21.7 shows the next five stages in the process of phagocytosis. Arrange them into the correct order. (1)

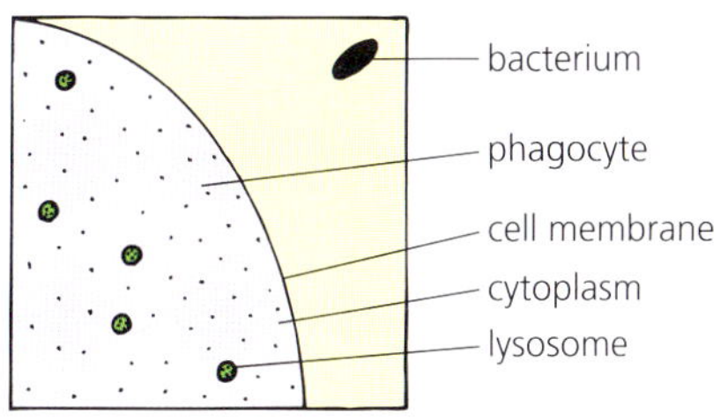

Figure 21.6

2 Figure 21.8 shows a simplified version of some of the events associated with the inflammatory response.
a) Match the following answers with blank boxes 1–6 in the diagram. (5)
A release of histamine by mast cell
B exit of phagocyte from blood capillary
C entry of microorganisms at cut
D attraction of newly arrived phagocyte to infected area
E action by phagocyte already present in connective tissue
F increased capillary permeability allowing increased flow of fluid out of capillary
b) *Pain*, *redness* and *swelling* are features of an inflamed area. Copy and complete Table 21.2 using these three words. (2)

→

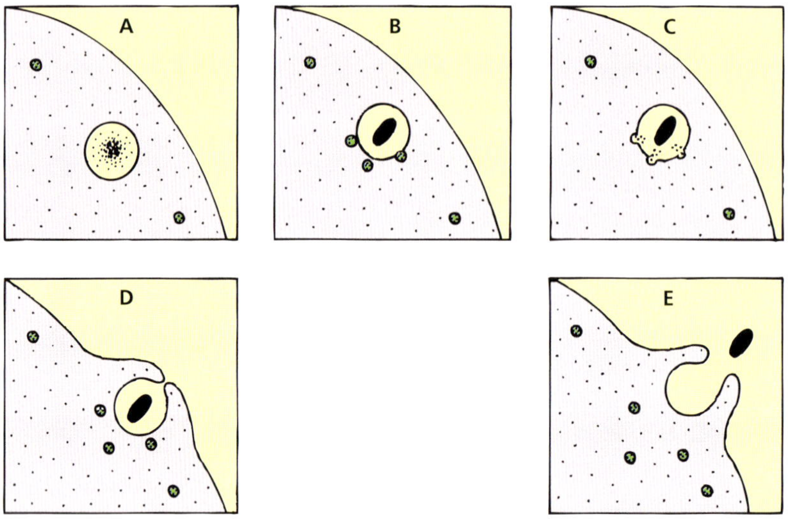

Figure 21.7

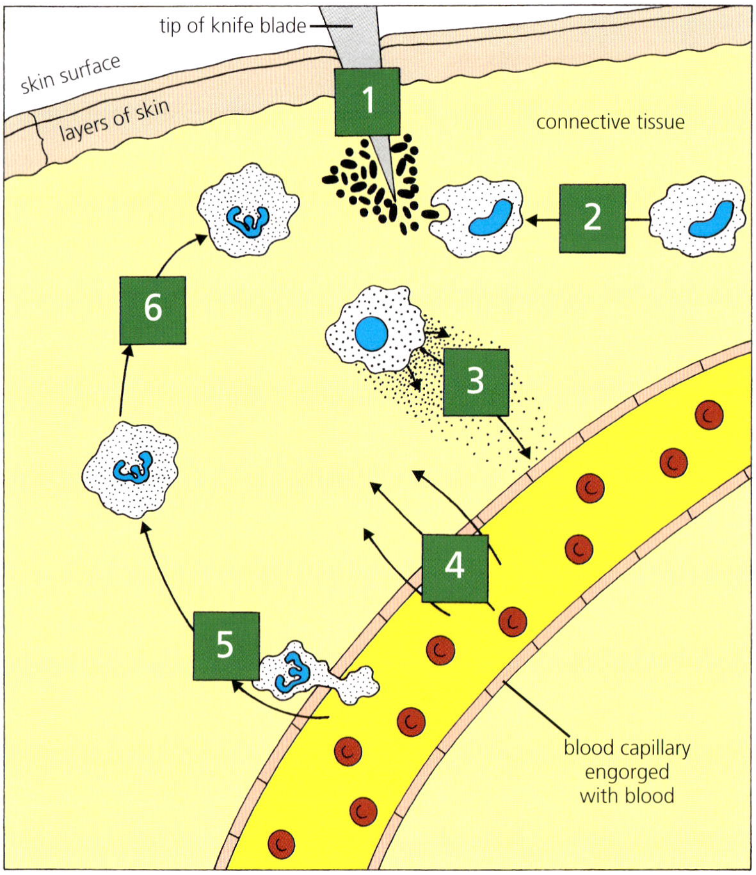

Figure 21.8

Feature of an inflamed area	Reason
	An increased blood supply is sent to the affected area
	Fluid is forced out of blood vessels into the tissues at the site of injury
	Swollen tissues press against nerve receptors and nerves

Table 21.2

3 Two measurements of white blood cells that are commonly made are:

- a count of the number of each type of white blood cell per microlitre (1×10^{-6} l) of blood
- a calculation of the percentage of each type of white blood cell.

Table 21.3 shows a set of normal values based on a large sample of healthy people. Table 21.4 shows some of the factors responsible for increasing the number and percentage of white cells in the bloodstream.

a) Which of the two ways of measuring white blood cells gives:
   i) an absolute value
   ii) a relative value?
   iii) Explain your answer. (3)

b) How many monocytes would normally be present in a litre of blood? (1)

c) With reference only to the information in Table 21.4, identify:
   i) the factor that could cause an increase in number of both monocytes and eosinophils
   ii) the factors that affect the neutrophil count but do not affect the others
   iii) the types of white blood cell that increase in number in response to leukaemia. (3)

d) Draw a bar chart of the percentage numbers of the white blood cells using mean values. (3)

Type of white blood cell	White blood cell count	Percentage
Neutrophil	2500–7000	50–70
Eosinophil	100–300	1–3
Monocyte	200–600	4–6
Lymphocyte	1700–3500	25–35

Table 21.3

Type of white blood cell	Factors responsible for increasing number and percentage of white blood cells
Neutrophil	Bacterial infection, rheumatoid arthritis, leukaemia, acute stress
Eosinophil	Allergic reaction, parasitic infection, Hodgkin's disease
Monocyte	Chronic inflammatory disease, parasitic infection, tuberculosis, viral infection
Lymphocyte	Bacterial infection, hepatitis, leukaemia, viral infection

Table 21.4

22 Specific cellular defences against pathogens

Lymphocytes

The third line of defence – the **specific** immune response – is brought about by **lymphocytes** derived from stem cells in bone marrow (see Figure 1.4, page 4). Some lymphocytes pass to the thymus (a gland in the chest cavity – see Figure 21.1) where they develop into **T lymphocytes (T cells)**. Those that remain and mature in bone marrow become **B lymphocytes (B cells)**.

Clonal populations

Any foreign molecule that is recognised by, and able to elicit a specific immune response from, a lymphocyte is called an **antigen**. Viruses, bacteria, bacterial toxins and molecules on the surfaces of transplanted cells and cancer cells can all act as antigens.

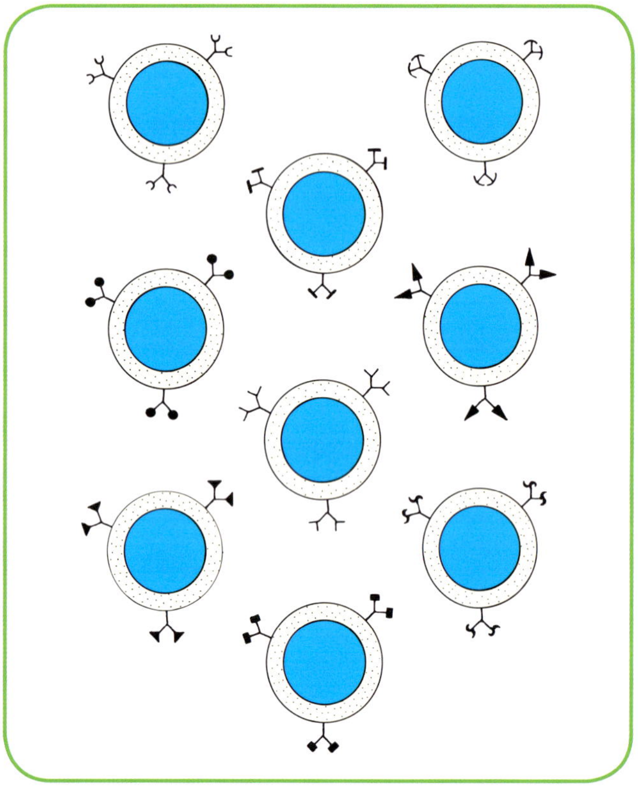

Figure 22.1 Pool of lymphocytes showing variety of antigen receptors

The body possesses an enormous number of different lymphocytes. Each lymphocyte has, on the surface of its cell membrane, several copies of a single type of **antigen receptor**. This antigen receptor is specific for one antigen and is different from that of any other type of lymphocyte (see Figure 22.1). Therefore, each lymphocyte is able to become attached to and be activated by only one type of antigen. When this occurs the lymphocyte responds by dividing repeatedly to form a **clonal population** of identical lymphocytes.

Although each lymphocyte can only be activated by one type of antigen, when taken as a group, all of the body's lymphocytes possess such an enormous range and variety of cell surface antigen receptors that almost any antigen is recognised by one of them.

B lymphocytes (B cells)

Antigens and antibodies

An **antigen** is a complex molecule, such as a protein, that is recognised by the body as non-self and foreign. The antigen's presence triggers the production of antibodies by B lymphocytes (B cells). An **antibody** is a Y-shaped protein molecule, as shown in Figure 22.2. Each of its arms bears a **receptor** (binding site) that is specific to a particular antigen.

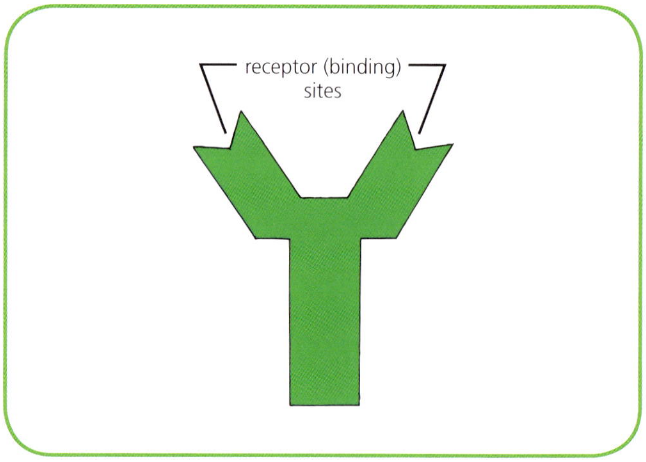

Figure 22.2 Antibody

Production of antibodies

A B lymphocyte specific to a foreign antigen responds to the presence of the antigen by multiplying to form:

- a clone of **activated B cells** which make antibodies for immediate use (each activated B cell may produce around 2000 antibody molecules per second during its 4–5-day lifespan)
- a clone of **memory B cells** capable of making antibodies in the future if required.

Once released into the blood and lymph systems, the antibodies are transported round the body and make their way to the infected area.

Action of antibodies

The antibodies recognise and combine with the antigens at the site of infection (see Figure 22.3). The binding of an antibody to an antigen does not in itself bring about the destruction of the pathogen. However, the formation of an **antigen-antibody complex** inactivates the pathogen (or its toxin) and makes it susceptible to phagocytosis.

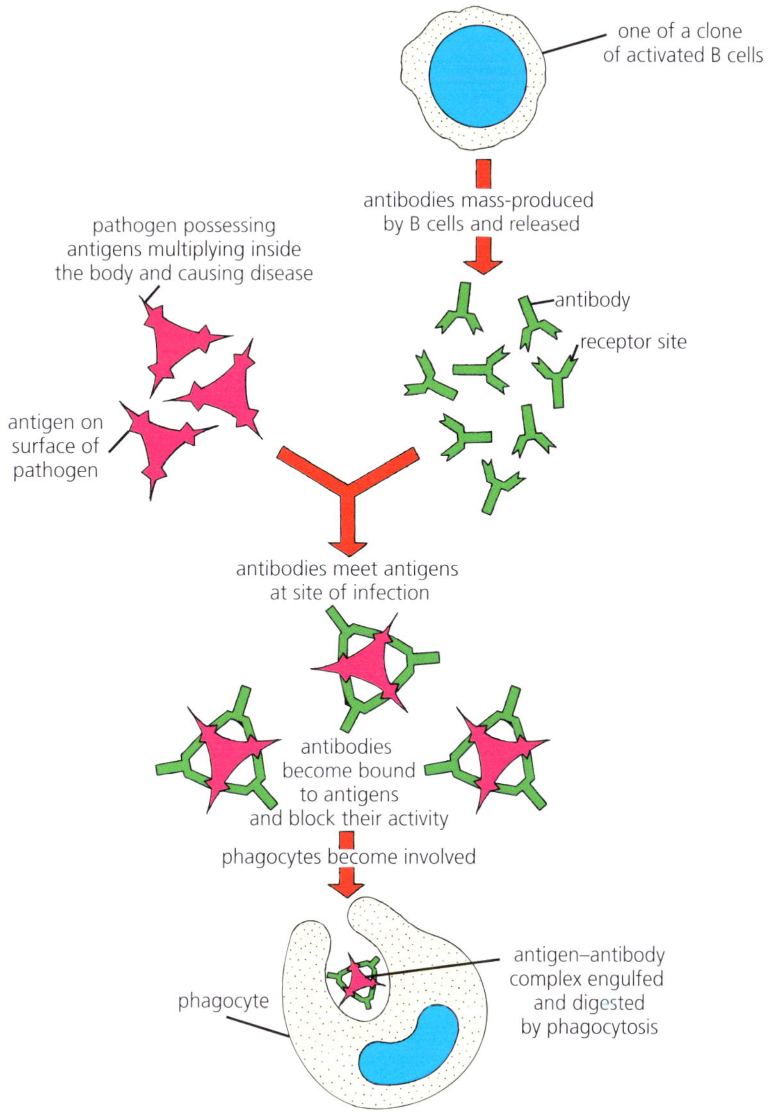

Figure 22.3 Action of antibodies

Allergy

The immune system responds to a wide variety of agents that are molecularly foreign to it. This enables it to defend itself against pathogenic bacteria, fungi, viruses, worms etc. However, sometimes it **over-reacts** by B lymphocytes responding to **harmless** substances such as pollen, dust or feathers, or even a helpful substance such as the antibiotic penicillin. Such hypersensitivity in the form of an exaggerated (and sometimes damaging) immune response is called an **allergic reaction** (see Case Studies on hay fever, anaphylactic shock and allergic asthma).

Case Study Hay fever

When airborne pollen grains (see Figure 22.4) enter the nose, throat and upper respiratory passages, they can act as an **allergen** by causing certain B cells to release antibodies. These become attached to mast cells in connective tissue causing the release of **histamine**. When stimulated in this way, the cells secrete excessive quantities of histamine, which produce the inflammatory response (see page 253). The sequence of events leading to this allergic reaction are summarised in Figure 22.5.

The symptoms typical of hay fever are:

- nasal congestion
- running nose
- red, itchy, watering eyes
- constriction of bronchioles.

They can be relieved by antihistamine drugs and other anti-inflammatory medication.

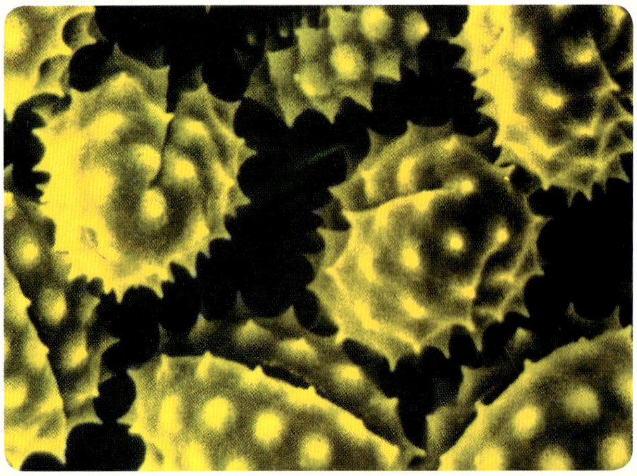

Figure 22.4 Pollen grains are essentially harmless but some of us react to them

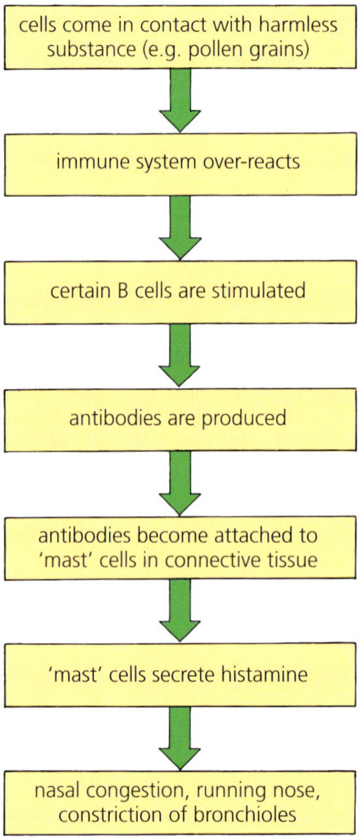
cells come in contact with harmless substance (e.g. pollen grains)
immune system over-reacts
certain B cells are stimulated
antibodies are produced
antibodies become attached to 'mast' cells in connective tissue
'mast' cells secrete histamine
nasal congestion, running nose, constriction of bronchioles

Figure 22.5 Events leading to an allergic reaction such as hay fever

Case Study Anaphylactic shock

Anaphylactic shock is a life-threatening allergic response to an allergen that has been injected (for example, penicillin or bee venom) or consumed (for example, peanuts). The person is so allergic to the antigenic substance that many mast cells respond and secrete large quantities of **histamine** and other inflammatory agents. This triggers sudden dilation of peripheral blood vessels, loss of much circulatory fluid to surrounding tissues and a drop in blood pressure. Death can occur within minutes of exposure to the allergen.

People who know that they are hypersensitive to such allergens make every effort to avoid them and should always carry a **preloaded adrenaline syringe** (see Figure 22.6) to counteract the allergic response and give symptomatic relief in an emergency.

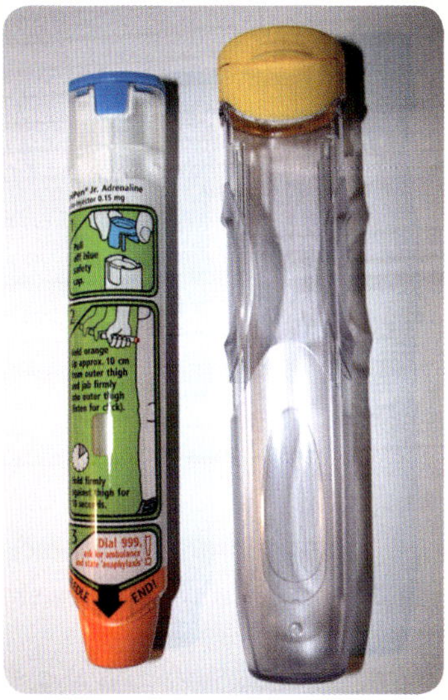

Figure 22.6 Pre-loaded adrenaline syringe

Case Study Allergic asthma

Asthma is a respiratory condition in which the affected person's air passages become narrower (see Figure 22.7). This makes it more difficult for the person to breathe. In addition to experiencing shortness of breath, the person tends to **wheeze**, especially after exercise. In extreme situations their chest becomes so tight that they feel as if they are going to suffocate.

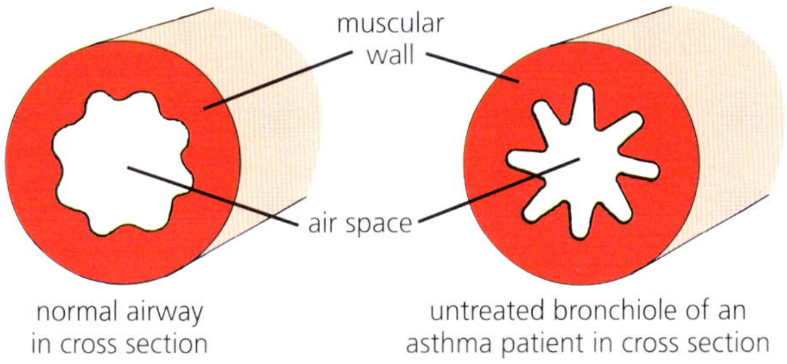

Figure 22.7 Effect of asthma on a bronchiole

An asthmatic attack can be caused by an **allergic reaction** to dust mites, pollen, animal fur and certain foodstuffs such as peanuts and wheat. It can also be brought on by nervous tension. In the UK, boys below the age of 10 are twice as likely to be affected as girls of the same age. People who have asthma are able to control the condition if they follow a management plan. Depending on the allergy, this might include:

- controlling dust mites
- avoiding foods to which they are allergic
- warming up gently before exercise
- using a bronchial dilator (see Figure 22.8) to inhale a drug that gives symptomatic relief by causing muscles in the bronchioles to relax and open the airways wider.

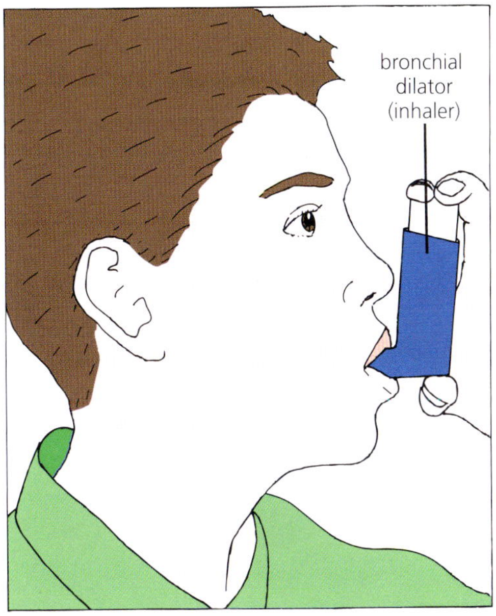

Figure 22.8 Bronchial dilator (inhaler)

Antigen-presenting cell

Once a phagocyte has captured and destroyed an invading pathogen, it normally presents fragments of the pathogen's antigen at its surface, as shown in Figure 22.9. Such a phagocyte is described as an **antigen-presenting cell**. Other cells in the body infected with the pathogen also become antigen-presenting cells.

T lymphocytes (T cells)

Action of T cells

Among the body's vast pool of T cells there will be a type that bears antigen receptors able to recognise and bind with the foreign antigens on the surface of an antigen-presenting cell such as the phagocyte shown in Figure 22.10.

When this happens, the T cell becomes activated, triggering the formation of:

- a clone of **activated T cells** for immediate use
- a clone of **memory T** cells for future use if necessary.

The activated T cells move to the site of infection and attack infected cells as shown in Figure 22.11.

Apoptosis

The T cells release proteins which diffuse into the infected cells and induce them to produce self-destructive enzymes. These break down the cell's DNA and vital proteins, causing the cell to die. This process of programmed cell death is called **apoptosis**.

Once a T cell has killed one target cell, it disengages from that cell and moves on to destroy another infected cell.

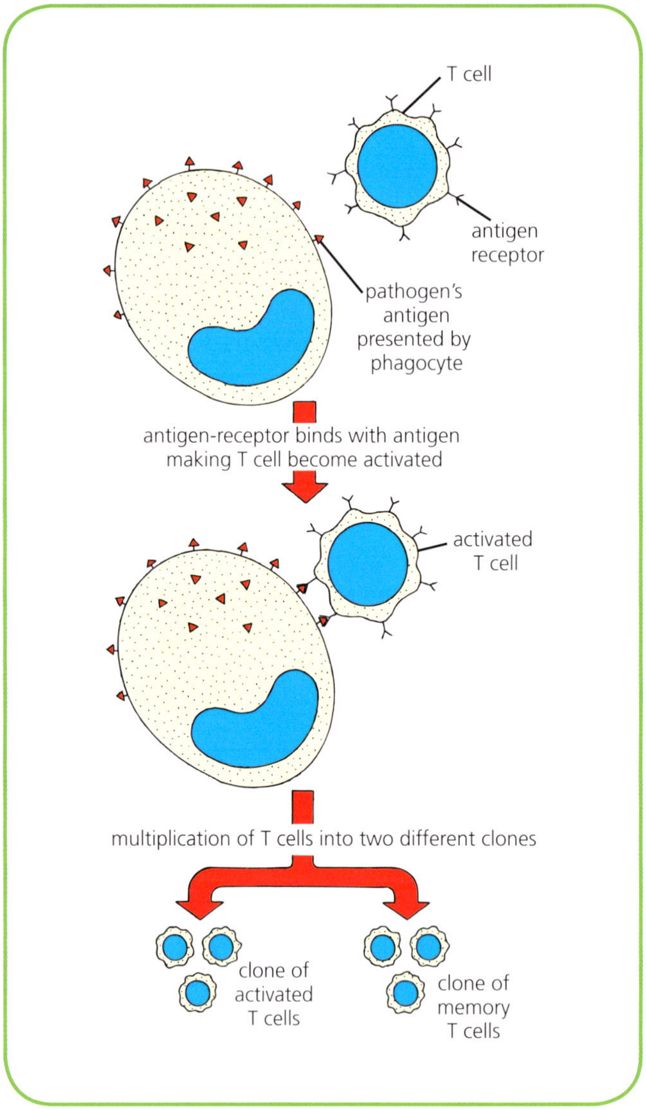

Figure 22.10 Activation of a T cell

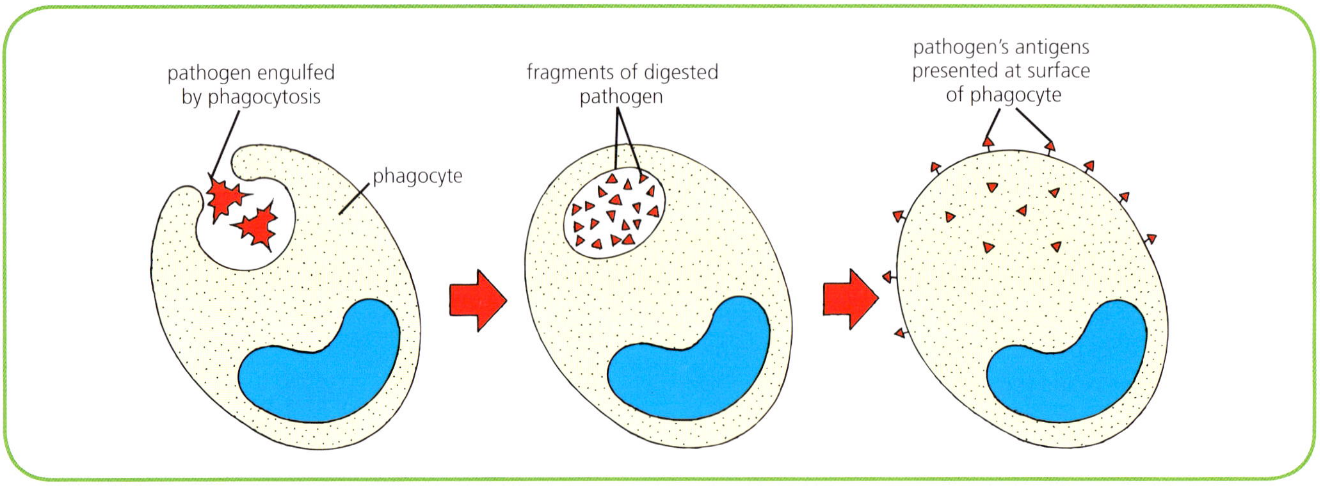

Figure 22.9 Phagocyte becoming an antigen-presenting cell

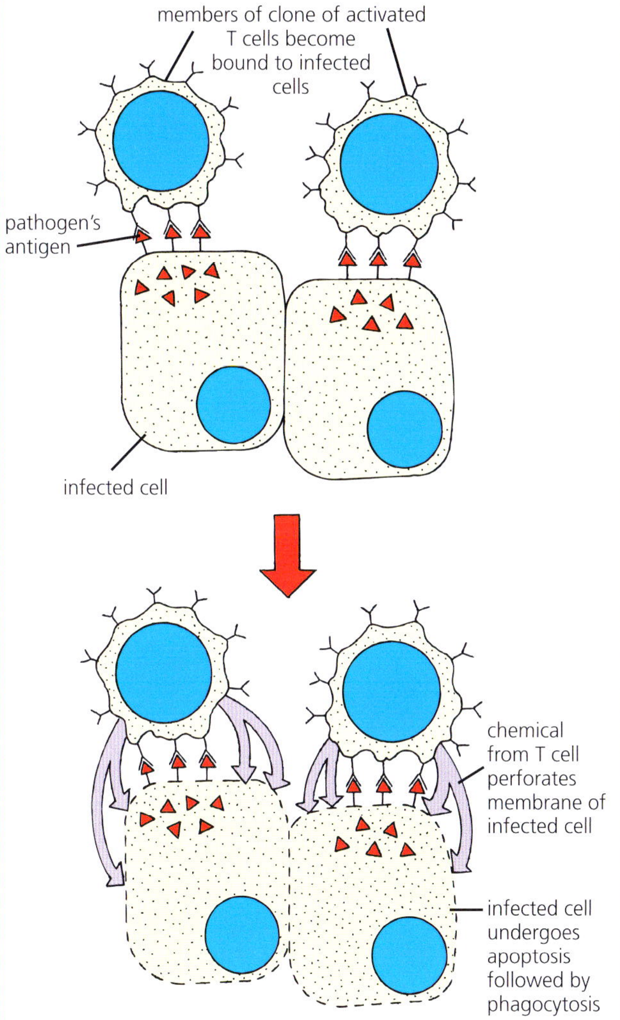

Figure 22.11 Destruction of infected cells by T cells

An infected cell's membrane is not destroyed by apoptosis. Therefore its cell contents and pathogenic antigens remain enclosed and are not dispersed. Instead, the dead cell, which has shrunk, becomes engulfed and digested by a phagocyte.

Recognition of self and non-self

Each person's body cells are different because they possess a combination of cell surface proteins (their 'antigen signature') that is unique to that person. It is of critical importance that a person's lymphocytes do not regard that person's own body cells' surface proteins as antigens and attack them. Normally this does not happen because any lymphocyte bearing an antigen receptor that would fit a body cell surface protein is **weeded out** and rendered non-functional or destroyed by apoptosis.

Surviving viable T lymphocytes are able to distinguish between:

- self-antigens on the surfaces of the body's own cells (and therefore take no action)
- non-self-antigens on the surfaces of infected cells or cells not belonging to the body (and therefore initiate an immune response).

This ability to **recognise self** and **non-self** means that normally there are no lymphocytes acting against the proteins on the surfaces of 'self' body cells.

Autoimmunity

Sometimes the body no longer tolerates the antigens that make up the self message on cell surfaces. Such a failure in the regulation of the immune system leads to T lymphocytes launching an attack on the body's own cells. This process is called **autoimmunity** and it is the cause of **autoimmune diseases** (see Case Studies on rheumatoid arthritis and type 1 diabetes).

Case Study Rheumatoid arthritis

Rheumatoid arthritis is an autoimmune disease that causes chronic **inflammation** of the **synovial membranes** in joints. The membrane swells up and the cartilage and bone underneath are gradually destroyed (see Figure 22.12). They are replaced by fibrous tissue that, in advanced cases, joins the two bones together making the joint immovable.

Rheumatoid arthritis is a painful, disabling condition that can result in substantial loss of mobility. It is experienced by about 1% of the population (with women being three times more likely to be affected than men) and onset occurs most frequently between the ages of 40 and 50.

→

Role of cytokines

The cause of rheumatoid arthritis is unknown but cytokines are known to play a key role in its progression. **Cytokines** are chemical messengers that allow cells to communicate with one another. When a certain combination of cytokines occurs in a person's synovial joint, it promotes an **immune response** and white blood cells are stimulated to migrate to the joint. This creates a state of chronic inflammation that is followed by damage to bone and cartilage.

Treatment

Anti-inflammatory drugs and painkillers are used to suppress the symptoms. Immunosuppressant drugs may be used to inhibit the immune response in order to prevent irreversible, long-term damage to the joint's bone and cartilage.

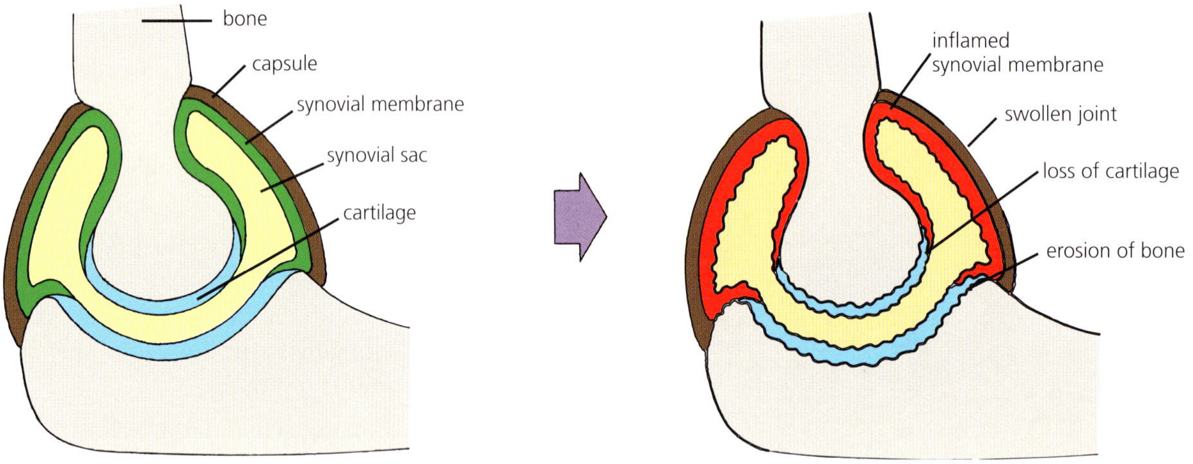

Figure 22.12 Effect of rheumatoid arthritis on a joint

Case Study Type 1 diabetes

Type 1 diabetes (diabetes mellitus) is an autoimmune disease where **insulin-producing** beta cells in the pancreas are attacked and destroyed by **T cells** from the body's immune system.

A continuous supply of insulin is essential for regulation of blood glucose concentration (see page 191). Therefore, people with type 1 diabetes must inject insulin on a regular basis or risk diabetic shock and death. Poorly controlled diabetes increases the risk of further problems such as blindness and kidney disease.

The inheritance of particular cell surface proteins that make up a person's 'antigen signature' is associated with susceptibility to this autoimmune condition. However, studies of identical twins have shown that where one had type 1 diabetes, the other had it in only around 40% of the cases studied. This suggests that, in addition to inherited factors, environmental factors also play a part in this autoimmune disease.

Immunological memory

Primary and secondary responses

When a person is infected by a disease-causing organism, the body responds by producing antibodies. This is called the **primary response** (see Figure 22.13).

Due to a latent period elapsing before the appearance of the antibodies, this primary response is often unable to prevent the person from becoming ill.

If the person survives, exposure to the same antigen at a later date results in the **secondary response**. This time the disease is usually prevented because:

- antibody production is much **more rapid**
- the concentration of antibodies produced reaches a **higher level**
- the higher concentration of antibodies is maintained for a **longer time**.

Memory cells

The secondary response is made possible by the presence of **memory cells**. These are B and T lymphocytes specific to the antigen and produced in response to the body's first exposure to it. When the body becomes exposed to the disease-causing microorganism for a second time, the memory cells quickly proliferate and differentiate, producing clones of T cells and antibody-forming B cells.

Immunodeficiency disease

An immunodeficiency disease results from the absence or failure of some component of the immune system which leaves the person susceptible to infection.

AIDS and HIV

AIDS (acquired immune deficiency syndrome) is a deficiency disease caused by **HIV** (human immunodeficiency virus).

HIV infection

HIV attacks T lymphocytes. It becomes attached to specific receptors on the T cell's surface (see Figure 22.14).

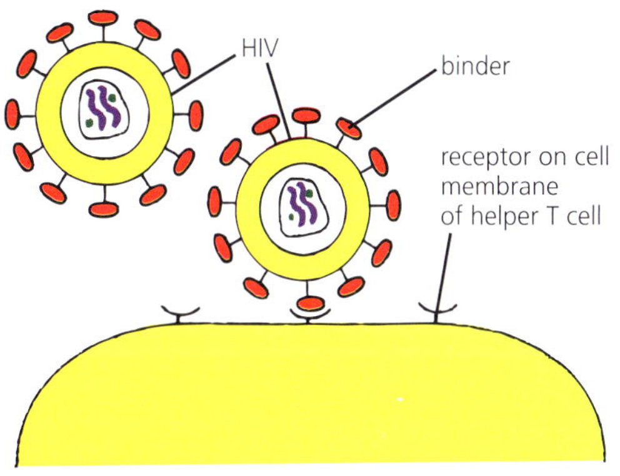

Figure 22.14 Attachment of HIV to a helper T cell

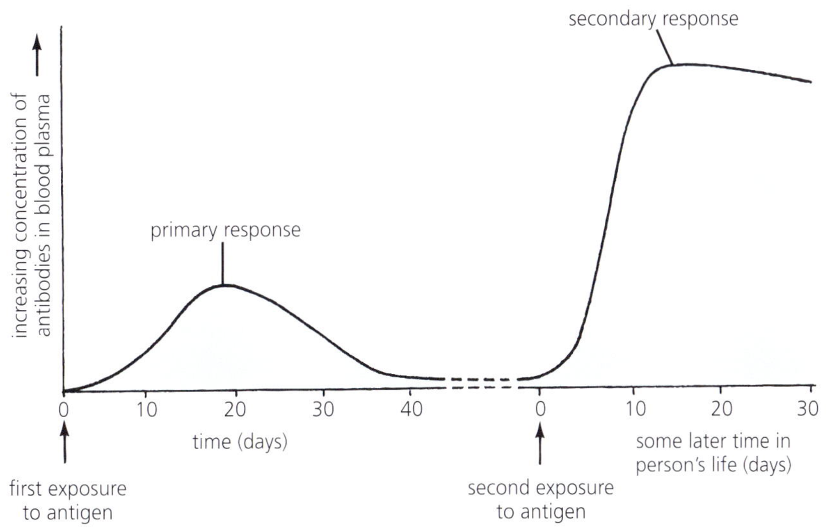

Figure 22.13 Primary and secondary responses

The coat surrounding the HIV particle fuses with the membrane of the T cell and the virus enters the cell (now the host cell). Viral DNA becomes incorporated into the host cell's DNA where it can remain dormant for many years before directing synthesis of new viral particles inside the host cell. These escape from the T cell by **budding** (see Figure 22.15) and move off to infect other cells.

B lymphocytes do make **antibodies** in response to HIV but these are ineffective against viral particles 'hiding' inside T cells. As the number of healthy, uninfected T cells gradually drops, the body's immunological activity decreases, leaving the person susceptible to serious **opportunistic infections** such as pneumonia and rare forms of cancer. At this point, after several years of infection by HIV, the person has an extremely weakened immune system and is suffering from AIDS.

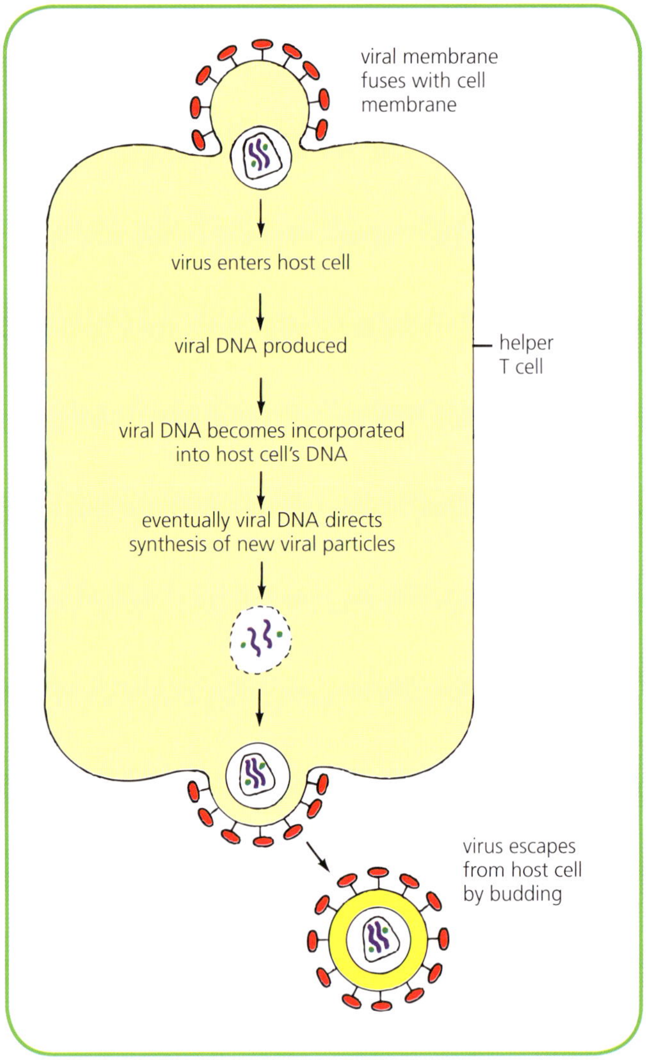

Figure 22.15 Life cycle of HIV

Case Study Control of HIV

Public health measures

An opportunity for HIV to be transmitted arises when a body fluid such as blood, semen or breast milk containing HIV from one person comes into contact with the mucous membranes or bloodstream of another person. Shared use of non-sterile needles by intravenous drug users and unprotected sex account for most cases of AIDS.

Public health measures to control the spread of AIDS set out to:

- raise public awareness of the problem (see Figure 22.16)
- educate people about how the virus is spread
- supply drug addicts with sterile needles while trying to persuade them to seek treatment for their addiction
- promote the practice of safe sex and the use of condoms.

Figure 22.16 Raising awareness

In the UK, screening of blood and blood products for HIV has eliminated, almost completely, the chance of the virus being transmitted via blood transfusions and blood products.

Drug therapies

At present there is no cure for AIDS. Some drugs do slow down the onset of AIDS but they are expensive and not available to all HIV-positive people, especially those living in developing countries.

Drugs developed to disrupt the action of HIV are called **anti-retrovirals**. They are designed to target different stages of the HIV life cycle by acting as:

- reverse transcriptase inhibitors
- DNA-synthesis inhibitors
- protease inhibitors (which prevent key steps in the synthesis of HIV proteins from occurring).

Combinations of these drugs, accompanied by medicines to treat opportunistic infections, prolong the life of a person with AIDS but do not offer a cure. Production of a successful vaccine has so far eluded scientists because the genetic material in HIV **mutates** frequently, forming many **new variants** with different antigenic properties.

Testing Your Knowledge

1 a) Name two types of lymphocyte. (1)
   b) Which of these is involved in the specific immune response to invasion by a pathogen? (1)

2 a) i) What is meant by the term *antigen*?
   ii) Give TWO examples of antigens. (3)
   b) If each lymphocyte can only recognise one specific antigen, how is it possible that lymphocytes offer effective protection against a vast variety of pathogens? (2)

3 a) From each of the following pairs, choose the words that apply to the term *allergic reaction* and then use all three to explain what the term means. (3)
   underreacts/overreacts, hypersensitive response/hyposensitive response, normally harmful substance/normally harmless substance
   b) Explain what is meant by the term *autoimmunity*. (2)

4 a) Define the term *apoptosis*. (1)
   b) Outline the series of events that takes place when an activated T cell binds to an infected cell. (3)

5 Why are individuals with AIDS extremely vulnerable to opportunistic infections? (2)

Applying Your Knowledge and Skills

1 Figure 22.17 shows an antibody complex in action.

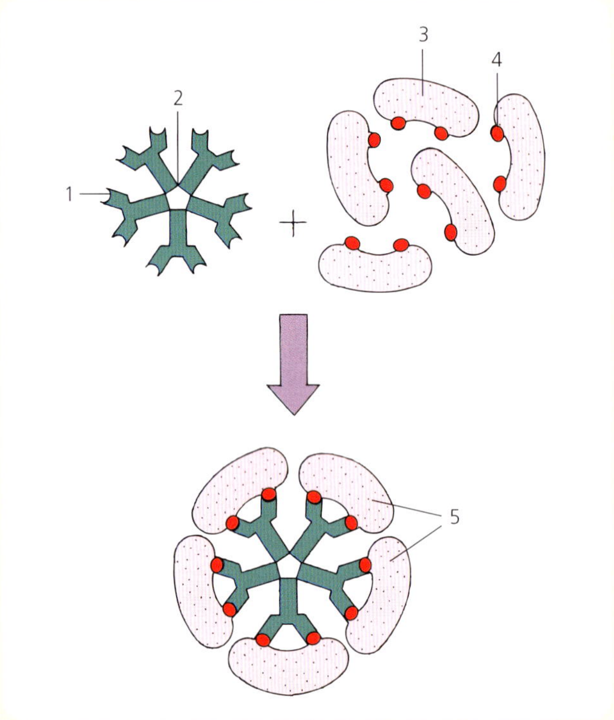

Figure 22.17

Match labels 1–5 with the following answers. (4)

A antibody complex
B antigen on surface of bacterium
C pathogens inactivated by antibody complex
D pathogenic microorganism
E receptor site on antibody

2 Figure 22.18 shows a bar chart of results from a survey carried out on 30 000 people to estimate the incidence of asthma in a country. Each bar represents a mean value with a 95% confidence level whose range is indicated by error bars.

a) On average, what percentage of
  i) males aged 55–64 had asthma?
  ii) females aged 35–44 had asthma? (2)

b) By how many times was the percentage of boys aged 5–8 with asthma greater than that of men aged 75+ with asthma? (1)

c) By how many percent was the number of women aged 25–34 with asthma greater than the number of girls aged 2–4 with asthma? (1)

d) At what age was there the least difference in percentage of asthma cases between the two sexes? (1)

e) What general conclusion can be drawn about the percentage of males with asthma compared with females with asthma in this sample group at age: **i)** 2–15, **ii)** 25–54? (2)

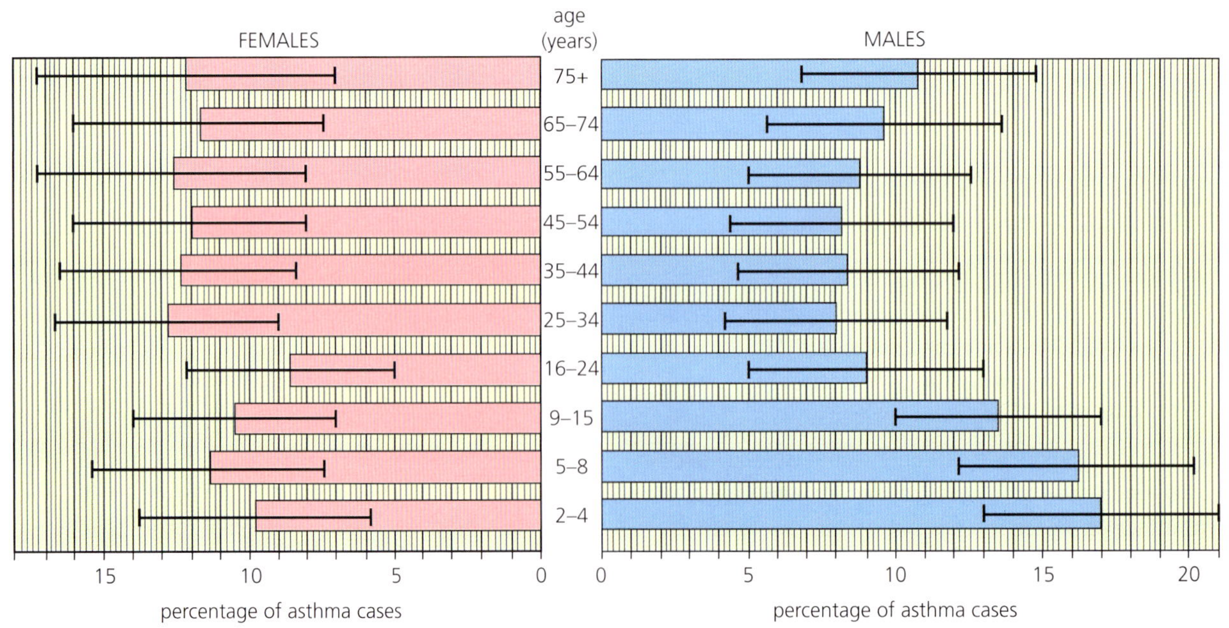

Figure 22.18

f) Decide whether each of statements **i)–vi)** below is true or false and then use T or F to indicate your choice. Where a statement is false, give the data that should have been used in place of that in bold print. (6)

Based on the information in the bar chart, health care experts could be 95% certain that the number of asthma cases for the whole population would be:

i) between **13% and 21%** for 2–4 year-old males

ii) between **7.2% and 15.2%** for 5–8 year-old females

iii) between **4.8% and 12.8%** for 25–34 year-old males

iv) between **8.4% and 16.4%** for 35–44 year-old females

v) between **5.0% and 12.6%** for 55–64 year-old males

vi) between **7.6% and 14.0%** for 65–74 year-old females.

3 Figure 22.19 shows a flow diagram of part of the specific immune response. Copy the flow diagram and complete it using the boxed answers that follow it. (4)

4 Table 22.1 refers to antibody proteins called immunoglobulins found in human blood. The graph in Figure 22.20 refers to the sequence of events that occurs in response to two separate injections of a type of antigen into a small mammal.

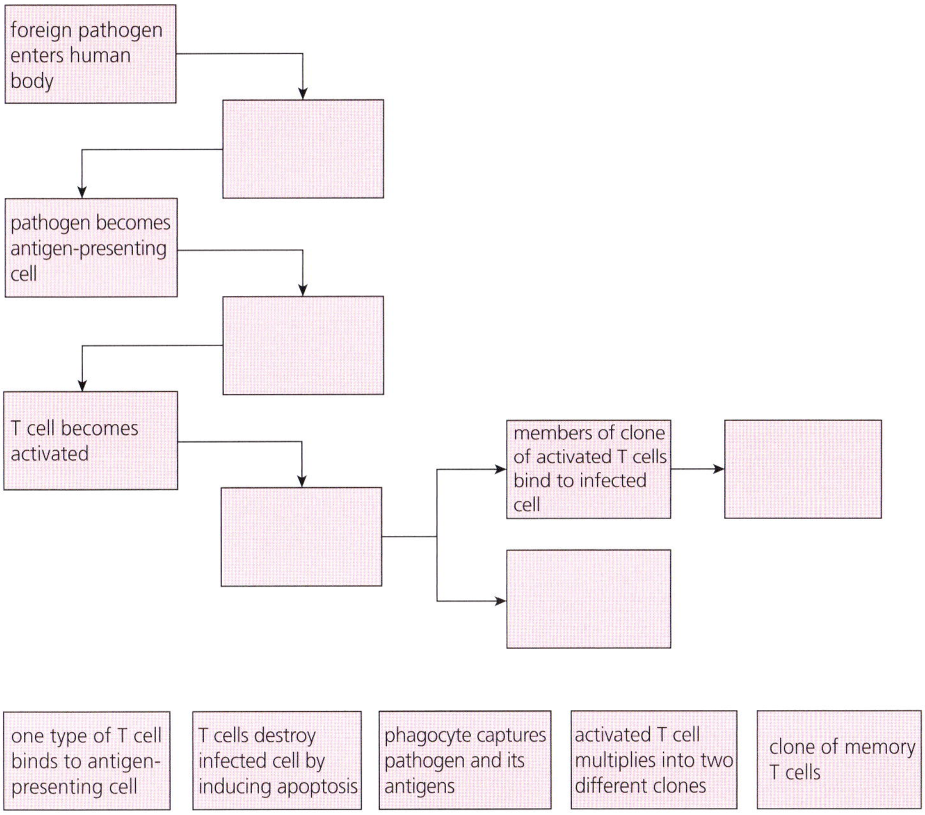
foreign pathogen enters human body
pathogen becomes antigen-presenting cell
T cell becomes activated
members of clone of activated T cells bind to infected cell
one type of T cell binds to antigen-presenting cell
T cells destroy infected cell by inducing apoptosis
phagocyte captures pathogen and its antigens
activated T cell multiplies into two different clones
clone of memory T cells

Figure 22.19

	Immunoglobulin (Ig)				
	IgA	**IgD**	**IgE**	**IgG**	**IgM**
Molecular weight	170 000	184 000	188 100	150 000	960 000
Normal serum concentration	1.4–4.0 g/l	0.1–0.4 g/l	0.1–1.3 mg/l	8.0–16.0 g/l	0.5–2.0 g/l
Ability to cross placenta	No	No	No	Yes	No

Table 22.1

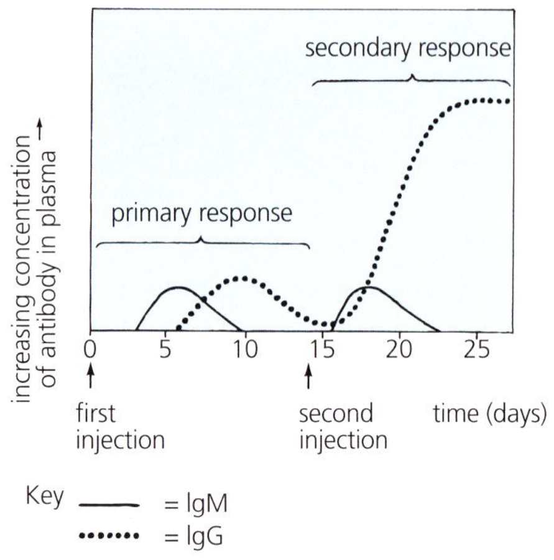

Figure 22.20

a) i) Which immunoglobulin in the table would be found in the blood of an unborn baby?

ii) Suggest why these antibodies are only needed by the baby for a few months after birth. (2)

b) Of the five types of immunoglobulin molecule, which is the **i)** largest, **ii)** rarest? (2)

c) State the normal serum concentration of IgA in mg/ml. (1)

d) With reference to IgM and IgG, state ONE feature common to both the primary and secondary response shown in the graph. (1)

e) With reference to IgG, state THREE differences between the primary and the secondary response. (3)

f) Antibodies such as IgG are now known to be produced by the activity of long-lived lymphocytes. With reference to the graph, suggest why the latter are called *memory cells*. (1)

5 The graph in Figure 22.21 refers to a person infected with HIV.

a) i) What happens to the relative concentration of HIV between 6 months and 1 year after infection?

ii) Suggest why. (2)

b) i) What relationship exists between the relative HIV concentration and relative helper T cell concentration from 2 years after infection onwards?

ii) Explain why. (2)

c) i) Which type of white blood cell makes antibodies?

ii) Why does the relative antibody concentration remain constant between years 1–9 after infection yet the relative HIV concentration increases? (2)

d) i) At which of the following times after infection would this person be most likely to be affected by AIDS?

A 6 months **B** 1 year, 3 months
C 4 years, 6 months **D** 10 years

ii) Explain your choice of answer. (2)

e) Why has it proved impossible so far to make people immune to HIV by vaccination? (1)

6 Give an account of the role played by B lymphocytes in the defence of the body. (9)

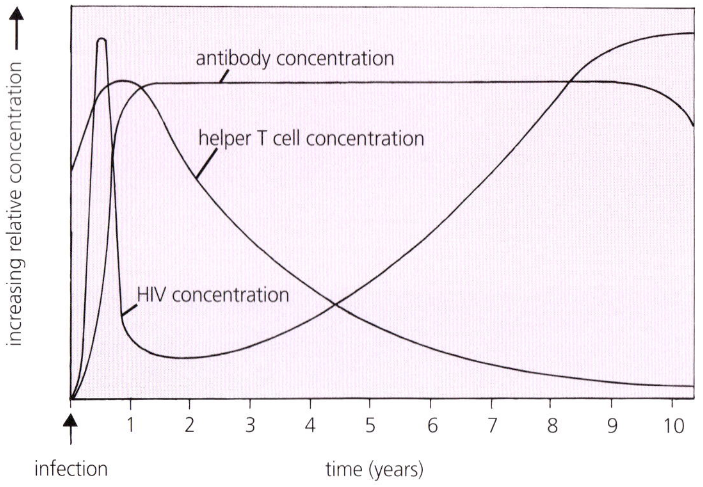

Figure 22.21

What You Should Know Chapters 21–22

activated	cytokines	membrane
AIDS	dilate	memory
allergic	distinguish	non-specific
antibody	epithelial	own
antigen	faster	pathogens
apoptosis	harmless	permeable
autoimmune	histamine	phagocytosis
bloodstream	immune	receptor
cells	immunological	specific
chemical	infection	susceptible
clonal	inflammatory	tolerate
complexes	lymphocytes	weakened

Table 22.2 Word bank for Chapters 21–22

1 The human body uses its ______ system to protect itself against ______, some toxins and cancer cells.

2 The body surface and cavity linings are covered with ______ cells that provide physical defence against infection and produce secretions that give ______ defence.

3 The body responds to an injury by making an ______ response. ______ released by mast cells causes blood vessels to ______ and capillaries to become more ______. Enhanced migration of phagocytes to the damaged site is accompanied by the rapid delivery of clotting elements.

4 Certain specialised white blood cells display ______ responses to pathogens. These phagocytes destroy pathogens by ______.

5 Phagocytes release cell-signalling molecules called ______ which attract more phagocytes to the site of ______.

6 The ______ immune response is brought about by B lymphocytes (B ______) and T ______ (T cells).

7 A foreign molecule able to elicit a specific response from a lymphocyte is called an ______. When an antigen binds to a ______ on the type of lymphocyte to which it is specific, the lymphocyte becomes ______ and divides, forming a ______ population.

8 Each clone of B cells produces one type of ______ specific to one type of antigen surface molecule on a pathogen. These antibodies are secreted into the ______ and transported to the site of infection.

9 The subsequent formation of antigen–antibody ______ inactivates the pathogen and makes it more ______ to phagocytosis.

10 T cells recognise pathogenic antigens on the cell ______ of an infected cell and destroy it by inducing ______.

11 Specific proteins present on T cells enable them to ______ between the body's ______ cells and cells bearing foreign antigens.

12 Failure to ______ the body's own antigens (that make up the 'self message' on cell surfaces) leads to an ______ disease. Over-reaction by the immune system to a ______ substance results in an ______ reaction.

13 Some of the T and B cells formed in response to antigens persist as ______ cells. If the body is exposed to the same antigen, these cells produce new clones, which give a ______ and greater ______ response than during the first exposure.

14 HIV attacks and destroys T cells, causing a ______ immune system and leading to the development of ______.

23 Immunisation

Immunisation

Immunisation is the process by which a person develops immunity to a disease-causing organism. **Active** immunity refers to the protection gained as a result of the person's body producing its own antibodies.

Naturally acquired immunity

If a person survives infection by a pathogen, subsequent exposure to the same antigen at a later date results in a secondary response (see page 265) which prevents the disease from recurring. The person has acquired immunity as an immunological memory by **natural** means.

Artificially acquired immunity

Vaccination is the method of immunisation by which a weakened or altered form of the pathogen or its toxin is deliberately introduced into the body by injection, ingestion or nasal spray in order to act as an **antigen** and initiate the **immune response** (also see Research Topic – Forms of antigen used in vaccines).

Adjuvant

Normally the antigen is mixed with an **adjuvant**. This is a chemical substance makes the vaccine more effective and enhances the immune response. In each case the antigen induces the production of B and T cells and the formation of antibodies but does not cause the disease. Some B and T cells persist in the body as **memory cells**. These initiate the secondary response if the person is exposed to the normal disease-causing antigen at a later date. The person has acquired immunity as an immunological memory by **artificial** means.

Research Topic: Forms of antigen used in vaccines

Table 23.1 gives examples of the various forms of antigen used in vaccines for several different diseases.

Form of antigen in vaccine	Examples of diseases to which active immunity is acquired
Dead pathogens	Hepatitis A and poliomyelitis
Parts of pathogens	Hepatitis B and HPV (human papilloma virus)
Weakened pathogens	Rubella, mumps and measles
Inactivated bacterial toxin	Diphtheria and tetanus

Table 23.1 Antigens in vaccines

Herd immunity

When most of the members of a population have been immunised by vaccination against a pathogen, the probability of the few remaining non-immune individuals coming into contact with an infected individual becomes very low. Under these circumstances, non-immune individuals are protected because the normal chain of infection has been disrupted. This form of protection, given indirectly to the non-immune minority by the immune majority, is called **herd immunity** (see Figure 23.1).

The greater the percentage of individuals in the population who are immune, the lower the chance that a non-immune person will come into contact with an infected person. Herd (community) immunity provides protection for **vulnerable sub-groups** of the population. These include people who must not be vaccinated because of a medical condition such as an immune disorder.

Mass vaccination

Herd immunity resulting from mass-vaccination programmes has successfully reduced the spread of diseases and even eradicated some (see the Case Studies on tuberculosis, poliomyelitis and smallpox).

Herd immunity threshold

For herd immunity to be effective, only a minority of the population can be left unvaccinated. The percentage of immune individuals in a population above which a disease no longer manages to persist is called the **herd immunity threshold**. Its value varies from disease to disease (see Table 23.2) and depends on factors such as:

- the extent of the pathogen's **virulence** (its capacity for causing disease)
- the vaccine's **effectiveness**
- the **density** of the population.

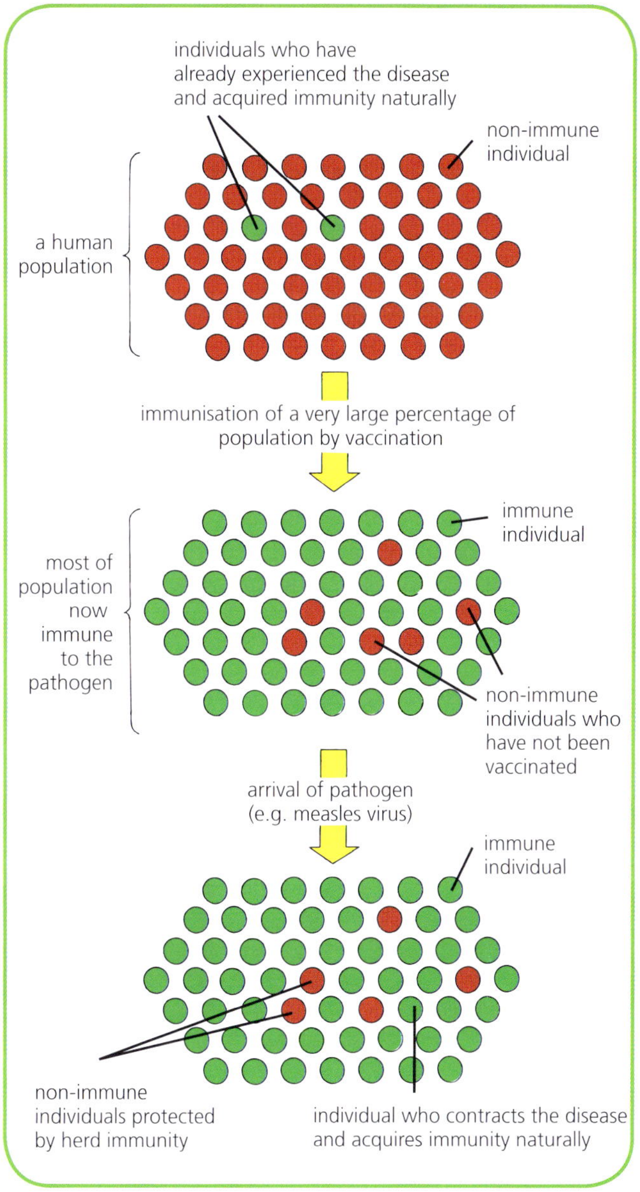

Figure 23.1 Herd immunity

Case Study Tuberculosis mass vaccination programme

Tuberculosis (TB) is caused by a bacterium that is inhaled in droplets released by an infected person during coughing. The disease most commonly affects the **lungs** but many other organs can also become infected. In its later stages, sputum containing blood is coughed up. This stage of the disease was formerly called **consumption**. Tuberculosis used to be a common cause of death in the UK. A close correlation existed between incidence of the disease and poor social conditions. Poverty-stricken people eating a poor diet and living in overcrowded conditions with poor sanitation were much more likely to develop the disease than wealthier members of society. As social conditions gradually improved with time, the death rate decreased, as shown in Figure 23.2.

Vaccination

A programme of **mass vaccination** (accompanied by **antibiotic treatment** for infected people) was begun in the UK in the 1950s. The vaccine was routinely administered to school children aged 10–13 years. It has been so successful in achieving **herd immunity** over the years that it is no longer delivered to everyone. Instead, it has been replaced by **targeted vaccination** for those infants, school children, health care workers and older people considered to be at greatest risk.

In recent times the number of cases of TB has begun to rise again as it gains a foothold among problem drug and alcohol users and homeless people with an extremely low quality of life and very poor general health.

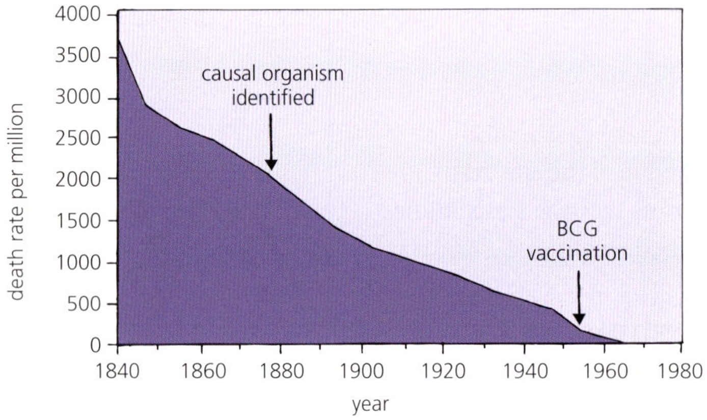

Figure 23.2 Decline in death rate from tuberculosis

Case Study Poliomyelitis mass vaccination programme

Poliomyelitis (polio for short) is a disease caused by a virus. Its principal mode of transmission is the faecal–oral route, but it can be passed on in exhaled droplets. In severe cases of the disease, the virus attacks **motor neurons** in the spinal cord and hindbrain. This often leads to **paralysis** of limbs. In very severe cases, the disease can be fatal.

A summer epidemic of the disease developed in the UK in 1947 and then recurred in subsequent years. Therefore concerted efforts were made to develop a **vaccine**. The first type containing dead virus was introduced in 1956. It reduced the incidence of the disease among vaccinated children to about 25% of that of non-vaccinated children. In 1962 an improved vaccine containing **attenuated** (weakened) virus was introduced. It was administered orally rather than by injection and has proved to be so effective that **herd immunity** has now been established and polio has been almost completely eradicated in developed countries such as the UK (see Figure 23.3). Experts have calculated that an infant immunisation rate of 80–86% must be maintained to keep polio in check. It is for this reason that polio vaccine is given to babies aged 2 months.

It must be kept in mind, however, that this successful outcome in the battle against polio was not due solely to the mass vaccination programme. In the UK, over the years, ever-improving standards of living and hygiene, including effective means of sewage disposal, have also played their parts in wiping out the disease. Poliomyelitis is still common in many developing countries that lack mass vaccination programmes and effective sanitation.

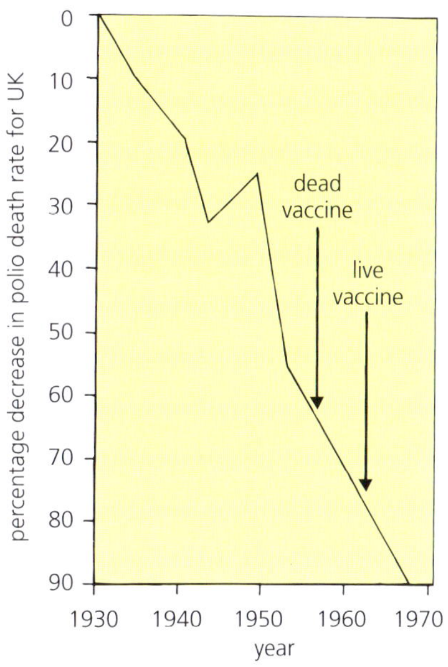

Figure 23.3 Effect of vaccination against polio

Case Study Smallpox mass vaccination programme

Up until the end of the eighteenth century, **smallpox** was widespread in the UK. This infectious disease caused severe fever and was fatal in about one out of every five cases. Survivors were left permanently scarred. It was known at that time that smallpox could sometimes be prevented by deliberately inoculating people with pus from a pustule of a person experiencing a mild form of the disease. However, this method of immunisation was not reliable and often produced the fatal form of the disease.

In 1796, a British doctor called Edward Jenner decided to act on observations that milkmaids who had been afflicted by **cowpox** (a similar, but milder, non-fatal disease) were immune to smallpox. He inoculated a healthy boy with cowpox. Once the boy had recovered, Jenner inoculated him with what would normally have been a deadly strain of smallpox virus. Fortunately for everyone concerned, the boy did not contract smallpox, showing that he was immune. The science of artificially acquired, active immunity had begun.

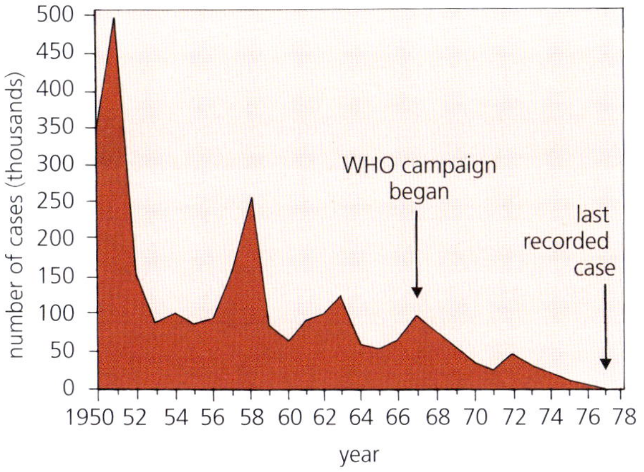

Figure 23.4 Worldwide eradication of smallpox

Eradication of smallpox

Free vaccination against smallpox became available in the UK in the 1840s and was made compulsory for babies 10 years later. In Britain and other developed countries, the death rate gradually decreased to a low level. However, it was not until many years later that one of the greatest triumphs in medical history was achieved. This was the **complete eradication worldwide** of smallpox which was brought about by a World Health Organization (WHO) programme begun in 1967. It involved vaccinating as many people as possible shortly after birth and quickly homing in on fresh outbreaks of the disease and then vaccinating all known and suspected contacts. This **surveillance-containment campaign** was so successful that the last recorded case of smallpox occurred in Somalia in 1977 (see Figure 23.4).

Public health medicine

In many countries, the **public health policy** for combating a number of common diseases is to use **mass vaccination** programmes that create herd immunity to them. In the UK, for example, a person's vaccination schedule normally begins around the age of 2 months (when they are vaccinated against diphtheria, tetanus, poliomyelitis, influenza and whooping cough) and continues for many years.

Absence of herd immunity

In some **developing** countries where the majority of the population are **impoverished** and **malnourished**, it may not be possible to introduce a programme of widespread mass vaccination. Under these circumstances herd immunity cannot be established.

In a **developed** country, herd immunity for a vaccine-preventable disease (e.g. measles) may be compromised if parents believe **adverse publicity** about the vaccine and refuse to have their children vaccinated. Under these circumstances the level of herd immunity can slip below its threshold value. As a result, the incidence of the disease among non-vaccinated individuals will increase rapidly.

Antigenic variation

Within a population of pathogenic microorganisms, new strains arise continuously by mutation. These new strains are described as demonstrating **antigenic variation** if they have antigens on their surface that are different from those of the original strain. A new strain of the pathogen showing antigenic variation is **genetically and immunologically distinct** from its parent strain(s) and succeeds because it enjoys a selective advantage.

Influenza virus

Production of new antigens enable the influenza virus, for example, to avoid the effects of the human body's immunological memory. This allows it to re-infect the person because its new antigens are not recognised by their memory cells (see Figure 23.5). It is for this reason that influenza remains a major public health problem. At-risk individuals need to be vaccinated every year with a new version of the vaccine to give protection (see Figure 23.6).

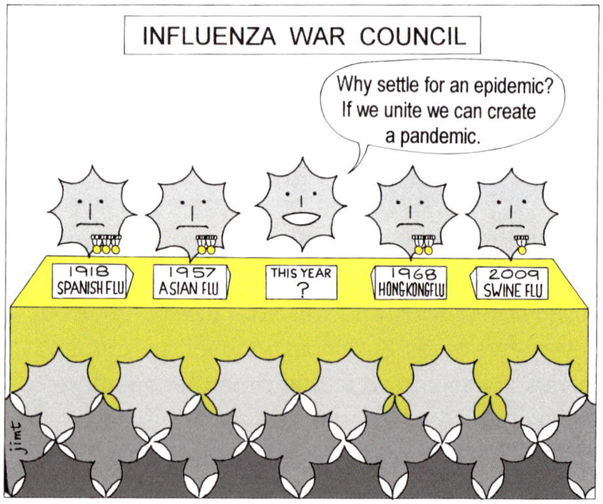

Figure 23.6 Epidemic or pandemic?

Related Topic

Comparison of herd immunity thresholds

Table 23.2 shows herd immunity thresholds for several diseases.

Disease	Mode of transmission	Herd immunity threshold (%)
Diphtheria	Airborne droplets of saliva	85
Measles	Airborne	83–94
Mumps	Saliva and airborne droplets	75–86
Poliomyelitis	Faecal–oral route	80–86
Rubella	Airborne droplets	80–85
Whooping cough	Airborne droplets	92–94

Table 23.2 Estimated herd immunity thresholds for vaccine-preventable diseases

1
Influenza virus arrives …
antigen (surface protein)
virus enters body
antigen
antibody
The person develops the disease. Antibodies are made and eventually the disease is contained as antibodies bind to antigens. Memory cells are produced.
2
If the identical strain of influenza virus arrives the next year…
antigen
virus enters body
Memory cells recognise the antigens on the virus and trigger antibody production. Antibodies bind to antigens and prevent reinfection.
3
If a newly mutated strain of influenza virus arrives the next year…
new version of antigen
virus enters body
Memory cells do not recognise the new antigen. Antibodies from before do not fit new antigens. The person develops the disease. Antibodies and memory cells specific to this new antigen are eventually made, the person survives and so on …

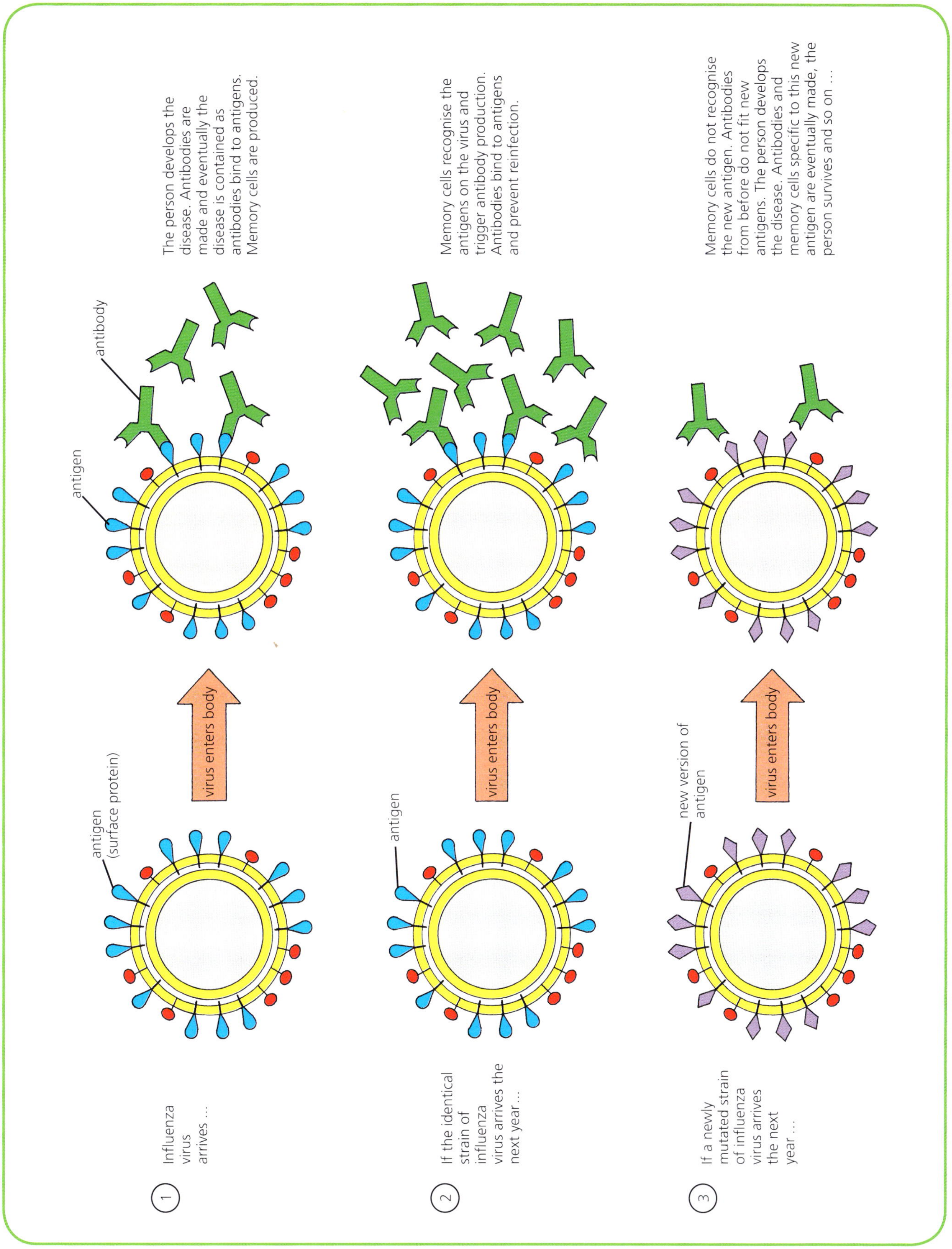

Figure 23.5 Effect of antigenic variation in influenza virus

Testing Your Knowledge

1 Briefly describe how active immunisation can be acquired by artificial means. (2)

2 a) Explain how a minority of people in a population can be protected from an infectious disease even if they have not been immunised against it. (2)

b) Identify TWO factors that affect the herd immunity threshold of an infectious disease. (2)

c) Give TWO examples of situations where herd immunity to an infectious disease cannot be established, and explain why in each case. (4)

3 a) By what means does antigenic variation arise in a population of a pathogenic microorganism? (1)

b) Explain why at-risk individuals need to be vaccinated against influenza every year. (2)

4 Decide whether each of the following statements is true or false and then use T or F to indicate your choice. Where a statement is false, give the word that should have been used in place of the word in bold print. (4)

a) The more **virulent** a pathogen, the higher the percentage of the population that needs to be vaccinated to establish herd immunity.

b) The creation of herd immunity is particularly important in **sparsely** populated environments.

c) Some pathogens can change their **antibodies** and evade the effect of the host's immunological memory.

d) An **adjuvant** is a substance mixed with an antigen in a vaccine to enhance the immune response.

Applying Your Knowledge and Skills

1 The data in Table 23.3 refer to the disease pertussis (whooping cough) in a European country.

a) Plot the data as two line graphs on the same sheet of graph paper with one *x*-axis and two *y*-axes. (4)

b) i) During which years were there 22 000 notifications of the disease?

ii) What was the percentage uptake of the vaccine in 1982? (2)

Year	Number of notifications of disease	Uptake of vaccine (%)
1965	34 000	No vaccine available
1967	31 000	No vaccine available
1969	32 000	80
1971	28 000	80
1973	29 000	80
1975	30 000	40
1977	48 000	32
1979	35 000	44
1981	28 000	54
1983	25 000	58
1985	22 000	64
1987	15 000	74
1989	31 000	78
1991	13 000	84
1993	4 000	86
1995	1 000	90

Table 23.3

→

c) i) Describe the pattern of uptake of vaccine during years 1973–77.
ii) What effect did this have on incidence of the disease? (2)

d) i) Describe the pattern of uptake of vaccine during years 1977–92.
ii) In general, what effect did this have on incidence of the disease? (2)

e) i) Which year required the introduction of a new vaccine for pertussis?
ii) Suggest why. (2)

2 Table 23.4 shows the immunisation schedule recommended for children in the UK.

a) How many doses of i) pertussis vaccine, ii) pneumococcal conjugate vaccine would be received by a person who completes the schedule? (2)

b) A child who has completed the full schedule would have received a total of five doses of vaccine against which diseases? (1)

c) Of which vaccine(s) would the same child have received fewest injections? (1)

3 The graphs in Figure 23.7 show the death rates in a European country for two diseases.

Age	Vaccine	Number of injections
2 months	Diphtheria + tetanus + pertussis + polio + hib	1
	Pneumococcal conjugate	1
3 months	Diphtheria + tetanus + pertussis + polio + hib	1
	Meningitis C	1
4 months	Diphtheria + tetanus + pertussis + polio + hib	1
	Pneumococcal conjugate	1
	Meningitis C	1
12–13 months	Measles + mumps + rubella	1
	Pneumococcal conjugate	1
	Meningitis C + hib	1
3–5 years	Diphtheria + tetanus + pertussis + polio	1
	Measles + mumps + rubella	1
12–13 years (girls only)	Human papillomavirus (HPV)	3
13–18 years	Diphtheria + tetanus + polio	1

Table 23.4

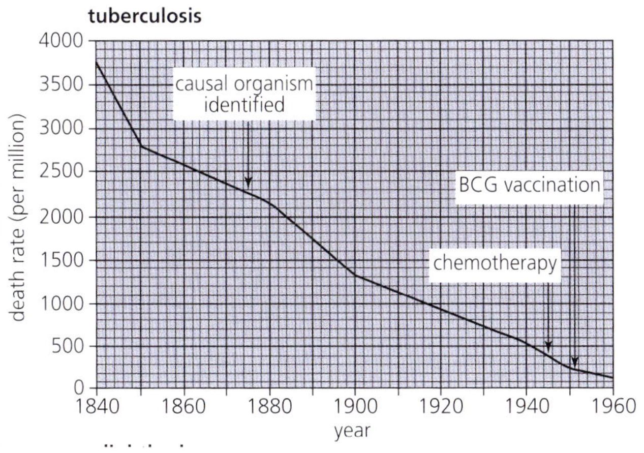

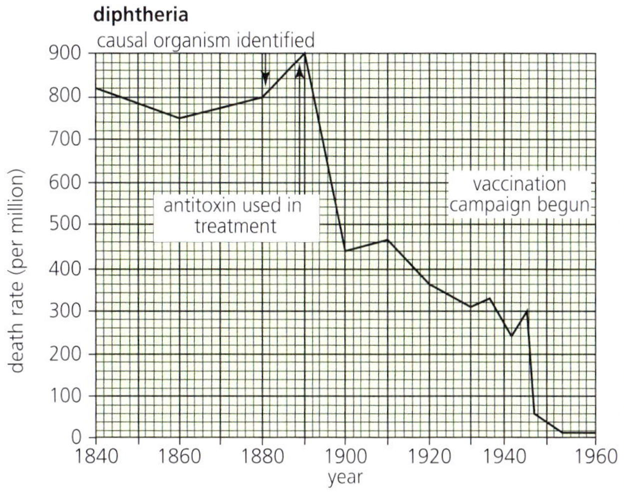

Figure 23.7

a) For which disease did an early drop in death rate occur:
   i) as a result of medical intervention?
   ii) in the absence of medical intervention? (2)
b) Name TWO factors that could account for the decline in death rate from a disease in the absence of medical intervention. (2)
c) i) By how many times was the death rate from tuberculosis greater in 1850 than in 1930?
   ii) Compared with the death rate from diphtheria in 1890, what percentage reduction had occurred by 1920?
   iii) In which year did 2 people per 1000 die of tuberculosis?
   iv) How many people per 1000 died of diphtheria in 1880? (4)
d) A rise in the number of cases of tuberculosis was recorded during 2009 among homeless people in Britain. Suggest why. (1)

4 Each graph in Figure 23.8 shows the number of reported cases of smallpox in a particular country over a period of time.
a) Which country is:
   i) developing?
   ii) developed?
   iii) Give a reason for your choice of answers. (2)
b) At the start of the vaccination campaign in each country, medical experts suspected that the system of reporting had been inadequate and that many cases had previously gone unreported. In what way do the data in the graphs provide evidence to support this view? (2)
c) i) What was the long-term effect of the vaccination campaign in each case?
   ii) Why have scientists been unable, so far, to repeat this success story with a vaccine for malaria? (2)

5 Read the passage and answer the questions that follow it.
Each influenza virus particle contains a genome composed of eight genes (segments), some of which code for antigenic surface proteins. The three types of influenza virus (A, B and C) that exist differ in the makeup of their genome and in the structure of their surface proteins. Type A infects humans and many other animals including pigs, ducks and chickens. Types B and C infect humans but not pigs, ducks or chickens.

Variation in the structure of its surface antigens enables virus type A to evade the host's immune system. This antigenic variation arises in the following two ways:

- by *antigenic drift* resulting from natural mutations that occur continuously and alter the viral genotype
- by *antigenic shift* resulting much less frequently when the genetic material from two different strains of the virus combine to form a new strain.

Figure 23.9 shows an antigenic shift in influenza virus type A that occurred in 1957. A human strain of virus type A and an avian (bird) strain of virus type A infected the same host cell simultaneously. This resulted in the formation of a new variant with a

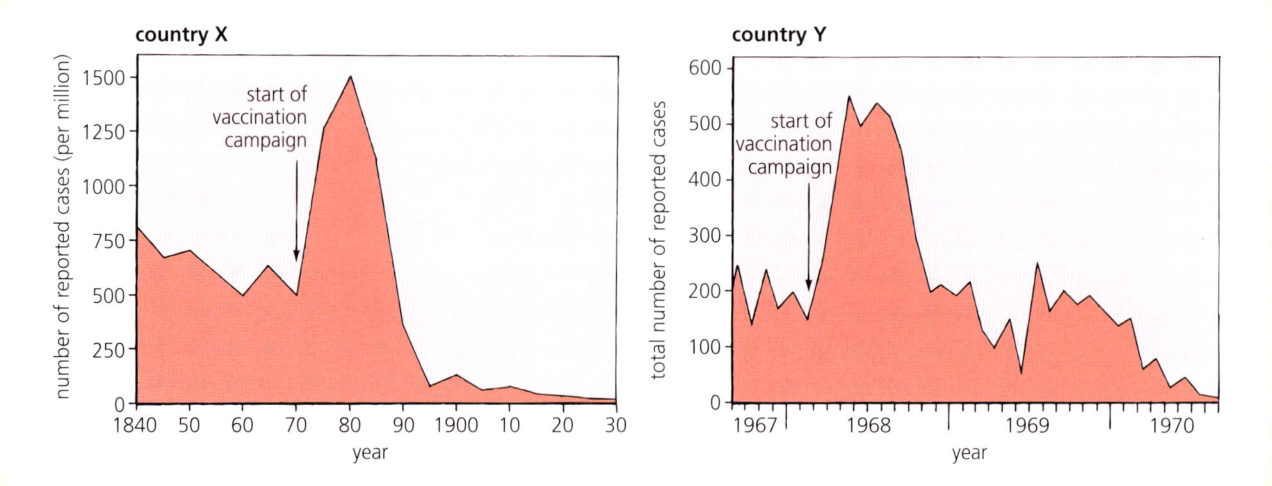

Figure 23.8

combination of genetic material and surface antigens different from the original strains. The new strain was so successful that it caused a pandemic called Asian flu. Scientists agree that it is only a matter of time until antigenic shift results in the production of another highly virulent strain of influenza with the potential to cause a new pandemic.

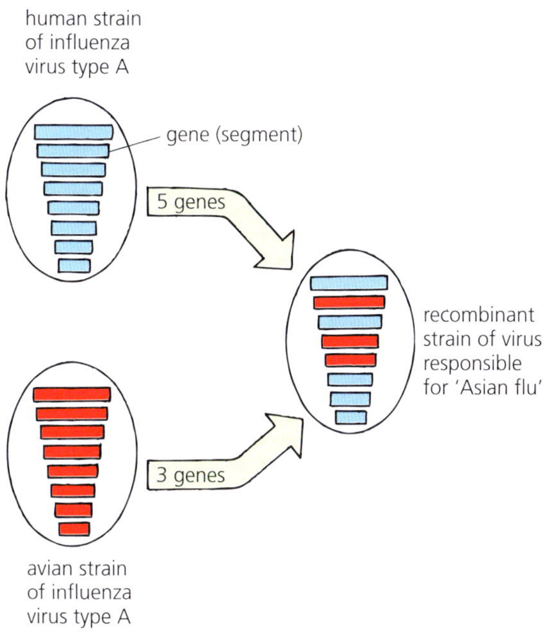

Figure 23.9

a) What is the difference between antigenic shift and antigenic drift? (2)

b) Copy and complete the following paragraph using the answers that follow it. (4)

A new influenza ______ is needed every year because all the strains of the ______ are continuously undergoing genetic ______ as a result of ______. Therefore one or more ______ strains appear each year able to resist ______ that blocked the ______ by the ______ viral strain.

(antibodies, drift, infection, mutation, new, previous, vaccine, virus)

c) Choose the answer that correctly completes the following statement. (1)

The new strain of virus formed by antigenic shift differs from the original strain in:

A genotype only **B** phenotype only

C genotype and phenotype. (1)

d) Antigenic drift affects influenza virus types A, B and C but antigenic shift only affects virus type A. Explain why. (2)

e) Using coloured pencils, copy and complete Figure 23.10, which shows how the type A influenza virus that caused the 1968 Hong Kong flu pandemic arose. (3)

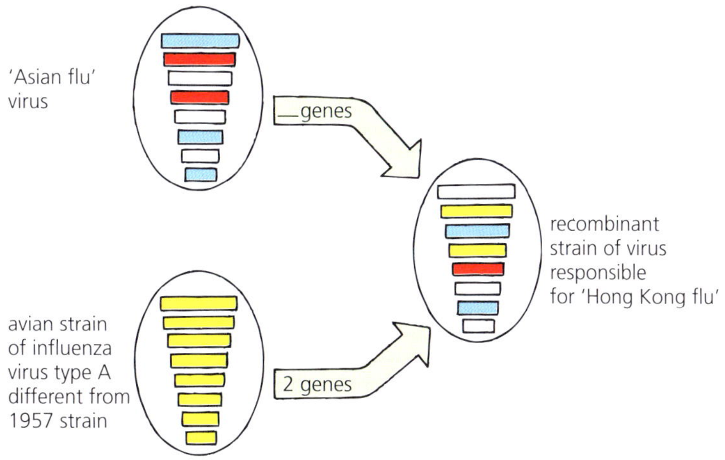

Figure 23.10

24 Clinical trials of vaccines and drugs

Clinical trials

Like other new pharmaceutical medicines, vaccines must be subjected to **clinical trials** on humans to establish that they are **safe** and **effective**. Only then can they be licensed for use.

Protocol for clinical trial

Before a clinical trial is carried out, the potential treatment undergoes extensive testing on cells and on animals in the laboratory. If the new treatment works on them, approval for the next stage is sought from the regulatory authority. This group checks that the clinical trial's proposed design involving humans matches international **protocol** (a procedural method whose design and implementation meet certain agreed standards).

Phases in the clinical trial

Once the protocol has been approved, testing on humans can take place. The three phases that make up a clinical trial are shown in Figure 24.1.

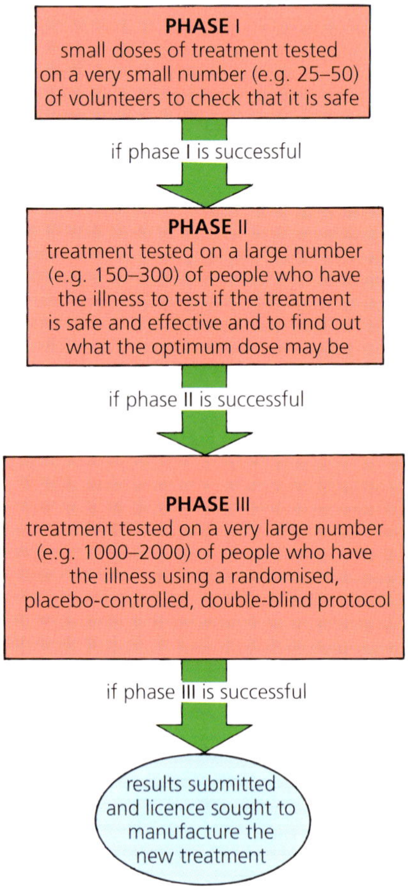
PHASE I
small doses of treatment tested on a very small number (e.g. 25–50) of volunteers to check that it is safe
if phase I is successful
PHASE II
treatment tested on a large number (e.g. 150–300) of people who have the illness to test if the treatment is safe and effective and to find out what the optimum dose may be
if phase II is successful
PHASE III
treatment tested on a very large number (e.g. 1000–2000) of people who have the illness using a randomised, placebo-controlled, double-blind protocol
if phase III is successful
results submitted and licence sought to manufacture the new treatment

Figure 24.1 Phases in a clinical trial

Design of phase III

In phase III of the trial, the target population is split into two groups – those in the **test group** who will receive the treatment and those in the **control group** who will not. The protocol employed at this stage is:

- placebo-controlled
- double-blind
- randomised.

Placebo effect

Instead of the treatment, the members of the control group are given a **placebo**. This is a 'sham' treatment that takes the same form as the real treatment except that it lacks the active ingredient being tested. This procedure is carried out to assess the **placebo effect**, that is the effect from receiving the treatment that does *not* depend on the active ingredient in the real treatment. For example, some patients receiving the placebo may show an improvement in their condition.

This could be a result of the psychological effect of:

- thinking that they were receiving the real treatment
- receiving expert attention from health care staff
- expecting the treatment to be effective.

The use of the placebo allows a **valid comparison** to be made between the test group and the control group to assess the effect of the new treatment. If the control group had not been given the placebo, then there would be no way of knowing how many members of the group receiving the real treatment showed improvement in their condition for one of the above 'placebo effect' reasons and not as a result of the active ingredient present in the new treatment itself.

Double-blind trial

A **blind trial** is one in which the human subjects do not know whether they are receiving the active treatment or the placebo. A **double-blind trial** is one in which neither the subjects nor the doctors know who is receiving what.

A double-blind trial is used at phase III to **eliminate bias** (an irrational preference or prejudice). For example, if the trial was not double-blind, then a doctor's belief in the value of the new treatment could, consciously or subconsciously, affect their behaviour towards a patient if they knew who was receiving which 'treatment'.

Randomisation

Normally the gender, age and other relevant details of each subject taking part in phase III of the trial are entered into a computer. This then puts each person into one or other of the two groups **at random**. This procedure further **eliminates bias**.

In its absence a doctor might subconsciously avoid putting more seriously ill patients into the group receiving the new treatment. Therefore, at the end of the trial the new treatment would appear to be more effective than it really was because the members of the test group would have begun in better health than those in the control group.

Experimental error

The computer also ensures that the composition of the two groups is as **similar** as possible. Figure 24.2 shows this process in a very simple way. In the test population about to be split up, there are more females than males. The computer ensures that this difference is reflected in the two groups formed. Similarly, among males there are more older than younger subjects. Again this difference is maintained in the two groups formed and so on. This process reduces **experimental error** to a minimum.

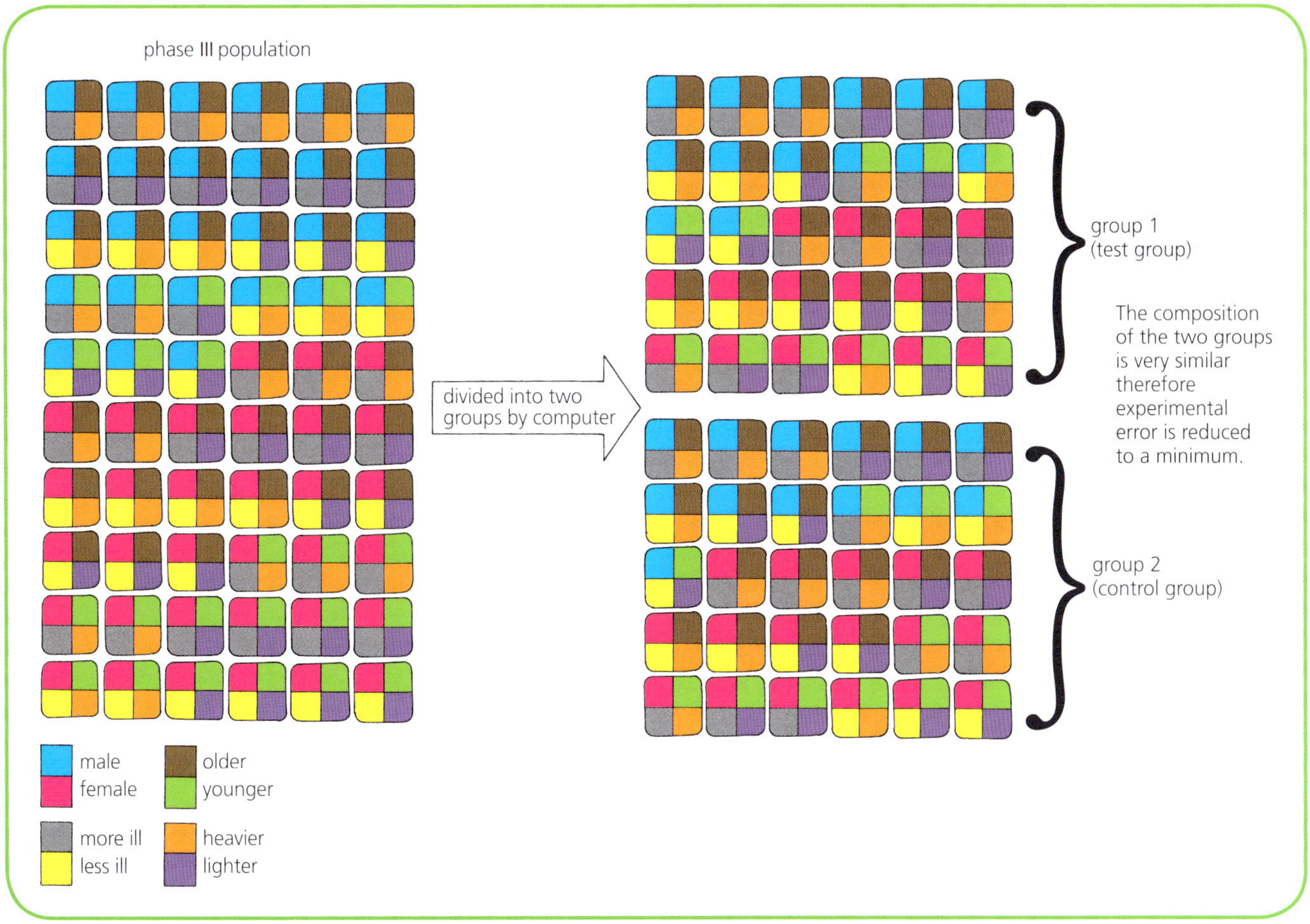

Figure 24.2 Using a computer to form test and control groups

If the process were not adopted, one group might receive, for example, an atypically large number of older subjects who are heavier in weight and more seriously ill. This could invalidate the results. Experimental error is also reduced by using a very **large sample** population. (The patient in Figure 24.3 has completely misunderstood the reasons for the protocol adopted in a clinical trial.)

Statistical analysis

It is also important to use a very large population of patients at phase III so that the results obtained can be subjected to **statistical analysis** with confidence. The results for the two groups can then be compared to find out if significant differences exist between them that indicate that the new treatment is effective. If so, the researchers would then seek a licence to manufacture it.

Figure 24.3 A misunderstanding

Related Activity

Examining a graph of clinical trial results

Figure 24.4 shows the results from a phase III clinical trial on a new to drug for the relief of migraine. This bar chart includes **error bars**. These allow a comparison to be made between the results of the various treatments to determine if they are **significantly different** from one another. If the error bars (based on 95% level of confidence) do not overlap, the difference between the results of the two treatments being compared is regarded as being significant.

In this case, it can be seen that the new drug's upper error bar does not overlap with the lower error bar of the earlier drug. This shows that, in this trial, the new drug was more effective than its predecessor. The results also show that both drugs were more effective than the placebo and that the placebo was no more effective than no treatment. (Also see Appendix 3 for further information on error bars and significant difference.)

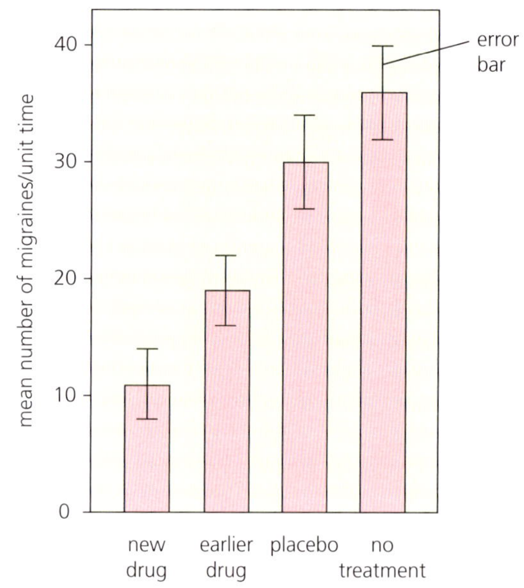

Figure 24.4 Graph of results of clinical trial

Testing Your Knowledge

1 Copy and complete Table 24.1. (6)

Feature of design of clinical trial	Reason for inclusion of design feature
Randomised	
Double-blind	
Placebo-controlled	

Table 24.1

2 With reference to the test population used in a clinical trial, identify TWO practices employed to reduce experimental error to a minimum. (2)

Applying Your Knowledge and Skills

1 Read the passage and answer the questions that follow it.

Clinical trials of a new drug

A large pharmaceutical company designed a new drug, Q, to treat moderate-to-severe allergic asthma in patients whose condition was barely or inadequately controlled by inhaled corticosteroids. During the development process, the company ran a clinical trial.

Phase I involved trying out drug Q on a small number of healthy volunteers who received financial incentives. In phase II, Q was administered to a large number of unpaid people with asthma who continued to use their inhalers when necessary. Phase III took the form of a placebo-controlled trial involving a very large number of people with asthma who continued to inhale corticosteroids as required. Half received drug Q and half received a placebo.

The results of phase III showed that patients treated with Q over a 48-week period experienced significantly fewer asthma attacks and made much less use of their inhalers than the control group. At the end of the trial, 45% of patients receiving Q were able to discontinue steroid treatment compared with 7% of the placebo group. The results also indicated that Q was well tolerated and that the frequency of adverse effects was low and similar to that of the control group.

a) Give THREE differences between the phase I and phase II stages of the clinical trial described in the passage. (3)

b) What is the reason for including the control group in phase III? (2)

c) What is the evidence in the passage that drug Q is 'fit for purpose'? (2)

d) i) What is a *placebo*?

ii) Suggest why 7% of the placebo group were able to discontinue the use of inhaled corticosteroids at the end of the phase III clinical trial. (2)

e) i) In general, would drug Q be better as an addition or an alternative to inhaled corticosteroids for people with allergic asthma?

ii) Justify your choice of answer. (2)

f) Elderly people consume more than one third of all the drugs prescribed in the UK, yet they are normally excluded from phase I of a clinical trial of a new drug. Suggest TWO possible reasons for this apparent discrimination. (2)

2 In some placebo-controlled, clinical trials, the phase III test population is divided at random into three groups, as follows:

- the natural history group **(N)** who receive no treatment of any kind and whose condition is allowed to run its natural course
- the placebo group **(P)** who receive a placebo that convincingly simulates the actual drug but lacks the active ingredient
- the active group **(A)** who receive the drug containing the active ingredient.

→

Complete the blanks in the following statements using the letters **N**, **P** or **A**.

a) The extent of the placebo effect is indicated by the difference in results between __ and __. (1)

b) The effectiveness of the drug's active ingredient is indicated by the difference in results between __ and __. (1)

c) The overall effect of the treatment, the drug and its active ingredient is indicated by the difference in results between __ and __. (1)

3 Table 24.2 shows the results for phase II of a clinical trial on an influenza vaccine.

a) Present the data as a bar chart, including error bars. (See Appendix 3 for help.) (4)

b) i) Based on these results, should this clinical trial proceed to phase III?

ii) Explain your answer. (2)

Time from vaccination (days)	Relative viral load in blood plasma (units)	
	Vaccine group	Control group
1	39 ± 6	51 ± 8
2	38 ± 6	48 ± 7
3	23 ± 5	31 ± 5
4	12 ± 3	18 ± 4

Table 24.2

What You Should Know Chapters 23–24

antigens	experimental	poor
bias	herd	randomised
clinical	host	rejected
comparison	immunity	threshold
density	influenza	toxin
effectiveness	mass	vaccination
evade	non-immune	virulence

Table 24.2 Word bank for Chapters 23–24

1 Weakened or altered forms of an infectious pathogen or its _____ are used as _____. These are administered to people by _____ so that they will develop _____ to the disease but not develop the disease.

2 Within a population where most individuals are immune to an infectious disease, vulnerable _____ individuals are protected from it by _____ immunity.

3 The percentage of immune individuals in a population above which a disease no longer persists is called the herd immunity _____. It depends on the pathogen's _____, the vaccine's effectiveness and the population's _____.

4 Herd immunity can be difficult to establish if the country is too _____ to afford _____ vaccination or if the vaccine is _____ by a large percentage of the population.

5 By altering their antigens, some pathogens are able to _____ the immune responses made by their _____.

6 Antigenic variation in the _____ virus makes it necessary to keep developing new vaccines.

7 The safety and _____ of new vaccines must be established by _____ trials before they can be licensed for use.

8 A clinical trial is _____ and double-blind to eliminate _____ and placebo-controlled to allow a valid _____ to be made. _____ error is reduced by using a very large number of people.

Appendix 1

The genetic code

First letter of triplet		Second letter of triplet: A	G	T	C	Third letter of triplet
	A	AAA	AGA	ATA	ACA	A
	A	AAG	AGG	ATG	ACG	G
	A	AAT	AGT	ATT	ACT	T
	A	AAC	AGC	ATC	ACC	C
	G	GAA	GGA	GTA	GCA	A
	G	GAG	GGG	GTG	GCG	G
	G	GAT	GGT	GTT	GCT	T
	G	GAC	GGC	GTC	GCC	C
	T	TAA	TGA	TTA	TCA	A
	T	TAG	TGG	TTG	TCG	G
	T	TAT	TGT	TTT	TCT	T
	T	TAC	TGC	TTC	TCC	C
	C	CAA	CGA	CTA	CCA	A
	C	CAG	CGG	CTG	CCG	G
	C	CAT	CGT	CTT	CCT	T
	C	CAC	CGC	CTC	CCC	C

Table Ap 1.1 The DNA bases grouped into 64 (4^3) triplets
(A = adenine, G = guanine, T = thymine, C = cytosine)

Abbreviation	Amino acid
ala	alanine
arg	arginine
asp	aspartic acid
asn	asparagine
cys	cysteine
glu	glutamic acid
gln	glutamine
gly	glycine
his	histidine
ile	isoleucine
leu	leucine
lys	lysine
met	methionine
phe	phenylalanine
pro	proline
ser	serine
thr	threonine
trp	tryptophan
tyr	tyrosine
val	valine

Table Ap 1.2 Key to amino acids

Appendix 2

Box plots

The data in Table Ap 2.1 refer to the birth weights of babies in three different groups. Each group contains 15 babies selected at random from a large number of individuals. The mothers of group A were non-smokers, those of group B smoked 20 cigarettes per day while pregnant and those of group C smoked 40 cigarettes per day while pregnant. It is difficult to compare the variability in birth weight between the three groups from the data table alone.

A **box plot** is a way of presenting information that allows differences between groups, sets, populations, etc. to be compared easily. Each box plot shows the **median**, which is the **central value** in the series of values when they are arranged in order.

Baby number	Birth weight of baby (kg)		
	Group A	Group B	Group C
15	3.98	3.71	3.42
14	3.75	3.53	3.30
13	3.72	3.49	3.29
12	3.69	3.45	3.24
11	3.62	3.32	3.20
10	3.55	3.27	3.18
9	3.46	3.18	3.15
8	3.38	3.10	3.01
7	3.24	3.06	2.96
6	3.15	2.97	2.92
5	3.12	2.90	2.88
4	3.04	2.86	2.84
3	3.00	2.82	2.78
2	2.96	2.77	2.66
1	2.74	2.53	2.38

Table Ap 2.1

A box plot also displays the **upper quartile** (in this case the value 25% above the median) and the **lower quartile** (the value 25% below the median). The maximum and minimum values are called **upper and lower whiskers**. Figure Ap 2.1 shows how the data for group A are converted into a box plot.

Figure Ap 2.2 (page 289) shows group A's box plot drawn alongside those for groups B and C. The box plots give a clear, visual representation that allows the variability between the three groups to be compared more easily than by studying the table of data alone.

In this case, the box plots show, at a glance, the depressant effect of smoking on the birth weight of babies.

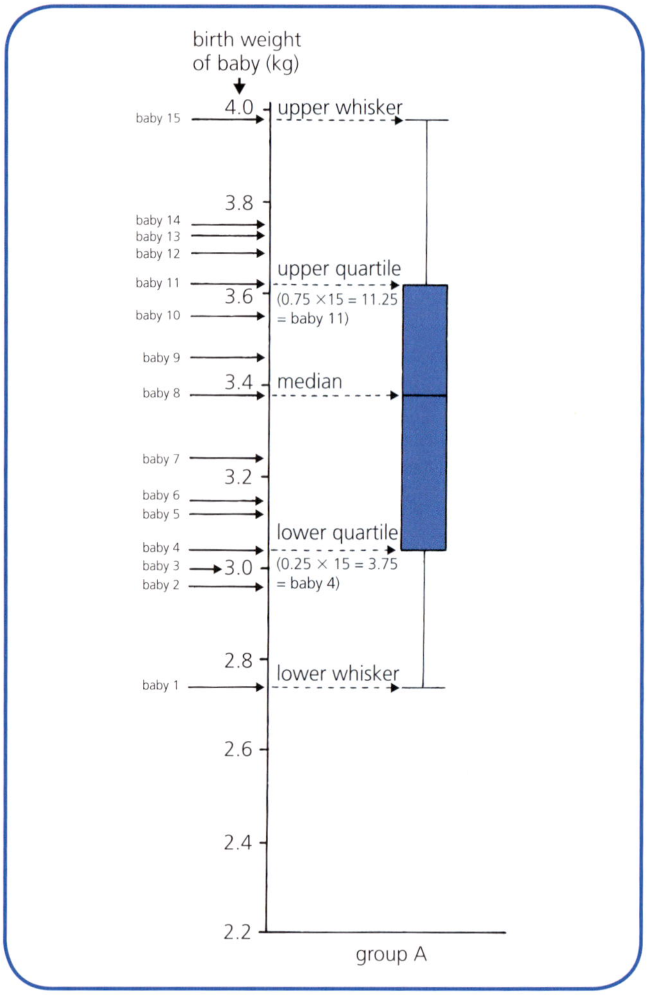

Figure Ap 2.1

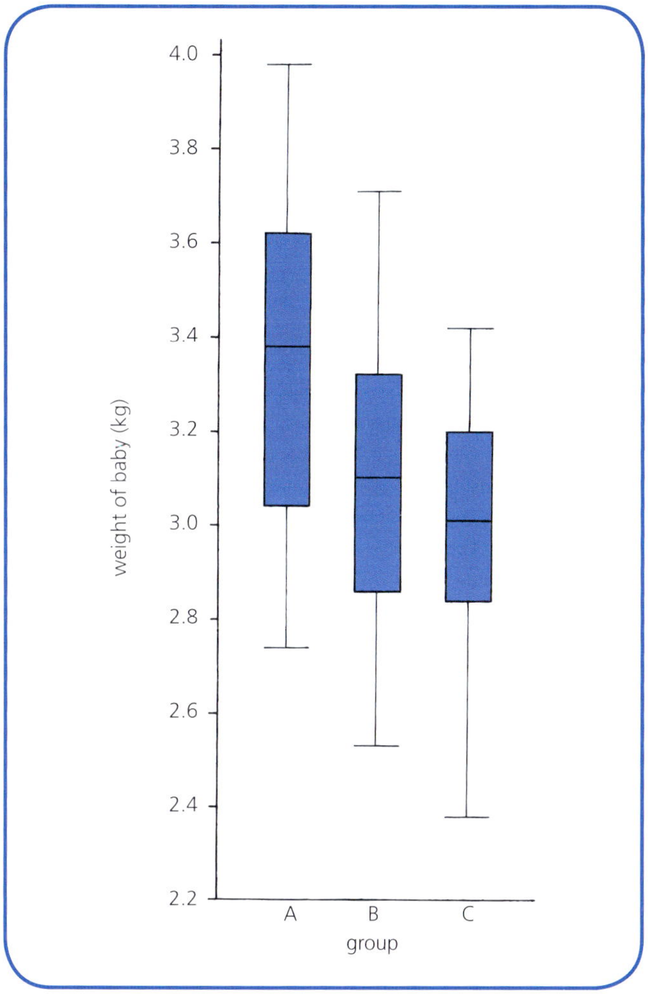

Figure Ap 2.2

Appendix 3

Statistical concepts

A scientist needs to organise the data collected as results from an investigation into a manageable form from which conclusions can be drawn.

Mean

The **mean** is often referred to as the average. It is the most widely used measure of the **central tendency** of a set of data. It is found by adding up all the values obtained and dividing them by the total number of values. For example, for the two populations of British miners shown in the scatter graphs in Figure Ap 3.1 (page 290), the mean for population A = 11 830/70 = 169 cm and the mean for population B = 12 530/70 = 179 cm.

Range

The **range** is the difference between the two most extreme values in a set of data. For example, for population A the range = 180 – 158 = 22 cm and for population B the range = 192 – 164 = 28 cm.

Standard deviation

Standard deviation is a measure of the spread of individual data values around their mean and shows how much variation from the mean exists. A normal distribution of results can be divided into intervals of standard deviation as shown in Figure Ap 3.2 (page 290). 68% of the values fall within plus or minus one standard

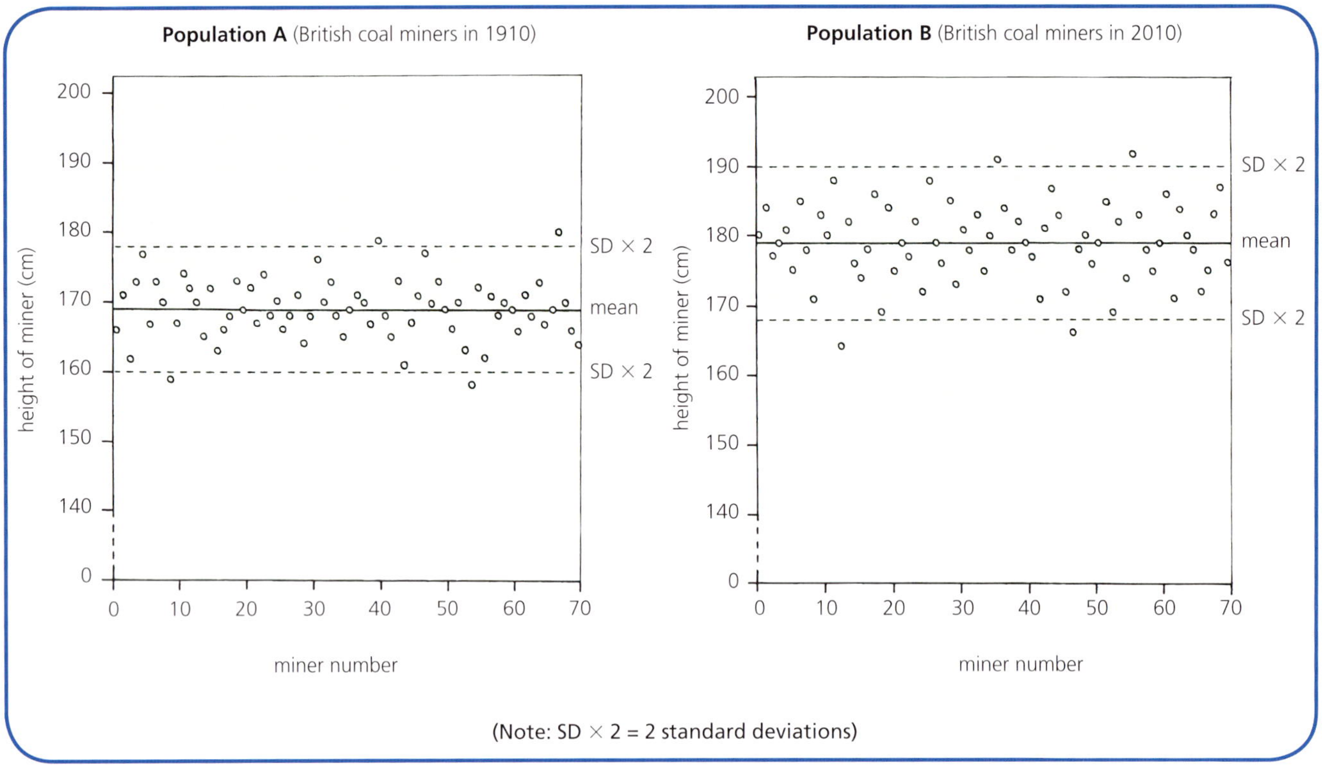

Figure Ap 3.1

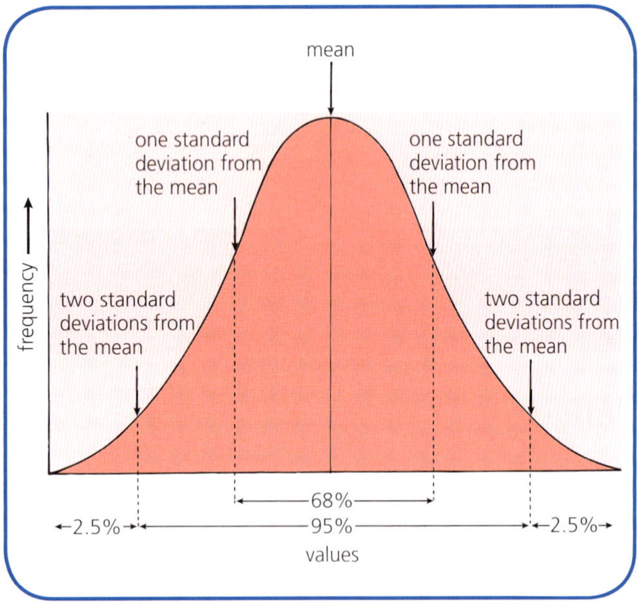

Figure Ap 3.2

deviation from the mean; 95% of the values fall within plus or minus two standard deviations from the mean.

The standard deviation of a set of data is calculated using a mathematical formula (often with the aid of an appropriate calculator or computer software). The deviation (as two standard deviations above or below the mean) for population A in Figure Ap 3.1 equals 9 cm. This low level of deviation reflects the clustering of the values around the mean, with 95% of values lying within the range 160–178 cm.

The deviation (as two standard deviations above or below the mean) for population B in Figure Ap 3.1 (page 291) equals 11 cm. This higher level of deviation reflects the wider spread of the values around the mean, with 95% of values lying within the range 168–190 cm.

Quality of data

In a properly designed scientific investigation, several **replicates** of each treatment are set up to allow for experimental error. These replicates produce results with a **central tendency** around the **mean**. A set of results that are **clustered** around the mean indicates data of **high quality**. A comparable set of results (from a replicate of the same treatment) that are widespread are of lower quality.

Significant difference

In biology, an experiment is carried out to test a hypothesis. Once results have been obtained, the scientist needs to know whether these data (which rarely conform exactly to the expected outcome)

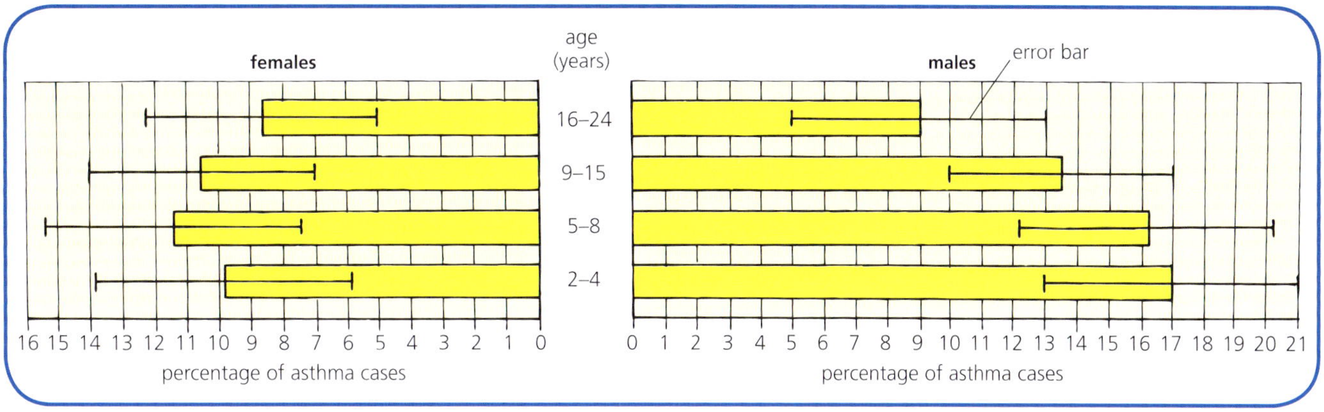

Figure Ap 3.3

support the hypothesis or not. A **significance test** (a type of statistical analysis) can be used to find out if the observed differences between two sets of data are **statistically significant** or simply the result of **chance**.

Error bars

When a bar chart of mean values of data is drawn, it is often important to be able to show variability on the chart. This can be done using **error bars**. These are lines that extend outside and inside each bar and indicate how far from the mean value the true error-free value is likely to be. Error bars can be based on aspects of variability such as 95% level of confidence and standard deviation.

Figure Ap 3.3 shows a bar chart of the results from a survey carried out on several thousand young people in a country to estimate the incidence of asthma. Each bar represents a mean value with a 95% level of confidence whose range is indicated by error bars. Based on the information in the bar chart, health care experts could be 95% confident that the percentage number of asthma cases for the whole population would be between 13% and 21% for 2–4-year-old males, between 7 and 14% for 9–15-year-old females, etc.

Error bars also allow a comparison to be made between two means to determine if they are **significantly different** from one another. If their error bars (based on 95% level of confidence) do not overlap, the difference between the two means is regarded as being significant.

Figure Ap 3.4 shows a bar chart of the results from Table 12.1 on page 139 of mean concentration of urea in the blood plasma of non-pregnant women (NP), pregnant women (P) and pregnant women with pre-eclampsia (PE). Each bar represents a mean value with its variability indicated by error bars. The mean for PE is seen to be significantly different from those for both NP and P, which are not significantly different from one another.

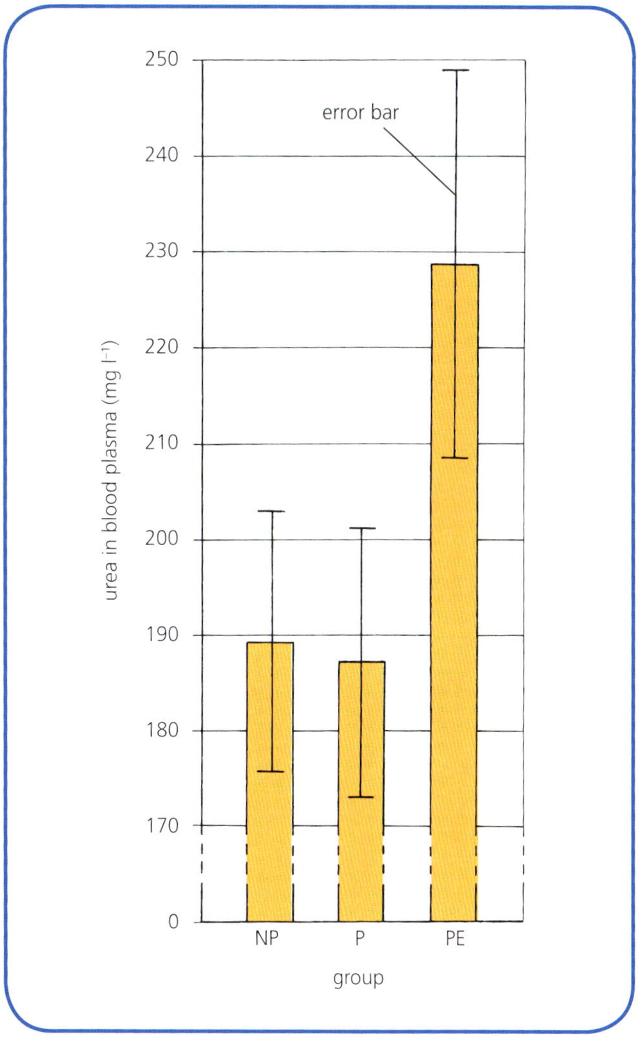

Figure Ap 3.4

Appendix 4

False positives and negatives

A **false positive** is a result that indicates that the outcome of an investigative procedure is a positive result when in reality the outcome for the set of conditions being tested is negative.

A **false negative** is a result that indicates that the outcome of an investigative procedure is a negative result when in reality the outcome for the set of conditions being tested is positive.

Table Ap 4.1 shows data from an investigation into the effectiveness of ultrasound imaging on the antenatal detection of inherited malformations in babies born in a region of the UK.

The results in row 3 of the table are examples of **false positives** because the procedure (screening for malformations) has produced results indicating that these fetuses had inherited malformations when in fact the babies were found to be normal at birth.

The results in row 4 are examples of **false negatives** because the procedure (screening for malformations) has produced results indicating that these fetuses had not inherited malformations when in fact the babies were found at birth to possess them.

Row	Category	Year		
		2001	2005	2009
1	Total number of births	36 433	33 292	29 779
2	Number of babies born with malformations	790	785	762
3	Number of babies reported antenatally as having malformations but normal at birth	151	119	52
4	Number of babies reported antenatally as being normal but born with malformations	487	464	398

Table Ap 4.1

Testing Your Knowledge Answers

Chapter 1 Division and differentiation in human cells

Testing Your Knowledge 1

1 a) The genetic material becomes doubled by replication and is then shared out equally between the two daughter nuclei formed at mitosis. Therefore each cell formed receives an identical copy of the full set of chromosomes. (2)

b) A haploid cell contains a single set of chromosomes whereas a diploid cell contains a double set of chromosomes as matching (homologous) pairs. (2)

c) A cell involved in reproduction. (1)

d) The genetic material in a germline cell becomes doubled by replication and then undergoes meiosis, a form of nuclear division, which results in the formation of four haploid gametes each containing a single set of chromosomes. (2)

2 a) Cellular differentiation is the process by which an unspecialised cell becomes altered and adapted to perform a special function as part of a permanent tissue. (2)

b) It has cilia, which sweep dirt in mucus up and away from the lungs making the cell well suited to its function. (1)

c) During differentiation most genes including those that code for insulin were switched off, so the goblet cell only expresses the genes left switched on that control the characteristics of that type of cell, such as the secretion of mucus. (2)

3 a) They can reproduce themselves while remaining undifferentiated. They can differentiate into specialised cells when required to do so. (2)

b) i) Embryonic and tissue stem cells

ii) Embryonic in an early embryo; tissue in bone marrow (4)

c) Embryonic (1)

Testing Your Knowledge 2

1 a) i) Leukaemia

ii) Bone marrow (2)

b) Parkinson's disease (1)

c) Bone marrow cells can only produce more bone marrow cells (and not nerve cells) because many of their genes are switched off. (2)

2 Some people believe that a human embryo even in its very early stages of development is already a person and that it is morally wrong that it dies when stem cells are extracted from it. (2)

3 They divide uncontrollably and do not respond to regulatory signals. (2)

Chapter 2 Structure and replication of DNA

Testing Your Knowledge 1

1 a) i) 4

ii) Adenine (A), thymine (T), guanine (G) and cytosine (C) (3)

b) Hydrogen (1)

c) Each base can only join up with one other type of base: A with T and G with C. (1)

2 a) i) and ii) See Figure AnT 2.1. (2)

b) Antiparallel (1)

3 a) Double helix (1)

b) i) Base pairs

ii) Sugar–phosphate backbones (2)

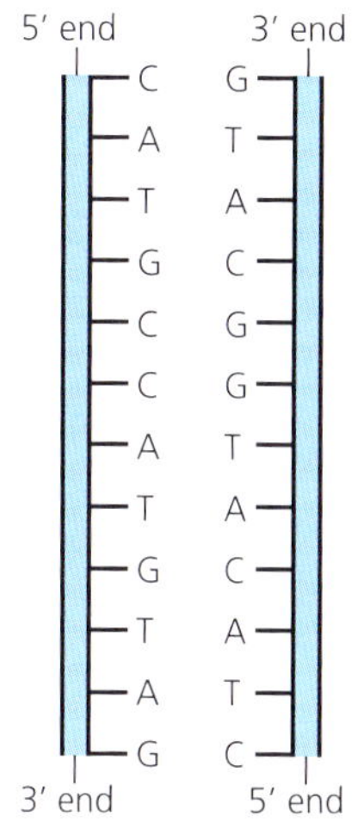

Figure AnT 2.1

Testing Your Knowledge 2

1 a) T (1)
   b) F – cytosine (1)
   c) F – thymine (1)
   d) F – hydrogen (1)
   e) T (1)

2 1 = b), 2 = f), 3 = e), 4 = c), 5 = a), 6 = d) (5)

3 a) DNA, the four types of nucleotide, appropriate enzymes and an energy supply (4)
   b) DNA replication ensures that an exact copy of an individual's genetic information is passed on from cell to cell during growth and from generation to generation during reproduction. (2)

4 a) Many copies of a DNA sample. (1)
   b) A piece of single-stranded DNA complementary to a target sequence at the end of the DNA strand to be replicated. (2)
   c) To break hydrogen bonds between base pairs and separate the DNA strands. (1)
   d) To allow the primer to bind to its target sequence. (1)
   e) It is heat-tolerant. (1)

Chapter 3 Gene expression

Testing Your Knowledge 1

1 A molecule of DNA is double-stranded and contains deoxyribose sugar and the base thymine whereas a molecule of RNA is single-stranded and contains ribose sugar and the base uracil. (3)

2 a) They differ by the sequence of the bases in their DNA. (1)
   b) 3 (1)

3 a) See Figure AnT 3.1. (2)

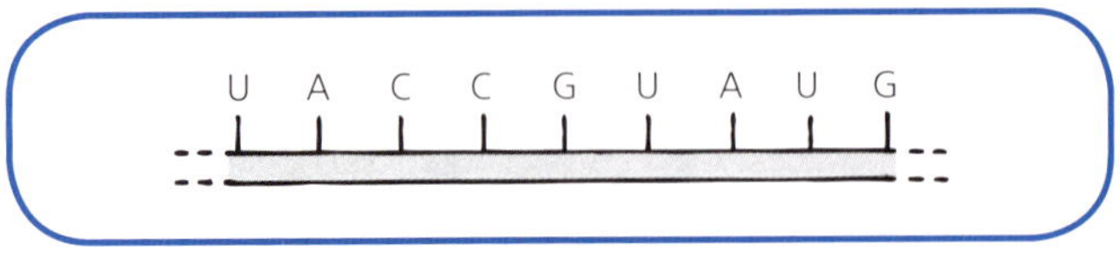

Figure AnT 3.1

   b) RNA polymerase (1)

4 a) An exon is a coding region of DNA; an intron is a non-coding region. (1)
   b) Introns (1)
   c) Splicing (1)

Testing Your Knowledge 2

1 a) 1 (1)
   b) An amino acid molecule (1)

2 a) One of many tiny, roughly spherical structures in a cell's cytoplasm (where translation of genetic information into protein occurs). (1)
   b) i) 3
      ii) To a codon on mRNA (2)
   c) Peptide (1)
   d) It is discharged from the ribosome and reused. (2)

3 a) See Table AnT 3.1. (2)

Stage of synthesis	Site in cell
Formation of primary transcript of mRNA	Nucleus
Modification of primary transcript of mRNA	Nucleus
Collection of amino acid by tRNA	Cytoplasm
Formation of codon–anticodon links	Ribosomes

Table AnT 3.1

   b) Ribosomal RNA (rRNA) (1)

4 a) Codons (1)
   b) Transcription (1)
   c) Intron (1)
   d) Anticodons (1)
   e) Ribosome (1)

5 a) 20 (1)
   b) Polypeptide (1)
   c) The sequence of bases in DNA (1)
   d) Arranged in long parallel strands or folded and coiled into a spherical shape. (2)

Chapter 4 Mutations

Testing Your Knowledge

1 A mutation is a change in structure or composition of an organism's genome. A mutant is an individual or allele affected by a mutation. (2)

2 a) Substitution, insertion and deletion (3)
   b) i) Insertion, deletion
      ii) Substitution (2)

3 a) Deletion (1)
   b) Translocation (1)
   c) Duplication (1)
   d) Adverse (1)

Chapter 5 Human genomics

Testing Your Knowledge

1 a) The sequence of nucleotide bases all the way along the DNA of a genome. (1)
  b) It can be used to relate information about genes to their functions. (1)
2 a) It is a fusion of molecular biology, statistical analysis and computer technology. (1)
  b) They would look for protein-coding sequences that were the same as those present in known genes and for sequences lacking stop codons. (2)
3 a) It is the branch of genomics involved in sequencing the genomes of individuals and analysing them using bioinformatics tools. (2)
  b) They will be prescribed with the most suitable drug and the correct dosage as indicated by their personal genomic sequencing profile. (2)

Chapter 6 Metabolic pathways

Testing Your Knowledge 1

1 a) Metabolism is the collective term for the thousands of enzyme-controlled chemical reactions that occur in a living cell. (2)
  b) One breaks down complex molecules to simpler ones and normally releases energy; the other builds up simpler molecules into complex ones and consumes energy. (2)
2 They lower the activation energy needed for the chemical reaction to proceed. They speed up the reaction. They remain unchanged at the end of the reaction. (3)
3 a) The chemical structure of the protein of which the enzyme is made and the bonding between its component amino acids. (1)
  b) The chemical attraction between them. (1)
  c) Induced fit (1)
  d) The shape of the active site ensures that the reactants are correctly orientated so that the reaction can take place. This is made possible by the fact that the enzyme decreases the activation energy needed by the reactants to reach the transition state. (3)
4 a) Quantity of chemical change that occurs per unit time. (1)
  b) i) Initially it causes an increase in rate but at higher concentrations no further increase in rate occurs.
    ii) At low concentrations of substrate there are not enough molecules of substrate to occupy all the active sites on the enzyme. At higher concentrations of substrate, all the active sites on the enzyme molecules are occupied. (4)

Testing Your Knowledge 2

1 a) Its molecular shape is similar to that of the substrate. (1)
  b) i) It brings about an increase in the rate of the reaction.
    ii) Substrate molecules eventually outnumber those of the competitive inhibitor causing more and more sites on the enzyme molecules to become occupied with substrate rather than inhibitor. (3)
2 Non-competitive. (1)
3 a) i) P
    ii) Q (2)
  b) i) Q
    ii) R (2)
  c) Left to right (1)
  d) i) If a high concentration of R built up some of it would bind to some molecules of enzyme X and slow down the conversion of P to Q.
    ii) It keeps the pathway under finely tuned control. (3)

Chapter 7 Cellular respiration

Testing Your Knowledge

1 a) Adenosine triphosphate (1)
  b) ATP has three phosphate groups whereas ADP has two. (1)
  c) ADP + P_i + energy → ATP (2)
2 a) Two molecules of ATP are used during the energy investment phase so the net gain is only 2 ATP. (1)
  b) As soon as oxaloacetate is formed, it combines with acetyl CoA to form citrate. Therefore there is never very much present at any given moment. (1)
3 a) G (1)
  b) E (1)

c) C (1)
d) E (1)
e) G (1)
f) G and C (1)
g) C (1)
h) G, C and E (1)

Chapter 8 Energy systems in muscle cells

Testing Your Knowledge

1 **ATP** is used to transfer energy to cellular processes (such as protein **synthesis** and transmission of nerve **impulses**) that **require** energy. (4)

2 Normally ATP molecules are being regenerated from ADP and P_i at the same rate as ATP molecules are undergoing breakdown to release energy. Therefore the quantity remains fairly constant. (2)

3 See Table AnT 8.1. (3)

Feature	Fast-twitch muscle fibre	Slow-twitch muscle fibre
Major storage fuels used	Glycogen	Fats
Relative number of mitochondria	Small	Large
Relative concentration of myoglobin	Low	High

Table AnT 8.1

Chapter 9 Gamete production and fertilisation and Chapter 10 Hormonal control of reproduction

Testing Your Knowledge

1 a) i) Seminiferous tubules
ii) Testosterone (2)
b) i) Seminal vesicles
ii) It supplies sperm with the energy they need for the mobility that enables them to reach and fertilise ova. (2)

2 a) Follicle (1)
b) Corpus luteum (1)

3 See Table AnT 10.1. (8)

Hormone	Site of production	One function of the hormone
FSH	Pituitary gland	Stimulates the development and maturation of each follicle
LH	Pituitary gland	Brings about development of the corpus luteum
Oestrogen	Ovary	Stimulates secretion of LH by the pituitary gland
Progesterone	Ovary	Promotes vascularisation of the endometrium

Table AnT 10.1

4 a) F – follicular (1)
b) T (1)
c) T (1)
d) F – ovulation (1)
e) F – pituitary (1)
f) T (1)

Chapter 11 Biology of controlling fertility

Testing Your Knowledge

1 a) Men are continuously fertile. This means that sperm are produced at all times throughout any given month. Women, on the other hand, are cyclically fertile. This means that one or more eggs are released and available to be fertilised only during a short period of time in any given month. (2)
b) i) 1–2 days
ii) Thinner consistency of cervical mucus and increase in body temperature. (3)

2 a) It is the introduction of semen into the female reproductive tract by some means other than sexual intercourse. (1)
b) The woman's partner has a low sperm count and several samples need to be collected before use. The woman's partner is sterile and she chooses to receive semen from a donor. (2)

3 a) C, F, D, A, E, B (1)
b) The woman is given hormonal treatment. (1)
c) A = To allow cell division to occur. B = To allow a second attempt at implantation if required. (2)

4 a) Barrier (1)
b) Chemical (1)
c) Endometrium (1)
d) Progesterone (1)
e) Tubal ligation (1)

Chapter 12 Ante- and postnatal screening

Testing Your Knowledge 1

1 It comprises a series of tests used to identify the risk of the fetus having inherited a disorder. (1)

2 a) i) 8–14 weeks
ii) 18–20 weeks (2)
b) A dating scan is used to determine the stage of the pregnancy. An anomaly scan allows the fetus to be checked for serious abnormalities. (2)
c) Ultrasound imaging (1)

3 A screening test detects signs associated with a certain condition which help to assess the degree of risk of the fetus developing the condition. A diagnostic test is definitive in that it produces results that establish for certain whether the fetus is affected by the condition or not. (2)

4 Amniocentesis uses fetal cells from amniotic fluid and is carried out at weeks 14–16 in the pregnancy. Chorionic villus sampling uses cells from the placenta and is performed as early as 8 weeks into the pregnancy. (2)

Testing Your Knowledge 2

1 a) The trait tends to skip generations. The trait is expressed in some of the offspring of a consanguineous marriage such as between cousins. (2)
b) All people with the trait are homozygous recessive. (1)

2 a) Many more males are affected than females (if any). None of the sons of an affected male shows the trait. (2)
b) All people with the trait are homozygous recessive. (1)

3 a) Within a few days of birth, the baby's blood is tested for the presence of excess phenylalanine. (1)
b) In PKU, a mutation leads to the formation of an altered version of an enzyme that is non-functional and unable to convert phenylalanine to tyrosine. (2)
c) They are placed on a restricted diet containing the minimum quantity of phenylalanine needed for normal growth. (1)

Chapter 13 Structure and function of arteries, capillaries and veins

Testing Your Knowledge

1 a) F – jugular (1)
b) T (1)
c) F – artery (1)
d) T (1)
e) F – pulmonary (1)
f) F – vein (1)

2 a) The wall of an artery is thicker than that of a vein. Valves are present in veins but not in arteries. (2)
b) Veins carry blood towards the heart, arteries carry blood away from the heart. (1)

3 a) It is the liquid consisting of plasma and small, dissolved molecules that is squeezed out of capillaries during pressure filtration. (2)
b) Carbon dioxide (1)
c) It is returned to blood capillaries by osmosis and it is absorbed into the lymphatic system via thin-walled lymphatic vessels. (2)

4 a) When the vessels are pressed periodically during muscular contraction, the lymph is pushed along the lymph vessels. (1)
b) Valves (1)
c) Two lymphatic ducts (1)

Chapter 14 Structure and function of the heart

Testing Your Knowledge 1

1 See Table AnT 14.1. (8)

Heart chamber	Type of blood contained	Where it has come from	Where it is going to
Right atrium (RA)	Deoxygenated	Body	RV
Right ventricle (RV)	Deoxygenated	RA	Lungs
Left atrium (LA)	Oxygenated	Lungs	LV
Left ventricle (LV)	Oxygenated	LA	Body

Table AnT 14.1

2 An AV valve is situated between an atrium and a ventricle and prevents backflow of blood from ventricle to atrium. On the other hand, an SL valve is located at the origin of a large heart artery such as the aorta and prevents backflow of blood from the artery into the ventricle. (2)

3 Stroke volume is the volume of blood expelled by each ventricle on contraction. Cardiac output is the volume of blood pumped out of a ventricle per minute. Heart rate (pulse) is the number of heartbeats that occur per minute. (3)

Testing Your Knowledge 2

1 a) Systole means the contraction and diastole the relaxation of the heart during each heartbeat. (2)
b) See Table AnT 12.1. (4)

	Atrial systole	Ventricular systole
State of atrial wall	Contracted	Relaxed
State of ventricular wall	Relaxed	Contracted
State of AV valves	Open	Closed
State of SL valves	Closed	Open

Table AnT 12.1

2 a) i) Sino-atrial node
ii) It initiates electrical impulses which make cardiac muscle cells contract at a certain rate. (2)
b) i) Atrio-ventricular node
ii) Ventricle walls
iii) Ventricular systole (3)

3 a) It is a display on an oscilloscope of the pattern of the heart's electrical activity. (1)
b) i) 3
ii) 2 (2)

4 a) i) Ventricular systole
ii) The blood entering the aorta has just been pumped out of the heart by the ventricle contracting at full force. (2)
b) Sphygmomanometer (1)
c) It is a major risk factor for problems such as coronary heart disease in later life. (1)

Chapter 15 Pathology of cardiovascular disease

Testing Your Knowledge

1 a) It is the formation of plaques called atheromas beneath the endothelium in the walls of arteries. (2)
b) Its wall becomes thicker and loses its elasticity. (2)

2 a) C, A, D, B (1)
b) i) Stroke
ii) Heart attack (2)

3 a) It is a component of cell membranes. (1)
b) i) By being attached to low-density lipoprotein (LDL).
ii) By being attached to high-density lipoprotein (HDL). (2)
c) They inhibit an enzyme essential for the synthesis of cholesterol in liver cells. (1)

4 a) F – narrower (1)
b) F – embolus (1)
c) T (1)
d) F – arteries (1)
e) T (1)

Chapter 16 Blood glucose levels and obesity

Testing Your Knowledge

1 a) i) They take in more glucose than normal.
   ii) Their walls become thicker but weaker. (2)
 b) Retina and kidneys (2)

2 a) i) Insulin
   ii) Glucagon
   iii) Pancreas
   iv) Liver (4)
 b) See Table AnT 16.1. (3)

	Type 1 diabetes	Type 2 diabetes
Typical body mass of person	Normal or underweight	Overweight or obese
Ability of pancreatic cells to produce insulin	Absent	Present
Possible treatment	Insulin and careful diet	Weight loss, diet control and insulin (in some cases)

Table AnT 16.1

 c) i) The capacity of the body to deal with ingested glucose.
   ii) To diagnose diabetes. (2)

3 a) It is a condition characterised by the accumulation of excess body fat relative to lean tissue. (1)
 b) $\text{BMI} = \frac{\text{body mass}}{\text{height}^2}$ (1)
 c) Lose weight and take regular exercise. (2)

Chapter 17 Divisions of the nervous system and neural pathways

Testing Your Knowledge

1 a) Brain and spinal cord (2)
 b) Peripheral nervous system (1)

2 a) A sensory pathway carries nerve impulses from receptors to the CNS; a motor pathway carries nerve impulses away from the CNS to effectors. (2)
 b) A receptor is a sense organ; an effector is a muscle or gland. (2)

3 a) Sympathetic and parasympathetic (2)
 b) i) Sympathetic brings about an increase and parasympathetic a decrease in cardiac output.
   ii) Sympathetic brings about an increase (dilation) and parasympathetic a decrease (constriction) in width of bore of bronchioles. (4)

4 The body becomes aroused ready for 'fight or flight' by the action of the sympathetic nerves. As a result, rate of blood flow to the heart increases, rate of peristalsis decreases and rate of breathing increases. (4)

Chapter 18 Cerebral cortex

Testing Your Knowledge

1 a) i) The right cerebral hemisphere
   ii) The left cerebral hemisphere (1)
 b) i) A bundle of nerve fibres
   ii) It acts as a link between the two cerebral hemispheres, allowing information to be transferred from one to the other. (2)

2 a) Visual, auditory and motor (3)
 b) The visual area receives impulses from the retina and interprets them as images. The auditory area receives impulses from the cochlea and interprets them as sounds. The motor area sends motor impulses to skeletal muscles. (3)

3 Intelligence, personality and imagination. (3)

Chapter 19 Memory

Testing Your Knowledge

1 a) 7 (1)
 b) Limited (1)
 c) 30 seconds (1)
 d) Displacement and decay (2)
 e) Chunking is the organisation of lengthy material into several small pieces called chunks so that they can be memorised, for example, splitting up an eleven-digit phone number into three or four parts. (2)

2 a) Encoding, storage, retrieval (1)
 b) The primacy effect results from rehearsing the first few objects seen and transferring them from the STM to the LTM. The recency effect results from the fact that these objects are still in the STM. (2)

3 a) It is the process of repeating a piece of information over and over again. (1)
b) It extends the time spent by the information in the STM and increases its chance of being transferred into the LTM. (1)

4 a) Organisation is the sorting of information into logical categories that are more easily transferred from STM to LTM. Elaboration involves analysing the meaning of the item to be memorised and noting its features and properties. (4)
b) These processes ensure that it has been filed under many categories associated with many contextual cues, any one of which may trigger a 'memory circuit' when required. (1)

Chapter 20 Cells of the nervous system and neurotransmitters at synapses

Testing Your Knowledge 1

1 a) See Figure AnT 20.1 (3)

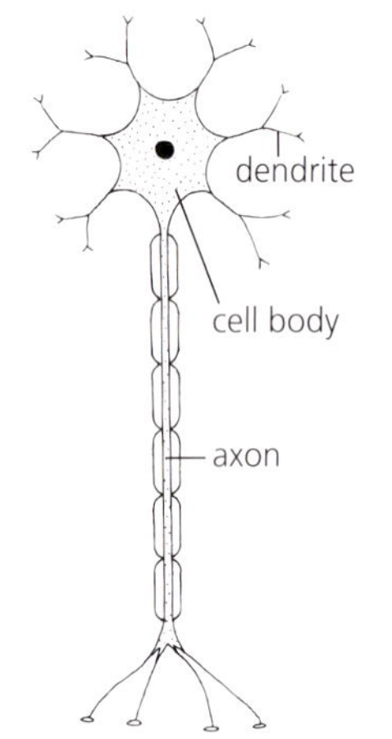

Figure AnT 20.1

b) The cell body is the control centre of a nerve cell's metabolism. A dendrite is one of several nerve fibres which receive nerve impulses and pass them towards a cell body. An axon is a single nerve fibre which carries nerve impulses away from a cell body. (3)

2 a) It greatly increases the speed. (1)
b) The neurons responsible for this control are not fully myelinated until the child is about 2 years old. (1)

3 a) 1 = membrane of dendrite
2 = synaptic cleft
3 = synaptic terminal
4 = axon (4)
b) i) Vesicle containing neurotransmitter
ii) Acetylcholine/noradrenaline
iii) Receptor molecules on the membrane of the dendrite
iv) Right to left
v) Acetylcholine is broken down into non-active products by an enzyme and the products reabsorbed by the presynaptic membrane OR noradrenaline is reabsorbed directly by the presynaptic membrane.
vi) Mitochondrion. It supplies the neuron with the energy needed for anabolic processes. (8)

4 It means the cumulative effect of a series of weak stimuli which together bring about a response. (2)

5 A *converging* neural pathway is one in which impulses from several sources are channelled towards and meet at a common destination. A *diverging* neural pathway is one where the route along which an impulse is travelling divides, allowing information to be transmitted to several destinations. A *reverberating* neural pathway is one in which neurons later in the pathway have axon branches that connect with neurons earlier in the pathway. (6)

Testing Your Knowledge 2

1 a) Endorphins (1)
b) A lengthy period of vigorous exercise; severe injury (2)

2 a) Dopamine (1)
b) Increased (1)
c) Agonist (1)
d) Antagonist (1)
e) Inhibiting (1)
f) Reward (1)
g) Sensitisation (1)

Chapter 21 Non-specific body defences

Testing Your Knowledge

1 a) i) Mucus
ii) Acid
iii) Mucus traps pathogens and acid kills many pathogens. (4)
b) Cancer (1)

2 a) Cells in connective tissue closely related to white blood cells (1)
   b) i) An extra blood supply is sent to the injured site. Capillaries leak fluid into the surrounding tissues.
      ii) Inflammation
      iii) It promotes the enhanced migration of phagocytes and the speedy delivery of blood clotting chemicals to the site of injury. (5)
3 a) Antibody production is specific. Phagocytosis is non-specific. (1)
   b) It is the process by which phagocytes engulf and digest pathogens. (2)
4 a) T (1)
   b) F – increased (1)
   c) F – lysosomes (1)
   d) T (1)

Chapter 22 Specific cellular defences against pathogens

Testing Your Knowledge

1 a) B and T lymphocytes (1)
   b) Both types (1)
2 a) i) A complex molecule recognised by the body as non-self and foreign.
      ii) Virus and bacterium (3)
   b) Because the body possesses a huge number of different lymphocytes each with a set of antigen receptors different from the others. (2)
3 a) An allergic reaction occurs when the body *overreacts* to a normally *harmless* substance by making a *hypersensitive* response. (3)
   b) When the body fails to tolerate the antigens on its own cell surfaces and attacks its own cells, this situation is called autoimmunity. (2)
4 a) Apoptosis is the name given to the process of the programmed death of a cell. (1)
   b) The activated T cell releases proteins which diffuse into the infected cell. These induce the production of self-destructive enzymes which cause the death of the infected cell. (3)
5 Because the HIV virus has weakened their immune system by destroying many of their T cells. (2)

Chapter 23 Immunisation

Testing Your Knowledge

1 It can be acquired by receiving an antigen that initiates the immune response but does not cause the disease. (2)
2 a) When most of the population have been immunised against the pathogen, there is a low chance of the pathogen coming into contact with the minority of non-immunised people. (2)
   b) How virulent the pathogen is. How effective the vaccine is. (2)
   c) When widespread vaccination is impossible because the country is impoverished. When the vaccine is rejected by a large percentage of the population who believe that it may be harmful. (4)
3 a) Mutation (1)
   b) Because the virus mutates and produces new antigens that the body has no immediate defences against. (2)
4 a) T (1)
   b) F – densely (1)
   c) F – antigens (1)
   d) T (1)

Chapter 24 Clinical trials of vaccines and drugs

Testing Your Knowledge

1 See Table AnT 24.1. (6)

Feature of design of clinical trial	Reason for inclusion of design feature
Randomised	To eliminate bias occurring when the population is divided into two groups
Double-blind	To prevent both doctors and subjects from knowing who is getting the drug and who is getting the placebo
Placebo-controlled	To assess the effect from receiving the treatment that does not depend on the actual active ingredient in the treatment

Table AnT 24.1

2 The test population is divided into two groups that are as similar as possible with respect to age and gender. The test population used is very large. (2)

Applying Your Knowledge and Skills Answers

Chapter 1 Division and differentiation in human cells

1 W = zygote, X = embryonic stem cell, Y = tissue stem cell, Z = specialised cell (3)

2 a) i) = T
ii) = P
iii) = S
iv) = Q
v) = U
vi) = R (5)
b) B (1)
c) i) Cow
ii) Because it is considered inappropriate to use cells that contain even a tiny amount of cow material to repair human tissue in this way. (2)

3 a) Nuclear transfer technique (1)
b) Because she is a genetic copy of another sheep. (1)
c) i) White
ii) Because her genetic material came from a white-faced sheep. (2)
d) i) A
ii) The DNA that she received came from a sheep not a ram. Therefore she could not have received a Y chromosome necessary to become a male. (2)

4 a) Jill (1)
b) i) Unconvincing
ii) Because some embryos are lost naturally, this does not justify using embryos for stem cell research. (2)

5 a) i) 8.3
ii) 6.2 (2)
b) i) 477 per million
ii) 0.052% (2)
c) i) Region A. 2006 is the only year that the trend is not the same as the country as a whole.
ii) It shows a much greater overall decrease in lung cancer deaths per 100 000 population. (3)

6 a) See Figure AnKS 1.1. (3)

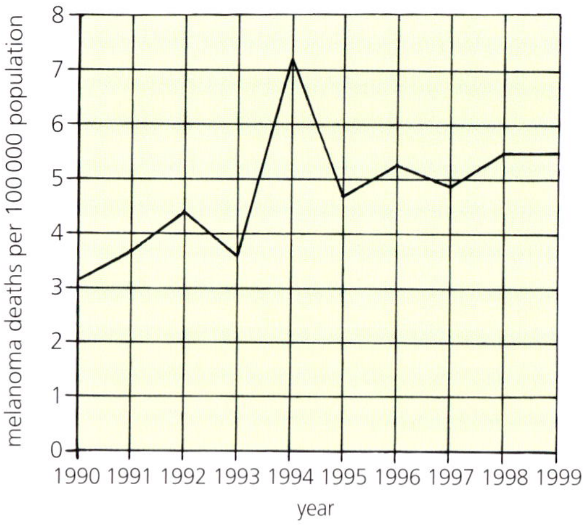

Figure AnKS 1.1

b) Dependent variable = melanoma death rate; independent variable = time (1)
c) An increase in number of melanoma deaths per 100 000 population. (1)
d) i) 1994
ii) Although the trend is upwards, the value for 1994 seems excessively high compared to the others. In addition, no such jump is present in the all Europe data which otherwise mirror, at a lower level, the data of the northern European country. (3)
e) 55 (1)
f) i) 37.5
ii) 8% (2)
g) i) B
ii) Although the overall trend is upwards, the values fluctuate slightly so the next value is more likely to be the slightly lower one than one that varies greatly from the previous value. (2)
h) More precautions taken; earlier diagnosis (2)

Chapter 2 Structure and replication of DNA

1 a) X = 22.0; Y = 0.98 (2)

b) i) The number of adenine bases in DNA equals the number of thymine bases and the number of guanine bases equals the number of cytosine bases. (A : T = 1 : 1 and G : C = 1 : 1).

ii) Yes

iii) Because the percentage of A is always very nearly equal to the percentage of T but not close to that of G or C. Similarly, the percentage of G is always close to the percentage of C but not close to that of A or T. (3)

c) C (1)

2 a) 30% (1)

b) 3200 (1)

3 a) i) 1 = chromosome; 2 = DNA; 3 = base

ii) 1

iii) 3 (5)

b) i) 10 000 : 1

ii) Because this is a constant reliable measurement whereas length measured in μm varies according to degree of coiling. (2)

4 a) See Figure AnKS 2.1. (6)

b) i) 20 000 minutes

ii) During replication, many replication forks operate simultaneously which ensures speedy copying of the DNA. (2)

5 See Figure AnKS 2.2. (4)

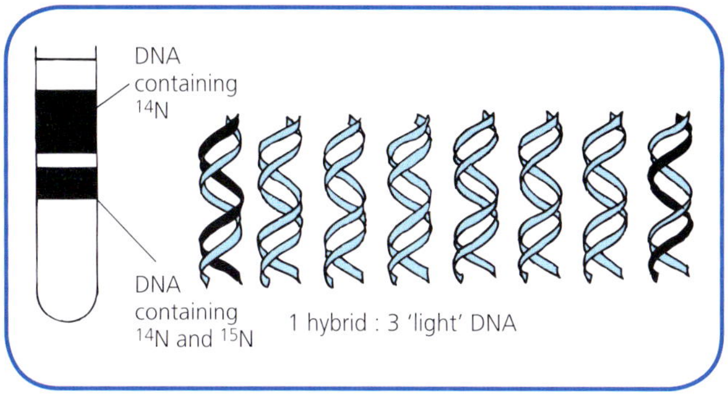

Figure AnKS 2.2

6 a) i) Semi-logarithmic

ii) To accommodate the very high numbers involved. (2)

b) 23 (1)

c) 10 (1)

d) i) 1000 000 000

ii) One billion (2)

e) See Figure AnKS 2.3. (4)

7 a) R and V (1)

b) Q and T (1)

c) i) Yes

ii) They have 50% of their DNA bands in common with the parents of P. (2)

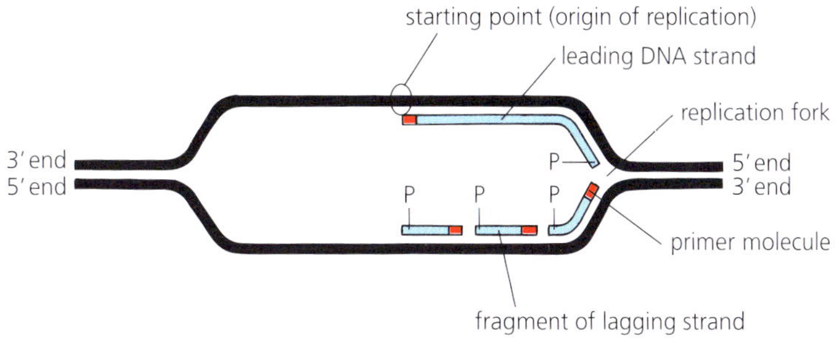

Figure AnKS 2.1

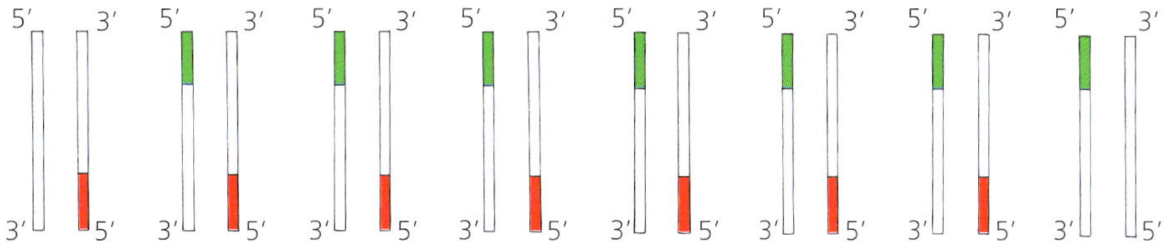

Figure AnKS 2.3

d) i) No
ii) They have no DNA bands in common with R and V. (2)

8 See core text pages 21–8. (9)

Chapter 3 Gene expression

1 a) 1 = C, 2 = T, 3 = T, 4 = A, 5 = U, 6 = A, 7 = G, 8 = C, 9 = G (2)
b) P = transcription and release of mRNA; Q = translation of mRNA into protein (1)
c) See Table AnKS 3.1. (2)

Amino acid	Codon	Anticodon
Alanine	**GCG**	CGC
Arginine	CGC	**GCG**
Cysteine	**UGU**	ACA
Glutamic acid	GAA	**CUU**
Glutamine	**CAA**	GUU
Glycine	GGC	**CCG**
Isoleucine	**AUA**	UAU
Leucine	CUU	**GAA**
Proline	**CCG**	GGC
Threonine	ACA	**UGU**
Tyrosine	**UAU**	AUA
Valine	GUU	**CAA**

Table AnKS 3.1

d) CAA (1)
e) U = proline, V = glutamine, W = glutamine acid, X = cysteine, Y = arginine, Z = isleucine (2)
f) i) ACACUUGCGGGC
ii) TGTGAACGCCCG (2)

2 a) X = U; Y =G (2)
b) 1 (1)
c) UAA, UAG and UGA (3)
d) i) Phenylalanine
ii) Threonine
iii) Glycine (3)
e) UUA, UUG, CUU, CUC, CUA and CUG (2)
f) Glutamine (1)

3 See core text pages 42–45. (9)

4 See Figure AnKS 3.1. (1)

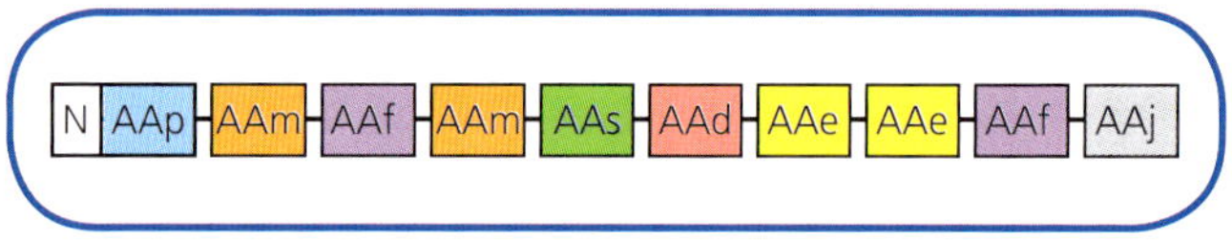

Figure AnKS 3.1

5 a) Casein contains them all. Group 2 rats gained weight throughout the experiment. Zein lacks two essential amino acids. Group 1 rats lost weight throughout the experiment. (4)
b) i) Zein
ii) Their diet could have been changed to casein or to zein supplemented with the two essential amino acids that it lacks. (3)
c) 35g (1)
d) 20% (1)

6 a) i) Lower molecular weight
ii) This is suggested by the fact that they have travelled the greatest distance from the negative electrode. (2)
b) i) Alpha-2-globulins
ii) Iron-deficiency anaemia (2)
c) i) D
ii) Because gamma-globulins also increase in concentration for other reasons such as response to viral invasion. (2)

Chapter 4 Mutations

1 a) i) Mutations (%)
ii) Dosage of X-rays (2)
b) As the dosage of X-rays increases so does the percentage of mutations. (1)
c) i) C
ii) B (2)
d) 0.1 per million cells (1)

2 a) Deletion
b) Substitution
c) Insertion (3)

3 a) i) Substitution
ii) A nucleotide with base A has been replaced by one with base T, making triplet AAC become triplet ATC. (2)
b) i) glutamic acid – serine – leucine – threonine
ii) glutamic acid – serine (2)
c) i) Nonsensical
ii) The full functional protein would not be expressed because the mutation would result in the transcription of stop codon UAG. (2)

4 See Figure AnKS 4.1. (4)

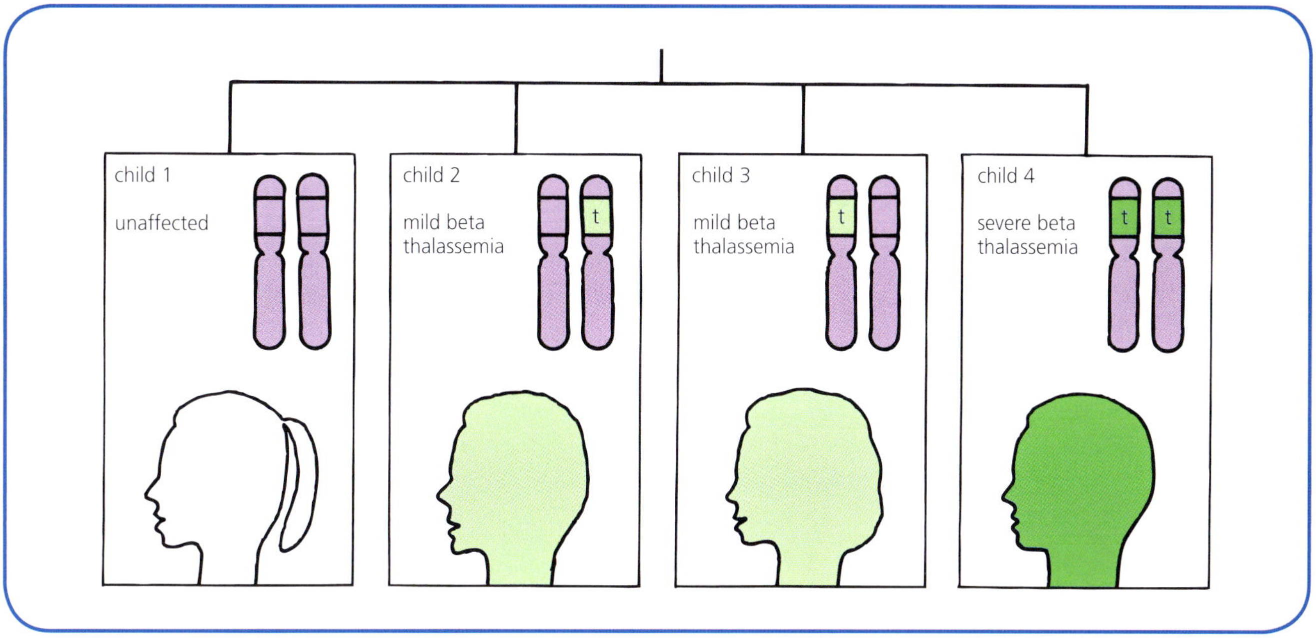

Figure AnKS 4.1

5 See Table AnKS 4.1. (8)

Genetic disorder	Type of single-gene mutation responsible	Effect of mutation on structure of protein expressed	Effect of mutation on functioning of protein	Effect of mutation on phenotype of untreated, affected individual
Phenylketonuria (PKU)	Substitution	Missense results and a molecule of arginine is replaced by a molecule of tryptophan	The protein expressed in non-functional	Normal development of the brain is prevented by toxins formed from the breakdown of excess phenylalanine
Cystic fibrosis	Deletion	Loss of a codon results in the frameshift effect which alters the sequence of many amino acids in the protein	The protein expressed is non-functional	Congestion of lungs and pancreas by extremely thick, sticky mucus

Table AnKS 4.1

6 a) The mutated gene is no longer able to code the correct message for the production of its particular enzyme. Lack of the enzyme prevents the pathway from proceeding normally. (2)

b) i) Q

ii) R

iii) T (3)

c) i) All the excess phenylalanine has been converted to tyrosine.

ii) The person with PKU is unable to make the enzyme needed to convert phenylalanine to tyrosine.

iii) The tyrosine has been converted to other metabolites. (3)

7 a) Cell 1 = deletion; cell 2 = duplication (2)
b) i) Cell 1
ii) Essential genes would probably have been lost. (2)

8 See core text pages 57–62. (9)

Chapter 5 Human genomics

1 AACCGATCAGCGCAGCGCTT
GATCAGATCGCGCTAG (1)

2 a) Site 4 (1)
b) 5 (1)
c) i) 7 and 12
ii) 5 and 9
iii) 8 (3)
d) 17 (1)
e) i) CTTATG
ii) 45% (2)
f) 10 (1)
g) 4 and 11 (1)
h) Increase the number of people sampled and include more sites in the study. (2)

3 a) i) 10^7 m
ii) 10^4 km. Ten thousand kilometres (2)
b) i) No
ii) It is based on the genomes of several people. (2)

4 a) TACTGGTACT (1)
b) ATGACCATGA (1)

5 a) See Table AnKS 5.1. (4)

Alleles of gene present in genome	State of enzyme	Person's metabolic profile
Two null alleles	Non-functional	**Poor**
One null allele and one inferior allele	**Partly functional**	**Intermediate**
One or two normal alleles	**Fully functional**	Extensive
More than two copies of normal allele	Highly functional	**Ultra-rapid**

Table AnKS 5.1

b) Duplication (1)
c) i) Poor metabolisers
ii) Their bodies will be so slow to clear the drug that it may do them harm. (2)
d) i) Ultra-rapid metabolisers
ii) Their bodies would remove the drug so quickly that it would not have time to bring about the desired effect. (2)
e) If the personal genome sequencing becomes routine then knowledge of a person's DNA profile may enable doctors to customise medical treatments to suit an individual's exact requirements. (2)

Chapter 6 Metabolic pathways

1 a) i) 5
ii) 3 (2)
b) Some of I would be converted to G by enzyme 5 and then G would be converted to H by enzyme 4. (2)
c) i) H could become L and M by the action of enzyme 8 and then L and M could become J and K by the action of enzyme 7.

ii) $\text{H} + \text{I} \xrightarrow{\text{enzyme 6}} \text{J} + \text{K} \xrightarrow{\text{enzyme 7}} \text{L} + \text{M}$

iii) $\text{G} \xrightarrow{\text{enzyme 4}} \text{H} \xrightarrow{\text{enzyme 8}} \text{L} + \text{M} \xrightarrow{\text{enzyme 7}} \text{J} + \text{K} \xrightarrow{\text{enzyme 6}} \text{H} + \text{I}$ (3)

d) It allows finely tuned control and prevents build-ups and bottlenecks. (1)

2 a) P and S (1)
b) i) Q, S, P, R
ii) R, P, S, Q (2)
c) B (1)

3 a) i) Concentration of substrate
ii) Independent
iii) It caused an increase in reaction rate. (3)
b) Concentration of enzyme (1)
c) i) A
ii) C
iii) B (3)
d) More enzyme could be added. (1)

4 a) i), (ii) and **(iii)** See Figure AnKS 6.1. (4)

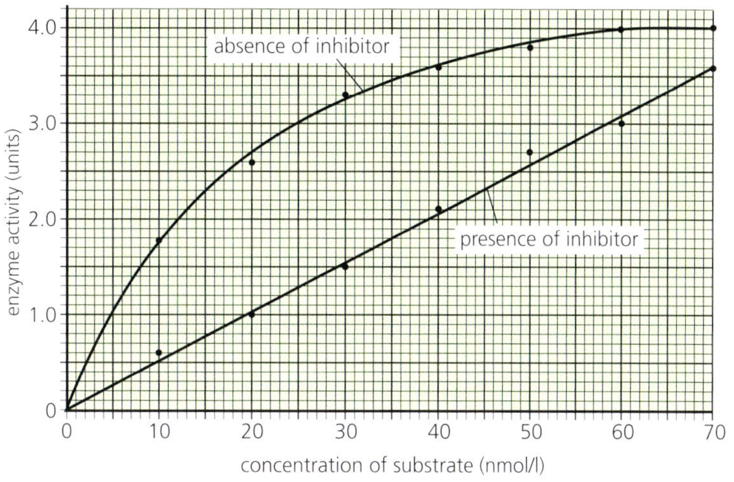

Figure AnKS 6.1

b) A (1)
c) 3 times (1)
d) i) 61.54%
ii) 10% (2)
e) There would always be a few enzyme sites blocked by the inhibitor. (1)

5 a) 1, 2 and 3 (1)
b) Substrate concentration (1)
c) 4, 5 and 6 (1)
d) Experiment = 4, 5 and 6; controls = 1, 2 and 3 (2)
e) i) Iodine solution
ii) Non-competitively
iii) If it had been a competitive inhibitor, the inhibitory effect would have decreased as substrate concentration increased and this would have resulted in some yellow colour appearing in tube 6 and maybe a faint yellow colour in tube 5. However, iodine completely inhibited the enzyme at all concentrations of ONPG showing that it acted non-competitively. (4)

6 a) i) Carbamyl phosphate and aspartate
ii) Carbamyl aspartate and phosphate
iii) Cytidylic acid (3)
b) i) The concentration of carbamyl phosphate will increase.
ii) Fewer molecules of P will be free to act on carbamyl phosphate. (2)
c) i) Decreased
ii) There will be so little cytidylic acid present that very few molecules of enzyme P will be affected by the negative feedback process. (2)
d) All 3 (1)

7 a) See core text pages 82–83. (3)
b) See core text pages 79–80. (3)
c) See core text page 84. (3)

Chapter 7 Cellular respiration

1 a) See Figure AnKS 7.1. (4)

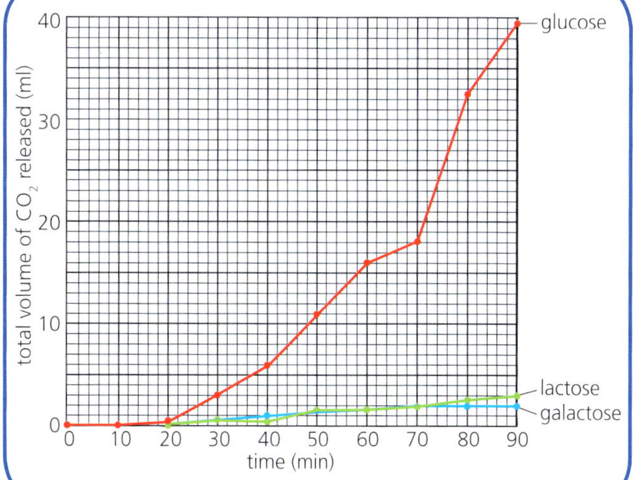

Figure AnKS 7.1

b) i) The result at 70 min
ii) It is much lower than would be expected from the general trend. (2)
c) 6400% (1)
d) It is able to make very good use of glucose but not able to make good use of galactose or lactose. (1)
e) i) It is hardly able to break lactose down.
ii) If it had been able to do so, glucose would have been released from lactose and rapidly used as a respiratory substrate. (2)
f) Repeat the experiment. (1)

2 a) and b) See Figure AnKS 7.2. (4)

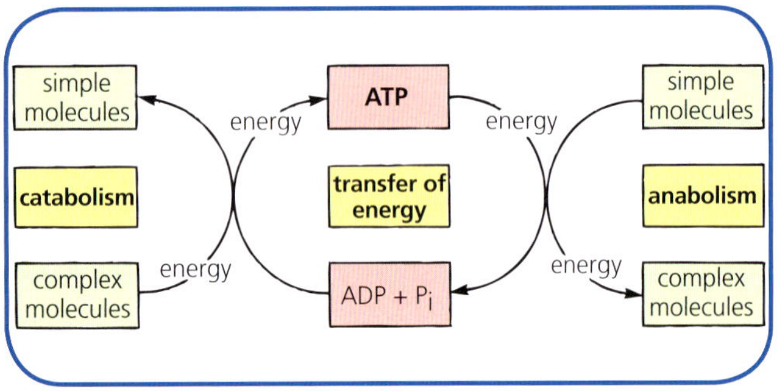

Figure AnKS 7.2

c) i) C
ii) A
iii) C
iv) A (4)

3 a) See Table AnKS 7.1. (5)

Stage of respiratory pathway	Principal reaction or process that occurs	Products
Glycolysis	Splitting of glucose into [pyruvate]	[ATP], NADH and pyruvate
[Citric] acid cycle	Removal of [hydrogen] ions from molecules of respiratory [substrate]	[CO_2], [NADH] and ATP
[Electron] transport chain	Release of [energy] to form ATP	ATP and [water]

Table AnKS 7.1

b) Glycolysis (1)
c) Electron transport chain (1)
d) Citric acid cycle and electron transport chain (2)

4 a) i) Intermembrane space
ii) A flow of electrons from NADH and $FADH_2$ pumps H^+ ions across the membrane against a concentration gradient. (3)
b) i) ATP synthase
ii) The return flow of H^+ ions to the region of lower H^+ ion concentration via molecule X makes part of it rotate and catalyse the synthesis of ATP. (3)
c) By stopping electron flow, cyanide brings the movement of H^+ ions to a halt therefore no ATP is synthesised and the organism lacks access to energy and dies. (2)

5 a) Repeat the experiment with several concentrations of the substrate (succinic acid) as the independent variable factor. (1)
b) If low concentrations give little or no colour change in the presence of malonic acid but higher concentrations do bring about decolourisation of DCPIP, then this shows that malonic acid is less effective at higher concentrations of substrate and is acting as a competitive inhibitor. (2)

6 a) 56% (1)
b) 1267.2 kJ (1)
c) Synthesis of protein from amino acids; contraction of muscles (2)

7 See core text pages 101–2. (9)

Chapter 8 Energy systems in muscle cells

1 a) See Figure AnKS 8.1. (3)

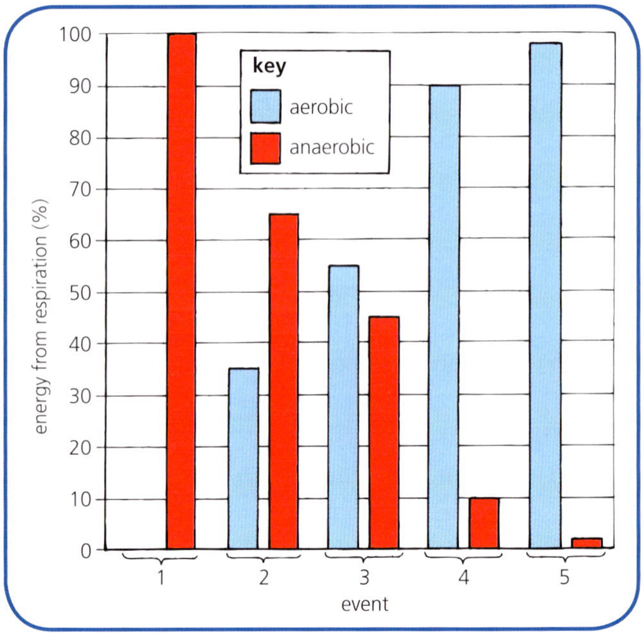

Figure AnKS 8.1

b) The longer the event, the larger the volume of oxygen breathed in. The longer the event, the greater the percentage of energy obtained from aerobic respiration. The longer the event, the more energy expended. (3)

c) i) Event 1 = 2 kJ/m; event 5 = 0.33 kJ/m

ii) 6 times (3)

2 a) i) 1.08 mg cm^{-3}

ii) 12.18 and 12.45 (2)

b) i) B

ii) The start of the steep rise in lactate concentration that occurs at this time indicates anaerobic respiration is occurring during intensive exercise. (2)

c) i) 5.5 times

ii) A

iii) 66.67% (3)

Chapter 9 Gamete production and fertilisation and Chapter 10 Hormonal control of reproduction

1 a) K, E, G, A, C, D, J, L (1)

b) See Table AnKS 10.1. (8)

2 a) D, A, E, C, B (1)

b) i) D, A and E

ii) Ovulation

iii) LH

iv) Pituitary gland (4)

c) i) Corpus luteum

ii) Progesterone and oestrogen

iii) Inhibitory effect (preventing release of LH) (4)

3 a) See Figure AnKS 10.1. (3)

b) 22, 23, 24 (1)

c) 8th April (1)

Letter in Figure 10.7 indicating accessory gland	Name of this accessory gland	Example of substance secreted by accessory gland which contributes to fertilisation	Way in which named substance contributes to fertilisation
B	Seminal vesicle	Hormone-like compound	Stimulates contractions of uterus which help sperm to reach oviduct and meet egg
I	Prostate gland	Enzymes	Maintains lubricating fluid at optimum viscosity for sperm mobility

Table AnKS 10.1

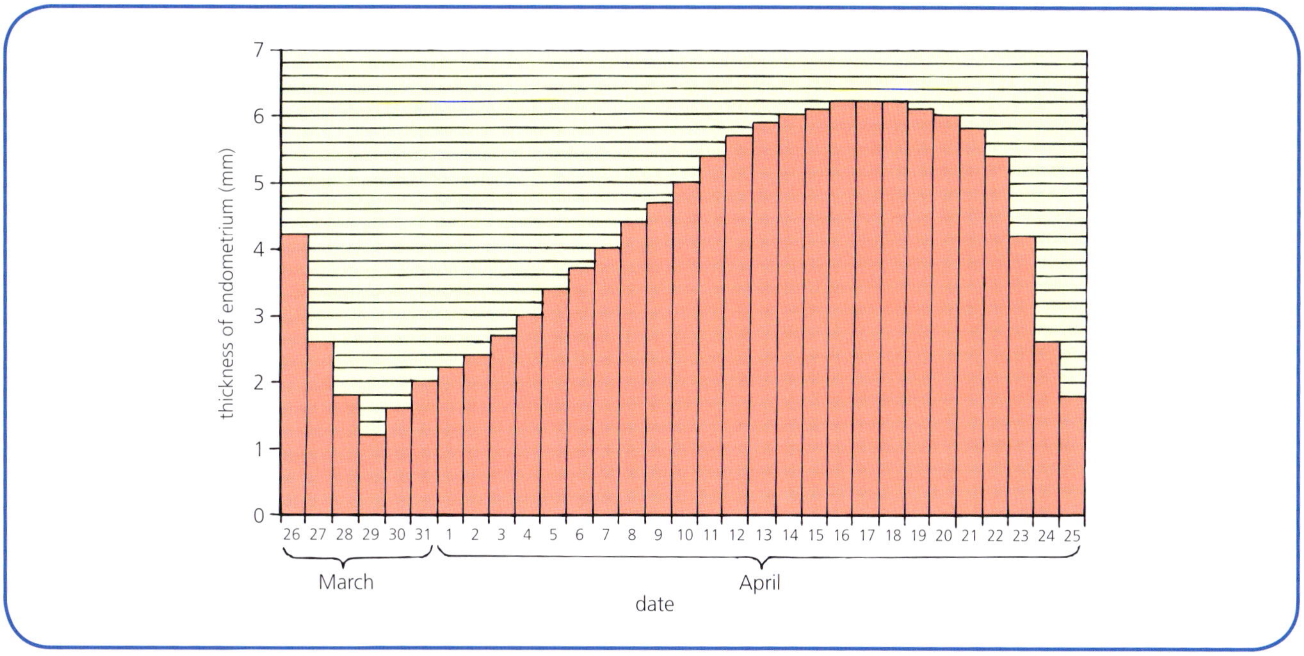

Figure AnKS 10.1

d) i) High
ii) Low
iii) High
iv) Low (4)

4 a) V = seminiferous tubule, W = blood capillary, X = interstitial cell, Y = germline cell, Z = sperm (5)
b) X (1)
c) ICSH (interstitial cell-stimulating hormone) (1)
d) It is exerted by negative feedback control. As the concentration of testosterone builds up in the bloodstream, it reaches a level where it inhibits the secretion of FSH and ICSH by the pituitary gland. This leads in turn to a decrease in testosterone concentration which is soon followed by resumption of activity of the pituitary gland and so on. (3)

5 a) See core text page 121. (4)
b) See core text pages 121–2. (5)

Chapter 11 Biology of controlling fertility

1 a) See Figure AnKS 11.1. (3)
b) B (1)

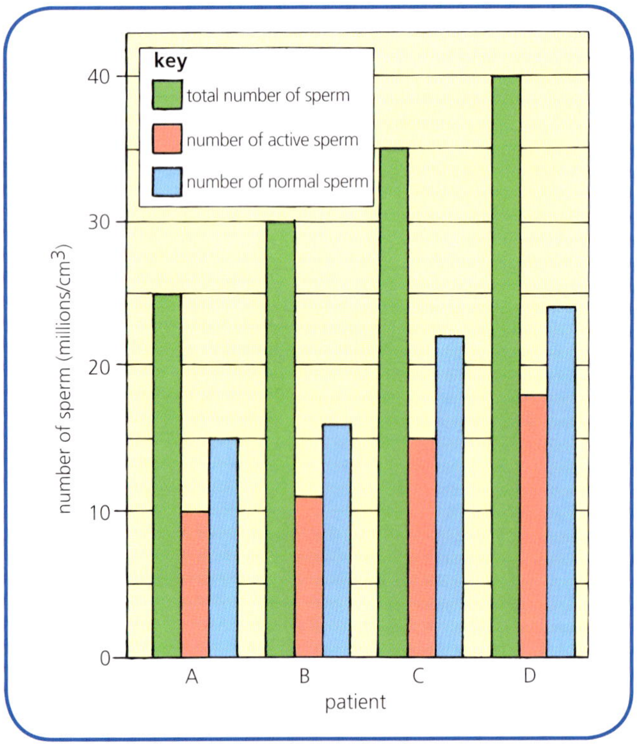

Figure AnKS 11.1

2 a) Sperm are unable to leave the man's body since both of his sperm ducts have been cut and tied. (1)
b) Compared to younger men, middle-aged men are more likely to already have a family and not wish to father any more children. (1)

3 These questions are intended to stimulate debate. There are no 'correct' answers to them.

4 A = 3, B = 2, C = 5, D = 6, E = 4, F = 1 (5)

5 See core text pages 126–9. (9)

6 a) i) 19–22 September approximately
ii) At this time her body temperature rises by 0.5°C showing that she is entering the luteal phase of the cycle that follows ovulation. In addition, this time is approximately two weeks before the start of menstruation which alternates fortnightly with ovulation. (3)
b) Her mucus would be thin and watery at this time. (1)
c) Menstruation occurred two weeks later. (1)
d) i) 17–20 approximately
ii) The concentration of progesterone would remain at a high level so the graph would not drop from the 29th September onwards. (2)
e) i) The increased concentration of progesterone exerts negative feedback control. Secretion of pituitary hormones by the pituitary is inhibited. In the absence of FSH no new follicles mature and ovulation fails to occur.
ii) Placebo pills are taken during the fourth week to allow levels of progesterone and oestrogen to drop and menstruation to occur.
iii) So that they get into the habit of always taking the pill and are therefore less likely to forget to take it during the three weeks that matter. (4)

Chapter 12 Ante- and postnatal screening

1 a) 5′-nucleotidase and alkaline phosphatase (1)
b) Bilirubin, albumin and GGT (1)
c) In a normal pregnancy, they remain unaltered so if they rise this indicates a problem. (1)
d) i) Serum bile acids
ii) Alkaline phosphatase
iii) Alkaline phosphatase level rises during a normal pregnancy therefore a rise may not be indicating a problem. The level of serum bile acids does not rise normally so it does indicate a problem. (3)
e) To ensure that the level of bile serum acids is not artificially elevated following the absorption of digested food into the bloodstream. (1)

2 a) i) 0.5 in 1000 = 1 in 2000
ii) 1 in 1000
iii) 10 in 1000 = 1 in 100 (3)
b) The germline cells of older women are more prone to mutation at gamete formation. (1)

3 a) Down's syndrome (1)
b) i) 32%
ii) 4% (2)
c) i) 4%
ii) 28% (2)
d) i) 3 MoM
ii) 30% (2)
e) i) 2 MoM
ii) 24% (2)
f) i) No
ii) 8% still occur at this level of MoM. (2)

4 a) The mothers of fetuses 2 and 5 are not over the age of 35 yet both had a fetus with Down's syndrome. (1)
b) Despite having a high NT value, some fetuses develop into babies without Down's syndrome. (1)
c) 10 (1)
d) 77.78% (1)

5 a) i) Autosomal recessive
ii) The trait is expressed relatively rarely.
iii) If the trait had been autosomal dominant then the two normal parents would not have been able to have children who were affected. If the trait had been sex-linked recessive then there would be far fewer or no females with the condition. (4)
b) See Figure AnKS 12.1. (9)

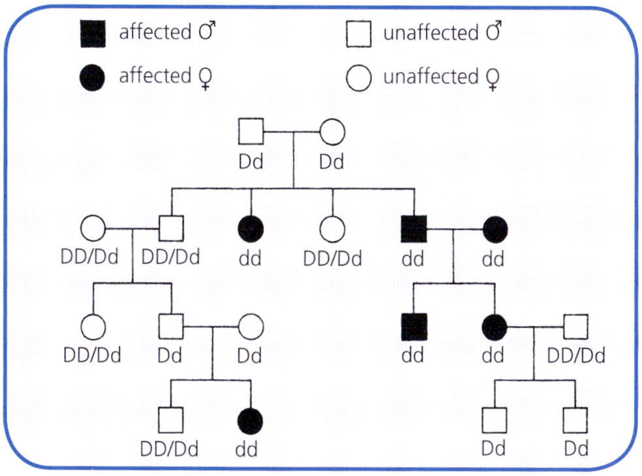

Figure AnKS 12.1

c) i) 0%
ii) 100% (2)
d) i) No chance
ii) 1 in 2 chance (2)
e) i) 1 in 2 chance
ii) 1 in 2 chance (2)

6 a) i) Hh
ii) hh (2)
b) i) Neither is old enough yet to show a phenotypic expression of the disorder which would indicate the presence of the H allele in their genotype.
ii) A = 3 in 4, B = 1 in 2, C = 1 in 2, D = no chance (5)

7 a) 2, 6 and 10 (1)
b) 1 in 2 chance (1)
c) i) 1 in 4
ii) 1 in 2 (2)

Chapter 13 Structure and function of arteries, capillaries and veins

1 a) Pulmonary vein, left atrium, left ventricle, aorta, renal artery (5)
b) Jugular vein, vena cava, right atrium, right ventricle, pulmonary artery (5)

2 a) and b) See Figure AnKS 13.1. (8)

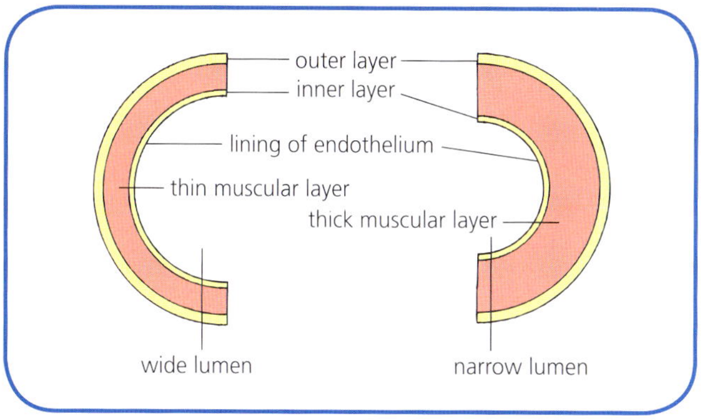

Figure AnKS 13.1

c) i) Veins possess valves whereas arteries do not.
ii) They prevent backflow of blood. See Figure AnKS 13.2. (4)

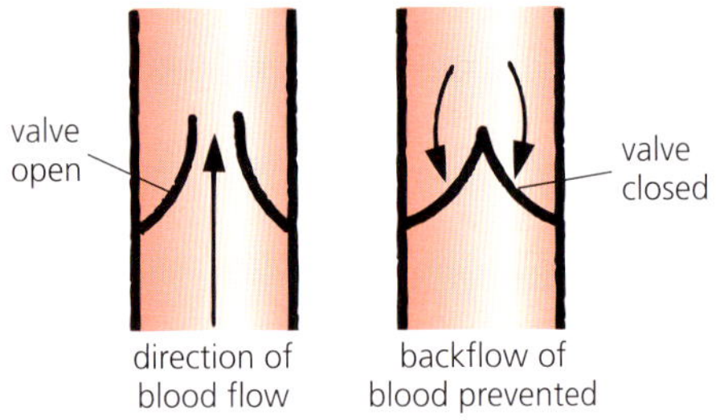

Figure AnKS 13.2

3 Capillary → venule → vein → artery → arteriole → capillary → venule → vein → artery → arteriole → capillary (4)

4 **a)** **i)** Increase
ii) Decrease
iii) The skeletal muscle is working hard and needs plenty of glucose and oxygen which are supplied by the bloodstream. Absorption of digested food is less important during strenuous exercise. (4)
b) **i)** Skin
ii) Kidneys (2)
c) **i)** Brain
ii) The energy demand by brain cells is continuous and steady regardless of the level of activity occurring elsewhere in the body. (2)
d) Vasoconstriction reduces blood flow to a body part because muscle in the wall of the arteriole supplying the body part contracts making the bore of the tube become narrow; vasodilation has the opposite effect. (2)

5 **a)** D (1)
b) D (1)
c) A (1)
d) C (1)

6 **a)** 1 = vein, 2 = artery, 3 = venule, 4 = arteriole, 5 = capillary (5)
b) Higher at W; lower at X (1)
c) **i)** Tissue fluid
ii) When blood arrives in a capillary bed it undergoes pressure filtration and plasma is squeezed out of the vessels. This liquid bathing the cells is called tissue fluid.
iii) It supplies them with dissolved oxygen, useful ions and soluble food molecules.
iv) Tissue fluid contains little or no protein. (4)
d) Z = lymphatic vessel. It absorbs tissue fluid (now called lymph) and returns it to the blood circulatory system via the lymphatic system. (2)
e) D (1)

7 See core text pages 159–60. (9)

Chapter 14 Structure and function of the heart

1 **a)** CO = HR × SV (1)
b) **i)** 5.76 l/min
ii) 100 beats/min
iii) 100 ml
iv) 120 ml (4)
c) Person **(iv)** is fitter. The larger stroke volume indicates that their heart muscle is more powerful. (2)

2 **a)** **i)** Ventricular systole
ii) The atria only have to pump blood a short distance to the ventricles but the ventricles have to pump blood to the lungs and body. (2)
b) **i)** X = atrial diastole; Y = ventricular diastole
ii) Relaxed (2)
c) **i)** 3
ii) 75 beats per minute (2)
d) See Figure AnKS 14.1. (3)

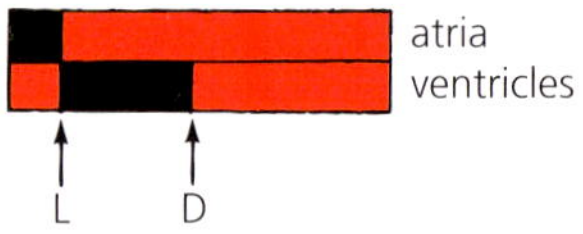

Figure AnKS 14.1

3 **a)** **i)** Right = 26 mm Hg; left = 120 mm Hg
ii) The wall of the left ventricle is thicker than that of the right ventricle. This enables the left ventricle to exert the higher pressure needed to pump blood all round the body. (2)
b) **i)** 0 mm Hg
ii) 80 mm Hg
iii) 20 mm Hg
iv) 10 mm Hg (4)
c) 0.1 s (1)
d) 15–0.4 s (1)
e) During diastole the pressure of blood in the pulmonary artery returns to 16 mm Hg where it started. (1)

4 a) See Figure AnKS 14.2. (4)

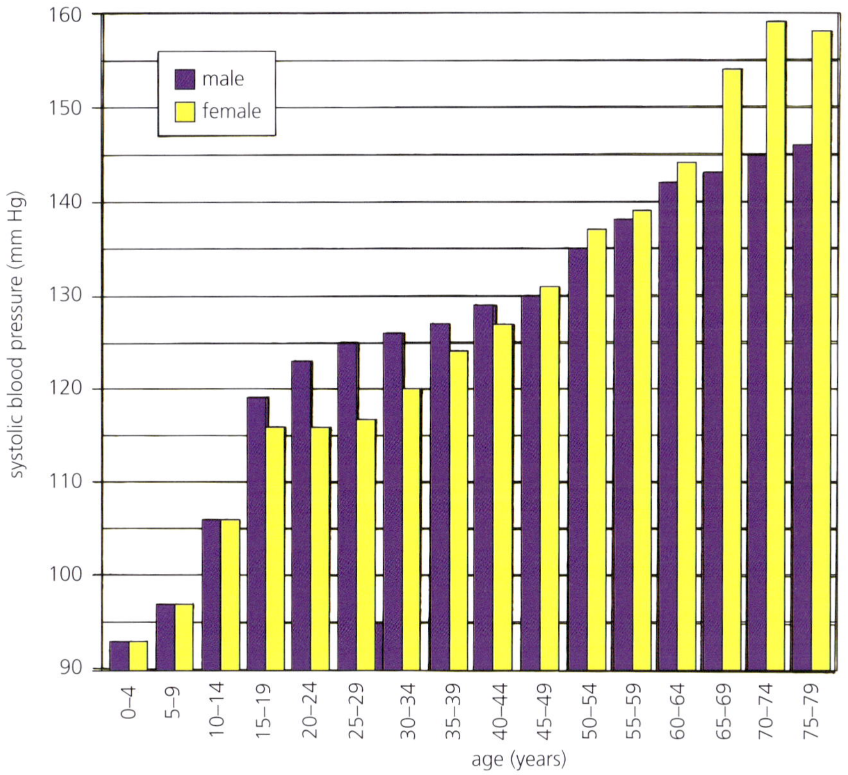

Figure AnKS 14.2

b) i) Blood pressure rises with increase in age.

ii) It is possible that increase in age is accompanied by increased level of stress in lifestyle (and possibly increased intake of unnecessary salt). (2)

c) When females reach adolescence, their blood pressure remains lower than that of males but after menopause it catches up again. (1)

5 1 = increases, 2 = open, 3 = aorta, 4 = stretched, 5 = reservoir, 6 = relax, 7 = decreases, 8 = shut, 9 = recoil, 10 = body (9)

6 a) i) Z

ii) X

iii) Y (2)

b) i) B

ii) A

iii) B's waves are further apart than normal but remain coordinated whereas A's waves are uncoordinated. (4)

7 a) See Table AnKS 14.1. (6)

Part of circulatory system	Blood pressure (mm Hg)	Drop in pressure in this part of system (mm Hg)
Left ventricle	100	0
Aorta	**100**	**0**
Large arteries	95-100	**5**
Small arteries	85-95	**10**
Arterioles	**35-85**	**50**
Capillaries	15-35	**20**
Venules	6-15	**9**
Small veins	**2-6**	**4**
Large veins	1-2	**1**
Venae cavae	0-1	**1**

Table AnKS 14.1

- **b) i)** Arterioles and capillaries
  - **ii)** 70 mm Hg
  - **iii)** The arterioles and capillaries are narrow in diameter and therefore offer resistance to blood flow causing the drop in pressure. (3)

8 a) See core text pages 167–8. (5)
- **b)** See core text page 168–70. (4)

Chapter 15 Pathology of cardiovascular disease

1 Men always suffer a higher death rate than women.
The death rate increases with age.
The death rates are all decreasing with time. (3)

2 $1\ \text{mmol}\,l^{-1} = 386.6\ \text{mg}\,l^{-1}$
$1\ \text{mmol}\,l^{-1} = 38.66\ \text{mg}\,\text{dl}^{-1}$
$1.56\ \text{mmol}\,l^{-1} = 1.56 \times 38.66\ \text{mg}\,\text{dl}^{-1}$
$= 60.31\ \text{mg}\,\text{dl}^{-1}$ (desirable level of HDL-cholesterol)
$3.88\ \text{mmol}\,l^{-1} = 3.88 \times 38.66\ \text{mg}\,\text{dl}^{-1}$
$= 150\ \text{mg}\,\text{dl}^{-1}$ (borderline level of LDL-cholesterol) (4)

3 a) 20 mg (1)
- **b)** $0.75\ \text{mmol}\ l^{-1}$ (1)
- **c) i)** 20 mg
  - **ii)** 80 mg (2)
- **d)** H (1)
- **e)** E and H (1)
- **f) i)** E
  - **ii)** It produces the greatest decrease in LDL-cholesterol at the lowest concentration of dose. (2)

4 The greater the decrease in level of LDL-cholesterol, the greater the expected percentage decrease in incidence of CVD. The older the patient, the lower the expected percentage decrease in incidence of CVD. (2)

5 a) i) U
  - **ii)** N (2)
- **b) i)** M = Hh, affected
  - **ii)** X = hh, unaffected (2)
- **c) i)** S
  - **ii)** Genotype could be HH or Hh. (2)
- **d) i)** 1 in 2
  - **ii)** 1 in 2 (2)
- **e)** Person V has inherited the condition from his father, person P. This would not be possible if the trait were sex-linked. (1)

6 See core text pages 181–182. (9)

Chapter 16 Blood glucose levels and obesity

1 a) See Figure AnKS 16.1. (3)

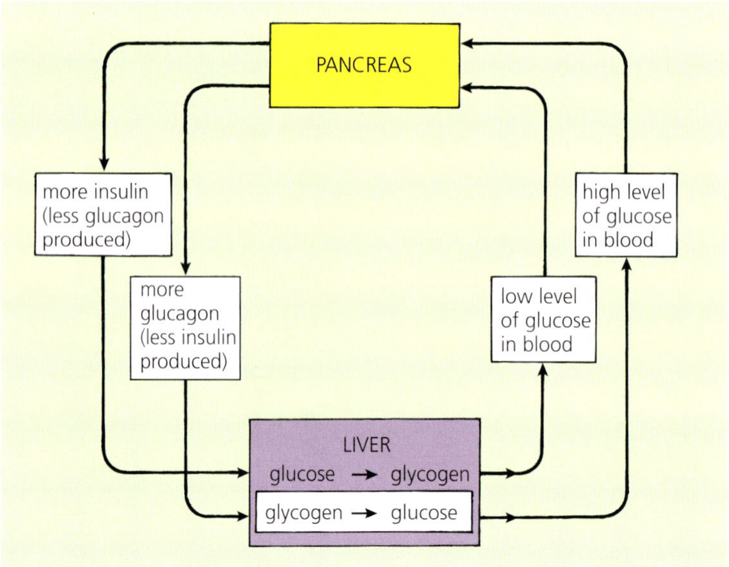

Figure AnKS 16.1

b) The diagram has been drawn as two interrelated circuits to show that a **physiological** factor under **homeostatic** control is constantly wavering on either side of its **normal** value. When it **deviates** from the norm, it is returned to this value by negative **feedback** control. If it overshoots the mark, a **reverse** set of mechanisms is triggered which returns the factor to its norm. If it now overshoots the mark in the opposite direction, the opposite set of **responses** is made and so on. (6)

2 a) i) Between 07.00 and 08.00

ii) Homeostasis (2)

b) i) 08.00

ii) They both increased.

iii) Time is needed for glucose in the blood to reach the pancreas and for the receptor cells to respond and release more insulin. (4)

c) i) Suppresses

ii) The concentration of fatty acids drops. If insulin promoted the breakdown of fat, the concentration of fatty acids would increase. (2)

d) i) See Figure AnKS 16.2.

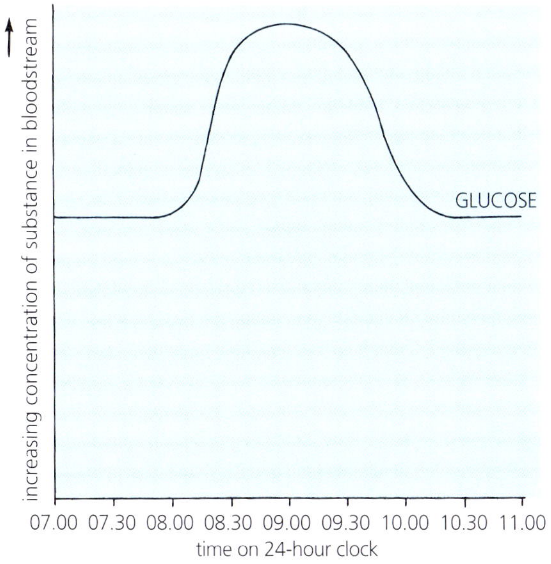

Figure AnKS 16.2

ii) After ingestion of glucose the maximum value of blood glucose concentration reached would be much higher. The blood glucose level would have only shown a slight decrease by 11.00 hours. (4)

e) The babies of diabetic mothers receive more glucose (which promotes growth). Their mother's blood is rich in glucose because she produces insufficient insulin to store her excess glucose as glycogen. (1)

3 i) 25 weeks

ii) 10 weeks (2)

4 a) 8 risk points (1)

b) Joe = 18% 10-year CHD risk whereas the average for 49-year-olds is 11%. (1)

c) To reduce his LDL-cholesterol level and to stop smoking. (1)

5 a) 50% (1)

b) i) By a horizontal line inside the box

ii) 1 = 68 kg, 2 = 76 kg, 3 = 86 kg (2)

c) i) 3

ii) 1 (2)

d) An actual value (1)

e) 42 kg (1)

f) 1 (1)

g) i) On average, more men than women are becoming obese.

ii) Less regular exercise taken nowadays because people live a more sedentary lifestyle. (2)

Chapter 17 Divisions of the nervous system and neural pathways and Chapter 18 Cerebral cortex

1 See Figure AnKS 18.1. (5)

2 a) Sensory nerve impulses are received by the brain and interpreted as indicating an impending crisis. Many impulses are transmitted via sympathetic nerves to certain parts of the body. This results in preparations being made for 'fight or flight' such as increased heart rate and dilation of air passages. Extra energy becomes available to cope with the crisis. After the crisis, many impulses are transmitted via the parasympathetic nerves. This results in decreased heart rate, constriction of air passages and increased rate of peristalsis as the body calms down. (4)

b) It is possible that they would sink into a coma. (1)

3 a) i) The muscle will contract.

ii) It will increase.

iii) Less blood will flow to the gut allowing more to be diverted to skeletal muscles where it is needed. (3)

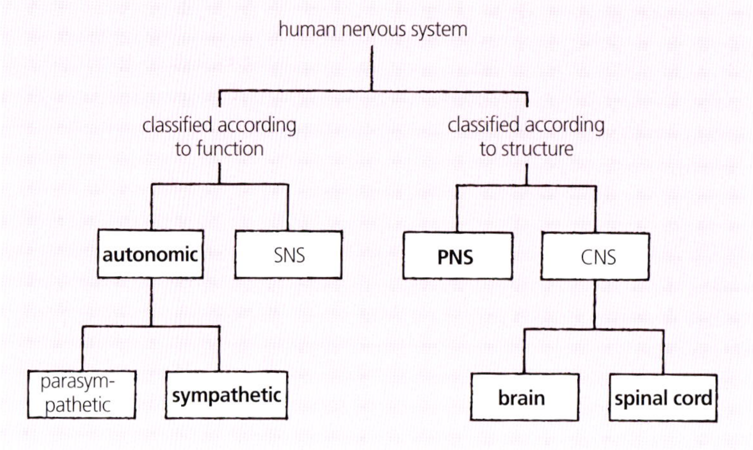

Figure AnKS 18.1

b) i) They will make the muscle contract and close the sphincter valves.
ii) Parasympathetic nerve impulses sent to the same muscles.
iii) It would be of advantage when the body is at rest and digesting a meal because it would enable the sphincters to open and allow food to pass through.(4)

4 i) A. The right side of the object becomes an image on the left side of the brain where the speech motor area is located.
ii) D. The left side of the object becomes an image on the right side of the brain which also controls movement of the left hand. (4)

5 a) 3 and 5 (2)
b) i) Reading a book silently
ii) Reading a book out loud (2)
c) 3 → 4 → 1 → 2 (1)
d) i) No effect
ii) The person would be unable to speak. (2)

6 a) i) 74.06%
ii) 12.04% (2)
b) Inherited factors play a major part because there is a higher incidence of schizophrenia amongst twins sharing all their genetic material than amongst those sharing only some of it. (1)
c) i) 4
ii) 1
iii) Survey 4 is the most reliable because it considered the largest number of twin pairs; survey 1 is the least reliable because it considered the smallest number of twin pairs. (4)

Chapter 19 Memory

1 a) As the number of letters in a series increases, the percentage of students able to remember the series decreases. (1)
b) i) 9 letters
ii) 2 (2)
c) i) 4 letters
ii) 5% (2)
d) i) No
ii) The graph of the results is symmetrical. (2)
e) i) To avoid using sequences of letters that would act as chunks and be easily remembered.
ii) To avoid the introduction of a second variable factor.
iii) To increase reliability. (3)

2 Four digits can be arranged into a large enough number of combinations to make each PIN number different from the others yet at the same time be short enough to be easily remembered. (2)

3 Person **b)** will be faster because they will be familiar with the first four codes that will act as chunks. They will only need to memorise the last four digits. Person **a)** is confronted with fourteen unfamiliar digits. (2)

4 a) To prevent them from rehearsing the letters that they will be asked to recall. (1)
b) i) 35
ii) 4 (2)
c) They would be allowed to rehearse the letters in between attempts to recall them. (1)

d) i) Effect of lack of rehearsal on memory.
ii) It leads to a decline in effectiveness of the encoding of memories.
iii) Lack of rehearsal allows items in the STM to be displaced and forgotten before they can be encoded and stored in the LTM. (3)

5 See Figure AnKS 19.1. (3)

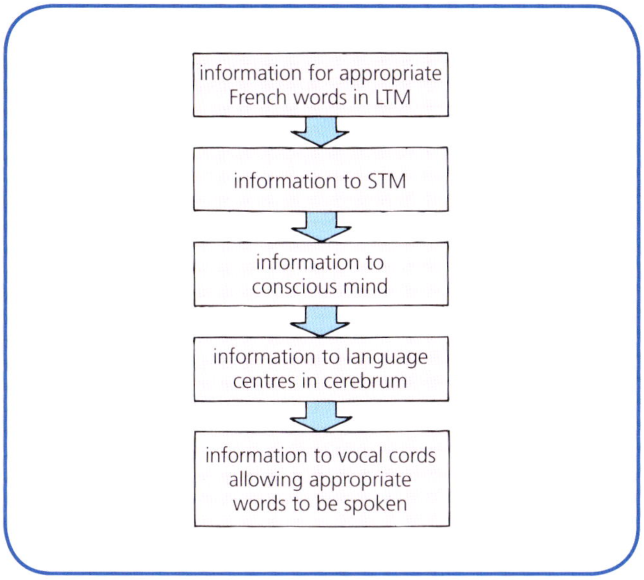

Figure AnKS 19.1

6 a) Attention
b) Groups
c) Repeating
d) Meaning
e) Visual, unusual
f) Overlearn
g) Short, long
h) Rest, recreation (10)

Chapter 20 Cells of the nervous system and neurotransmitters at synapses

1 a) X = sensory neuron, Y = inter neuron, Z = motor neuron (3)
b) Somatic, involuntary (2)
c) Brain (1)

2 See Figure AnKS 20.1. (5)

3 E, B, C, F, D, A (1)

4 a) = B
b) = D
c) = A
d) = C (3)

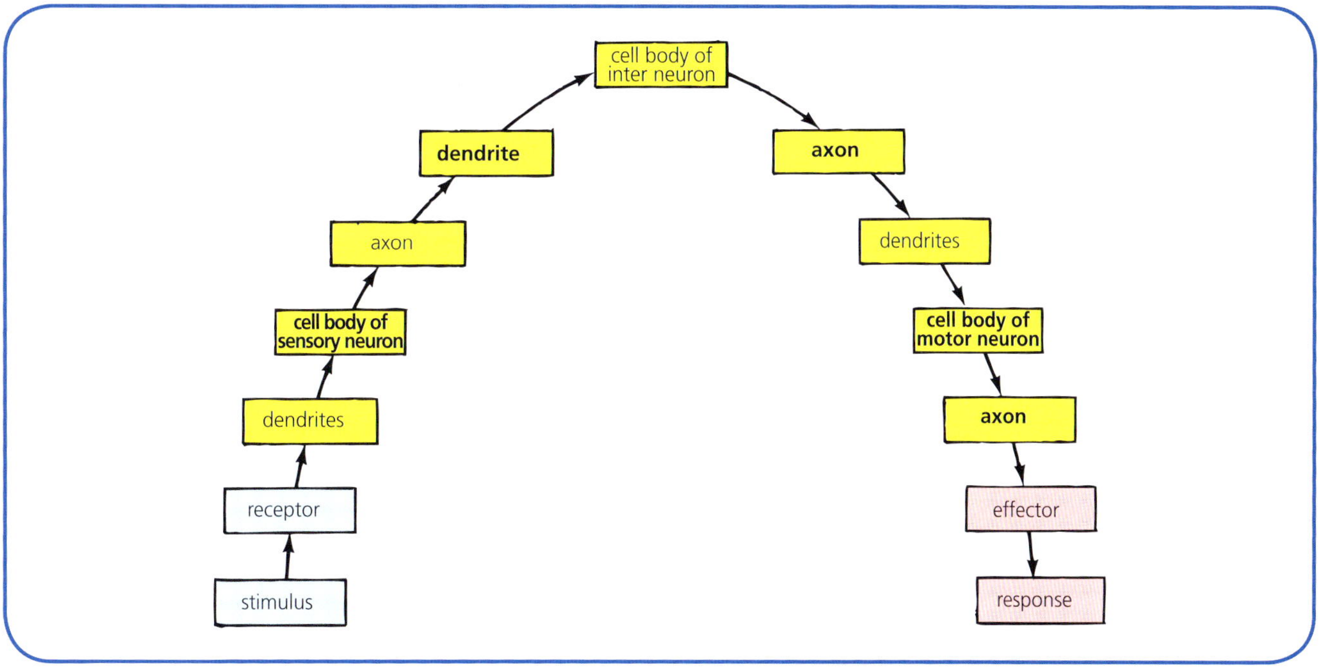

Figure AnKS 20.1

5 a) X = cone, Y = rod (2)
b) 1 and 3 (1)
c) Compared with cones, rods are much more sensitive to light and are able to transmit weak nerve impulses in dim light. Several of these impulses from convergently arranged rods are needed for the postsynaptic membrane to reach threshold. (3)

6 a) See core text pages 232–234. (5)
b) See core text page 237. (2)
c) See core text page 236. (2)

7 a) i) 6
ii) No
iii) The error bars overlap. (3)
b) i) 20
ii) Yes
iii) The error bars do not overlap. (3)
c) A prolonged period of laughing can elevate the pain threshold. (1)
d) Repeat the experiment but also take blood samples, before and after, from the members of both groups and analyse these for the presence of increased levels of endorphins. (2)
e) Repeat the experiment with each person in isolation when viewing the video. (1)

8 a) i) X
ii) Y (1)
b) An agonist mimics a neurotransmitter and stimulates specific receptors to transmit nerve impulses. Drug X must be the agonist because an increase in its concentration brings about increased stimulation of receptors. An antagonist binds to specific receptors and blocks the action of the neurotransmitter. Drug Y must be the antagonist because an increase in its concentration brings about decreased stimulation of receptors. (2)
c) i) 8
ii) 8×10^{-9} (2)
d) Drug Y is competing with the natural neurotransmitter for receptor sites on the postsynaptic membrane. But however high the concentration of drug Y, a few receptor sites will still become occupied by the natural neurotransmitter. (2)

Chapter 21 Non-specific body defences

1 E, D, B, C, A (1)

2 a) 1 = C, 2 = E, 3 = A, 4 = F, 5 = B, 6 = D (5)
b) See Table AnKS 21.1. (2)

Feature of an inflamed area	Reason
Redness	an increased blood supply is sent to the affected area
Swelling	fluid forced out of blood vessels into tissues at site of injury
Pain	swollen tissues press against nerve receptors and nerves

Table AnKS 21.1

3 a) i) White blood cell count
ii) Percentage
iii) Absolute refers to a value that is an actual number. Relative refers to a value that relates or compares two numbers. (3)
b) 1 microlitre (1×10^{-6} l) contains 200–600 cells. Therefore, 1 litre contains $200–600 \times 10^{6}$ cells $= 2–6 \times 10^{8}$ cells. (1)
c) i) Parasitic infection
ii) Rheumatoid arthritis and acute stress
iii) Neutrophil and lymphocyte (3)
d) See Figure AnKS 21.1. (3)

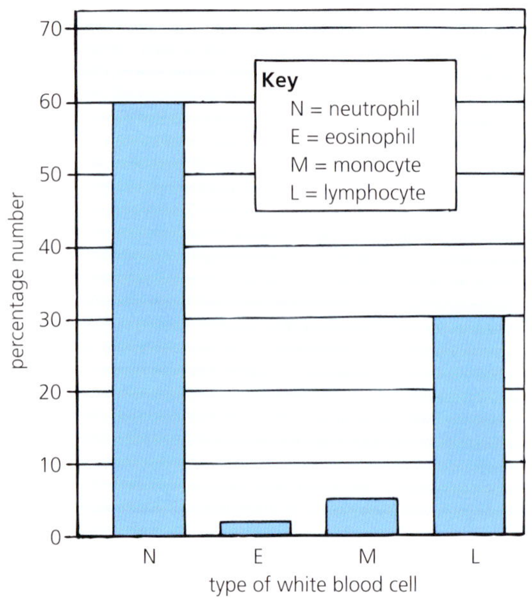

Figure AnKS 21.1

Chapter 22 Specific cellular defences against pathogens

1 1 = E, 2 = A, 3 = D, 4 = B, 5 = C (4)

2 a) i) 8.8%
ii) 12.4% (2)
b) 1.5 (1)
c) 3% (1)
d) 16–24 (1)
e) i) There are more males with asthma.
ii) There are more females with asthma. (2)
f) i) T
ii) F, 7.4 and 15.4
iii) F, 4.2 and 11.8
iv) T
v) T
vi) F, 7.4 and 16.0 (6)

3 See Figure AnKS 22.1. (4)

4 a) i) IgG
ii) The baby's own immune system makes antibodies after a few months. (2)
b) i) IgM
ii) IgE (2)
c) 1.4–4.0 mg/ml (1)
d) The concentration of IgM increases before that of IgG in both the primary and the secondary response. (1)
e) During the primary response, the concentration of IgG takes a longer time to begin to rise than during the secondary response. The highest concentration of IgG reached during the primary response is less than that reached during the secondary response. The concentration of IgG decreases after reaching its maximum level in the primary response but remains level at its highest concentration in the secondary response. (3)
f) Since the response to the second injection was faster than that to the first, this suggests that certain lymphocytes already 'knew what to do' from the previous time. (1)

5 a) i) Decreases
ii) Immune response is working. (2)
b) i) Inverse relationship
ii) HIV is destroying helper T cells. (2)
c) i) B lymphocytes
ii) HIV is not detected by the immune system because the virus is inside helper T cells. (2)
d) i) D
ii) AIDS does not occur until most of the immune function is lost and normally this takes many years (ten in the case of the person represented by the graph). (2)
e) Because HIV shows great antigenic variation. (1)

6 See core text pages 258–9, 265. (9)

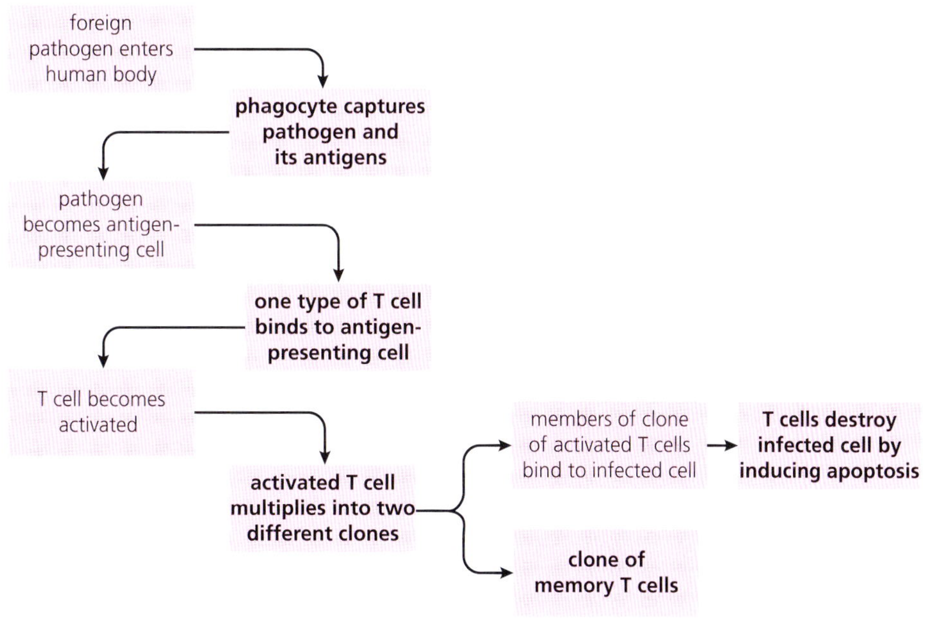
foreign pathogen enters human body
phagocyte captures pathogen and its antigens
pathogen becomes antigen-presenting cell
one type of T cell binds to antigen-presenting cell
T cell becomes activated
activated T cell multiplies into two different clones
members of clone of activated T cells bind to infected cell
T cells destroy infected cell by inducing apoptosis
clone of memory T cells

Figure AnKS 22.1

Chapter 23 Immunisation

1 **a)** See Figure AnKS 23.1 below. (4)
b) **i)** 1985, 1988 and 1990
ii) 56% (2)
c) **i)** Decreased
ii) Increased (2)
d) **i)** Increased
ii) Decreased (2)
e) **i)** 1989
ii) A new strain of the pathogen evolved which evaded the immunity that the people had developed. (2)

2 **a)** **i)** 4
ii) 3 (2)
b) Diphtheria, tetanus and polio (1)
c) Measles, mumps and rubella (1)

3 **a)** **i)** Diphtheria
ii) Tuberculosis (2)
b) Good food and improved quality of housing (2)
c) **i)** 4
ii) 60%
iii) 1882
iv) 0.8 (4)
d) People sleeping 'rough' in cold, damp conditions become susceptible to respiratory infections including tuberculosis because their resistance is low. (1)

4 **a)** **i)** Y
ii) X
iii) Vaccination began earlier and eradication was achieved earlier in X. (2)
b) This is supported by the fact that the start of the vaccination campaign was followed each time by an apparent surge in cases when in fact this high level probably existed all along. It is hardly likely that it was caused by vaccination. (2)
c) **i)** Almost complete eradication of the disease
ii) Many strains of the pathogen exist and it is able to change the antigenic proteins present on its surface. (2)

5 **a)** Antigenic drift results from mutations that occur naturally and continuously. Antigenic shift results from the occasional combination of genetic material from two different viral strains forming a new strain. (2)
b) A new influenza **vaccine** is needed every year because all the strains of the **virus** are continuously undergoing genetic **drift** as a result of **mutation**. Therefore one or more **new** strains appear each year able to resist **antibodies** that blocked the **infection** by the **previous** viral strain. (4)
c) C (1)
d) Antigenic drift results from natural mutations and these affect the genetic material of all organisms including influenza viruses A, B and C. Antigenic shift involves the combination of

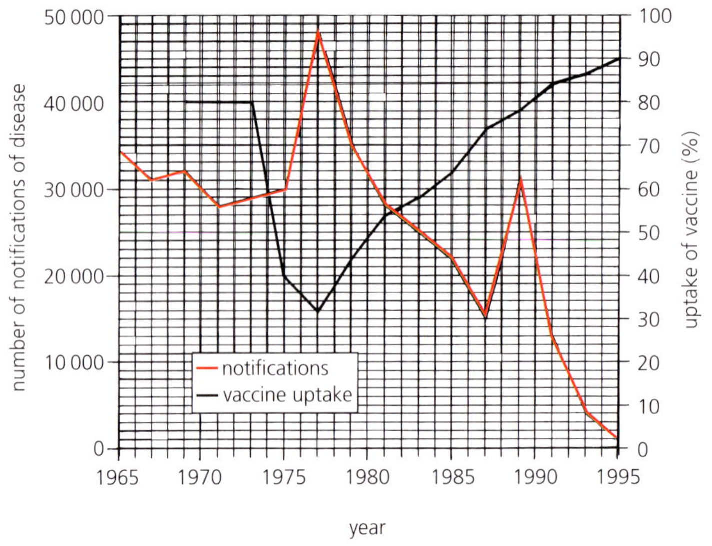

Figure AnKS 23.1

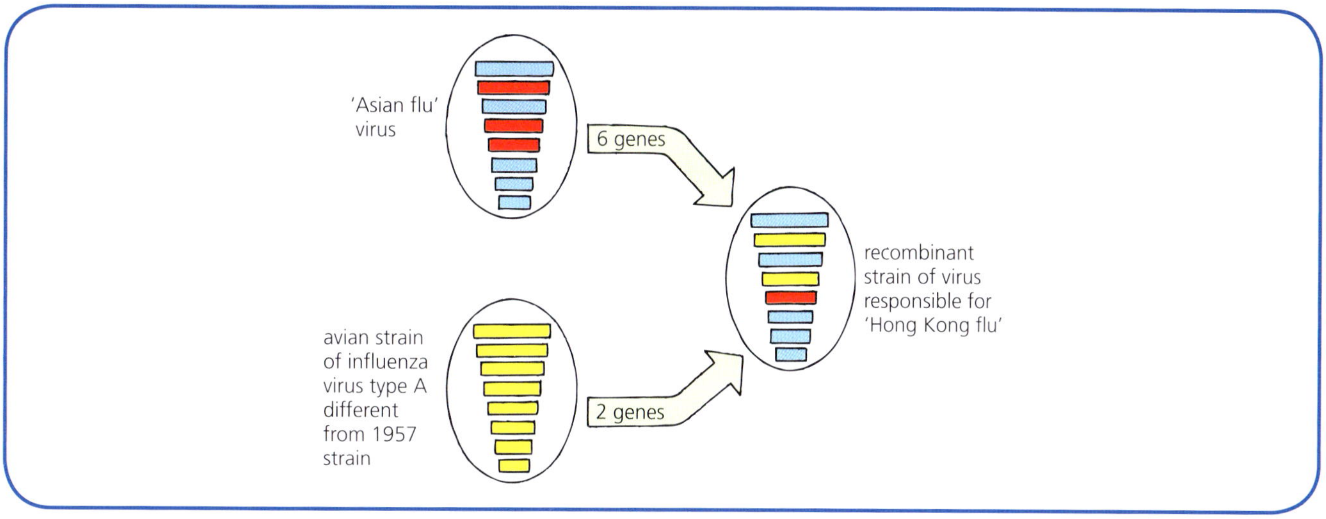

Figure AnKS 23.2

genetic material from two (or more) strains of the same virus from different hosts. Unlike B and C, influenza virus A can infect both humans and birds and therefore opportunities arise for antigenic shift to occur when two different strains of type A virus meet. (2)

e) See Figure AnKS 23.2. (3)

Chapter 24 Clinical trials of vaccines and drugs

1 a) Phase I used a few, paid, healthy people whereas phase II used many, unpaid people with asthma. (3)

b) So that any improvements in people receiving Q can be attributed to Q if the same improvements are absent from the control group. (2)

c) The results of phase III showed that patients on Q had fewer asthma attacks and used their inhalers less often than the control group. (2)

d) i) An inactive copy of the drug

ii) They had gained a psychological benefit from taking the placebo or their condition had just happened to improve. (2)

e) i) Addition

ii) Although the condition of many people improved, less than half were able to give up inhaled steroids. (2)

f) On average, elderly people's health is poorer than that of young people so a new drug might affect them adversely. Elderly people use so many medicines that the data produced would be unreliable. (2)

2 a) P and N

b) A and P

c) A and N (3)

3 a) See Figure AnKS 24.1. (4)

b) i) No

ii) The error bars overlap showing that there is no significant difference between the drug and the control. (2)

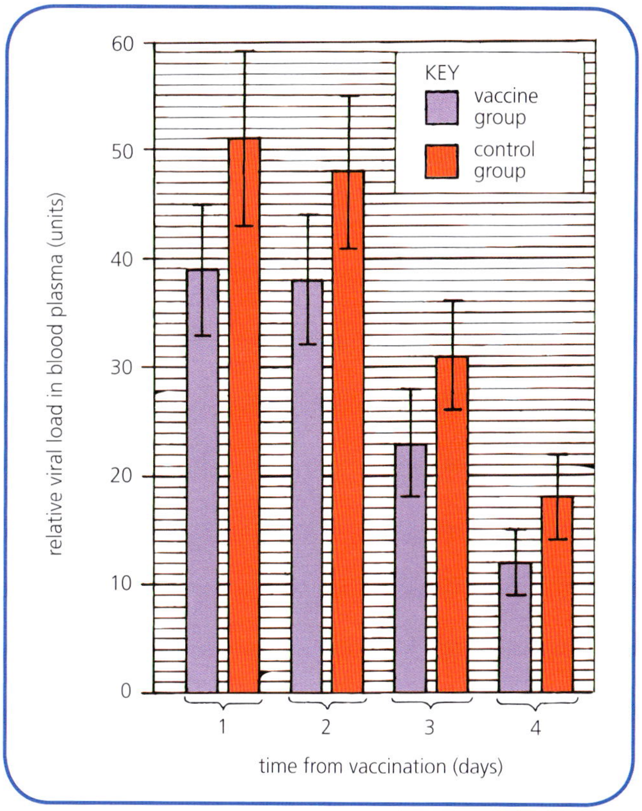

Figure AnKS 24.1

Index